CONFLICT IN THE CATHOLIC HIERARCHY:
A STUDY OF COPING STRATEGIES IN THE HUNTHAUSEN AFFAIR, WITH PREFERENTIAL ATTENTION TO DISCURSIVE STRATEGIES

Timothy P. Schilling

ISBN: 90-70660-43-1

Limited edition: 300 copies

Cover design: Wilco Telderman
Printed by Labor Grafimedia BV Utrecht, The Netherlands

CONFLICT IN THE CATHOLIC HIERARCHY: A STUDY OF COPING STRATEGIES IN THE HUNTHAUSEN AFFAIR, WITH PREFERENTIAL ATTENTION TO DISCURSIVE STRATEGIES

CONFLICTEN BINNEN DE KATHOLIEKE HIËRARCHIE: EEN STUDIE NAAR STRATEGIEËN IN HET HANTEREN VAN DE KWESTIE HUNTHAUSEN, MET BIJZONDERE AANDACHT VOOR DISCURSIEVE STRATEGIEËN.

(met een samenvatting in het Nederlands)

Proefschrift

Proefschrift ter verkrijging van de graad van doctor aan de Katholieke Theologische Universiteit te Utrecht op gezag van de Rector Magnificus, Prof.dr. H.W.M. Rikhof, ingevolge het besluit van het College voor Promoties in het openbaar te verdedigen op vrijdag, 10 januari 2003, des middags te 12:30 uur

door

Timothy Peter Schilling

Geboren op 26 augustus 1965, te Lafayette, Indiana, U.S.A.

Promotor: Prof. Dr. A. J. Baart

For Janke

TABLE OF CONTENTS

APPENDICES:

LIST OF TABLES, FIGURES AND BOXES

CHAPTER ONE

INTRODUCTION

1.1 A Capsule Summary

The Roman Catholic Church is one world Church made up of many local churches. Since its inception, the leadership of the Church has sought to forge an internal unity that transcends the diversity of its membership. Over the course of centuries, the Pope and other bishops of the Church have served as symbols and proponents of this desired unity. The Pope in union with the college of bishops constitutes the hierarchy which guides the Church and is responsible for its adherence to "one Lord, one faith, one baptism."

When conflicts arise within the Catholic hierarchy, the unity of the Church is called into question. The reality of this threat is easily demonstrated by historical reference to the Reformation and to the Roman Catholic-Orthodox Catholic separation. But it is also seen in more contemporary examples, as in Archbishop Marcel Lefebvre's post-Vatican II conflict with the Holy See, which resulted in the departure of Lefebvre and many of his followers from the Church.

Conflicts such as the Rome-Lefebvre conflict may be described as "center-periphery" conflicts: the central authority in Rome is pitted against the authority of the local Church, and the authority of the Pope is placed in opposition to the authority of one or more local bishops. (Following Rahim 1992, I define conflict as an *interactive process manifested in incompatibility, disagreement or dissonance within or between social entities*.) Center-periphery conflicts are not the only kind of conflict to arise within the hierarchy. Conflicts may arise within the bounds of the organizational center (as in conflicts among bishops serving in the Roman Curia) or they may take place on the periphery (as in conflicts within a national or regional conference of bishops). But center-periphery conflicts are notable for the way they dramatize, in an especially clear way, the tension that exists generally in the Church between central and local control.

Since the Second Vatican Council, several cases of center-periphery conflict have come before the public eye. Apart from the Lefebvre case, one thinks of such highly publicized cases as the Holy See's exchanges with the Dutch Cardinal Bernard Alfrink, with the American Archbishop Raymond Hunthausen, and with the French Bishop Jacques Gaillot. Typically, such cases have been assessed from journalistic and theological perspectives, but systematic descriptions focusing on the conflict handling *as such* have been lacking. Whereas the surface issues and a number of relevant theological questions have received consideration, one is hard pressed to find accounts that identify and break down the strategies employed to manage the conflicts. At best we have a sketchy picture of how participants seek to advance their own interests strategically in the course of such conflicts. The present case study is designed to address this information gap.

This investigation attempts to make the handling of center-periphery conflict more transparent by conducting an exploratory and descriptive case study of a recent empirical example of the phenomenon. The empirical example I have chosen for study is the conflict between the Holy See and Seattle Archbishop Raymond Hunthausen, which took place during the years 1983-1989. (A brief summary of the case follows in section 1.7.) I have selected this case because it is recent enough in time to be reflective of current conflict-handling patterns within the hierarchy (many key figures from the case, including Pope John Paul II, Cardinal Ratzinger and Bishop Donald Wuerl, still hold office) and accessible to a variety of forms of information gathering (the extent to which the conflict handling came into the open is unusual). The case is also fascinating for being something of an extreme example. Not only did it draw a remarkably high level of public attention, especially in the American Church; it was exceptional, too, for the degree of polarization it demonstrated between the points of universal and local leadership in the Church. Another intriguing dimension of the case is the effectiveness with which Hunthausen defended his own position in the conflict. Although the Vatican, almost by definition, has the upper hand in the management of such conflicts, Hunthausen was able to achieve something that at first glance would appear to be unlikely in the handling of center-periphery conflict: he pressed the Vatican into a limited retreat. Though neither Hunthausen nor representatives of the Holy See were ever inclined to speak of winning or losing the conflict, there is reason to believe that both parties lost in substantial ways, as did the institutional Church. While it is striking that Hunthausen managed to resist Vatican imperatives without being forced from office, and also to induce Rome to retract sanctions it had already imposed at his expense, Roman priorities appear to have prevailed in the long run. No local bishop has so boldly made the case for local priorities in the years since. Though Hunthausen may in a limited sense have "won" simply by holding his ground, the Vatican appears to have sent a message that has been heard loud and clear by other bishops in ensuing years: the final say rests with the center. The loss for the institutional Church, as I see it, is that the opportunity for a more robust dialogue between center and periphery in the post-Vatican II era has been missed amid the center's fear of losing control and the college of bishops' constrained approach to conflict handling. Why I hold these conclusions should become clear as I present the findings from my intensive study of the Rome-Hunthausen case.

First and foremost, my intention here is to describe how the principal parties (that is, Hunthausen, members of the hierarchy representing the Holy See and, to a lesser extent, bishops participating as third parties) managed the conflict strategically, with special attention going to their use of language. The research falls within the realm of practical theology, with practical theology understood to be an interdisciplinary field that draws extensively on the techniques of the social sciences. Though at no point in this research do I theologize explicitly, I do believe that this study of the Church organization can offer direct benefits to the Church's own process of ecclesiological discernment.

I have oriented my study by articulating a guiding question: *What coping strategies are observable in center-periphery conflict discourse?* This question indicates the phenomenon under consideration (center-periphery conflict), the data I intend to examine (discourse samples), the type of results I am seeking (coping strategies), and the exploratory and descriptive nature of the research. I will expound upon this question's components later. By answering the guiding question, I hope to bring us to a clearer understanding of how center-periphery conflicts in the Church are managed in practice.

1.2 Center-Periphery Conflict in the Church
There is nothing new or surprising about leadership conflicts in the Church. From the beginning of its existence, the life of the Church has been shaped by divergent viewpoints, various kinds of party alignments, and debates that have ranged from the amicable to the violent (Hume 1999, 6; Reese 1996, 25; McBrien 1992, 44; Cooke 1989, 3; O'Connor 1986, 79; Ashby 1955, 5). Nor, given the actual and potential costs to the Church through losses of

membership, material resources or prestige, should we be surprised to find that Church leaders might want to curb the likelihood for conflict to arise. Some observers have gone so far as to assert that an aversion to conflict prevails generally among Church leaders (Van der Ven 1996, 280-281; Stevens 1994, 7; Laeyendecker 1967, 307).

Understandably, Church leaders concerned to promote harmony within the Church organization will tend to downplay the image of Jesus as controversialist, who promises to bring division, and to disrupt peace rather than to establish it (cf. Luke 12:51, Matthew 10:34). Nonetheless, conflicts have not disappeared from the life of the Church, because conflicts are intrinsic to social life itself. Indeed, in an age of democratization, globalization and efficient information technologies, one might say that conflicts within the Catholic Church are more visible than ever, especially when those conflicts involve the hierarchy. The challenge for the Church appears to be not to rid itself of conflict altogether, an unrealistic goal, but to manage conflict in productive rather than counterproductive ways.

Present-day intraecclesial conflicts touch the membership of the Catholic Church more immediately, directly and (in some instances) extensively than they have in the past, thanks in part to developments in information technologies (Reese 1996, 2; Hanson 1987; Hume 1989, 185; Seidler and Meyer 1989, 5. See also: Soukup, Plude & Philibert 1995; *Aetatis Novae* 1992). Moreover, such conflicts gain widespread attention because they surface questions concerning freedom and authority which are of interest even to those who are not part of the Church's membership (Quinn 1996, 14; K. A. Briggs 1992, 1).

In a context of modernity, conflicts are more quickly and widely publicized than ever before, thanks to the facility of information technologies. With the arrival of global and instantaneous transmissions has come the participation of a broad public in conflictual matters as the conflicts themselves unfold. Thus recent disputes between the Vatican and certain bishops, and between the Vatican and certain theologians -- to name just two among many forms of intraecclesial conflict -- have drawn countless others, Catholic or not, into the conflict process. These new "participants" in the conflict, varying in the extent of their involvement, reside the world over. The Vatican exchanges with Bishop Gaillot of France in 1995 and with the theologian Leonardo Boff of Brazil in 1985, to cite just two examples, both received worldwide press coverage, eliciting comment from Catholics and non-Catholics alike. Conflicts between the Vatican and representatives of the local Church have taken on an increased significance for the Church universal because the whole Church now has more opportunity than ever to watch and speak to the process, and to be affected by it. In an information age, such conflicts become a performance of identity (cf. Tjosvold & Johnson 1983, 2-3; Bartholomaus 1978, 97; C. L. Briggs 1996, 3; Cheney 1991, 88; Cox 1988, 4) wherein questions of who the Church is and who it seeks to be are made manifest in the words and actions of the participants.

Apart from the fact that intraecclesial conflict is much publicized in our time, it is also not surprising that such conflict gets attention in light of the widespread (especially in Western countries) contemporary focus on local and individual autonomy. Intraecclesial conflict reveals in a vivid way present-day societal tensions between the claims of unity versus those of diversity -- or, to put it another way, the claims of institutional authority relative to individual or group autonomy (Ashby 1955, 10). One aspect of the heritage of the Enlightenment has been a readiness to question the self-evidence of institutional authority (be it governmental, religious, corporate or of another sort), particularly when the insights of individual reason run counter to the will of the institutional authority. The Church, being one of the world's most readily recognized bearers of institutional authority, naturally draws attention to itself when it experiences conflict within its ranks. Such conflict symbolically demonstrates for the public the current "state of the question," as far as the Church is concerned, in matters of unity and diversity, authority and obedience, and institutional identity relative to individual freedom (Granfield 1987, 1; McKenzie 1969, 11; Ashby 1955, 10). It also poses a challenge to non-ecclesiastical institutions to clarify their own stand on these issues.

Since the Second Vatican Council -- to limit the historical scope of our discussion -- the world has had many opportunities to watch the Church cope with internal conflicts taking place at all levels of the organization. Cases involving the Vatican, however, tend to garner the most attention because the papacy serves on a day-to-day basis as the highest decision-making entity in the Church and as a focal point of the Church's unity. Typically, a conflictual matter must be fairly significant, even globally significant, for the Vatican to become involved at all.

The Holy See's conversational partners in intraecclesial conflicts come from all regions of the world. Conflicts between the Holy See and local bishops – center-periphery conflicts -- are among the more noteworthy kinds of conflict experienced within the Church because both parties lead significant sectors of the Church membership. Such conflicts hold a special significance for the life of the Church as a whole, since the leadership of the pope in union with the bishops greatly determines the course that the Church will take. Conflicts between Rome and a local Ordinary pit two primary symbols of the Church's unity one against another. Bishops, like the Pope himself, symbolize and have responsibility for the unity of not only their own diocese, but of the universal Church as well. Conflicts between the Pope (or papal office) and members of the episcopacy are perilous for the Church as a whole, in that they may produce doubt, fractiousness and antagonism within the ranks of the faithful (Reese 1996, 25). Catholics and non-Catholics alike may be alienated by the sight of two successors to the apostles in tense or oppositional relationship.

Such conflicts are often painful for those involved. The principal parties and those loyal to them may experience anxiety and disillusionment as a result of the proceedings (Bernardin 1987, 256). In addition, intrahierarchical conflicts may interfere with the Church's progress toward its own stated goals. Conflict that is poorly managed can diminish the Church's institutional vitality, making those inside and outside the Church unready to hear the message the Church wants to proclaim (Quinn 1996, 14). One should note my distinction here between the desire to see conflicts managed well and the desire for its disappearance from ecclesial life altogether. The latter does not orient this research. One of my presuppositions is that conflict can contribute positively to Church life (Hume 1999, 6; Halverstadt 1991, 3; Granfield 1987, 3; Lee and Marty 1964, 5). The Church has a clear interest in seeing the best possible outcomes emerge when conflicts do arise. Thus it makes sense for the Church to seek to better understand, in general and specific ways, how such conflicts develop, how they typically unfold, and how they can most rationally be managed in light of the Church's own ultimate objectives.

Since the Second Vatican Council, we have seen conflicts involving the primacy and episcopacy resolved in various ways. In some cases, the disputes have been resolved with both parties achieving some of their stated objectives and indicating at least a minimal level of satisfaction: the Hunthausen case seems to be an example of this. In others, as in the Lefebvre and Gaillot cases, unwanted final conditions were forced by one party on another and significant dissatisfaction was expressed publicly by one party or both afterward.

The three cases of center-periphery conflict I have just mentioned, though isolated examples, demonstrate that the Vatican ordinarily has the upper hand in such conflicts. In each case the Vatican took power away from the bishop in question: Hunthausen had certain powers of governance removed that were later restored; Lefebvre was excommunicated; Gaillot was reassigned to an inactive See. One should not, however, overlook the power that individual bishops wield vis-à-vis the papacy, particularly when the individual bishop has the sympathy of other bishops. Historically, bishops have shown great resourcefulness in conflicts with the papacy, achieving personal (or local) objectives despite contrary Vatican preferences. This has been true even when a bishop's position has been decisively sanctioned. As cases in point, Bishop Gaillot has found creative ways to continue to spread his views (via the internet) despite being reassigned to an inactive diocese, and Archbishop Lefebvre resisted the Vatican's lead for years before being decisively removed.

The fact that intrahierarchical conflict can be costly for the Church is amply demonstrated by these few examples. When Archbishop Lefebvre was excommunicated, many loyal followers left the Church with him. Such disaffection among Catholics, though less drastic in the Hunthausen and Gaillot cases, was also readily apparent in the outcry heard in the bishops' own dioceses and beyond. Unity among the leaders of the Church is critical to the maintenance of unity among those they seek to serve.

Maintaining this unity has never been easy. Quite literally, the Church faces a world of challenges within its own ranks. Roughly one billion persons across the globe call themselves Catholic, but they do so according to widely varying cultural viewpoints and individual experiences (Marzheuser 1995; Fitzpatrick 1987). How is it possible to join and hold such a diversity together within a single organizational unity? How can individual bishops respect the specific realities of life in their own diocese while integrating the same into the life of the Church universal? How can the Pope address the needs of the many and at the same time act to foster oneness? And when the Pope and a bishop find themselves in disagreement, how do they know when to listen and when to speak, when to yield and when to stand firm?

1.3 The Problem of Limited Information About Center-Periphery Conflict Handling
Ideally, when evaluating intrahierarchical conflicts in the Catholic Church, one could consult a comprehensive body of existing concerning such conflicts. But in fact, even more general studies of *intrachurch* conflict are fairly limited, especially those done from a social scientific-organizational management perspective (among those recognizing the problem are Kniss and Chaves 1995, 172; Gangel and Canine 1992, 11; Vaillancourt 1980, 3). Moreover, wide ranging agreement about terms and models is lacking, and empirical studies are rare. Kniss and Chaves (1995, 173), who give specific attention to Christian intradenominational conflict, have observed that, between 1965 and 1995, the study of such conflict "has left many interesting and important questions unanswered."

Among the writings of the past few decades that lend insight concerning intraecclesial conflict in general are Van der Ven 1996, Stevens et al. 1994, Gangel and Canine 1992, Halverstadt 1991, Lee 1989, Seidler and Meyer 1989, Shawchuck 1983a and 1983b, Bacher et al. 1983, Bossart 1980, Fray 1969 and Laeyendecker 1967. Though none of these treats Catholic intrahierarchical conflict in particular, the works introduce concepts that have relevance for the present research.

Various aspects of intrahierarchical conflict management (as seen from a social scientific or journalistic perspective) have been discussed in a limited number of works that I have found to be especially helpful. These include Reese 1996, Reese 1992, Byrnes 1991, Cheney 1991, Cooke 1989, Reese 1989, Hanson 1987, Hebblethwaite 1986, Kolbenschlag 1986, Lawler 1986, Nichols 1982, Vaillancourt 1980 and Greeley 1979. I have also found orientation for this study in works that have examined the handling of particular cases of conflict within the hierarchy. Among these: Van Schaik 1997, Cox 1988, Coleman 1978 and Congar 1976.

Although my interest here is not directly theological, theological literature has certainly broadened my knowledge of the Church organization, its mindset and practice. Works that have been helpful in this way are too numerous to mention, but at a minimum I would single out the reflections on conflict treatment offered by the (U.S.) National Conference of Catholic Bishops (1989) and Danneels (1987), and the discussions of papal-episcopal relations found in Buckley 1998, Quinn 1996, Schatz 1996, Granfield 1987 and Tillard 1983. Granfield 1987 is a good example of a theological work that uses empirical examples to examine the sharing of power and authority between pope and bishop. But Granfield's interest is with the limits of papal power and not with conflict handling as such.

1.4 A Social Scientific Approach: The Church as Organization

While empirical studies of Catholic intrahierarchical conflict are not abundantly available, it is possible to draw insights from studies of leadership conflicts in other organizations (Watkins 1991, 689; Seidler and Meyer 1989, xi; Vaillancourt 1980, 3). One starting point of the present research is the presumption that leadership conflicts in the Church can be compared with leadership struggles in other organizations.

In many respects, the Church is an organization comparable to other organizations (cf. Reese 1996, 1; Van der Ven 1996, 89; Thung 1996, 343; Watkins 1991; Safranski 1985), but we should not lose sight of features which make the Church unique among organizations (Tracy 1991, 23; Wilson 1982, 17). The Church is a particular kind of *religious* organization that can be distinguished from other religious organizations. Granfield (1987, 58) writes that the Church "is a society with no counterpart because of its unique origin, means, patterns of interaction, and goals."

> The Church is a unique combination of several elements: human and divine, visible and invisible, temporal and transcendent. It is both a mystery, a part of God's "hidden plan" (Eph. 1:19), and a social institution (Granfield 1987, 58. See also Reese 1996, 4-5).

One way the Church is like other organizations is in its experience of internal conflicts. Tjosvold and Johnson (1983, 1) have made a case for the ubiquity of conflict within organizational life in general: "To be alive is to be in conflict. To be effective is to be in conflict. Organizations cannot function without conflict and members of organizations cannot interact without conflict." (See also Fraser and Hipel 1984, 3.) On the basis of the Church's capability of being compared with other organizations, and its being like other organizations in its experience of internal conflicts, we may presume that social scientific studies of leadership conflicts in other organizations will have some relevance to our investigation of intrahierarchical conflict. Therefore, one of the initial points of orientation of this research is engagement with terms, categories and models that have emerged from social scientific studies of intraorganizational conflict.

1.5 Gaining Insight into Center-Periphery Conflict by Means of a Case Study

Given the complexity of the phenomenon I have chosen to study and my desire to study the phenomenon in the richness of its social context, I have determined to undertake a case study. (My perspective on case study research derives primarily from Denzin and Lincoln 2000, Yin 1994, Yin 1993 and Hutjes and Van Buuren 1992. For the definition of a case study and a detailed discussion of how I apply this method, see chapter five.) Observable cases of center-periphery conflict are relatively rare, and the variables which have impact on the transpiration of this phenomenon (societal factors, organizational factors, personal factors) are large in number and not easily separated out from one another. Therefore it is not a simple matter to isolate variables for comparison (in a laboratory setting, for example) or to conduct comparisons across many cases. Conducting a case study offers the advantages of helping us to see the interrelationship of multiple (at times too many!) variables at once and in their natural context (to the extent that I have accurately reconstructed it). Another advantage to pursuing a case study strategy, especially of the exploratory and descriptive kind I have undertaken here, is that it makes room for a wide range of types of findings to emerge. In my examination of the Rome-Hunthausen conflict, summarized briefly at the end of this chapter, I have found myself led in various directions I did not expect to go, to my mind a positive development.

At an early stage of this research I formulated an intention to compare the findings emerging from my study of the Rome-Hunthausen case with another case, that of the Vatican's exchanges with Cardinal Alfrink of Utrecht during the early post-Vatican II years. The Alfrink case suggested itself because of apparent similarities in the conflict-handling styles of Hunthausen and Alfrink (and similar kinds of tensions in the local Church) but with differing outcomes from the conflict with Rome. For practical reasons, this intention did not come to fruition. (Investigation of the Hunthausen case proved to be demanding enough by itself.) But I continue to believe that it would be a worthy research pursuit to take the theoretical framework developed in this study and make comparisons across cases of center-periphery conflict.

1.5.1 The Formulation of Expectations through a Process of Theoretical Sensitization

Prior to confronting data from the case itself, I have engaged in a lengthy process of theoretical sensitization, the results of which are presented in chapters two through five. The purpose of doing so has been to become acquainted with the state of the question in regard to center-periphery conflict and to gain some initial points of orientation for our investigation. This effort has taken as its major topics the structural make-up of the Church organization (chapter two) and the context of modernity that contains the Church (chapter three). At the end of chapter three I advance a limited number of expectations about center-periphery conflict handling, given the Church's organizational structure and societal placement. These include expectations about the hierarchy's approach to center-periphery conflict in general, its perspective on the use of power, and seven specific coping strategies center-periphery conflict participants are likely to apply. Chapter four carries the process of sensitization a step further by offering a descriptive theory of conflict handling in general. Chapter five completes the process of sensitization by providing a set of reflections, taken from the discipline of critical discourse analysis, that help us to conceptualize links between applications of language and power.

1.5.2 A Discourse-Oriented Approach to the Case Study

Organizational conflicts are typically made manifest in language use. Language use is at the heart of our ability to interact as persons, and as such, it is also an inescapable dimension of conflict experience (C. L. Briggs 1996, 3; Jandt 1973, 2). One cannot wage conflict, or resolve it, or understand it, without being able to send messages, and receive and interpret them. Language is not the only medium of conflict conduct: behaviors other than speaking and writing also determine the course of a dispute. But by studying the language used in a conflict one may gain much insight into the nature of the conflict and the patterns of its resolution.

In the present case study I place a priority on discerning how language is used to cope with the center-periphery conflict. It is my view that close attention to the language used by Church leaders in conflict situations reveals much about what interests are at stake for these leaders (and for the Church as an institution) and what means they consider appropriate to secure those interests. On the other hand, language is not the only medium for the strategic management of conflict, and one cannot tell the whole conflict story by speaking only of texts. Conflicts will also be carried out by persons through nonverbal means, as for example through the use of body language, attire, symbols, etc. Therefore, my attention does not go exclusively to discourse products, but my overall concern remains at the level of conflict handling.

As a means to distill and analyze (on a micro level) the language used in hierarchical conflicts, I employ a social-linguistic method of recent origin, *critical discourse analysis* (CDA). CDA (Fairclough 1995; 1992; 1989) is a method for illuminating how language use relates to social practice and social change. A fundamental premise undergirding the method is the belief that texts negotiate sociocultural contradictions and differences between groups (Fairclough 1995, 7). Embracing this perspective, I have studied texts produced by members of the hierarchy participating in the Rome-Hunthausen conflict as a way of gaining deeper insight into how the parties have defended and advanced their own interests.

1.5.3 Conflict Analysis As a Tool for Bringing Coherence to the Case Study
Having drawn up my own picture of the Rome-Hunthausen conflict in this study, it has been helpful to make comparisons with existing theories of social conflict as a means for clarifying my thinking about the case. Rahim 1992 was especially useful at an early stage of the research. In a later stage I found it profitable to draw on the work of Pruitt and Rubin (1986), whose focus on conflict participant's aspirations and perceptions fits well with my own focus on individual actors' (bishops') participation in conflict situations. Pruitt and Rubin also provide a set of expectations concerning the appearance of particular strategies in particular stages of conflict, which has enhanced my ability to make distinctions within the conflict experience.

1.5.4 Interview with a Conflict Insider
The view of the Rome-Hunthausen conflict presented here has been substantially benefited by my contact with someone who viewed the Rome-Hunthausen conflict from the inside: Very Rev. Michael G. Ryan, former chancellor and vicar general of the Seattle Archdiocese under Archbishop Hunthausen. During two two-hour interviews I conducted with him in 2001, Fr. Ryan shared his own perspective on the conflict experience. His information rounded out my own understanding of the conflict in a number of ways: by providing a full account that was not influenced by my own theories (in an open-structured component to the interview), by supplying missing information that helped me to reconstruct the case (in a semi-structured interview component), and by allowing me to hear Fr. Ryan's opinion of certain theories I had developed (in a validational interview component). Because of the sensitive nature of the interview materials, Fr. Ryan and I have agreed that the interview will not be reproduced in

full in this context, but he has given me permission to reproduce selected portions of the transcribed text. I have taken advantage of this opportunity and the results are presented near the end of this study. I am most grateful for Fr. Ryan's cooperation.

1.5.5 Documentation Supplied by a Chancery Employee from the Conflict Years
A second source of information that has immeasurably benefited this research is a collection of documentation gathered by one who worked for the Archdiocese of Seattle during the years of the Rome-Hunthausen conflict. While working as an administrative assistant at the archdiocesan chancery, Ms. Janice Wasden Price began compiling scrapbooks of documentation relevant to the Hunthausen case. Included in her collection of eight scrapbooks spanning three years are newspaper clippings from a wide range of sources (*The Progress*, the *National Catholic Reporter*, the *Wanderer*, the *New York Times*, the *Washington Post*, the *National Catholic Register*, the *Seattle Post-Intelligencer*, the *Seattle Times*, the *Seattle Weekly* – in other words, sources representing viewpoints right and left, secular and Catholic), internal office memoranda, photos, letters from conflict participants, mailing lists, invitations to events of various kinds, buttons in support of Hunthausen and more. Ms. Wasden Price's collection added a depth and breadth to my own reconstruction of the case that could not otherwise have been achieved. I owe a heartfelt debt of gratitude to her for her provision of these materials. In the near future Ms. Wasden Price's materials, which amount to a kind of time capsule from the Rome-Hunthausen conflict, will be made available to other researchers at an as-yet-undetermined academic institution.

1.6 Findings from the Case
The primary findings identified through this research are a general perspective on, and specific coping strategies applied within, one empirical example of center-periphery conflict. These findings are presented in unfolding fashion in my reconstruction of the case itself and in my subsequent reflection on the case thereafter, as aided by several validation techniques. Ultimately these findings boil down to my understanding of the strategies used to achieve, maintain and apply power in a given case of conflict within the Church hierarchy. My intention is to offer a description of what I have found in the Rome-Hunthausen case, after having viewed it through a lens of language and power.

Though I write from the perspective of a Catholic believer who is concerned for the future of the Church, I do not attempt in this analysis to account for how God works through Church leaders' efforts at conflict management. My intention has been to describe as precisely and correctly as possible what actually happened in the selected case. For the sake of relevant disclosure, I admit that I am predisposed to believe that all people, bishops included, are motivated by a will to power, which will color their handling of conflict situations. Having said that, I recognize too that certain strains of Church teaching point to the dangers of wanting and possessing power and that the ideal of emptying oneself – of becoming powerless -- is proposed by the Church (as in the image of Jesus in Philippians, chapter two). My assessment of the Rome-Hunthausen case takes a neutral view of power (power is necessary and can be put to good or bad ends) and does not speculate about the inner motivations of individual bishops, but simply takes for granted that bishops possess ample powers that they will apply – probably for a mixture of selfish and selfless reasons – in conflict situations. While I hold that God is somehow at work in the conflict handling process, I confront obvious limits in being able to say exactly how. Limiting myself to the evaluative framework of organizational management, however, it does seem clear to me that center-periphery conflicts can be managed more effectively than they are, in light of the Church's own stated goals.

1.7 Relevance of the Study

This study is relevant in theoretical, practical and theological terms. Its theoretical relevance lies in its provision of a clearer understanding of how conflicts within the Church hierarchy work, identifying societal and organizational pressures that bear on such conflicts, resources available for managing the conflicts, and a variety of strategies that may be applied by bishops in their pursuit of personal and organizational objectives. At most, I offer a mini-theory of center-periphery conflict here, but it is a useful first step toward a more comprehensive grasp of the phenomenon.

The practical relevance of the study lies in the consistent grounding of theory in knowledge of actual practice. In the course of this investigation all theoretical suppositions are measured against the available empirical evidence. The result is a picture of what strategies tend to be applied in center-periphery conflict and the effects thereof. Given that center-periphery conflicts are likely to recur in the future – the structural tension between center and periphery will not go away – the findings here can contribute to the more effective handling of such conflicts in the future.

The theological relevance of this study lies not in its advancement of a theological reflection on center-periphery conflict – no such reflection is offered – but in the foundation it lays for future theologizing. Before exploring the theological implications of intrahierarchical conflict for the life of the Church, one needs to have a clear picture of what such conflict involves. Though my focus here stays with questions of language and power, which at no point are put in theological perspective, these are crucial concepts that need to be addressed in any valid, comprehensive ecclesiology.

1.8 Summary of the Hunthausen Case

By way of introduction, I offer the following summary of the Rome-Hunthausen conflict.

In 1983, the Vatican pro-nuncio to the United States, Archbishop Pio Laghi, informed Archbishop Hunthausen that the Vatican wished to conduct a visitation of the Seattle Archdiocese, the purpose of which was to assess the merits of complaints made about the Archbishop's management of affairs within the Archdiocese. Hunthausen agreed to this request. Subsequently, the Holy See sent Washington, D.C. Archbishop James Hickey to Seattle to carry out the visitation, during which time he met with priests, religious and laypersons within the Archdiocese. Hickey also studied documents which had been issued by the Archbishop and the Archdiocese. Hickey then reported his findings to the Vatican.

Hunthausen received word of the Vatican's conclusions from the visitation by means of a September 1985 letter from Joseph Ratzinger, Cardinal Prefect of the Congregation for the Doctrine of the Faith. The letter concluded the visitation and summarized Rome's findings. The letter mixed praise of Hunthausen's loyalty to the Church and his leadership as a bishop with some specific criticisms of his management of the Archdiocese. The Vatican concluded that among the abuses taking place in the Seattle Archdiocese at that time were: instances in which divorced persons were allowed to remarry within the Church without an annulment; a failure to assert the legitimate authoritativeness of the teaching of the magisterium; overuse of general absolution; common intercommunion at weddings and funerals; inadequate distinctions made between the roles of priests and laypersons; Church employment of laicized priests; and insufficient expression of Church teachings on homosexuality.

In December 1985, the Vatican appointed Donald Wuerl auxiliary bishop in Seattle. Though not publicly announced at the time of Wuerl's appointment, it later came to light that Rome's intention was for Hunthausen to delegate to Bishop Wuerl "special faculties," giving Wuerl final authority in five areas of responsibility. Wuerl would oversee: (1) the tribunal, (2) liturgical decisions, (3) priestly formation, (4) decisions concerning former priests, and (5) moral decisions in matters of medical ethics and the ministry to homosexuals. News of the Vatican intention for Wuerl to have special faculties became public in September of 1986, when Archbishop Hunthausen announced that he himself had only recently come to understand that he was supposed to give Wuerl final authority in these areas.

News of the special powers Wuerl was to receive led to many protests within the Archdiocese of Seattle and beyond. Priests, religious and laypersons expressed their dismay and openly questioned the rightness and legality (according to Church law) of such a transference of authority.

In answer to the public debate that arose in response to Hunthausen's disclosure of Wuerl's faculties, the papal pro-nuncio, Archbishop Laghi, issued a chronology in October of 1986, which presented the Vatican's view of the affair up to that point. Some weeks thereafter, during a closed session of the National Conference of Catholic Bishops (NCCB) November 1986 meeting, Hunthausen offered his own perspective on the events that had transpired. Having heard both sides, the NCCB found itself divided in opinion.

The controversy persisted in the aftermath of the bishops' meeting. On February 9, 1987, the pro-nuncio announced that the Vatican had appointed a three-man commission (made up of Cardinal Bernardin of Chicago, Cardinal O'Connor of New York and Archbishop Quinn of San Francisco) to resolve the matter. In May of 1987 the commission, issued its assessment report simultaneous with the Vatican-approved implementation of their recommendations. Hunthausen was restored to full power, Wuerl was reassigned to another diocese (not yet named at the time), and Bishop Thomas J. Murphy of Great Falls-Billings, Montana, was appointed Coadjutor Archbishop of Seattle. Murphy had the right of succession to Hunthausen but no special powers. The commission itself continued in existence until the April of 1989, with the purpose of helping Hunthausen to further address the problems identified through he visitation process.

CHAPTER TWO

CENTER-PERIPHERY CONFLICT IN ORGANIZATIONAL CONTEXT

2.1 In Search of Propositions to Orient the Exploration

Center-periphery conflict is by no means a blank slate. Any number of information sources stand ready to clarify various aspects of this phenomenon for us and to suggest the sorts of coping strategies we can find employed therein. My confrontation of the empirical example has been given direction by a preliminary literature study. In chapters two and three I bring the results of that study together in the articulation of a set of coping strategies I expect to find applied in cases of center-periphery conflict (summarized in sections 3.5-3.5.3). These expected findings do not amount to full-blown hypotheses that are subsequently tested. Rather, they serve as propositions to orient the exploration and set it underway. Presenting them here also allows me to be upfront about my presuppositions when addressing the empirical evidence.

Three main questions focus the discussion of the current chapter. They are

(1) What is center-periphery conflict?
(2) Who participates in center-periphery conflict?
(3) And how does the organizational culture (type of organization, organizational goals, resources available to leaders, etc.) condition the choice of coping strategies in center-periphery conflict?

In chapter three I take up the question of how societal pressures are likely to condition the choice of coping strategies in center-periphery conflict.

2.2 Center-Periphery Conflict

Leadership conflicts in the Catholic Church are one among numberless kinds of conflict experienced by human persons. Conflict itself is a fundamental theme of human existence. Human persons have always experienced conflict -- in their quest to survive and prosper in the world, in their relationships with others, and within themselves. Nisbet (1969, 86) has written that, "of all experiences in social and political life, conflict is surely one of the deepest seated and most universal." Conflict is the dynamic principle of social change. In my study of conflicts within the Catholic hierarchy, I share the presumption of Stevens et al. (1994, 15) that conflicts are common, normal and necessary, even for the Church, and that they have the potential to benefit as well as harm the Church.

Rahim (1992, 34) notes that there is no generally accepted definition of conflict (see also Aubert 1963 and Fink 1968). Pruitt and Rubin (1986, 4) define conflict as *"perceived divergence of interest, or a belief that the parties' current aspirations cannot be achieved simultaneously."* With this definition they take into account the "psychological under-pinnings" of social confrontation, as well as the concretely manifested dimensions of the conflict (resource deployments, counter-deployments). I find Pruitt and Rubin's overall perspective on conflict -- especially their emphasis on strategic choice -- and the definition they offer, to fit well with my decision to give special attention to the calculated pursuit of personal and organizational interests in center-periphery conflict handling. Attention to strategic choice has advanced the understanding of leadership conflicts in other types of organizations and I believe the same will hold true in regard to Church center-periphery conflicts. It is my intuition that bishops entertain notions of personal and organizational interest (which are sometimes compatible and sometimes incompatible) and that these interests come to be reflected in aspirations that the bishops pursue, at times harmoniously and at times conflictually, in relation to the aspirations of other Church leaders. A full discussion of Pruitt and Rubin's theory of conflict handling follows in chapter four.

In this study my concern is with a specific type of conflict: center-periphery conflict. By this I mean *conflict taking place within the Church hierarchy between the central leadership position (Rome, the papacy) and one or more peripheral leadership positions (the local churches, the other bishops).* It is manifested in a perceived divergence of interest between the Pope and other operatives of the Holy See and one or more local bishops and their representatives. Though members of the hierarchy are not the only ones involved in or affected by such conflicts, my focus here lies exclusively with how these persons approach the handling of such conflicts.

2.3 Participants in Center-Periphery Conflict

Center-periphery conflict within the hierarchy may be seen as a conflict that engages two principal parties – the center party (the Pope and his representatives) and the peripheral party (the local bishop and his representatives) – and various kinds of third parties (my focus is on the involvement of other bishops). In the sections that follow, I will describe in general terms the role that these parties play in the life of the Church organization.

2.3.1 The Center Party: The Pope and His Representatives

The Pope stands at the top of the leadership structure of the Church. He is the center of the center party and is surrounded by a large number of functionaries who help him to carry out his responsibilities. As "pastor of the universal Church" and successor to the Apostle Peter, the Pope's position and power are unrivalled in the Church. He enjoys "supreme, full, immediate and universal ordinary power in the Church, which he can freely exercise" (Canon 331, *Code of Canon Law*). At the Second Vatican Council, the Council Fathers emphasized the importance of a collegial type of governance of the Church, whereby the Pope has leadership over but also shares responsibility with all of the bishops of the Church. To a degree, the practice of collegiality has been enhanced in the post Vatican II Church (cf. Nichols 1997, 245; Granfield 1994, 9; Watkins 1991, 690-691; Seidler and Meyer 1989, 5; Gannon 1988, xi; Safranski 1985, 44; Vaillancourt 1980, 12), but one should avoid overstating the extent of this change (Nichols 1997, 247, 286; Watkins 1991, 700; Granfield 1987, 7; Hanson 1987, 62; Safranski 1985, 44).

Though the Pope guides the Church in company with the entire college of bishops, he stands as first among equals as the head of the college, with the power to appoint and depose other bishops. Canon 333 states, "There is neither appeal nor recourse against a decision or decree of the Roman Pontiff." Only the Pope has the power to call an ecumenical council which manifests the most authoritative type of new teaching that the Church can proclaim. The Pope also possesses a unique power to teach infallibly in matters of faith and morals. Besides serving as the foremost leader of the universal Church, the Pope serves as the Bishop of Rome, and the political leader of the Vatican City State. The Pope holds office for life, though he can resign his office if he so chooses.

In carrying out his duties the Pope is aided by the Vatican bureaucratic apparatus known as the Roman curia. Current usage applies the term Roman curia to those helping the Pope govern the Church, but not to those involved in governing Vatican City or the diocese of Rome. The curia consists of agencies, or "dicasteries," which gather and process information, advise the Pope and implement his decisions (Reese 1996, 106-139). Among the dicasteries are the Secretariat of State, nine congregations, eleven councils, three tribunals and other offices.

Reese (1996, 175) likens the Secretariat of State to a combination of the U.S. State Department and the White House Staff. "It coordinates the work of other Vatican offices and handles any issue that does not fall into some other offices jurisdiction."

The nine pontifical congregations and eleven councils in the present-day curia are as follows: the Congregation for the Doctrine of the Faith, the Congregation for the Oriental Churches, the Congregation for Divine Worship and the Discipline of the Sacraments, the Congregation for the Causes of Saints, the Congregation for Bishops, the Congregation for the Evangelization of Peoples, the Congregation for the Clergy, the Congregation for Institutes of Consecrated Life and for Societies of Apostolic Life, the Congregation for Catholic Education; the Council for the Laity, the Council for Promoting Christian Unity, the Council for the Family, the Council for Justice and Peace, the Council for Unum, the Council for Pastoral Care of Migrants and Travelers, the Council for Pastoral Assistance to Health Care Workers, the Council for the Interpretation of Legislative Texts, the Council for Interreligious Dialogue, the Council for Culture, the Council for Social Communications.

Reese (1996, 112) notes that the basic structure of congregations and councils is the same. Each has a defined area of competence, a committee membership appointed by the Pope for renewable five-year terms, and a chair, who is also appointed by the Pope for a renewable five-year term. Members of congregations are cardinals and bishops only, but councils may include laypersons. The chair of a congregation is known as its "prefect," while the chair of a council is its "president." Only cardinals serve as the prefect of a congregation. A council president does not need to be a cardinal, but very often cardinals fill this role. Reese observes that congregations existed before councils and in general enjoy more prestige and authority than the councils.

Three tribunals act on behalf of the Holy See. The Apostolic Penitentiary deals with excommunications reserved to the Holy See. The Roman Rota hears appeals of lower courts of the Church. The Apostolic Signatura is the supreme court of the Church.

Cardinals play an important leadership role in the Church (the college of cardinals elects a new pope in "conclave" upon the death or resignation of the previous pope), but it is necessary to note that the office of cardinal does not constitute an intervening level of authority between pope and bishop, in the sense that bishops answer to cardinals who in turn answer to the Pope (Safranski 1985, 46). Cardinals are nominated by the Pope. Though one need be only a priest and not a bishop at the time of appointment, in the Church of the present day cardinals are automatically made bishops at the time of their appointment. Cardinals normally assume high-level administrative functions on behalf of the Church, either in Rome (leading curial dicasteries, for example, or presiding over ecclesiastical commissions) or in other dioceses. It has become a papal custom to elevate bishops of large and important sees to the rank of Cardinal. At the request of the Pope, cardinals may gather in forums known as "consistories" to advise the Pope. Cardinals are required to submit their resignation to the Pope at age seventy-five. He then decides whether to accept it. Only cardinals under eighty years of age at the beginning a conclave can participate in the election of a new pope.

Apart from the offices of the Roman curia, the Holy See depends on representatives called "nuncios" to maintain relations with local governments and with local Church leaders around the world. Nuncios, who are archbishops, represent the Holy See, not the Vatican City State. They normally have the status of ambassador in the country of their posting. Reese (1996, 230) describes nuncios as "the eyes and ears of the Holy See in a country." The focus of the nuncio's diplomatic efforts is on the welfare of the local Church and on the foreign policy goals of the Holy See, which center on human rights, economic justice and peace (Reese 1996, 231). Nuncios are especially influential with the Holy See in the intermediary role they play in the selection of a new bishop to fill a vacant see. Having received candidate recommendations from bishops in the province that contains the vacant see, the nuncio investigates the diocese and the candidates and then submits a list of three nominations to either the Congregation for Bishops or the Congregation for the Evangelization of Peoples. The congregation then makes a recommendation to the Pope, who appoints the bishop (Reese 1996, 235).

2.3.2 The Peripheral Party: The Local Bishop
Local bishops represent the position of peripheral power in the Church organization, though they also share leadership responsibilities for the Church universal. Most commonly, their power base stands at a distance from the center and is in constant tension with the center (though the degree of tension varies). Some bishops may much more truly represent positions of peripheral power in the Church than others. It is possible to identify local bishops who so strongly identify with the central power in Rome that they hardly represent the peripheral position (that is, a legitimate power distant from Rome's) at all. Harder to imagine, though still conceivable, is the Pope who so downplays the power of the center in favor of local autonomy that he may no longer be considered a defender of centralized power. In any case, my attention here goes to cases that do seem to be true instances of center-periphery tension. I am interested in conflicts in which the structural tension in the Church between center and periphery is manifest in intentional (though perhaps less than transparent) advocacy.

Like the Pope, local bishops have operatives who work on their behalf and who contribute to the power of the peripheral party. Sometimes a bishop is accompanied by one or more other bishops (auxiliary bishops, a coadjutor bishop) who help with the governance of the diocese. But in general, and sharply in contrast with the pope's Roman curia, a bishop's staff is made up of clergy, religious and lay persons who, by any measure, are less powerful in the Church organization than center party operatives.

As the ordinary of a particular church, a bishop's responsibility is to the people of his own diocese, but it is also to the Church universal. All bishops are understood to be successors of the Apostles, standing in union with the Roman Pontiff (successor to the Apostle Peter in his role of leadership) to lead the Church universal. The entire body of bishops is known as the college of bishops. The college of bishops, under the leadership of the Pope, enjoys full and supreme power and authority in the Church (*Lumen Gentium*, arts. 22-23, in Abbot 1966).

Bishops are the chief teachers, priests and ministers of governance of the local Churches. The Catholic Church considers them, in their capacity as bishop, to be Vicars of Christ in their own right, and not simply vicars or agents of the Pope (*Lumen Gentium*, art. 27, in Abbot 1966). Nonetheless, the bishop's power is always exercised in company and agreement with that of the other bishops and the Pope. Canon 381.1 of the *Code of Canon Law* declares that "a diocesan bishop in the diocese committed to him possesses all the ordinary, proper and immediate power which is required for the exercise of his pastoral office except for those cases which the law or a decree of the Supreme Pontiff reserves to the supreme authority of the Church or to some other ecclesiastical authority." Thus a bishop's power, though extensive within the Church (he enjoys an especially wide latitude within his own diocese, where his powers are not separated as in civil society), has limits. This is especially true in relation to papal power, which supersedes the local ordinary's power, since the Pope serves as the chief guardian of unity. Reese (1989, 57) notes that a local bishop has, for example, no authority to rewrite liturgical texts or ceremonies, ordain women or consecrate a bishop without Vatican approval. Nor may he issue legislation contrary to laws passed by a higher authority, namely the Pope or the national bishops' conference.

Bishops may exercise their authority collectively in a variety of forums. They do so most prominently and powerfully in an *ecumenical council*, convened by the Pope, which assembles all of the world's Catholic bishops to formulate teachings and decisions binding on the whole Church. The Second Vatican Council, 1962-1965, is the most recent example of this. *Synods* are another forum in which bishops exercise their authority collectively. A synod's role, however, is advisory to the Pope and not deliberative, unless the Pope declares it otherwise (Reese 1996, 43). Bishops may also gather in national or regional *episcopal conferences* to address matters of concern and pastoral applications within that national or regional context. Bishops' conferences sometimes serve as channels of communication between local bishops and the Holy See, or between local bishops and bishops in other parts of the world (Reese 1992, 228).

As the leader of a diocese, a bishop presides over a diocesan hierarchy. (An archbishop is the ordinary of an archdiocese, which is the lead diocese in an ecclesiastical province.) A bishop (or archbishop) may be assisted by one or more auxiliary bishops (helper bishops, without right of succession) or by a coadjutor bishop (a helper bishop with right of succession) in his administration of the diocese. Normally, these assistant bishops arrive in response to a request for help which the ordinary himself has made (Canon 403, Code of Canon Law), but occasionally such bishops are imposed on a bishop despite his wishes (Reese 1989, 15). In some cases, an auxiliary or coadjutor bishop may be equipped with special faculties of governance in a diocese (Canon 403, *Code of Canon Law*). Generally speaking, a bishop fully determines who serves in the diocesan structure beneath him. Others who serve in the diocese derive their authority from him (Safranski 1985, 47).

Though structural arrangements vary somewhat from diocese to diocese, common positions within a diocesan hierarchy include: a vicar general (always a priest), who assists the bishop in the overall governance of the diocese; other episcopal vicars (always priests), who assume other leadership responsibilities assigned by the bishop; a chancellor (may be a priest, religious or layperson), who maintains the diocesan archives and performs other assigned duties; a finance council (composed of clergy, religious or laity); a presbyteral council (council of priests); a chapter of canons (all priests), responsible for liturgical functions in the cathedral and other duties; and a pastoral council (made up of priests, religious or laypersons). A number of the above-named advisory functions, especially those that include possibilities for the participation of laypersons, are the product of innovations in Church teaching that emerged at the Second Vatican Council. Lawler (1986, 26) has noted that members of the bishop's staff often play an important intermediary role in press communications, by distilling the bishop's message for public consumption.

2.3.3 Third Parties

Other bishops may become involved in center-periphery conflict as third parties – that is, parties who cannot be said to fall decisively within the orbit of the principal parties to the conflict. Third parties enjoy a significant degree of autonomy in regard to the conflict itself. They may participate of their own initiative (friendship or an interest in the issues may be a motivating factor), or they may become involved through an invitation from either the center or periphery party. Their involvement may be informal or formal, behind the scenes or in the open. Participation in an advisory capacity is the likeliest form of their participation.

Though officers of the Roman curia and papal nuncios commonly act as communications intermediaries between the Pope and local bishops, I am not inclined to treat these as true third parties. As I have already suggested, they are better understood as extensions of the center party. Auxiliary bishops and / or a coadjutor bishop assigned to assist a diocesan ordinary have a greater possibility for being considered legitimate third parties, though much depends on the circumstances of their appointment. For while auxiliaries and coadjutor bishop normally must obey the ordinary, they may also have special obligations or responsibilities to Rome which keep them from aligning themselves within the periphery party. Vatican appointees (visitors, special commissions, etc.) also fall into a gray area. They may be treated as representatives of the center party or as third parties, depending on the degree of autonomy guaranteed by the circumstances of their appointment.

National or regional bishops' conferences are likely to at least provide support and advice in cases of center-periphery conflict. Such groups do not have the legal status of an intermediary power in the Church between pope and bishop. At most, they are in a position to function in a consultative fashion.

Many other persons or groups outside of the Catholic hierarchy also play third party roles in center-periphery conflict. These include members of the clergy and Religious congregations, lay Catholics, journalists and other media commentators, advocacy groups, political officials and any number of others who may have a stake in the conflict outcomes. Since my concern here is with the conflict-handling tactics of the hierarchy, my attention will go to these other third parties only when their participation appears to have direct bearing on the hierarchy's behavior.

2.4 Organizational Role and the Choice of Coping Strategies

The choice of coping strategies in center-periphery conflict will reflect social pressures and conditioning that apply within the organizational and societal context. I have already introduced the question of the organizational context by considering key roles of leadership that members of the hierarchy bear on behalf of the Church organization. Now this picture needs to be filled in with further depictions of the Church organization, with attention going specifically to the type of organization the Church is, its goals, and the means by which members of the hierarchy coordinate and control resources to achieve those goals. In the section that follows, I consider these aspects of the Church organization and reflect on how each relates to the handling of center-periphery conflict. Once this treatment of the Church's internal functioning is complete, I then turn, in section 2.5, to analyze how elements of the encapsulating societal context are likely to influence the choice of coping strategies in center-periphery conflict.

2.4.1 The Church as Organization

Center-periphery conflict may be characterized as an leadership problem occurring in the immediate context of the organization that is the Church. To comprehend the organization as context, we need a basic grasp of the type of organization the Church is, its leadership structure, goals, resources, and means of coordination and control. In light of the size of the Catholic Church, its complexity (Reese 1996, 109; Safranski 1985, 43), its long history, and the multitude of cultures in which it exists, my organizational description will be far from complete. But I hope at least to capture some of the most prominent aspects of the Church's organizational life.

2.4.1.1 Organization Defined

Organizations, according to Morgan (1990, 5), "involve bringing together human beings and physical resources in a co-ordinated and controlled mechanism in order to achieve certain objectives, otherwise impossible." He proposes that the central issue in the study of organizations is "the tension between actors and individual subjects with their own goals and interests and the organization as a structure of control and co-ordination which is trying to guide those actors to act 'for' the organization as a system" (Morgan 1990, 7-8). McGuire (1997, 203), following Coleman (1956, 46), observes that members of religious organizations are not exempt from experiencing conflicting loyalties, or "cross pressures," which complicate their participation in the organization.

It is not difficult to conceive of the Catholic Church as an entity seeking to achieve certain objectives through coordination and control of its human and material resources (McGuire 1997, 166). Moreover, Morgan's concern with the role of individual actors within the organization would seem to be highly relevant for our study of the role that hierarchical members play in guiding the participation of other individual members who affiliate with the organization that is the Church. In this latter aspect, Morgan's approach appears compatible with Cheney's (1991, 83-84) notion that bishops engage in a process of "managing multiple identities" in their leadership of the Church. (I will return to this concept later.)

In forthcoming pages I classify the Church as a *type* of organization and then turn to consider the separate components of Morgan's definition of organization as they apply to the Church. Thus I describe the means by which the Church *coordinates and controls* human and physical *resources* for the sake of achieving certain *objectives*.

2.4.1.2 Classification of the Church as a Type of Organization

Through much of the twentieth century, discussions of organizations made heavy use of Weber's (1958) concept of bureaucracy, and observers of the Church have not been shy about applying this concept as well (Seidler and Meyer 1989, 17; Boff 1986, 1; Safranski 1985, 43). But as Scherer (1988) asserts, exclusive use of this concept is unsuitable for describing organizations that affirm values or involve strong commitments, as religious organizations do. Others have noted the more general difficulty of accounting for the organizational behavior of the Church, which is, at once, "a social phenomenon and a sacred system" (Ashbrook 1965, 397).

In answer to this problem, Scherer employs a fourfold typology to characterize the Catholic Church as an organization. Scherer's typology includes four generic complementary models of organizing, which he offers as "ideal" constructions (or, exaggerations for the purpose of theoretical clarity). "Real" organizations will contain mixtures of elements of two or more models (Scherer 1988, 477). Scherer's ideal types of organization are *political-economic market*, *bureaucracy*, *clan* and *mission*.

Scherer's typology is not the only one that can help to clarify the Church's functioning as an organization. Thung (1976) observes that an organization's relationship with the environment can be the basis for an organizational typology (cf. Parsons 1965, and a subsequent applications along this line in Van der Ven 1996, which draws on Parsons' work and Mintzberg 1979). Another basis for an organizational typology that Thung points to is the means of compliance employed within the organization (cf. Etzioni 1961). Dulles (1974), working within the theological discipline of ecclesiology, has also provided a set of "models" -- *hierarchy*, *herald*, *sacrament*, *mystical communion*, *dialogue*, and the more recently added *community of disciples* (Dulles 1982,7-9) -- which reveals various "ways of being Church." All of these approaches make unique contributions to our understanding of the Church's organizational life.

My choice to use Scherer's typology has to do with its concreteness (over and against the Parsons and Etzioni typologies) and its applicability to a wide range of organizational structures (as opposed to Dulles' scheme, which is not empirically but ideologically interpreted). I find that Scherer's four types readily call to mind familiar organizational examples in a way that Parsons' (adaptation, goal achievement, integration, latency) and Etzioni's (utilitarian, coercive, normative) more abstract typologies do not. (Scherer argues for mid-range theories, which are "general but not too general" -- p. 478.) Examples of a market, a bureaucracy, a clan and a mission come easily to mind, an advantage when making comparisons. By virtue of their concrete associations, we also keep in touch with the fact that an organization is a complex social entity that still must function in the real world.

A description of each of Scherer's four ideal types follows.

A **political-economic market** type of organization has a flat, coalitional structural shape. Its authority source is buyer-seller competition and votes by participants. It is characterized by a high permeability to environment and is in fact dominated by this permeability. Its control strategy involves withdrawal and renegotiation and popular or market demand. It embraces a rationality that is technical, short-term in its focus, and influenced by collective behavior. Its operational hallmarks are rapid turnover, wheeling dealing and contractualism. Scherer identifies stock exchanges and federations as among its illustrative organizations.

A **bureaucratic** type of organization has a tall, interlinked hierarchical structural shape. Its authority source is procedural authorization. Its level of permeability to environment is moderate to low. Its control strategy is one of surveillance via hierarchy and rules. It is marked by a rationality that is technical and long-term in its orientation. The operational hallmarks of a bureaucracy are rule-procedure books, litigation and boundary maintenance. As illustrative organizations, Sherer offers the general category of federal bureaus, with the specific example of the (US) Internal Revenue Service.

A **clan** type of organization has a generational and territorial structural shape. Its authority source is seniority, group consensus and family-like trust. Its permeability to environment is frequently low. Clan-type organizations adopt control strategies of socialization and informal sanctions. A rationality based on traditionalism and feeling more important is operative. Operational hallmarks include ceremony and rituals, low turnover and stigma at exit. Among the illustrative organizations Scherer cites are political machines and mafia. Another example could be the political power exercised by extended families such as the Kennedys.

A **mission** type of organization has the structural shape of a charismatic retinue. Its authority source is ideology, charisma and a transcendent call. A control strategy of group esprit and intrinsic values is operative. Its type of rationality is substantive. The operational hallmarks of a mission-type organization include an overriding commitment to particular goals and commitments of awesome sacrifice. Illustrative organizations include religious orders and strategic force operations such as the CIA.

Scherer emphasizes that organizations are not static or fixed entities but instead exist as constant, ongoing processes, and again, no one type accounts perfectly for any actual organization. The four models give us perspective on how organizations "come to terms with the 'functional imperatives' of organized life: openness to environment (market), efficiency and control (bureaucracy), member loyalty (clan), and height of purpose (mission)" (Scherer 1988, 483). In Scherer's (1988, 492-494) view, the Church is "a bureaucratized mission-clan - - or even lots of mini-ethnic subclans (and low in technical rationality), but now deemphasizing bureaucratic control in favor of openness to the market."

As evidence of its bureaucratic character, Scherer cites the Catholic Church's hierarchical leadership, its system of canon law and ecclesiastical courts, its high system awareness and attention to boundary maintenance (see also Safranski 1985 and McDonough 1997). Clanlike features include ethnic connections to the Church and transgenerational membership retention. Mission qualities appear in the Church's "unapologetic particularism" (its habit of speaking of itself as "the" Church), its rising emphasis on social action and ecumenism, and its religious orders, which serve as "task forces for mission." Finally, market characteristics of the Church (i.e., emphases on rational, free exchanges between autonomous entities; cf. Young 1997, Moore 1994, Finke and Stark 1992), while traditionally less recognized as hallmarks of the Church (Seidler and Meyer 1989, 8), are showing an increased presence, or at least acknowledgement, in competitive, voluntaristic contexts (Bevvino 1995, Scherer 1988, 489-490; see also Gannon 1988, xi).

Scherer's contribution lies more with the provision of the classifying types than with his description of the Church according to type. In my opinion he does right to introduce the clan type (in addition to the more commonly applied three other types) into discussions of how to characterize the Church as organization, for this type helps to clarify the highly personal kinds of attachment (inclusion) and alienation (exclusion) that people feel toward the Church. All four types, taken together, help us to see how the Church is multifaceted and in some sense contradictory in its impulses. This depiction of the Church in reference to four organizational models allows us to see that the Catholic Church is both inwardly and outwardly directed. It is inwardly directed in its desire to guide members' behavior and strengthen their ties to the Church (objectives well suited to the bureaucratic and clan models). It is outwardly directed in its attention to its environment (market model) and its concentration on a purpose that goes beyond the survival of the organization itself (mission model). While one should not equate these objectives exclusively with the models I equate them with here, they are nonetheless useful lenses through which we can glimpse the big picture of the Church as an organization.

Less helpful is Scherer's statement that the Church is "deemphasizing bureaucratic control in favor of openness to the market." While it does appear that the Church of the modern world is conscious of a need to compete for "customers" in a social marketplace of beliefs, one wonders where Scherer sees evidence of bureaucratic control being deemphasized (he does not elaborate). I would be more inclined to argue the opposite: that bureaucratic control is being reemphasized to enhance the Church's position in the marketplace. But that is a topic for another study. For our purposes here, it is enough to say that each type reveals distinctive aspects of the Church's functioning, and that different types of functioning will be applied more prominently at different times and in different places and cultures. Thus, I am content here to describe the Church as a bureaucracy-clan-market-mission organization (the types are alphabetized) whose dominant operational mode varies. Seen as a whole, the Church operates as a unique and changeable mix of these types, and organizational tensions may well arise as a result of mutual incompatibilities between the various modalities.

To take it a step further, this typology of the Church organization is relevant to our exploration of center-periphery conflict in two ways. First, it provides insight into realities that are given for members of the hierarchy (given in the sense of being realities already in place when those members arrive on the scene). That is, the Church *is* a certain way: it has elements of and functions as a bureaucracy, a clan, a market and a mission. Second, the typology provides a set of operational modalities which can be drawn upon for the sake of advantage. By operating according to one modality versus another, Church leaders help to determine what can be accomplished, and in what fashion, by the Church organization. In cases of center-periphery conflict, participant parties may have good reason to choose one operational modality over another as they pursue interests on behalf of themselves and the organization.

In the first table below I summarize some of the likely consequences from organizational operations according to each type. Though I characterize these consequences as advantages or disadvantages for the Church organization, I realize that this determination can only be made in a final sense in light of what one's objectives are. In the second table, I offer a glimpse of how certain modes of operation may stand in tension with one another.

Consequences of Functioning According to Organizational Type:
Advantages (+) and Disadvantages (-)

Bureaucracy	+ Adds rationality, efficiency, fairness, predictability
	- Functions impersonally and indirectly; bureaucracy can become end in itself
Clan	+ Fosters strong personal ties within Church, unity, continuity
	- Undervalues contributions of outsiders; exit cost is high; creates suffocating climate
Market	+ Church reads environment well; competes well; adapts well
	- May lose sight of identity, mission by catering to "consumers"
Mission	+ Focuses and motivates Church membership to pursuit of goals
	- Exacts high cost of participation; organizational zeal is hard to sustain

TABLE 2.1

Potential Incompatibilities Between Operational Modalities

Bureaucracy versus Clan	The rational, impersonal orientation of bureaucracy clashes with the clan's preference to make decisions of the basis of personal ties
Bureaucracy versus Market	The complex, multi-layered, slow-changing structure of bureaucracy proves a hindrance to market adaptability and response to potential members or clients
Bureaucracy versus Mission	Bureaucracy's emphasis on rationality, consistency and fairness in the carrying out of procedures stands in tension with the (ultimate) goal orientation of those who operate out of a mission perspective
Clan versus Market	The clan's tendency to draw sharp distinctions between those inside and outside the "family" interferes with market-directed plans that give priority to the perspectives (wishes, fears) of potential members / clients
Clan versus Mission	The clan's tendency to protect the "family" above all else challenges a mission orientation that may posit another organizational goal as higher
Market versus Mission	A tendency to cater to the dictates of the marketplace challenges the Church's ability to pursue its mission with integrity

TABLE 2.2

Being acquainted with these operational modalities (according to organizational type) can possibly help us to better understand the dynamics of center-periphery conflict.

To the extent that the Church functions as a **bureaucracy** it both empowers and constrains the hierarchy, but we should notice that the forms of empowerment and constraint differ according to office. In many respects the Pope stands above the Church bureaucracy. Not only does the Pope possess the highest powers to teach, judge and govern the Church, he also enjoys the freedom to exercise these powers independently even of the other bishops. (An example is his power to teach infallibly in matters of faith and morals.) The Pope does not "answer" to bureaucratic structures in the same way that other bishops and lower-power parties in the Church do. He can bypass layers of the bureaucracy to resolve individual problems directly (bypassing a bishop, for example, to rein in a troublesome priest). This is not to say that the Pope is not constrained by the bureaucratic machinery of the Church. Clearly, he is dependent on the bureaucracy to carry out his wishes, and there may be any number of problems that arise between his decrees and the pastoral implementation thereof. But he is not constrained to the extent that a local bishop is, who may find himself frustrated as he awaits a curial or papal decision to resolve some matter that transcends his authority. (An example is the bishop who must wait patiently for an answer to his request for an auxiliary bishop, or who receives an unwanted answer.)

We should keep in mind, however, that the bureaucratic machinery of the Church is an asset to Pope and other bishops alike, serving as a preferred means whereby Church resources may be organized toward the achievement of Church goals. Contrary to popular stereotypes, bureaucracies can contribute to organizational effectiveness as well as inhibit it. Well-trained functionaries, central offices and codified procedures all may serve to enhance efficiency and productivity. The Pope and other bishops oversee layers of bureaucracy which serve to extend their personal power.

In cases of conflict involving the Holy See and a local see, we will want to pay attention to how the bureaucratic power of the Roman curia plays a role, for this layer of bureaucracy serves as a complex and ambiguous intervening power between Pope and bishop. Although the curia does not (on the surface, at least) operate independently of the wishes of the Pope, the relationship between the will of the Pope and the actions of the curia is never clear. As an example, curial congregations regularly release teaching documents that are not the work (the writing) of the Pope himself. While such writings emerge with the Pope's approval, it is hard to know what parts of that particular teaching are most important to him and in what matters he would or would not readily invest his authority and "political capital." Another example is provided by occasions when the Congregation for the Doctrine of the Faith questions the writings of a particular theologian. When does this initiative come originally from the Pope and when is it the product of the Congregation? The secrecy which commonly attends curial functioning prevents our knowing. Because of this secrecy, the Pope has the option of distancing himself from curial operations when it is advantageous to do so. He can choose to remain "above the fray" and not directly involve himself in a matter wherein the curia is taking what appears to be heavy-handed action. In cases of center-periphery conflict, we can expect that the bureaucratic power contained in the Roman curia will provide the Holy See with significant advantages over the local see. But curial interventions can have a down-side as well. In popular consciousness, the curia is often perceived negatively because of its controlling power and lack of transparency. In democratic-minded contexts, a local bishop can draw on this perception as a way of shoring up support for his own position.

Besides looking at the involvement of the curia, we should also be prepared to examine the role played by other bureaucratic resources in cases of intrahierarchical conflict. A local bishop oversees his own diocesan curia, which provides him with logistical and communications support. In cases of conflict that involve the local and universal Church, we can expect that other layers of the Church bureaucracy will also be a factor: presumably, the papal nuncio to the local country and the national or regional conference of bishops will participate in the dialogue.

The challenge for the Church when the Church functions primarily as a bureaucracy is that bureaucracies have the tendency to get stuck in routine ways of handling problems. This is acceptable when the problems and their solutions are standard, but less felicitous when creative solutions are needed to unfamiliar problems. Cases of intrahierarchical conflict may present the Church with the difficulty of discerning where and when the bureaucratic machinery is serving the ultimate ends of the Church, and where and when that machinery needs refinement.

Inasmuch as the Church is a **clan**, it makes use of family-like bonds and places a premium on seniority, consensus, loyalty and trust. It can be encouraging for a bishop or Pope to be able to count on these strong relational supports. Families "look out for their own," and this can be reassuring in the face of outside threats. It is not unusual to hear talk of the "fraternity" of bishops and to hear the phrase "brother bishops" in reference to intrahierarchical relations. In conflict situations, this notion of familial connection can help to prevent conflicts from escalating unnecessarily. At the same time, it is clear that conflicts within families can be among the hardest to resolve because of the intimacy and trust which are placed at risk, and because of the significance of the relationship as a whole. Sometimes real problems within families are not addressed out of a desire to protect the family or out of a fear of losing the relationship altogether. Such ties can be constricting or even suffocating. Members of the hierarchy are not immune to such pressures as they face one another in conflict.

When members of the hierarchy operate upon the assumption that Church is a social entity in competition with other social entities in a pluralistic environment, as in the **market** model, they come up against fundamental choices that must be made. One such choice concerns how costly participation should be for Church members. Making the costs of Church affiliation (in the form of time, talent and money) high has a tendency to produce fewer but highly-committed Church members. Making the costs low has a tendency to bring in larger numbers of less-committed members.

Such decisions relate directly to the hierarchical member's ecclesiological viewpoint, and specifically to his view of the extraecclesial world. For those who see the Church as possessing a monopoly on the truth over and above the unchurched world, competition is directed toward the goal of dominating the market at the expense of unworthy competitors. Compromise with "worldly" ways is untenable and acceptable only as an unavoidable fact of life. Their attitude toward the Catholic flock will be to "set the bar" of belonging to the Church high, knowing that this may cost the Church some members in the short-run, but believing this to be the only way for the Church to prevail in the long-run. For those who see the Church as holding a privileged but not exclusive possession of the truth, competition will mean seeking advantage for the Church's position while being open to learning from competing traditions. Church leaders adhering to this view will not see active interchange with other belief systems as a danger, but as an opportunity for the Church. Their attitude toward the flock will be to make room for their freedom and worldly experience, believing that God is speaking through these encounters as well as through ecclesiastical structures.

Differences of opinion about how the Church should proceed within the competitive environment that contains it can be a source of intrahierarchical conflict or an aggravating factor therein. While the portraits of diverging viewpoints I have just drawn are exaggerations -- at the Second Vatican Council, most bishops showed at least some degree of openness to the world and none overtly held the position that Church is just one tradition among many -- differences of emphasis in ecclesiological perspective do affect how members of the hierarchy relate to one another and to those Catholics under their leadership. These difference can influence the course a conflict takes, but even more importantly relate to the Church's organizational continuity and its adaptability to its social environment.

Scherer locates the keys to **mission** activity in a shared ideology, the power of charisma, and the recognition of a transcendent call. The Church as mission finds its origin and empowerment in the charismatic figure of Jesus, his proclamation of the kingdom of God, and his call to his followers to bring all people to God. The Church leadership understands its own role (at least in an official way) as one in which this divine call is answered by shared efforts to proclaim and build this same kingdom of God through the personal commitments and witness of all believers. The charismatic dimension of this activity did not leave the earth permanently with Jesus but has been passed on in the Holy Spirit, who empowers the work of the Church in the world (cf. Suenens 1975, 21-32). For Church leaders in conflict, we can presume that they will feel encouraged to the extent that they place confidence in this spiritual empowerment. Church teaching holds that all things are possible with God. Embracing this belief can enable Church leaders to address all sorts of problems with courage and hope. But awareness of God's empowerment can also cloud the judgment of Church leaders. Hubris is but one danger that comes with the determination that one is an agent of God. Without humble and clear-sighted discernment, members of the hierarchy may not be able to discern when their own ego is at the fore rather than the will of God. Moreover, the transcendent orientation of the Church may invite a neglect of more mundane matters that need attention, including the earthly problem-solving steps that need to be taken in a conflict. The perspective of eternity may cause Church leaders to rule out possibilities of compromise unnecessarily, and to dominate conflict situations at the expense of the other party.

To sum up the main points of this section: Center-periphery conflict is a problem of organizational leadership taking place in a particular kind of organization: therefore, we need to have some sense of what sort of organization we are talking about. Scherer's typology helps us to see the Church's functioning more clearly through descriptions of the Church as a bureaucracy, a clan, a political-economic market and a mission. At various times the Church will act more according to one type or another, but all will continue to apply. Each organizational type comes with its own type of conflict and conflict handling. Within a bureaucratic mindset, conflicts will be seen as bureaucratic problems lending themselves to bureaucratic solutions; within a clannish mindset, the implications for the "family" will be assessed, and a solution will be sought within the family; and so forth. Seeing the Church in light of these organizational dimensions helps us grasp particular ways that members of the hierarchy may be empowered and constrained as they manage intrahierarchical conflicts. It also helps us to locate certain sources of center-periphery conflict, which may be rooted in internal clashes of organizational culture.

2.4.2 Organizational Goals of the Catholic Church

Organizations do not exist whenever people assemble. Rather, organizations come into being when people join together to achieve goals they could not achieve individually (Demerath and Hammond 1969, 173). Typically, an organization has an identifiable reason for existing and this reason is associated with the accomplishment of particular goals that the organization has set for itself. Granfield (1987, 58) writes that "the most important element in every institution is the directing idea of the work to be realized." When speaking of an organization's goals, we can distinguish between ends and means. (A desired end is, of course, a goal, but a means can be a (short-term) goal as well.) For a car manufacturer, for example, the end may be profits and the means may be organizational efficiency. Ideally, an organization would enjoy agreement about what its ends are and what means are needed to secure those ends. But no actual organization enjoys full agreement about ends and means all the time – and identifying the alternations of means and ends can be highly confusing. In the case of the Church, goal setting and goal achievement are problematic, and both may be sources of conflict within the Church.

The first difficulty is that the Church's ultimate goals are not self-evident. While one can formulate the ultimate goals of the Church in ways that will claim widespread agreement (I will provide an example in the pages that follow), one cannot avoid the fact that these goals can be formulated in more ways than one, and may be reformulated over time. (Indeed, at the Second Vatican Council one finds a normative impulse toward reformulation in the concept of *ecclesia semper reformanda*.) There is no brief "mission statement" or standardized set of "core values" that the Church proclaims, in the fashion of modern corporations. In their place stands a collection of Sacred Scriptures and a two-thousand year tradition of Church teaching, with neither source of authority lending itself to simple summary. Cheney (1991, 35) acknowledges this complexity when he observes that the Church is neither monolithic nor unchanging (see also Nichols 1982). Moreover, the Church may be described as an "omni-purpose" organization that is concerned with the whole of life (Thung 1976, 123; but see also Vallier 1969, 149). Thus, while one may speak of the ultimate goal of the Church being *to unite all people with God*, or *to bring salvation to all*, or *to fully participate in the establishment of God's kingdom on earth* -- to name just three possibilities -- it is not clear whether these are distinct goals, overlapping goals or simply one and the same goal expressed in three different ways. Nor is it obvious whether one formulation should be preferred over another. In short, disagreement may arise within the Church about what the Church's ultimate purposes are and / or about how best to express those purposes.

The challenge for the Church is to find good, acceptable procedures to (re)express and (re)formulate its goals in new contexts. This poses problems for the Church because not only is it difficult to assess the linkage between immediate or short-term means and ultimate goals, it is also hard, if not impossible, to know how worldly actions relate to spiritual purposes. In other word's, if the Church's goal is to unite all people to God, how can we know what concrete actions to take toward that goal, and how can we know if our spiritual and material efforts harmoniously contribute to reaching the goal (Demerath and Hammond 1969, 174)? And what is one to do about valid but conflicting goals? Thung (1976, 114-124) treats these problems in her extended study of Church operations. Following March and Simon (1966), she distinguishes between *operational* and *non-operational* goals that the Church may choose to pursue. Operational goals lend themselves to rational decisions about whether and to what extent they are served by a particular course of action. They are short-term, concrete, and susceptible to realization through calculative action. Non-operational goals, on the contrary, are abstract and offer an orientation for the long-term, but the means to their achievement is not made clear by rational calculation.

Because agreement about non-operational and operational goals is not automatic within the Church, we can expect that this will be a source of conflict within the Church (and not, as one might hope, a stable frame of reference for resolving conflicts!), especially within the hierarchy, which bears a unique responsibility to lead the Church and make decisions on its behalf. Presumably, members of the hierarchy will express a high level of agreement about the Church's non-operational goals. This is because the abstractness of non-operational goals allows divergent interpretations to attach themselves to the same terms, while preserving the appearance of unity. Hence, members of the hierarchy, who have a clear stake in appearing unified, may agree about the (non-operational) goal of demonstrating God's love on the earth, but quietly disagree about what they mean by that concept more concretely. (When does love mean tolerance and when does it mean correcting others?) At this level in our analysis of center-periphery conflict discourse, we will want to pay attention to how non-operational goals are articulated. Whereas we can expect agreement about the abstract, ultimate goals of the Church, we may nonetheless find clues about what those goals imply for the daily life of the Church by looking at the particular terms or images the conflict participants employ. Does, for example, the bishop or Pope prefer to talk about unity or salvation? If one or more terms are settled upon by conflict participants (to describe the Church's ultimate ends), do they attach divergent associations (connotations or images) to those terms in their exchanges? And by extension, do these associations clearly suggest operational goals that should be pursued to the sake of the ultimate organizational purposes?

Within intrahierarchical conflict discourse, we can expect to find more outright disagreement about means than about (ultimate) ends. Though bishops and the Pope may want to keep both sorts of disagreement under wraps, it is safer to disagree about the route to the destination than about the destination itself. Such disagreements are more palatable because they concern more optional or disposable *means* rather than ultimate matters of organizational identity and purpose. (An intriguing problem, one I will not pursue here, concerns the perspective that sees the journey itself – i.e., the successive choice of means – as the end.) We can expect, therefore, that in cases of intrahierarchical conflict, there will be more open disagreement about operational goals than about non-operational goals. At the same time, it will be interesting to discern how operational and non-operational goals are identified in the exchanges and how they appear to relate one to another in the minds of the conflict participants.

2.4.2.1 The Church's Ultimate Goal: Uniting All People to God

Having said that (1) the Church, like other organizations, employs various means to achieve certain designated ends; and that (2) the relationship between means and ends is both subtle and complex; and that (3) discernments about appropriate means and ends can invite conflict, I now propose to provide a general overview to help us to see more clearly what is at stake in cases of center-periphery conflict and how the pursuit of goals relates to conflict behaviors. After consulting a key work of Church teaching, I offer one possible way of expressing the Church's goals that I believe sums up much of what the Church is about. This expression of the Church's ultimate purposes contributes to our comprehension of the Church's direction and world view.

Though the Church's goals do not easily reduce to a self-sufficient, simple formula, it is possible to identify key organizational goals of the Church by consulting multiple, classic pronouncements the Church itself has offered. But how is one to select from among the two millennia of Catholic teachings to identify the Church's core issues of purpose? Fortunately, the Church itself has already confronted this problem in significant ways. Repeatedly through its history, the Church has seen a need to reflect on and give new voice to its teaching and its place in a changing world. In the twentieth century, one can find examples of such ongoing reflection in papal encyclicals, the documents of pontifical congregations and councils, the 1983 revision of the *Code of Canon Law*, the 1992 issuance of the *Catechism of the Catholic Church*, and most prominently and authoritatively, in the documents of the Second Vatican Council, 1962-65. Like the First Vatican Council of the previous century, 1869-70, and in the tradition of the ecumenical councils of the early Church, Vatican II brought the college of bishops together, under the headship of the pope to make decisions about Church doctrine and practice binding on the whole Church. Dulles (1988, 135) states that the Second Vatican Council "provides the most complete discussion of the finality of the church that can be found anywhere in the official utterances of Roman Catholicism." In our effort to perceive the Church's organizational goals in the modern world, the teachings of Vatican II are a likely source of illumination.

To be fair, even the Vatican II documents do not lend themselves to simple summaries of what the Church is about. Nonetheless, two conciliar documents in particular offer insight into the Church's understanding of its own internal organization and engagement with the world. They are, respectively, *Lumen Gentium* (or, Dogmatic Constitution on the Church) and *Gaudium et Spes* (or, Pastoral Constitution on the Church in the Modern World). In a forthcoming section I will consult *Gaudium et Spes* for insight into the Church's perceptions of its place in the modern social context, but for now my attention goes to *Lumen Gentium*, which lends valuable perspective on the Church's organizational goals.

While other documents of the Council focus on particular aspects of the life of the Church, or with particular activities, or with the relation of the Church to outside groups, only *Lumen Gentium* takes the whole Church as its principal focus (Dulles 1966, 10). Promulgated in 1964, *Lumen Gentium* has the status of a Dogmatic Constitution, the most solemn form of conciliar teaching. Given its subject matter, its authority as an official teaching of the Pope and bishops in unison, and its impact on the life of the contemporary Church, I believe that *Lumen Gentium* provides a worthy resource for illuminating the central goals that the Church proposes to pursue.

Admittedly, other sources (some of which I have named above) could be used to conceptualize the Church's organizational goals. But I find several advantages in choosing *Lumen Gentium* as my primary resource for this task. First, it reflects the direct input (and agreement) of the entire hierarchy, as opposed to a segment of the hierarchy, as is the case in papal encyclicals, curial documents, the 1983 *Code of Canon Law* and the 1992 *Catechism of the Catholic Church*. (Dulles 1966, 11 notes that it was approved by 2,151 bishops in Council, with only 5 opposing, and was immediately promulgated by Pope Paul VI.) Second, it represents the *most recent* reflections of the entire hierarchy gathered in Council: thus it has the advantage over earlier ecumenical councils of being able to take the insights of those previous councils into account. Third, for my own immediate purposes, documents that post-date the Hunthausen affair (1983-89), such as the 1992 *Catechism*, cannot be said to have informed the handling of that case. Thus, while they may serve to shed light in other ways, they are less useful for my purposes than other sources.

Dulles (1966, 11) introduces *Lumen Gentium* by observing that the document "sets forth, with conciliar authority, the Church's present understanding of her own nature." Furthermore, it describes the Church's orientation "toward a goal beyond history" -- a goal focused on a future time when "God will be all in all." But let us turn now to the document itself. (I will be consulting the Abbott 1966 English translation. Citations of the document will be indicated by the abbreviation LG followed by the article number.)

That *Lumen Gentium* directly addresses the Church's aspirations becomes clear at the outset of the document. Article one declares the intention of the Council "to set forth... the nature and encompassing mission of the Church." Article two tells us that "at the end of time she will achieve her glorious fulfillment."

We are not left to wonder of what that mission consists. Article one states:

> By her relationship with Christ, the Church is a kind of sacrament of intimate union with God, and of the unity of all mankind, that is, she is a sign and an instrument of such union and unity.

This mission follows from the plan of God himself, who created the world with the intention of dignifying humankind "with a participation in his own divine life" (LG 2). These professions deserve elaboration, in the light of our focus on the Church as a unique kind of organization. My first observation is that the Church here is described as a "sign" and an "instrument," which is to say, the Church is not an end in itself. It points to and seeks to bring about something beyond itself. Secondly, the end that is served by the Church is a twofold unity wherein "all mankind" is united intimately with God. Finally, the work of the Church is divinely sponsored. The Church is a "sacrament" by virtue of its relationship with Christ. Hence, the organizational instrumentality is understood in specifically religious terms. (In the theology of the Church, a sacrament "effects what it symbolizes." In this case it signifies and effects union with God.)

In a further passage, *Lumen Gentium* presents the mission of the Church in the language of trinitarian theology.

> When Jesus rose up again after suffering death on the cross for mankind, He

manifested that He had been appointed Lord, Messiah, and Priest forever (cf. Acts 2:36; Heb. 5:6; 7:17-21), and He poured out on His disciples the Spirit promised by the Father (cf. Acts 2:33). The Church, consequently, equipped with the gifts of her Founder and faithfully guarding his precepts of charity, humility, and self-sacrifice, receives the mission to proclaim and to establish among all peoples the kingdom of Christ and of God. She becomes on earth the initial budding forth of that kingdom. While she slowly grows, the Church strains toward the consummation of the kingdom and, with all her strength, hopes and desires to be united in glory with her King. (LG 5, in Abbott 1966, 18.)

Here the Council fathers assert once again that union with God is the ultimate aim of the Church. In this case, that goal is envisioned according to the metaphor of the building up of the kingdom of Christ and of God. The Church, empowered by Christ and the Holy Spirit, becomes the initial budding forth of God's kingdom. At the consummation of the kingdom, all of the faithful will be unified among themselves and with God, in accordance with the Father's plan. At that time, the Church will shine forth as "a people made one with the unity of the Father, the Son, and the Holy Spirit" (LG 5).

The image of the "People of God" (LG 9-17), which is central and highly developed in *Lumen Gentium*, further expresses the Church's concern to unite the human family with God.

It has pleased God, however, to make men holy and save them not merely as individuals without any mutual bonds, but by making them into a single people, a people which acknowledges Him in truth and serves Him in holiness. (LG 9)

The People of God is not meant to be composed of a select few. Rather, "All men are called to belong to the new People of God" (LG 13).

In the light of these declarations, **I propose that we see the overarching goal of the Church organization as a matter of joining all people to God**. Clearly, there are other ways that one can, drawing on *Lumen Gentium*, formulate the Church's ultimate goal. Some may, for example, favor the expression "salvation" (as in, "the Church is called to follow the same path [of Christ] in communicating to men the fruits of salvation" -- LG 8) over my preferred "unity." These and others offer viable alternatives for illuminating the Church's organizational activity. I would argue, however, that in many cases the variance in terms has more to do with angles of viewing than with actual differences in the phenomena viewed. In other words, I believe "saving souls" and "uniting souls to God" amount to much the same thing.

My reason for favoring the unity expression over the alternative is that it has certain advantages for the present study of intrahierarchical conflict. Specifically, I find three advantages. First, I believe the unity formulation is a legitimate expression of Church teaching and of a widely-held view within the Church. It provides a credible point of orientation from which we can make sense of the Church organization. Second, the unity formulation sharpens our perception of the organizational roles, generally, of the hierarchy itself. Bishops and the Pope, as we shall see in the forthcoming discussion of their offices, have express responsibilities to symbolize and establish a unity within the Church that is ultimately directed toward the achievement of human unity with God. Third, the concept of unity is centrally and inescapably relevant to center-periphery conflict. At the heart of center-periphery conflict is the quality of the relationship that exists -- unified or not? -- between the Pope and local bishop and between the Church of Rome and the local Church. Hanging in the air of the conflict is the question of whether, and in what sense, any and all parties are united with God.

Because of its abstractness and quality of ultimacy, the goal of uniting all people (among themselves and) with God can be understood to be a non-operational goal of the Church. It is my view that all of the organizational activity of the Church relates to this ultimate goal (though, at times, only in a superficial way), because this is the Church's reason to be. As such, we can expect that Church leaders will make decisions on behalf of the Church which implicitly and explicitly acknowledge this goal. We can expect, too, that the *language* used by Church leaders will acknowledge this goal. In the more specific matter of center-periphery conflict, we may presume that the Church's goal to join all people to God will always be in the background and will often be in the foreground of such conflicts. Even in a case of conflict that appears to involve only personal issues, bishops and the Pope, by virtue of the unity their offices symbolize and promote, will have bearing on the Church's ability to achieve its professed goals.

How one understands this non-operational goal of unity will inevitably be a source of conflict within the hierarchy. This is so because unity is open to various interpretations: Is it a matter of establishing *uniformity* within the beliefs and practices of the faithful (which are taken to be outward proofs of oneness), or does unity allow for a bounded form of diversity. In other words, how much conformity within the community is required for unity to be present? Individual bishops are likely to differ among themselves in their answer to this question. Another, related problem is the difficulty of knowing when the unity achieved is truly a unity with God.

Having introduced the question of the Church organization's ultimate goal(s), let us now turn to the matter of operational goals for the sake of that end.

2.4.2.2 Operational Goals for the Sake of the Ultimate Goal: Steps Toward Humankind's Union with God

It is impossible to account for all of the objectives that the Church pursues in keeping with its chief aspiration of uniting humanity with God. More feasible is to point out some of the main strategies it embraces. As in my analysis of the long-term goal of the Church, I turn to *Lumen Gentium* for clarification on this matter.

Some conclusions about these strategies can be drawn on the basis of passages already cited. We have seen, in a passage quoted from article one, that the Church is to be a "sign" (as well as an "instrument") of union and unity with God. I take this to mean that the Church must not only point the way toward union with God but must also in some sense symbolize or reveal such a union in the here and now. A further passage makes this explicit.

> God has gathered together as one all those who in faith look upon Jesus as the author of salvation and the source of unity and peace, and has established them as the Church, that for each and all she may be the visible sacrament of this saving unity. (LG 10)

The Church, therefore, has the God-given charge of demonstrating and promoting a unity that is meant for all in its earthly practice. Thus, a first operational goal we can assume the Church will pursue is simply to get as many people as possible to affiliate themselves with the Church and to interrelate in satisfying and harmonious ways within the Church. This is, of course, an operational goal that is still fairly high on the ladder of abstraction (What does it mean to "affiliate" with the Church? What does "unity" look like?), but it does put us in touch with well-known organizational practices, such as making the organization visible and attractive (marketing), inviting new members (recruiting), finding ways to enhance commitment and participation once members are in the door (promoting loyalty), and handling dissensus (conflict management). Though God and not the Church is ultimately the source of saving unity with God, the Church understands itself to be the supremely privileged, though not the only, vehicle directed to that end. As such, it believes that **growing the Church and managing it well will be positive short-term steps toward the ultimate goal** of bringing all persons to intimate union with God. Doing so rationally presents no contradiction to the Church's mission or beliefs.

Structurally, the implication for the Church is that all local Churches within the Church should contribute to the unicity of the Church. *Lumen Gentium* (14) states that within the universal Church, the particular Churches (local Churches) "hold a rightful place. These Churches retain their own traditions without in any way lessening the primacy of the Chair of Peter. This **Chair presides over the whole assembly of charity and protects legitimate differences, while at the same time it sees that such differences do not hinder unity but rather contribute toward it.**" In this vision of participation, unity does not of necessity equal uniformity.

> In virtue of this catholicity each individual part of the Church contributes through its special gifts to the good of the other parts and of the whole Church. Thus through the common sharing of gifts and through the common effort to attain fullness in unity, the whole and each of the parts receive increase. Not only, then, is the People of God made up of different peoples but even in its inner structure it is composed of various ranks. This diversity among its members arises either by reason of their duties... or by reason of their situation and way of life... (LG 13)

Thus, while trying to bring all people into union and unity with God, the Church, officially at least, recognizes, values and needs the diversity of its membership. Organizational energy, according to *Lumen Gentium*, is to be spent not on fitting all of these different people into the same mold, but rather on establishing a harmonious whole that benefits both the individual and the Church entire. The operational challenge for the Church is to find ways of incorporating diversity on a global scale (consisting of the variety of ways that Catholicism is understood and practiced in all of the world's regions) into something that can genuinely be called a unity.

Two further operational goals related to the building up and unification of the Church are expressed in the charges to preach the gospel and celebrate the sacraments. *Lumen Gentium* 17 tells us that the Church has received from the apostles "as a task to be discharged even to the ends of the earth" a mandate to "proclaim the saving truth."

> Hence she makes the words of the Apostle her own: "Woe to me, if I do not preach the gospel" (1 Cor. 9:16)... By the proclamation of the gospel, she prepares her hearers to receive and profess the faith, disposes them for baptism, snatches them from the slavery of error, and incorporates them into Christ so that through charity they may grow up

into full maturity in Christ." (LG 17)

In concrete terms, effectively preaching the gospel involves reading and understanding the wisdom of the Scriptures and proclaiming the riches found there in a way that can be appreciated by modern hearers. The sacramental system of the Church (not just the sacraments themselves, but the whole structure of meaning that contains them) is the apparatus whereby participation in the Church is most clearly realized. The seven sacraments of the Church (baptism, confirmation, Eucharist, reconciliation, anointing of the sick, holy orders, matrimony) are practices wherein, in the eyes of the Church, God's presence is manifested and the bonds between human persons and God are strengthened. Article eleven of *Lumen Gentium* states that "It is through the sacraments and the exercise of the virtues that the sacred nature and organic structure of the priestly community is brought into operation." At the summit of this sacramental system is the Eucharist. "(I)n the sacrament of the Eucharistic bread the unity of all believers who form one body in Christ... is both expressed and brought about" (LG 3). (For a description of the function of each sacrament individually, see LG 11.) Thus, we can expect that, among its operational goals, the Church will seek to **preach the gospel as persuasively as possible** and to **safeguard and maximally employ its sacramental system**. By safeguard, I mean that the Church will want to guarantee the continued use and integrity of the sacraments. (A potential source of contestation: Of what does a valid and effective celebration of the sacraments consist?). By maximally employ, I mean that the Church will want to celebrate the sacraments wherever and whenever appropriate, extending them to as many people as possible.

Another major operational goal of the Church is **to maintain and enhance its forms of social outreach to all people**, regardless of Church membership. Here I mean to call attention to the practical means the Church employs to reach out to and serve others through the efforts of Catholic missionaries, social service agencies, educational and health care institutions and many other operations which bring the Church's mission and message to the world. These tools provide explicit and more subtle means of evangelizing those whose connection to the Church is tenuous or nonexistent. Inasmuch as the Church desires to bring all of humanity into union with God, it must have such means that enable it to reach out to those outside the fold and perhaps incorporate them into the life of the Church. The other side of this same goal derives from the Church's perception, well articulated at Vatican II, that God is present outside of the Church as well as within it. The challenge for the Church, then, is not simply to share its wisdom about God with others, but to continue to go in search of God and to be prepared to learn from the encounter with God, *wherever* God may be found.

Though the discussion of operational goals that the Church pursues could continue indefinitely, I will conclude it now by offering one further observation. Because God is holy, the approach to union with God is a journey of growth in holiness (cf. LG 11: "the Church, embracing sinners in her bosom, is at the same time holy and always in need of being purified, and incessantly pursues the path of penance and renewal"). Church teaching holds that in order to draw closer to God, one must (through God's power) draw ever nearer to God and be continually remade in greater likeness to God. The implication for the effectiveness of the Church organization is that **decision-making on behalf of the Church in the here and now must show signs of an evolving, intimate relationship with God.** In the short run, if Church leaders are not, or appear not to be, consistently committed to their own growth in holiness (and admittedly, careful, deep-level discernments are needed to perceive whether this is in fact the case) and to the Church's growth in holiness, then the confidence of other Church members will be tested. Those outside the Church will question the credibility of the

Church's message whenever Church members appear to act in ways contrary to the gospel. In the long run, the ability of the Church to fulfill its ultimate purpose will be threatened. (Failure on this level is better expressed with the language of theology than of organizational science.) This is not to suggest that there is no room for error, sin or disunity in the life of the Church, or that the presence of these shortcomings inevitably precludes the Church's realization of its purpose. But it is to say that a credible relationship between short-term means and long-term ends is essential. In cases of intrahierarchical conflict, this expectation should have a bearing on participants' behavior.

More generally, we can expect that the six above-mentioned operational goals of the Church -- growing and enhancing the Church organization, finding ways to establish unity amid diversity within the Church membership, effectively preaching the gospel, preserving and promoting the sacramental system, practicing social outreach, striving for holiness -- will be relevant in cases of center-periphery conflict. We can suppose that members of the hierarchy will be pressed in their role as organizational leaders to implicitly or explicitly acknowledge these operational goals and to take action on behalf of their achievement (or give the appearance thereof).

We can also suppose that differing opinions about how one should go about pursuing these operational goals and about how they relate to the ultimate aims of the Church will be a source of conflict within the hierarchy. We should not expect Church members, in practice, to pursue these goals in fully committed and uniform fashion. Like other human institutions, the Church is a collectivity of persons, each of whom has a personal view of his or her role within the institution and a limited power to affect its course (Lambrecht 1987, 54). Not all Church members will show an equal readiness to work collaboratively for the achievement of any given objective of the Church. Some may even work, intentionally or not, in opposition to the Church's stated goals (Yinger 1963, 170). But by focusing on the Church's clear and pronounced concern for uniting people to one another and to God, we gain valuable insight into the Church's organizational orientation. In cases of center-periphery conflict, we have the opportunity to observe how the leaders' actions in such conflicts can promote or hinder the Church's progress toward this goal.

2.4.3 Church Resources
Organizations pursue their chosen goals through the employment of human and material resources. In this section I will consider the human and material resources available to the Church as it pursues its goals.

2.4.3.1 Human Resources
As the world's largest religious organization, the Catholic Church is exceedingly rich in human resources. Counting more than one billion persons as members at the beginning of the twenty-first century the Church enjoys marvelous opportunities for accomplishing goals of all kinds. But as with any organization, one should not lose sight of the fact that people do not stop being fully *people* when they belong to the Church. That is to say, they do not reduce to being cogs in an organizational machine once they are members (Morgan 1990, 18).

Motives
Church members (including Church leaders) vary in their life experience, attitudes and reasons for participating in the Church organization (Argyle and Beit-Hallahmi 1975). And they are susceptible to any number of influences that exist independently of the Church, be they family, friends, other people, personal desires, economic needs, the media, or countless

other influences within their total social and cultural environment (Boulding 1962, 110). On the other hand, Church members also *have influence over* their environment and can use this on behalf of or against the wishes of the Church. In short, it is not a simple matter to coordinate the human resources of the Church for the sake of accomplishing the Church's goals. It is more than challenging to enlist people's involvement so that the Church moves toward its designated goals and not in some other direction.

Church leaders will be like the leaders of other organizations in showing a fundamental desire to save face (Brown and Levinson 1987), first for themselves as individuals and then for the organization as a whole. This desire will consistently inform the decisions Church leaders make in the course of leading the organization.

Both Fichter (1954) and Ashbrook (1965) provide helpful distinctions which classify the participation of Church members in the Church according to type, and give us a glimpse of the mixture of motivations that may lead people to practice as Catholics. Fichter observes that the membership of Catholics in the Church may be characterized as institutional or personal. Institutional membership entails participation based on factors such as baptism, place of residence, race and nationality. Personal membership focuses more on one's intentions and the quality of one's religious practice. Ashbrook also provides a twofold typology of Church involvement. Participation may be either voluntary expression of personal moral commitment, or it may be a more burdened kind of participation, undertaken grudgingly or calculatively, as a way of gaining advantages that accrue from membership in the Church.

While these fairly simple distinctions cannot by themselves account for the complexity and ambiguity of Church members' motivations and involvement, they do help us to recognize the challenges that face Church leaders (whose own participation is ambiguous) who seek to coordinate and control the human resources of the Church. Though the professed mission of the Church may be to bring all people, through God's power, to salvation in God, the Church itself acknowledges that not all members (Church leaders included) are equally invested in this mission, and some may even sin against it (*Lumen Gentium* 8; de Lubac 1963, 170-197). One temptation facing Church leaders is to promote organizational continuity, and one's own retention of authority within the organization, for its own sake, at the expense of the Church's mission (Schillebeeckx 1981, 75-76; Yinger 1963, 172; Weber 1958, 228-229).

Space / Means
Thus far I have been making use of a rather general distinction between Church members and Church leaders (who are also members). At the heart of this distinction, which is not meant to be a hard and fast distinction in the present usage, is the fact that Church members are not equal in their power to direct the organizational movement. Though all members have some power in the Church, this should not divert our attention from the fact that power to guide the Church is concentrated at the top, in the hierarchy. The portrait of the leadership structure of the Church already presented gives some sense of who has authority over whom in the Church.

Authority -- power perceived to be legitimate (Etzioni 1961; Berger 1967) -- is especially important in the Church because of the Church's normative orientation (Reese 1989, 54; Vaillancourt 1980, 4; Szafran 1976, 339; Etzioni 1961). In normative organizations (see also section 2.4.4), social control is maintained through the manipulation of symbolic and moral power (Szafran 1976, 339). Vaillancourt (1980, 5) finds that physical compensations and sanctions are rarely available to religious organizations operating in secular, pluralistic contexts: "Consequently, ideological rationalizations and spiritual compensations and sanctions (i.e. psychic coercion) are more commonly relied upon." In sum, those with authority in the Church will be concerned to manipulate symbolic and moral power so that, internally, the Church's resources will be directed to the attainment of the Church's goals. Church leaders will also want to be externally focused, using symbolic and moral power to foster an environment receptive to the Church's efforts.

We should not go further without acknowledging the profound difficulty that faces Church leaders as they seek to bring themselves and those they lead -- and ultimately even those outside of the Church, too -- into union with one another and with God. Such a transcendent purpose holds promise of realization only in the perspective of the Church's faith in the Holy Spirit of God who sustains the Church. And yet, though this confidence in the Holy Spirit is surely comforting to those who hold authority in the Church, it does not free them from their responsibility to do their part in bringing about God's kingdom. Therein lies the challenge. How do Church leaders know if they are doing what they ought to do to carry out God's mission for the Church? And how does one measure the progress (Reese 1989, ix) of these efforts?

A partial answer to this problem can be found in Church's leaders' attention to the extent with which people *identify with* the Church. While Church leaders are not in a position to judge the condition of people's faith, they can find any number of outward signs of people's willingness to affiliate with the Church and its mission. High levels of Church membership (as expressed in baptism and the reception of other sacraments, parish registration, membership in other Catholic groups, etc.) and Church commitment (as expressed in financial contributions, participation in Church ministries, support for Church-backed political positions, etc.) are reassuring to both "worldly"-type and "spiritual"-type Church leaders. For worldly-type leaders (that is, those strongly focused on the Church's effectiveness and success in the world), these signs of identification with the Church demonstrate the Church's continuing importance in the world. This continuing importance may be of interest to them for selfish reasons (their own prestige and power are enhanced through their connection to the Church) or selfless reasons (the Church's worldly advancement puts it in a better position to alleviate suffering in the world). For spiritual-type Church leaders (that is, those strongly focused on a salvation experienced on the plane of the spirit rather than on the plane of bodily / earthly life), high levels of Church membership and commitment can be comforting as well, because they may be interpreted as outward signs that the Holy Spirit is indeed at work in the Church.

My point in drawing this simple sketch of Church leadership and participation is to introduce the matter of *identification and identity* into our discussion of how human resources fit with the Church's organizational life. When people choose to identify with the Church, they increase the sum total of human (and material) resources that the Church can put to the achievement of its goals. Even more significantly, as I have already noted, in some (provisional) sense increased membership is itself a reflection of *the goal* of the Church, since the Church's mission is to bring all of humankind into union with God and the Church believes itself to be a privileged, unparalleled means by which people come into that union.

Hence, Church leaders clearly have a stake in inducing people to identify with the organization that is the Church. But this, too, is a complex matter, for as Cheney (1991, 13-18) observes, people take on shared identities because they have an *interest* in doing so -- and as I observed previously, people are mixed in their motivations and interests, and the Church is a voluntary organization (Reese 1989, 54). The task for Church leaders, then, is to convince people that their interests are best served by participating in the shared identity that is the Church, and to see that interests contrary to the mission of the Church do not keep the Church from carrying out its mission.

In Cheney's (1991, 15) words, "The Roman Catholic Church, as a transnational bureaucratic organization, has been fundamentally engaged in the management of identities throughout most of its history... Continually the Church has sought to balance its universal, or catholic, identity with local and particular concerns while encouraging individuals, the faithful, to derive a sense of self from allegiance to the Church." This task of managing identities is largely a rhetorical enterprise, whereby Church leaders use language to persuade Church members to make decisions in accord with the leaders' preferences (Cheney 1991, 8).

As an example, Cheney cites the US bishops' production of the pastoral letter on nuclear arms (*The Challenge of Peace: God's Promise and Our Response*, 1983). That production process shows the (US) hierarchy managing multiple identities through language for the sake of the Church's mission. In the course of composing and disseminating the document, the bishops had to balance interests associated with their identities as individual bishops, as members of the national bishops' conference, and as members of the worldwide college of bishops. At the same time they had to speak to and "manage" the identities of others implicated in their statement, including: American Catholics, the Vatican, the Reagan Administration, nuclear pacifists, the public at large (Cheney 1991, 10).

Establishing connections with key audiences is especially important in conflict situations. Gangel and Canine (1992, 215-218), in their study of conflict management in churches, emphasize the role played by audiences.

> The mere presence of an audience (including psychological presence) motivates bargainers to seek positive, and avoid negative, evaluation -- especially when the audience is important to the bargainers. The external audience helps to keep the bargaining process honest. The effect of the negotiator's behavior before a watching world provides a check-and-balance-system so that grave injustices are less likely to occur.
>
> The particular audience we desire to influence plays a large part in what motivates us.... In many ways, negotiators view themselves as representatives of a larger body of people. This real or imagined audience serves as a reference point for what we will use as bargaining chips and how we will engage in this process.

Having this in mind, it is worth our while to identify key audiences that participants in center-periphery conflict will want to reach. I have listed the audiences roughly in order of their potential power to affect the conflict outcome.

Key Targets of Persuasion in Center-Periphery Conflict

Actor	Audiences he will be concerned to persuade
The Pope / **Papal Representative**	His conflictual partner(s) (the local bishop) Bishops of the local bishop's country The apostolic nuncio or delegate in the local bishop's country Officers of the Roman curia Bishops of the world Catholics in the local bishop's diocese (especially priests) Catholics in the local bishop's country
The local bishop	His conflictual partner(s) (the Pope, papal representative) The apostolic nuncio or delegate in his own country Officers of the Roman curia Bishops of his own country Bishops of the world Catholics in his diocese (especially priests) Catholics in his country

TABLE 2.3

A few words of explanation are in order here. Obviously the most important party to reach in a conflict is the opposition, so there should be no surprise in my placement of the conflictual party at the top of each list. Thus the Pope has a primary interest in gaining compliance from the local bishop. The next most important party for the Pope to influence are fellow members of the episcopacy in the local bishop's country. Within the universal college of bishops, those of the periphery party's own country are among the most likely to support him (the periphery party), since they share his national identity and, probably, much of his experience. Since the Pope does not want to see a local conflict turn into a regional conflict, he must make sure that those other bishops align with his position and not with that of the local bishop. At the same time, those bishops are likely to be in a good position to persuade the local bishop himself. Therefore, the Pope can obtain a significant strategic advantage if he can get these bishops to put pressure on his conflictual partner. A local bishop may show a readiness to listen to his countrymen when he is not so inclined to listen to Rome.

Probably the Pope will have to do little work, perhaps none at all, to convince his curia and nuncio to line up with his position in a conflict with a local bishop. But I place these officials next on the list to be persuaded for the simple fact of their profound influence on the organizational life of the Church. The Pope's own effectiveness is enhanced to the extent that these officials are in tune with his wishes. These highly-placed leaders are also in a position to interfere significantly (though likely in hidden ways) with his efforts if they become so inclined. Besides keeping bishops in line in the country in question, the Pope will also want to keep the rest of the world's bishops in harmony with his position. This will be especially necessary if the conflict seems inclined to grow to be a regional rather than a local conflict. When other bishops of the world show their support for the Pope they remind independence-oriented bishops of their connection to the universal Church.

Catholics in the local diocese and in the nation in question are in a position to put pressure on the local bishop. If they line up behind the local bishop, he will surely be encouraged, if not emboldened. The support of local priests is crucial if a local bishop has any notion to defy Vatican wishes, because the priests take the bishop's (or Rome's) case to the people locally. For this reason, the Pope will want to remind these Catholics of their "Roman" identity.

Not listed on my list of audiences for the pope to persuade, but nonetheless highly relevant, is the **news media**. The news media is indeed an audience to be persuaded, but it is more fundamentally significant as an arena of conflict handling. The news media functions as something of a wild card, by virtue of its power to influence events and shape perceptions about them – a power that has only increased in recent years as more and more channels of information processing have opened up. Reports issued through the news media affect not only the opinions of the public at large (Crowley & Mitchell 1994, 11) -- which in turn put pressure on the bargaining positions of the parties in conflict -- they also directly affect the perceptions of the parties themselves in regard to the behavior of the opposing party (Robbins 1992, 178; Salazar 1996; Hubbard 1997). Once a center-periphery conflict becomes public, the news media will play a crucial role in the conflict handling. Obviously, the Pope prefers to have media coverage be as favorable as possible. In contrast with the target audiences listed above, all of whom are Church members that the Pope and other Church leaders prefer to keep as compliant participants in the life of the Church, members of the media may or may not be Church members, and may even be hostile to the Church (Quinn 1999, 54). Given the multiplicity and variety of media venues, managing press messages in regard to a given conflict is a highly challenging task (Soukup 1996, viii). Nonetheless, in conflict situations media outlets are valued for their ability to reach a variety of audiences and even a mass audience quickly.

As for the audiences that the local bishop will be concerned to persuade in center-periphery conflict, the Pope clearly tops the list. Not only is he, in structural terms, the prime conflictual partner in center-periphery conflict; he is also the one person who can single-handedly exercise power to definitively resolve the conflict. In short, if the local bishop can win over the Pope, he wins the conflict. After the Pope, the local bishop will be most concerned to persuade those who are in a position to persuade the Pope. The apostolic nuncio or delegate to the local bishop's country is the most likely go-between in a conflict situation, and the Pope can be expected to consult this representative to discern what exactly is at hand in the local church. Similarly, members of the Roman curia will likely have some say in conflictual exchange between the Holy See and a local ordinary. Hence, the ordinary will want to seek a favorable hearing and advocacy from among those who hold high office at the Vatican. Another possible source of support for the periphery party lies with other bishops outside the Vatican, especially those who reside in the local bishop's own country. If the local bishop can persuade a significant number of his countrymen that he has a legitimate case to make against Rome, he can gain considerably more leverage in the conflict. In and of itself, a unified national hierarchy is not guaranteed to prevail against Rome (consider the failure of the Dutch hierarchy's resistance to bishop appointments in the early 1970's; on the other hand, consider the successful intervention of the Brazilian hierarchy on behalf of theologian Leonardo Boff in 1986). But a local bishop's position is much stronger when he has (preferably many) allies within the hierarchy. In general, one can expect a local bishop to generate at least a certain amount of support for his cause among his priests and the other people of his diocese. The key issue here seems to be how great in number and how passionate these supporters are. The risk for the Vatican in the Lefebvre case was quite evident: if Lefebvre would go, a great many of his people would follow. (In the end, they did.) A bishop, therefore, who shores up his support among the local faithful is a more formidable opponent for Rome than is one whose support is sparse and / or lukewarm. Finally, a local bishop involved in center-periphery conflict will want to take his case to a broader audience (Catholics elsewhere) and the news media is, again, a prime vehicle for doing so.

In the course of my analysis of the Rome-Hunthausen conflict, I will be concerned to identify which audiences appear to be targeted in particular and which end up playing the most crucial role in the conflict handling.

To round out this discussion about the hierarchy's challenge of managing the human resources of the Church – particularly in conflict situations – I would like to add one final observation. Bishops, as coordinators of the Church's human resources, tend to be people "in the middle" in more senses than one (cf. Reese 1989, 345; Cheney 1991). As leaders of the local Church and of the Church universal, they must continually address the tensions that exist between personal and organizational priorities, and between local and global needs. From the perspective of the total Church organization, the assertion of "local" or subgroup interests can be threatening because they pose the possibility of the organizational mission and identity being subverted by a narrow faction (Cheney 1991, 169; Van der Ven 1996, 365; Morgan 1990, 81). Alternatively, however, too much control from a top-down, total organization perspective endangers the positive results of creativity and organizational dynamism that can emerge from grass roots efforts. But bishops are also "middlemen" in their capacity as ambassadors of the Church to the world. In this role they must keep sight of the extra-organizational constituencies that affect and are affected by the Church, for the Church's mission relates to all human persons.

2.4.3.2 Material Resources

As a means to achieve designated objectives, organizations employ not only human resources but material resources as well. In the legal parlance of the Church, these material resources are known as "temporal goods" (Canons 1254-1310, *Code of Canon Law*). Temporal goods consist in the material means (such as finances, property, etc.) necessary for the Church to pursue "its proper ends." Among the ends that are "especially proper" to the Church are "to order divine worship; to provide decent suport for the clergy and other ministers; to perform the works of the sacred apostolate and of charity, especially towards the needy" (Canon 1254). In order to obtain necessary funds, local ordinaries have discretionary powers to impose "a moderate tax" (Canon 1263) and special collections (Canon 1266) on those under their authority. Additionally, bishops "in view of their bond of unity and charity and in accord with the resources of their dioceses," have a responsibility to provide resources of support to the Apostolic See (Canon 1271). The Pope is considered "the supreme administrator and steward of all ecclesiastical goods" – i.e., temporal goods (Canon 1273). Diocesan bishops have a responsibility to "supervise carefully the administration of all the goods which belong to the public juridic persons" subject to them (Canon 1276).

In short, the Church sees fit to acquire any sort of material resource necessary to carry out its mission (Galbraith 1986, 215), with due respect for civil law shown in the acquisition and use of such goods (Canon 22). And indeed, in practice, the Church possesses and employs a range of material resources so vast that it cannot be fully accounted for. Some of these resources are more visible than others. For example, it is commonly known that the Church regularly takes up financial collections, undertakes capital fund drives and owns impressive properties such as Church buildings, land, office buildings, schools, hospitals, newspapers, radio and TV stations and works of art. But even these more visible signs of the Church's wealth as an organization are only surface markers of extensive resources in the same realms that are not open to view. Occasionally the financial wherewithal of the Church is underestimated, perhaps as the result of the Church's being constituted as a voluntary, religious organization. As a case in point, after the US Bishops released their 1987 pastoral letter on the economy (*Economic Justice for All*), the criticism was heard that the bishops had insufficient experience in money matters to speak competently thereof. But in fact, American bishops oversee multi-million dollar budgets for their dioceses (Reese 1989, 150) and the budget for the Bishops' Conference itself runs in the tens of millions of dollars (Reese, 1992, 271). Budgets managed by the Holy See account for hundreds of millions of dollars (Reese 1996, 202-229).

Without temporal goods, the Church cannot carry out its work. Without money the Church cannot buy food for the poor or pay for missionaries to preach the Gospel in remote areas. Even something as simple -- and fundamental -- as regular celebration of the Eucharist comes with accompanying costs (compensation for priests, maintenance of church buildings, liturgical supplies, etc.). Thus Church leaders have a vested interest in obtaining funds and other instruments for the sake of the Church's mission. At the same time, the need to obtain temporal goods also places Church leaders in a position of dependence on those who can supply the necessary resources (Henrici 1994, 53; Bassett 1979, 29; Cereti 1979, 15). Therefore, the Church is in a position to influence (for example, funding some activities and not others: cf. Vaillancourt 1980, 267) or be influenced through its reliance on material resources. On the parish level, pastors are dependent on the contributions of parishioners to meet operating costs. Within a diocese, the bishop is dependent on parish contributions to the diocese to meet its costs. And on a global scale, the Holy See is dependent on the contributions of the world's dioceses to make ends meet and conduct its pastoral activity. Bishops and the Pope are best understood to be the guardians and administrators of ecclesiastical goods (ownership applies only to a limited number of personal possessions), with canonical expectations (see, for example, Canon 1267.3) about proper stewardship governing their use of Church goods.

Financial leverage may prove to be a relevant question in cases of center-periphery conflict, especially where a rich local or national Church is involved. (Reese 1996, 225 reports that in its 1992 Peter's Pence collection – an annual discretionary fund assembled for the Pope – the US donated $23 million of the $67 million total collected, and the top ten nation contributors gave 78% of the world's total amount.) No bishop wants to lose his financial wherewithal in his own diocese by alienating contributors (thus he will be careful about how he comes across to his people), and Rome will be reluctant to see dwindling returns from a local Church that is normally a financial mainstay (thus the Pope will be careful about how he comes across to the people of the particular churches and their bishops). The desire to preserve or enhance one's financial stability is potentially a source of conflict, but also an inducement to the maintenance of harmony. The command of ample material resources is potentially a strategic advantage to be employed in center-periphery conflict handling, especially where direct lines of financial dependence apply.

2.4.4 Means of Coordination and Control
Morgan envisions organizations as entities in which resources are brought together "in a co-ordinated and controlled mechanism" to achieve desired goals. In this section I will discuss means by which the Church coordinates and controls its human and physical resources.

Church leaders vary in the degree of their authority (legitimized power) to control and coordinate Church resources, with members of the hierarchy possessing the highest level of authority, and the Pope possessing this authority supremely so. Vaillancourt (1980, 264-268), drawing on Weber, Etzioni, and French and Raven, provides a useful classification of eight kinds of control exercised by "upper-echelon officials in the Catholic Church." Vaillancourt's eight types of power are described below, together with examples he provides.

Before confronting the Vaillancourt material, allow me first to interject two prefatory comments about power itself. First, unless otherwise specified, my use of the term power in this study is congruent with the classic definition offered by Weber (1959, 180): it is the ability to realize one's will, even in the face of resistance. Second, as I stated in chapter one, my view of power itself is essentially neutral, much in the manner of Yinger (1963, 170), who wrote that "power is found in all human relations and is *per se* neither good nor evil." With this in mind, let us now turn to Vaillancourt's scheme for classifying employments of power by high-level Church leaders.

1. *Ecological power*, based on the physical control of material environmental conditions. Examples: use of territory, buildings or real estate to control people through domination of their environment, as in the case of convent walls or the placement of bureaucratic offices.

2. *Remunerative power*, based on material or nonmaterial rewards or compensations. Example: Funding favored activities.

3. *Coercive power*, based on physical or psychic violence. Examples: burning at the stake, torture, imprisonment, banishment, blackmail, removal from office, denouncement.

4. *Social power*, based on the use of structural-organizational or psycho-sociological mechanisms. Examples: peer-group pressures, rumors, co-optation, social ostracism, socialization, use of mass media, nepotism, selective recruitment.

5. *Legal power*, based on juridical, administrative or bureaucratic norms, procedures and maneuvers. Examples: secrecy rules in hierarchical activities, censorship through the *nihil obstat* and the *imprimatur*.

6. *Traditional power*, based on the use of traditional symbols, rituals, ideas and sentiments. Examples: confirming loyalties through liturgies; appeals to practices and documents popular or prevalent in previous times.

7. *Expert power*, based on professional, technical, or scientific or purely rational arguments. Examples: recourse to experts in theology or sociology to bolster one's position; Church leaders teaching as experts.

8. *Charismatic power*, based on exemplary or ethical prophecy. Examples: calls for social justice and equality, giving away Church possessions for certain causes. Personal charisma may be replaced by charisma of office or "routinized" (Weber) in other ways. Through routinization, charismatic power is made more predictable, by linkage with or transformation into legal, traditional and expert power.

Vaillancourt (p. 268) finds that the types can be organized into more general categories of the way power is exercised. Types 1-3 exemplify the use of "raw power" or "the carrot-and-stick approach." Types 4-8 are more "normative" employments of power, "often referred to as authority rather than power because of the greater degree of legitimacy which they connotate." Finally, the normative group can be further organized. Types 4, 5 and 6 demonstrate a "manipulative" approach, whereas 8 and 9 are more oriented to "persuasion" and rational-ethical appeals to human intelligence, freedom and initiative. Vaillancourt concedes that more than one category may aptly describe a given instance of power use by a

Church leader, but argues that the scheme is nonetheless useful for analysis that goes beyond concrete historical description.

It is unfortunate that Vaillancourt does not offer us a clear definitional key for distinguishing between raw and normative uses of power. The heart of the matter, apparently, concerns the crossing over from applications of power which are grounded in the superior possession of strength or resources, and which are only minimally dependent on processes of negotiation or references to external sources of authority for their effectiveness, to applications of power that are more the product of free choice and rational agreement between the parties involved. Making distinctions between raw and normative uses of power can be particularly difficult because the use of raw power (removing a bishop from office, for example) can be fully "legitimate" (by virtue of being sanctioned by Church law and tradition, for example). Making distinctions can also be difficult because a given act may demonstrate power of several kinds at once (e.g., appointing a man bishop demonstrates remunerative power, but it also draws on social, legal and traditional power). This difficulty of making distinctions will need to be confronted on a case-by-case basis.

Below is a schematic diagram which helps us to see how Vaillancourt distinguishes between types of power applied by high-level Church leaders.

Kinds of Control Used by Upper-Echelon Officials in the Catholic Church
(cf. Vaillancourt 1980)

Raw Power	Nonargumentative	1. Ecological Power
		2. Remunerative Power
		3. Coercive Power
Normative Power	Manipulation	4. Social Power
		5. Legal Power
		6. Traditional Power
	Persuasion	7. Expert Power
		8. Charismatic Power

TABLE 2.4

As Vaillancourt's typology suggests, the Church's character as a primarily normative organization does not prevent it from using forms of power that are "raw" or coercive. Though uses of this kind of power are more limited and less physically drastic than they once were (Vaillancourt's examples of coercive power include types of coercion, such as burning at the stake, torture, imprisonment, that are not practiced by the Church of the present day), it is still possible to find the carrot-and-stick approach in acts such as the naming of bishops, the removal of Church officials from office, excommunication, and public "silencing." Here the perspective of Habermas becomes relevant (cf. De Roest 1998, 217). Empirical sanctions available to organizational leaders stand in the background of collective attempts to determine organizational goals through a reasoning process that has reference to legitimate organizational norms.

There are trade-offs for the Church organization when Church leaders choose to employ one type of power rather than another.

Generally, in almost any religious organization, attempts to use coercive or remunerative means of control lead to alienation, aggressiveness, and loss of commitment on the part of the membership. If purely normative means are used, especially the nonmanipulative normative means that respect the members' freedom, then the officials tend to lose their importance in the organization, because of the renewed interest in participation this strategy brings forth. There are then also fewer, but more committed members. For officials who want to keep their grip over an organization but who cannot openly use coercion and remuneration to do so, the tendency is to use the more manipulative of the normative means of control, those which Weber characterizes as "psychic" or "hierocratic" coercion. (Vaillancourt 1980, 264-265)

The challenge for Church leaders is to decide when to apply which type of control over Church resources for the sake of achieving organizational goals (assuming that is what the leaders want). Members of the hierarchy may use power in a disinterested fashion (for the sake of the Church itself) or for motives of personal advantage (protecting official privileges, seeking career advancement, etc.). Presumably, their motives will often be mixed. If Vaillancourt is correct in the passage quoted above, members of the hierarchy will be careful about applying power in a "raw" fashion, because this leads to the alienation of other Church members. (Such an approach would also seem to be in tension with the operative goal of charitably allowing for legitimate differences within the Church.) At the same time, members of the hierarchy will also be reluctant about applying nonmanipulative, normative means, which actually diminish the hierarchy's control of the Church organization in favor of greater member freedoms and control. The most likely strategy, then, for members of the hierarchy to adopt if they wish to retain their own power without alienating other Church members is to employ manipulative types of normative control which involve the internalization of the control of Church members. This third option results in Church members being controlled without perceiving they are being controlled. (Schellenberg 1982, 229, writes: "Coercion can occur through simple obedience to authority, especially if the persons involved see no other choice as effectively available.")

In center-periphery conflict, we are concerned with how certain members of the hierarchy use means of coordination and control in relation to other members of the hierarchy. Presumably there will be agreement about maintaining hierarchical privileges in general, but members of the hierarchy are not equal in their possession of power, and thus we can expect that tensions will arise (perhaps out of view) around questions of who controls whom (and to what degree), and the legitimacy of this arrangement. The center party has the possibility of legitimately using raw power over and against the periphery party and any (intrahierarchical) third parties because structurally such powers have been entrusted to the center party by Church law and tradition. Thus, the center party can exercise such powers against lower-power intraecclesial parties and still be perceived as legitimate in doing so – but damage can come as a result, as in the form of hindered relations or harms to the appearance of the Church. The opposite – the periphery party using raw power against the center party -- is a much less real possibility, because of the potential costs to the peripheral party for doing so. And such use is not generally perceived as legitimate within the Church. The periphery party, therefore, must seek to advance its position through applications of manipulative and nonmanipulative normative power. The center party can also, of course, employ these same types of power in an attempt to control the periphery party. An interesting dynamic to observe in center-periphery conflict is how the center and periphery parties employ psychic coercion in relation to one another. Do applications thereof differ from how psychic coercion is used to control Catholics who are not members of the hierarchy?

In order to take this discussion to a more concrete and specific level, let us now turn to the eight specific types of power which Vaillancourt identifies and consider how each may take shape within the dynamics of center-periphery conflict.

2.4.4.1 Potential Applications of Distinct Types of Power in Center-Periphery Conflict

Ecological power, in Vaillancourt's conception, is control manifested directly through domination of material environmental conditions. He notes, for example, that some branches of the Roman curia are located at a distance from the Vatican and thus have disadvantages of proximity and access in their relations with the pope. This example is helpful because it highlights the importance of the physical distance that lies between Rome and the rest of the world's sees. Taking advantage of the fact of separating distance (especially by maintaining control over one's own territory) is a likely way for parties to center-periphery conflict to employ ecological power.

Both the center party and periphery party exercise territorial control. In cases of center-periphery conflict, we can expect that each party will seek to exploit its territorial advantage and to minimize the territorial advantage enjoyed by the opposing party. By territorial control I mean the fullest sense in which a local bishop has control over the material and human resources of a diocese and the Pope has control over the diocese of Rome and all other dioceses around the world.

The center party enjoys a high level of control over Church life in the Vatican city state and the diocese of Rome. It enjoys a lesser but still high level of control over the remainder of the world's dioceses. The periphery party enjoys a high level of control over the life of the local Church in question, but little control elsewhere.

The center party can exploit its territorial advantage (employing ecological power) to keep the periphery party removed from those who make decisions which directly affect the periphery party. Most bishops do not have frequent or easy access to the Pope or to the Vatican offices where key decisions are made. (Papal nuncios and officials of the Roman curia play important gatekeeper roles.) Invitations from the Vatican and news of its operations are rarely forthcoming, and the bishop who ventures to Rome under his own volition faces an imposing architectural setting (Hebblethwaite 1986, 1-11) which houses an equally imposing bureaucracy. These obstacles must be confronted by a bishop who wants to influence the decision making there.

On the other hand, a local bishop can employ ecological power by reinforcing his dominance of his territory – especially by cultivating local loyalties in various ways -- at the expense of Roman preferences for that local church. Rome can only observe goings-on in the world's dioceses from afar (Goddijn 1975, 47). It cannot monitor situations there first-hand and must rely on local observers (Safranski 1985, 57) and the cooperation of the bishop himself to remain apprised of local conditions.

Nonetheless, certain general strategies enable the Vatican to counteract the local bishop's territorial control. One such strategy is the *ad limina* visit. By (canonically) requiring local bishops to journey to Rome once every five years for a visit "to the threshold" of the tombs of Sts. Peter and Paul, the Vatican temporarily closes the distance between itself and local sees, and thus makes the periphery more accountable to the center. During these visits the bishops provide a comprehensive account of current conditions in the local Church. This obligation to close the distance between Rome and the local diocese is one-directional. Bishops have a responsibility to come to the Pope, but papal visits to a bishop's see are normally portrayed as an honor that the Pope bestows on the local Church, not as any kind of obligation (cf. May 1987, 254). Papal visits to local sees, however, may also be understood as a strategy whereby the center asserts control over the local Church. Melady (1999) demonstrates persuasively how such visits serve to lay claim symbolically to the Pope's rule over the local church. The orchestration of such events is an intriguing example of how environmental trappings may convey and reinforce presumptions of one's power. Another way for the Pope to "visit" a local church is to conduct an apostolic visitation of that church. This amounts to an investigation of conditions in the diocese carried out by a papal representative. This is typically a means for reining in a bishop or diocese that appears to be getting out of Rome's control. (See below under "coercive power.")

A local bishop has few opportunities to diminish the Pope's territorial control over the diocese of Rome or over other dioceses not his own. Therefore, his best option for asserting ecological power in center-periphery conflict appears to be to take advantage of his control of his own territory and exploit Vatican fears that many of the faithful of that local church could be lost to the Church if the local bishop's wishes are not respected.

Remunerative power is another type of power which can serve strategic purposes in center-periphery conflict (Henrici 1994, 53-54). This too is a type of power which is more available to the center party than the periphery party.

The Pope is in a position to reward bishops in various ways. The power of appointment is an obvious example of this. Bishops hold their office by virtue of a Pope's having approved their appointment. (The Pope can also remove bishops from office.) In addition, the Pope has the power to further advance careers through his right to make bishops into archbishops, cardinals, papal ambassadors and curial officials. He can also reassign a bishop to lead a more prominent see. Thus, career-minded bishops have incentives to please the Pope (and those bishops and curial members who are close to the Pope). A further power of appointment that can be employed as a form of remuneration is the Pope's power to appoint an auxiliary or coadjutor bishop to assist a bishop his management of a local diocese. It is common for bishops of larger sees to request this form of assistance because the demands of office are so great.

The power of appointment is not the only means the Pope has of rewarding bishops. The Pope also has great power to convey and confer visibility and prestige. He may do so by choosing to visit a bishop's diocese, by including the bishop in inner circles of decision-making, by praising the bishop publicly, or by other means.

Local bishops can also exercise a remunerative power over the Pope, though in a much more limited way. One means to do so is through financial contributions (Lernoux 1986, 16). The papacy is dependent on money supplied by the world's dioceses to do its work. While this flow of money does not have a measurable impact on the Pope's own personal financial well-being, it is something that the Pope must attend to because it directly affects the ability of the papacy to carry out its leadership role within the Church. Bishops also have the ability to remunerate the Pope by enhancing his power and prestige locally. This can be done by frequently citing his teachings, praising him, and working hard to promote causes the Pope has embraced.

When analyzing cases of center-periphery conflict, we will want to ask whether either party appears to have leverage with the other thanks to rewards given in the past, bestowed in the present, or promised for the future. It is unlikely that this form of power will show itself in a blatant way, at least not in the public discourse, because of its raw nature. For the most part, a Pope's more tangible powers of remuneration (e.g., offering the bishop a prestigious appointment) and a bishop's (e.g., through financial contributions or strengthening the Pope's control locally) will be reward powers that are taken for granted by the parties involved. They are long-term rather than immediate in their orientation. The most likely form of remuneration to appear in conflict discourse may well be expressions of approval and agreement which go beyond standard politeness conventions. These signs of approval and agreement are significant because not only do they signal increased possibilities of power, prestige and future rewards for the one shown approval, but more basically they appeal to the basic human desire for approval. Such approval is an incentive to compliance. To gain compliance from the other party is to "win" at least something in the conflict.

Coercive power is another form of power available to the papacy and episcopacy which can be applied in intrahierarchical conflicts. The 1983 *Code of Canon Law* states explicitly (canon 1311) that "the Church has an innate and proper right to coerce offending members of the Christian faithful by means of penal sanctions." Though the actions are infrequently taken, a Pope can limit a bishop's powers, silence him, publicly humiliate him, remove him from office, move him from one place to another, and excommunicate him from the Church. The Vatican may also initiate an "apostolic visitation," essentially an investigation of a local diocese, which calls into question the condition of the diocese and its leadership (Granfield 1986, 28-30). These types of coercive power are not reciprocal (see also Hoose 2001, 78 and Gaillardetz 1992, 133 on the use of coercive power by the Holy See over and against local bishops). An ordinary's subordinate position does not allow him to impose penalties on the Roman Pontiff (cf. canon 1333.3.1).

Though the Church's legal structure does not enable a bishop to sanction the Pope, a bishop may nonetheless exercise coercive power vis-à-vis the Pope. Perhaps the most obvious, and significant, potential for this lies in the bishop's influence over his own diocese. In light of the Church's prioritization of universal unity as a goal, Rome has an interest in seeing that no portion of the Church falls away. A diocesan bishop has the potential to fracture the Church's unity -- not only within his own see, but also beyond it -- by challenging directives from Rome. At the very least this will present an embarrassment to Rome. If Catholics in other areas perceive that Rome is being heavy-handed in its treatment of a local Church, this may cause them to re-evaluate their own commitments. Thus an ordinary can coerce the Holy See by taking advantage of the Pope's dependence on his own cooperation and that of the people in the local Church (cf. Granfield 1986, 73-74).

We can expect that when members of the hierarchy employ forms of coercion they will try to hide their use of this raw form of power. In many cases, merely suggesting (threatening) the possibility of taking any of the actions listed above can serve as a tactic of coercion. Both the center and periphery parties are in a position to use coercive power in this way, holding out the possibility of loss of control for the other. (If you do X, I can no longer guarantee Y.) Withholding rewards (for example, refusing to make the archbishop of an important see a cardinal) is another understated way to apply pressure for desired behaviors and punish undesired behaviors. The Pope, for example, could decide not to make the archbishop of an important see a cardinal. Going the other way, a local bishop might raise funds on behalf of the Holy See in a less than enthusiastic way. Public criticism, too, can be a means to force desired behaviors, but typically one will have to listen closely to hear these negative words. Rarely are the pope and bishops critical of one another in the open. More commonly, one would expect such opinions to be voiced by surrogates (such as curial or diocesan officials), though occasionally the principals themselves will offer critiques in veiled language. Such criticism gives permission to other parties to join in the criticism, which can come as an unwelcome form of public pressure. In center-periphery conflict situations, employing heavy-handed coercive means may be a way of quickly gaining compliance, but just as likely it will serve to throw oil on the fire. Especially when the coercion involves a loss of face for one party at the expense of the other (as for example, in cases where a Pope publicly humiliates a bishop), the organizational costs may exceed the short-term gains.

Social power, which focuses on personal desires for belonging and acceptance, is also likely to be applied in center-periphery conflict. Social power within the Church draws on the desire that people may feel to be accepted within the Church or one of the social circles within the Church. Church leaders, in view of their responsibility to maintain the identity and boundaries of the Church, have disproportionate power (relative to other Church members) to determine who feels welcome and who feels unwelcome in the Church. We can presume that participants in center-periphery conflict will use their ability to manipulate social power when it suits their purposes. But we should also keep in mind that members of the hierarchy, while greatly able to apply social power, are themselves intensely susceptible to social power as they carry out their duties on behalf of the Church.

Members of the Catholic hierarchy are products of highly intensive processes of organizational socialization, and their status as bishops (archbishops, cardinals, Pope) reflects an unusual level of personal commitment to the religious organization, as exemplified in promises of celibacy and obedience and heavy personal investments in education and training (Hanson 1987, 356; see also Etzioni 1961, 102-103). I point this out because the pronounced quality of their organizational affiliation makes them both well-versed in the means of socialization practiced by the organization (and thus able practitioners of the same), and unlikely candidates to disaffiliate with the organizational culture. Etzioni (1961, 202), following Argyris (1957, 94-95) writes: "The higher the rank, the greater we would expect the average commitment to be."

To put it another way, bishops are experts in "the Catholic way of doing things" and are strongly inclined both to do things the Catholic way themselves and to encourage others to do the same. Granted, it is not a simple matter to characterize this Catholic culture of social interaction, but some observations can be made.

One observation that is in order is that bishops are not equally "Romanized." Some bishop are more Romanized – that is, more attuned to the culture of the center party -- than others, by virtue of their educational curriculum vitae, their theological-ecclesiological views, their ecclesiastical ambitions, etc. Although all bishops become bishops by virtue of a Vatican appointment, bishops' levels of connectedness to Rome will vary greatly. Some bishops have established Vatican connections even prior to their consecration as bishops, by having studied in Rome (Hanson 1987, 171), or by having served as a priest in an administrative or diplomatic post that has put them in touch with the Holy See. Once a bishop, one may pursue (or avoid) Vatican ties to a greater or lesser extent, by means of his level of participation in bishops' synods, his assumption of national or international leadership roles, his handling of his required *ad limina* visit to Rome every five years, his personal contacts, his promotion of Roman causes locally, and other means. This can make a difference in cases of center-periphery conflict because we can expect that bishops with stronger ties to the Vatican will have more resources to draw on in such conflicts, in the form of personal connections at the Vatican, greater good will and greater knowledge of Vatican processes of decision making, than will bishops who have weaker ties to the center. (But NB: The case of Cardinal Alfrink suggests that strong Roman ties carry a local bishop only so far in a conflict with the Holy See. Cf. Van Schaik 1997.)

As a general principle, we can expect that all bishops will be conditioned by social power and will employ social power to keep up the appearance of the Church. In order to maintain the impression of unity and harmony, certain strategies are likely to be preferred for the handling of intraorganizational tensions. Among these are (1) the use of *familiar structures of engagement*, (2) the practice of *courtesy*, and (3) the employment of *techniques of extenuation*, particularly silence or secrecy. It should come as no surprise to find any or all of these strategically applied in center-periphery conflict. Before considering how the center party and periphery party are likely to use such strategies oppositionally in center-periphery conflict, I will consider predispositions about the use of these strategies which apply to both parties.

Like the leaders of other organizations, Church leaders should want to save their own face and that of the organization by showing that they can manage organizational conflicts productively. A common strategy for achieving this is the use of "tried and true" methods to handle internal conflicts. Familiar structures of engagement counteract the unpredictability and dangerousness of conflicts by placing them in known and limiting contexts. Thus a conflict becomes managed by means of reference to a chain of command, an existing legal structure (canon law), and various unwritten protocols of communication and politeness. Even more important than the structures themselves is the pre-existing tacit agreement (cf. Chomsky 1987 on "the manufacture of consent;" see also Lukes 1974, 23) that dictates which kinds of issues come up for discussion in the first place, and which rules for carrying on discussions are accepted without question. Organizational standards of thought and conduct are strongest when they are accepted as "common sense" (Fairclough 1989, 2-4). Thus Church leaders have a stake in promoting belief in the rightness of the Church's means and ends. Much of this will take the form of public relations and communications work. Conflicts will be most easily dispensed with by not giving them the occasion to arise in the first place and, when they do, having strong incentives in place to ensure that conflicts are handled in predictable ways which are known to generate desirable outcomes.

Another way we can expect Church leaders to keep up the appearance of the Church in the case of high-level conflicts is through the use of courtesy. An absence of critical commentary and harsh words in hierarchical exchanges suggests that all is well in the governance of the Church. Fraternal deference expressed within the papal-episcopal ranks shows that the topmost leadership of the Church is united and harmonious (and therefore stronger) as it takes up the challenges that the Church faces. Bishops are noted for their demeanor of politeness. Hanson (1987, 293) has spoken of "the usual (even exaggerated) courtesy that pertains among episcopal collegiality." While politeness offers the obvious advantage of keeping conversations civil and ongoing -- an advantage that should not be taken lightly -- some commentators have noted that the hierarchy's persistent desire to appear harmonious and act nonconfrontationally is problematic. Indirect language, silence or bureaucratic procedural moves may be used to avoid allowing conflicts to surface or to avoid certain issues altogether (see Reese 1996, 248; Quinn 1996, 16; K. Briggs 1992, 93-94; Reese 1992, 178-179; Reese 1989, 358; Bartholomaus 1978, 105). These approaches to the handling of conflict have the potential to be counterproductive for the Church by inviting the escalation of conflicts whose real issues have not been addressed early on.

Techniques of extenuation are a third likely means whereby participants will keep up the appearance of the Church in center-periphery conflict. Church observers frequently comment on the role that silence and secrecy play in Church governance (Stanley 2000; Melady 1999, 35; Quinn 1999, 56-58; Thomas 1997; Reese 1996, 4; Henrici 1994, 53; Granfield 1987, 93; Hanson 1987, 70; Hebblethwaite 1986, 128-129; Greeley 1979; McKenzie 1969, 31). Secrecy, in general, is sometimes viewed with suspicion, since, as Simmel (1950, 331) concedes, "the immoral hides itself for obvious reasons." But the use of secrecy is not by itself cause for alarm, and Bok (1984, 18) notes that it is "indispensable" for human life, enabling self-protection and autonomy (see also Martinson 1998, 15; Simmel 1950, 330). The desire for transparency, therefore, is not always ethically preferable (nor is it necessarily efficacious for all forms of conflict handling), and in some cultures secrecy is much more usual than in others. The most basic way we can expect secrecy to apply in center-periphery conflict is in regard to the fact of conflict itself. Conflicts can be, at a minimum, embarrassing for the Church, and so Church leaders have reason to want to keep leadership conflicts out of public view altogether. In cases where this is not entirely possible, there may be efforts to minimize the number of aspects of conflict that are revealed (participants, contested issues, processes of decision making). Intrahierarchical conflicts may be hidden through various means, including: closed meetings, non-public correspondence, silence, verbal obfuscation, secret archives, and the maintenance of policies of institutional exclusivity (priests must be male and celibate) that, a priori, limit access to institutional realms and conversations.

Thus far I have suggested that members of the hierarchy are heavily invested in and conditioned by the Church organizational culture. Generally speaking, they will be inclined to perpetuate the culture that has conditioned and rewarded them, with the implication that in cases of leadership conflict they will want to save the face of the Church and its hierarchical structure. I have also pointed to three strategies of conflict handling (the use of familiar structures of engagement, courtesy and extenuating techniques) through which social power may be applied to keep up the appearance of the Church and its hierarchy. Having offered these observations, however, I must note, too, that there are reasons to expect that the center and periphery parties will not apply these three strategies uniformly in case of center-periphery conflict. Among the reasons for this are that (1) the use of the strategies benefits the center party more than the periphery party and (2) both center and periphery party may occasionally foresee advantages to be reached by forgoing use of these usual approaches to conflict handling.

As the party of higher power and rank, the center party benefits more from these strategies of conflict handling, which maintain current distributions of power, than does the periphery party. The periphery party also benefits (privileges of membership in the hierarchy are retained), but to a lesser degree. Use of the familiar structures of engagement in conflict favors the continuance of current arrangements of power which are slanted in favor of the higher-power center party. Use of courtesy and secrecy keep conflicts from coming into the open and thereby enlisting the support of influential third parties or of the Church faithful in general. By controlling the machinery and keeping the machinery out of sight, the higher-power party is able to reduce the possibility that the machinery will be reconfigured. Hanson (1987, 44-45) has noted that "the Vatican holds an enormous advantage in any closed bureaucratic struggle" with local bishops.

In the same passage, however, Hanson also notes that breaking with expected protocols of conflict handling can be a source of power to a local bishop who is in the lower-power position. Providing news "leaks" or making confidential documents available for public consumption has proven to be an effective means through which opposing bishops have countered the Vatican's advantage by gaining public support. A member of the hierarchy always has, in conflict situations, the possibility of *avoiding* the preferred organizational ways of doing things (e.g., by questioning the validity of canonical strictures or undermining the chain of command). He may also choose *not* to be courteous (e.g., by failing to observe diplomatic protocol or by publicly challenging a fellow bishop) or *not* to maintain ordinary standards of secrecy. This potential *not to save* the face of the Church or of the other party is a considerable means of leverage available to the lower-power party in center-periphery conflict. (The other side of the coin here is that the periphery party also faces the incursion of greater *costs* if it decides to abandon social expectations, and this may make it less likely than the center to part from the normative conventions. The center can punish and ostracize the periphery for such activity, but the center needs not fear punishment – or at least, the Pope himself needs not fear punishment.)

It should not be surprising that the periphery party will be inclined to circumvent disadvantageous arrangements of power when necessary, but we should not overlook the likelihood that the center party will also occasionally forgo use of expected protocols for the sake of realizing specific advantages within the conflict. For example, the Vatican is also in a position to leak news which damages the opposition party, and it may drop the practice of courtesy in regard to a bishop who has crossed acceptable lines of behavior. Because the familiar structures of engagement, courtesy and secrecy generally favor the position of the center party, however, my expectation is that the periphery party will be more likely to forgo use of these practices than will the center party.

One can also conceive of occasions in center-periphery conflict when nonstrategic reasons (that is, reasons which are not about seeking advantage over the opposition party) for breaking with conflict-handling protocols are put forth. For example, a member of the hierarchy may break with the standard ways on the grounds of principle or out of the feeling that his own or others' use of those ways has betrayed him.

To summarize the contents of this long section succinctly: a member of the hierarchy (himself the product of intensive social conditioning) may employ social power in center-periphery conflict either by reinforcing the Church's prevailing social identity and cohesion, or by threatening to undermine or acting to undermine the same.

Legal power, like social power, both constrains and empowers the parties to center-periphery conflict. Within the Church organization, members of the hierarchy possess powers (which are sanctioned by Church law) to contribute to the making of Church laws and to act as interpreters and enforcers of Church law. Members of the hierarchy are also *subject* to the laws of the Church. At the same time, members of the hierarchy are subject to the laws and legal culture of society as well (and their immersion in the legal structures of society will influence the way that they understand and enforce laws of the Church: as in perceptions of rights, fairness, justice, etc.). In some cases, Church leaders may have control or influence over the legal structures of society, but this is exceptional rather than usual in modern times.

In center-periphery conflict we can expect to see participants pursue their own interests by employing the powers guaranteed them by Church law. We can also expect that they will be limited by constraints imposed by Church law. But whereas questions of Church law almost by definition apply in cases of center-periphery conflict, legal power that is based on the laws of society are more likely to inform such conflict in less transparent ways.

The Pope and other bishops of the Church exercise powers to make laws and govern and judge the Church in accord with the prescripts of the *Code of Canon Law*, and they oversee other administrative agents and tribunals who help them with this work. Canon law itself is understood to be a means by which the Church carries out its mission (John Paul II 1983, xi).

As should already be obvious, members of the hierarchy are not equal in their possession of legal power. A Pope, for example, can depose a bishop, but the reverse is not also true. Moreover, certain judicial decisions made at the level of a local diocese can be appealed to Rome and may be overturned at that level. The Pope possesses the highest power of judgment in the Church: There is "neither repeal nor recourse" against his decision or decree (Canon 333). A Pope's power to make law also goes beyond that of a bishop. An outstanding example is the recent revision of the *Code of Canon Law* itself, a work which incorporated the contributions of bishops (and other theological experts), but which was instigated by decree of one Pope (John XXIII) and finally approved and promulgated by another (John Paul II). Still, it is not true to say that the pope is "above the law," even in regard to Church law. And it would be a mistake to overlook the legal power that bishops themselves possess, especially in overseeing the local churches. Granfield (1987) provides a helpful analysis of the legal limits on primatial power in the Church. While conceding the tremendous official autonomy that accompanies the papal office, Granfield observes that the Pope is nonetheless constrained by various forms of natural law, divine law and ecclesiastical law in his leadership of the Church.

The normative character of the Church suggests that members of the hierarchy will want their actions to be legal in fact, or at least appear to be legal. The Church sets forth its laws as the product of ongoing discernment in continuity with the divine law of Revelation communicated through the Old and New Testament traditions (John Paul II 1983, xiii). Thus a strong presumption prevails which sees a connection between legality and ethical rightness. A bishop or Pope who acts in agreement with the law can make the case, explicitly or implicitly, that he is conducting himself in a morally proper way.

We can expect that members of the hierarchy will use their knowledge of the legal structures of the Church not only to pursue their preferred course of action but to justify it. Presumably, center-periphery conflict participants will manipulate Church structures and procedures to advantage and they will also invoke the correctness of their relationship to legal authorities -- be they impersonal (specific laws or Church teachings) or personal (officers of the Church) – to justify their actions.

In center-periphery conflict the center party has a clear advantage of ecclesiastical legal power over the periphery party. To a great extent the periphery party must work within a legal system that is controlled by the center party. To nullify this advantage and achieve objectives opposed by the center party, two likely options for the employment of legal power present themselves to the periphery party. One is to work cleverly within the ecclesiastical legal system as it exists to make it work in one's own favor. (I rule out the possibility of trying to change the controlling system in a short-duration conflict.) This can be done through skillful bureaucratic maneuvers, tactics of delay, creative interpretations of applicable laws, and most especially, perhaps, through appeals to alternative sources of legal authority recognized within the Church tradition. Another option is to appeal directly to the Pope himself, in order to try to separate him from a position that members of his curia have taken.

The other general possibility is to appeal to legal standards or powers which lie outside of the Church organization. This strategy has become more viable since the Second Vatican Council, when the Church recognized sources of authority outside of the Church which have a legitimacy that is independent of the Church. One way this strategy could apply – but this is in fact more an application of social power than of legal power – is by the periphery party drawing attention to the contrast between ecclesiastical and societal legal orders. From a given cultural viewpoint, the Church's legal order may compare unfavorably with the societal legal order. Thus, proponents of Western-style democracy, inside the Church and out, have criticized the Church for non-democratic practices that are written into canon law, such as the top-down secretive process for naming bishops and the exclusion of women from holy orders. Conceivably, a local bishop could play off these cultural resentments to heighten his own popularity while putting pressure on the Vatican. But this is a risky strategy because the bishop may ultimately lose power within the Church by appearing too closely aligned with extrecclesial groups.

Traditional power is another means of coordination and control available to Church leaders. The effectiveness of this type of power rests on the force of habit (Russell 1986, 21). Because a form of social practice or thought has been consistently embraced over time (within recent memory, at least), it gains acceptance as a "fact of life," or as "a given." The strength of a position based on tradition is the unlikelihood of its being challenged: the everyday routine can solidify into "an inviolable norm of conduct" (Weber 1958, 296; see also Weber 1962, 59).

Church leaders can reinforce established traditions actively by practicing those traditions and invoking them symbolically, and passively by not challenging the traditions. An emphasis on tradition as a unifying element – various traditions coalesce in one overriding, consistent tradition -- is one of the hallmarks of Catholicism. All of the central aspects of Catholicism, including its sacred documents, its teachings, its patterns of worship and its social commitments, are the products of tradition(s) and are legitimized by tradition(s). Hence there is nothing surprising in the fact that members of the hierarchy would apply traditional resources and make appeals to traditional authorities when leadership decisions are at hand.

Considering the richness and variety of Catholic traditional life, it is also not surprising that members of the hierarchy sometimes find themselves in disagreement about how the traditions of Catholicism relate to present circumstances (Congar 1985, 23; Dulles 1985, 86-87). The pluralism that characterizes the history of Catholic thought and practice invites parties in conflict to emphasize those traditional concepts and practices which most reflect their own viewpoint. Indeed, one of the essential tasks of the Catholic hierarchy (itself a traditional responsibility, and one that involves significant power) is to discern which Church traditions are most telling for the contemporary Church. I will not here enter into the complex and contentious question of the "immutability" of certain Church teachings, but will simply acknowledge that, throughout its history, claims have been made on behalf of the Church that on essential issues its teaching has remained internally consistent and "unchanging" (cf. Gaillardetz 1997, 101-128). Within this perspective, new Church teachings never reverse earlier Church teachings but simply reflect a deeper understanding of the question that the Church is communicating. For our purposes here, it is only necessary to acknowledge that

Church teaching has been formulated in a multitude of ways and has been translated into practice in even more various ways.)

When analyzing cases of center-periphery conflict, we will want to observe which traditional resources each party chooses to emphasize (see also the discussion in section 3.2.2, below). How does a bishop or Pope explain his choices? Does he invoke God? Jesus? The Holy Spirit? The teaching authority of the Church? Apostolic tradition? Does a bishop make mention of the current Pope? His fellow bishops? Does the speaker carry on as though his own authority is self-evident? Another matter to examine, especially in written communications, is the range of documentary authorities cited. Variances in ecclesiology can be signalled by a Church leader's tendency to cite, for example, recent papal encyclicals rather than the documents of Vatican II, or Canon Law rather than Scripture.

Traditional power can also be called upon and expressed in nonverbal ways (Bartholomaus 1978, 96). Members of the hierarchy may symbolically invoke the traditional power of their office through things as simple and direct as the clothing (clerical garb varies in its level of refinement, as does liturgical vesture: cf. Noonan 1996) and jewelry (such as papal and episcopal rings) they wear. What is important to note is not so much the attire itself, but how the attire or other marker of traditional power – as in physical posture or gesture (kissing the Pope's ring) -- relates to its context. Does it draw attention to distinctions of rank? (For examples, see Hanson 1987, 95-97 and Bernstein and Politi 1996, 515.) Is it meant to elevate feeling in a gathering, giving the impression a critical mission is underway? (Melady 1999 depicts John Paul II's deployment of markers of traditional power, such as the Mass and established ecclesiological images, in the course of his pastoral visits. Melady also shows that the traditional markers themselves evolve, as in the case of papal pastoral visits, which John Paul II has undertaken much more extensively than previous popes.)

Members of the hierarchy may also draw upon the power of tradition by refraining from using certain elements or by playing off of its symbolic markers. For example, a bishop may present himself in democratic fashion as a "man of the people" (or as one who possesses the "common touch" – cf. Bourdieu 1991, 68). This can be achieved in part by wearing simple clerical clothing or non-clerical attire, not insisting on highly deferential treatment, presiding at low-key rather than "high Church" liturgies, making frequent visits to the poor and bereaved, not employing his power in a highly authoritarian fashion, etc. These acts of forbearance are themselves underwritten by long-standing, active traditions in the Church, which call for austere living and devotion to those in need (Franciscan spirituality is an example). While the bishop does not stop being a bishop (member of an elite) when he adopts this manner of conduct, to many people he will look better for his willingness not to take advantage of his advantaged position.

In center-periphery conflict we can expect that the center party will have more of a stake in proclaiming a traditional unicity for the Church (i.e., the idea that one consistent, permanent tradition guarded by Rome applies in the Church) and that the periphery party will be more likely to advance a view of tradition that is pluralistic and evolutionary. The reason for this is that it is easier for the Holy See to preside over the Church if variations of thought and practice are kept to a minimum. On the other hand, local bishops have an easier time in leading their own particular churches if they have the freedom to accommodate local preferences for thought and practice. Presumably both sides will draw on arguments from within the tradition (magisterial teachings, theological reflections) in order to make their case with the other. Thus, Rome will find advantage in arguing that Church tradition, according to the traditional understanding (singular) that has been handed down, is one and the periphery party will have reason to hold that Church tradition (the teachings and practices which have been handed down over time) have always made room for local variations of thought and practice, within limits. The critical question, for our own purposes, is how each party invokes tradition for strategic advantage within the conflict handling.

Expert power is one more type of power available to participants in center-periphery conflict. Expert power may be utilized when members of the hierarchy act as experts themselves -- based on their education, experience or practical competence in matters of Church governance, theology, spirituality, etc. It may also be applied through Church's leaders' command of resources of expertise at their disposal (documentation, advisers, etc.). Expert power subsists both in the actual possession of expertise and in the *perception* that one is an expert. Recognition as an expert legitimizes one's judgments. In technical matters, people normally prefer the judgment of an expert over that of someone less tutored. (Though we should be careful to notice when being labeled an "expert" becomes a liability, as in cases of populist backlash against elite parties.) Consequently, members of the hierarchy can employ expert power by possessing and acting upon education, experience and competence, and also by taking advantage of the perception that they possess these faculties.

While it is safe to say that every member of the hierarchy will be able to draw on expert power, it is difficult to generalize about the specific education, experience and competencies each will possess. Training and experience will vary. All bishops have studied theology and some are theological experts. But only a small minority have theological expertise comparable to that of full-time scholars of theology. Canon law is another area in which some bishops may be considered experts, but again this constitutes only a small portion of the episcopacy. At best, one might say that all bishops are experts on Catholic life and culture in general, and the great majority (those who are diocesan bishops) might also be deemed experts on local Church life and governance. The Pope, and those cardinals and bishops who collaborate with him in the Vatican, will have an advantage of knowledge over other members of the hierarchy in regard to the functioning of the topmost layers of the Church bureaucracy, for only they are privileged to view its workings on a day-to-day basis.

Expert power, by definition, is an elite possession. Experts are set apart as a result of the perception that they have wisdom and abilities others do not. In regard to the hierarchy, one must wonder if the fact that they are already set apart from the general populace (through celibacy, ordination, and the mystique associated with being a "successor to the apostles") does not bolster the impression that they are also exceptional in their possession of expertise. In any case, expert power is always relative to the knowledge possessed by the perceiver. Expert power (like all power) does not exist if it is not recognized. To the general populace, bishops may be experts in theology and may draw on the consequently available expert power. Professors of theology, however, may concede less expert power to the bishops, since their own theological training is extensive and may exceed that of the bishop in question.

In cases of center-periphery conflict we can expect that participants will take advantage of expert power when the possibility arises. Thus they will draw on the knowledge resources (both theoretical and practical) they possess and they will try to gain allies by cultivating the perception that their knowledge is superior. Since center-periphery conflicts engage matters of Church teaching and practice, we can expect that there will be competition to provide more compelling interpretations of what is at stake in the conflict and what authoritative precedents apply. In the contemporary Church this may take the form of disagreements about the legacy of Vatican II or about how Church law relates to the situation at hand.

As I suggested above, there may be other factors (such as inaccessibility) which reinforce perceptions of one's expertise. Superior power, for instance, can give the impression of superior knowledge. One may encounter operative perceptions that the people in charge must know better *because* they are in charge. This would seem to be a factor in disputes about Church governance. One can imagine that the population at large will assume that the Vatican knows better than local Church officials in debates about which precedents of Church tradition apply to given circumstances and which possible course of action will be best for the universal Church. In some cases of conflict with the Vatican, a local bishop may enjoy expertise advantages of his own. He, and not the Curia, is the expert on the local Church and local situation. He sees on a daily basis how the people of the local Church think and act and how they respond to various pastoral initiatives. This can help him to communicate his viewpoint more convincingly in the local (if not the global) context. (We might speak here of a clash between theoretical and practical experts.) Since the Vatican has a vested interest in not alienating the local Church, this presents itself as a significant advantage for the local bishop. The use of expert power in media exchanges can also influence of the course of center-periphery conflict.

Apart from demonstrating superior expertise in conflict situations, one may also adopt a strategy of undermining perceptions of the opposing party's expertise. Possibilities for carrying out this strategy include: casting doubt on the opponent's possession of expertise (Are his credentials or arguments suspect?) or, contrarily, conceding the opponent's expert status while fanning popular sentiments of distrust for experts (by suggesting that it is better to be good than to be smart).

Charismatic power is the final type of power Vaillancourt identifies in his discussion of how upper-echelon officials exercise control in the Church. Vaillancourt observes that this kind of power may emanate directly from a person, in the form of exemplary or ethical prophecy, or may be routinized in an office (cf. Weber 1959, 297). We can expect that pure charisma will be more strongly influential than routinized charisma (Etzioni 1961, 204). By linking charismatic power to, or transforming it into, legal, traditional and expert power, charismatic power can be made more predictable.

In its most basic form, charismatic power appears in the uniqueness of personality. A person possesses certain charisms or "gifts," such as eloquence, boldness, spiritual insight, etc., which make him (or her) attractive or persuasive to others. When the power of these gifts is intensively persuasive, perceivers may come to believe that they are of divine origin. The notion of priest as *alter Christus* in the Church offers a dramatic example of how charisma undergoes routinization in the Church. In this case the uniqueness and unprecedented quality of Jesus' last supper with his disciples comes to be replaced by the priest presider's strict adherence to repeated patterns in the Eucharistic liturgy. Charismatic power that is attached to a particular person rather than to an office can be dangerous for the Church because it displays power that is independent of the Church's institutional power. A popular bishop in a conflict with the Vatican has the possibility of taking many of his followers with him out of the Church if the conflict proves irresolvable. On the other hand, charismatic power in the hands of one who remains firmly within the institutional Church can be a tremendous institutional asset. Many commentators have noted how Pope John Paul II has used his personal charisma in this way (cf., for example, Melady 1999, Hanson 1987). In studies of center-periphery conflict, we should maintain a distinction between transferable and nontransferable forms of charismatic power.

We can expect to find charismatic power in both its nontransferable-personal form and transferable-routinized form in cases of center-periphery conflict. Participants will differ in the amount of personal charismatic power they possess, but every bishop will have access to the routinized charismatic power that comes with his office. A mystique surrounds the persons holding the highest offices of the Church. Several elements contribute to the public perception of the specialness of these officials, including: their authority as rulers, teachers and judges of the Church; the traditional-historical link to Christ's apostles; and symbolic enhancements in the form of official promises (celibacy and obedience), formal attire and ritual (especially liturgical) roles.

Charismatic power of the personal, nontransferable type may function in unforeseeable ways in center-periphery conflict. Because of its potential to mobilize followers and sway antagonists, it can trump the use of other, more predictable kinds of power (such as organizationally-routinized coercive power) by opposing parties. This is especially true when charismatic power is employed through the mass media. But note too: charismatic power of the highly personal variety can be fleeting in its persuasiveness – today's media hero may well be tomorrow's has-been – and audience appeal does not always translate into support for one's policies, as Greeley (1979, 39) has noted. In cases of center-periphery conflict we will want to observe the forms of charisma and its applications. What is the source of the charisma? (Is it a distinctly religious kind of charisma, rooted in perceptions of the possessor's closeness to God? Or does it appear grounded in more secular kinds of appeal, such as personal attractiveness, strength, mysteriousness, etc.?) How does the possessor convey his charisma? (Through writing? Public speaking? Conversation? Does he use the mass media?) And, are the ends achieved through charismatic power more beneficial to the individual or to the organization?

Conclusions

In this section I have described eight types of power whereby members of the hierarchy coordinate and control the organization that is the Church. I have also pointed out select ways these powers, given their possibilities and limits, can serve strategic purposes within center-periphery conflict. By way of a summary, I offer the following table, which shows the *types of power* that members of the hierarchy can be expected to employ, certain *means* by which the power can be applied, my *expectations* concerning applications in center-periphery conflict, and a set of *questions* to guide the examination of the Rome-Hunthausen case.

Anticipated Applications of Power in Center-Periphery Conflict

Types	Means of Application in Church	Expectations for Application in Center-Periphery Conflict	What to examine in the Rome-Hunthausen Case
1. Ecological Power	One may employ ecological power by preserving separating distance between self and other (by refusing to offer or accept invitations, by using bureaucratic rules or officers as gatekeepers). Another application of ecological power involves maintaining control over one's own territory (ensuring that clerical and popular support is firm). Finally, one may attempt to establish control over the opposing party's territory (through surveillance, as in ad limina visits, appointments of helper bishops and nuncios, etc., but also through symbolic assertions of control over territory, as in papal visits).	Center and periphery are separated by distance (a fact that offers advantages to both parties). Rome has more opportunities for closing the distance (through papal visits or requiring the local bishop to come to Rome). The Vatican has jurisdiction and control over diocese of Rome; its jurisdiction and control apply to other local churches as well, but to a lesser extent in practice. The local bishop strongly controls his own local church but has little influence over the other territory overseen by Rome. The greatest source of leverage for the local bishop appears to be the possession of strong support within the local church, which Rome will be reluctant to alienate.	Does Hunthausen go to Rome? Does the Pope go to Seattle? What is the role of the papal nuncio? What if the function of ad limina visits, if they took place? What is the function of helper bishop appointments? Where there other ways that Rome was able to monitor Hunthausen's leadership in Seattle? Did Hunthausen find ways of crossing over into and having influence within the center party territory? Were symbolic means of establishing control over the other party's territory applied on either side? What was the level of Hunthausen's support within his own archdiocese, and did this prove to be a significant advantage to him?
2. Remunerative Power	The Pope can apply remunerative power through his power of appointment (providing bishops with auxiliary bishops, assigning bishops to more prestigious sees, making bishops cardinals, giving bishops curial assignments). The Pope can also remunerate by conferring prestige (by praising a bishop, visiting his diocese, including him in inner circles of decision making). Local bishops are more limited in their ability to remunerate the Holy See (possibilities: financial contributions, promoting the prestige of and causes of the papacy in the local church).	The center's ability to remunerate the periphery (especially over the long run) is an important advantage in its favor in center-periphery conflict. A local bishop will be reluctant to lose favor or the possibility of future rewards from Rome. The local bishop's ability to reward the Pope is not as great, but the Pope has incentive to see that the local bishop continues to provide financial contributions and a favorable picture of Rome in the local church. This gives the periphery some influence over the center. The most likely forms of remuneration to come from either side are public expressions of praise and agreement.	How has Rome remunerated Hunthausen in the past? Are any remunerations from Rome to Hunthausen being applied or in the offing in the present? Does Hunthausen appear to have ambitions for higher office or closer ties to Rome? How has Hunthausen remunerated the Holy See in the past (has Seattle been a key financial contributor)? What would Rome like to see from Hunthausen at the time of the conflict and in the time beyond it? To what extent does Rome confer visibility and prestige on Hunthausen? To what extent does Hunthausen praise and support the Pope and his causes?

3. Coercive Power	The Pope can coerce a local bishop by criticizing him, investigating him (apostolic visitation), limiting his powers (taking faculties away), withholding reward, silencing him, removing him from office, reassigning him and excommunicating him from the Church. He can also employ coercion by (explicitly or implicitly) threatening any of the above actions. Local bishops do not enjoy similar, legally sanctioned means for penalizing the Pope, but they have the opportunity to coerce Rome by taking actions (or threatening to take actions) that embarrass Rome, limit its resourcefulness or jeopardize its relationship to the local church.	In center-periphery conflict, Rome is likely to draw on its wide assortment of coercive powers to try to bring about compliance from the periphery party. We should expect that it will do so, however, in ways that minimize the appearance of heavy-handedness. (In other words, Rome will want the coercion to appear legitimate and respectful of rightful freedoms of the periphery.) The local bishop is likely to employ significantly more limited tools of coercion, in particular the threat of non-cooperation and of bringing embarrassment to Rome. Coercive kinds of criticism may be carried out by surrogates representing both parties to the conflict.	Did Rome (the Pope) apply specific kinds of observable sanctions against Hunthausen, and if so, which? Did Hunthausen sanction Rome, and if so, how? Did the threat of imposing penalties serve the conflict handling strategy of either side? What techniques were used to make the imposition of penalties more acceptable to the other party and to outside observers?
4. Social Power	Social power focuses on needs for belonging and acceptance. Bishops are heavily conditioned to feel attached to and protective of the Church. Some bishops may be more oriented toward the center ("Romanized") than others. As a reflection of their socialization, we can expect bishops to manage intraecclesial tensions through the use of *familiar structures of engagement* (Church laws, chain of command, communications protocols, recognizable forms of "common sense"), *courtesy* (deferential language, indirectness, euphemisms, etc.) and *techniques of extenuation* (silence, secrecy, limits to access). At times, a party may find advantage in forgoing social expectations (by breaking from politeness or secrecy, for example).	The existing social conventions in the Church favor those who have the most power according to the conventions. In center-periphery conflict, this means that the more powerful center party has a stronger incentive to maintain the existing social norms and the periphery may have more reason to abandon or challenge such norms (in order to gain more power; but NB, such activity brings great risk for the periphery party, and so we should not expect this choice to be made lightly). In center-periphery conflict, we can expect, therefore, that both parties will use familiar structures of engagement and standard forms of politeness and will pursue their disagreements quietly (secretly, politely) in order to keep up their own appearance and that of the Church. Presumably the periphery party will be the first to break from the prevailing social expectations (by offering open criticism, departures from secrecy, etc.).	How "Romanized" do each of the conflict participants appear to be (by virtue of their education, ties to the Vatican, theology, etc.), and does this prove to be an advantage? Do the center and periphery parties apply the expected forms of conflict handling (familiar structures of engagement, courtesy techniques of extenuation), and if so, how does this advantage or disadvantage them? Does either party forgo social expectations in the conflict handling at any point? If so, how (who goes first), and what is the result? Do membership factions (within or without the Church) play a role in the conflict handling, and if so, how? Are the center or periphery party able to apply social pressure by appealing to outside groups?

5. Legal Power	The center and periphery parties can be expected to conform to the laws of the Church and to apply the powers legally entrusted to them. The papacy has legal jurisdiction over the world's particular churches and can force compliance (through threat or application of sanctions) as necessary. . The periphery party has no recourse of appeal to a decision of the Holy See: in Church disputes, the Holy See legally holds the ultimate powers of legislation, enforcement and judgment. The center party can enhance its advantage in contested matters by entrusting their handling to opaque bureaucratic processes that the center controls. To advance its own position, the periphery party can attempt to work cleverly within the existing system (through tactics of argumentation and delay, direct appeals to the Pope, or appeal to other legal standards recognized within the Church), but it is unlikely to bring change to the system itself in the short run. Alternatively, the periphery party may appeal to legal powers and traditions existing outside the Church.	We can expect that the center party will attempt to handle center-periphery conflicts quietly and at low cost, by applying the legal means at its disposal. This suggests that it will try to deal with contested matters behind the scenes using existing offices and procedures of the Church bureaucracy. Presumably the center party will apply legal penalties to the periphery party in an ascending order of severity, as necessary, to gain compliance. We can expect that the periphery party will attempt to work within the legal structure of the Church to advance its own position (through argumentation, recruitment of well-placed allies, tactics of delay and bureaucratic manipulation) before it makes appeal – in the face of the failure of the above-named efforts – to extraecclesial sources of legal authority.	Which legal powers does Rome apply in its conflict with Hunthausen (commands, bureaucratic processes, sanctions, surveillance, etc.)? Which representatives of the Holy See apply these powers, and what is their legal status (curial officials, nuncios, appointees)? Does Rome try to contain the conflict entirely within its bureaucratic apparatus? Do applied penalties increase progressively in accord with a need to gain compliance? Which legal powers does Hunthausen apply? Which forums for legal contestation apply (courts, bureaucratic offices, informal private settings, public gatherings)? Which sorts of legal arguments do both sides advance? How does Hunthausen attempt to advance his cause within the existing legal system? Does he appeal to extraecclesial sources of legal authority, and if so, which and how? Is the expectation of great legal advantage for the center-party born out in the Rome-Hunthausen exchanges? Why or why not?

| 6. Traditional Power | Traditional power has to do with ingrained habits of thought and practice. Traditions may be actively reinforced by symbolic invocation and applications in practice. One also finds a passive form of support for traditions in the choice not to challenge the traditions. Members of the hierarchy have powers which are bestowed to them through tradition (they are understood to be successors to the apostles and to have standard powers of leadership that have been recognized over time). Thus, they have a vested interest in maintaining certain traditions. An ongoing tension in the Church concerns whether the Church's "Tradition" is one or pluralistic. The means for applying traditional power may be verbal (preaching, teaching, giving orders) or nonverbal (as in certain liturgical acts, choices of setting and attire, uses of body language, etc.). Church leaders may resist certain traditions of thought or practice for various reasons (including to increase their own power), but normally we should expect them to point to a particular strand of tradition as justification for doing so, since respect for tradition is a central aspect of life in the Catholic Church. | Tradition favors the primacy of the papacy in the Catholic Church. Thus, we should expect to find strong support within the Holy See for doing things in the Church as they have been done in the past. Local bishops are also well served by conservatism in Church matters, so we should expect the periphery party, too, to challenge the status quo only reluctantly. One difference we can anticipate in center-periphery conflict is a greater inclination for the center party to emphasize the unicity of Church tradition and a greater inclination for the periphery party to emphasize notions of plurality (allowing for diversity and shared leadership within the Church). Again, challenges to tradition will be made on the basis of references to tradition. | Do representatives of the Holy See emphasize the unicity of tradition, and if so, how (words, actions)? Do any representatives of the Holy See actively challenge existing traditions, and if so, which and how? Does Hunthausen argue for a pluralistic view of Church tradition? If so, does he appeal to traditional concepts when doing so? (Which?) In which forums do communications take place (at the Vatican, in public or private meetings, during liturgies, in correspondence, during ad limina or pastoral visits, etc.)? How do the conflict parties position themselves (their identity, their relationship to the Church) through their employment of religious language (images of God, references to the Church, invocations of Church teaching or theology)? |

| 7. Expert Power | Church leaders may apply their own expertise (grounded in education, experience or practical competence) or command employments of expert power by others (advisers, theologians, canon lawyers). The key to the effectiveness of expert power is that one be perceived to know more (be more competent) than another party. Bishops (and especially bishops closely associated with Rome) will be assumed to be experts on various aspects of Church life (theology, Church law, etc.). But the perception that one is an "expert" can also have a down side: elitist connotations associated with expertise can repel some persons or groups. Thus, it is possible to paint one's opponent as an expert in a negative way and to argue that it is better to be good than to be smart. | The center party will automatically enjoy an advantage in perceptions of its expertise in many Church matters (especially in disputed matters of Church teaching or canon law). The center party can also call on a multitude of highly-placed experts in support of its positions on matters of Church teaching or governance. The local bishop will be presumed by many to have a superior knowledge of conditions within his own local church and will be assumed to be closer to the people. In center-periphery conflict we can expect that the center party will operate on the assumption of its superior knowledge in Church matters, and that the periphery party will counter by emphasizing its own superior awareness of people's everyday experience, especially in the local church in question (perhaps even to the point of fostering negative feelings concerning Vatican "experts"). | Does Rome demonstrate its expertise in obvious ways? If so, how and in which domains? Does Rome call upon experts to help make the case on its behalf? (Who and how?) Does Hunthausen presents himself as an expert of some kind, and if so, what kind of expert and how does he do this? Does Hunthausen foster feelings of mistrust toward experts on the center party side? If so, how does he do this, and to what effect? |

8. Charismatic Power	Charismatic power may emanate directly from a person or may be routinized in an office. Bishops, by virtue of their office, enjoy high levels of routinized (transferable) charismatic power (mystique and authority that come from, among other things, their traditional link to the apostles, their right to confer sacraments, the symbolic trappings of their office, their powers of Church governance). Beyond this, they may also enjoy some level of personal charisma, which they can apply to advantage (embodied in traits such as eloquence, personal strength, integrity, etc.).	The center party enjoys a higher level of routinized charismatic power than does the periphery party, and this will likely work to its advantage in center-periphery conflict. If mystique surrounds the office of a local bishop, it is much more so the case of the office of Pope, who is understood to be the successor to Peter and able to speak infallibly on questions of faith and morals. Moreover, while there are thousands of bishops around the world, there is only one Pope, and he carries out his duties amid the magnificence of Rome. In addition the routinized charisma of the papal office commands significant levels of respect around the world, whereas a bishop's mystique will know its strongest effects within the bishop's own diocese. An uncertainty in center-periphery conflict handling is how much personal (nontransferable) charisma the party representatives possess and are willing to apply in the conflict. Personal charisma can carry one a long way in conflict. If the local bishop is highly charismatic, this may serve him well in the conflict handling (assuming of course his own personal charisma is not offset by the Pope's or that of some other center party representative).	How do the center and periphery parties apply the routinized charisma they possess, and to what effect? Does Pope John Paul II employ his own personal charisma within the conflict, and if so, how? Do any other Vatican representatives try to apply their own personal charisma in the conflict handling, and if so, how? How much personal charisma does Hunthausen show, and how does this contribute to his conflict handling?

TABLE 2.5

These descriptions bring to a close my account of key aspects of the internal arrangement of the Church organization. To review: the chapter survey has included an introduction of roles within the hierarchy, a definition of organization, a classification of the Church as a type of organization, a presentation of organizational goals of the Church, a look at Church resources (both human and material), and an analysis of the means of coordination and control whereby Church leaders (members of the hierarchy) direct resources toward the achievement of the designated goals. The purpose of this chapter has been to gain insight into organizational factors (structures, pressures) that will be relevant to the management of center-periphery conflict. The discernments articulated here serve to sensitize the reading of the Rome-Hunthausen, presented hereafter in chapters six to eight.

Before proceeding to the consideration of the case, however, there is more theoretical (sensitising) ground to be covered. Organizations, and organizational leadership conflicts, do not function in a vacuum. They must be appreciated in societal context. Therefore I turn now to an assessment of the societal pressures that have direct bearing on the Church organization and on Church center-periphery conflicts.

CHAPTER THREE

CENTER-PERIPHERY CONFLICT IN SOCIETAL CONTEXT

3.1 Points of Orientation

The choice of coping strategies in center-periphery conflict will reflect the societal as well as the organizational context. Since the Church is a global organization, we need to see it in the fullness of the context that is the modern world. This is, needless to say, an imposing task. While it cannot be achieved comprehensively here, it is possible to highlight some especially relevant aspects of the societal context which are likely to affect how members of the hierarchy conduct themselves in center-periphery conflict. In this chapter I pursue three main questions:

(1) What attitudes do the hierarchy bring to worldly engagement?
(2) What characteristics of the modern world are especially relevant for leadership of the Church?
(3) What do the answers to the two previous questions imply for the handling of center-periphery conflict?

The answers to these questions should provide us with a fuller sense of how the Church engages the world and a clearer set of expectations about the conduct of center-periphery conflict.

I understand organizations to be "open systems" (cf. Weverbergh 1992, Likert 1967) wherein resources are drawn from the environment and products are released into the environment. Obviously not all of the goods ("products") that the Church produces are tangible and quantifiable, though some are (e.g., Church buildings, schools, hospitals, and services rendered through these facilities; Christians themselves can also be considered, though the usage is crude, to be "products" sent forth into the environment). But the open systems lens is useful for avoiding the temptation to analyze organizations independently of these processes of environmental interchange.

Parsons, working from this same perspective, helps us to see more clearly the interchange between an organization and its environment. He perceives organizations to be subsystems of society that contribute to the functioning of society (Thung 1976, Parsons 1959). Parsons well-known AGIL typology categorizes organizations according to the functions they carry out in society. Organizations focused on economic production (e.g., businesses) primarily fulfill *Adaptation* functions. Organizations which are oriented to political goals and exercise power in the political sphere (e.g., governmental organs, credit banks) are especially oriented toward *Goal achievement* functions. Organizations that adjust conflicts and facilitate cooperation for the sake of maintaining institutionalized roles and functioning (e.g., courts, political parties) primarily serve *Integrative* functions. Cultural and educational organizations (e.g., churches and schools) are mostly ordered to the maintenance of patterns of social interaction. As such they fulfill a *Latency* function. All organizations carry out all of these functions in some degree, but the accent varies sharply with organizational type (Thung 1976, 47-48. See Van der Ven's 1996, 63-83 use of Mintzberg 1979 for a further application (AGIL / LIGA) of Parson's typology to the Church).

An important contribution from Parsons' perspective to our own understanding is that the exchange between Church and society is not simply a one-way exchange, wherein the Church seeks to manipulate its social environment for the sake of furthering its own ends. Society, too, (if I may speak of the social environment as a single entity; perhaps it is better to speak of other groups and individuals within society) engages the Church and draws benefits from the Church's presence, while feeling the effects of the Church's activity in myriad ways. In Parsons' (stability oriented) scheme, the Church serves as a source of social stability and meaning-provision within the world. This role gives the Church influence even with those who stand outside its membership. But the Church is only one organizational system among others in the social environment. These other systems may have interests that are either compatible or in competition with those of the Church (Thung 1976, 113). Only in the context of this total, dynamic interplay can we properly discern the opportunities and challenges that spur the Church as it pursues its mission. I will now consider a range of attitudes which have informed the hierarchy's management of the Church's progress within its social environment. Thereafter I will offer some commentary on the type of environment wherein the Church finds itself.

3.2 The Hierarchy's Attitudes Toward Worldly Engagement
Like other organizations, the Church *is influenced by* its environment, but also *has influence on* its environment (McGuire 1997, 160; Thung 1976, 111-114; Safranski 1985, 1-2). Analyzing these patterns of interaction is complicated because the Church is a complex entity changing over time, and its social context is still larger, more complex, and also changing. Thus far we have accumulated data revealing aspects of the Church's internal functioning. Now we direct our attention to the ways the Church engages the human culture that contains it. Considering the diversity of cultures within which the Church functions, this is no easy task. But we can at least depict the modern societal context in broad strokes, and see the Church's engagement of human society in an ongoing diachronic perspective.

Historically, the Church has perceived its engagement with "this world" (Robinson 1977, 13-29) with marked ambivalence. Citing the creation account of Genesis 1:1-2:3, the Church has understood the world to be God's creation which he saw to be "good." But scripture also describes the "fall" (Genesis 3), a term that through subsequent theological development has come to signify the world's estrangement from God. According to Church teaching, Christ's intervention in the world (symbolized by his cross and resurrection) overcomes this estrangement. Through Christ the world is restored to rightful relationship to God. Nonetheless, until final establishment of "a new heaven and new earth," the world remains a sinful and dangerous place. Hence, while affirming that "God so loved the world that he gave his only Son" (John 3:16), the New Testament also offers warnings about the world ("Do not love the world" -- 1 John 2:15; "The whole world is under the power of the evil one" -- 1 John 5:19; cf. Robinson 1977, 22). Taking up Jesus' charge to "make disciples of all nations" (Matthew 28:19) and to be his witnesses "to the ends of the earth" (Acts 1:8), the Church has conceived itself to be, simultaneously, of the world, in opposition to the world and sent to the world. More recently, especially since the Second Vatican Council, it has also understood the world to be the place where God's presence is active even outside of the Church (cf. the doctrine of *Missio Dei*).

In practice, the Church has sought to make use of the potentiality it has found in its social environment. Thus it has proclaimed its gospel message to Christians and non-Christians alike, employing existing languages and techniques of persuasion, prevailing organizational strategies and other material and non-material resources. It has done so from positions of social advantage and disadvantage, with neither stance proving unproblematic for the Church's mission. As the Church has sought to bring all people into the fullness of union with God, it has at times found itself in social contexts that have opposed the Church organization (as in the Church's early struggle with the Jewish leadership and the Roman government in Palestine) and at other times in social contexts that have actively promoted the Church organization (as in the centuries of Christendom). (Thung 1976, 111, following Thompson and McEwen 1958, envisions a continuum along which the Church dominates or is dominated by its environment.) Cultural resistance has often, paradoxically, served to enhance the Church's "mission effectiveness." In the old saying, the blood of martyrs is the seed of the Church. Courage demonstrated by Church participants in times of persecution has proven to be a compelling example for those inside and outside the Church: impressed by the heroic witness, many have been drawn to the Church and established deep(er) commitments to it. In reverse fashion, and also paradoxically, cultural endorsements of the Church, while normally welcomed by the Church leadership (and membership) have increased Church membership over the centuries, but sometimes at the expense of deep internal commitments. When many cultural advantages accompany Church membership, it is not surprising that some will join the Church for the sake of realizing social (rather than expressly religious) goals. Possessing the power to dominate the social environment has also brought temptations of complacency and malfeasance to the Church at times (as in the Inquisition, the pre-Reformation selling of indulgences, evangelization by force in Latin America, etc.).

These historical examples demonstrate that the Church's effort to achieve its organizational goals (see sections 2.4.2, 2.4.2.1 and 2.4.2.2, above) has manifested a variety of stances toward the world it finds itself in, and in particular toward persons, practices and beliefs standing outside the Church. In order to clarify the range of possible stances Church members may adopt in regard to perspectives arising independently of the Church ("worldly" perspectives), I present the following scheme of ideal types, sketched for this occasion. This scheme distinguishes a set of options available to members of the hierarchy as they guide the Church in its worldly context.

Stances of Openness to Church and World:
A Range of Positions Available to the Hierarchy

Change Church according to world			*Change world according to Church*	
-2	-1	0	+1	+2
Radical	**Liberal**	**Centrist**	**Conservative**	**Reactionary (Radical)**
Openness to world always improves Church (makes Church redundant)	Openness to world often improves Church	Openness to world sometimes improves Church	Openness to world rarely improves Church	Openness to world never improves Church
Action: Flee Church; Overcome Church	Action: Reform Church	Action: Dialogue	Action : Reform world	Action : Flee world; Overcome world

FIGURE 3.1

By "world" in this scheme, I mean realities of earthly life which the Church does not control. This draws on the old pejorative meaning of world, whereby Church and world stand opposed, but I make use of this meaning for clarity of contrast only. I do not hold the view that the Church and its worldly context can in fact be distinguished in a tidy way. The essential question here is, *How open are members of the hierarchy to systems of thought and practice which contrast with the usual systems of thought and practice of the Church, and how is their level of openness manifested in their own leadership?* The positions I identify are placed along a spectrum. As one moves to the left, non-Catholic thought and practice is increasingly appreciated and the willingness to change the Church is increasingly plausible. As one moves to the right, non-Catholic thought is increasingly perceived as threatening and the openness to changing the Church is ever smaller. A description of each position on the spectrum follows. (Note: the terms used to identify the five positions on the spectrum above -- radical, liberal, centrist, conservative and reactionary -- appear commonly in discussions of Church and secular politics, and their meanings vary with context. I wish to signify with these terms only the ideas expressed in the diagram above and in the descriptions below, and nothing further. They are, for my own purposes, primarily handy markers for distinction. The term "radical," as commonly used, could fit at both ends of the spectrum I have constructed. For the sake of clarity, I assign it to the left end, as distinct from "reactionary" on the right.)

The **radical position** bespeaks a deep distrust of the Church and a fully committed openness to the extraecclesial world. According to this stance, secular wisdom normally surpasses that possessed by the Church. This is in fact an exit position from the Church organization or a position of very marginal membership. It may also be the position of those who wish to undertake revolution in regard to the Church, or pursue its abolition. It is not a position we can expect to find among members of the hierarchy.

The **liberal position** characterizes those who stand committed to the Church organization while training their gaze beyond it in search of insights that can improve the Church. Persons adopting this stance believe that the extraecclesial world has much to offer the Church. Though they show little inclination to leave the Church, they are prepared to admit the Church's shortcomings and to substantially remake the Church in light of "worldly" discoveries. One can find members of the hierarchy who hold this viewpoint, but they are rare.

The **centrist position** describes Church members who are decisively committed to the Church but are open to dialogue with the world. Such persons operate from an assumption of the Church's correctness but are willing to concede that occasionally the Church falters and at times wisdom drawn from outside the Church can benefit the Church. Statements of principle are more likely to emerge from this position than concrete actions undertaken to transform the Church, but concrete change is not ruled out. It is likely that many bishops will fall in this category.

The **conservative position** foresees little chance that the incorporation of extraecclesial perspectives will benefit the Church. Persons operating from this position are reluctant to search out and apply to the Church insights not traditionally accepted by the Church: on the contrary, insights not traditional to the Church are typically perceived to pose a threat to the Church. Thus, in general (some exceptions may be allowed), changing the Church according to the wisdom of the (extraecclesial) world is not acceptable. Many bishops will fall in this category.

The **reactionary position** is the position of those who find the Church to be fully self-sufficient (a *societas perfecta*) and the extraecclesial world to be wholly insufficient. For these persons, the separation between the Church and the world outside its borders must be maintained at all costs. Contact with non-Catholic viewpoints is conscientiously avoided. The only options for the Church are combat against the world (overcoming it through material or spiritual efforts) or total disengagement from (flight from) the extraecclesial world. Because of the extremity of this position and its impracticality, we can expect it to be only very rarely adopted by bishops.

Having envisioned a range of options for Church member openness and responsiveness to Church and world, the question remains, What is the hierarchy's official perspective (position) on this matter? Though this question cannot be answered definitively, I do believe that Church teaching articulated at the Second Vatican Council goes a long way toward providing an answer.

3.2.1 *Gaudium et Spes* Reveals Operative Attitudes Toward Worldly Engagement

In my earlier discussion of the organizational structure of the Church, I consulted the Vatican II document *Lumen Gentium*, which sheds light on how the hierarchy understands the Church's internal functioning. I now turn to another document of the Council, *Gaudium et Spes* (otherwise known as the *Pastoral Constitution on the Church in the Modern World*), for its valuable articulation of how the hierarchy views the Church's functioning in relation its global social context. This document, promulgated in 1965, has been exceptionally influential in the thinking of the post-Vatican II Church as the result of its timeliness, its authoritative status (it is a teaching of the entire college of bishops in union with the Pope), and its comprehensive treatment of a topic that had not previously been addressed in a separate document at a prior Ecumenical Council (Campion 1966, 183-184).

Gaudium et Spes, as much as or more than any other document, expresses the official stance of the conciliar / post-conciliar Church in regard to the modern world. It is not the only or most recent authoritative statement which applies (subsequent papal encyclicals, curial documents, bishops' conference letters, and the *Catechism of the Catholic Church* (1992) have also taken up this topic, often with apparently less openness to the world), and many positions taken in *Gaudium et Spes* were contested both during and after the Council. But *Gaudium et Spes* does reflect attitudes toward worldly engagement which have remained relevant and officially sanctioned within the Church throughout the post-conciliar era. Examination of the document gives us a glimpse of how positions associated with the ideal types identified above are conceptualized and, at the same time, embraced or rejected in hierarchical discourse. Moreover, the document provides justification for the view that the hierarchy's attitudes toward worldly engagement tend to fall within the centrist or conservative positions, and occasionally within the liberal position, but rarely within the radical or reactionary positions.

On the whole, *Gaudium et Spes* reveals a centrist stance toward extraecclesial thought and practice. The emphasis in the text on openness to the world ("earthly matters and the concerns of faith derive from the same God" (36)) is persistently coupled with a presumption of the Church's own privileged insightfulness. Thus, while God is acknowledged to be present in the fullness of human activity (and not simply in the witness of the Church), and while the obligation to delve into worldly affairs and to engage contrary viewpoints (92) is affirmed, the Church retains the authority and responsibility to distinguish "earthly progress" from "the growth of God's kingdom" (39).

At times, the document's prioritization of reading the "signs of the times" gives the document a liberal cast – as in the observation that the Church seeks "to uncover, cherish, and ennoble all that is true, good, and beautiful in the human community" (76). But I would argue that the document only leans in this direction, while remaining firmly in the centrist, and occasionally in the conservative, position. The outward gaze is ordinarily justified by the intention to learn how the Church can better serve humanity, but not vice-versa. The possibility of restructuring Church thought and practice according to extraecclesial perspectives is not really considered. Hence, the document discusses the Church's role to serve the human community by: witnessing to the truth (3); offering assistance in fostering brotherhood (3); responding to perennial questions about this life and the life to come (4); offering recommendations for building up human society (11); helping the human community to form a correct conscience (16); and promoting the pursuit of authentic freedom (17). But contrary examples are rare. Worth noting are the document's recognition that misconceptions and sinfulness exist within the ranks of the Church (19, 43); its acknowledgement that the Church depends on forms of expertise arising outside of the Church as it seeks to penetrate the truth (44); and its declaration that the Church's conversational partners should include all persons, holding all manner of divergent viewpoints (92).

In one sense, evidence of conservative positioning can be found throughout *Gaudium et Spes*, especially in its presumption that the Church understands those outside the Church better than they do themselves, and in its express intention to reform the world according to Churchly understandings. The secular world, for all of its knowledge and resourcefulness, will never obtain a truly coherent, comprehensive and deep insight into reality so long as it excludes Christ from its comprehending. Modern technologies and institutions will always be lacking so long as they fail to perceive that reality itself is God's ongoing act of creation and that humanity finds its dignity and fulfillment through its being created in the image of God. In keeping with this viewpoint, *Gaudium et Spes* again and again makes distinctions between concepts that are partially grasped within a secular framework and more perfectly grasped within a Catholic framework. One sees this sort of distinction at work when the Council fathers write that the Church depicts "man's *true* situation" (12) and "directs the mind to solutions that are *fully* human" (11) (my emphasis). In other words, *Gaudium et Spes* frequently mixes signs of its attentiveness to secular developments with (polite) expressions of disapproval.

But to truly embody the conservative position as I have defined it above, the document would need to show a decided wariness of the extraecclesial world: the world outside the Church would need to be presented as more threatening and less promising. That simply is not the case in *Gaudium et Spes*. The concern here lies with threats to humankind -- war, slavery, hunger, poverty, illiteracy, social strife (4) -- which the Church can help to address, not with threats posed to the Church by engagement with the world.

For the same reason, *Gaudium et Spes* cannot be said to articulate a reactionary viewpoint. The reactionary intention to disengage from the (extraecclesial) world is expressly rejected. (See, for example, articles 34, 39, 40, 43, 62, 93.) On the contrary, Christians are "stringently bound" to attend to this world and the welfare of their fellows persons (34).

At the opposite end of the spectrum, the option of radical openness to the world is also rejected. No inclination to flee the Church in search of a better world shows itself, nor are there any outright admissions that superior forms of thought and practice drawn from outside the Church should be used to remake the Church.

In my opinion, the range of attitudes toward worldly engagement discernible in *Gaudium et Spes* reflects a range of attitudes acceptable within the hierarchy in the conciliar and post-conciliar periods. I take the document to be a form of empirical evidence of the hierarchy's way of thinking at a particular time (over 85% of the world's bishops approved its promulgation in 1965) and a statement of norms intended to inform post-conciliar decision-making. As such, it provides a general indicator of attitudes likely to be operable in center-periphery conflict in the decades immediately following the Council (at least through the time of the Hunthausen case, I would hold, since Hunthausen, Cardinal Ratzinger and Pope John Paul II were all present at the Council). Admittedly, positions taken during the Council have been contested in the post-conciliar years (see Kasper 1989, 166-167; Dulles 1988, 19), but attitudes expressed within this contestation have tended to remain within the range of acceptable attitudes toward worldly engagement (that is, according to the centrist, conservative or liberal positions, but not the radical or reactionary positions) suggested by *Gaudium et Spes*. (The Lefebvre case may be the exception which proves the rule. Arguably, Lefebvre's attempts to reverse teachings of the Council can be seen as an example of adoption of the reactionary position. His effort was rejected by the papacy and received little support from the rest of the hierarchy.) To sum up, then: it is my expectation that, in cases of center-periphery in the years since the Council, one is likely to find bishops holding centrist, conservative and, more rarely, liberal positions regarding worldly engagement, but significantly less likely to find bishops (openly, at least) holding radical or reactionary positions, because the Council did not endorse these latter positions.

3.2.2 Openness to the World and the Invocation of Authority
The attitudes toward worldly engagement held by participants in center-periphery conflict will be relevant to the handling of such conflicts in several ways. Most essentially, participants' attitudes toward the Church-world encounter will determine which sources of authority can be called upon and which kinds of argument can be advanced in center-periphery conflict. In conflict, it is advantageous to be able to call on sources of authority which are closer to oneself than to the opposing party (in other words, sources of authority which one controls and / or which are associated with one's own position of authority). This is an important issue, because the sources of authority which apply in center-periphery conflict are "given" only in a limited sense (cf. Gaillardetz 1997, 26-28): to a large extent they are contested in the course of the conflict itself. Moreover, the number of potentially relevant sources of authority increases dramatically when the door is opened to consideration of extraecclesial sources of authority.

Authority is largely a question of point of view. Even when agreement exists about which authorities should be recognized (e.g., the hierarchy agrees that God's authority is supreme), understanding of the nature of this authority typically is pluriform (thus, one bishop sees the God of justice, while another sees the God of mercy and forgiveness). So we are left with certain questions. Which sources of authority will be invoked when? How will they be invoked? And how will these invocations be received by the opposing party?

What is crucial in the perspective of Vatican II as articulated in *Gaudium et Spes* is the openness to the possibility of recognizing extraecclesial sources of authority. By suggesting that the Church can learn from experience taking place outside its walls, the hierarchy has conceded the relevance of extraecclesial points of reference: other systems of thought and practice (science and technology, other religions, cultural systems, etc.) have something to offer the Church. Though the door to this possibility is opened cautiously, it is nonetheless opened: one would be hard pressed to interpret *Gaudium et Spes* otherwise.

The implication for the handling of intrahierarchical conflicts is that a range of intraecclesial and extraecclesial concepts of authority can be drawn upon to support one's position. Even two parties referring to the same object and using only descriptors endorsed by the Church will not necessarily characterize the object in the same way. Hence: God may be invoked as sovereign ("Almighty God," "the Lord") but also as suffering servant; the Church may be described as a "fortress" or as "a pilgrim people;" and the world may be presented in terms of praise or rejection.

In regard to center-periphery conflict handling, we can expect to find struggles over definition. It is highly likely, in the first place, that both parties to center-periphery conflict will attempt to justify their position in the conflict with reference to sources of authority traditionally recognized in the Church (God, the Bible, Church teaching, etc.). Second, given the multiple sources of authority (recognized by the Church) that can be invoked, and the various ways each of these sources of authority can be called upon, we can expect that such invocations will be put to strategic use in center-periphery conflict and will be matters under contestation. Third, we should also not be surprised to see the invocation of extraecclesial sources of authority, especially when one party (most likely the periphery party) is having difficulty advancing its position with more usual kinds of Church-recognized authority. (In other words, if a party is losing the conflict debate when it is limited to an ecclesiastical reference frame, it can attempt to expand the reference frame to include secular perspectives that may be more advantageous to its position.) I see greater likelihood for the periphery party to look for extraecclesial authoritative supports simply because the center party has a significant advantage when it comes to calling upon sources of authority that are strongly associated with the Church. The center party normally (formally) gets the last word on how God, the Bible, Church teaching, etc. are to be understood by Catholics. Given an unpromising outcome in such an exchange, the periphery party may well find reason to look for other grounds on which to make its case.

3.3 Characteristics of the Modern World Pertinent to Church Leadership
The Church hierarchy leads the Church organization in the societal context which is the modern world. Having identified a possible range of stances toward the "world" that we can expect members of the hierarchy to adopt, we are left with the question: What sort of world is it that Church leaders and the Church itself encounter empirically? My assumption is that the handling of center-periphery conflict is conditioned by the societal as well as the organizational culture. Therefore, it is necessary to spend time considering which aspects of the societal culture appear to be especially pertinent to the handling of center-periphery conflicts.

Gaudium et Spes itself, of course, highlights certain characteristics of the modern world. The list of characteristics below is culled from the document. It provides an introduction to aspects of modernity which the Church hierarchy has found to be relevant to its own mission. (Article numbers appear in parentheses.)

Characteristics of the Modern World Noted in *Gaudium et Spes*

1. Profound and rapid change in the world of human experience (4, 5)
2. The extension of human power through scientific advances and technology (4, 33)
3. A newfound abundance of wealth, resources and economic power (4) (coupled with the

persistence of hunger, poverty, illiteracy)

4. An unprecedented awareness of freedom (4)
5. New forms of social and psychological slavery (4)
6. A vivid sense of global human interdependence (4, 23, 33, 84)
7. Continuing political, social, economic, racial and ideological disputes (4)
8. The threat of totally-destructive war (4, 79, 80); dependence on arms stockpiling for war deterrence (81)
9. A growing exchange of ideas among peoples (4, 54) alongside problems of communication (4)
10. A search for human betterment that excludes spiritual concerns from the process (4); "spiritual agitation" (4-5)
11. A failure to adjust permanent values to new situations (4)
12. Uneasiness as people are buffeted between hope and anxiety (4)
13. A scientific and technological orientation (5)
14. The extension of human self-knowledge through history, biology, psychology, social sciences (5)
15. The replacement of a "rather static" concept of reality with a "more dynamic, evolutionary" one (5)
16. Changes in traditional local communities such as families, clans, tribes, villages (6)
17. Spreading industrialization (6, 54) causing changes in economic and social conditions
18. Urbanization (6, 54)
19. New and more efficient media of social communication (6)
20. Migration leading to social change (6)
21. Social ties that fail to produce positive personal and social developments (6)
22. The growing social influence of young people (7)
23. Dissatisfaction with existing institutions, laws and modes of thinking (7)
24. Newly critical religious thinking leading to the rejection of magical or superstitious practices (7)
25. The abandonment of religious practice by growing numbers of people (7)
26. An inability to synthesize modern practical thought -- a loss of a comprehensive view of reality (8)
27. A concern for practicality and efficiency at the expense of moral demands (8)
28. Conflicts resulting from social, racial, economic inequalities (8)
29. A universal moral belief that cultural benefits can and should be extended to all (9)
30. An ever-increasing number of people raising questions about the meaning of human life (10)
31. Widespread atheism ("among the most serious problems of this age") (19) often in systematic forms (20, 34)
32. New forms of (mass-) culture (20, 54); widely uniform customs and usages (54)
33. Progress in the methods of production and in the exchange of goods and services (63)
34. A growing divide between economically advantaged and disadvantaged countries (63, 66)
35. Increasing diversification of forms of private ownership and dominion over material goods (71)
36. Advocacy for protection of personal rights through political-juridical order (73)
37. Problems stemming from rapid population growth (87).

BOX 3.2

These characteristics of the modern world identified in *Gaudium et Spes* can be organized according to four main themes. First, there is an **unprecedented quality to life** in the modern world: the extent and rapidity of scientific, social, economic, political and cultural change makes this age different from those that have preceded it. Second, **secular scientific thinking and techniques** have been especially important contributors to the modern world's wondrous advantages (increased knowledge, resources, power and communications capacities; more egalitarian and participative social-political structures) and dangers (the threat of totally-destructive war, new forms of social and psychological slavery, rapid population growth, social unrest, moral-spiritual dislocation). Third, the **development of the human person and human social groups through secular scientific thought and techniques** (we understand people better through biology, psychology, sociology, etc.; we encounter one another socially in new ways through industrialization, urbanization, migration, new communications media, etc.) – a positive development – has sometimes come without equally intense and rapid forms of moral and spiritual development. Fourth, as a result, **a spiritual agitation characterizes the modern age**, a situation of opportunity and danger. Amid the turbulent change (old ways of doing things no longer apply, traditional communities dissolve, trusted institutions are displaced) humanity has lost its moorings and gives expression to its lostness in disaffection, atheism and failures of hope.

At times, there is tension between the viewpoints expressed in *Gaudium et Spes*. Thus, for example, the document speaks of the loss of a comprehensive view of reality (see no. 26 above) and of a societal concern for practicality and efficiency coming at the expense of moral considerations (no. 27) while commending society's advocacy of the extension of cultural benefits to all (no. 29). It is hard to know whether this contradiction lies with the world perceived or with the perceiver. In either case, the document reflects a recurrent tension between the impulse to appreciate and more negatively evaluate modern conditions.

And what is the Church's empirical response to this modern world to be? According to *Gaudium et Spes*, it is to carry out the Church's mission (*Lumen Gentium*'s description of the Church as "a sacramental sign and an instrument of intimate union with God, and of the unity of all mankind" is explicitly invoked: see article 42, but also my own discussion of the Church's goals in chapter two), informed by an open but critical attentiveness to what is transpiring within the world.

3.3.1 Elaboration of the Description of the Modern World
Before considering how the handling of center-periphery conflict relates in specific ways to the Church's societal context, it is to our advantage to further specify that context. I have already summarized certain themes in the Church's perception of the modern world. These themes can be pursued fruitfully by consulting writings of the sociologist Anthony Giddens. Giddens' perspective both confirms and challenges concepts of the modern world put forth by the Church.

In works such as *The Consequences of Modernity* (1990) and *Modernity and Self-Identity* (1991), Giddens probes the nature of modernity and its consequences for social life. For Giddens (1991, 14-15), "modernity" refers very generally to "the institutions and modes of behaviour established first of all in post-feudal Europe, but which in the twentieth century increasingly have become world-historical in their impact. 'Modernity' can be understood as roughly equivalent to 'the industrialised world', so long as it be recognised that industrialism is not its only institutional dimension."

Giddens is but one among several writers of recent decades who have illuminated major aspects of modernity, and who might well serve our purpose of clarifying the empirical societal context that contains the Church. (C. Taylor and J. Habermas present themselves as likely alternatives.) But I am impressed by the fact that Giddens is at once influential (his work has at times been ground-breaking) and representative in his thinking (if one compares the overview of thinking about modernity in Van der Loo and Van Reijen 1997, one finds that much of Giddens' thought resonates with generally accepted findings). Moreover, Giddens is articulate on themes that appear highly relevant to my own study, such as the modern world's loss of confidence in providential reason and the modern organization's need to engage in reflexive monitoring.

If we take in turn each of the four themes I highlighted from *Gaudium et Spes*, we find that Giddens speaks to each of those themes in his own work. (Though Giddens writes at a later date – the two works I cite were published twenty-five years after Vatican II – his concern with the period of modernity as a whole takes in and remains relevant to center-periphery conflict handling in the postconciliar period.) Giddens comments on the pace, scope and profoundness of the changes that mark the modern world (1990, 6; 1991, 16) and points to the role of scientific thought and technology in creating this "runaway world." Giddens also echoes the views that science and technology have set before humanity great benefits and great dangers (1990, 7-10) and have transformed the way people live, interact socially and understand their humanness (1990, 112-124). Finally, Giddens shares the view that modern people suffer from various forms of "existential anxiety" (1991, 35-69) and that traditional communal networks and institutions which once would have helped people to manage this anxiety have been replaced or are being replaced (cf. his concept of "disembedded relations").

But there are differences, too, between Gidden's account of life in the modern world and that given by the Catholic hierarchy at Vatican II. From his later vantage point, Giddens seems to be even more impressed by the rate and scope of change in modern life, and this is understandable because he has had more time to observe how computer technology and other scientific developments have revolutionized the contemporary world. Giddens is also in a position to see better how scientific advances have created new benefits (e.g., global information systems networks) and dangers (e.g., foreseeable ecological disasters) not discussed in the conciliar document. In regard to the third and fourth themes, Giddens does not make a case, as the Church does, for addressing the crises of modern life in a specifically spiritual or religious way, but he does acknowledge that people's loss of their bearings in matters of faith and life philosophy amounts to a moral problem.

Additionally, there are other perspectives that emerge in Giddens' study of modernity that do not appear in the Vatican II account. In *Gaudium et Spes* one finds a healthy respect for what Giddens refers to as "providential reason." Providential reason is the faith, associated with the Enlightenment period, that reason enables humankind to gain increasing knowledge and control over its worldly environment, to the increasing benefit of humanity. The conciliar document proposes, of course, that such reasoning will go astray to the extent that it is not open to the wisdom that comes through faith in God. Nonetheless, the optimism concerning the world and the potential for continuing human progress (despite the seeming disproof offered by the two world wars) is a remarkable feature of *Gaudium et Spes*. Knowledge in this context continues to function as a manageable tool. The tool may be misused, but knowledge can potentially be harnessed for human purposes. Giddens (1991, 27), on the contrary, finds that confidence in providential reason has been undermined and totally mistaken (following Beck 1986). Not only is there much evidence to show that knowing more does not necessarily make people better (more "enlightened"), but new knowledge (cf. chaos theory in physics and deconstruction in linguistics) also has the potential to undermine the foundations on which current knowledge is based (or even to question the possibility of "knowledge" altogether). Thus, while language is a stabilizing force, permitting the reenactment of social practices across generations (1991, 23), it can also be a source of fragmentation and destabilization.

For an organization such as the Church, which places a premium on the authority of tradition, the challenges posed by these aspects of modernity are clear. At the time of the Council, the Church saw itself as a centrally relevant institution whose language and practice needed to be updated and aired out -- for the sake of organizational effectiveness, but also for the sake of faithfulness to its own tradition. Certain important aspects of tradition had come to be neglected (e.g., episcopal collegiality, the role of the community in the celebration of the Eucharist, the role of the laity). The Council expressed the Church leadership's belief that these traditional elements needed to be polished and brought into the light. But even more fundamentally, the Council expressed the conviction that Church tradition, and the Church itself, is a living thing in the world, and not something closed, static or already completed. What did not seem to be up for grabs at the time of the Council was the authority of tradition itself. Though authority was being questioned in highly public ways by the time the Council closed -- in the form of war protests, civil rights protests, insurrections against colonial governments, student rebellions of various kinds -- the thrust of much of this discussion favored replacing existing orders with more just and accountable orders. As such, they may be seen as further expressions of confidence in providential reason. But anti-institutionalism itself (an attack on tradition-oriented bearers of authority per se) was limited to the social fringe and had not yet found mainstream expression (as it would in the 1970's-'80's-'90's preoccupation with New Age religions that promoted spiritual searching outside of institutions). And members of the intellectual elite had not yet been captivated by deconstructionist theory, which holds (somewhat disingenuously) that language does not ever truly cohere, since signs cannot be fixed to meanings. Similarly, public confidence in the steady advance and manageability of science had not yet faced the Pandora's box posed by biomedical advances (consider the challenges posed by cloning, in vitro fertilization, genetic engineering, etc).

I do not want to exaggerate the extent to which public confidence in science, reason, tradition (even religious tradition) and institutions has been corroded. People continue to put faith in reason, institutions and God, and to believe that human progress is possible. But we should not overlook significant ways that the social climate has changed in the period that concerns us in this study. Giddens is right to point out that in modernity one chooses between "possible worlds" (1991, 29) in a non-authoritarian way ("bricolage" as task), and this has never been more true than in recent decades. The separation of time and space (through maps and clocks synchronized globally) and the disembedding of social institutions (lifting social relations out of local contexts through mechanisms such as symbolic tokens -- e.g., money, diplomas, credentials -- and expert systems) has placed modern persons in a social setting that is much global as local. Giddens describes an ongoing "dialectic of the local and global" (1991, 22). In premodern times one had a much easier time accepting local realities as fixed and stable reflections of the way things are. But modern technology, communications, economic possibilities, travel and processes of cultural mutuality and democratization have confronted modern peoples with, quite literally, "a world of possibilities" and tremendous pressure to consume. For much of the world's population, personal identity is less inevitable and more a product of choice than it ever has been. Knowing more about other cultures, religions, ways of thought and practice, modern peoples have to consciously discern which aspects of their own cultural-personal identity they will retain and nurture. All the while, of course, one encounters the threat of finding no sure footing at all. It is this public that the Church has sought to embrace and serve in its recent history. The challenge for Church leaders is imposing. How does the Church successfully enter into this dialectic of the local and global? How does it offer a sure place to stand for modern people without becoming fixed (calcified) and irrelevant as an institution? How does it address the "paradox" of modern benefits which are intrinsically and tensely related to accompanying dangers? (cf. Van der Loo and Van Reijen 1997, 48). And how does it promote confidence in a given religious tradition when one has a world of belief systems to choose from (including the possibility of not "believing" in anything)?

Before leaving Giddens, I want to call attention to one more aspect of his thought that is especially instructive for our purposes here. Giddens perceives four institutional dimensions of modernity: industrialism, capitalism, surveillance and the industrialization of war. Of these four, I will comment on his notion of *surveillance* (cf. Foucault 1977), because it has an especially direct bearing on Catholic intrahierarchical conflict. In Giddens view, reflexive monitoring is constitutive of modern social life. Ours is a "risk society" (1991, 28; cf. Beck 1986), because all activities are subject to contingent happenings and entail risk (some with potentially disastrous consequences). Science and technology have provided ever more means for monitoring risk but this ability to monitor conditions and calculate risks has also created an ever-more-anxious focus on risks. Modern life has come to be characterized by a "calculative attitude," wherein we constantly evaluate the risks associated with the open courses of thought and action available to us. Constant informational inputs make us aware of risks we might otherwise have ignored (in a less "wired" world). And tools for monitoring can pose threats in and of themselves. For example, the internet that lets us better keep track of the world also lets the world keep better track of us.

The difference between pre-modern and modern practices of human reflexivity is that "in pre-modern civilizations reflexivity is still largely limited to the reinterpretation and clarification of tradition" (1990, 37), but in the context of modernity this reflexivity

> is introduced into the very basis of system reproduction, such that thought and action are constantly refracted back upon one another. The routinisation of daily life has no intrinsic connections with the past at all, save in so far as what "was done before" happens to coincide with what can be defended in a principled way in the light of incoming knowledge. To sanction a practice because it is traditional will not do; tradition can be justified, but only in the light of knowledge which is not itself authenticated by tradition. (1990, 38)

It is not just individuals who demonstrate this calculative attitude. Organizations, too, practice reflexive monitoring and must continually face the possibility of radical doubt concerning the organization's choice of direction and reason to be. Giddens (1991, 16) notes that organizations, a prototypically modern social form, are distinctive not primarily for their size or bureaucratic character but for the reflexive monitoring that marks their awareness of contingency. Management science is a contemporary phenomenon, whereby organizational leaders attempt to rationally anticipate and manage risk to the advantage of the organization (and themselves within it). This sort of monitoring includes attention to the micro-, meso- and macro-level dynamics of the organization. Organizational leaders want to know what is happening in individual-level exchanges that involve organizational members, but they also want to be able to see how the organization functions internally as an organizational whole and externally in relation to its environment. Gaining this total perspective requires constant information gathering and assessment and a readiness to integrate useful findings into the organization's operations. Church leaders are no less susceptible to this tendency of organizational reflexivity than are leaders of any other organization. It is simply the way organizations function and survive in modern times.

To sum up, Giddens introduces several concepts which enhance our understanding of the modern societal context which contains the Church. His heightened emphasis on the rate, scope and profundity of change in modernity and on the social volatility following from scientific and technical developments lends depth of perspective to the Church's more confident, optimistic assessment of the modern context. His assertion that trust in providential reason has been undermined and mistaken, leaving social fragmentation and destabilization in its wake, sharpens our sense of the difficulty facing the Church as it carries out its mission in the world. The authority of a tradition-based organization faces serious challenges when tradition itself is suspect. Giddens' commentary on the "dialectic of the local and global" points to the need for a paradigmatic shift in thinking in the Church (which may or may not be underway). Whereas previously the task for Rome was to link and establish a high level of uniformity within clearly-distinct, locally-grounded local churches (this task being an operational approach to the attainment of "unity"), now these local units are no longer local in the sense they once were. The rest of the world intrudes upon local settings (in the form of ideas, consumer goods, media products, travelers, immigrants, etc.) and the multitude of localities presses upon the world (local ideas, goods, persons do not stay local: they circulate globally). Church members' ties to specific localities are increasingly tenuous, and an awareness of pluriformity in the Church and in the world suffuses the Church. It is not clear how the post-conciliar Church intends to address these problematic realities. Finally, Giddens points to the strategy of "surveillance" practiced by organizations in modern times. Organizations monitor conditions and calculate risks in order to survive and thrive in their social environment. This approach serves a pressing need in the absence of confidence in providential reason. On the one hand, the Church itself remains a standard bearer in the cause of providential reason. Essentially its position is that, while secular forms of providential reason (faith in humanity, faith in science) have been unmasked, the one true form of providential reason – personal participation in the divine plan for the world – remains. So let us get back to it. But the question remains: to what extent is this even possible (and what shape should it take) in the modern world? This is a real question because the loss of faith in providential reason is alive within the Church as well as outside it. Techniques of surveillance, long practiced by Church leaders, offer options for maintaining the Church organization as such (one can make rational calculations directed toward the perseverance and growth of the Church), but how does this calculative attitude fit with the abandonment to God proper to faith? Do the premises which inform the practice of surveillance contradict the Church's professed confidence in God's good care of the world?

3.4 Attitude Toward Worldly Engagement As an Influence on Conflict Handling

Center-periphery conflicts are ecclesiastical events and worldly events at the same time. As such, we can expect the choice of coping strategies in these conflicts will have much to do with the way participants view the Church-world encounter. In section 3.2 I discussed a range of attitudes which can serve to characterize the hierarchy's approach to extraecclesial thought and practice in the conciliar and post-conciliar era. Subsequently, with reference to Church teaching promulgated at Vatican II (section 3.2.1-3.3), I stated that centrist and conservative attitudes are most likely to be operative in center-periphery conflicts, with liberal attitudes appearing rarely, and radical and reactionary positions appearing very rarely (since these positions stand in tension with the officially adopted stance of a guarded openness to the world that privileges the position of the Church). Finally, having thereafter identified some of the characteristic features of life in the modern world, I would now like to invite consideration of how the adoption of the above-named attitudes is likely to play into the handling of center-periphery conflict.

3.4.1 The Radical Stance in Center-Periphery Conflict

The radical stance favors the full reconciliation of the Church to the world, or the abolition of the Church altogether. The Church possesses truth only to the extent that it correctly understands and correctly acts within the world. Thus the Church is to be judged according to worldly understandings and not the other way around. From this viewpoint the Church is not the only or even the most highly privileged vehicle of salvation (whatever salvation means from a worldly perspective). Rather, the Church is one system of thought and practice (perhaps an especially compelling or helpful system) among many. The radical is constantly faced with a need to justify his continued participation in the Church, since it is one among a multitude of legitimate options for living a meaningful, satisfying life. Because this is by definition a fringe position in regard to the Church, and an uncertain one in regard to continued participation, one is unlikely to find a bishop holding this position. However, were a bishop to in fact hold this attitude, one could easily imagine that he would soon find himself in conflict with Rome and with others in the Church, because this viewpoint is dangerous for the perseverance of the institutional Church.

In center-periphery conflict, a bishop holding radical views could be expected to invoke extraecclesial forms of authority at the expense of intraecclesial forms of authority and to suggest that the Church's mission must also be justifiable according to extraecclesial standards. Because this perspective is not widely shared in the hierarchy, the radical bishop would likely have difficulty mustering the support of other bishops. Also, the official ideology and legal structure of the Church does not recognize this perspective. As a result, he would have little opportunity to exercise intraecclesial forms of coercive power.

One advantage to the radical position in center-periphery conflict is that, when such views are genuinely held, one has little to fear from the possibility of being put out of office or out of the Church, since one recognizes other options for living a satisfying life. Thus, one can approach the handling of the conflict fearlessly. Another advantage to the radical position is that it will find much support from persons and groups outside the Church. This can put pressure on the Church (and one's opponents in particular) from without. Unfortunately for the radical who would hope to prevail in such a conflict, it appears that extraecclesial support does not matter nearly so much as intraecclesial support in center-periphery conflict. Typically, the only outcome we should expect from a center-periphery conflict involving a bishop who holds the radical viewpoint is that the bishop will be removed from the Church, or at least removed from significant leadership responsibilities. The most interesting test case would involve a radical Pope, since he would challenge accepted standards of thought and practice from the position of highest power. It is hard to know what the outcome of such a case would be.

3.4.2 The Liberal Stance in Center-Periphery Conflict

The liberal stance inclines toward modernization of the Church according to the best insights of the world. Though an assumption of the Church's privileged status underwrites this position (the Church is to be preferred to other ways to God), notions that the Church is the exclusive bearer of truth or the possibility of salvation are rejected. Moreover, the interconnectedness of the world makes it obligatory to attend to and make use of perspectives arising outside the Church.

The liberal's openness to extraecclesial perspectives means that certain aspects of modernity which could be perceived as threatening are not necessarily perceived in that way. Hence, the global pluriformity in systems of thought and practice is likely to be viewed positively, as more an opportunity than a danger. Similarly, uncertainties surrounding issues of authority (What authority do traditional institutions, traditional beliefs, traditional ways of doing things have in modern time? What new sources of authority have emerged?) can be welcomed as promising occasions from which improved systems of thought and practice can develop. Even social fragmentation can be optimistically assessed as an early stage in the construction of new social configurations, wherein local ties and territorial concerns are no longer obstacles to cross-cultural, transglobal interconnectedness. And the progress of scientific knowledge can be taken to be one more means through which humanity deepens its awareness of God's presence.

It is important to remember, however, that the liberal stance, for all its openness to other perspectives, privileges the viewpoint of the Church. Therefore, the aspects of modernity cited above are interpreted according to concepts familiar within Catholic tradition and they are applied to the Church in ways designed to benefit the Church. The liberal desires the perseverance of the Church and sees realization of that goal as dependent on the Church's ability to adapt to changing times. From the liberal viewpoint, change in the Church is a necessary strategy for survival and the successful accomplishment of the Church's goals. Change is to be embraced purposefully and related to Catholic tradition, which is understood to be both pluralistic and evolving.

In center-periphery conflict a strength of the liberal position is its possibility of appealing to constituencies inside and outside the Church, because it makes use of intraecclesial and extraecclesial perspectives. The position attracts those inside and outside the Church who place a premium on the relevance and viability of the Church in its societal context. The liberal stance's openness to extraecclesial sources of authority can be both an advantage and a disadvantage. It can be an advantage by its possibility of appeal to a wider range of sources of authority, but it can be a disadvantage by exposing one to the criticism from within the Church that one is not being faithful to the Church's traditional understandings. Because the liberal view advocates changing the Church, it appeals to those who desire change and inspires resistance in those who fear change.

3.4.3 The Centrist Stance in Center-Periphery Conflict
The centrist stance presumes the privileged status of the Church in the world but acknowledges that the Church must pay close attention to developments outside its own walls. What distinguishes the centrist position from the liberal and conservative positions is that while the liberal position argues for changing the Church according to worldly knowledge and the conservative position argues for changing the world in accord with standards determined by the Church, the centrist position recognizes the reasonableness of both of these options and tries to hold them in fruitful tension. Ideally, the centrist position is bipartisan, drawing on the best insights of the liberal and conservative stances and uniting members of those camps, but it has also has the possibility of being bipolar (counterproductively directed to two incompatible positions at once). Because the centrist position is not decisively oriented toward change in one direction or the other, it tends to favor strategies of reflection, dialogue, discernment and incremental action for change.

The centrist position is skeptical toward all "extremism" inside and outside the Church. Centrists are more mistrustful of extraecclesial thought and practice than liberals, but are less confident of the self-sufficiency of the Church than conservatives. So centrists look for a golden mean balancing traditional ways of doing things in the Church with a readiness to change the Church as necessary (implementing the right changes at the right times). Because they make a point of conceding the legitimacy of a wide range of viewpoints, centrists have the possibility of forging alliances and drawing support from many different camps inside and outside the Church. That is, they are "consensus" oriented. This same centrism can be a liability, in that the commitments made, insofar as they are ideological in nature, are seen to be weak commitments, and they draw weak commitments in return. Thus, centrists are in a better position to avoid making enemies than to garner support based on commonly held ideological positions.

In center-periphery conflict centrists are likely to recognize the legitimacy of various competing viewpoints and to employ the strategies of reflection, dialogue and discernment in conflict handling. Centrism may also translate into strategies of avoidance or indifference, pluralism or integralism, depending on the circumstances of the conflict handling. Centrists will emphasize organizational continuity, with change being an option only if preceded by much aforethought and implemented cautiously. In conflicts between liberal and conservative parties, centrists are well placed to serve as intermediaries.

3.4.4 The Conservative Stance in Center-Periphery Conflict
The conservative stance presumes the superiority of the Church's system of thought and practice over other systems of thought and practice. Accordingly, it advocates bringing other systems in line with the Church's through domination (actively seeking to conform the world to the Church) or resistance (avoiding the negative influence of extraecclesial perspectives). Though God's activity outside the Church may be conceded in principle, only the Church, from the conservative viewpoint, is capable of correctly reading the signs of God's presence. Moreover, there is no question of the Church being one among many ways to God. If not the only way to God, then the Church is the most perfect way.

The conservative stance does not recognize extraecclesial sources of authority. Church tradition is authoritative by virtue of its being uniquely so endowed by God, and it is understood to be constant, coherent and transparent. Church tradition provides a rock of certainty within a modern world that has lost its bearings by placing hope and trust in ideologies that are unworthy of such confidence (secular humanism, scientific progress, non-Catholic religions and spiritualities). Just as threatening are "nihilistic" ("postmodernist") perspectives which emphasize the ambiguity and uncertainty of existence and which refuse to accept the concept of objective truth and the possibility of privileging one viewpoint above others. The task of the Church begins with the need to maintain the strength of the Church organization against threats from the outside. A premium is placed on demonstrations of Church loyalty and the employment of tried and true ideas and practices in carrying out the mission of the Church. Because external elements are perceived as threatening, there is a tendency to establish clearly-marked borders between the Church within and the Church without. To outsiders, what is appealing about a conservatively-disposed Church is the prospect of finding a safe haven from the turbulence and dangers of the world. What is less appealing is the potential constriction – the loss of freedom -- which is the price of belonging to such a Church.

In center-periphery conflict we can expect that a strength of the conservative stance will be its appearance of being unquestionably Catholic. This encourages a bold and active approach to conflict handling. Because conservatives draw on clearly-recognizable forms of Church-based authority, their loyalty is unlikely to be questioned, whereas the stance of those who suggest the relevance of extraecclesial sources of authority will be suspect by comparison. We can expect that conservatives will seek advantage over and against opponents in center-periphery conflict by drawing on established forms of power within the Church which tend to maintain the current order. These include Church law, bureaucratic procedures and the system of hierarchical rank. Keeping up the appearance of the Church as self-possessed, certain in its mission, and unfazed by internal or external threats will be a priority for conservatives in conflict situations. We can expect to see strong emphasis on maintaining the appearance of harmony and of peaceable acceptance of the prevailing distribution of power. A disadvantage to the conservative stance in center-periphery conflict is the vulnerability to the attack from centrists or liberals that one is out of touch with the times and operating from a cloistered perspective. The conservative view of the Church's encounter with the world is difficult for many outside the Church to accept because the outsider's own view is not seen as credible by the conservative. For this reason, centrists and liberals are better placed to summon extraecclesial support.

3.4.5 The Reactionary Stance in Center-Periphery Conflict

The reactionary stance values the wisdom and experience of the Church alone: it does not recognize the legitimacy of viewpoints not traditional to the Church. The Church is understood to be entirely self-sufficient. There is no need to change it. From the reactionary standpoint the Church is the only way to God and all other ways are false. These false alternatives are to be walled off from the Church. The only options for the Church in regard to extraecclesial thought and practice are combat or flight. As I have already noted, the extremity of this position puts adherents at odds with the teaching of the Second Vatican Council, which stressed the need for the Church to bring a critical openness to the modern world. The extremity of the position also makes its pastoral implementation more than challenging. Thus Rome has reason to want to avoid naming bishops who incline toward reactionary opinions. My presupposition is that only a small portion of the hierarchy operates according to the reactionary stance.

In center-periphery conflict a reactionary can be expected to claim that only his viewpoint is legitimate. All other visions of Church and world (from within the Church and from without) are faulty and therefore dangerous. We can expect this single-mindedness because extraecclesial perspectives are automatically dismissed and, since in the reactionary's view the Church can only be one way, clearly knowable, for all time, Church-based world views other than his own are also ruled out. This single-mindedness is likely to be disadvantageous in center-periphery conflict. Though such certainty and strength of conviction can be attractive to others, the inflexibility of the reactionary position makes it difficult to draw in those holding opposing viewpoints and to maintain ties for long periods of time with those who have similar convictions. The reactionary's extreme, inflexible position also makes him susceptible to attacks which paint him as a representative of the lunatic fringe. One advantage to the reactionary position in center-periphery conflict is that the reactionary can claim he is more truly adherent to Catholic tradition (which is thought to be constant and not pluralistic) than anyone else, because he makes no room for anything other than (his version of) Catholic tradition.

3.5 Summary of Expectations for the Handling of Center-Periphery Conflict

At the beginning of chapter two I suggested that examination of the organizational and societal context of center-periphery conflict could illuminate participant approaches to the handling of such conflicts. Consequently, in chapters two and three I have worked through a process of theoretical sensitization in regard to those contexts. I am now prepared to articulate a set of conflict-handling expectations for center-periphery conflict. The expectations are the outcome of the theoretical sensitization. The expectations will orient our approach to the empirical example soon to be considered, the Rome-Hunthausen conflict.

I will now summarize the main assumptions I have drawn through this process of reflection. The assumptions are expressed in terms of a *general stance toward conflict handling*, a *perspective on the use of power* and a list of *particular coping strategies that I consider highly likely to be applied* in cases of center-periphery conflict. An elaboration follows.

3.5.1 The General Stance toward Conflict Handling

My expectation is that **all members of the hierarchy participating in center-periphery conflict will strive to save the face of and enhance the power of the Church organization and themselves**. Admittedly, this is a complex formulation, since it involves two tasks (saving face and enhancing power) and two objects (the Church and oneself), which I choose not to separate out. My reason for not separating out these distinct dimensions of the expectation is that I believe them normally to be intertwined and frequently indistinguishable, not only for an outside observer but also for the conflict participant himself. Saving face is closely related to the acquisition and maintenance of power, whether one is talking about an organization or an individual. And in the case of bishops, I believe that, in general, they will be so strongly conditioned to identify with the Church organization that they will ordinarily associate the organization's appearance and power with their own. This is not to say that individual bishops will never pursue power at the expense of the Church organization or attempt to look good without concern for how the Church looks, but it is to say that – especially in cases of center-periphery conflict, where their relationship to the Church is in question – they will normally be inclined to pursue both sets of objectives at the same time.

As justification for formulating my expectation about the general stance toward conflict handling in this way, I would refer to the findings I have already presented in chapters two and three. From chapter two, I would point in particular to my descriptions of: (1) the privileges and powers that accompany membership in the hierarchy (sections 2.3-2.3.3), those being personal advantages accruing from their organizational role that we can expect bishops to want to preserve; (2) the intensive process of socialization bishops undergo on the way to assumption of their office (see the discussion of social power in section 2.4.4), a factor producing a strong tendency to identify with and protect the Church organization; (3) the mixture of motivations that all Church members, including bishops, show in their affiliation with the Church (sections 2.4.1.1 and 2.4.3.1), with the consequence that their participation shows ambivalence and varying degrees of egocentrism and selflessness; (4) the clannish side of Church life (2.4.1.2), and of clerical life in particular, which positively reinforces faithfulness to the Church "family" and punishes betrayals thereof; (5) the pressure to meet the (non-operational) organizational goal of uniting all people to God (2.4.2.1) through the operational means of growing the Church (2.4.2.2) and marketing it effectively (2.4.1.2); and finally, (6) the enticement of reward for bishops who strengthen the Church and give it an attractive appearance (see the discussion of remunerative power in section 2.4.4); (7) the threat of sanction that exists for bishops who fail or refuse to save face for the Church or work for the enhancement of its power (see "coercive power" in section 2.4.4).

From chapter three I would highlight my observations that: (1) bishops are much more likely to privilege the perspective of the Church over the perspective of the "world" (3.2.1) and will show a natural tendency to protect the Church organization (its power and appearance); and (2) bishops will attempt to defend and advance the Church's position within society through by means of "reflexive monitoring" (3.3.1), a process that attends directly to the Church's organization's power and appearance.

All of these factors, taken together, lead me to believe that bishops involved in center-periphery conflict – a situation where the appearance and power of organization and individual are at stake – will be strongly predisposed to attend to the Church's appearance and power and their own appearance and power.

3.5.2 Perspective on the Use of Power

Bishops have access to multiple kinds of power as they carry out their role of coordinating and controlling the Church. In section 2.4.4, I discussed how distinct kinds of power can be applied, in ordinary tasks of governance and in the context of center-periphery conflict. My assumption is that certain strategies for employing power (strategies for coping with the conflict) are especially likely to come to the fore in center-periphery conflict handling. I discuss these strategies in the next section (3.5.3). Before doing so, I see the necessity of offering a number of observations that articulate my expectations for how power, in general, will be applied in center-periphery conflict. These observations follow.

Primarily, my expectation concerning the use of power in center-periphery conflict is that the use will reflect the general stance toward conflict handling I have just discussed (in section 3.5.1), and much of the same reasoning applies (bishops will want to protect their own power and prestige, which is closely associated with the power and appearance of the Church organization; they are strongly conditioned to act in this way; potential rewards and punishments apply; etc.) Simply put, my expectation for the use of power in center-periphery conflict is that **members of the hierarchy will strive for (the appearance of) legitimacy in their employments of power**. This concern for legitimacy flows from the general concern for the appearance of the Church and is the natural byproduct of leadership of an organization whose ordinary means for generating member compliance are normative rather than raw. In a normative organization, power acquisition and power maintenance are dependent on perceptions of legitimacy. Thus the concern for legitimacy also serves the interest of enhancing the Church's and one's own power. By having their applications of power look "good" (at a minimum, *legal* according to ecclesiastical and civil standards; but preferably also *fair, just, charitable*), members of the hierarchy heighten the likelihood of preserving and increasing power for themselves and the Church.

In section 2.4.4 I noted (following Vaillancourt 1980) the balancing act that faces bishops when applying power in their organizational leadership role: applying power in too "raw" a fashion (forcing compliance) has the tendency to alienate Church members because it appears out of step with Church ideals, such as respecting legitimate diversity while pursuing unity (2.4.2.2); but applying normative power in a fashion that is highly respectful of members' ability to decide for themselves carries the risk that the role of the hierarchy itself will become irrelevant. Accordingly, members of the hierarchy will typically opt to employ power in ways that are in some fashion normative but still strongly controlling (drawing on social pressures, traditional habits for practice, legal guidelines that the hierarchy itself has established, etc.). This essentially is what I am getting at when I assert that members of the hierarchy will strive for the (appearance of) legitimacy when applying power in center-periphery conflict. The power employment needs to be strong enough to work (gain the desired compliance), but it should look legitimate so as to go unchallenged. Strategically, as far as the bishops' own interests are concerned, there is reason to have the use of power look as legitimate as possible – that is, as I suggested above, not simply legal, but ideally, even charitable.

My expectation, as articulated in detail in section 2.4.4, is that members of the hierarchy will apply multiple kinds of power in center-periphery conflict (any and / or all of the somewhat artificially distinguished types discussed in that section) and that these employments of power will be intertwined in complex ways. As for how, specifically, we can anticipate the various types of power being applied empirically, I would refer one to the observations offered in

2.4.4 and to the discussion of coping strategies in the next section). Before taking up that task, I will introduce one final assertion into this perspective on the use of power. My intuition is that *the degree of "rawness" of the power applied in the conflict handling is likely to increase in the face of resistance from the other party*. To put it another way, I would expect the see the first attempts to generate compliance be made through normative approaches that are respectful of the other's freedom (and which have a greater appearance of legitimacy to Church members), and more coercive approaches applied when desired ends are not achieved through normative means. A further exploration of this view is forthcoming, in my introduction of a particular theory of conflict handling in chapter four.

3.5.3 Likely Coping Strategies

Conflict within the Church hierarchy sets before those involved an assortment of dangers and opportunities. The risks at hand apply to both the conflict participants and the organization itself. Therefore we can expect that the participants, being organizational leaders and persons concerned for their own well-being, will have a natural inclination to want to employ the powers available to them to achieve satisfying outcomes from the conflict. My assumption is that this attempt to move from the current position, A, to the desired position, B, will to some degree involve rational planning (a bishop decides *how* he wants to approach the other party and the conflict realities), but will also be reflective of social conditioning that is not necessarily in the foreground of one's thinking when the plan is made (a bishop chooses a particular approach out of habit or unacknowledged desires or fears).

I believe that the term "coping strategy" captures certain distinct operative means whereby participants in center-periphery conflict attempt to manage (calculatedly and intentionally, but also according to subconscious influences and impulses) the conflict productively. The word "strategy" implies that the approach to (or avoidance of) the people and problems is *orchestrated*, in the sense that it takes into account the actions and reactions of allies and adversaries insofar as they relate to the desired outcomes. (Here I draw on the definition of strategy offered by Tropman and Ehrlich 1997, 280.) In other words, bishops will reflexively choose from among various powers available to them which powers they will apply and in which forms, factoring in what the effects of their own actions will be (and making adjustments over time), for the sake of emerging as advantageously as possible from the conflict situation.

At the same time, there will also be a sense in which their conflict handling is not orchestrated (by themselves at least): realities beyond their control, and perhaps not to their liking, will be imposed upon them, and they will be left to come to grips with these realities. Drawing on their own resources and shortcomings and conditioned ways of thinking and acting, they must deal with or "cope with" the challenges at hand. Qualifying the word strategy with "coping" reminds us that conflicts tend to be difficult (center-periphery conflicts are, in any case), may even be irresolvable, and may be "managed" by means of conflict participant behaviors that are as much impulsive re-actions as they are thoughtfully chosen actions.

Incorporating the concepts I have just specified, I define a **coping strategy** as *an orchestrated attempt to manage conflict as advantageously as possible.*

Based on arguments I have already presented in preceding chapters, I believe that a number of specific coping strategies likely to be employed in center-periphery conflict can be identified. In general, my reasons for anticipating the use of these particular coping strategies are that: (1) they draw on powers members of the hierarchy have available to them; (2) bishops are conditioned to use the strategies; and (3) personal advantages are likely accrue from doing so. I will now describe seven coping strategies that I consider especially likely to find application in center-periphery conflict.

1. Show deference to the structural order and mindset of the Church

Bishops directly benefit from current norms of thought and practice in the Church organization. A local bishop may not benefit nearly so much as the Pope does by this arrangement, but he benefits greatly nonetheless. For this reason, we can expect members of the hierarchy to be strongly disposed toward maintenance of the prevailing norms. By maintaining these norms, bishops guarantee the continuance of their own power and prestige: they protect present rewards (social approval and perquisites of office) and possible future rewards (higher appointment), avoid potential punishments (loss of power, ostracization), and honor the process of education and socialization that has shaped them and to which they have made considerable personal investments (belief, time, obedience, celibacy). Since bishops will be disinclined to alienate themselves from the organization which has so amply rewarded them, my expectation is that in center-periphery conflict participants will tread softly where the Church itself is concerned. At a minimum, they will be respectful of the Church's thought and practice in their words and deeds, and this with an almost inviolable consistency. (NB: I use the expression "structural order and mindset of the Church" above as a kind of catch-all. My intention is not to argue that there is one single order and mindset which can be specified, but that rather, one can linguistically suppose / propose that there is, and use this supposition to advantage.) Very commonly, bishops will speak highly of the Church as a whole, of what the Church has to offer the world, and of other Church leaders (especially those superior in rank). Essentially, this can be thought of as a strategy of *reassurance*. In center-periphery conflict it amounts to one member of the hierarchy conveying to another his trustworthiness: I am not a radical (or reactionary); I am not a threat to the continuance of the Church or of the hierarchy. This is not to say that criticisms of the Church or proposals for reform are ruled out altogether, but it is to say that such challenges will be voiced with justifying references to existing Church traditions and beliefs.

In terms of concrete *tactics*, one might find this strategy applied in any or all of the following ways in center-periphery conflict: by refraining from criticism of Church thought and practice and of its leaders; by using euphemisms to describe problems in the Church; by consistently invoking familiar ecclesiastical terminology (jargon, official titles, theological words) and thought (Church doctrines); by praising the Church and its leaders; and (perhaps above all) by obeying one's superiors. This last item, obedience, is perhaps the one key difference we can expect to find in applications of the strategy between the center and periphery parties. Ultimately, the periphery must answer to the center, but the reverse is true in only a very limited (and perhaps in only a theoretical) sense. The Pope is the local bishop's superior. Thus, there will be deference shown mutually between center and periphery – an honoring of the concept of shared power ("collegiality") within the hierarchy – but the periphery will need to bow much more deeply.

Before moving on, I should say a word about the distinction between strategies and tactics. In common parlance, tactics are the concrete means for carrying out a strategy. I retain that distinction here (cf. Pruitt and Rubin 1986, 3).

2. Associate one's own efforts with the best interest of the Church

My justification for anticipating use of this strategy closely follows the reasoning for anticipating the use of the Church deference strategy, described above. In center-periphery conflict, the Church itself is a mandatory reference point. As the most prominent leaders of the Church, members of the hierarchy are widely expected to be its foremost defenders, and they experience strong social incentives to meet this expectation. Therefore, it is in their interest to claim that the actions they take, in conflict situations but also more generally, are oriented toward the good of the Church. By adopting this strategy in center-periphery conflict, they *legitimize* their own actions and, at the same time, *deflect suspicions* that they may be putting their own interest ahead of all else. The latter is especially important because, given the Church's normative character, its proclaimed ideals must be honored in Church discourse.

All members of the hierarchy participating in center-periphery conflict can be expected to employ this strategy to some degree. What is interesting about this strategy is that it can be used to defend contrary viewpoints and in association with divergent traditions within the Church. The center and periphery are both likely to say that they are acting for the good of the Church, even while advocating very different courses of action.

Potential tactics for carrying out this strategy include: making frequent reference to the Church, refraining from criticizing the Church (through silence, the use of euphemisms, indirect language, etc.), and especially, expressly linking oneself to the effort to achieve recognized goals of the Church.

3. Minimize the appearance of conflict
I have characterized the ultimate goal of the Church, following one pronounced tradition within its own teaching, as a matter of bringing about humankind's unity with God. The presence of conflict in the Church is a sign that the achievement of this goal is not at hand. One can argue, of course, that conflict is a necessary step on the way to resolution in unity, but still, I would hold that for most observers the presence of conflict in the Church negatively contrasts with their impression of how the Church is supposed to be (what it is supposed to be about). Therefore, my expectation is that bishops will want to avoid giving the impression that the Church is unhappily divided within itself (this to save face for the Church organization). In particular, bishops will want to convey the impression that the hierarchy itself is functioning harmoniously, not only for the sake of the appearance of the Church as a whole, but as a means for preserving the power of the hierarchy itself, which will seem stronger if it is not beset with internal contestation.

Primarily, this strategy is a public relations strategy meant for outsiders. The point of it is not that there *be* no conflict within the hierarchy – I consider conflict to be an unavoidable feature of organizational leadership – but rather that outsiders be given limited access to the center-periphery conflict handling and that, on the whole, they receive the impression that the conflict poses no great threat to the Church organization or to the strength of the hierarchy. My assumption is that an unspoken pact will be operative between members of the hierarchy, whereby contention is allowed but ordinarily only in private. When public revelations of the conflict are unavoidable, these will, as much as possible downplay the extent and seriousness of the conflict and will emphasize the solidarity existing between the members of the hierarchy involved.

Though here I speak of an implicit agreement that applies between all members of the hierarchy participating in the conflict, I anticipate too that this strategy will at times serve one party at the expense of another. Since the center party benefits the most from the appearance of unity – the sight of one local church going its own way might inspire others to do the same -- it will be especially strongly disposed to keep the conflict handling out of view. Conflict handling in private limits the periphery's power to call on public support for its position and to recruit allies from within the hierarchy itself. On the other hand, the periphery party has incentive to minimize the appearance of conflict in its desire to protect its own reputation. Being openly in conflict with Rome is likely to be an embarrassment for a local bishop. Keeping the conflict out of sight does not necessarily produce an advantage for him in the process of conflict negotiation, but it does bring security to his position by maintaining the appearance of loyalty, thus increasing the likelihood of his not losing power.

Tactics serving the strategy of minimizing the appearance of conflict may well include: conducting conflict negotiations in secret; refusing to publicly acknowledge the existence of conflict (silence, denial); and using euphemisms to improve the appearance of one's relations with other parties, understate the gravity of the problems, or overstate the degree of harmony or prospects for resolution.

4. Show fraternity

The Catholic hierarchy often refers to itself as a brotherhood of bishops. Individual bishops, beyond having much in common with one another by virtue of the office they hold -- with its distinctive mystique (divine sanction), powers, obligations and involved preparation process -- also share responsibility for leading the Church. By their office and their shared responsibility for governance, bishops are bonded together and set apart from the rest of the Church. They are separated to a lesser extent from clerics, who typically enjoy significant powers of governance at the parish level and who share in the mystique of ordination, and to a greater extent from those who are not ordained and not canonically commissioned to govern. The notion of brotherhood, or "fraternity," suggests that the bond between bishops is a familial one: in other words, it goes deeper than rationally chosen, voluntary association. It is not simply something that one just happens to enter into or abandon. To stay within the metaphor, it is a matter of blood.

This way of conceiving of itself shapes the way members of the hierarchy interact with one another and it also shapes the way the hierarchy as a whole relates to the rest of the Church and world. The implication for center-periphery conflict handling is that bishops involved in such conflicts will *show fraternity*, which is to say that *they will implicitly and explicitly acknowledge their bond to fellow bishops, a bond that will both empower and constrain them.* The phrase "show fraternity" suggests a number of conflict handling tendencies at once, some of them competing. I choose this somewhat ambiguous expression advisedly. The verb "show" has multiple meanings. I want to highlight two of those meanings at once in my usage here: to *point out* and to *reveal*. My expectation for center-periphery conflict is that bishops will almost always *make a show of* their relationship of fraternity: that is, they will point out or point to, for all interested parties, the fact that they are "brothers" (doing so because they are conditioned to, because they want to keep up appearances, because there are social advantages to be gained, etc.). They will call one another "brother bishop(s)," they will invoke the concept of episcopal fraternity (and the related concept of collegiality), they will show a pronounced level of graciousness and respect toward one another in public, and so on. At the same time, they will also unavoidably *reveal* the bond that episcopal fraternity implies. With this I mean they will take advantage of their insider status to assume privileges not available to outsiders, but they will also at times struggle within the suffocating confines of the brotherhood. Among the advantages to belonging to the fraternity are rewards, protections and the loyal support and understanding of fellow bishops (so long as one does, oneself, show loyalty to the Church and to the hierarchy). The disadvantages of belonging include restrictions on freedom – of thought, speech, action – which follow from the expectation to guard the interests of the "family" (see my discussion of clannishness in section 2.4.1.2).

My expectation is that the center party, having more say over the management of "family matters" will emphasize the bond of fraternity in order to remind the periphery of its duty of loyalty (which serves the center party's interest). The periphery party, on the other hand, will show fraternity as a means of retaining privileges and avoiding ostracization. The risk both sides face is that betrayal of the brotherhood is always possible, if unlikely, and betrayal by an insider can do great damage to the culture of the closed off realm. The threat of betrayal has the potential of being employed to gain concessions from an opposing party.

A variety of tactics, some already suggested, could be employed to carry out the strategy of demonstrating fraternity. These include: referring to other bishops as "brother bishops" in public; invoking the concept of episcopal fraternity (and related concepts such as bondedness, collegiality, etc.); showing a heightened level of graciousness and deference toward other bishops (in comparison with what is shown toward those who do not belong to the hierarchy); showing what appears to be genuine kinds of trust and friendship toward other bishops; conducting substantial intrahierarchical exchanges in private; symbolically drawing distinctions (through attire, use of technical language, liturgical action, closed meetings, etc.) between the knowledge and experience of the bishops and the knowledge and experience of others; indicating (one bishop to another) what the limits of acceptable thought or action are.

5. Practice courtesy
The use of courtesy, beyond being serviceable as a tactic in other strategies, can also serve as a strategy in its own right (see, especially, the discussion that has preceded in section 2.4.4). That is, courtesy may be employed in orchestrated fashion for the sake of achieving designated conflict goals. Courtesy is to be expected in intrahierarchical communications in general. Bishops are strongly conditioned to use various forms of politeness to save face for the Church and the hierarchy. Courteous discourse creates the impression for outside observers that harmony reigns within the hierarchy (a condition conducive to the achievement of greater kinds of unity). Courtesy also acknowledges and reinforces hierarchical roles and distinctions of power. At a minimum, the use of courtesy prevents the giving of offense. In more targeted applications it may serve as a tool for ingratiating oneself with or restricting the movement of the other party. (Note: under most circumstances, given the purposes of this study, I feel free to use the terms politeness and courtesy interchangeably, as synonyms. Courtesy, however, is my preferred term because it carries a stronger connotation of outreaching graciousness that I believe is relevant to relations between bishops.)

As I have just suggested, in center-periphery conflict we can expect to find courtesy applied on two levels. The first level is the level of courtesy as a given (courtesy applied habitually): the use of politeness that is simply expected from any member of the hierarchy, by means of which one symbolically (primarily linguistically, but in other ways too) demonstrates respect for the Church and acknowledges one's own place in the Church's social order. On this level, the strategy is defensive in nature, and will find application in almost any public exchange between members of the hierarchy. One shows courtesy in this sense because one is socially conditioned to do so, the use of courtesy demonstrates one's mastery of (mostly unwritten) Church rules, and not employing courtesy will probably lead to penalizing repercussions. Tactics functional on this level include: avoiding criticism of the Church and Church leaders; using honorary titles (thus maintaining established social boundaries); showing respect for and carrying out the wishes of superiors; honoring formality rules; and using euphemisms and other forms of indirect language to give an untroubled appearance to troubled situations.

But one can also expect to see more premeditated applications of courtesy in center-periphery conflict as well. Such applications will go beyond matter-of-course adherence to politeness rules, by consciously attempting to manipulate courtesy for gain. One likely possibility is the use of courtesy to create a climate of good will (through tactics of ingratiation, praise, self-diminishment, shows of common feeling, etc.), wherein concessions or cooperation can be achieved. Another likely possibility is the employment of courtesy as means of putting up a good appearance for outsiders (courteous behavior suggests a party is reasonable and charitable). Finally, one can also expect to see courtesy employed as a means of reducing conflict tensions (euphemisms and indirect language can save face for the other party).

6. Employ secrecy

Secrecy (cf. section 2.4.4.1) is a strategy that we can expect members of the hierarchy to employ as a matter of course in specific operational domains (which may apply in center-periphery conflict situations). But, as with courtesy and fraternity, we can also expect that they will employ secrecy in a more intentional fashion for the sake of advantage. Secrecy is a strategy of restriction. It is a primary means whereby members of the hierarchy limit access to designated sources of information, decision makers and decision making forums. Secrecy can be used by the hierarchy in relation those outside the hierarchy (in a circle-the-wagons approach), but it can also be used by one bishop or group of bishops in relation to another.

There are numerous operational domains within the hierarchy where secrecy is the norm: in the matter of bishop appointments, for example, or in deliberations of the Roman curia. In center-periphery conflict bishops will ordinarily adhere to the standard secrecy rules and protocols that apply. Thus, sensitive, high-level organizational matters will be handled in private (through personal meetings and confidential correspondence), in keeping with the charge to protect the appearance of the Church and to minimize the appearance of conflict; internal documents will be archived; restrictions will be placed on press communications; and so forth. Bishops will conform to such expectations out of habit (one tends not to question – or even notice – social processes that are always handled in the same way) and a responsiveness to social pressure. They will also do so out of a desire to protect privileges and the possibility of future awards, and avoid potential punishments.

Conflict within the hierarchy poses a challenge to the maintenance of the usual secrecy standards, because it is likely that one party will have a greater stake in the use of secrecy than the other. Often, the party benefiting the most from secrecy is the center party, which holds the balance of decision making power. In general, we can expect that both parties will be prepared to uphold the usual standards of secrecy so long as it does not disadvantage them to do so. Once secrecy places a party at a disadvantage (the periphery party sooner than the center party?), however, we should expect that it will show resistance to the use of secrecy. The extent to which a party might actually forgo the use of secrecy is unclear.

Tactical applications of the strategy of secrecy might well include: refusing to acknowledge that a conflict exists; minimizing (even insider) access to the conflict handling; keeping the conflict handling out of sight (by keeping silent about it and limiting its handling to private meetings, private correspondence, phone calls); hiding the identity of conflict participants (through silence or linguistic techniques that hide agency); lying; limiting press contacts (refusing interviews, offering minimal press conferences, providing little information in writing); and archiving sensitive documents.

7. Recruit allies

The concept of alliance, in and of itself, suggests a lack of self-sufficiency. The value of allies is the possibility they offer of enabling one to achieve what could not be achieved independently. In center-periphery conflict, it may be possible to accomplish one's objectives without the support or cooperation of others (this is especially true where the Pope is concerned), but ordinarily we can expect that formal and informal types of alliance will contribute to the conflict handling and resolution. We can also expect that a party will be more strongly inclined to construct alliances when the conflict handling is proceeding disadvantageously for the party in question.

In center-periphery conflict, the most powerful ally one can have is the Pope, since the Pope always has the possibility of overruling other participants in intraecclesial matters. Beyond the Pope, one finds powerful allies in the persons of other bishops. Presumably, the more that the Pope and (ideally many) other bishops are on one's side, the stronger one's position will be in center-periphery conflict. A conflict participant's position within the hierarchy will greatly determine the degree of support he can give. Officials of the Roman curia have the advantage of being on the inside of top-level discussions and decision making processes, and they also have a level of access to the Pope that most of the world's bishops do not enjoy. On the other hand, curial officials (as a whole) are commonly viewed with suspicion by local bishops because they exercise power in non-transparent ways that have decided consequences for local bishops. Thus there are certain kinds of power, rooted in popular appeal, that Roman curial officials do not automatically command. Leading bishops within the national hierarchy can serve as important allies in center-periphery conflict, as can the membership and leaders of national and regional bishops' conferences. This kind of support can be especially important for defending the position of a local bishop.

In my discussion of center-periphery conflict I will limit use of the term "allies" to members of the hierarchy, but of course there are other parties who can play an influential role in the conflict handling (2.3.3). Third parties who may help shape the course the conflict takes include: the news media (which may help create popular support for a cause, which in turn puts pressure on the members of the hierarchy participating); members of a bishop's staff; the local clergy, religious and laity. Primarily, my expectation for center-periphery conflict handling is that participants will first attempt to handle the conflict successfully without recruiting allies. (Conflicts have the appearance of being more manageable when fewer participants are involved.) When seemingly insurmountable difficulties are encountered, then a party will show more readiness to recruit allies from within the hierarchy. Bishops can be expected to recruit allies by means of direct personal contact with other bishops and the cultivation of popular support which strengthens the appearance of his own position.

On a tactical level, we can anticipate seeing any or all of the following expedients applied: consulting with and drawing on the support of friends within the hierarchy; looking for agreeable intermediary contacts within the hierarchy who are well positioned to influence a targeted party; using persuasive argumentation to win potential allies; appealing for support by going directly to the people (of one's own diocese, the broader Church); appealing for support through the news media.

Summary Table of Strategies Likely to Be Applied in Center-Periphery Conflict

Strategy	Expectations	Possible Tactics
1. Show deference to the structural order and mindset of the Church	Both the center and periphery parties will be strongly disposed to defer to existing organizational structures and norms. Even when resisting existing structures or norms, parties will want to give the appearance of deference at least. This is a strategy of reassurance, a means for demonstrating trustworthiness.	Refraining from criticism of Church thought and practice and of its leaders; using euphemisms to describe problems in the Church; invoking familiar ecclesiastical terminology (jargon, official titles, theological words) and thought (Church doctrines); praising the Church and its leaders; obeying one's superiors.
2. Associate one's own efforts with the best interest of the Church	All participant in center-periphery conflict are likely to use this strategy, but perhaps in defense of competing viewpoints.	Making frequent reference to the Church; refraining from criticizing the Church (through silence, the use of euphemisms, indirect language, etc.); expressly linking oneself to the effort to achieve recognized goals of the Church.
3. Minimize the appearance of conflict	In keeping with the organizational goal of unity, the hierarchy will strive to avoid appearing divided to outsiders. Members of the hierarchy will conduct conflict handling, as much as possible, in private, and may choose to avoid conflict issues altogether; when conflict discussions must come into the open, bishops will put the best face they can on the conflict. The center party will have a stronger incentive to minimize the appearance of conflict because it benefits the most from the appearance of unity. The periphery party will minimize the appearance of conflict primarily to prove its loyalty.	Conducting conflict negotiations in secret; refusing to publicly acknowledge the existence, relevance and / or importance of conflict (silence, denial); using euphemisms to improve the appearance of one's relations with other parties, understate the gravity of the problems, or overstate the degree of harmony or prospects for resolution.
4. Show fraternity	Membership in the brotherhood of bishops will bring privileges (of inclusion) and restrictions of movement (following from the fear of exclusion). The center party will emphasize the concept of fraternity in order to secure the continuing loyalty of the periphery. The periphery will demonstrate fraternity as a means of retaining privileges and avoiding punishments. The threat of betrayal can be used by either party to advantage.	Referring to other bishops as "brother bishops" in public; invoking the concept of episcopal fraternity (and related concepts such as bondedness, collegiality, etc.); showing a heightened level of graciousness and deference toward other bishops (in comparison with what is shown toward those who do not belong to the hierarchy); showing what appears to be genuine kinds of trust and friendship toward other bishops; conducting substantial intrahierarchical exchanges in private; symbolically drawing distinctions (through attire, use of technical

		language, liturgical action, closed meetings, etc.) between the knowledge and experience of the bishops and the knowledge and experience of others; indicating (one bishop to another) what the limits of acceptable thought or action are.
5. Practice courtesy	We can expect to find bishops apply courtesy on the habitual level but also in more premeditated fashion for gain. The use of courtesy signals a bishops acknowledgment of his place in the Church social order, but it can also be used in conscious strategic fashion: to ingratiate oneself with the other part, give a good appearance to outsiders or to reduce conflict tensions.	Matter-of-course (defensive) courtesy: avoiding criticism of the Church and Church leaders; using honorary titles; showing respect for and carrying out the wishes of superiors; honoring formality rules; and using euphemisms and other forms of indirect language to give a positive appearance to problematic situations; diminishing oneself. Tactics seeking advantage: using praise, shows of common feeling, etc. to create a climate of goodwill, thereby inducing concessions or cooperation; demonstrating politeness to give a good appearance (of reasonableness, charity) to outsiders; using euphemisms, indirect language, etc. to reduce conflict tensions.
6. Employ secrecy	Secrecy is an ordinary practice in specified domains of Church operations. Bishops can be expected to adhere to conventions of secrecy (as in bishop appointments and curial deliberations). In center-periphery conflict we can expect that bishops will embrace secrecy conditionally. We can expect that members of the hierarchy will abandon secrecy or resist it when it places them at a disadvantage. How far they will go in their abandonment of secrecy is unclear.	Refusing to acknowledge that a conflict exists; minimizing even insider access to the conflict handling; keeping the conflict handling out of sight (by keeping silent about it and limiting its handling to private meetings, private correspondence, phone calls); hiding the identity of conflict participants (through silence or linguistic techniques that hide agency); lying; limiting press contacts (refusing interviews, offering minimal press conferences, providing little information in writing); and archiving sensitive documents.
7. Recruit allies	The Pope has the possibility of having his way by acting unilaterally in center-periphery conflict, but the same is not true of other participants (including those others on the center side), thus we can expect that the formation of alliances will be a key component of the conflict handling and its resolution. The Pope is the most valuable person to have as an ally. Other desirable allies include Roman curial officials and leaders of episcopal conferences. Though the primary focus here is on allies within the hierarchy, other	Consulting with and drawing on the support of friends within the hierarchy; looking for agreeable intermediary contacts within the hierarchy who are well positioned to influence a targeted party; using persuasive argumentation to win potential allies; appealing for support by going directly to the people (of one's own diocese, the broader Church); appealing for support through the news media

	allies can also play an important role in the conflict handling, including the media, leaders of the local Church and the mass membership of the local / national / international Church. Bishops are likely to first try to manage conflicts successfully by themselves before turning to others for help.	

TABLE 3.3

The foregoing presentation of strategies that we are likely to encounter in center-periphery conflict handling is not meant to be exhaustive. The list, rather, specifies strategies that, in my view, have a high probability of application because bishops are conditioned to use them (a conditioning that is reinforced through potential rewards and punishments).

An important matter for our consideration – and this can perhaps best be pursued in the confrontation of the empirical example itself – is the possibility of foregoing or resisting any of the above-named coping strategies as a means for handling the conflict advantageously. I do not anticipate that participants in center-periphery conflict will see advantage in foregoing or resisting strategies one (show deference to the structural order and mindset of the Church), two (associate one's own efforts with the best interest of the Church) or four (show fraternity), because this would seem to create a dangerous cleavage between the bishop's personal identity and the organization that guarantees his position of power. But I can well imagine that there will be occasions wherein participants foresee and pursue advantage by renouncing, or threatening to renounce, strategies three (minimize the appearance of conflict), five (practice courtesy) or six (employ secrecy). Any of these strategies can work to the direct disadvantage of a party – providing an incentive for resistance -- but adherence to the strategies themselves is not self-evidently required (perhaps we can say it is very strongly recommended?) for one who wishes to remain in good standing as a member of the hierarchy.

Thus far we have considered organizational and societal pressures on center-periphery conflict handling, a process that has led to the formulation of a number of coping strategies we are likely to find applied in center-periphery conflict. Of necessity, this discussion has taken place on a general level. But we should not lose sight of the fact that center-periphery conflicts are highly specific events which, while likely conforming to a limited number of general patterns, will also be uniquely shaped by the personalities and configuration of developments that comprise the particularity of the conflict. Ideally, to understand choices made in conflict situations, we would have access to the personal history of the conflict participants. In the limits of the presents study, it is not possible to produce this sort of comprehensive analysis. But we should at least be conscious that the absence of such information will likely cause some interpretations to be less than fully accurate or complete.

Apart from being conditioned by society, their role within the Church organization, their personal history and physiological / psychological makeup, participants in center-periphery conflict will also be shaped in their decision-making by the immediate situational context of the conflict itself. One party may choose coping strategy X because it seems a rational response to the opposing party's choice of coping strategy Y. For this reason we need a theoretical framework to help us interpret the dynamics of conflict negotiation in organizations. The following chapter provides such a framework.

CHAPTER FOUR

PERSPECTIVES FROM CONFLICT THEORY

4.1 Search for an Applicable Theory

In order to recognize and understand the coping strategies applied in center-periphery conflict, we need an operative idea of conflict itself and of what typically makes up a conflict. Although conflicts are natural and normal developments within organizations, they are not everyday events – at least, Church center-periphery conflicts are not. Within the Catholic Church, manifest conflict at the topmost level diverges from what is ordinarily a more placid experience of leadership and decision making. The dynamics of conflict situations can be distinguished, in their intensity and in the opportunities and dangers they bring to light, from the pattern of day-to-day leadership situations. Thus far I have presented a picture of the Church's usual situation as a specific kind of organization pursuing its goals in the context of modernity. In this chapter I will present a descriptive theory of social conflict that enables us to see conflicts (as integrated wholes) in terms of the strategic activity that comprises them.

My search for a theory that would serve the purpose just specified has brought me into contact with a wide variety of studies of social conflict. Especially helpful by way of their provision of a composite overview of the field have been Pruitt and Carnevale 1993, Gangel and Canine 1992, Rahim 1992, Väyrynen 1991, Rahim 1990, Dahrendorf 1988, Shawchuck 1986b, Fraser and Hipel 1984, Schellenberg 1982, Tjosvold and Johnson 1983, Himes 1980, Schelling 1980, Zartman 1978, Snyder and Diesing 1977, Filley 1975, Mack and Snyder 1973, Patchen 1969, Fink 1968, Gamson 1968, Iklé 1968, Simmel 1966, Coser 1964, Boulding 1962, and *The Journal of Conflict Resolution* (1956-present). Consultation of these and other works has shown that not all theoretical approaches to the handling of conflict suit the purposes at hand equally well. Among the reasons for not choosing certain approaches: some rely on mathematical models that are not easily transferable, e.g., Schelling 1980, Zwartman 1978, Patchen 1969; some offer conflict models that are more static than dynamic, e.g., Rahim 1992; some are focused exclusively on nation states and not organizations, e.g., Iklé 1968 and Snyder and Diesing 1977; some are grounded in problematic ideological standpoints, e.g. Dahrendorf 1988; some are more prescriptive than descriptive, e.g. Shawchuck 1986b.

In particular, I have found myself in need of a descriptive perspective that not only specifies how conflicts hold together (preferably employing terminology and models that are standard enough to allow for cross comparisons within the field of conflict theory), but also gives special attention to the concept of strategy and to the role (motivations, actions) of individual participants in the conflict. Since I am attempting to identify *coping strategies* applied in center-periphery conflict and to integrate these into a coherent account of the conflict as a whole, I have sought a conflict theory that relates the picture of the entire conflict to the choices of opposed decision makers who, in more or less intentional fashion, attempt to achieve designated goals while taking into account the conditions of the decision making environment, and especially the actions and reactions of other conflict participants. In the work of Pruitt and Rubin (1986: *Social Conflict: Escalation, Stalemate, and Settlement*) I have found such a perspective.

4.2 Pruitt and Rubin on Conflict Handling

Pruitt and Rubin's theory satisfies the needs identified above by providing an integrated picture of conflict handling in general (it "transcends the various levels and arenas of society" – p. 187) that is focused on the role of strategic choice. Their descriptive, social psychological approach is built around a few basic observations. Actors act according to personal "interests" (feelings about what is basically desirable), translating their interests into "aspirations" (actions toward a goal). Those aspirations at times clash with the aspirations of others. The handling of this clash (which strategies of conflict management are adopted) depends largely on the relative levels of concern for one another's outcomes and the perceived feasibility of success in obtaining desired outcomes. And finally, conflicts tend to play out in stages of escalation, stalemate and settlement.

For the purposes of our own study, Pruitt and Rubin's perspective offers the following advantages: 1) it focuses on *individual behavior* (which fits with my attention to the behavior of individual bishops); 2) it foregrounds the concept of *strategy* (in a way compatible with my own understanding, as articulated in section 3.5.3); 3) it identifies possible *tactics* that may serve given strategies; 4) it helps us to associate strategies with distinct *stages* of conflict; 5) it descriptively accounts for the *whole of the conflict experience*; and 6) it offers insight into the role of *third parties*. In short, it supplies us with a necessary referential framework (based on studies of how parties commonly behave in conflict), by means of which we can better grasp our chosen case. Just as importantly, Pruitt and Rubin supply these advantages in a straightforward and highly accessible presentation. Complexities are honored without being allowed to overwhelm the interpretive process. Though all of the conflict writings mentioned in the previous section offer valuable reflections (models, theories, insights, etc.) in their own right -- with many employing terms and ideas that are functionally equivalent to (or viable alternatives to) those offered by Pruitt and Rubin -- I have decided that more coherence can be brought to my own work by concentrating on the single approach I have found to be most advantageous. Given that Pruitt and Rubin's theory is in fact well within the mainstream (like countless others, for example, they draw heavily on Blake and Mouton's (1964) "managerial grid"), I trust that this decision will not lead me toward idiosyncratic conclusions.

Practically speaking, I will use their theory as follows. In this chapter I will summarize their theory and highlight aspects that may prove especially relevant to our study of center-periphery conflict. It is fair to say that this chapter continues the process of theoretical sensitization carried out in chapters two and three, in that it supplies orientating concepts for our confrontation of the empirical example. After having confronted the Rome-Hunthausen case, I will revisit Pruitt and Rubin's theory to see how the theory and the empirical example shed light on one another.

But first, a general overview of Pruitt and Rubin's approach.

4.2.1 Sources of Conflict

Conflict, according to Pruitt and Rubin, is found in almost every realm of human interaction, but not all interaction necessarily involves conflict (p. 6). Thus there is no surprise that conflict should arise in the context of decision making on behalf of the Church.

The results of conflict can be positive or negative. Among the positive functions of conflict identified by Pruitt and Rubin are (1) its role in nourishing social change; (2) its ability to (creatively) reconcile people's legitimate interests; and, by virtue of the first two functions, (3) its power to foster group unity. (The potential for conflict to serve the purposes of group unity is, of course, highly pertinent to our study of Church center-periphery conflict.) Along this same line, Coser (1956, 31), following Simmel (1955), observes that conflict facilitates socialization by helping to establish and maintain group boundaries, by allowing for the ventilation of hostilities, and by establishing and maintaining the balance of power. Robbins (1992, 182-183) notes that conflict can improve organizational performance (see also Tjosvold & Johnson 1983, 8-9). And Janis (1982) asserts that it counteracts "groupthink" and the too-ready acceptance of decisions based on weak assumptions. The negative functions of conflict, however, are also familiar. Pruitt and Rubin point out that conflict is fully capable of "wreaking havoc on society" (p. 7). Within organizations, Rahim (1992) has asserted that conflict can damage communication, create distrust and suspicion, and diminish levels of organizational loyalty and performance. In short, organizations, the Church included, have strong reason to want to manage conflicts so that functional outcomes emerge to the exclusion of dysfunctional outcomes.

Pruitt and Rubin understand conflict to be "perceived divergence of interest." "Interests" are "people's feelings about what is basically desirable" and they "tend to be central to people's thinking and action, forming the core of many of their attitudes, goals and intentions" (p. 10). Interests translate into "aspirations." One aspires toward a particular "goal," which is "the more or less precise end toward which one is striving." At the same time, knowing that not all goals are fully achievable, one envisions a minimally acceptable level of achievement – a "standard" in regard to the goal. Achievement below the standard is considered inadequate by the aspiring party. Conflict arises when one party perceives that satisfaction of its aspirations precludes satisfaction of the other party's aspirations, and vice-versa.

For Pruitt and Rubin, three elements converge to produce conflict: "Party's level of aspiration, Party's perception of Other's level of aspiration, and the apparent lack of integrative alternatives" (p. 13). All three elements must be present for conflict to arise.

Determinants of Party's level of aspiration (based on realistic or idealistic considerations) include: Party's past achievements (raising aspirations); Party's perception of own advantage in strength (raising aspirations); normative justification (underwriting Party's aspirations in the face of incompatible aspirations by Other); invidious comparisons (leading to a rise in aspirations); formation of struggle groups (bringing a rise in aspirations).

When Other's aspirations are low or flexible they do not threaten Party, thus precluding conflict. But Party may perceive that Other's objectives are too high to be compatible with his own, with conflict as a result. Among the circumstances that may invite Party to perceive that Other's aspirations are incompatibly high are hard experience with frustration at the hands of Other and distrust of Other's motives based on other knowledge.

Pruitt and Rubin call alternatives satisfying both parties' aspirations "integrative solutions" (p. 18). The perception that such alternatives are not at hand is the third element that must be present for conflict to develop. The perception that such integrative solutions are not available may be rooted in a realistic assessment (mutually-desired resources may in fact be scarce), but it may also be the product of a negative view of the other party which makes one reluctant to investigate solutions creatively.

4.2.2 Strategic Choice
When faced with perceived divergence of interest, a party must decide how it will proceed. Party has a high aspiration, so does Other, and the two appear to be incompatible. What now?

Pruitt and Rubin, building on the work of Blake and Mouton (1964, 1979) and others (see p. 28) posit five strategic options:

1. **Contending:** Trying to prevail; pursuing one's own aspirations without regard to opposing party's aspirations.
2. **Problem solving:** Trying to satisfy own and other party's aspirations. Agreements reached through problem solving may take the form of an integrative solution or a compromise.
3. **Yielding:** Lowering one's own aspirations as a form of concession.
4. **Inaction:** Doing nothing; temporarily withdrawing from the efforts to resolve the controversy.
5. **Withdrawal:** Removing oneself permanently from the conflict handling process.

Pruitt and Rubin call the first three strategies "coping strategies" (p. 3) because they involve "some relatively consistent, coherent effort to settle conflict." These contrast with inaction and withdrawal, which are not considered to be coping strategies because they are approaches of pause or abandonment. Note that Pruitt and Rubin's definition of "coping strategy" differs from my own, stated earlier in section 3.5.3. By my definition, all five of the above-named strategies have the possibility of being coping strategies, since each can serve as an orchestrated attempt to manage conflict advantageously. From this point forward in the study, I will not retain Pruitt and Rubin's concept of coping strategy but will stay with my own.

One should also note that the five general strategies identified by Pruitt and Rubin function on a lower conceptual level than the context-specific strategies I identified at the end of chapter three. Whereas the five strategies listed above can account for activity in any social conflict, my effort in this study is to identify coping strategies that are highly specific to Church center-periphery conflict. Therefore, at a later point in this presentation (see section 5.4), I will distinguish between the five general coping strategies and more specific kinds of coping strategies that in some sense reflect the more general strategies.

Most conflict situations call forth a combination of the above-named strategies. The authors propose two theoretical notions which help us to understand why a given strategy is adopted. The first is summarized in a *dual concern model* (pp. 28-35). The second is conceptualized as the *perceived feasibility perspective* (pp. 35-41). The two theoretical notions focus on distinct and separate determinants of strategic choice. An explanation of each follows.

The dual concern model (see figure below) recognizes two types of concerns: *concern about one's own outcome* (abscissa) and *concern about other's outcome* (ordinate). These concerns range from indifference (the zero point of the coordinate) to very great concern.

> The two concerns in this model are defined as follows: Concern about own outcomes means placing importance on one's own interests – one's needs and values – in the realm of the dispute. People with a strong concern about their own outcomes are highly resistant to yielding; in other words, their aspirations tend to be rigid and high. Concern about the other's outcomes implies placing importance on the others' interests – feeling responsible for the quality of the other's outcomes. This concern is sometimes genuine, involving an intrinsic interest in the other's welfare. However, it is more often instrumental, being aimed at helping the other in order to advance one's own interests. (p. 28)

The Dual Concern Model
(Pruitt and Rubin, 1986)

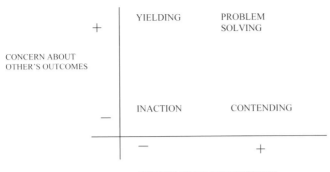

FIGURE 4.1

The dual concern model holds that: *problem solving* is encouraged when there is a strong concern about both own and other's outcomes; *yielding* is encouraged by a strong concern about only the other's outcomes; *contending* is encouraged by a strong concern about only one's own outcomes; *inaction* is encouraged when concern about both parties' outcomes is weak. The model makes no prediction about when *withdrawing* is embraced as a strategy. Pruitt and Rubin believe that compromising need not be seen as a separate strategy. They understand it to be the product of less-than-robust problem solving or of simple yielding by both sides. (Variants on the dual concern model have been applied to the study of Church-based conflicts. See, e.g., Van der Ven 1996 and Gangel & Canine 1996.)

The strength of concern for one's own outcome varies with the person and situation, but certain determinants can be identified (pp. 29-31). These include: the importance of values affected by the outcomes; the relative importance of other outcomes pursued at the same time; one's own fear(lessness) regarding conflict itself. Concern for the outcome for one's group (and not just for oneself) is also a significant determinant of the strength of one's own concern.

Determinants of concern for the other party's outcomes include: existing interpersonal bonds, kinship, group identity; and one's having acted altruistically in the recent past. These determinants tend to foster genuine concern. Instrumental concern for the other's outcomes is fostered by the perception that one is dependent on the other party (the other is seen as capable of delivering rewards or punishments). The authors note that while personal bonds and dependencies usually foster concern for the other's outcome, they can also, under certain conditions produce antagonisms that reduce this concern.

One's decision about whether to problem solve, contend, yield, do nothing or withdraw in a conflict situation is determined not only by the level of concern for oneself and the other party. It is also determined by perceptions of cost and benefit related to the implementation of a particular strategy. This is where the *perceived feasibility perspective* proves helpful.

For a strategy to be adopted, it must be perceived as minimally feasible. (In regard to center-periphery conflict, socially-conditioned organizational roles and perceptions about what the Church and societal culture allow are likely to be important influences on feasibility conceptions.) If a strategy appears to have no or little chance of success, another will likely be chosen. Pruitt and Rubin focus on the perceived feasibility of three strategies in particular: problem solving, contending and inaction.

Pruitt and Rubin (p. 36):

> **Problem solving** seems more feasible the greater the *perceived common ground* (PCG). PCG is a party's assessment of the likelihood of finding an alternative that satisfies both parties' aspirations. The more likely it seems that such an alternative can be found, the more feasible problem solving appears to be. PCG is greater (1) the lower Party's own aspirations, (2) the lower Other's aspirations as perceived by Party, and the (3) the greater the perceived integrative potential (PIP) – that is, Party's faith that alternatives favorable to both parties exist or can be devised.

At a given point of negotiation, the existence of some strategic alternatives is known and the availability of others is suspected. The *perceived integrative potential* is high when there are known alternatives that provide high benefit to both parties. It is moderately high when the prospect of developing such alternatives is likely. It is low when one sees little chance of coming to mutually beneficial alternatives. As conditions contributing to PIP, the authors identify: (1) faith in own problem-solving ability; (2) momentum – i.e., prior success at reaching agreement in the current controversy; (3) availability of a mediator; (4) other's perceived readiness for problem solving – which is sometimes a function of trust.

Contending seems more feasible when the Other's resistance to yielding appears low. Contentious behavior is invited when the Other appears to be easy to dislodge. The feasibility of contending also hinges on Party's apparent capacity to employ contentious tactics and of Other's apparent capacity to resist (power versus counterpower). "In a stable long-term relationship, each party's capacity to employ contentious tactics tends to be matched by the other's level of resistance, so that there is relatively little advantage to either party in employing contentious tactics" (p. 40).

Potential costs of contending – including the instigation of a conflict spiral and the alienation of the other party – act as deterrents against the choice of contentious action.

Time pressure is the key to the feasibility of adopting the strategy of **inaction**. As time pressure increases, the feasibility of inaction decreases. In the face of time pressure, **yielding**, which is the fastest means to move to agreement, appears to be the most commonly adopted strategy (p. 41; cf. Pruitt and Drews 1969.) Normally, contending and problem solving are adopted in situations of time pressure only when there is heavy resistance to yielding.

Pruitt and Rubin concede that the dual concern model and perceived feasibility perspective do not go far in explaining why people choose to **withdraw** from a conflict, but they do observe that people, apparently, withdraw from conflict handling when the benefit they expect to receive falls below their minimal aspiration.

4.2.3 Applications of Strategy
Pruitt and Rubin identify a variety of ways that parties carry out the strategies of contending (pp. 44-61) and problem solving (pp. 139-164).

Among the lighter tactics of contending are *ingratiation, gamesmanship, persuasive arguments* and *promises*. (NB: Where Pruitt and Rubin speak of "tactics," I prefer to speak of *specific* coping strategies that can be distinguished from the more general classification of five strategies presented above. I reserve the term tactic for micro-level techniques of social interchange, as in elements of text construction, symbolic acts, nonverbal gestures, etc. See sections 5.4 and 5.5.) Ingratiation involves the use of guile to soften up the opposing party for later concessions. It may be carried out by means of flattery, opinion conformity, granting favors, or self-presentation (showing one's positive side). Gamesmanship seeks to "ruffle the feathers" of the opposing party, thereby lowering the opponent's resistance to yielding. The authors offer the example of taking time when the opponent is in a hurry, and observe that the key to the success of gamesmanship is not raising the suspicion of one's own deviousness. Persuasive arguments attempt to win cooperation by reasoning. One may, for example, persuade the other party that one has a legitimate right to a favorable outcome. Promises offer reward in return for compliance.

Heavier means of contention include *threats* and *irrevocable commitments*. Threats send a message that one will punish noncompliance. Pruitt and Rubin cite studies (p. 53) demonstrating that threats are more likely than promises to elicit compliance. Irrevocable commitments are threats that assume the following form: "I have started doing something that requires adjustment from you and will continue doing it despite your best efforts to stop me." As in the game of "Chicken," one enters into a test of will with the other party, with the loser being the first party to change course. If neither party gives in, both lose. One of the interesting features of irrevocable commitments is the attempt to place the locus of control for avoiding a negative outcome squarely on the shoulders of the other (as has been seen in classic examples nonviolent resistance).

In contrast with the strategy of contention, which seeks one's own advantage without regard to the wishes of the other, problem solving seeks to address the concerns of both parties. Getting started with problem solving may be difficult because showing one's interest in this strategy may telegraph weakness. At the heart of the strategy is the effort to *identify and discuss the true issues dividing the parties. Creatively envisioning alternatives* may enable parties to identify conflict solutions that bridge their opposing interests. Though problem solving has the best chance of success when both parties apply the strategy, a single party may apply the strategy individually, and it is also possible for a third party to do the problem solving.

Since all of the above-named forms of contending and problem solving are common to the handling of social conflict in general, we can expect that they may also turn up (in context-specified ways) in Church center-periphery conflict. Though none of the strategies stand out as being inevitably relevant to intrahierarchical conflict handling, one can imagine that the strategy of ingratiation may in some ways play into bishops' (presumed) orientation toward courtesy, that persuasive argumentation is likely to fit well with the normative-rational aspect of the Church organization, and that promises and threats relate to bishops' powers of remuneration and coercion.

The strategies of contending, problem solving and yielding may be practiced more or less "vigorously" (p. 42). Contending is more vigorous as heavier actions are taken. Problem solving is more vigorous as the investment of creativity rises. Yielding is more vigorous as one drops one's aspirations further and further. The vigorousness of strategic action has much to do with the level of concern for one's own and the other party's outcome. High concern for both party's outcomes makes problem solving more vigorous. High concern only for one's own outcome leads to vigorous contending. If concern for one's own outcome is weak, higher concern for the other party's outcome leads to more vigorous yielding. Typically, parties who have adopted a coping strategy begin by applying the strategy less vigorously. They gradually apply the strategy with greater vigor if earlier efforts have not achieved agreement. This "gradualism" ensures that a greater price than necessary will not be paid to reach designated goals.

4.2.4 Conflict Stages: Escalation, Stalemate and Settlement

Pruitt and Rubin invoke various metaphors to clarify the way social conflicts tend to hold together in sequence (pp. 183-184). One metaphor is that of the three-act play. In the first act (Escalation) conflict builds. In the second act (Stalemate) the conflict gets to the point where it seems unwise to escalate further and a stage of transition is reached. In the third act (Settlement) one finds the denouement, the resolution to the conflict. This metaphor, they note, fits many conflicts but also tends to oversimplify. As an example, the symmetry of the three-act play metaphor neglects the fact that it is much easier to move up the escalation ladder than to move back down. This is because people are more prone to retaliate when challenged than to reciprocate when they are treated well. Thus, conflict spirals are more readily achieved than benevolent circles that relieve escalation.

It might be better, the authors propose, to employ the image of a valley or canyon to speak of conflict. One descends into conflict (analogous to escalation), crosses to the other side (stalemate), and makes the effort of climbing up the other side. This image allows for the fact that it is often easier to get into conflict (gravity helps us to descend into the valley) than to get out of it. This image works better for the visualization of conflict if one envisions a rather expansive valley, with intermittent ascents and descents before emerging on the other side – since conflicts tend to vary in their levels of intensity and contention over time, rarely following a simple line of descent-ascent.

Another helpful image sees the conflict sequence as a tree of many branches. Here the changes that occur in conflict – visualized in the progression from trunk to branch to sprig to leaf – are accounted for in an image that captures something of the complexity of turns a conflict can take.

I call forth these metaphors because they illuminate our own task of determining how center-periphery conflicts hold together, but to do so in a way that does not overlook important elements of the experience. I will now discuss what, according to Pruitt and Rubin, the stages of escalation, stalemate and settlement look like and what sorts of coping strategies and tactics we can expect to find applied in each stage.

During conflict **escalation**, certain incremental transformations take place which tend to be mirrored by the two parties (pp. 64-65). As a result of these transformations, the conflict is intensified in ways that persist and are often difficult to undo. Pruitt and Rubin identify five types of transformation that typically occur during conflict escalation.

Transformations That Occur During Escalation

1. **Light→Heavy.** Gentle tactics are supplanted by heavier counterparts.
2. **Small→Large.** Issues proliferate and there is a tendency for parties to become more and more absorbed in the struggle and to commit ever-increasing resources in order to prevail.
3. **Specific→General.** Specific issues tend to give way to general issues and there is deterioration in the relationship between the parties.
4. **Doing well→Winning→Hurting the other.** Interest in doing well is replaced by decidedly competitive objective and, finally, after continued escalation, by the objective of hurting the other.
5. **Few→Many.** Conflicts that begin with a small number of participants often grow, as collective efforts arise at the prospect of one party's failure.

A conflict can be said to escalate when any or all of these five transformations takes place. (But NB: the transformations are often subtle and hard to notice.) Conflicts which have escalated tend to stay escalated, at least for a time, because, as has been noted, it is harder to de-escalate conflict than to escalate it.

It is possible to specify conditions that increase or reduce the likelihood of conflict escalation.

> The likelihood of escalation is increased by high perceived power, low perceived integrative potential, and high aspirations, particularly if these conditions exist on both sides. The likelihood of escalation is reduced (and hence the situation tends toward stability) in the presence of conflict-limiting norms and institutions, fear of escalation, bonds between potential antagonists, and bonds to third and fourth parties who can be expected to oppose the conflict. (p. 86)

Pruitt and Rubin draw our attention to **three models** (pp. 89-6) **that clarify why conflicts escalate**. The *aggressor-defender model* distinguishes between an "aggressor" party who has one or more goals that place it in conflict with a "defender" party. The aggressor ordinarily starts with lighter tactics but moves to heavier tactics if these do not work. The defender merely reacts, escalating his response in line with the aggressor's escalation. Escalation continues until the aggressor wins or gives up trying. The *conflict spiral model* holds that escalation results from a vicious circle of action and reaction: one contentious act begets another, in back-and-forth fashion. The *structural change model* holds that the use of conflict tactics leads to changes (psychological changes, changes in groups and collectives) in the parties and the communities that contain them. These changes invite the continuation and escalation of the conflict.

Though not all conflicts escalate over an extended period of time, we can explain why some conflicts do (pp. 111-125). One reason for this is that during intensifying conflict, the relationship between the two parties may pass a psychological or collective threshold beyond which return to the original state of relationship appears to be impossible. Moreover, negative attitudes and perceptions toward opposing parties tend to endure, aided by processes of selective perception (one sees only what fits a need or preconception), by self-fulfilling prophecies (one's expectation of the other party's behavior invites that behavior) and by the emergence of autistic hostility (one stops communicating or interacting with a disliked party). Another reason for the perpetuation of conflicts is the vested interest that some may have in continuing it. Participation in conflict provides social benefits (e.g., newfound status or a sense of purpose) that some may be reluctant to relinquish. Finally, one may become overcommitted to and entrapped in a given conflict. This occurs when parties invest more resources in waging the conflict than seems reasonable by external standards. Being hesitant or unwilling to concede this overinvestment, one persists in the escalation with the hope of still winning and thereby saving face.

Stalemate in conflict (pp. 126-138) comes when neither party can or will escalate the conflict further (the point of maximum conflict intensity has been reached), nor will either party take steps toward agreement. One may still see contentious activity during the period of stalemate, but this does not contribute to escalation and it is less significant than the change in the parties' outlook that is at hand. Pruitt and Rubin recognize four major reasons for the emergence of stalemate: the failure of contentious tactics, the exhaustion of necessary resources, the loss of social support and unacceptable costs.

Since contention as a means of resolution is ruled out at the point of stalemate, the parties are left with four ways out of the conflict. Inaction offers little promise because the parties are already at an uncomfortable impasse and prefer to move beyond it. Yielding offers the potential for a quick resolution, but one or both parties may not be in a position to yield because they are entrapped by their commitment of resources and / or a need to save face. (Pruitt and Rubin point out, p. 30, that representatives are usually more reluctant to yield than are individuals bargaining on their own behalf, because representatives want to please their constituents. This finding may be relevant the choices bishops' make in center-periphery conflict.) If both parties yield and come to agreement by this means, we call it a "compromise." Withdrawal entails a reversion to the status quo. Depending on whether the status quo is advantageous or disadvantageous to a given party, such a solution may be considered a form of victory or defeat in the conflict. Lastly, the strategy of problem solving holds out the possibility of yet obtaining a resolution that is beneficial to both parties. Power equality between the parties and the apparent chance of success are factors favoring the adopting of problem solving methods at this point. The presence of an influential third party may also encourage the decision to engage in problem solving. Trust in a third party mediator can substitute for trust between the parties.

Settlement is the stage of actively taking steps toward resolution. It is characterized by the use of problem solving and often involves third-party intervention (p. v). Three broad classes of outcomes result from successful problem solving: compromise, agreement on a procedure for deciding who will win (such as voting, or submitting to a judge or arbitrator's decision) and integrative solutions.

Types of integrative solutions include: expanding the pie (increasing the available resources); non-specific compensation (Party gets what it wants, Other is repaid in an unrelated coin); logrolling (each party concedes on issues that are of low priority to itself and high priority to the other party); cost cutting (Party gets what it wants, Other's costs are reduced or eliminated); bridging (neither party achieves its initial demands, but a new option is devised that satisfies the most important underlying interests of those demands). There are distinct advantages to the achievement of integrative solutions. Specifically, integrative solutions lead to more stable relationships between the parties in the long run and the broader communities containing the conflictual parties are benefited as well by this stability.

The authors point out that parties do not always understand the nature of the interests underlying their own preferences. Hence, the clarification of applicable interests is seen as an important step in integrative problem solving.

Third parties (pp. 165-182) may be instrumental in the process of settling the conflict. A third party is "an individual or collective that is external to a dispute between two or more others and that tries to help the disputants reach agreement." Pruitt and Rubin note that the mere presence of a third party is likely to change the relationship between the disputant parties and, in many cases, to benefit that relationship by diverting energies otherwise given over to escalation. At other times, however, a third party may disturb the progress toward agreement. Thus third-party intervention is not a panacea in conflict resolution. Third parties may take on formal or informal roles, individual or representative roles, invited or uninvited roles, impartial or partial roles, advisory or directive roles, interpersonal or intergroup roles, and content- or process-oriented roles. Effective third-party intervention can take the form of modifying the physical and social structure of the dispute, altering the issue structure of the dispute, and increasing the parties' motivation to work energetically for resolution.

When assessing center-periphery conflict outcomes, we will want to look not only at type of outcome and the consequences for the parties themselves – did both parties "win" in the form of an integrative solution, did one party win at the expense of the other, did both yield to reach a compromise, did both lose – but also, and more importantly, at the consequences for the organization. Is the Church better or worse off for the way the conflict was handled? What are the long-term effects of such an approach likely to be?

4.3 Use of the Conflict Theory to Illuminate the Case

This chapter has supplied us with an integrated way of thinking about social conflicts and their management. My purpose in discussing the work of Pruitt and Rubin has been to sensitize myself -- and the reader -- in preparation for the confrontation of the evidence from the case, as presented in chapters six to eight.

Since I am in search of coping strategies that characterize the handling of center-periphery conflict, I am indebted to Pruitt and Rubin for their provision of a way of thinking about the role of strategic choice in conflict handling and their identification of a number of specific strategies that may be employed. When we turn to consider the empirical example, we will want to keep the concepts and strategies identified in this chapter in mind along with the strategies and expectations summarized at the end of chapter three. In chapters six-eight I draw specific connections between the case materials and the theoretical resources previously provided, commenting on the "conflict functionality" of participants' words and actions.

In chapter nine I will revisit Pruitt and Rubin's theory in more cohesive fashion, using their framework in support of my own understanding of how the conflict in its entirety holds together.

CHAPTER FIVE

METHODOLOGY FOR THE CONFRONTATION OF DATA

5.1 Overview

There are three main components to this research. The first component is a process of theoretical sensitization that generates expectations for what we may find (which coping strategies we will find applied) in Church center-periphery conflict. The second component is the confrontation of the theory-based expectations with the empirical data (the evidence from the case itself). The third and final component is the process of drawing and reflecting on conclusions emerging from this confrontation. The purpose of the present chapter is to complete the work of theoretical sensitization (with reference to the concepts and methods of critical discourse analysis) and to offer a nuts-and-bolts description of how I have carried out the analytical tasks associated with confronting the empirical data and drawing and assessing conclusions.

5.2 Application of Case Study Method

My understanding of what a case study is follows the two-part technical definition of Yin (1994, 13), which is reproduced below.

1. A case study is an empirical inquiry that
   - investigates a contemporary phenomenon within its real-life context, especially when
   - the boundaries between phenomenon and context are not clearly evident.
2. The case study inquiry
   - copes with the technically distinctive situation in which there will be many more variables of interest than data points, and as one result
   - relies on multiple sources of evidence, with data needing to converge in a triangulating fashion, and as another result
   - benefits from the prior development of theoretical propositions to guide data collection and analysis.

Yin's definition helps us to see when the case study approach is appropriate and what it looks like in practice. For the sake of tying the current study to this definition, one will note that this is an empirical inquiry that investigates a contemporary phenomenon (center-periphery conflict management) within its real-life context (immediate, organizational and societal). The boundaries between the conflict handling phenomenon and the multiple layers of context are often ambiguous. There are countless variables of interest (factors influencing the conflict handling) but relatively few data points available for study (cases of center-periphery conflict which can readily be analyzed). The research relies on multiple sources of evidence (original documents; newspaper, magazine and scholarly journal accounts; other publications; the personal archive of one close to the conflict, which includes documents and ephemera; and an informational / validational interview), which converge in triangulating fashion. Finally, the research benefits from the prior development of theoretical propositions (see chapters two-four), which have served to guide the data collection and analysis.

5.2.1 Selection, Delimitation and Demarcation of the Case

The Rome-Hunthausen conflict is the primary unit of analysis in this case study. The conflict is an actual instance of the phenomenon of concern here, center-periphery conflict. I have selected the Hunthausen case with the understanding that it is a rare, contemporary example of a local bishop openly in conflict with the Holy See. Because of the large number of members of the hierarchy who participated in the controversy publicly, its recent occurrence, extended duration, and the high level of media attention it received, it is a case of center-periphery conflict that is especially accessible to research.

The Hunthausen case also offers the advantage of being one that is personally familiar to the researcher. Though I possessed no noteworthy insider information at the time the conflict was underway, I did enter the priestly formation program of the Seattle Archdiocese in 1987, the year in which the recommendations of the apostolic commission were accepted and implemented. Thereafter I was in a position to observe some of the lasting effects of the conflict as a seminarian (1987-1990) and as a lay ecclesial minister in the archdiocese (1994-2001). I was personally acquainted with Archbishop Hunthausen, much better acquainted with Archbishop Murphy (who oversaw the seminary program during my time), and have enjoyed friendships with many priests and other pastoral leaders of the archdiocese. Though it is common to think of personal familiarity and attachments as inducing bias, I think one can also rightly argue that a close-up view enables one to come to levels of understanding that are not obtainable from afar. Though I have not been privileged to see the workings of the Vatican in this same close-up way, I am happy to benefit from the writings of other researchers who have.

In chapter two I defined center-periphery conflict as *conflict taking place within the Church hierarchy between the central leadership position (Rome, the papacy) and one or more peripheral leadership positions (the local churches, the other bishops).* I noted along with my provision of the definition that my attention would be limited exclusively to how members of the Roman Catholic hierarchy engage in such conflict.

The Hunthausen case is the primary unit of analysis of this investigation in the sense that it conforms to this definition and can be judiciously compared with other phenomena that also conform to this definition. In the Hunthausen case, Hunthausen, as ordinary of a local church, occupies the peripheral position. The main actors in the center position are Pope John Paul II, Cardinal Ratzinger, Cardinal Gantin, Archbishop Laghi and Archbishop Hickey (see sections 5.2.1.2 and 5.2.1.3). Disagreement is clearly manifest between the center and periphery positions in the case.

5.2.1.1 Use of a Composite Source as an External Reference Point
Prior to undertaking an extensive study oneself, it is difficult to know where a case of conflict begins and ends and of what it consists. In my confrontation of the Hunthausen case I have benefited – especially early on -- from three descriptions of the affair that supplied key points of orientation by focusing my attention on matters I might otherwise have overlooked. These descriptions also acted as a check on my own judgments. Each of these sources discusses the case from a distinct vantage point and according to a specific explanatory purpose. Here below I identify and characterize these three sources. Thereafter I explain how I have employed them as a *composite source* that has helped me to delimit and demarcate the case.

- Kenneth A. **Briggs**, *Holy Siege: The Year That Shook Catholic America* (San Francisco: Harper, 1992).
- Thomas J. **Reese**, *Archbishop: Inside the Power Structure of the American Catholic Church* (San Francisco: Harper & Row, 1989).
- Patrick **Granfield**, *The Limits of the Papacy: Authority and Autonomy in the Church* (New York: Crossroad, 1987).

BOX 5.1

Briggs 1992 is a journalistic account that places the case in the context of contemporaneous events in the American Church. Reese 1989 discusses the Hunthausen affair in the course of his sociological study of the office of archbishop in the American Church. Granfield 1987 takes up the case in a theological look at limits on the power of the papacy. In the absence of any single, "definitive" version of the Hunthausen case that could serve as a point of reference, the composite source provides us with a body of information that includes contextualized descriptions of participants, events and interactions.

My use of the composite source respects the distinctiveness of the three accounts it contains. Thus I do not attempt to harmonize the three accounts. Instead I use the composite as a general information source, drawing on the total pool of data provided by the three works taken together. For this purpose, the works are, in a sense, placed end to end as I consider the information they contain. I also use the composite source as an indicator of key participants, the (observable) starting and ending points, critical turning points, and crucial documents emerging within the context of the conflict. To make these discernments, I treat the three works as roughly parallel accounts, looking for points of agreement and disagreement between them. Using the composite in this way has provided a way of getting a handle on the case initially and has given some direction to my approach to the data.

5.2.1.2 Identification of Key Participants in the Case
In this study I am concerned to identify those members of the hierarchy who participated in the Hunthausen case in a direct and consequential way. The composite source has been helpful for focusing attention on a limited number of members of the hierarchy who appear to have been directly involved. In certain respects, the identification of key participants is straightforward. The Pope, John Paul II, and the local (arch)bishop, Raymond Hunthausen, automatically qualify as key participants in this study, being the focal points of the center and periphery parties. The sources making up the composite source also show a high level of agreement about a number of other members of the hierarchy who played a significant role in the conflict. One finds below a list of the persons cited in the accounts of the composite source.

Members of the Hierarchy Participating, As Identified by the Composite Source

Member of the Hierarchy Participating	Identified in: Briggs	Reese	Granfield
Raymond **Hunthausen**, Archbishop of Seattle	x	x	x
Donald **Wuerl**, Auxiliary Bishop of Seattle	x	x	x
Bernardin **Gantin**, Cardinal Prefect of the Congregation for Bishops	x		
James **Malone**, Bishop of Youngstown, Ohio; NCCB President, 1983-1986	x	x	x
Pio **Laghi**, Archbishop, Papal Pro-Nuncio to the United States	x	x	x
James **Hickey**, Archbishop of Washington, D.C.; Apostolic Visitator	x	x	x
Thomas **Murphy**, Bishop of Great Falls- Billings, Montana; named Coadjutor Archbishop of Seattle, 1987	x	x	x
John **O'Connor**, Cardinal Archbishop of New York, Commission member	x	x	x
John **Quinn**, Archbishop of San Francisco, Commission member	x	x	x
Joseph **Bernardin**, Cardinal Archbishop of Chicago, Commission member	x	x	x
Pope **John Paul II**	x	x	x
Joseph **Ratzinger**, Cardinal Prefect of the Congregation for the Doctrine of the Faith	x	x	

TABLE 5.2

Of the twelve persons just named, ten are cited by all three accounts within the composite source as having played a significant role in the Hunthausen affair. The two exceptions are Cardinal Ratzinger, who is mentioned by name in two of the three accounts (Briggs, Reese) and Cardinal Gantin, who is mentioned in just one account (Briggs). (Cardinal Ratzinger's participation in the conflict is further evidenced by two letters he sent to Hunthausen during the conflict, both of which have been made public. Gantin's participation is chiefly associated with the letter he wrote to Hunthausen confirming the Vatican's intention for Hunthausen to provide Wuerl with special faculties, but see also the report of other involvement in the 9.19.86 *National Catholic Reporter*.)

At a minimum, all of the above-named bishops have been counted as "persons of interest" in my inquiry into the Rome-Hunthausen affair. Thus I have sought, using all of the evidence available to me, to determine the role they played in the conflict's unfolding and any apparent strategies they employed to cope with the reality of conflict.

5.2.1.3 Participants Identified by Other Sources
Beyond these members of the hierarchy recognized by the composite source, certain others who participated more or less directly in the affair can also be identified. In interviews given

on May 11 and May 18, 2001, Fr. Michael G. Ryan (see sections 9.7-9.7.4) noted that **Archbishop Francis Hurley** (Anchorage, Alaska) served as a close adviser to Archbishop Hunthausen during much of the conflict period.

Another person who advised Hunthausen, according to Hunthausen himself (cf. Hunthausen's address to the NCCB, November 11, 1986) was **Archbishop John Roach** of Minneapolis-St. Paul. After Hunthausen was approached by the Pro-Nuncio about the possibility of conducting a Visitation, Hunthausen called then (outgoing) NCCB President Roach for advice. Roach suggested that Hunthausen demand a "Bill of Particulars" from the Holy See to clarify what the visitation was about.

Ryan also called attention to the fact that Hunthausen kept the bishops of Region XII (Northwestern United States) apprised of developments along the way and consulted with them. Perhaps the most direct involvement of the bishops (eight of the twelve) occurred when they were interviewed by the assessment commission in Menlo Park, California on March 6-7, 1987. The bishops interviewed at that time were: **Archbishop William Levada** (Portland, Oregon), **Archbishop Cornelius Power** (retired, Portland), **Bishop Thomas Connolly** (Baker, Oregon), **Bishop Sylvester Treinen** (Boise, Idaho), **Bishop Elden Curtiss** (Helena, Montana), **Bishop Thomas Murphy** (Great Falls-Billings, Montana), **Bishop Eldon Schuster** (retired, Great Falls-Billings, Montana), **Bishop William Skylstad** (Spokane).

One other member of the hierarchy who played a peripheral role in the affair was **Bishop Nicholas Walsh**, Bishop Emeritus of Yakima, Washington and a former Auxiliary Bishop of Seattle. In October of 1986, Walsh made a trip to Rome of his own volition to offer his assistance in resolving the conflict.

Lastly, in a broader sense, one might consider any of those who participated in the floor debates of the November 1986 National Bishops' Conference meeting (see, e.g., those cited in the case narrative, but one could also identify other bishop commentators from newspaper accounts at the time). These interventions are perhaps best described as tangential forms of participation. In my examination of the case I have paid attention to the participation of all of the above-named bishops.

5.2.1.4 Alignments of Participants

Within the framework of my concept of center-periphery conflict, the identified participants can be associated with the center party, periphery party or third party positions. I envision the following set of alignments.

> **Center Party:** Pope John Paul II, Cardinal Ratzinger, the Papal Pro-Nuncio (Laghi), the Apostolic Visitator (Hickey), Cardinal Gantin, other bishops supporting the Vatican's position
> **Periphery Party:** Archbishop Hunthausen, other bishops actively supporting Hunthausen's position (e.g., Hurley)
> **Third Party:** Bishop Wuerl, Bishop Malone (and the US Bishops' Conference, including the Bishops of Region XII), the assessment commission (Bernardin, O'Connor, Quinn), Bishop Murphy, Bishop Walsh

The first criterion I have applied in determining the alignments is office. Clearly there is no room for disputing the placement of Pope John Paul II (as Pope, he is the representative of the center par excellence) or of Hunthausen (as the local bishop in question, he is the standard bearer for the periphery position). Cardinals Ratzinger and Gantin, as prefects of Roman curial congregations, are also decidedly within the center party camp by virtue of their office. There is also little reason to hesitate about Archbishop Laghi's placement. As papal pro-nuncio, he represents the Holy See in the land of his assignment. Though he represents the bishops of that country to the Pope at the same time, it is clear that his primary accountability is to the Pope.

Other placements are slightly less clear-cut. I have Cardinal Hickey, the Apostolic Visitor, in the center party position, but he might also be considered a third party. Is his office in this case his temporary appointment as Visitor or his more usual service the leader of a local church (Archbishop of Washington, D.C.)? Given this ambiguity, I have turned to a second criterion for determining alignments, which I will call functional affiliation. I have applied this criterion by asking two questions, side by side: (1) Can one identify strong reasons why a party might want to side with center over periphery, or vice-versa? And (2) does the party in practice appear to strongly favor one position over the other?

At the heart of this criterion is the question of (in)dependence. A true third party, as I understand it (see section 4.2.4), has the possibility of siding with either the center or periphery party, or remaining neutral or uninvolved. (Within limits, of course: no bishop can simply turn his back on the Holy See without consequence.) Those associated with the center and periphery positions, however, are clearly beholden to those positions for one reason or another, be it fear of sanction, hope for reward, social pressure, personal convictions, personal ties, or some other reason. Their being beholden will be reflected functionally, in their actions. On the basis of this second criterion, I place Hickey with the center party. His assignment originated in Rome and entailed investigating, in Rome's name, an archbishop and archdiocese that Rome was concerned about. Even if he had wanted to exercise a high degree of independence (whether he did or not, I cannot say), he would have been hemmed in by the fact that Rome expected his loyalty, he was but one person (in contrast, the later assessment commission consisted of three persons), his role was intended to be fully secret (even, to a large degree, with reference to Hunthausen himself), and he did not have the advantage of NCCB backing that encouraged the independence of later bishop participants (as the commission did).

Hunthausen, in my scheme, is essentially alone in his occupation of the periphery party position. Other bishops, representing their own local churches to some extent, but also coming forth as friends or admirers of Hunthausen or defenders of principle, did rally to his side, but this was rare and often took place in private. Most notably, one can point to the role of supporter and adviser taken up by Hunthausen's friend, Archbishop Hurley of Anchorage, and certain other bishops of the Northwest region.

I have identified a number of third parties above, some of whom were very directly involved in the conflict (Wuerl, Bernardin, O'Connor, Quinn, Murphy, Malone) and others who were tangential in their participation (the Northwest bishops and other members of the US bishops' conference). One might be tempted to place Wuerl in the center party position, since he was Rome's choice to fill the auxiliary bishop position (over local candidates that were proposed), was himself a Roman insider (after years of curial service), and received special powers of governance at Rome's directive, over and against Hunthausen's wishes. Certainly, Wuerl was viewed by many Hunthausen loyalists during and after the conflict years as a man of the center and not of the periphery. Nonetheless, I have categorized Wuerl as a third party. In terms of the criteria I have presented, his office in and of itself associates him with the local church. There is some ambiguity here because of the circumstances of his appointment (his appointment was tied to the visitation, he was ordained in Rome and not Seattle, etc.), but his day-to-day official responsibility after the fact of his appointment was to the local church and to his superior, the Archbishop, and was carried out within the social environment (with its own conditioning pressures) of the local church. Applying my second criterion, I would argue that while Wuerl might have had reason to feel a strong loyalty to Rome, he showed himself in practice to be sensitive to his responsibility to the local church. He never once openly opposed Hunthausen, he immersed himself in the life of the local church, and he wrestled (by his own account and by that of others) with the questions of loyalty that were placed before him. On this basis, then, I prefer to see him as a third party and not simply as one doing the bidding of the Holy See in Seattle.

Coadjutor Archbishop Murphy can also be treated as a third party. Like Wuerl, his appointment was marked by a decisive and unusual Roman intervention, but unlike Wuerl, Murphy had few obvious ties to Rome and he himself was already a bishop of the Northwest region. Thus, he was already in some sense acculturated to the local church and, if anything, he appeared to be more a man of the periphery than of the center. Murphy was in a sensitive position, since his appointment came with heightened expectations that his presence in Seattle would improve local conditions in accord with Rome's wishes. But as with Wuerl, Murphy seemed able to balance center and periphery concerns and work with both sides.

The apostolic commission of Bernardin, O'Connor and Quinn also finds placement in my scheme as a third party. In contrast with Hickey's appointment as Visitator, the commission's appointment came when there was social pressure to meet the needs of both the center and periphery parties. Though, like Hickey, the commission had a central role in the conflict as the result of a Vatican directive, its participation was also largely the result of the intervention of the NCCB on behalf of Hunthausen. As such, it had an informal mandate to represent the position of the local churches (local bishops) in America as well. In practice the commission showed itself to be ultimately accountable to Rome but also willing to defend certain interests of the periphery. The same might be said of the NCCB itself and of its president, Bishop Malone. The Northwest bishops (including Bishop Walsh) are understood here to be third party, tangential participants who balanced their obligations to Rome with feelings of loyalty to Hunthausen and to their own local churches.

5.2.1.5 Demarcations and Stages of the Conflict

As I have already pointed out, in order to carry out a case study, we need some idea of where the case begins and end. It is also helpful to have a skeletal description of the case to structure our approach to the case materials. My own reading of the case, which corroborates and is corroborated by the composite source, suggests that the case may be demarcated at eight critical points, each of which is signalled by a public pronouncement by a member of the hierarchy participating directly in the conflict. These eight points mark where the case enters and leaves public consciousness and six internal junctures -- key turning points initiating a marked rise or decline in the level of (observable) conflict intensity. Below is a description of each of the eight critical points of demarcation.

Main Demarcations of the Rome-Hunthausen Conflict

1. October 26, 1983: Archbishop **Hickey announces forthcoming Visitation** of Seattle. Case enters public awareness. Prior to this date the conflict may be considered to be latent and perhaps incipient since the year 1978, when a low-key exchange between Rome and Hunthausen first began (cf. Vatican Chronology).

2. December 3, 1985: Archbishop **Laghi announces Vatican appointment of Donald Wuerl** to serve as Auxiliary Bishop of Seattle. Speculation arises concerning the relationship of Wuerl's appointment to the visitation but this is not made clear by Rome or Hunthausen.

3. September 4, 1986: Archbishop **Hunthausen publicly declares Wuerl's possession of special faculties**. Beginning of period of high level of open conflict.

4. October 24, 1986: Laghi releases **Vatican Chronology** of recent events in Seattle. The report escalates conflict tensions.

5. November 11, 1986: Hunthausen addresses the National Conference of Catholic Bishops. Beginning of period of highest level of open conflict. NCCB meeting includes an extended discussion of the case and leads to the release of a neutral statement by conference president Malone. Period of stalemate follows the NCCB gathering.

6. February 9, 1987: Laghi issues brief written statement announcing **formation of apostolic assessment commission.** Settlement stage begins. Conflict handling takes place primarily in Hunthausen's exchanges with assessment commission. Tensions rise sharply shortly prior to resolution.

7. May 27, 1987: Assessment **commission releases its report. Hunthausen announces appointment of Murphy as Coadjutor Archbishop**. Beginning of period of steady decline in level of open conflict and level of public awareness of the conflict.

8. April 11, 1989: Archbishop **Laghi announces that the commission's review of the situation in Seattle is concluded**. Latency of conflict resumes.

BOX 5.3

Stages of the Rome-Hunthausen Case
(Preliminary Assessment Incorporating Numbered Demarcations)

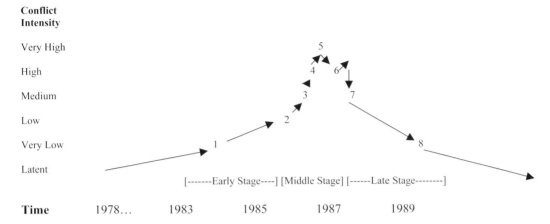

Key: 1 = Hickey and Hunthausen announce visitation
      2 = Laghi announces Wuerl appointment
      3 = Hunthausen announces Wuerl's possession of faculties
      4 = Laghi releases Vatican chronology
      5 = Hunthausen addresses NCCB
      6 = Laghi announces formation of assessment commission
      7 = Commission releases its report
      8 = Commission's oversight of situation in Seattle ends

FIGURE 5.4

The demarcations and stages presented above are open for discussion. But this scheme, based on my extensive reading of the case materials (texts produced by insiders and outside observers as well), serves a useful function by drawing our attention to the fact that the Hunthausen case evolves over time and varies in its intensity along the way. It also highlights the fact that there are concrete turning points and distinguishable periods (stages) of conflict handling. To gain an in-depth perspective on the reasoning justifying the selection / depiction above, I refer readers to the case narrative and analysis presented in chapters six-eight.

One matter of judgment concerns the latency and manifestness of conflict. How do we determine when a conflict has risen to the surface – and to whom is it perceptible? Primarily here I am concerned with public consciousness of the conflict. I presume that Hunthausen and his Roman counterparts felt themselves to be in tension sometime before the October, 1983 announcement of the visitation, and perhaps as early as 1978 (when, according to the Vatican chronology, Rome first started discussing its concerns with Hunthausen). Surely by May 1983, when Laghi approached Hunthausen about the Vatican's wish to have a visitation, or shortly thereafter, there must have been some felt tension, perceptible to the insiders but not to the public at large. For all practical purposes, the conflict left public consciousness (returned to latency) shortly after the release of the assessment commission report and the simultaneous implementation of its recommended solution (the reassignment of Wuerl and the instalment of Murphy, with an extended period of oversight by the commission itself). Little national attention went to the disbanding of the commission in April of 1989, and only a limited amount of attention in the Seattle archdiocese itself. By that time, it appears, most considered the matter long since resolved. For the principals themselves, however, and certainly for Hunthausen in particular, it is likely that tensions associated with the conflict have lingered ever since. Hunthausen's career had been on the line over a period of years. That is not something one walks away from easily.

As for the judgments of conflict intensity indicated in the descriptions of the points of demarcation and subsequently plotted on the graph: these refer to the conflict theory of Pruitt and Rubin (1986), and especially to their discussion of escalation and de-escalation. Pruitt and Rubin identify five transformations that occur during escalation (heavy tactics supplanting lighter tactics; the proliferation of issues; specific issues giving way to general issues; a shift from wanting to do well to wanting to hurt the other; an increase in the number of participants: see section 4.2.4, above). I have used these transformations as benchmarks for identifying periods of escalation in the Rome-Hunthausen case. All five of these transformations can be observed in what I have marked as the middle stage on the graph, the stage when the conflict reaches its highest level of intensity.

Note that I have graphed two peaks of conflict intensity: one in the middle stage (point 5) and one near the beginning of the late stage (the sharp rise and fall between points 6 and 7). The peak at point 5 signals the very public, heated confrontation which took place at the November 1986 U.S. bishops' meeting, where the Vatican and Hunthausen positions were debated. This is the occasion of greatest conflict intensity shown, more or less, openly. The second peak signals the intensity of conflict handling carried out in private, when Hunthausen and the assessment commission struggled to come to agreement.

One should note that the stages presented on the graph are labeled early-middle-late, rather than escalation-stalemate-settlement. I do this in order to roughly distinguish the periods of high and low conflict (rising-high-descending). In my reading of the case, the stages of escalation, stalemate and settlement cannot be broken out quite so neatly (as is seen by the brief but sharp rise in conflict intensity early in the settlement stage) and can better be accounted for in my detailed description and analysis of the case in the chapters ahead. The early-middle-late scheme gives us an oversimplified overview for the sake of introductory familiarity with the case. It also provides a helpful way of dividing up the long case narrative.

5.2.1.6 Selection of Documents for Analysis

Documents produced by members of the hierarchy participating in the Rome-Hunthausen conflict serve as an "embedded" unit of analysis (Yin 1994, 41-42) in the case study. Thus, while the case of conflict as a whole remains the primary unit of analysis, selected case documents provide us with an internal unit that can be assessed to determine which coping strategies have been employed empirically.

My rationale for choosing documents as an embedded unit of analysis is both theoretical and practical. In theoretical terms, I operate from the assumption that organizational conflicts are typically made manifest in language use. Language use is at the heart of our ability to interact as persons, and as such, it is also an inescapable dimension of conflict experience (C. L. Briggs 1996, 3; Jandt 1973, 2). One cannot wage conflict, or resolve it, or understand it, without being able to send messages, and receive and interpret them. Moreover, written texts serve to negotiate sociocultural contradictions and differences between groups (Fairclough 1995, 7). Language (written or spoken) is not the only medium of conflict conduct: behaviors other than speaking and writing also determine the course of a dispute. But by studying texts produced in conflict situations one may gain much insight into the nature of the conflict and the techniques employed in its management. In regard to center-periphery conflict, it is my view that close attention to the language used by Church leaders in conflict situations reveals much about what interests are at stake for these leaders (and for the Church as an institution) and what means they consider appropriate to secure those interests.

In a more strictly practical respect, my choice to focus on case documents as an embedded unit of analysis has to do with the relative availability of documents in comparison with other information sources. Factors of distance, cost and inaccessibility led me to rule out the possibility of basing my analyses on interviews with principal participants from the case. And other communications media (television, radio) were not employed as primary means for conducting the exchanges between the parties, so analysis of broadcast tapes did not appear to be a fruitful possibility. (Among the rare instances of the use of television by principals in the affair were the November 1986 NCCB press statement; the Hunthausen-Murphy press conference in June of 1987; and a September 14, 1986 broadcast of an interview with Hunthausen and Wuerl on the KOMO-TV program "Real to Reel," a program produced by the Seattle archdiocese. Real to Reel showed on Sunday mornings and typically had low viewership.) In contrast, public documents issued in the name of principal participants in the conflict offer the advantage of representing a range of positions in the conflict, as articulated by the hierarchy over time. Such documents, it seemed to me, offered the best opportunity to glimpse the case in its breadth and its depth. As such, I have tried to ensure that the documents selected for analysis be representative of the case as a whole. By representative, I mean that the selection of documents should reveal – to the fullest extent possible, given practical constraints – coping strategies employed by the center, periphery and third parties through the duration of the conflict.

Before selecting documents for analysis, one must become acquainted with the "archive" of documents relevant to the case that could conceivably be obtained (Fairclough 1992, 227). It is common for a researcher to find that many documents that could prove beneficial for a study are not within reach. There may simply be too many to collect, or documents may have disappeared or been destroyed, or perhaps they are being kept private by one party or another. (Thomas 1997, 235 points to the research difficulty created by "the inaccessibility of pertinent archival collections dealing with Vatican-American hierarchical relations after 1965.") Thus, an important step is to determine which documents are within reach. From these, then, a selection of documents can be made for analysis.

In regard to the Hunthausen case, I quickly determined that several documents of interest which are known to exist are not available for public consumption. An example is Cardinal Hickey's visitation report, which apparently even Hunthausen himself has never had the opportunity to read. Nonetheless, plenty of documents are available for our examination. I have identified the available archive of documents through consultation of the composite source, personal inquiries, and further reading of a wide range of sources including, in particular, the Seattle Archdiocesan newspaper (*The Progress*) and the national Catholic documentary resource *Origins*. This archive of documents potentially available for analysis is specified in Appendix 2.

In my initial selection of documents for analysis, I have chosen those documents identified as important to the case by two or more of the sources in the composite source. There are ten documents which meet this criterion. Hickey's visitation report is named in this list but must be omitted because it is not available for analysis. This leaves us with nine key documents.

My intention has been to read these documents, listed below, closely for signs of how participants have strategically engaged the conflict situation.

Primary Documents for Analysis

Document	Identified in: Briggs	Reese	Granfield
Early Stage			
1. Ratzinger, Letter to Hunthausen with Visitation findings, dated September 30, 1985	x	x	
2. Laghi, Letter to Hunthausen with Visitation findings, dated November 14, 1985	x	x	x
Middle Stage			
3. Hunthausen, Public announcement of Wuerl's faculties, released September 4, 1986	x	x	x
4. Laghi, Vatican Chronology, released October 24, 1986	x	x	x
5. Hunthausen, Response to Vatican Chronology, released November 12, 1986	x	x	x
6. Hunthausen, Address to NCCB, released November 12, 1986	x	x	x
7. Malone, Statement at NCCB meeting, released November 12, 1986	x		x
8. Laghi, Announcement of Commission appointment, released February 9, 1987	x		x
Late Stage			
9. Commission, Assessment Report, released May 27, 1987	x	x	x

TABLE 5.5

I believe this selection of documents provides us with a rich source of information regarding the ways center, periphery and third party participants approached the conflict as it unfolded. My own reading of the case confirms the judgment of the composite source that these documents are critical for an understanding of the case. Each one of them is associated with a key turning point in the case. (Fairclough 1992, 230 notes the advantage of choosing for analysis texts that emerge out of "moments of crisis," since these have an especially strong potential for revealing aspects of social practice that are under contestation.) Also arguing in favor of the above-named selection of documents is its representation of all three stages of the conflict and participants from each position (center, periphery, third).

5.2.1.7 Accounting for Intervening Developments

In the construction of this case study it has been necessary to use other materials beyond the nine texts identified above to draw up a picture of the conflict handling. While the documents themselves are highly revealing when analyzed closely, the success of this analysis depends on proper contextualization. Without a clear idea of the activity (including nondiscursive forms of strategic coping) and discourse that surround the select documents, we are likely to misread them and the conflict itself. For this reason, my presentation of the case narrative and analysis in chapters six-eight includes descriptions of the conflict developments prior and subsequent to the distribution of each document.

Producing these descriptions of conflict developments has presented a methodological challenge. Specifically, I have faced a two-part problem of selecting and interpreting evidence in order to accurately reproduce relevant events and exchanges from the conflict. The primary materials I was able to track down in support of this undertaking were other documents from the case produced by conflict participants, newspaper accounts from the time and miscellaneous other sources (magazine and journal articles, letters, internal memoranda, etc.). Having gathered together a rather substantial collection of such materials, I then set aside a limited number of documents (not the primary documents) produced by the conflict participants for use in a later control analysis of my findings from the discourse analysis of the nine documents already selected (see my discussion of this process later in this chapter and the control analysis itself in chapter nine). The remaining materials provided a fairly comprehensive information source about the case, which I used to reconstruct the case history. The single best source for following the history of the case proved to be the newspaper of the Seattle Archdiocese, *The Progress*. The Catholic documentary resource *Origins* was helpful for providing the integral text of a number of documents and for supplying other pieces of information as well. Among secular newspapers, the *Seattle Post-Intelligencer* offered the fullest and most detailed coverage of the case. Among national Catholic publications, the *National Catholic Reporter* offered the most comprehensive coverage of the case from beginning to end, and was invaluable in its provision of insider accounts of negotiations within the hierarchy. Numerous other publications also made valuable contributions to my ability to (re)tell this story, including the *Seattle Times*, the *New York Times*, the *Seattle Weekly*, the *Washington Post*, the *National Catholic Register*, the *Wanderer* and the Catholic journals of opinion *America* and *Commonweal.* I have already mentioned (in chapter one) the "time capsule" of materials I received from Ms. Janice Wasden Price, a chancery employee during the entire period of the conflict. Ms. Wasden Price's box of materials contained numbered and dated scrapbooks full of article clippings (many from the above named sources), photos, letters, campaign-style Hunthausen buttons, internal memoranda and more, which she assembled as the conflict progressed. Beyond filling in information gaps about the principal participants, this time capsule also offered an acquaintanceship with the ways that peripheral participants came to participate in the affair. Ms. Wasden Price, interestingly enough, tracked not only the activity of Hunthausen supporters (she herself was one) but also of Hunthausen opponents. As a result, she has left a highly informative, multi-dimensional record of the conflict. My own research has substantially benefited from her earlier efforts.

Securing a deep and broad base of evidence from the case was only the first step in the effort to characterize the events contextualizing the selected documents. The next step was to decide how to distill these materials. Which events, which quotations were to be singled out as especially revealing of how the conflict moved forward? What was worthy of mention in my conflict narrative apart from the findings from my analysis of the nine documents?

I made my selections according to three priorities. The first priority was to *ensure that key developments and issues mentioned in the composite source were addressed* in some fashion. The second priority was to *account for the full range of participants and debated questions highlighted in the other information sources*, even if these achieved only a singular appearance. (There were practical limits to how far I could apply this standard.) The third priority was to *mention words or deeds that appeared especially instrumental or influential within the conflict handling.* (According to a cross-referencing reading of the conflict as a whole, did the words or deeds generate direct responses, open up new issues, or serve as some sort of crystalization of, or turning point within, the conflict as a whole?)

5.2.1.8 Construction of the Narrative
In chapters six-eight I present a narrative of the case that is based on my findings from the

selected documents and the wide-ranging assortment of other materials. I am conscious of the fact that this narrative is already one level of interpretation: it is one way of telling the story out of countless other possibilities (based on one particular selection of evidence and one way of understanding the evidence). I do not apologize for this fact, since I see no way around the need for making some sort of coherent whole out of the jumble of possibilities, but I do believe it is important to acknowledge this reality. As a means for allowing other observers to judge the quality of my interpretation, and draw their own conclusions as necessary, I have tried to be as transparent as possible in my presentation of the narrative. Therefore, I have consistently identified the sources of quotations and I have tried to limit descriptions of actions to empirically verifiable dimensions. As much as possible, I have tried to save more "subjective" observations for the sections that are specifically focused on analysis (of the conflict functionality of words and deeds).

Any story teller will at times be tempted to include items that are interesting rather than (apparently) directly pertinent. I confess to have – hope to have – given in to this temptation on one or more occasions.

5.3 Discourse Analysis of the Selected Documents

Texts – and here I refer specifically to the selected documents, but also to the other written sources I have drawn on in constructing my own narrative account of the conflict – provide us with traces of the conflict we are studying, but no more than that. They cannot perfectly reproduce the fullness, ambiguity, dynamism and human complexity of actual conflict exchanges. We need to keep in mind that a given text takes shape in the process of its production, distribution and consumption, and realizes it full meaning within the contexts of an immediate interchange and broader organizational and societal frameworks. What is really of interest in this investigation are not the texts themselves but the social dynamics (the thought and practice) that the texts represent and carry out.

Practically speaking, in this research we require a method that allows us to move from textual evidence to the recognition of conflict coping strategies. The most central and crucial form of evidence drawn on here is the selection of documents produced by conflict participants themselves. Thus, for these documents, we need an analytical method that relates text constructions to social conflict. Critical discourse analysis is such a method. I will now offer a description of this method and my application thereof in this research. (Later in the chapter I will describe the method I have employed to analyze the conflict functionality of nondiscursive strategic developments and of other discursive developments not accounted for by the selected documents.)

I believe that the method of discourse analysis advanced by Fairclough (1989, 1992, 1995) serves our purposes well. I have employed Fairclough's method extensively in this study, using it as the intermediate step toward the identification of conflict coping strategies applied in the case. Fairclough's is one among several approaches to discourse analysis that offer viable application to the study at hand. These approaches are not mutually exclusive: some among them can be used in complementary fashion. A likely alternative and / or complement to the work of Fairclough is the well-developed approach of Van Dijk (1998, 1997a, 1997b, 1985). (But see also the range of other possibilities identified in Fairclough and Wodak 1997, 262-268.) Though my own work is much informed by the writings of Van Dijk, I take Fairclough as my starting point and general frame of reference. I became acquainted with Fairclough's perspective early in this investigation: the questions he raises (about how people acquire, maintain and employ power through discourse) and his suggestions for looking into those questions have shaped this research from the beginning. In a concise, compact presentation, Fairclough points to practical applications whereby one may relate particular texts to prevailing currents of social practice, and his focus on how power is applied discursively in social struggle fits well with my primary interest. (Fairclough, like Van Dijk but unlike certain other practitioners, emphasizes that the analysis of texts should not be isolated from the analysis of the institutional and discursive practices within which they are embedded. See Fairclough 1995, 9.) Thus, I take my lead from Fairclough, but supplement use of his method, as necessary, with the perspective of others (Van Dijk, but also, e.g., Brown and Levinson 1987, Caldas-Coulthard and Coulthard 1986, Brown and Yule 1983).

5.3.1 An Overview of Fairclough's Approach

"Discourse," in Fairclough's view, "is use of language seen as a form of social practice." "Critical discourse analysis" (CDA) is his method for analyzing how texts work within sociocultural practice (Fairclough 1995, 7). In the following passage, Fairclough provides a succinct description of his approach:

> [Critical discourse analysis] sees discourse -- language use in speech and writing -- as a form of 'social practice'. Describing discourse as social practice implies a dialectical relationship between a particular discursive event and the situation(s), institution(s) and social structure(s) which frame it. A dialectical relationship is a two-way relationship: the discursive event is shaped by situations, institutions and social structures, but it also shapes them. To put the same point in a different way, discourse is socially constitutive as well as socially shaped: it constitutes situations, objects of knowledge, and the social identities of and relationships between people and groups of people. It is constitutive both in the sense that it helps to sustain and reproduce the social status quo, and in the sense that it contributes to transforming it. Since discourse is so socially influential, it gives rise to important issues of power. Discursive practices may have major ideological effects: that is, they can help produce and reproduce unequal power relations between (for instance) social classes, women and men, and ethnic / cultural majorities and minorities through the ways in which they represent things and position people. So discourse may, for example, be racist, or sexist, and try to pass off assumptions (often falsifying ones) about any aspect of social life as mere common sense. Both the ideological loading of particular ways of using language and the relations of power which underlie them are often unclear to people. CDA aims to make more visible these opaque aspects of discourse. (Fairclough and Wodak 1997, 258)

In the current study my aim is to supply a description of how power was applied strategically, through language use, to manage a case of center-periphery conflict. As such, I aspire, in conformity with the agenda of Fairclough, to "make more visible" the discursive applications of power in that conflict that may be opaque. With Fairclough, I believe discursive events (such as the production, distribution and consumption of a text within an intrahierarchical conflict) dialectically engage conventions of language use on the institutional and societal level. Within that engagement, the discursive event shapes the institutional and societal context, but it is also shaped by the same. The challenge for the discourse analyst is to look at a particular discursive event and accurately account for how this mutual transformation takes place. Central to this challenge is the analyst's dependence on fixed or "frozen" reference points (a particular version of a particular text) to reveal social exchanges that are highly complex and constantly shifting (the situation, organization and society changes in its particulars from moment to moment). While no text can perfectly reveal the variety of social forces that are in play, astute, multifaceted analyses of discourse samples can provide valuable insight into the social forces that apply.

A key idea in Fairclough's approach holds that conceptions of "common sense" (cf. Gramsi 1971) are crucial to the maintenance of existing power arrangements. If groups in power can convince others that there is an inevitability or obvious rightness to the way things are, then less-powerful groups are not likely to act to change the prevailing arrangement. To put it another way, powerful groups remain in power to a large extent thanks to the fact that others take for granted their belonging there. As part of their taking for granted the power arrangement, less-powerful groups buy into ways of thinking and communicating that overtly and covertly reinforce the established social order. (See the discussion of traditional power in section 2.4.4.1 and my reference to "psychic" or "hierocratic" coercion in 2.4.4.) At the same time, there may be multiple ways in which lower-power parties do not take for granted their position of lower power and may actively seek to change their situation by challenging the existing patterns of thought, communication and action. What CDA tries to do is lay bare how such struggles show up in language events. (Note that key parts of Fairclough's work – see, e.g., Fairclough 1995, 91-92 – develop "within the framework of a Gramscian theory of power in modern capitalist societies as 'hegemony.'" While I acknowledge that this theoretical background is of interest, I choose not to explore it here, since Fairclough's primary value to this study is his identification of micro-level linguistic techniques used in applications of power. I believe that this practical benefit can be drawn from Fairclough's work without necessarily adopting, in its entirety, the view of society and history that he advances.)

Fairclough provides questions and organizing perspectives that help us to recognize traces of social contestation that show up in given texts. I will now discuss these questions and perspectives and describe my own employment of them in the consideration of the Rome-Hunthausen case.

5.3.2 Application of Discourse Analysis Within the Current Study
Before proceeding, I should add a word of caution. Discourse analysis is in some ways as much art as science. It is essentially of a form of literary criticism that relates given linguistic constructions to social practice. In order to build accountability into the process of analysis, I identify the text source, the specific questions put to each text, and the evidence used to justify particular assessments. Obviously, too, the quality of the analysis will depend on one's familiarity with the societal and institutional cultures (norms, practices, etc.) that apply. That is one reason for having spent so much time on these matters in chapters two and three.

My application of Fairclough's method involved a number of steps: (1) immersing myself in Fairclough's writings on discourse analysis; (2) reading, in survey fashion, all available materials concerning the Hunthausen case; (3) reading, in close fashion (highlighting, adding margin notes, etc.), all available documents produced by the conflict principals, except for those set aside for the control analysis; (4) summarizing in narrative and table form the results of the close reading of the nine selected documents (see chapter 9 and appendix v); (5) digitally producing readable versions of the selected documents with margin notes indicating identified strategies; (6) summarizing the strategies and tactics identified in the nine control documents.

Listed below are the analytical topics, suggested by Fairclough, that I have used to organize my ground-level consideration of each of the documents. The topics draw on Fairclough's approach, but they do not come from him as-is. Instead, they represent my distillation of key findings he offers. I use the topics as points of entry into each document and as a means to gain a coherent sense of the efficacy of its construction. With each document I describe those dimensions of the text indicated by the topic, with the help of a set of leading questions that relates to the topic. More than description, this is already a level of interpretation, wherein I identify elements in the construction of the document which appear be tactics within a broader strategy for coping with the realities of the conflict. Following the list of topics below is a description of what goes into each topical inquiry.

General Points of Inquiry Into Each Document
- Production
- Distribution
- Consumption
- Text Type
- Diction
- Usage
- Substructures of the Text
- Intertextuality

BOX 5.6

In the matter of **production**, Fairclough (1992, 78) notes that the position of "text producer" is less straightforward than it might seem to be. He invokes Goffman's (1981, 144) distinction between "animator" (the person who actually makes the marks on paper), "author" (the one who puts the words together) and "principal" (the one whose position is represented by the words) as a case in point. Consequently, when considering documents issued in the name of members of the hierarchy, we need to realize that ghost writers, editors or other commentators, and secretaries may all have shaped the text product that is eventually consumed. Other dimensions of production that we should be conscious of are the social constraints on production. Production is constrained by the available members' resources and by the governing social practice which determines how the members' resources are drawn upon. A member of the hierarchy will only produce the sort of text that he can conceive, and his conception of possibility will be shaped by the social world of which he is a part. It is worth our while to explore the constraints on production that apply. We should also keep in mind that text production is normally carried out with awareness that the text will be distributed, transformed and consumed in particular ways. "Producers within sophisticated organizations… produce texts in ways which anticipate their distribution, transformation, and consumption, and have multiple audiences built in to them" (Fairclough 1992, 79). A bishop, for example, who wants to pass on a particular message may choose certain phrases to appeal to certain audiences, avoid others because of their potential of being taken out of context (in the form of an undesirable sound bite), and authorize the formatting of his text into a press release for ease of handling by media outlets. To the extent that I can, with each document I delineate aspects of the document's production that are factors in the conflict handling.

Production
a. Who is the principal?
b. Who is the author?
c. Who is the animator?
d. Did any other persons influence the production process? Who, and how?

e. Are earlier drafts of the document known to exist? Specify.
f. Which constraints on production can be identified?
How is the production process relevant to the conflict experience?

The **distribution** of texts may be simple, as in the mailing of a single letter, or vastly more complex, as when a political leader's speech passes through multiple governmental and news media domains (television, radio, newspaper, internet) on the way to its consumption by various audiences (Fairclough 1992, 79). En route to its receivers, a text will make its way through "more or less settled chains of discursive practices" (Fairclough 1995, 13). It can be illuminating to observe what these chains are and how they shape the text in question. One should not overlook the fact that production and consumption processes also occur within the processes of distribution. The intermediaries who pass on texts from producers to consumers are themselves producers and consumers. They are producers in the sense that they re-produce the text they have received into some new arrangement and they are consumers in that they consume what they have received. The intermediaries of distribution will have their own unique interests to pursue as they pass on the texts they have received. Thus, the newspaper editor who receives a press release from a bishop may be more inclined to give the statement prominent coverage if the subject matter seems appealing for his paper's readership. The same text will be greeted differently by the editor of a diocesan newspaper who is dependent upon the bishop for his job. In my assessment of each document I note traces of the distribution process that appear in the documents themselves and which can be identified by reference to other sources. I also point out any transformations of the text that I am aware of which took place during the process of distribution. Beyond this, I reflect on how the text distribution process (so far as it is known: I consult available external sources) impinges upon the reception of the text at hand and the text producer's participation in the conflict.

Distribution
a. What are the known steps in the distribution process?
b. Who is involved in distribution of (various versions of) the text?
c. How does passage through the distribution process shape the text?
How is the distribution process relevant to the conflict experience?

Text **consumption** is a dialectical process that engages properties of the text itself and interpretive resources brought to bear by the one confronting the text (Fairclough 1995, 9). We should, therefore, be prepared to discern how elements of the text invite certain types of reception and how the (socially conditioned) personal resources of the text consumer predispose him or her to respond to the text in particular ways. Various factors independent of the text itself shape the reader's reception of the text. These include the social context in which the text is consumed (Private or public? Tightly or loosely controlled? Etc.) and the sort of reading of the text that is undertaken (Individual or collective? Perusal or close reading? Well-informed regarding the subject matter or not? Etc.). While one cannot know with certainty what goes on inside readers as they encounter the text, it is sometimes possible to gain insight in this matter by querying readers through surveys or interviews. Unfortunately, in the present study I am only able to do this in a limited way (as in the interview with Fr. Ryan). Still, it is possible to get some sense of responses that were desired (by looking at cues present in the text) and actual responses (by looking at texts written in response to the given text or by consulting other written sources which document responses). Specifying the social conditions of consumption is another challenging task, especially when one is talking about multiple (and even unknown) receiving parties and environments of reception. But we can at least suggest audiences who are likely targets for reception and those who are likely overhearers, and make observations about social factors that are likely to guide their consumption of the text. Because we are concerned with how members of the hierarchy employ language in the selected documents to cope with conflict, we will want to discern not only how texts appear to be received but also how they appear to be constructed for the sake of gaining particular sorts of reception which are advantageous for their position within the conflict.

Consumption
a. Who were the intended consumers of the text?
b. Who were the actual consumers of the text?
c. In which text formats (personal letter, newspaper, etc.) was the text consumed?
d. In which social environments was the text typically consumed?
e. Which social constraints on consumption can be identified?
How is the experience of consumption relevant to the conflict experience?

Fairclough's (1995, 13-15) use of the term **text type** stands in relation to his concept of *genre*. Whereas a genre, for Fairclough, is "a socially ratified way of using language in connection with a particular type of social activity (e.g. interview, narrative, exposition)," which exists on a rather abstract level, a text type is a configuration of genre(s) which instantiates the genre in a more situationally and historically specific, text-bound way. (In the background of Fairclough's view of genre is the informing contribution of Bakhtin 1986.) As an example, correspondent to the interview genre, one might find the following text types (ordered from most to least abstract): news interview, TV news interview, Channel 4 news interview. Text types and genres are ideal types – reference concepts against which actual texts can be compared – which stand in relation to societal and institutional orders of discourse. Flexibility is required when making use of these terms since no fixed, widely-agreed-upon list of genres or text types is available. (Fairclough himself provides no canon of text types.) In general, I will make use of the notion of text type as a tool for making comparisons with other texts. A producer's choice of a given text type signals a willingness or unwillingness to accommodate certain social expectations (politicians normally issue press releases, not internal memoranda). Departures from the expected approach (which can crop up internally within a given text as well) can hint of social arrangements under contestation. Thus my intention is to characterize the text type of the document with a single descriptive term or phrase, but also, when possible, to go beyond this to comment on ways the actual text is conventional or creative in regard to the text type that is invoked, and to suggest how the choice of text type fits within the conflict discourse that is underway.

Text Type
a. What name best characterizes the text type?
b. Which text properties invite this designation of text type? (These are conventional aspects of text type.)
c. Which properties of the text are creative (unconventional) in regard to the text type?
How is the application of text type relevant to the conflict?

Diction is a term I use in preference to Fairclough's "vocabulary." Though for the most part I employ it in the same way he does vocabulary, I prefer diction because it focuses on word choice (the act of selection), rather than on the full array of words one's personal knowledge makes available for use. This topic means to draw our attention to specific words which serve strategic purposes within the documents themselves and more broadly within the conflictual engagement. Not all words, of course, will be chosen with the same degree of intentionality. Whereas a text producer may introduce certain words within a text consciously for a decided purpose, the majority of assembled words will likely be there as the result of unreflective habits of text construction. These (apparently) unreflective inclusions are worthy of our notice because they reveal structures of thought that the text producer takes for granted – though caution is in order when we read motives into word choices.

Fairclough raises many pertinent questions about the wording of a text. Are the word choices in line with what one would expect, considering the text type, social situation, institutional domain, etc.? Do certain words stand out by virtue of being unusual, repeated, or centrally important to the discourse as a whole? What *experiential* values do words have? (What knowledge and beliefs do they convey? What classification schemes and vocabulary domains are drawn upon? How are ideological differences coded into the vocabulary? Do the meanings of certain words appear to be under contestation? Are there examples of "overwording" (an abundance of synonyms placed in proximity, perhaps indicating a preoccupation with some specific aspect of reality) or "rewording" (the systematic replacement of one word or set of words with another) (Fairclough 1989, 113-115)? Do certain words tend to collocate?) What *relational* values do the words have? (Do the word choices invite the reader into relationship? Are they distancing? Do euphemisms smooth over threats to relationship? Is the diction formal or informal?) What *expressive* values are communicated by the word choices? (How is social identity communicated through word choice?) Do any words have a particular *functionality* in relation to the (conflict) business at hand? What role do *metaphors* play, if any? These are the kinds of concerns which inform my study of the documents at the level of word choice. Keeping this range of questions in mind, I relate the document's diction to the conflictual context.

Diction

a. Which words stand out from the text, and why? (Possible reasons: repetition, unusual in context, ideologically contested, code word, metaphor, euphemism, crudity, eloquence, highly technical, jargon.)

b. From which social-discursive (sub-)domain(s) do the words in the text appear predominantly to be drawn? (Examples of domains: domestic life, work, recreation, church, politics, academics, etc. Examples of sub-domains of social discourse within the church could include liturgical prayer, private informal prayer, parish gossip, theological language (in its multitude of forms), church organizational language, canon law, etc.)

c. Which words are especially instrumental in the assignment of social identities?

d. Which words work to improve / maintain / detract from the quality of relationship between the parties to the communication?

e. Which words appear intended to manage certain issues of the conflict? How do these function?

How does the diction as a whole in the document relate strategically to the conflict?

Usage is a term I use (much in the way that Fairclough uses "grammar") to discuss how the text producer puts words together -- with implicit reference to grammatical rules -- to make sentences and join sentences in the document. In his method of critical discourse analysis, Fairclough gives substantial attention to how text construction on the grammatical level of the sentence serves social goals pursued by means of the text. There are myriad ways in which this can take place. Fairclough (1989, 111, 120-132) invites us to consider some possibilities through questions he raises, among which are the following. What *experiential* values do grammatical features have? (Does the construction of the sentence make *agency* unclear? Do the use of *nominalizations* – nouns or multi-word compound nouns which stand in for sentences articulating process – hide dimensions of causality? Are sentences active or passive?) What *relational* values do grammatical features have? (Which grammatical *modes* are employed – declarative, grammatical question, imperative? Are there important features of *relational modality*, expressing the authority of one participant in relation to another? (Here one gives special attention to modal auxiliary verbs, adverbs and tense.) Are the pronouns *we* and *you* used, and if so, how?) What *expressive* values do grammatical features have? (How is the writer's authority with respect to the truth communicated? (Again the use of modal auxiliaries, or the absence thereof, is often revealing.)

Fairclough (1992, 77; following Halliday and Hassan 1976, and Halliday 1985) uses the term "cohesion" to refer generally to ways that clauses are linked together into sentences, and sentences are linked together to form larger units in texts. Linkage may be achieved in various ways, including through the use of repeated words, near synonyms, words drawn from the same semantic field; through referring and substituting devices (pronouns, definite articles, demonstratives, ellipsis of repeated words, etc.); and through conjunctive words. Another aspect of cohesion worth considering is whether the linkage of clauses and sentences shows *coordination* or *subordination*.

For each document, I will note under the heading Usage constructive techniques, such as those identified above, which appear to carry out the document's social functionality.

Usage

a. Are agency (who acted?) and causality (which x caused effect y?) clarified, made ambiguous or hidden through sentence constructions? Which techniques of sentence construction (and/or sentence linkage) achieve this?

b. How are identities articulated through grammatical forms?

c. How are relational values signalled and pursued through elements of usage?

d. What expressive values do grammatical features have?

How does the usage function strategically within the conflict?

Beyond the level of the sentence we find larger **substructures of the text** which help to make up the structure of the text as a whole. This concept has reference to the text type and genre that the document instantiates. Certain expectations accompany the association of a document with a particular text type: we will expect to see familiar elements of text in a familiar arrangement. For example, when reading a newspaper article, we may well expect to see a headline, followed by identification of the author, and then the body of the article, divided into paragraphs. If it is a straight news story (as opposed, say, to a work of editorial comment), we may then anticipate finding key points of information in the first few paragraphs (answers to the questions who, what, where, when, how?), followed by subsequent paragraphs which take up the secondary topics or the main topics in greater detail. The expected elements will vary according to the text type. When familiar elements appear as expected, broader social understandings implied by the text type are drawn upon and reinforced. The inclusion of unexpected elements or the arrangement of text elements in unexpected ways may serve to challenge the presumed social order. The invocation of an alternate source of authority into the text at hand may produce a similar effect.

Fairclough's concepts of intertextuality and interdiscursivity are relevant here. One may find subsections of a given text which stand out because they refer to other texts or incorporate portions of the same. Or one may come upon the mingling of discourse types within a given text, as when a rather formal lecture begins with a humorous preamble. There is no fixed set of categories for distinguishing the sorts of substructures that may cohere in a single text, but by dialectically inquiring into the relations between the parts and the whole one can gain a more sophisticated sense of how the text functions within its social context.

Substructures of the Text

a. Which substructures of text organization can be identified?

b. How do these substructures relate to the structure of the text as a whole?

How do the identified substructures serve a strategic purpose, if any, within the conflict?

Having raised the question of **intertextuality**, let us consider further how that concept may come into play in our analysis of documents. I have already made a point of giving preferential treatment in my selection of documents to those documents that stand in manifest intertextual relationship to other documents. When such relationships are transparent, we have a ready opportunity to observe how the texts respond to and anticipate one another. The manner of this interchange says much about the social prerogatives which are operative within the conflict. My intention, however, is not to consider only manifest kinds of intertextuality, but also more implicit forms of the same. Fairclough (1992, 102) holds with Bakhtin (1986) that all texts are inherently intertextual. That is, a text marks a turn in a continual turn-taking of speakers (writers). It is made up of words others have used and has direct and indirect bearing on instances of future word use by others. By and large, intertextuality is implicit rather than explicit. When possible in this study, I will also consider instances of intertextuality that, while notable, are perhaps less than obvious. An important assignment in the study of intertextuality is to sort out the more prominent voices that speak in a text. We will want to attend to how the text producer incorporates these other voices (In a detached way? Ironically? Reverentially?). Intertextuality can be a source of ambivalence (Fairclough 1992, 105), since it may be difficult to know which voice is holding forth at any given point. In the course of my analysis, I draw attention to various elements of the selected texts that seem to indicate relationship with other texts (be they included in my document selection or not). In each case I will say something about what the nature of that relationship appears to be and how the interconnectedness factors into the total discourse of the conflict.

Intertextuality
a. Which external texts are explicitly invoked?
b. Which external texts are implicitly invoked?
How does the observable intertextuality function strategically in regard to the conflict?

Taken together, the reflections shared above serve both to sensitize our consideration of case materials and to provide us with methodological tools of discernment. They paint a picture of how power functions discursively and remind us that power cannot be studied independently of its applications.

5.4 Identification of Coping Strategies on the Basis of Documentary Evidence
Careful consideration of the select documents in light of the eight discursive-analytic topics helped me to come to a multi-dimensional view of how each document functioned within the conflict. (See the detailed presentation of findings in appendix v.) On this basis, I was able to think more clearly about how the texts served strategic purposes.

The most pertinent challenge was to discern, on the basis of the documentary evidence, which coping strategies were being applied by means of the text. In chapter three (3.5.3) I defined a coping strategy as *an orchestrated attempt to manage conflict as advantageously as possible*. I then went on to identify a set of expectations for the conflict handling. To refresh our memory, these were:

The General Stance toward Conflict Handling:
All members of the hierarchy participating in center-periphery conflict will strive to save the face of and enhance the power of the Church organization and themselves.
Perspective on the Use of Power:
Members of the hierarchy will strive for (the appearance of) legitimacy in their employments of power.

Likely Coping Strategies:
1. Show deference to the structural order and mindset of the Church
2. Associate one's own efforts with the best interest of the Church
3. Minimize the appearance of conflict
4. Show fraternity
5. Practice courtesy
6. Employ secrecy
7. Recruit allies.

This set of expectations needs refinement in light of the findings from the encounter with Pruitt and Rubin's conflict theory (chapter four). In section 4.2.3 I specified a number of possible strategies of contending highlighted in that theory. Though I do not accord these a status in my reflections that is equal to the expectations just listed (since they are not grounded in an in-depth reflection on the Church organization and culture), I do want to call attention to them once more, since they have served as a set of second-tier or background expectations. And indeed, as we will see in the confrontation of the empirical example, certain of these strategies cited by Pruitt and Rubin do prove relevant to the handling of center-periphery conflict.

Other Strategies (of Contending) That May Apply (Identified by Pruitt and Rubin):
1. Ingratiation
2. Gamesmanship
3. Persuasive Argumentation
4. Promises
5. Threats
6. Irrevocable Commitments

Pruitt and Rubin also identified certain techniques of getting to problem solving (section 4.2.3) that, while not construed as strategies per se, may prove relevant to center-periphery conflict management.

In the confrontation of evidence from the Rome-Hunthausen case, the following questions stand central. Did the expected strategies show up? If so, which tactics carried them out? Which, if any, other coping strategies were applied (by means of which tactics)? And how did application of the strategies relate to the question of power?

My initial assessments were written up as notes and rough checklists. These tracked my observations about the strategies and tactics that seemed to apply, along with my reasons for thinking so. The results of these assessments turn up in progressively refined form in the case narrative that follows and in the analyses subsequent to it. A fundamental problem concerns the decision to declare a loose set of discursive moves a *strategy*. How do we know that one supposed tactic relates to another in "orchestrated" fashion? (Each could simply be the product of habit, or the two could be coincidentally joined.) Strategy implies intentionality (though I lessen this a degree with the qualifier "coping"): How do we know when a party is really intending to move in certain direction as opposed to being carried along by events? And finally, when does a tactic become a strategy in its own right? (In practice I found it sometimes difficult to separate out uses of silence, for example, from uses of secrecy. Should silence be considered a strategy rather than a tactic?) There are no easy answers to these questions. In general, I have tried to stay close to the definition of coping strategy that I have offered and to explain my judgments as clearly as possible along the way. I have reserved use of the term strategy for what strike me as more *pronounced* approaches to conflict handling. Thus, not for one-time occurrences or for techniques applied in minor matters, but rather for repeated patterns (identifiable across time and in multiple documents) wherein several tactics appear to be directed, in converging fashion, toward the same chosen end. A further reason for applying the label coping strategy came when conflict moves could be tied to a party's *explicitly stated* value judgments and intentions. (Sometimes parties state clearly the goals they are pursuing and the means they have chosen to get there.) At this juncture I should stress that I have not sought to identify every single strategy applied in the conflict. Instead I have concentrated on locating those strategies that stand out because: (1) they are *applied repeatedly* (by more than one party on more than one occasion); (2) they appear *strongly related to the "culture" of the Church organization* (its prevailing ways of thinking and acting, especially inasmuch as these distinguish the Church from other organizations); and (3) they appear *decisively instrumental in the conflict handling and resolution itself* (i.e., I am particularly interested in strategies that seem to "make a difference" in how the conflict shapes up and is resolved). More minor applications of strategies do not necessarily show up in my narrative or analysis of the case.

In my analysis of the Rome-Hunthausen case documents, I distinguish between the *objective* apparently pursued by a conflict participant through *general* and more *specific (coping) strategies*, which are carried out on the level of the text by means of certain *text construction tactics*. The objective is the specific goal within the conflict context to be achieved by the issuance of the text: e.g., responding to an earlier attack made by the opponent. The general coping strategy is the overall conflict handling approach evidenced by the text as a whole, with the designation limited to a choice from among the five general strategies named by Pruitt and Rubin (see section 4.2.2). The specific coping strategies are the distinctive approaches that work within the general strategy: e.g., recruiting allies may be a specific strategy within the more general strategy of contending.

One will notice, when reading through the conflict analysis sections of chapters six-eight (both the document and intervening development sections), that the descriptions of strategic applications tend to be more condensed the further one goes. This is primarily a reflection of the learning process that is underway and my own desire to avoid redundancy. Thus, typically when a strategy is encountered for the first time in practice, I describe its use in detail. But later identifications of use, for the most part, call attention to the use without elaborating, unless new dimensions of potential in the strategy are revealed by that particular use. In such cases, I do offer a more detailed description. In general, however, I try to avoid what seems rather obvious and to avoid repeating lessons that have already been learned. When there are questions about whether a strategy has or has not been recognized in a particular section, the readers should consult the appropriate table in appendix v.

To sum up: for each of the selected documents I have identified the following elements. This information is presented in appendix v and in the case narrative and analysis of chapters six-eight.

Organizational Scheme for the Naming of Strategies and Tactics, Per Document

A. The main **tactics of text construction**, which realize the specific coping strategies identified. The techniques of critical discourse analysis are applied to identify these tactics. For each tactic identified I offer examples of constructions contained in the text that embody the tactic.

B. The **specific coping strategies** which contribute to the overall coping strategy in evidence in the document. Rather than noting all coping strategies in evidence, I typically highlight the strategies that appear to be most prominently applied.

C. The **general coping strategy** (one or more) applied through the production, distribution and consumption of the document. This designation is limited to a choice from among five options: contending, yielding, problem solving, inaction and withdrawal. NB: the focus here is on the strategy actualized through the composition and public release of the document itself, not on other strategies that may be evidenced by the document but not in fact applied through it.

D. The **objective** apparently pursued through issuance of the document. This is a brief summary statement that characterizes what the document is intended to achieve within the conflict context.

BOX 5.7

5.5 Assessment of the Conflict Functionality of Other Developments

Accounting for the strategic dimensions of other developments in the conflict – that is, for the rest of the conflict story, the parts not revealed by analysis of the selected documents – required the employment of another kind of assessment process. In chapters six-eight, one sees that extensive descriptions "flesh out" the skeletal description of the conflict provided by the findings from the documents. After writing these descriptions, it became clear that it was also necessary to say something about the conflict functionality of these prior, intervening and subsequent conflict developments. And obviously, since these descriptions were composite constructions based on other conflict documents, outside-observer descriptions, ephemeral materials, etc., they did not lend themselves to analysis according to precisely the same method I applied to the selected individual documents.

Most important, in my view, was the need to say something about how these other developments fit into the conflict picture as a whole. It would also be interesting to draw on these materials (as they cohered in the narrative description), to identify, as fully as possible, conflict tactics, specific coping strategies, general coping strategies and objectives, much as was done in the discourse analysis of the documents. The question was how to conduct such an analysis.

My answer to this challenge was to develop a two-pronged approach. First, I focused on the empirical referents that could be isolated in the narrative material. What actually happened, what actually was said? Identifying the empirical referents was never a straightforward matter, since newspaper accounts, for example, always offer interpretive descriptions of events, not the events themselves. The same is true of reproduced speech. (Is the quotation accurate? Is it the full text given? What was the context?) Nonetheless, plumbing the variety of information sources available to me, I was able to cross-reference my determinations about empirical referents discernible in the descriptions and thus render my judgments with greater confidence. Second, to interpret the strategic significance of the identified referents, I drew on the discussions of strategic negotiation in Pruitt and Rubin 1986. Taken together, these works provided a frame of reference that allowed me to characterize the conflict functionality of the contextualizing developments.

One finds in chapters six-eight, at the end of each description of intervening developments, a brief narrative description of the conflict functionality of those developments. A more detailed breakdown of my findings concerning those developments appears, in tabular form, in appendix v.

5.6 Cross-Site Analysis of Strategy Applications

After identifying conflict tactics, specific coping strategies, general coping strategies and objectives, as revealed by the selected documents and the analysis of the intervening developments, I prepared a table summarizing the findings (section 9.4). This table shows which strategies were applied by which parties at which stages of the conflict, allowing for various kinds of comparison and summation. It provides a first "complete" answer to the question, Which coping strategies are observable in center-periphery conflict discourse? Following the presentation of the table, I offer a detailed breakdown of the findings it represents, considering in turn each of the conflict expectations I had before confronting the empirical data from the conflict (re. general stance toward conflict handling, perspective on power, strategies to be applied), and what actually turned up, based on the evidence examined (including perspectives and strategies that were not anticipated).

5.7 Further Integration With Reference to Conflict Theory

Upon completing the description of the pool of strategic elements making up the conflict experience, I turned to the theory of conflict handling presented earlier (in chapter four) for help with the task of ordering the elements into an organized whole. In chapter ten I offer a reading of the Rome-Hunthausen case that relates the case events to the conflict theory concepts. Thus I have specified the *interests* that appear to have been at stake for each of the participants and the *goals* and *standards* governing their choice of conflict moves. There I have also characterized the participants' apparent *level of concern for one another* and the operative *perceptions of feasibility* informing the conflict moves.

The major part of the conflict theory reflection goes to a chronological description of the coping strategies applied (divided into stages) and to a qualitative account of strategy use. My analysis focuses on *party preferences for the use of a particular strategy* (Were there unbroken commitments to the use of a given strategy? Were there notable departures from a strategy one appeared committed to?), on *linkages between strategies* (e.g., Does use of one particular strategy generate the use of another particular strategy in response?) and on *strategies used in desperation*. I also assess the *vigorousness* of strategy applications and the range of *tactics* associated with each strategy.

Finally, the conflict theory reflection considers the case in terms of its stages, identifying *signs of escalation, stalemate and problem solving*, offering reasons for why the parties chose the conflict handling approaches they did when they did, and it presents an assessment of *outcomes*.

5.8 Ascertaining the Validity of the Findings

After viewing the case through the lens of conflict theory, we are left with a still more complete and coherent picture of what the conflict was about, how it took shape and which strategic means parties employed in pursuit of their own interests. But the question arises, How trustworthy are these findings? As tests of their validity, I have employed two techniques of control. One is a document-based control and the other is an informant-based control.

5.8.1 Use of Control Documents

To my mind, the most persuasive evidence that certain identified strategies were applied to manage the Rome-Hunthausen conflict comes from analysis of the documents issued by the participant parties themselves. Carefully attending to such documents reveals much about what was at stake for the participants and how they sought to secure their own interests. But the possibility exists that I have missed important findings by selecting documents that are nonrepresentative or by selecting too few documents, with the result that we have a too limited view of the coping strategies applied discursively. To guard against that form of misreading of the case, I have introduced a method for validating the findings from the document analysis.

The control method I have used is rather simple. At an intermediate point in the research process I set aside a number of documents produced by conflict participants for subsequent use for comparative purposes. These were documents I had looked over in my general reading for overview of the case, but which I had not exposed to any systematic close reading (of the kind that was being done with the nine selected documents). My intention for the documents was to read them at a later time in light of my findings from the discourse analysis of the selected documents to see how they corroborated, expanded upon or challenged the findings from the nine documents previously considered.

As much as possible, I wanted the selection of control documents to be representative of the case as a whole (all parties, all stages) and a random selection. These became my two criteria for selection of the control documents. First, I sought to have one document each representing each of the three parties in each of the three stages of the conflict (that is, nine in total). This proved not to be possible in every instance, since the center-party documents for the middle stage for the middle stage were either already analyzed (as part of the earlier selection of nine) or not available for analysis (not made public). Consequently, I analyzed a total of eight, and not nine, control documents. My second aspiration was to have my choices be random: i.e., as much as possible, undetermined by my own biases. For this reason, whenever possible (whenever more than one choice presented itself to represent a party and stage) I used a technique of random selection to make the choice of control documents.

My comparative analysis of the control documents was not a ground-up analysis, as was conducted with the original selection of nine documents. Instead, I conducted *two semi-closed readings of the documents*, focused on two sets of expectations, one positive and one negative. These expectations expressed, in specific formulations for each of my main findings, *what I fully expected to encounter in the control documents* and *what I did not at all expect to find there*. If my own findings were valid, I should find more of the same in the control documents and should not find anything that would seem to disprove my own view outright.

As it turned out, my findings were largely confirmed through the control analysis, but there were some obvious points of tension that led me to modify my conclusions. This analytical process and the presentation of its conclusions is set forth in chapter nine.

5.8.2 Use of the Fr. Ryan Interview for Validation Purposes

The second technique of control I applied to test my findings from the case was an interview with someone who directly participated in the affair. (Fairclough 1992, 238 suggests this as a possible technique of validation for findings derived from discourse analysis.) Thus, late in the research process, I asked Fr. Michael G. Ryan to sit for an interview organized into three components: an open-ended component, which invited him (see appendix vi for the question I posed) to give his own account of the affair as a whole (with rare inquiries for clarification); a semi-open component, wherein I asked specific informational questions to fill in gaps in my own knowledge; and a closed component, wherein I offered the questions and specified a range of potential answers. Though the third component in particular was designed for validational purposes – I asked Fr. Ryan to judge the credibility of certain conclusions I had come to in the research process (which at that point was three-quarters complete) – eventually, I was able to draw on all three components as checks on my own findings.

In chapter nine I present the results of the Ryan interview in the following order: first, I summarize the new information about the conflict gathered from the interview (i.e., information I did not find available in other sources); second, I describe the confirmations and disconfirmations of my own findings that the interview brought to the surface; third and lastly, I consider a possible additional coping strategy (one I had not earlier considered) that Ryan identified.

5.9 Conclusion and Evaluation

Chapter ten brings this investigation to a close. It presents my summary of findings from the Rome-Hunthausen case, offering my final answer to the question, What coping strategies are observable in center-periphery conflict? Answering this question of necessity entails a reflection on the *generalizability* of my findings, a matter that I pursue in chapter ten as well. Included, too, is an *evaluation* of the strength and weaknesses of this research project, and in particular of the suitability of the methods chosen to answer the central question. Finally, I briefly consider the *relevance* of my findings and the implications for the Church organization.

CHAPTER SIX

NARRATIVE AND ANALYSIS OF THE ROME-HUNTHAUSEN CASE: THE
EARLY STAGE (1978-SEPTEMBER 1986)

A. Early Developments in the Hunthausen Case (1978-September 1985)

According to the Vatican (see Archbishop Laghi's "Vatican chronology," document 4, below), one can trace the beginning of the Hunthausen case to 1978. From that year forward, "the Holy See, through the then Apostolic Delegation, ... corresponded with Archbishop Hunthausen on matters related to pastoral practices and the presentation of the Church's teachings. Through this exchange the Holy See sought the assistance of the Archbishop of Seattle in responding to the high volume of complaints that were sent to Rome by priests, Religious and faithful in the archdiocese."

In his response to the Vatican chronology (see document 5, below), Archbishop Hunthausen writes that "if there were substantial complaints I was never told who made them or who substantiated them and on what basis. Nor was I told till considerably after the Visitation was decided upon and announced to me ... what *some* of those complaints were."

These competing statements, and the absence of alternate sources of verification, leave us with uncertainty about when the Hunthausen case actually began as a case of perceptible conflict. When did Vatican representatives first become displeased with Hunthausen? When did Hunthausen first feel this displeasure (and perhaps return the feeling)? When did each party first consider itself to be in conflict with the other? These are important questions, but ones I cannot answer.

Certain early exchanges, which took place behind the scenes, have been publicly acknowledged by one or more parties, but contents of these exchanges remain mostly hidden. Hunthausen himself apparently first became aware of the Vatican's interest in conducting a visitation of Seattle in May of 1983, when the Papal Pro-Nuncio to the United States, Archbishop Pio Laghi, approached him about this at a meeting of the American bishops in Chicago. Hunthausen agreed at that time that a visitation could be undertaken with his support. Shortly after learning of the Vatican's wish to have a visitation, Hunthausen consulted with then president of the national bishops' conference John Roach, Archbishop of Minneapolis-St. Paul, who advised Hunthausen to request a "Bill of Particulars" specifying the reasons for the visitation (cf. Hunthausen's 11.12.86 address to the bishops' conference, document 6, below). Hunthausen reports that this request was refused. (He does not say by whom.) In July of that same year, Washington, D.C., Archbishop James Hickey was appointed Apostolic Visitor (cf. the Vatican chronology). It is also known that Hunthausen discussed the forthcoming visitation with Cardinal Joseph Ratzinger, Prefect of the Congregation for the Doctrine of the Faith, during Hunthausen's *ad limina* visit to Rome in September of 1983 (cf. Hunthausen response to Vatican chronology, document 5, below). No detailed descriptions of any of the events just cited is available for public inspection, though Hunthausen has said on the record that during the *ad limina* visit he expressed to Ratzinger his opposition to conducting the visitation in secrecy, and he also offered to invite Ratzinger or a designee to come to Seattle to inspect conditions for himself. "But my invitation and my point of view were not accepted." Finally, Ratzinger mentions (in his 9.30.85 letter to Hunthausen) and quotes from a 10.4.83 letter that the Congregation for the Doctrine of the

Faith sent to Hunthausen concerning the forthcoming visitation. This letter, too, has never been made public.

The first clear signal to the public that something was amiss in Archbishop Hunthausen's relationship with the Vatican was Hunthausen's joint announcement with Archbishop James Hickey of Washington, D.C. (on 10.26.83) that Hickey would be "visiting" the Archdiocese of Seattle, November 2-8, 1983 (*The Progress*, 10.27.83). This announcement was made necessary when word of the impending visitation leaked to the news media. (Hunthausen, by his own account, argued ahead of time against keeping the visitation secret. See his response to the Vatican chronology, document 5, below.) The news leak came to the attention of Hickey, who first consulted with Archbishop Laghi and then contacted Hunthausen about the need to make a public announcement. The origin of the leak is unknown. Hunthausen insisted that the leak came from the East Coast and not from Seattle (cf. Hunthausen's response to Vatican Chronology).

In his brief press statement Hickey said that he came "at the request of the Holy See and with the gracious welcome of Archbishop Hunthausen." Noting that "from time to time, Archbishop Hunthausen has suffered criticism regarding his pastoral ministry in Seattle," Hickey stated that the purpose of the visit was to "explore the views and opinions of informed members of the clergy, religious and laity so that [the Holy See] may evaluate the criticisms and support the Archbishop in his ministry." Hickey concluded his statement, saying:

> I go as a brother bishop to observe the situation at first hand and to offer appropriate fraternal assistance and support. I look forward to my days in the Northwest and a visit with my colleague, Archbishop Hunthausen.

Hunthausen's accompanying statement (*The Progress*, 10.27.83, p. 5) offered the following commentary:

> For my part, I must say that I welcome Archbishop Hickey's visit. As he indicated in his statement, many bishops these days are in the position of receiving criticism of the sort that calls into question the direction of their pastoral ministry and, in some cases, actually hinders that ministry.
> Recent articles in the national Catholic press have pointed to the fact that much of this criticism has come from reactionary elements within the church which seem bent on undoing the renewal begun in our church in the Second Vatican Council.
> Because my faith tells me that this renewal in the Church is the work of the Holy Spirit, and because I am convinced that our efforts here in this archdiocese are in keeping with the spirit and intent of the Council, I do welcome Archbishop Hickey's visit here. I believe it will help bring into focus both our strengths and our weaknesses in carrying out the renewal and, in so doing, that it will be of benefit not only to this archdiocese but to the church in the country and beyond as it seeks to renew itself.
> I ask your prayers for the continued guidance of the Holy Spirit now and in the days to come.

Early media speculation about the reason for the visitation focused on Archbishop Hunthausen's well-known opposition to the build-up of nuclear arms. Hunthausen had participated in highly public protests at the Bangor, Washington military base housing Trident nuclear submarines and was known for having labeled the base "the Auschwitz of Puget Sound." As an act of civil disobedience, Hunthausen had also taken the step, in 1982, of refusing to pay half of his income tax, the portion of the tax that would otherwise go for military spending. In subsequent years Hunthausen continued to withhold a portion of his taxes as a form of witness. In response, the government, with Hunthausen's cooperation, garnisheed that portion of his wages which had not been paid. This brand of activism had earned him many admirers and many detractors as well. Perhaps his controversial stance somehow had something to do with the visitation? Upon his arrival in Seattle, reporters put this question to Archbishop Hickey. But Hickey said the visit was not prompted by Hunthausen's stand on nuclear arms. When asked which areas *were* of concern, Hickey refused to elaborate. "Sometimes you do things in a quiet way," he said (*The Progress*, 11.10.83).

Hickey conducted the visitation assisted by Fr. William Coyle of Fargo, North Dakota. Together they interviewed, in private, more than 70 members of the clergy religious and laity (cf. Laghi letter of 11.14.85, document 2, below) at the chancery of the Archdiocese of Seattle. Hunthausen himself sat for an interview which lasted more than four hours. The interview was taped and later transcribed and submitted to Hunthausen for a review of its accuracy.

At the conclusion of the visitation, Hickey issued a press statement in which he said:

> I came as brother-bishop to brother-bishop to assist in reviewing the pastoral life of this important archdiocese. The Holy See asked me to come for a short time, to gather information and thus assist the Holy Father in his on-going evaluation and support of bishops throughout the world.
> I have observed the progress made in the Archdiocese of Seattle, and have gained, I believe, an insight into a range of viewpoints. I heard from so many who expressed admiration for Archbishop Hunthausen as a man of Gospel values, a bishop deeply committed to Christ and to the church. Concerns and criticisms expressed to me have been discussed with the archbishop. We are confident that these can be resolved in a spirit of mutual understanding and in harmony with the teaching and direction of the church.

Shortly before Christmas of 1983, Hunthausen received a letter from Cardinal Joseph Ratzinger, Prefect of the Sacred Congregation for the Doctrine of the Faith, dated 12.12.83. Ratzinger's letter informed Hunthausen that the Holy See had received Archbishop Hickey's report of his findings from the visitation. Ratzinger complimented Hickey for conducting the visitation "with exemplary objectivity and thoroughness and with a characteristically fraternal spirit" and he thanked Hunthausen for his "complete cooperation in this understandably difficult project." As for the contents of the visitation report itself, Ratzinger was not forthcoming but he pledged to give the report "the attentive study which [it] deserves, and which will obviously be necessary to overcome the specific problems which have been encountered." The visitation report has never been made public, and, according to his own testimony (cf. Hunthausen's 11.12.86 address to the U.S. bishops, document 6, below), Hunthausen himself has never seen the report.

Hunthausen published the Ratzinger letter in the January 26, 1984 issue of *The Progress*, the official newspaper of the Seattle Archdiocese (now known as *The Catholic Northwest Progress*), together with his own cover letter. Hunthausen wrote that he was publishing the letter, addressed to "My Dear People," "[I]n the interest of keeping you informed." Hunthausen closed the brief cover letter expressing "commendation and gratitude to Archbishop James Hickey for the wonderfully sensitive manner in which he carried out his difficult assignment."

Following publication of this letter from Cardinal Ratzinger, little stands on the public record to account for the exchanges between Hunthausen and the Holy See during the twenty-month period beginning in January, 1984 and ending in September, 1985. Ratzinger (in his letter of 9.30.85) mentions a 3.14.84 letter from Hunthausen to the Congregation for the Doctrine of the Faith, wherein Hunthausen discusses steps taken to correct the practice of contraceptive sterilization in local Catholic hospitals (one of the visitation issues). This Hunthausen letter has never been made public. Archbishop Laghi (in the Vatican chronology) mentions another letter, dated 9.11.85, from Hunthausen to Laghi, that discussed the visitation findings and the possible appointment of a helper bishop in Seattle to assist in problematic areas of archdiocesan life. This letter, too, has never been made public.

The official announcement of the visitation findings came to Hunthausen in the form of a 9.30.85 letter from Cardinal Ratzinger (see document 1, below). The Ratzinger letter closed the visitation process and identified a set of problems in the archdiocese that Hunthausen was expected to address. Hunthausen had received a preliminary briefing on the investigation findings from Laghi sometime before September 11 (cf. the Vatican chronology). A summary and analysis of the Ratzinger letter follows, in section 6.1. But first I will consider the conflict functionality of the developments just described.

A.a. Conflict Functionality of the Early Developments (1978-September 1985)

A critical question for our understanding of the conflict is what happened in the center and periphery party exchanges between 1978 and early 1983. During a later, more openly contentious, stage of the conflict, Laghi looks back and states that the Holy See had been trying for years (since 1978) to gain Hunthausen's cooperation in addressing the problems that were now being discussed in the open (cf. the Vatican chronology). Hunthausen challenges this claim (in his response to the chronology), saying that he had been ill informed of the nature of the complaints made against him and of the sources of the complaints. Since these prior exchanges took place in private forums (meetings, correspondence), there is no public build-up to the imposition of the visitation. To the outside observer, the visitation comes "out of the blue." By all accounts I have seen, this is how Hunthausen experienced it, too. In light of my expectation that parties will employ lighter means of inducing cooperation early in a conflict and will only use heavier tactics in the face of resistance, it is puzzling to see this conflict – in its public appearance, at least – beginning with the rather heavy sanction of a visitation (i.e., an investigation that serves as a means of territorial control). But if, say, Hunthausen had been intransigent for years, out of view, it might be easier to understand. Or perhaps Hunthausen simply did not understand what the Vatican wanted, or he found the requests to be out of line? Then again, maybe the action was about something else altogether (Hunthausen's nuclear arms stance?) and the prior history between the two parties had little to do with it. If we had more information about the earlier private exchanges, we could get a better handle on these questions. (A last possibility to consider is that the conflict theory is wrong, and we need not expect a build up to heavier tactics. Conceivably, the Vatican started with a heavy tactic because it did not want to waste time with lesser tactics.)

Once the problem between the two parties comes into the open, we see a number of strategies applied. The center party places a premium on *secrecy*. The Apostolic Visitor, Archbishop Hickey insists on conducting the visitation in secret and he publicly defends the use of secrecy. Even when the fact of the visitation is forced into the open by a news leak, the process itself is a secretive one, wherein the interviewees meet privately with the visitation team. The Holy See does at no point allow Hunthausen to see the visitation report that Hickey files. Hickey also stresses that this is a *fraternal* action. He comes as a "brother bishop" to support Hunthausen (in keeping with the strategy of *minimizing the appearance of conflict*; see also Hickey's comment about a "spirit of mutual understanding"). Hickey shows *courtesy* by using euphemisms to downplay the seriousness of the matter at hand and by praising Hunthausen. Finally, Hickey associates his own efforts with the good of the Church, saying that his purpose is "to assist the Holy Father in his on-going evaluation and support of bishops throughout the world." After Hickey files his report, the Congregation for the Doctrine of the Faith conducts its own internal process of assessment and response, to which Hunthausen has no access (another example of the strategy of *secrecy*). One should not overlook the length of time that Hunthausen was made to wait (*delay*) for a response: this was surely an unsettling experience. More unsettling still would have been the prospect of a helper bishop (auxiliary or coadjutor) appointment that would be tied to the visitation findings (a potential application of coercive *power*; cf. the Vatican chronology's reference to a 9.11.85 Hunthausen letter discussing this possibility).

The periphery party applies many of the same strategies but in different ways. Hunthausen claims to have resisted the Vatican's preference for *secrecy* in regard to the visitation (and Rome does not deny this claim) but he also cooperates in the use of secrecy (showing *deference* to the hierarchical order), much as he did in the exchanges prior to 1983. Hunthausen seeks *fraternal* support by consulting Archbishop Roach and he demonstrates fraternity in another way when he welcomes Hickey into his archdiocese (this is a sign of *courtesy* as well). By seeking out Roach, Hunthausen shows himself prepared to enlist powerful *allies*. Hunthausen's inclination to go public with news about the visitation also shows his readiness to seek out the support of others.

One strategy we see Hunthausen apply here is one not identified in my list of expected strategies: the use of *persuasive argumentation*. There is, of course, something rather self-evident in the thought that conflict participants would attempt to persuade one another with argumentation. Presumably this took place in the negotiations between Hunthausen and the Holy See prior to 1983, though we have no firm evidence that it did. Thus far in the case developments, the Vatican has shown little inclination to offer rational justifications for its positions in public. Hunthausen, on the other hand, uses persuasive argumentation to challenge the supposition that he has done something wrong. Many bishops are being criticized these days, he argues, and much of this criticism comes from "reactionary elements within the church." In defense of his own position, Hunthausen asserts that he has acted in keeping with the spirit and intent of the Second Vatican Council and in support of the project of "renewal" that is its heritage. In his argumentation, Hunthausen presents himself as one *acting on behalf of the Church*, whose well-being he equates with the concepts of renewal, Vatican II and the work of the Holy Spirit.

Key third parties at this stage of the affair are Roach, who advises Hunthausen in private, and the news media. Interestingly enough, Roach suggests that Hunthausen demand a "Bill of Particulars," something which does not exist within the Church's legal system. Such a concept only applies with reference to extraecclesial legal frames. This is an early marker in the conflict of how certain Church and societal perspectives stand in tension. Most notable in the media's involvement early on is the speculation about a possible relationship between Hunthausen's controversial political stance on nuclear arms and his trouble with the Vatican. Hickey quickly denies that the two matters have anything to do with one another. It is not surprising that the media would pick up on this theme. Certainly to the secular media, and to many Catholics as well, Hunthausen was best known for his political views, and the possibility of a story linking Roman intervention to Washington political intrigue offered a much more enticing than an account of intrachurch discipline matters. The question that remained was whether there was any truth to the conjecture.

In these early developments we find both the center and periphery parties working to save face for themselves, one another, and the Church organization. Rome wants to keep the conflict out of sight and to minimize its seriousness when public discussions are necessary (the strategy of *minimizing the appearance of conflict*). This is also an ideal way for it to have its own way in the conflict handling: thus, the policy of saving face by covering up the matter also serves its own possession of power. Hunthausen is in a more difficult position. Saving face by not having the visitation come into the open carries the risk of diminishing his power if he loses a hidden confrontation (where no allies are available to support him). Instead Hunthausen opts to push for public revelation of the investigation. Once it is in the open, he tries to put the best spin on it he can (he is being targeted by reactionaries). More innocent readings of the same developments, as offered by the principals themselves, have Rome wanting to keep the visitation secret in order to preserve Hunthausen's reputation (cf. the Vatican chronology) and Hunthausen wanting to go public in order to spare the Holy See from public criticism and as a matter of principle (cf. his address to the NCCB).

Rome's apparent *objective* in undertaking the visitation is to correct problems in a local church that are perceived to be a threat to that church and to the Church Universal. Toward that end it exercises *territorial control* (ecological power) and *coercive power* in the form of a visitation. Rome *legitimizes* this local intervention by first asking Hunthausen's "permission" and by publicly understating the seriousness of the situation with the help of euphemisms (the action is pursued to "support" Hunthausen). The technical means of a visitation is itself legitimized by Canon Law. Hickey also emphasizes the fairness of the process: a "range of viewpoints" was taken into account, many of which offered praise for Hunthausen.

In response, Hunthausen, too, exercises *territorial control*. He shores up his support locally by sharing his version of the matter through the press. Hunthausen's objective appears to be minimize his own loss of power and prestige.

One more unanswered question related to the early developments is who leaked the news of the impending visitation. Those opposed to Hunthausen might have had reason to do it because it reveals the shaming fact that he is being investigated. Those favoring Hunthausen (including Hunthausen himself) might have done it because it makes the conflict handling more transparent, diminishing the Vatican advantage of secrecy.

6.1 Document Number: 1
Ratzinger Letter Summarizing Visitation Findings (dated 9.30.85)
Source: *Origins*, 6/4/87, p. 41; *The Progress*, 5/28/87, p. 5

6.1.1 Summary of Contents:
After nearly two years of waiting to learn the outcome of the visitation conducted by Archbishop Hickey, Archbishop Hickey finally received his response, in a letter from Cardinal Ratzinger dated September 30, 1985. The express purpose of the letter, which bears the greeting "Your Excellency," is both performative and informative. The performative dimension is revealed in the first sentence:

> I am writing to bring to a close the Apostolic Visitation process, which was assisted by the visit of Archbishop James Hickey of Washington, D.C., to the Archdiocese of Seattle from November 2-8, 1983.

The rest of the letter is primarily informative, especially in regard to the findings which have emerged from the visitation. Ratzinger briefly describes the visitation process that has taken place, states that "this Congregation" has carefully reviewed the visitation materials, presents the findings, and commends them to Hunthausen for pastoral application. Ratzinger concludes by praising Hunthausen's patience and kindness during the visitation and by extending best wishes to him.

The bulk of the letter is taken up with fourteen numbered paragraphs of "observations" made by the Congregation for the Doctrine of the Faith, "which we hope will be received by you in the spirit in which they are offered and will be of assistance to you as Archbishop of Seattle." A summary of these observations follows. (I follow the numbering and lettering of paragraphs as they appear in the letter.

1. Ratzinger **praises Hunthausen** for his loyalty and conscientious efforts as a bishop. He notes the praise that others have offered about Hunthausen, describing him as "a man of Gospel values."

2. Ratzinger concedes that Hunthausen has "suffered from **exaggerated criticism and routine misunderstandings**." The Vatican assessment has sought to keep the criticisms and misunderstandings in perspective. The observations offered in this letter are meant to support Hunthausen's efforts to "promote the renewal of the Church in Seattle and to point out, at the same time, areas we consider are in need of correction and improvement."

3. A single-sentence **transitional paragraph** in which Ratzinger acknowledges Hunthausen's "commitment to the real service of the Lord and... His people. "It is with this background," Ratzinger writes, "that this Congregation wishes to outline these problems and to enlist your cooperation in resolving them."

4. This section is the first to discuss a specific problem identified: "the rather widespread practice of **admitting divorced persons to a subsequent Church marriage without prior review by your Tribunal**, or even after they have received a negative sentence." Ratzinger states that "such a practice lacks foundation in the Church's clear teaching." He urges Hunthausen to see that future teaching and practice in this matter conform to the prescriptions of Canon Law.

5. This section identifies other "basic doctrinal problems." Ratzinger uses lettered subpoints to list these problems:

a. "Clear and firm guidance" must be given to those in the Archdiocese who are reluctant to accept the **Magisterium's legitimate teaching authority** in matters of faith and morals.

b. The nature and mission of the Church should be taught in its entirety, showing it to be **more than a "merely social entity**, governed chiefly by psychological, sociological and political processes."

c. Hunthausen must work to ensure that **"faulty Christologies"** not be embraced within the Archdiocese.

d. Hunthausen must strive to achieve a "correct appreciation of the **sacramental structure of the Church**, especially as it provides for sacred ministry in the Sacrament of Holy Orders" by the priests, religious and laity of the Archdiocese.

e. Pastoral initiatives should be informed by an **adequate anthropology**.

f. Misunderstandings exist concerning the **role conscience plays** in moral decision-making. Hunthausen should collaborate with theologians and other advisers to determine how best to correct these misunderstandings within the local Church, but he should not hesitate to overrule unorthodox advisers.

6. This section addresses the problem of **contraceptive sterilizations** performed in local Catholic hospitals.

7. Church teaching holds that **first Confession should precede first Communion**. Hunthausen needs to put a stop to variations on this order within the Archdiocese.

8. The use of **general Absolution** within the Archdiocese must also be brought into conformity with Magisterial teaching.

9. **"Routine intercommunion"** is a problem in the local Church that needs correction.

10. A "carefully trained priest" should be appointed "to aid in the **supervision of sacramental and liturgical discipline**."

11. Hunthausen should show concern for **priests who have left the ministry**, but he should do so without allowing them to take on illegitimate ministerial roles. There are also restrictions on the ministerial involvements of their civilly married wives that apply and need to be addressed.

12. This section raises concerns about **questionnaires** distributed by the Archdiocese in 1976 and 1979. Ratzinger finds fault with the questionnaires for giving respondents the impression the process was "a kind of voting process on doctrinal and moral teachings."

13. Hunthausen's teaching within the Archdiocese should emphasize the "God-given dignity" of **women** without casting doubt on Church teaching excluding women from Sacred Orders.

14. In a final word about pastoral practice, Ratzinger writes: "The Archdiocese should withdraw all support from any group which does not unequivocally accept the teaching of the Magisterium concerning the intrinsic evil of **homosexual activity**." Ratzinger cites several documents setting forth this teaching and then chastises Hunthausen for a specific abuse: "The ill-advised welcome of a pro-homosexual group

The first of the three short paragraphs concluding the letter reminds Hunthausen that the purpose of bringing the above points to his attention is to assist him in his office as Archbishop. The penultimate paragraph of the letter asks "the Holy Spirit of Christ" to be with Hunthausen and with the people he serves. The final paragraph of the letter offers personal best wishes from Ratzinger to Hunthausen.

6.1.2 Conflict Functionality of the 9.30.85 Ratzinger Letter

Though shortly prior to receiving this letter, Hunthausen had been briefed by the pro-nuncio on what the visitation conclusions were, he was no doubt anxious to inspect this official report from Rome.

Ratzinger pursues several objectives at once with the letter. He marks formal closure of the visitation process; announces what the visitation has revealed; assures Hunthausen that the Holy See has been conscientious and fair in its assessment; and enlists Hunthausen's cooperation in solving the identified problems.

The letter, written under the letterhead of the Congregation for the Doctrine of the Faith, is businesslike in structure and tone, and even its more personal touches have a formal, perfunctory feeling to them. Thus Ratzinger addresses Hunthausen as "Your Excellency" (a politeness convention) and his words of praise for Hunthausen are often indirect, coming forth as opinions voiced by others: "Numerous people spoke of your laudable and conscientious efforts to involve the laity in the work of the Church... You have been repeatedly described as a man of Gospel values..."

The letter is unfailingly polite (strategy of *courtesy*). Not once does Ratzinger criticize Hunthausen directly. This is something of a feat, because the letter is full of bad news for Hunthausen (an abundance of problems in the archdiocese are identified), and that bad news amounts to a thoroughgoing critique of the pastoral ministry he has overseen. Ratzinger's politeness strategy involves first providing a cushioning layer of introductory comments which make a case for the Vatican's rationality and *fairness* (many were consulted, the information was carefully assessed, "extremist" opinions were dismissed out of hand), then *praising* Hunthausen ("There are many indications that you have striven with heart and mind to be a good bishop..."), and finally smoothing out the critique with *euphemisms* ("visit" / "visitation" for investigation; "it has been our purpose to *assist* you" – emphasis mine) and *sentence constructions that avoid the assignment of culpability* ("It is important that the nature and mission of the Church be taught in their entirety" – who has failed to do this?). A notable disjuncture in the letter lies in the fact that what praise there is goes to Hunthausen personally (with no direct blame), whereas the assessment of the archdiocese itself contains only criticism (and no praise).

Informing Ratzinger's letter is a vision of the Church which he expresses explicitly and repeatedly. This is an extended piece of rational *(persuasive) argumentation*, a demonstration of Ratzinger's personal possession of *expert power*. According to this vision, there is a clear, consistent and true teaching of the Church which can be known and passed on (the authentic tradition is singular). The duty of the hierarchy in relationship to this teaching is to defend it and pass it on untainted with error. (Contrast this with Hunthausen's emphasis on renewal, Vatican II and the "guidance of the Holy Spirit.") This is where Hunthausen has fallen short. As Ratzinger sees it, confusion and a lack of clarity about where the Church stands have been allowed to settle into many aspects of archdiocesan pastoral practice. Though Ratzinger is careful never to say that Hunthausen himself is directly responsible for these conditions, he is plain in his meaning that Hunthausen is responsible for "correction and improvement" in these areas. Whether the issues identified in this letter were what prompted the visitation in the first place and whether these are in fact the essential issues for the Vatican in pursuing this action (are there deeper, underlying reasons operative?) remains unknown at this point. What *is* known is that Ratzinger has set these problems forth as the relevant questions for the Vatican. This, Ratzinger proposes, is the business at hand, the set of issues which Hunthausen is to address in his leadership of the archdiocese and in his exchanges with the Holy See (Rome controls the agenda).

Notably, an issue that Ratzinger does not mention is Hunthausen's controversial stand on nuclear weapons. The only statement that approaches this matter at all is the apparently benign observation that Hunthausen's "concern for justice and peace is well known," a remark that comes in the middle of the one paragraph devoted to praise of Hunthausen. Is this evidence that the nuclear arms issue was indeed not of concern to Rome?

Despite Ratzinger's invocation of the Second Vatican Council, he acknowledges here no earthly forms of authority arising outside of the Church. On the contrary, extraecclesial sources of knowledge are depicted here as posing a threat to the proper catechesis and pastoral service of the faithful: "The Church should be understood as more than a merely social entity, governed chiefly by psychological, sociological and political processes," Ratzinger writes. "An anthropology which is dominated by the tentative conclusions of the human sciences could well undermine many pastoral initiatives, however well intentioned." Juxtaposed with the remarks about the limits of the "human sciences" is a catalogue of references to teachings of the magisterium, which offer the kind of sure teaching absent in the extraecclesial disciplines. Thus, if Hunthausen is unclear himself about the way forward, he is invited to have reference to the Congregation for the Doctrine of the Faith's 1976 Declaration on Sexual Ethics, the documents of the U.S. Bishops' Conference, the revised Code of Canon Law, the Congregation's 1975 Instruction, *Inter Insigniores*, etc. (These documents signal the Holy See's possession of superior *legal* and *expert power*.) The technical nature of this presentation highlights the fact that this is a communication between one bishop and another. It also underscores Ratzinger's view that this is an intraecclesial matter that Hunthausen is expected to address with intraecclesial resources.

With this letter the responsibility for further initiative is turned over to Hunthausen. Ratzinger speaks of his Congregation's involvement in the present-perfect tense ("In bringing all the above points to your attention, it has been our purpose to assist you as effectively as possible..."). Its present intervention is complete. Though no future involvement is mentioned explicitly, the possibility thereof is indicated when Ratzinger writes: "we hope [the observations] will be received by you in the spirit in which they are offered..."

Significantly, this communication to Hunthausen is carried out privately (the strategy of secrecy). The public is not privileged to know the contents of this exchange or the fact that it is taking place. Certain other matters are also kept quiet. Ratzinger refers to Archbishop Hickey's report, but, as Hunthausen himself will later point out, the contents of this report are kept even from Hunthausen. In addition, Ratzinger attributes agency in the affair to "the Holy See" (which has undertaken the visitation project) and "this Congregation" (which has reviewed the Visitation report): these collective terms allow Ratzinger to avoid naming the specific people involved in the decision making process (a linguistic tactic of secrecy). The

Pope's own role in the affair is left to speculation. Finally, we should also note Ratzinger's *silence* regarding the imminent appointment of an auxiliary bishop. Though this discussion was already underway between Hunthausen and Rome (cf. the Vatican chronology), Ratzinger makes no mention of such a possibility here.

B. Intervening Developments (October-November 1985)

Hunthausen requested that he be allowed to make the 9.30.85 Ratzinger letter public, but the Holy See refused this request (cf. *The Progress*, 5.15.86). Twenty months later, on May 27, 1987, the Holy See finally did release the letter, in conjunction with distribution of the assessment commission report (see document 9, below).

On October 9-10, 1985, Hunthausen and Laghi met at the apostolic nunciature in Washington, D.C. (cf. the Vatican chronology). According to Laghi, though Hunthausen was not allowed to see the Hickey report at this time, he was given the opportunity to respond to the visitation findings and seek clarification. Because Hunthausen continued to insist on having some way of publicly sharing the contents of the Ratzinger letter, the Apostolic Nunciature was commissioned by the Vatican to produce an alternate version of the Ratzinger letter, which Laghi would send to Hunthausen (see document 2, below). Hunthausen would be permitted to release this letter publicly. The Laghi letter is dated November, 14, 1985, six weeks later than the Ratzinger letter.

B.b. Conflict Functionality of the Intervening Developments (October-November 1985)

The preceding description accounts for the events that took place between Hunthausen's receipt of the Ratzinger letter (sometime before October 9, 1985) and Laghi's composition of a new letter (November 14, 1985), which recapitulates the Ratzinger letter and packages its message for public consumption. Little stands on the public record to inform us about the actual conflict handling that took place during this period of approximately five weeks, but we can make a few observations.

First, it is clear that the center party remains with its strategic preference for keeping the conflict handling out of public view (*minimize the appearance of conflict, practice secrecy*).
There are two levels to this secrecy: the secrecy that the Vatican practices over and against Hunthausen and the level that the Vatican and Hunthausen together practice over and against others. The Vatican practices secrecy over and against Hunthausen by continuing to refuse his requests to see the Hickey report. The Vatican and Hunthausen practice secrecy together by carrying out their negotiations in private (the Ratzinger letter, the one-to-one exchange between Laghi and Hunthausen) and by not sharing the substance of the conflict (i.e., the specific issues identified by Ratzinger).

Hunthausen *cooperates* with the Holy See's requirements for secrecy, but he also engages in a strategy of *resistance*. His cooperation is a sign of his *deference for the order and mindset of the Church* (he respects his superior's wishes). At the same time, it is apparent that the Vatican's use of secrecy works against him, since he can hardly refute charges he does not know. My presumption is that he used *persuasive argumentation* to try to obtain a copy of the Hickey report. This effort failed. He definitely used persuasive argumentation to convince the Vatican to provide him with a visitation findings summation that he could make public. Hunthausen presses the Vatican (the *general strategy of contending*) and the Vatican *yields*. What is unclear is why Rome does not want the Ratzinger letter released (especially since, at a later date, it does agree to release the letter) and why it subsequently gives in to

Hunthausen's request to be supplied with some alternative statement for public release. Evidently, the Vatican's commitment to secrecy was not unconditional, and it did not need to have its way on every issue. It would appear that maintaining a hermetical seal of secrecy was less important than warding off the possibility of increased resistance from Hunthausen. My guess is that this minor concession was made with an eye to avoiding unnecessary friction on the eve of the appointment of Donald Wuerl as auxiliary bishop.

The center party applies *ecological power* in its assertions of territorial control. The Congregation for the Doctrine of the Faith does not let Hunthausen see the Hickey report and it does not allow Hunthausen to publish the Ratzinger letter. Laghi functions as a *gatekeeper* between Hunthausen and Rome, and Hunthausen apparently has very limited *access* to the inner workings of the Congregation that is addressing his case. In the concession to provide Hunthausen with a visitation report for publication, one can recognize a minor employment of *remunerative power*. Hunthausen's use of power is harder to characterize, since we do not know the nature of the arguments he employs to persuade the Holy See to provide the report for publication. To some extent, he applies *social power* by showing that he is willing to abide by Church rules (adhere to the chain of command, limit the appearance of conflict): does his loyalty function as an investment with expected return, or as a bargaining chip?

6.2 Document Number: 2
Laghi Letter Summarizing Visitation Findings (11.14.85)
Source: *The Progress*, 11/28/85, p. 3; *Origins*, 12/26/85, pp. 458-459.

6.2.1 Summary of Contents
Laghi's letter begins with an announcement of the official closure of the Visitation. He **reviews the Visitation process** in language that is very close (there are many word-for-word agreements) to Ratzinger's description of the process. (An example of matching language: Laghi exactly reproduces Ratzinger's sentence, "In addition, he [Hickey] examined many pertinent documents, statements issued by the Archdiocese and letters.") But Laghi also departs from the content of the Ratzinger source letter, adding lines and omitting others. Thus, Laghi mentions a September 15, 1983 meeting between Hunthausen and the Visitator, but he does not mention the correspondence between Ratzinger and Hunthausen that Ratzinger cited in his own letter. (Indeed neither Ratzinger nor the Congregation for the Doctrine of the faith is named in this letter from Laghi to Hunthausen.)

Laghi then brings to Hunthausen's attention a set of "observations," which are arranged into four numbered sections. The **first section offers praise** for Hunthausen. Closely following Ratzinger's language, Laghi writes: "There are many indications that you have striven with heart and mind to be a dedicated bishop of the Church, eager to implement the renewal called for in the Documents of the Second Vatican Council." The section goes on to name positive examples of Hunthausen's leadership: his establishment of consultative bodies, his attention to the Council of Priests and Archdiocesan Pastoral Council (not mentioned in the Ratzinger letter), his accessibility, his evident embrace of Gospel values, his concern for "the suffering and aggrieved," his apostolic zeal and concern for peace and justice, and his loyalty to the Church and devotion to the Holy Father.

A **second section of praise** follows, the contents of which did not appear in the Ratzinger letter. This paragraph focuses on the time Hunthausen has given to fostering the morale of his priests and religious, on his development of local lay leadership, and on his attention to the matters of prayer and preaching.

Section number three declares that **Hunthausen has suffered exaggerated criticisms** and declares, as did the Ratzinger letter, that the observations to follow are not based on the testimony of "strident critics" or "obviously biased" publications. Nor are they meant to encourage "extreme" groups (Ratzinger referred to "extremist" groups) seeking to undermine Hunthausen's authority.

Section four, finally, presents the Vatican's "**concerns**" (Ratzinger spoke of "problems" at a comparable point in his own letter). Laghi structures this section with an introductory sentence that asks Hunthausen's assistance in addressing the concerns "in a way that will contribute to the spiritual well-being of the Archdiocese of Seattle." The concerns are listed in five lettered subsections. Rather than attempting to summarize what is itself a rather concise summary, I will reproduce this list here.

    a.   The need to bring into clear focus – working together with priests, religious and theologians -- certain teachings of the Church and their implications for the pastoral practice of the Archdiocese. These include the role of the conscience in making moral decisions, the role of the Magisterium in giving definitive guidance in matters of faith and morals; the nature and mission of the Church, together with its sacramental and hierarchical structure; an anthropology which provides an authentic understanding of the dignity of the human person; and a Christology which correctly reflects our Catholic faith concerning Christ's divinity, His humanity, His salvific mission, and His inseparable union from the Church.

    b.   In particular, the need to present more clearly the Church's teaching concerning the permanence and indissolubility of marriage and to ensure that the Archdiocesan Tribunal, both its constitution and practice, conforms with all the prescriptions of the revised Code of Canon Law.

    c.   Greater vigilance in upholding the Church's teaching, especially with regard to contraceptive sterilization and homosexuality.

    d.   The need to ensure that pastoral practice regarding the liturgical and sacramental ministry of the Archdiocese is in accord with the Church's universal norms, especially in the celebration of the Eucharist. This includes, for instance, routine intercommunion on the occasion of weddings or funerals. Such a need also involves the Sacrament of Reconciliation, mentioning particularly the proper sequence of first confession / first communion and regulations regarding general absolution.

    e.   The need to review the ongoing education of the clergy and the selection and formation of candidates for the priesthood, and to be clear that laicized priests are excluded from certain roles in accord with the rescripts of their laicization.

This group of lettered subpoints recapitulates numbered sections 4-14 in the Ratzinger letter.

Laghi closes by commending Hunthausen for his "loyal cooperation and kindness" during the visitation and during the month's since, while the Holy See reviewed the visitation materials. He acknowledges Hunthausen's "continuous efforts to promote genuine growth and renewal" in the archdiocese and thanks Hunthausen on behalf of "the Church" for what he has accomplished. He expresses his confidence that Hunthausen "will be able to address effectively" the concerns articulated in the letter and he offers his own assistance and support toward that end.

6.2.2 Conflict Functionality of the 11.14.85 Laghi Letter

The fact that this letter was produced at all represents a concession by Rome to Hunthausen's wishes, though only a partial concession, since Hunthausen was not was not allowed to release the Ratzinger letter itself.

A close comparison of the two letters offers a rare opportunity to discern Vatican priorities when tailoring a message for public consumption. Here we have a glimpse of how the Vatican addresses the same issues in separate private and public forums. Revealing, too, is the intermediary role played by the pro-nuncio, who effectively "translates" the message for the local culture and public at large.

In my summary of the contents of the Laghi letter, above, I have already noted some key differences from the Ratzinger letter that preceded it. The Laghi letter is *shorter* (about half as long as the Ratzinger letter); *warmer in tone* (Laghi greets Hunthausen with "Archbishop Hunthausen," instead of the officious-sounding "Your Excellency," and he changes Ratzinger's list of "problems" into a list of "concerns"); *more generous with praise* (Laghi adds several passages of praise, including an entirely new paragraph); *more sparing of criticism* (Laghi condenses Ratzinger's detailed discussion of problems, with examples, into a list of thumbnail descriptions); and *more plain-spoken* (Laghi minimizes the use of Church jargon and technical terms; e.g., all names of curial documents are omitted). My impression of these changes is that they are designed to make the message friendlier and easier to understand, and thus more palatable to the average American Catholic.

When comparing the experience of reading the Ratzinger letter with the experience of reading the Laghi letter, one gets the sense from the former that Hunthausen is being "called on the carpet" for problems stemming from his leadership, whereas the latter depicts Hunthausen as a well-regarded and trusted collaborator who the Holy See is actively engaged in supporting. In other words, it is one thing for the Holy See to challenge the competence of one of its own bishops in private, but another thing to do so in front of the bishop's own people and in front of other bishops who might fear being subjected to the same.

I have already noted certain ways that the 9.30.85 Ratzinger letter was secretive (being a private correspondence; refusing to name decision makers). This letter from Laghi, though purportedly meant to be revealing, is, ironically, more secretive than the Ratzinger letter in an absolute sense. For one thing, as I have already pointed out, it hides crucial details of the Vatican's complaints against Hunthausen. For another, it hides the involvement of the Congregation for the Doctrine of the Faith, which is never mentioned. Laghi refers only to the activity of "the Holy See." This term is highly ambiguous. An apostolic visitation can only be undertaken on the Pope's order, but the precise role of the Pope and members of key congregations remains unclear. And despite the fact that the appointment of an auxiliary bishop would follow this letter by just two weeks, no mention of that prospect appears here.

Apparently, at this point in the exchanges between Rome and Seattle, Rome remains firmly committed to its policy of conducting its business in Seattle in a quiet way. Hunthausen, for his part, has cooperated with the use of secrecy but has also resisted its use at least twice: first, in regard to the conduct of the visitation itself and, second, in regard to distribution of the visitation findings. The provision of the Laghi letter for public consumption appears to be an attempt by the Holy See to appease Hunthausen and enlist his further cooperation. Thus far, Hunthausen has offered no public challenge to or criticism of the Vatican. But surely the Vatican could conceive of that possibility.

C. Intervening Developments (November 1985-September 1986)

Hunthausen released the Laghi letter to the press on November 27, 1985 and published it himself in the 11.28.85 issue of *The Progress*, together with his own cover letter (dated 11.26.85) introducing the Laghi letter. In his cover letter Hunthausen thanked Laghi for the letter, which afforded "the opportunity to share with you [the letter is addressed to "Dear Friends in Christ"] the results of what was a highly-publicized event in the life of our Church." Hunthausen said he had looked forward to having such an opportunity for a long time. Hunthausen also thanked the Pro-Nuncio and the Holy See for having supported and affirmed his ministry in the archdiocese. Hunthausen noted that areas of his ministry had been singled out for affirmation, but that "areas of concern" had been identified as well. The concerns had been presented to him in a "fraternal and constructive spirit," Hunthausen said, and he accepted them in the same spirit. (Perhaps an oblique answer to Ratzinger's request that Hunthausen receive the observations in the spirit in which they were offered?) Hunthausen pledged to deal with all of the concerns and observed that in some cases he had already taken "appropriate action." In the remainder of his letter Hunthausen made a plea to all the people of the archdiocese to cooperate with him in this effort, acknowledging his own limitations and admitting his dependence on the people of the archdiocese. Hunthausen brought his plea to conclusion with an extended metaphor built on images of family and pilgrimage.

> In closing, I want to say several things. First, I wish to acknowledge my own limitations as a person and as an archbishop. Because of this, I am particularly dependent on your prayers, your support, your advice, and your constructive criticism. At the same time, for the sake of the unity and well-being of the Church, I call those of you who have supported me and those who have stridently criticized me to join together to build up this Church. To the extent we fail to do this, we wound and, in many cases, do serious harm to our unity in Christ.
>
> Lastly, as the Second Vatican Council so aptly acknowledged, we are a pilgrim people. We are on a journey. In some cases, we are, as a human family and a Christian family, facing difficulties and challenges that have never been faced before. For this reason, I need to remind myself as I remind all of you of the reassuring words of our God that are found time and time again throughout the pages of Scripture: "Do not be afraid." We need not be afraid because the Lord is with us on each step of our journey. Knowing that, and knowing, too, of your deep faith and loving support, I take courage for the future and look forward to the journey we will continue together.

On December 3, 1985, Archbishop Laghi announced that Pope John Paul II had appointed Fr. Donald Wuerl, a priest of the Diocese of Pittsburgh, auxiliary bishop of Seattle. (Wuerl, at the time of his appointment, was serving as executive secretary to the papal representative for the study of seminaries in the United States. Prior to that, from 1969 to 1979, he had served in Rome as secretary to the late Cardinal John Wright, prefect of the Vatican Congregation for the Clergy.) Immediately following this announcement, Hunthausen and Wuerl issued their own statements acknowledging the appointment (*The Progress*, 12.5.85, p.3). Hunthausen declared that the news brought "joy" to him personally and he expressed his assuredness that it would do the same "to the entire church in Western Washington." He also professed his gratitude "in a special way ... to our Holy Father, Pope John Paul II, for his response to my request for assistance in carrying out my pastoral ministry as archbishop of this large and growing church." Hunthausen's praised Wuerl's background and credentials ("He has served the church with distinction both within his own diocese of Pittsburgh and at the international level, as evidenced by his 10 years as an official of the Congregation for the Clergy in Rome") and he expressed own certainty that Wuerl would "bring many blessings to the church here in Western Washington." In his own statement, Wuerl described the experience of being named auxiliary bishop as "joyful and humbling... an honor and a privilege..."

> I am very happy to be called to serve such a distinguished archbishop and so vibrant a church. The Archdiocese of Seattle is a fruitful and vigorous part of Christ's vineyard and I eagerly look forward to the challenge of this new pastoral assignment as well as the opportunity to work with so many clergy, Religious and laity who so deeply love Christ and his church.
>
> ....
>
> From a loving heart I respectfully express my affectionate gratitude to our Holy Father for this sign of his confidence. I beg the prayers of the bishops, priests, deacons, Religious and laity of both Seattle and Pittsburgh that God will bless and prosper my efforts. And I enthusiastically pledge to the holy church of Seattle whatever gifts with which I have been graced by the Holy Spirit, but most of all, my faith, my

hope, and my love.

The same issue of *The Progress* (12.5.85) that carried the statements regarding Wuerl's appointment also offered a *Progress* interview with Hunthausen (pp. 4-5). Therein Hunthausen answered questions about the Laghi letter and Wuerl's appointment.

Archbishop, what is your reaction to Archbishop Laghi's letter?

I would have to say that my overall reaction is one of gratitude. I indicated this in a letter I sent to our people last week. The reason I say this is that Archbishop Laghi's letter was something that I personally asked for. It was sent in response to my own request, and not for any other reason.

Most often in situations of this sort, as I understand it, the bishop is the only one to receive information regarding the findings of a visitation. I do not think that this approach would be appropriate for our archdiocese and so, from the very beginning – from the time I first learned of Archbishop Hickey's visitation and up to the present moment – I have always maintained that it would be terribly important for me to be able to share with all our people as fully as possible the results of Archbishop Hickey's evaluation. I felt that I owed this to our people since I knew that the results of this visitation, whatever they were, would involve all of us because it is together that we are church…

Do you regard the letter as a fair analysis of the condition of the church here in the archdiocese and of your own ministry as archbishop?

I don't believe that's what it was intended to be. The visitation was undertaken in order "to evaluate certain allegations" regarding my pastoral ministry, to borrow Archbishop Laghi's words. In view of that, I don't believe it would be fair to expect his letter to be a thorough or comprehensive analysis of the conditions of the church here or of my own ministry as chief pastor, for that matter. The visitation had a limited purpose and, for that reason, so does the letter concluding it. When I say "limited," however, I do not mean for a minute to imply unimportant. Obviously, the areas listed by Archbishop Laghi are of very real importance.

….

Archbishop, the appointment of Father Wuerl as auxiliary bishop comes right on the heels of the closing of the visitation. Is there a connection?

To answer that, I first need to say that for several years now – ever since Bishop Nicholas Walsh was forced to retire for reasons of health – I have been asking the Holy See for an auxiliary bishop. For that matter, the Holy See recognized such a need in this archdiocese long ago when, back in 1956, Bishop Thomas Gill was appointed to serve as the first auxiliary bishop of this archdiocese. Since that time, of course, the archdiocese has grown by leaps and bounds and the demands placed on me, both with regard to pastoral ministry and archdiocesan administration, have increased immeasurably. So there is no question about our need for an auxiliary bishop.

Having said that, I think it is only fair for me to say further that the delay we experienced before an auxiliary bishop was appointed had to do with the decision which was made to undertake a visitation here in this archdiocese. It doesn't seem surprising that the Holy See would wait for that visitation to be concluded before making its choice of a suitable candidate to serve here as auxiliary bishop. And I would judge that the Holy See's choice of Father Donald Wuerl was certainly guided by some of those things that were learned during the process of the visitation.

Could you say something about the responsibilities of an auxiliary bishop?

An auxiliary bishop serves as a helper to the Ordinary in the carrying out of his pastoral ministry. Frequently, this involves such things as the celebration of the sacrament of Confirmation and the making of parish visitations. There are a number of other areas in which the auxiliary bishop can be of assistance, too – for example in the administration of the archdiocese.

….

How will Bishop-elect Wuerl assist you, Archbishop?

I have already spoken of some of the ways he will be able to help me in my pastoral and sacramental duties. In addition, I look forward to drawing on his valuable experience as we address those areas of concern outlined in Archbishop Laghi's letter. Obviously, these matters will continue to constitute a significant part of our agenda as church, and I am pleased to know that Bishop-elect Wuerl's background and training will suit him especially well to help us deal with them.

Pope John Paul II ordained Wuerl a bishop in Rome on January 6, 1986. The 2.6.86 *Progress* shows a picture of the Pope, Hunthausen and Wuerl together in Rome and reports that they met on January 7. No further information regarding the meeting is offered. Wuerl arrived in Seattle and assumed his duties on January 26.

Before Wuerl's arrival in Seattle, Hunthausen read the 9.30.85 Ratzinger letter with the visitation findings to his presbyteral council (sometime late in 1985) and to the priests of the archdiocese (January 23, 1986). According to one priest present at the January gathering, the purpose of the meeting itself was for the clergy "to hear the letter and get out their anger and frustration" prior to Wuerl's arrival (Source: National Catholic News Service story, printed in the 5.15.86 *Progress*.) The same priest said that clergy reaction at the meeting was one of "great anger at the process."

Wuerl celebrated his first Mass in the Archdiocese on January 30. At the start of that liturgy, Fr. Michael G. Ryan, archdiocesan vicar general and chancellor, read the letter from Pope John Paul II appointing Wuerl.

> The letter explained that "our brother bishops who share with us the responsibility of governing the Church of God are frequently burdened by many and serious matters in the carrying out of their ministry, so they seek assistance from this Apostolic See in order that they might more freely exercise their offices and attain the greater good of the souls whom they govern."
>
> The pope's letter continued, "we have willingly heard the request of our venerable brother, Raymond Hunthausen, Archbishop of Seattle, and grant him an auxiliary bishop."
>
> "There is one pastor of the Christian flock, Jesus Christ," the letter said. "Therefore, beloved brother, be at one with the Archbishop for the good of the sheep so that this sign of unity might remain untarnished and so that through it, all might recognize that the flock is one and that all are called to be members of this flock." (*The Progress*, 2.6.86)

Wuerl's appointment came as the result of an extended behind-the-scenes discussion between Hunthausen and the Holy See (represented by Laghi: other participants are unknown) about appointing a bishop to serve in Seattle who would have special powers to address the problem areas of the archdiocese identified in the visitation report. Apart from a few excerpts, the contents of these exchanges have not been revealed. We do know that Wuerl was not a candidate Hunthausen himself recommended, since Wuerl was essentially unknown to Hunthausen when he was named. The Vatican chronology (document 4, below) reports that at least three options of appointment were considered: the appointment of a coadjutor with full power, the temporary appointment of an administrator, and the appointment of an auxiliary with special faculties from the Holy See. Both the Vatican chronology and Hunthausen's response to the chronology make reference to a letter, dated 12.2.85, which Hunthausen sent to Laghi. According to both accounts, this letter was pivotal in that it conveyed Hunthausen's acceptance of a plan whereby Wuerl would come to Seattle as an auxiliary bishop with special powers of oversight in regard to the problem areas. (I will come back to this in a moment.) Two months after the implementation of this arrangement, in March of 1986, it became apparent that Hunthausen and the Holy See had different ideas of what Hunthausen had agreed to in that letter. Whereas the Holy See understood Hunthausen to have agreed to its intention for him to grant final power in the designated areas to Wuerl (as opposed to the faculties being granted by Rome), Hunthausen argued (in his response to the Vatican Chronology) that he had "agreed to give substantive authority without, however, relinquishing my ultimate authority." In other words, Hunthausen understood that he would be commissioning Wuerl to oversee handling of the areas of concern, but he himself would retain final decision-making power in those areas.

Wuerl understood his role in the same way that the Holy See did. At first, however, according to the accounts of both Hunthausen and Wuerl (see their joint interview in *The Progress*,

9.11.86), the discrepancy in their understandings did not come to light and the two worked together compatibly. The public record offers no reports of personal friction between the two, either early on or later, during the most intense phase of the conflict. On the contrary, both normally went out of their way to show politeness and respect to one another. What finally did bring the discrepancy to light was a disagreement that arose between Hunthausen and Wuerl, in March of that year, about the position the archdiocese should take in regard to a proposed ordinance being considered by a local county board (*National Catholic Reporter*, 9.19.86). Hunthausen decided he would support the proposal, which sought to uphold job rights for minority groups, including homosexuals. Wuerl voiced his opposition to taking such a stand and asserted that the nature of the question put it within those areas where he had final say. At this point it became clear that Hunthausen and Wuerl understood Wuerl's role in Seattle differently. Both proceeded to seek clarification from the Holy See.

Six months later, after Hunthausen and Wuerl had sought and received clarification from the pro-nuncio and from the Vatican about what powers Wuerl was in fact to have, and after news of Wuerl's special faculties was made public, Hunthausen was asked how he could have been mistaken in such a consequential matter. He replied:

> My conversations with Archbishop Laghi about the visitation and how it might be concluded and what some of the consequences of that would be engaged us in the possibility of an auxiliary bishop with special faculties. That was always presented as one of the possibilities that we might try to work with.
>
> I resisted that, quite frankly, because I felt it was fraught with real difficulties. It would create, as it has created in the minds of many people, a sense of division in the authority of the church and I wondered whether it was workable. I seriously wondered whether it was workable and I felt that it would be better if we avoided it.
>
> And so when Bishop Wuerl's appointment was determined, I had come to believe from my conversations with Archbishop Laghi, that his appointment would be as auxiliary bishop. Of course I was aware of the concerns in these special areas and I indicated that I was open to, clearly, not only his involvement in these special areas, but in the whole governance of the archdiocese.
>
> But I was also absolutely convinced that I was to retain final authority in all aspects of the governance of the archdiocese. I felt that was our understanding. I honestly and truly felt that was our understanding. (*The Progress*, 9.11.86, p. 3)

On a still later occasion (in his response to the Vatican chronology, to which I have already alluded), Hunthausen elaborated and offered further support for his contention that this was a case of honest misunderstanding. He cited an epistolary exchange with Archbishop Laghi, which took place just prior to the announcement of Wuerl's appointment.

> In a crucial letter dated December 2, 1985, which I wrote to Archbishop Laghi, I agreed to give substantive authority without, however, relinquishing my ultimate authority. These are the words I used: "(this arrangement) will not impinge upon my ultimate authority as Ordinary of this archdiocese." I went on to quote the Code of Canon Law to make the matter unmistakably clear. Archbishop Laghi's response stated: "While this does not lessen your authority as the local Bishop, it is understood that this action is being taken at the specific instruction of the Holy See." For this reason, it troubles me greatly not only that a great misunderstanding could have later ensued, one that in the end I was informed was mine, but also that it would later be suggested publicly that I might have acted in bad faith. I did not.

Laghi has never challenged Hunthausen's assertion that this exchange took place, nor has he challenged the accuracy of the quotations. But the complete texts of these two letters have never been made public.

Hunthausen and Wuerl's requests for clarification from the Holy See were pursued through letters which Hunthausen and Wuerl wrote separately to the pro-nuncio, and through a meeting both had with Laghi during a June gathering of the U.S. bishops, in Collegeville,

Minnesota. The contacts with Laghi and a later letter received (on July 1, 1986) from Cardinal Bernard Gantin, head of the Congregation of Bishops (*National Catholic Reporter*, 9.19.86), confirmed that Hunthausen was to have given Wuerl final say in the areas of concern.

Once no room for doubt remained, Hunthausen granted the faculties to Wuerl, effective August 1. On September 3, 1986, Hunthausen and Wuerl held a press conference to announce Wuerl's possession of faculties in the designated areas.

C.c. Conflict Functionality of the Intervening Developments (November 1985-September 1986)

The full implications of the apostolic visitation, whose conclusions are first communicated openly with the release of the 11.14.85 Laghi letter, do not become clear to the public until the announcement of Wuerl's possession of special faculties the following September. Apparently, even Hunthausen himself only gradually comes to understand the visitation's full cost to himself. As far as the public's involvement in the controversy goes, this period amounts to the calm before the storm. Though press accounts voiced suspicions about the relationship between the visitation and Wuerl's appointment at the time of his appointment, both Hunthausen and Wuerl explicitly sought to allay fears that Wuerl's appointment posed any kind of threat to Hunthausen's authority.

At the time he releases the Laghi letter, Hunthausen knows that the appointment of a bishop to Seattle is imminent and he knows that this bishop is supposed to help him address the visitation issues. Based on the later reports of Laghi and Hunthausen, it is clear that the nature of the appointee's power is under contestation. All of the options under consideration by the Vatican (as cited in the Vatican chronology) have Hunthausen turning over some degree of authority to make binding decisions. Hunthausen, on the other hand, says he is ready to commission the auxiliary with special powers of oversight but not with any form of final say in archdiocesan matters. Hunthausen and Laghi carry out this negotiation (*persuasive argumentation*) in *secret*. At the time of Wuerl's appointment, Hunthausen and Laghi believe they have an agreement both can live with, but with time this proves an illusion.

Though the appointment of an auxiliary bishop is often a form of *remuneration* practiced by Rome, providing local ordinaries with valued assistants, in this case the appointment is *coercive* in two ways. First, it involves a *loss of power* by Hunthausen; and second, it takes the public appearance of a *second symbolic intervention by Rome* (after the visitation). Hunthausen is to relinquish power to one who, by all appearances, is a Roman insider and, at the very least, is a Seattle outsider and not one of Hunthausen's own choices for the post. Wuerl had been a seminarian in Rome; he had served most of his years of priesthood in Roman curial posts; and, in a somewhat exceptional move, the Pope called him to Rome for his ordination. Symbolically, Rome asserts *territorial control* over Seattle by having the Pope ordain Wuerl instead of Hunthausen and then sending Wuerl to serve in Seattle on the heels of the visitation.

Hunthausen, up until the time that he makes Wuerl's faculties known, adopts *a two-front approach to the conflict handling*. In *public* he shows a *respectful conformity* to Rome's wishes, but in *private* he shows a willingness, as necessary, to *resist* the Roman agenda. His challenge to the Vatican's intention for Wuerl to have special faculties is the third prominent example we have seen of this (if we can trust Hunthausen's own reports), after resisting Vatican preferences of secrecy regarding the visitation process and the visitation findings. Notably, Hunthausen attempts to make Canon Law work in his favor (*legal power; strategy of persuasive argumentation*) by specifying a particular canon that should not apply in his case, thereby protecting himself against an undesirable arrangement. In public, at the time, we hear nothing of these negotiations. Hunthausen releases the Laghi letter summarizing the visitation findings, thanks the pro-nuncio and the Holy See (in his cover letter) for having supported and affirmed his ministry (strategy of *courtesy*), and refers to the "fraternal and constructive spirit" at work (*fraternity*).

This same cover letter from Hunthausen includes a notable employment of *God talk*. Earlier texts from the conflict have been, for the most part, perfunctory in their use of language that refers specifically to (Catholic) Christian beliefs. Most commonly we have seen what I would call *pious interjections*: that is, conventional, predictable invocations of God's name(s) or requests for God's blessing, often appearing at the end of statements or letters. These can be thought of as forms of simple reassurance, whereby the speaker proves that he belongs to the Catholic community and knows what is expected of him as a leader of that community. My point here is not to discount the sincerity of the pronouncements, necessarily, but to note that habit and the need to signal belonging are among the reasons for their use. (We can think of pious interjections as a minor employment of *traditional power*.)

In the case of this open letter from Hunthausen to the people of his archdiocese, however, we see Hunthausen engaging in a form of God talk that is rather involved and, apparently, *conscientiously applied for a strategic purpose* (*strategic God talk*). The passage quoted in the narrative above presents the final paragraph of Hunthausen's letter, wherein he refers to a specific doctrinal reference frame (the Second Vatican Council), invokes two specific conceptions of God (the God who speaks through Scripture and the Lord who is with us on our journey), and offers two images for God's people (they are a "pilgrim people" and a human and Christian "family"). This passage accomplishes several things at once. Most crucially, it elevates the experience at hand (ultimately, what is at stake is the "unity and well-being" of the Church itself) and invites the people of the archdiocese to join with Hunthausen in facing the difficulties that lie ahead. Rather than being a power struggle within the confines of the hierarchy, which parishioners can conveniently ignore, the present conflict becomes here an unprecedented challenge that *all of us* are facing together – a journey, a *pilgrimage*, where the Lord himself is our companion. By means of this rhetorical device, Hunthausen has greater stature, so too do the people, and the people have an incentive for supporting the Archbishop in the future. Note the presumptions undergirding the passage: there is something to fear (disunity perhaps?) but we need not be afraid; we are already on the journey together ("knowing… your deep faith and loving support, I… look forward to the journey we will continue together"); and the Lord is with us. As much as an invitation to join in the cause, this is praise (flattery) for having already so nobly committed oneself.

Hunthausen's reinforces the strength of the message with a self-deprecating presentation of self. He acknowledges his limitations as a person and as an archbishop. This discursive approach, as we will see in later statements, is typical of Hunthausen. He shows a strong tendency to personalize his message by foregrounding his own identity (I call this strategy *assertion of personal identity*), even when the content of his words purports to self-effacement. On a tactical level this shows up in his preference for use of the first person, his readiness to share personal thoughts and feelings, and his habit of calling upon his own experience as a framework for the discussion of conflict issues. Hunthausen's use of this strategy stands out when we compare it with the Ratzinger and Laghi letters summarizing the visitation findings. In those texts we gain little sense of *who* the letter writers are, or of how the conflict affects them on a personal level.

It is striking to compare the foreboding that marks the Hunthausen letter of 11.26.85 with the statements he and Wuerl issue just a week later, which acknowledge Wuerl's appointment as auxiliary bishop. Both speak of their joy at the news and both employ effusive words of praise and gratitude (*show deference to the order and mindset of the Church; minimize the appearance of conflict; act fraternally; practice courtesy*). Hunthausen's statement is more restrained than Wuerl's, but it has its own moments of pietistic hyperbole, as when Hunthausen writes that Wuerl's appointment "brings joy to me personally as I am sure it will to the entire church in Western Washington." Wuerl's statement brims with ameliorating modifiers ("I am *very happy* to be called to serve *such a distinguished* archbishop and *so vibrant* a church" – emphasis mine) and expressions of gratitude and self-effacement. When Wuerl describes the Archdiocese of Seattle as "a fruitful and vigorous part of Christ's vineyard," with "so many clergy, Religious and laity who so deeply love Christ and his church," one can only assume that Wuerl has a personal knowledge of Seattle that Cardinal Ratzinger lacks!

In the same issue of the *Progress* (12.5.85) where the Hunthausen and Wuerl statements convey unreserved approval of Wuerl's appointment, one finds the interview with Hunthausen that addresses the matter of a possible connection between Wuerl's appointment and the visitation. It is unclear why Hunthausen decides to release this interview. Perhaps he had concluded that speculation about the relationship between Wuerl's appointment and the visitation was inevitable and he would be better off if he confronted that question directly. (Hunthausen says as much at a later date: cf. *The Progress*, 9.11.86.) Two interesting features of the interview are Hunthausen's statement that the visitation itself and the Laghi summary serve a "limited purpose" (addressing "certain allegations," but not giving a complete picture of the archdiocese or of Hunthausen's leadership) and his declaration that Wuerl's responsibilities are confined to offering various kinds of *assistance* (pastoral, sacramental, administrative) to Hunthausen. Thus, Hunthausen relativizes the visitation and its findings (they do not tell the whole story) and he denies that Wuerl's appointment comes at a cost to himself (*persuasive argumentation; secrecy*).

Obviously, Hunthausen does not tell as much as he knows about Wuerl's role at this point. Nine months later, Hunthausen admits this and offers a justification for not having been more forthcoming.

> [Bishop Wuerl's] appointment here shortly after the formal conclusion of the Apostolic Visitation made it inevitable that people would wonder whether, in appointing him as my auxiliary, the Holy See had not also intended for him to have some specific additional responsibilities with reference to the findings and conclusions of the visitation. As a matter of fact, it did, but at the time of his appointment, both Bishop Wuerl and I, along with the Apostolic Pro-Nuncio, judged it best to make no public announcement to that effect. The importance of making Bishop Wuerl's transition to the archdiocese as smooth as possible and of assuring him of the best possible climate for beginning his ministry among us seemed to outweigh any possible good that might have been realized by giving a full public acknowledgment of all of the specifications surrounding his appointment as auxiliary bishop. (*The Progress*, 9.11.86)

Clearly, there is a dividedness at work in Hunthausen's approach to *secrecy*. On the one hand he argues against the use of secrecy and resists it. (In his interview comments Hunthausen states explicitly that he pushed to have the visitation findings brought into the open.) But on the other hand, he cooperates with Vatican directives for its use and also employs it of his own volition (rationalizing his decision to do so).

Shortly prior to Wuerl's arrival in Seattle, Hunthausen further demonstrates the ambivalence in his approach to secrecy when he reads the 9.30.85 Ratzinger letter, with its summary of visitation findings, to the priests of the archdiocese in a closed session. (Did Hunthausen have permission from Ratzinger or Laghi to do this? It is possible, but doubtful.) A later account of this meeting (*The Progress*, 5.15.86) says it was marked by anger and frustration, which priests directed toward the visitation process and its conclusions. In actuality, if not in intention, this meeting seems to have betrayed the objective of "making Bishop Wuerl's transition to the archdiocese as smooth as possible." Over time, Wuerl would be confronted with suspicion and, in some cases, outright hostility.

During Bishop Wuerl's first liturgy in Seattle, we encounter a rare discursive intervention from the Pope himself during the affair. It is interesting to see what the Pope says in this statement commissioning Wuerl and what he does not say. At most, one finds an oblique mention of the visitation and hint of the intention for Wuerl to have special powers. The Pope speaks of bishops being "burdened by many and serious matters in carrying out their ministry *so that* [emphasis mine] they seek assistance from this Apostolic See..." This could refer to the problems identified in the visitation and consequent need for special help, or, more neutrally, it could refer to the ordinary ministerial overload that bishops encounter and the way that auxiliaries help them to handle this workload. In any case, the purpose of Wuerl's being there is to allow Hunthausen to "more freely exercise" his office and "attain the greater good of the souls" he governs. Thus does the Pope associate (*persuasive argumentation*) his act of appointment with the *best interest of the Church*.

The language of the statement as a whole is highly abstract, which fits its intended liturgical context of reception (a bishop's inaugural Mass is no place for polemics) and which allows the Pope to signal meanings without spelling them out (strategies: *courtesy*; *minimize the appearance of conflict*). The Pope places a premium on *unity* in his statement. He counsels Wuerl to "be at one with the Archbishop" so that "this sign of unity" (the episcopal office) might remain untarnished and the unity of the flock will not be jeopardized. The message to Wuerl seems to be to tread carefully in managing his relationship with Hunthausen. The message to both bishops together seems to be to guard the unity in the Church.

Hunthausen and Wuerl themselves, in the time that they worked together, consistently showed *deference* to one another and gave the appearance of personal compatibility, even after they declared their power-sharing arrangement unworkable. Once it became clear they were at odds in their understanding of who was to have final say in the areas identified by the visitation, they pursued clarification quietly and according to the hierarchical chain of command (*deference to the order and mindset of the Church*). When word came back from Rome – the Congregation for Bishops had jurisdiction at this point, not the Congregation for the Doctrine of the Faith – Hunthausen submitted (*yielded*) and granted the faculties to Wuerl.

CHAPTER SEVEN

NARRATIVE AND ANALYSIS OF THE ROME-HUNTHAUSEN CASE: THE
MIDDLE STAGE (SEPTEMBER-NOVEMBER 1986)

7.1 Document Number: 3
Hunthausen 9.3.86 Press Statement Announcing Wuerl's Special Faculties
Source: *Origins,* 9/18/86, pp. 250-251.

7.1.1 Summary of Contents:
Rather than summarize Hunthausen's brief statement, I will reproduce it in full:

> I am aware that for quite some time speculation has taken place, both in printed form and in less formal ways, regarding the roles and responsibilities of Bishop Donald Wuerl. His appointment here shortly after the formal conclusion of the apostolic visitation made it inevitable that people would wonder whether, in appointing him as my auxiliary, the Holy See had not also intended for him to have some specific additional responsibilities with reference to the findings and conclusions of the visitation. As a matter of fact, it did; but at the time of his appointment both Bishop Wuerl and I, along with the apostolic pro-nuncio, judged it best to make no public announcement to that effect. The importance of making Bishop Wuerl's transition to the archdiocese as smooth as possible and of assuring him of the best possible climate for beginning this ministry among us seemed to outweigh any possible good that might have been realized by giving a full public acknowledgement of all the specifications surrounding his appointment as auxiliary bishop.
>
> However, at the time of his appointment, I did not understand the nature and extent of Bishop Wuerl's role. After considerable discussion with the Holy See, it was confirmed that it was the understanding of the Holy See in December 1985 when appointing Bishop Wuerl that he not only assist me by assuming a general oversight and responsibility for these five areas (identified in the apostolic visitation), but that he actually be delegated by me to have complete and final decision-making power over them. The clarification of this decision took place in June at the Collegeville (Minn.) meeting of bishops, where I met with the apostolic pro-nuncio. It was subsequently confirmed to me in a letter dated July 1, 1986.
>
> Once I received this clarification, I not only took steps to carry out the wishes of the Holy See, but also arrived at the conclusion that it was important to share these matters with my close collaborators in the ministry and administration of the archdiocese.

7.1.2 Conflict Functionality of the 9.3.86 Hunthausen Press Statement
Laghi (in the Vatican chronology, see document 4, below) would later characterize this press statement from Hunthausen as a "surprise announcement," but Hunthausen contested that description (in his response to the Vatican chronology, document 5). Hunthausen:

> The record will show… that I repeatedly made the point in my conversations and exchanges with Archbishop Laghi at Collegeville this past summer, that, in the then unlikely event that I would agree to accept the special faculties arrangement according to the manner in which they were being understood by the Holy See, I would have no choice but to make this matter known to all my priests and close collaborators since it would be absolutely essential for them to know to whom they were accountable and from whom they would receive orders and directives. I never left the slightest doubt about this matter since I knew that to have acted in any other way would have resulted in a chaotic situation with regard to the governance of the Archdiocese.

Whether the announcement indeed came as a "surprise" to the Holy See is perhaps a moot point. More obvious and pertinent is Rome's displeasure that Hunthausen has again *resisted* the policy of *secrecy*. But one should be careful not to categorically associate the Vatican with the practice of secrecy and Hunthausen with the practice of openness. As is apparent from the contents of this statement, Hunthausen, too, could find reason for actively practicing secrecy. Hunthausen counts himself among those (the others being Wuerl and Laghi) who "judged it best to make no public announcement" regarding "all the specifications surrounding [Wuerl's] appointment as auxiliary bishop." Moreover, Hunthausen's word choices are, willingly or not (perhaps it's the product of unconscious episcopal habit?), complicit in the persistent refusal to name Vatican agents. Four times Hunthausen refers to "the Holy See," but not once does he say whom exactly he means with this (The Pope? Ratzinger? Gantin? Others?). Indeed, the pronoun he uses to refer to the Holy See is "it" – the Holy See is not people acting, but something more akin to an impersonal force.

Interestingly, this communication is brief, matter-of-fact, and – on the surface, at least – non-contentious. The contents can be boiled down to: I misunderstood; now I understand, and I am making corrections accordingly. Hunthausen articulates no protest here (though no profession of loyalty appears either) and presents his own involvement in the affair up to this point as having been thoroughly cooperative (*show deference to the order and mindset of the Church*; *minimize the appearance of conflict*). Hunthausen also makes no attempt to tell his side of the story in regard to the visitation and Wuerl's appointment. But there is a subtext, which I have already noted: by making a public statement ("I... arrived at the conclusion that it was important for me to share these matters..."), Hunthausen chooses to go his own way, rather than hold with Vatican preferences. Thus, the text seems to speak at one time of Hunthausen's loyalty and obedience and of his willingness, if necessary, to challenge the Holy See.

Hunthausen makes a strong argument when he points out that it would be administratively dysfunctional for priests not to know whom they were accountable to. (How exactly *did* the Vatican envision this working?) Hunthausen says he shared this view with the Vatican and made clear that, if a division of power were imposed, he would have to make the details of the new arrangement known to his priests. Thus, his stated justification for making this announcement. At the same time, however, Hunthausen must have been aware that sharing this news would cause an uproar. Apparently, either Hunthausen saw some advantage in the instigation of controversy or he tolerated it as a necessary side effect of meeting his communicative objective.

Perhaps the most striking absence in the statement is anger. Hunthausen here announces that the Vatican has taken power from him in five key areas of oversight – in other words, he is on the receiving end of a humiliating disciplinary measure (*coercive power*) -- but Hunthausen presents this in neutral language as a misunderstanding that, thanks to Vatican "clarification" is now clarified. Surely Hunthausen felt anger. The question is how the anger was channeled, at the time and thereafter.

D. Intervening Developments (September-October 1986)
It did not take Hunthausen long to begin to share his version of recent events in detail. Simultaneous with or shortly following the release of the 9.3.86 press statement, Hunthausen circulated at least five other texts that commented on Wuerl's faculties and the past and present situation in the archdiocese. These texts were a chronology of recent events (accompanying the press statement announcing Wuerl's faculties), three explanatory letters of like content (directed to the chancery staff, the priests of the archdiocese and the people of the archdiocese) and an interview conducted with Hunthausen and Wuerl (published in the *Progress*).

The chronology (hereafter referred to as the *Seattle* chronology, to distinguish it from the better-known Vatican chronology) was published under the title "Chronology" (cf. *The Progress*, 9.11.86 and *Origins*, 9.18.86) but its full title in the original press release was "Chronology of Events Related to Apostolic Visitation and Appointment of Auxiliary Bishop Donald W. Wuerl to the Catholic Archdiocese of Seattle." The text is structured around five dates and presents no introductory or concluding commentary. The five focal points are the announcement of the visitation, the visitation itself, Hunthausen's announcement of the visitation findings, Hunthausen's announcement of Wuerl's appointment, and Wuerl's ordination. These events are described in the third person in a matter-of-fact tone and with little elaboration.

The Seattle chronology precedes the better-known Vatican chronology (see below, document 4) in time. One has to wonder whether the Apostolic Nunciature's decision to release a chronology of its own was inspired by the archdiocese's issuance of a text of this genre. On the surface, the Seattle chronology is a benign document. It offers no information that was not previously available and little in the way of argumentation. The thumbnail sketch of the visitation and post-visitation events in language avoids criticism of Hunthausen or the Holy See. The chronology was released as an informational "backgrounder" to the press, providing a context for interpreting the accompanying press statement. The Vatican chronology, distributed seven weeks later, does not appear to offer direct counterpoint to the Seattle chronology. The Vatican chronology is a much more lengthy and contentious document, which responds to the whole of the case that Hunthausen was making publicly at the time.

In contrast with the terse, muted quality of Hunthausen's announcement of the faculties and the neutral language of the Vatican chronology, the letters Hunthausen released shortly after his press statement regarding Wuerl's faculties are full of feeling and include an impassioned plea to his readers. The following passage appeared (with minor amendments) in all three versions of the letter:

> In writing to you about these matters, critical as they are for all of us, I feel it is important for me to tell you that I continue to feel honored and deeply privileged to be able to serve this Church as its Archbishop and to be able to do so in close collaboration with Bishop Wuerl and with each of you. Our relationship, which has come to mean so very much to me personally, will, I know, continue to grow stronger and closer as the days unfold. More than ever I will depend upon your close collaboration and prayers. Among the duties that are mine as your Archbishop, none are more important or more sacred than the preaching and teaching of the saving Gospel of Jesus Christ and of witnessing to that Gospel, to the very best of my ability, by all I say and do. I am firmly committed to doing this, but I cannot do it alone. None of us can. We can only do it with the strength that comes from God's grace. We can only do it in union with each other and with the Church Universal.

Here Hunthausen enlists the personal support of the people of his archdiocese, in language that is explicitly religious. Other notable features common to Hunthausen's letters include: an argument in favor of open disclosure ("Not to have [publicly disclosed Wuerl's faculties] would have deprived all the key people within our organization of the most vital sort of information imaginable"); a declaration that Wuerl possessed uncontested authority in the designated areas ("Bishop Wuerl now enjoys complete and final authority… for each of the five areas"); and their inclusion of Hunthausen's acknowledgment of his own personal suffering ("the long days and complex events which have brought us to this particular moment as a church have been extremely trying and agonizing ones for me"). What comes to the fore is Hunthausen's humanity and vulnerability.

The letters are not the only example of Hunthausen's readiness to take his case to the public. The same issue of *The Progress* containing his open letter to the people of the archdiocese

(9.11.86) also carries an interview that Hunthausen and Wuerl gave to *Progress* editor Bill Dodds. In the interview the bishops explain how they came to realize the divergence in their understanding of Wuerl's role and how they intend to proceed in light of the clarification now received. Both emphasize that the misunderstanding had been genuine and that they acted "in good faith." Hunthausen extended that characterization of good faith to others involved in the visitation, but noted at the same time that he had questioned the process.

> We hear the expression all of this has been very "unjust." I don't know whether I'd use the word. I can't tell people what word to use.
> I think it's important for me to say that from the very outset I have been aware that at each step along the way the individuals who have been involved have been doing what they felt they were charged to do. And I feel that they have done that with a sense of responsibility, a sense of fidelity to the church.
> I've questioned the process. Methods that somehow seem to be in place to get at concerns in the church or dioceses. I've seriously wondered whether there has to be something better.
> I feel that even with the best of intentions there's such a potential for hurting people and bringing about divisiveness.

Wuerl, for his part, explicitly challenged those who would claim the process was unjust, but he agreed with Hunthausen's suggestion that the process was a painful one.

> We can disagree with how things turned out. We can disagree even with some of the process along the way, but I think it's important for the good of the church, as the unity we are and for what we understand the church to be, to always say this is not an injustice, not an evil thing, not a denial of basic human rights.
> Those are really strong words and very strong judgments on the character of the people involved. I wouldn't get into that type of judgment.
> I certainly would support the archbishop that the process as it was carried out turned out to be very painful. I would associate myself completely with the archbishop in attempting to address any future use of this specific process.

The public reaction to Hunthausen's announcement was swift and pronounced. On September 7, the *Seattle Times* described responses of support, opposition and bafflement among local Catholics. The September 8 *Seattle Post-Intelligencer* said, "Western Washington Catholics remained confused and uncertain about a power shift in their archdiocese…" One week after Hunthausen's announcement (9.12.86), the *National Catholic Reporter* wrote, hyperbolically, that news of the power-sharing arrangement had "rocked Northwest Catholics, triggering a burst of outrage from clergy, religious and laity alike." In its issued dated September 20, the Jesuit journal *America* observed "the clergy and lay leadership in Seattle are angry and confused at what has been done to their archbishop."

Though apparently in the majority among Catholics locally and media writers nationally, supporters of Hunthausen were not the only ones to speak out. Many persons – in the Seattle archdiocese and around the country -- sent letters to newspapers expressing approval for the Vatican's disciplinary action against Hunthausen. Some of these letters enumerated his failings. And conservative Catholic publications such as *The Wanderer* consistently challenged the positions of Hunthausen and his advocates.

Activists mobilized quickly on Hunthausen's behalf. Briggs (1992, 17) speaks of "a torrent of protest by the most active elements in the Seattle church…" A Seattle group calling itself Concerned Catholics organized a petition drive with the intention of gaining 25,000 signatures in favor of the restoration of full authority to Archbishop Hunthausen. (The September 25, 1986 issue of *The Wanderer* characterized the actions of Hunthausen's supporters as "a campaign of resistance to the Vatican's action.") Throughout the archdiocese (and shortly thereafter in places beyond the archdiocese), supporters held rallies, organized prayer meetings and discussion forums, and initiated letter-writing campaigns on behalf of the archbishop.

Members of the hierarchy were less quick to speak out on the affair or to take sides publicly. On September 22, the bishops of the Northwestern US issued a two-sentence statement saying that they unanimously supported "the efforts of Archbishop Hunthausen and Bishop Wuerl in their process to deal with the present situation in Seattle, to help the church in Seattle to move beyond this moment and to continue to build up the unity of the church – a unity within the local church in Seattle and with the Universal Church" (*The Progress*, 9.25.86). Some cautious expressions emerged from a gathering of bishops in Portland, Oregon (where new archbishop William Levada was installed on September 22). Spokane, Washington Bishop Lawrence Walsh commented that "the fact that [we bishops are] not doing all kinds of things [publicly in regard to the situation] is not an indication of a lack of concern." Portland's outgoing archbishop, Cornelius Power said, "I think what you want to ask me about, I don't want to talk about." And Cardinal Bernard Law, while describing the Vatican's involvement as "legitimate," expressed his hope that pain would give way to unity in the case.

The apostolic pro-nuncio was present at the same gathering. The *Oregonian* newspaper (9.24.86) quoted Archbishop Laghi as saying that the Vatican's reassignment of powers in Seattle was "not to be interpreted as a slap in the face." Laghi went on to say, "The Archdiocese of Seattle has done many things very well. But we have to contain all those energies in a straight line. We are not a uniform church, but we are one church." Another report (*The Seattle Times*, 9.23.86) quoted Laghi as saying: "We admit diversity. But what we don't admit, though, is isolation, or particularly we don't admit, I would say, a kind of separation." Hunthausen and Wuerl were also present but did not speak to the press. (At approximately the same time – see the 9.19.86 *National Catholic Reporter* – two Vatican officials shared their views. Monsignor Marcello Costalunga, under secretary of the Congregation for Bishops, called the removal of Hunthausen's powers a "disciplinary" action, and one that was not necessarily permanent. Vatican spokesman Joaquin Navarro-Valls characterized the Holy See's action as a "regular" procedure according to canon law. He held out the possibility of the action being reversed, "if discipline is restored in the archdiocese."

Perhaps the most significant and, by various accounts (see the 9.26.86 and 10.10.86 issues of the *National Catholic Reporter* and the 9.18.86 issue of *The Progress*), intense exchange of views to take place in the first weeks after Hunthausen's announcement of Wuerl's faculties occurred during two meetings (Sept. 12 and 26) of Hunthausen and Wuerl with 250 priests of the archdiocese in a closed session. (According to the *National Catholic Reporter* article, a videotape of this meeting was made of the first meeting for the archdiocesan archives, but the current chancellor of the archdiocese reported on 11.2.01, in answer to my request, that no such videotape is in the archives currently.) Among the discussion points at the first meeting was whether the Vatican action against Hunthausen could be considered just. Many priests in attendance expressed the view that the action was "unjust." One week later Bishop Wuerl wrote a letter to the priests of the archdiocese (which he released for publication in the 9.25.86 *Progress*; see also *Origins*, 10.9.86), responding again to that specific charge (see his 9.11.86 *Progress* interview statement above) and reflecting more generally on the recent developments.

In his letter, Wuerl writes:

[….] When I view the visitation and its results it is clear to me that the person of the archbishop and the sincerity of his ministry were never challenged, much less attacked. The letter bringing closure to the visitation speaks of the archbishop in high praise, noting that he has "striven with heart and mind to be a good bishop of the church." This I know you believe and I can affirm from my own experience to be true.

Nor at issue, Wuerl continues, "Are the many good and positive things happening in the archdiocese." What *is* at issue are "certain practices and aspects of the archdiocesan administration that the Holy See indicated need attention." Wuerl's recommendation to the priests was to "move forward to address the concerns that prompted the faculties in the first place."

Any timeline for the continuance of the faculties is intrinsically tied to our success in addressing the concerns of the visitation. The purpose of these faculties is to help the archbishop. Once the reason for the faculties no longer exists, it seems to me neither does the need for the faculties.

As for the justness of the visitation process, Wuerl writes:

You may recall that I was asked repeatedly at the Friday meeting to denounce the visitation process as "unjust." This, as I said, I cannot do. The fact that the process indicated in the September 30, 1985, letter of Cardinal Ratzinger is a process with which we Americans may be unfamiliar or uncomfortable does not of itself make the process "unjust."

Before closing, Wuerl declares the intention that he and Hunthausen had reached jointly to go to Rome "for a forthright discussion with the proper authorities on the issues, process of the visitation, and the reaction in the archdiocese." (This suggestion had been made to Hunthausen and Wuerl at their gathering with the archdiocesan presbyterate on 9.12.86.) He also offers a brief theological reflection that holds out hope for finding "a redemptive aspect to our sorrow, humiliation and pain."

One week after Wuerl wrote his letter, and two weeks after the archbishop and auxiliary met with the priests of the archdiocese, the presbyterate met again with the bishops (on 9.26.86). The archdiocesan pastoral and finance councils were also present for this meeting, as were the chancery department heads. In the course of this meeting some especially heated exchanges between Wuerl and others in attendance took place. According to a (10.10.86) *National Catholic Reporter* account, Wuerl accused some priests of "fomenting a divisive current against the process he and Hunthausen were trying to follow to resolve the conflict," a challenge that some priests interpreted to be a threat. At this meeting Hunthausen and Wuerl formulated more concretely their plan to go to Rome, though no date was set for the trip. (In fact, such a trip would never materialize.)

A key question Wuerl raised in his letter to the priests -- one that tended to be underplayed in secular and liberal Catholic press coverage at the time (which focused on the "justice" of the visitation process) – concerned the practical progress toward addressing the concerns identified by the visitation. For some months, at least since April of 1986, Wuerl had served with Chancellor (Very Rev. Michael G.) Ryan and Director of Administration (Rev. Michael J.) McDermott on a committee that Hunthausen had established to review the 9.30.85 Ratzinger letter and find concrete ways of responding within the archdiocese. A major focus of the committee's work was identifying the parties with responsibility in the areas of concern and engaging them in a discussion of how to approach specific problems. In an internal memorandum to "Designated Leaders in the Archdiocese of Seattle" (exact recipients unknown), dated September 29, 1986, Hunthausen reported on the work of this committee and passed on a copy of an assessment the committee had submitted to him on April 29, 1986.

(Copies of both of these documents are available in the Wasden Price collection.) In that same document, Hunthausen made clear that oversight of the process of addressing the visitation concerns was now entrusted almost entirely to Wuerl. (The public record is only minimally revealing of Hunthausen's effort to address Rome's specific pastoral concerns prior to Wuerl's arrival, but see Ratzinger's reference, in his 9.30.85 letter, to a 3.14.84 Hunthausen letter – never made public -- wherein Hunthausen discusses the steps he has taken to correct the practice of contraceptive sterilization in local Catholic hospitals.)

On October 1, the group calling itself Concerned Catholics met with Hunthausen and Wuerl and presented to Wuerl 13,500 signatures it had collected calling for the restoration of full power to Hunthausen. The petitions were given to Wuerl and not sent directly to Rome (*Seattle Post-Intelligencer*, 10.2.86) because the group believed that Rome would listen only to Wuerl's voice in this matter. Participants in this meeting said that, while the meeting itself was cordial, Wuerl shared his view that press coverage had been detrimental in the Seattle situation thus far and that, unless the "decibel level is lowered" in Seattle, the Vatican might yet take sterner action against Hunthausen.

By the middle of October, commentators nationally were speculating that the controversy would command center stage at the November meeting of the national bishops' conference (cf. *National Catholic Reporter*, 10.17.86). Since the Laghi letter of the previous November, which had summarized the visitation findings, no official pronouncements on behalf of the Holy See had been issued to clarify Rome's position. According to the *National Catholic Reporter* (10.31.86), Laghi came under increasing pressure to make public the Vatican's version of development in the case. On 10.27.86, Laghi released a document that served this purpose.

It is revealing to consider the process whereby Laghi's Vatican chronology (document 4, assessed below) was released. The account in the 10.31.86 *National Catholic Reporter* identifies several of the participants involved and the interests at stake. Because it is highly detailed and the only relevant source I can find on this matter, I will quote this particular article at length.

> Laghi, under growing pressure to make public the Vatican's version, had initially worked out a plan with [NCCB President James] Malone. According to that plan, Laghi's chronology was to be released to the U.S. bishops and the press along with a Malone cover letter that at one point contained an endorsement of the pro-nuncio's chronology, a source said.
> But after conversations with other bishops, Malone decided to maintain a neutral approach.
> He convened a teleconference Oct. 23 of the NCCB executive committee during which it was decided that the U.S. bishops would distribute the Laghi chronology only if an accompanying Hunthausen chronology were included.
> The bishops scrupulously wanted to maintain neutrality on the matter, but at that point ended up forcing Laghi to change his approach in handling the matter, one source said. "They wanted to be fair and acted in a very American way," he added.
> At first, Laghi agreed with the changed plan, but he later telephoned Malone to say that under the circumstances the Vatican Embassy would release the document on its own.
> It was not clear whether all committee members participated in the Oct. 23 conference call. The committee is made up of Malone, NCCB Vice President John May of St. Louis, Boston Cardinal Bernard Law, Washington Auxiliary Eugene Marino and Rockville Center Bishop John McGann.
> Laghi had shared his chronology with Hunthausen, who, another source said, made it clear to both Laghi and Malone that he disagreed with aspects of the apostolic pro-nuncio's version. Hunthausen asked Malone and Laghi not to distribute it. Hunthausen, one source said, thought that making the document public at this time would distract attention from the work of the Nov. 10-12 annual U.S. bishops' meeting and would cause further division in the church.

But a major concern among the U.S. bishops for not wanting to release the chronology without an accompanying Hunthausen chronology was the potentially awkward position it would place Hunthausen in. He would have to respond publicly to the disputed points or say nothing at all. On the one hand, responding publicly, the source noted, would have placed him visibly at odds with Laghi. On the other hand, not replying would have allowed the appearance of accepting Laghi's chronology as fact.

The critical factor in these initial deliberations was that the bishops appeared to remain neutral, even if it meant requesting Laghi to change his approach to publicizing the chronology. Malone last week referred calls on the matter to the NCCB communications department.

Russell Shaw, NCCB spokesman, said Oct. 23 that there had been "a tentative plan" to distribute the chronology but that "there followed a series of consultations involving officers of the conference, Archbishop Hunthausen and Archbishop Laghi" and that "the outcome of those conversations was that the bishops' conference would not distribute the document as prepared."

The next day, however, an NCCB spokesperson said the chronology would be available to the press Oct. 27 with a one-day embargo.

This abrupt reversal, according to sources, including one Catholic conference member familiar with the case, came after the following sequence of events.

Chicago Cardinal Joseph Bernardin received a call from Laghi, who told Bernardin of the Vatican's distress over the NCCB decision not to release the Laghi chronology as initially planned.

Bernardin told Malone that Laghi had spoken with the prefect for the Congregation for the Doctrine of the Faith Cardinal Joseph Ratzinger and prefect for the Congregation for Bishops, Cardinal Bernardin Gantin, and that "it was the request of the Holy See" that the NCCB distribute the chronology. The cardinal discussed with Malone ways in which the chronology could be released that would both satisfy the Vatican and maintain the independence of the NCCB. Bernardin suggested that Malone again convene an NCCB executive committee meeting.

Malone then called Laghi, who relayed the Vatican "request." A second hastily called conference took place and the decision to distribute the Laghi chronology was made.

Under the latest terms of the agreement between Laghi and Malone, the chronology will be distributed with a Malone cover letter stating that the document is being distributed "at the request of the Vatican and authorization of the Holy See." One observer noted that implicit in this NCCB position was the desire to separate the bishops from the chronology. Another source said it was the intention of the bishops to go along with the Vatican request but to continue to stand back from the chronology, giving Hunthausen "room to maneuver."

Several sources said the Vatican and Laghi's office have been "deluged" in recent weeks with Hunthausen support letters. One source said this had "irritated" at least some Vatican officials; another, however, said it was pushing them to answer critics' complaints that it had failed to explain adequately what exactly led to the Vatican move to give Seattle Auxiliary Donald Wuerl final authority in several ecclesial areas in the archdiocese.

A spokesperson for the Seattle archdiocese said Hunthausen was "discouraged" by the developments and had not yet decided how he would respond.

D.d. Conflict Functionality of the Intervening Developments (September-October 1986)

The events just described take us from Hunthausen's announcement of Wuerl's possession of faculties to Laghi's distribution of the Vatican chronology. We can characterize this period in terms of a few key actions and reactions. It begins with a public relations offensive from Hunthausen, who announces the faculties, justifies his actions and strongly asserts his own personality. Hunthausen's statements generate a public reaction. An outcry arises among the priests and people of the Seattle archdiocese, and some supporters begin to campaign on Hunthausen's behalf. Fellow U.S. bishops offer a muted response and seek to minimize the appearance of conflict. Two Vatican officials briefly comment on the case and observe that the action taken in Seattle was disciplinary and perhaps temporary. In the course of the controversy that brews, the priests of the archdiocese ask Bishop Wuerl to denounce the visitation. Wuerl refuses, defending the Holy See's actions. Rather than agreeing to challenge Rome, Wuerl attempts to engage in problem solving by directing attention to the issues identified in the visitation and showing his willingness to go with Hunthausen to Rome to discuss the current situation. But tensions remain high between Wuerl and many of the priests. As the public debate grows more heated, the pro-nuncio prepares the Holy See's statement of response. Laghi works behind the scenes to have the Vatican statement (chronology) endorsed by the U.S. bishops' conference. The NCCB leadership strives to maintain neutrality. Eventually, through the intervention of Cardinal Ratzinger, a compromise is reached. The NCCB releases the document not with an NCCB endorsement but with a statement that it was being distributed "at the request of the Vatican and authorization of the Holy See."

Notice that the field of participants increases dramatically as the result of Hunthausen's announcement. The NCCB begins to play a significant *third party* role in the affair at this point, though initially the conference's involvement is limited to hidden negotiations involving its executive committee (NCCB President James Malone, NCCB Vice President John May of St. Louis, Cardinal Bernard Law of Boston, Auxiliary Bishop Eugene Marino of Washington, Bishop John McGann of Rockville Center). Individual bishops also weigh in with their own opinions, though in very guarded ways. (I mentioned Walsh, Power and Law, but one could identify numerous others.) Moreover, the involvement of certain officers of the Roman curia comes into the open for the first time: Cardinal Gantin, prefect of the Congregation for Bishops; Monsignor Marcello Costalunga, under secretary of the same Congregation; and Vatican spokesperson Joaquin Navarro-Valls. Bishop Wuerl, for his part, begins to engage the conflict issues more actively in public. Finally, Cardinal Bernardin (himself a past president of the NCCB) plays an important intermediary role between Rome and the present leadership of the conference in the matter of the release of the Vatican chronology. Beyond the increasing activity by members of the hierarchy, we also see a sudden rise in the level of press coverage of the affair and in the involvement of other concerned parties (lay persons, priests, Religious).

There are two main thrusts to Hunthausen's activity during this period, with some contradiction between the two. The main thrust is his public relations offensive, which reveals Wuerl's possession of faculties and justifies Hunthausen's actions up to this point. By disclosing Wuerl's faculties, Hunthausen *resists* the Vatican's preference for *secrecy*, taking the matter out of the confines of the *bureaucracy* and into the open. Hunthausen's arguments of self-justification (*persuasive argumentation*) emphasize his own loyalty (embodied in his good working relationship with Wuerl: *fraternity*), good faith and good intentions (*deference to the structural order and mindset of the Church; associate one's own efforts with the best interest of the Church*). The implication is that Hunthausen is an innocent who has been wronged. (Possibly one may locate incipient forms of strategies here. Is Hunthausen portraying himself as a *victim*? Apparently so. Is he *demonizing* those who have acted against him? If so, only with very subtle indications.) In his delivery of these messages, Hunthausen adopts a businesslike and measured tone. He explains the current situation, a necessary practical task for moving forward with leadership of the archdiocese, and pleads for support from the people of the archdiocese (*territorial control*) by *asserting his own identity* (vulnerable, of good will, a victim) and making ample use of *God talk*. Ironically, Hunthausen's act of disclosure *reveals the conflict* and *escalates* it, but it does so in language that *emphasizes unity and harmony*.

The other thrust of Hunthausen's activity during this period is his behind-the-scenes effort to convince Laghi not to release the Vatican chronology. In this case, the center moves for openness (abandons *secrecy*) and the periphery resists. (In secret, Hunthausen argues for secrecy.) Though Hunthausen does not achieve his overt objective – Laghi releases the chronology anyway – his resistance may have been a factor which kept the NCCB administrative board from going so far as to endorse the chronology.

The production and release of the Vatican chronology appears to be a direct response not so much to the announcement of faculties in and of itself, but to the debate that erupted in response to Hunthausen's announcement and subsequent elaborations. Prior to releasing the chronology, Laghi says little about the affair in public, but his comments at Archbishop Levada's installation show him struggling to find words to dampen the controversy. The Vatican's action was not intended to be a "slap in the face," he says (*minimize the appearance of conflict*). Seattle has done "many things very well," *but* "we have to contain all those energies in a straight line." We are not a uniform church, *but* we are one church. We admit diversity, *but* we don't admit isolation or separation. The chronology itself will prove to be less balanced and more decidedly critical in its judgments.

Strikingly, at the same time that Laghi asserts that the redistribution of power was not a slap in the face for Hunthausen, two Vatican officials offer statements on the record that send mixed signals regarding this question. Congregation for Bishops Under Secretary Costalunga says the act was "disciplinary" but not necessarily permanent, and Vatican spokesman Navarro-Valls says the action was a "regular" (*legal*) one, but has the possibility of reversal. What is surprising here is that Costalunga, in particular, speaks on the record, since he sits on the critical congregation in Rome (the one that gave the final clarification on the faculties question, but also that his message contradicts Laghi's. Here the center party speaks with three voices, not one, and it is difficult to know how to interpret the statements that the disciplinary action could be reversed. Is this simply a tactic (*leaks?*) to quiet controversy, or does the Vatican have some concrete plan under consideration?

Clearer, in a strategic sense, is Laghi's back room attempt (*secrecy*) to get a seal of approval for his account of the case from the NCCB. The chronology itself is a rhetorical effort to achieve *legitimacy* (through *argumentation* justifying the Vatican's actions); Laghi seeks further legitimacy by having it accredited and distributed by an influential third party. At the same time, Laghi seeks to secure that party as an *ally*. This struggle is crucial because winning over the NCCB would take away Hunthausen's only likely source of support within the hierarchy. It would isolate Hunthausen as one out of step with the Church leadership.

By seeking the endorsement within the forum of the NCCB executive committee, Laghi saves himself time (he does not have to wait until the gathering of the entire body in November) and he limits the number he has to persuade to five or fewer. But the *number of participants* in this negotiation *increases* as it bogs down. Hunthausen is involved from early on thanks to Laghi's decision to show him the chronology in advance of its release. (Why does Laghi do this? Strategically, it seems to work to his disadvantage.) When it appears that the NCCB will not be distributing the document at all, Laghi consults with Ratzinger and Gantin in Rome (they possess more *coercive power*), who make clear their desire to have the NCCB circulate the document. This leads Laghi to call on another bishop (cardinal) to intervene: Bernardin (*recruit allies*). Bernardin calls Malone, Malone calls Laghi, and then Malone reconvenes the executive committee to come to a new decision. The result is a *compromise*, wherein the NCCB maintains neutrality on the content of the statement but serves the Vatican's wish that it be the vehicle of distribution.

This is the first time in the conflict that we see the Vatican making a concerted effort to gain third party support. Hunthausen's effort to do so has been apparent from a much earlier time. This suggests that the Holy See now finds itself lacking the ability to resolve the conflict with resources it already possesses. Through news media projections the conflict has become rapidly enlarged and amorphous. The direct appeal of the Vatican raises the stakes for other bishops who might choose to take a stand in the affair, since the lines are now more clearly drawn. Individual bishops, as we see in the statement of the Northwest bishops and the comments of those present at Archbishop Levada's installation, show a high degree of caution (as in Power's refusal to comment), but they also offer hints of where they stand (Walsh speaks of the bishops' "concern" about the situation, implying some level of support for Hunthausen, whereas Law's remark about the legitimacy of the Vatican action suggests more of an affiliation with the center party.) The NCCB executive committee's firm decision to remain neutral, even after the preference of Ratzinger and Gantin is made known (it yields on the distribution question but not on the endorsement question), suggests that the bishops' conference enjoys a significant degree of autonomy and does not feel compelled to slavishly follow Rome's lead.

Bishop Wuerl is at this point tightly wedged between the positions of the center and periphery parties. Certain priests of the archdiocese want him to denounce the visitation process as unjust, and Hunthausen himself leaves open the possibility of taking this stance himself (which he later does, in his NCCB address). But fidelity to Rome requires Wuerl to defend the visitation. Wuerl resolves this dilemma of dual (conflicting) loyalties by asserting the "justice" of the proceedings but acknowledging that the process was "painful." He also declares himself ready to go with Hunthausen to Rome to discuss the current state of affairs and the criticisms of the process that have arisen. Thus, Wuerl appears to engage in *problem solving*.

Perhaps the hardening tension between Wuerl and many priests of the archdiocese is what leads Hunthausen later (in his NCCB address) to call the present arrangement in the archdiocese "unworkable." It is intriguing that Wuerl, like the Vatican officials just days before him, foresees a chance of Hunthausen's faculties being restored. ("Once the reason for the faculties no longer exists, it seems to me neither does the need for the faculties." Does Wuerl possess inside information at this point, or is he just following the lead of the curial officers public pronouncements?) Noteworthy, too, is Wuerl's emphasis on the importance of concretely addressing the Vatican concerns identified through the visitation process. This is a question that is largely neglected in much of the press coverage (mostly supportive of Hunthausen) of the time. Hunthausen establishes a process for addressing the concerns, but it may have been difficult for Rome to gauge Hunthausen's level of commitment to this process. Uncertainty about this could have been a source of tension between Hunthausen and Rome.

In general, the priorities of the third party (member-of-the-hierarchy) participants at this point seem to be, first, cautiously to avoid getting oneself into trouble and, to second, signal one's own position in a nonaccountable (indirect way). By holding out for neutrality, the NCCB executive committee and other bishops support Hunthausen in an intentional (surreptitious) way, or by default. Rome has made clear its wish for the American bishops to side with the Holy See. Openly criticizing Rome or defending Hunthausen would be problematic for individual bishops own relations with Rome. Thus, neutrality is the most Hunthausen can hope for from his fellow bishops at this stage, and he gets it.

7.2 Document Number: 4
Laghi, The Vatican Chronology (10.24.86)
Source: *The Progress*, 10/30/86, pp. 2-4; *Origins*, 11/6/86, pp.362-364.

7.2.1 Summary of Contents:
The text carries the title, "A Chronology of Recent Events in the Archdiocese of Seattle," and consists of four numbered sections divided into lettered paragraphs. All four sections highlight key points related to the visitation from the Vatican perspective. The document contains no stand-apart introductory or concluding material.

Section 1, *Decision for an Apostolic Visitation of Seattle*, opens the chronology with a reference to 1978, when the Vatican began a correspondence with Hunthausen about "pastoral practices and the presentation of the church's teachings" in the Archdiocese. The Vatican-Hunthausen correspondence arose as the result of letters of complaint that the Vatican had received about Hunthausen's pastoral leadership.

Laghi asserts that the Vatican interest in the matter developed out of its concern for the well being of the universal Church. The text explicitly denies that the Holy See's action had anything to do with Hunthausen's stance on "nuclear weapons and the payment of taxes." According to the chronology, Hunthausen agreed certain abuses exist and needed correction. Though Hunthausen took some corrective actions, the Vatican continued to receive "substantiated complaints" about ongoing abuses. At the prompting of "certain bishops" who saw the need "to clear the air," the Vatican decided to conduct an Apostolic Visitation of Seattle.

Section 2, *Preparation for the Apostolic Visitation*, identifies two Vatican priorities in the affair: (1) building up the local Church in harmony with the universal Church, and (2) protecting Hunthausen's good name. Thus publicity was kept to a minimum and the Vatican sought to inform Hunthausen and enlist his cooperation throughout.

The chronology then describes Archbishop Hickey's consultation with Hunthausen prior to his conduct of the Visitation. Together they reviewed the forthcoming procedure and the doctrinal and pastoral issues in question. Hickey also discussed with Hunthausen specific letters of complaint of which Hunthausen was already aware. As part of this process, Hunthausen was allowed to suggest persons to be interviewed. Laghi notes at the end of section 2 that Hunthausen insisted that a public announcement of the Visitation be made.

Section 3, *The Visitation*, describes the Visitation process, including its information sources (public documents, personal interviews with persons of the Archdiocese, an extensive interview with Hunthausen himself) and its findings ("five areas of concern" remained after the information gathering). According to the chronology, "the testimony of 'unfriendly witnesses' added little to the data on which the criticism of the Holy See was based." The areas of concern are identified with brief titles (The Tribunal, The Liturgy, Health Care, Homosexuals, Inactive Priests, Clergy Formation) followed by descriptions of the problems encountered. (NB: Laghi speaks of five areas of concern but names six.)

Laghi ends this section by presenting the overarching conclusion of the visitation that, though the Holy See judged Hunthausen "to be an effective bishop in many respects," it nonetheless "considered him lacking the firmness necessary to govern the archdiocese." Laghi continues, "The archbishop would dissent from such a judgment," but Hunthausen said in a 9/11/85 letter to the pro-nuncio that he could begin to understand why the Vatican might want to consider appointing an auxiliary bishop in light of its holding that viewpoint.

Section 4, *The Decisions After the Visitation*, begins with a reference to an October 9-10,

1985 meeting at the apostolic nunciature, at which the visitation findings were discussed with Hunthausen again. (Apart from Hunthausen, the chronology does not identify the meeting participants.) Of concern to the Holy See was Hunthausen's "interpretation of the importance of these matters and the inadequacy of his response..." Laghi says Hunthausen "did not dispute the facts" revealed by the Visitation.

While considering Hunthausen's request for an auxiliary bishop, the Holy See examined options that would enable the auxiliary bishop to assist Hunthausen in the five "problem areas." Paragraph c. of this section cites Canon 403.2 of the Code of Canon Law, which would enable the Holy See to grant special faculties. However, the chronology states, Hunthausen agreed in a 12/2/85 letter to a compromise whereby he himself would grant the faculties to the auxiliary bishop. For more than six months after Bishop Wuerl's arrival, the agreed-faculties were not given. Laghi allows, "This could be attributed to a misunderstanding or misinterpretation on [Hunthausen's] part." After clarification from Rome, Hunthausen granted the faculties and went public with a statement that the act was "mandated by Rome." In closing, Laghi makes clear that the Vatican is displeased with Hunthausen for "portraying this whole process as a one-sided affair."

7.2.2 Conflict Functionality of the 10.24.86 Vatican Chronology

The Vatican chronology is an attempt to make the Vatican's case with the public, with the American bishops being, apparently, the primary intended audience. Unlike in his letter reporting on the visitation findings, Laghi here does not write in his own name or identify an intended readership. Instead, he constructs this text to read as an objective chronicle of events. The overall thrust of the document is to explain and justify the Vatican's actions (from the beginning to the present) and to simultaneously undermine Hunthausen's position. It is a surprisingly open -- and contentious – expression of the Vatican's unhappiness with one of its own bishops. Here the Vatican shows a willingness to abandon the polite language of episcopal graciousness when it deems necessary.

Laghi's narrative and organizational structure depicts the Vatican interventions as reasonable and carefully managed (*persuasive argumentation; legitimize use of power*). His four sections offer a rationale for Vatican action at each stage of the affair, with one step logically following another. The repeated pattern in the chronology is one of the Vatican discerning a problem (which has arisen on the Seattle side), assessing it and responding to it. Thus, the Vatican received complaints about conditions in Seattle (problem), discussed these with Hunthausen (assessment), and sought his assistance in improving the conditions (response). The complaints continued and Hunthausen's own documented responses were worrisome to the Vatican (problem), discussions with other bishops suggested a need to "clear the air" (assessment), and the Vatican decided -- here reportedly at the suggestion of other bishops – to conduct a visitation (response). The Vatican foresaw a challenge in maintaining intraecclesial harmony and Hunthausen's good name (problem), "consequently, it was determined [assessment] that publicity would be kept to a minimum…" (response). The visitation showed Hunthausen was "lacking the firmness necessary to govern the archdiocese" (problem), so the Vatican discussed with Hunthausen the possibility of appointing a bishop with special powers to Seattle (assessment), whereupon Wuerl was appointed (response). When Hunthausen finally gave to Wuerl the special faculties, he claimed he was forced to do so by Rome (problem), an act, together with its ensuing publicity, that has been deemed "regretful" (assessment) by Rome. Therefore, the Vatican has authorized production and release of this chronology (response). The repetition of this pattern leaves one with an impression of the Holy See as a responsible adult managing an inattentive or willful young charge. It is surely no coincidence that the Holy See applies to Hunthausen just the sort of disciplinary limit setting that he has, in the Vatican's view, failed to implement in his local Church.

What is most remarkable in the chronology is the abandonment of the policy of *courtesy*. My own reading of the document finds twelve assertions within the document that can be characterized as *face threatening* for Hunthausen. I present these in the list that follows.

1. Complaints about pastoral practice in the Seattle Archdiocese have been a concern to the Vatican for a long time (since 1978). The volume of such complaints has been "high," and they have come from a cross-section of the archdiocese (priests, religious and laypeople). Rome became concerned about this situation in light of its own responsibility for "the well-being of the Universal Church..." (par. 1.a.)
2. Hunthausen himself agreed there were "abuses." (par. 1.b.)
3. Complaints continued despite the fact that the matters had been brought to Hunthausen's attention. (par. 1.c.)
4. The "documented responses" of Hunthausen were themselves of concern to Rome. (par. 1.c.)
5. "Other bishops" suggested the need for a visitation of Seattle.
6. Key euphemisms are dropped in the chronology. Thus, Laghi calls the visitation an "investigation" (par. 3.b.) and the "areas of concern" are identified here as "problems" (par. 3.b.).
7. "The Holy See considered [Hunthausen] lacking the firmness necessary to govern the archdiocese" (par. 3.c.).
8. Hunthausen's "interpretation of the importance" of the visitation findings "and the inadequacy of his response" were of concern to the Vatican. (par. 4.a.).
9. Even more drastic power-sharing arrangements in Seattle had been considered, including the appointment of an auxiliary with full power and the appointment of an administrator. (par. 4.b.)
10. Hunthausen failed to give Wuerl the faculties in a timely manner after agreeing to do so. (par. 4.d.)
11. Hunthausen mischaracterized the granting of faculties as having been "mandated by Rome." (par. 4.e.)
12. Hunthausen's public announcement of the faculties came as an unwelcome "surprise" to Rome, one that misrepresented the matter of faculties as a "one-sided affair." (par. 4.e.).

These breaches in the language of politeness send a clear signal that the Holy See has lost patience and is frustrated with Hunthausen (*revealing the conflict instead of hiding it*). Here Laghi (*contentiously*) lays blame for Hunthausen's troubles right at his own doorstep: "the inadequacy of his response" to problems which had been pointed out to him – since 1978 -- was a decisive factor leading to the Vatican's actions.

Laghi identifies two recent sources of the Holy See's irritation with Hunthausen: his "surprise announcement" making the news of Wuerl's faculties public (breach of *secrecy*), and his declaration that the faculties were "mandated by Rome." Laghi justifies the Vatican preference for silence in the affair generally by calling them expressions of concern for the good of the Church (*associate one's efforts with the best interest of the Church*) and Hunthausen's reputation (*deference to the order and mindset of the Church; courtesy; fraternity*). (As for the Vatican's refusal to supply Hunthausen with a copy of Archbishop Hickey's visitation report, Laghi attributes this to promises of confidentiality which had been made to visitation interviewees.) In the question of Rome's mandating the giving of faculties, Laghi shows a willingness to engage Hunthausen directly by contesting his interpretation of events: "In fact, a more precise description would have been that this was the agreement reached between Archbishop Hunthausen and the Holy See after much discussion and effort to support him." This is an intriguing and potentially revealing point of contention. Simply put, Laghi says Hunthausen was not forced to give over the faculties: this was something he agreed to (*legitimize use of power*). But Hunthausen's own testimony over time consistently attests to his resistance to give the faculties. It is hard to imagine that Laghi experienced Hunthausen's "agreement" to surrendering these powers as something Hunthausen entered into willingly. So the question is: Did Laghi hear in Hunthausen's agreement only what he wanted to hear; or did Hunthausen so desire to present himself as cooperative that he gave the impression that he freely agreed to surrendering the powers; or was some other kind of failure to communicate at hand?

Regardless of what had been the case, with the release of this document the Vatican shows its readiness to criticize Hunthausen publicly, to test his base of support and look for support of its own in an open forum. Distribution of the document *escalates* the conflict.

E. Intervening Developments (October-November 1986)

Once the chronology was released, its highly critical tone and content was not lost on outside observers. The 10.28.86 *New York Times* noted that the chronology "was studded with references that could embarrass the Archbishop, something regarded as uncommon in a document about a functioning archbishop." A 10.31.86 article in the *National Catholic Reporter* carried the title, "Laghi's perspective seen as blaming Hunthausen." The article observed that the chronology: placed the onus for the entire affair on Hunthausen; challenged Hunthausen's version of the special faculties discussion; said that other U.S. bishops had recommended the visitation; mentioned complaints received from within the archdiocese; and portrayed Hunthausen as a weak leader, unable to govern the archdiocese effectively. The same issue of the NCR offered editor Tom Fox's comment that, through its release of the chronology, "the Vatican played hardball again."

Attention in the press quickly turned to how the matter would be addressed at the forthcoming meeting of the National Conference of Catholic Bishops, November 10-13 in Washington, D.C. (See the 10.30.86 *New York Times*, the 11.7.86 *National Catholic Reporter* and the 11.9.86 *National Catholic Register.*). On November 6, the bishops released their agenda (cf. *The Progress*, 11.6.86) for the meeting: the Hunthausen case was scheduled for discussion in a closed-door session on November 11.

Hunthausen's first public response to the Vatican chronology was measured. In a statement released on 10.27.86, Hunthausen wrote that the chronology, "prepared by Archbishop Pio Laghi… and released at the direction of the Holy See, is an attempt to condense into three-and-one-half pages of print an extremely complex network of events, meetings, conversations and exchanges of correspondence which took place over a period of several years."

> […] In my judgment, a fair description of just the context in which all these events took place, let alone of the underlying issues themselves, would require considerably more space than that given. And it goes without saying that a much longer and more detailed document would be required in order to report adequately and faithfully the precise unfolding of each individual development in all its complexity. I prefer not to do this—at least not at the present time or in this particular forum.
>
> For the present, I will simply let it suffice to say that my understanding of a number of statements, interpretations and conclusions that are set forth in Archbishop Laghi's "Chronology" differs significantly from his.
>
> My respect for Archbishop Laghi and for the office he holds, as well as my personal loyalty to our Holy Father, prompt me at this time to reserve the making of more specific comments and judgments to other more appropriate forums. One of those forums may be the Executive Session of the forthcoming meeting of the National Conference of Catholic Bishops, where I have been given an indication that I will have an opportunity to speak.

Hunthausen closed his statement with an "earnest plea." "[L]et us help break the cycle of tension that now exists by making every sincere effort in word and action to rise above any contentious spirit, and let us do all we can to preserve the bond of unity that is ours as faithful members of the church, committed always to witnessing to the truth in love."

By this time, a number of themes had emerged repeatedly in the local and national media discussion of the case. Examples of these themes appear in the 10.30.86 *New York Times*, which observed: "Hunthausen has become a favorite of liberal church activists in the United States, who say the church in Rome is out of touch with most American Catholics in matters of birth control, homosexuality and other social issues." (The Hunthausen case was often linked spoken of in conjunction with the Vatican's August, 1986 revocation of Fr. Charles Curran's license to teach theology, another controversy that received considerable attention as an example of a Vatican crackdown on the U.S. church.) But, the same article went on to note, "Hunthausen also has his detractors. Thrust into the limelight in 1982 when he withheld part of his income taxes to protest the arms race, Archbishop Hunthausen has been criticized for both his political and religious stances… Conservative Catholics in Seattle say his interpretation of liturgy and the Gospel are out of line. They criticize him for allowing a homosexual group to sponsor mass at St. James Cathedral." Other writers, especially in Catholic publications, focused on ecclesiological questions of relationship: between the Church Universal (symbolized in Rome's centrality) and the church in the U.S., and between the bishop of Rome and the American bishops. How was Church unity being affected by the case? How autonomously could the American episcopal conference function in cases where it found itself at odds with Rome? Finally, some writers (cf. *The New York Times*, 11.10.86; but also note this same view was expressed by Hunthausen's Vicar General, Michael G. Ryan as early as 1985, cf. *The Progress*, 12.5.85) raised the question of why Hunthausen and Seattle were being singled out. Such pastoral problems could be located in any number of other American dioceses. (Briggs 1992 offers a detailed presentation, in narrative form, of the speculations and arguments that permeated contemporary American discussions of the case.)

Beyond these specific perspectives, it is safe to say that in the fall of 1986 many shared the view of Archbishop Hurley of Anchorage, who said, "It is no longer a question of Archbishop Hunthausen of Seattle. It's a question of the state of the church."

As a means of presenting his case to his fellow American bishops, Hunthausen prepared two texts in anticipation of the November 10-13 gathering. One text was a detailed response (see document 5, below) to points raised by the Vatican chronology. The other was an address to the bishops that Hunthausen intended to deliver orally (document 6, below). The bishops would already have in their possession a copy of the Vatican chronology, which had been distributed earlier.

The conference itself opened on the morning of November 10 with an address by the outgoing NCCB President, Bishop James Malone of Youngstown, Ohio. Malone was finishing his three-year term as conference president. Malone offered an assessment of the current state of the Church in the United States, which called attention to the vitality of parish life and to vitality within the episcopal conference itself (the latter demonstrated by collegiality within the conference and a willingness to offer critiques of American culture). Malone also highlighted certain challenges facing the American Church, specifically: how to manage questions concerning the relationship between the local and universal Church, the role of women in the Church, the celebration of the Eucharist in the face of a declining number of priests and the relationship between the teaching office of bishops and that of theologians. Malone made reference to the Hunthausen case in the context of his remarks about the relationship between the Church universal and Church local. He spoke of "a growing and dangerous disaffection of elements of the church in the United States from the Holy See."

> Some people feel that the local church needs more freedom. Others believe that more control is in order. Some feel that appeals to authority are being exercised too readily. Others applaud what they perceive to be a return to needed central control. Wherever you stand, this division presents the church in the United States with a very serious question: How will we move to address this developing estrangement, to strengthen the cognitive and affective bond between the church here and the Holy See? We do not exist alone. We cannot exist alone. We are a communio. We are a church.
>
> We all know that in recent weeks the situation in the Archdiocese of Seattle has exemplified these concerns. Tomorrow we shall take up this matter in our executive session. Let me be very clear about the reasons for doing so.
>
> We recognize that our conference of bishops has no competence to interject itself into the special relationship between the Holy Father and a local bishop. Nor have we any intention of engaging in a retrospective review of events which have already occurred and which have been placed on the public record.
>
> The purpose therefore of addressing this matter in our executive session is simply this: to offer fraternal support to Archbishop Hunthausen and Bishop Wuerl in their future efforts to minister to the church in Seattle. We look to this as a constructive expression of the collegial spirit which unites us with one another and with the Holy Father."

Following Malone's address, the Apostolic Pro-Nuncio spoke to the body, presenting first a few remarks of his own and then reading a message of Pope John Paul II to the bishops. In his own remarks Archbishop Laghi drew attention to the significant role he himself had played in the naming of a many (almost one-third) of the bishops present.

> As I look out over this assembly, permit me to express satisfaction at the presence of so many who have been appointed to the hierarchy during my tenure as papal representative. We have not yet reached the "magic number" of 100, but we are not yet far from it."

Laghi then proceeded to read the Pope's message, which did not address the Hunthausen case specifically, but did speak to issues directly pertinent to it. Calling himself, "the first servant of the church's unity and universality," the Pope offered some reflections on the Petrine ministry and then noted three instances in which he was currently engaged in trying to serve and collaborate with the U.S. bishops.

> The very mystery of the church impels us to recognize that the one, holy, Catholic and apostolic church is present in each particular church throughout the world. And since the successor of Peter has been constituted for the whole church as pastor and as vicar of Christ (*Lumen Gentium*, 22), all the particular churches – precisely because they are Catholic, precisely because they embody in themselves the mystery of the universal church – are called to live in communion with him.
>
> Our own relationship of ecclesial communion – *collegialitas effectiva et affectiva* – is discovered in the same mystery of the church. It is precisely because you are pastors of particular churches in which there subsists the fullness of the universal church that you are, and must always be, in full communion with the successor of Peter. To recognize your ministry as "vicars and delegates of Christ" for your particular churches (Lumen Gentium, 27) is to understand all the more clearly the ministry of the chair of Peter, which "presides over the whole assembly of charity, protects legitimate variety and at the same time sees to it that differences do not hinder unity but rather contribute to it" (*Lumen Gentium*, 13).
>
> To promote the universality of the church, to protect her legitimate variety, to guarantee her Catholic unity, to confirm the bishops in their apostolic faith and ministry, to preside in love – all this is what he successor of Peter is called by Christ to do. This Petrine service by the will of Christ is directed to the good of the universal church and all the ecclesial communities that compose her.
>
> For that reason I endeavor to be of service to all the bishops of the church, so that together as one college, each of us having a different role, we can all serve the Church of Christ in the distinctive ministry assigned to us as bishops.

The specific ways named by the Pope to exemplify his recent – and forthcoming – efforts to be of service to the American bishops were the apostolic visitation of American seminaries he had commissioned, his establishment of the Pontifical Commission for Religious Life, and his plan to make a pastoral visit to the United States, September 10-18, 1987.

Having heard these opening speeches (see *Origins*, 10.20.86 for the full text of each), the bishops then moved on to other business in their afternoon session of September 10 and their morning session of September 11. The most important business undertaken during this time was the election of new officers of the bishops' conference. (Archbishop John May of St. Louis was elected the new President and Archbishop Daniel Pilarczyk of Cincinnati was elected Vice President. Both were described as Church "moderates" in most press accounts.)

On the afternoon of September 11, the bishops began a closed executive session to discuss the Hunthausen case. A copy of Hunthausen's response to the Vatican chronology and his address to the bishops was provided to each bishop at the beginning of the session, along with an initial draft of a statement by Bishop Malone (see discussion of document 7, below). Malone opened the session with a prayer. The bishops were then given twenty minutes to read the three documents.

E.e. Conflict Functionality of the Intervening Developments (October-November 1986)

Between the distribution of the Vatican chronology and Hunthausen's detailed response to it two weeks later at the NCCB meeting, we see the center party press the critical third party (the NCCB) while Hunthausen offers a first response and prepares to make an all-out defense of his position.

Despite the highly critical tone and content of Laghi's chronology, Hunthausen's initial response is measured and polite (*courtesy; deference to the order and mindset of the Church*). Hunthausen professes respect for Laghi and his office and personal loyalty toward the Holy Father. He characterizes his conflict with Laghi as a matter of differing understandings. Rather than attack individual points in the chronology, Hunthausen suggests (*persuasive argumentation*) that Laghi has oversimplified a highly "complex" matter. Hunthausen does not leave it at that but indicates a specific time when he will answer Laghi's assertions, most probably at the forthcoming NCCB meeting. It is not hard to find reasons for why Hunthausen might choose not to fire back immediately with a contentious response to the chronology. For one, many news media commentators and Church members were already voicing ample criticisms of Rome, lessening the need for him to make certain arguments himself. For another, by showing restraint and once again declaring his loyalty, Hunthausen protects his own appearance as a faithful and non-threatening Church leader. Moreover, the critical audience to persuade at this time is the bishops' conference: Hunthausen would have reason to presume they would prefer to hear from him directly and in private.

Once the NCCB meeting starts, Conference President Malone makes clear his (the conference leadership's) desire to confront challenges facing the American Church, not the least of which is a "growing and dangerous disaffection of elements of the church in the United States from the Holy See." But just as clear is Malone's intention not to let the discussion get out of hand. Malone states unequivocally that the NCCB has "no competence to interject itself" between Hunthausen and the Holy Father, and it will not engage in a review of "events which have already occurred and which have been placed on the public record." (From the viewpoint of this study, his reference to the contents of the public record is ironic. That may be the most problematic issue of all: what was and was not on the public record.) The purpose of the discussion of the case *would be*, according to Malone, to "offer fraternal support to Archbishop Hunthausen and Bishop Wuerl in their future efforts to minister to the church in Seattle" (*act fraternally; associate oneself with the best interest of the Church*). As we will see (section F., Intervening Developments), a number of *procedural controls* govern the debate of the Hunthausen case, but in his speech Malone already points to one type of restriction – the format of the meeting itself. The consideration of the Hunthausen case will take place in "executive session." Reese (1992, 174-175) explains that, while most of the NCCB's work takes place in the open (i.e., in the presence of reporters), the bishops "meet in executive session without the press at least once every time they gather… By making these sessions a regular event, the bishops can meet to discuss issues and problems privately without signalling a major crisis." Reese adds, "Topics that tend to be treated in executive session are sensitive or controversial." By assigning discussion of the Hunthausen case to the executive session of the gathering, the NCCB leadership ensures the privacy (*secrecy*) of the discussion, keeping infighting out of public view.

The center party also shows a decided interest in controlling the NCCB debate. Laghi, in a rare public reference to his own political power in the Church, reminds the assembled bishops that he has played a role in the appointment (power of *remuneration*) of almost one-third of the men in the room. He then reads Pope John Paul II's message to the conference, which tells the bishops that they are, "and must always be, in full communion with the successor of Peter." In and of itself, the Pope's message – a standard feature of NCCB meetings – amounts to a *symbolic intervention* of the center party into the territory of the periphery (*territorial control*). But the Pope makes this still more explicit with repeated assertions of papal primacy. Because the Pope "has been constituted for the whole church as pastor and as vicar of Christ… all the particular churches… are called to live in communion with him." Though the Pope makes no specific reference to the Hunthausen case, his ecclesiological reflection (*God talk*) leaves no room for doubting where the bishops' accountability lies. Ecclesiastical communion requires all to come to Rome: there is no discussion of the other way around.

The Pope presents his role as one of divinely sanctioned service – service offered in effective and affective collegiality (*fraternity*) for the "good of the universal church" (*associate self with the best interest of the Church*). It is hard to ignore, however, that the concrete examples of his own service that the Pope identifies -- the apostolic visitation of American seminaries (a process that Bishop Wuerl played a key role in), the establishment of the commission for religious life, and the Pope's imminent pastoral visit to the U.S (in September of 1987: this will become an increasingly important question as the conflict progresses) -- are all forms of *surveillance*. The term surveillance has a sinister ring to it, but it effectively highlights the fact that all of these activities are means by which the Pope can monitor local conditions (monitoring and being of service are not, of course, mutually exclusive). Notably, the Pope quotes the statement of *Lumen Gentium* about the responsibility of the Petrine ministry to protect "legitimate variety" in the Church. This seems to make room for pluralism in the Church, but the power to determine what is legitimate and what is not remains with Rome.

7.3 Document Number: 5
Hunthausen's Detailed Response to the Vatican Chronology (11.11.86)
Source: *The Progress*, 11/13/86, pp. 15-16; *Origins*, 11/20/86, pp. 406-408

7.3.1 Summary of Contents:
This statement, together with the written text of Hunthausen's 11.11.86 address to the NCCB

(see document 6, below), provides the "more specific comments and judgments" regarding recent events that Hunthausen promised in his 10.27.86 press statement. Though the response to the chronology and the address work together, they differ in their focus. Whereas this document takes its lead from the contents of the chronology, the address considers the history of the conflict and its central issues more generally.

Hunthausen's response to the Vatican chronology contains introductory remarks, four numbered sections, and some brief concluding remarks. The numbered sections group various difficulties Hunthausen has with the Vatican chronology under headings that tell us what, specifically, Hunthausen objects to in that document. The headings of the numbered sections are self-explanatory: "1) The Chronology contains some misleading things;" "2) The Chronology contained some new learnings;" "3) The Chronology contained some disappointing things;" "4) The Chronology also contains some very real inaccuracies."

Hunthausen's *introductory remarks* pick up where he left off in his earlier press statement, arguing that the Vatican chronology failed to do justice to the complexity of the present circumstances. He also asserts that his own recollection of prior transactions differs from that presented in the chronology. In Hunthausen's opinion, the Vatican chronology tried to do either too much or too little: it either tried to say too much in too little space or failed to address some of the "deep, underlying problems which are at stake."

Section one provides three examples of how the chronology is "misleading." Hunthausen observes that if "substantial complaints" were made about his leadership of the archdiocese, he himself was "never told who made them or who substantiated them and on what basis." Hunthausen also asks why, if his own responses to Vatican inquiries were a strike against him (even as far back as 1978), he was never informed of this at the time. Another misleading point for Hunthausen is the Vatican suggestion that Hunthausen erred by describing the handing-over of special faculties as an act "mandated by Rome." Hunthausen challenges this point on two grounds. He says first that he did not use the phrase "mandated by Rome," and that, second, even if he had it would have been, essentially, an accurate description of the interaction.

Section two focuses on ways that the chronology came as a revelation to Hunthausen. Prior to its release, he writes, he was unaware that Rome's dissatisfaction with Seattle's priestly formation program centered on its admissions practices. Nor did he know of Rome's specific concerns about the Archdiocesan Continuing Education program for priests before he encountered this item in the Vatican chronology. Hunthausen writes that he wishes he had had this information sooner. In this section Hunthausen also learned for the first time that the Holy See judged him to lack the "necessary firmness" to run the Archdiocese.

Section three identifies "disappointing things" Hunthausen discovered in the Vatican chronology. Among these are the intimations that Hunthausen did not carry out his promise to award the special faculties to Wuerl, and that he had acted intransigently and in bad faith. Hunthausen argues that such was not the case, that he had made it clear to the Vatican that he would be willing to resign his office, or to yield certain powers to Wuerl (without giving Wuerl final authority in these areas), but that he would not agree to a solution that would leaving him pretending to have powers he no longer possessed. Hunthausen emphasizes that he made his position on these matters quite clear to the Vatican all along. His decision to stay on as Archbishop, he writes, was influenced by the advice of colleagues, who persuaded him it would be the best choice for the local Church.

Section four highlights two inaccuracies Hunthausen perceives in the Vatican chronology. Hunthausen challenges the Vatican statement that he *insisted* on a public announcement of the Apostolic Visitation. He offers the alternate characterization that he expressed to the Holy See his "earnest desire" that, if a Visitation were necessary, it be conducted in a spirit that was "open and positive and constructive." A second inaccuracy Hunthausen identifies is the notion that his public announcement of Wuerl's special faculties *surprised* the Vatican. This could not have been the case, Hunthausen writes, because "I repeatedly made the point in my conversations and exchanges with Archbishop Laghi... that, in the then unlikely event that I would agree to accept the special faculties arrangement... I would have no choice but to make this matter known to all my priests and close collaborators..." Hunthausen is at pains throughout this section to show that secrecy is counterproductive for the Church and is not in keeping with the spirit of the Second Vatican Council. He raises the question, too, of how on a practical level it could be expected to work. "I also find it difficult to understand how anyone could ever have believed that keeping the Special Faculties a secret could possibly have worked in the first place. If nothing else, the early history of the Visitation to which I have just referred should have clearly indicated otherwise."

Hunthausen *concludes* the statement with a request for a "review of all these matters" by the NCCB. He expresses his intention to offer additional perspective in his oral remarks before the group and thanks the bishops for their attention.

7.3.2 Conflict Functionality of Hunthausen's 11.11.86 Response to the Vatican Chronology

Hunthausen's primary aims with this text appear to be to refute specific Vatican attacks (*persuasive argumentation*), assert his own personal integrity (*personal identity*) and call on his fellow American bishops to identify with and support his cause (*recruit allies*). With the release of its chronology, the Vatican has begun an open argument. Here Hunthausen takes up the challenge and engages the argument.

The claims in the Vatican chronology – that Hunthausen had not corrected the problems in his archdiocese, that he had failed to hand over faculties after agreeing to, that he had broken with the Vatican preference for secrecy, etc. -- put Hunthausen on the defensive. Most of Hunthausen's energy here goes to responding to those claims, but he opens up some new lines of argument as well.

Hunthausen makes clear that he is appealing here first and foremost to the American bishops. Not only does he address them directly, but he also identifies with them and makes a point of mentioning Archbishop Laghi in only the most respectful (*courteous*) terms ("...it frankly embarrasses me to be engaging in this form of exchange of information. I have the greatest respect and admiration for Archbishop Laghi and appreciate his time and efforts to resolve this matter.") Hunthausen is fully aware that individually and collectively the bishops are concerned not to place themselves in a precarious position by seeming to oppose the Holy See (*deference to the order and mindset of the Church*). Hence, Hunthausen tells the bishops that he did not make a point-by-point response to the chronology earlier because that "would only have escalated an already tense situation" and caused "further confusion for our people" (*minimize the appearance of conflict*).

Hunthausen is at pains to avoid presenting this is a personal attack on Laghi ("the matters which I will set forth herein are in no sense an attack on his person or his integrity"). In order to excuse Laghi, Hunthausen points to the limits of the human mind: "That our recollections and interpretations differ in some important respects should not be so surprising when one considers that we are both attempting to present in capsule form a very long and complicated series of events." Hunthausen, at the same time, professes himself to be just as concerned about *saving face* for the Holy See.

> From the very outset of these events, which now go back some three-and-one-half years, I have been concerned about adverse publicity for the Holy See. I expressed this concern in my earliest correspondence and in all my conversations with the Holy See, with Cardinal Ratzinger, Archbishop Laghi, Archbishop Hickey, and even with the Holy Father himself. It was always my deepest desire and my strongly expressed wish that, whatever steps might be taken to address certain concerns in Seattle, that they be taken in a way that would strengthen and cement our relationship with the Holy See, and not in any sense detract from it.

Ironically, Hunthausen's concern to avoid negative publicity for Rome caused him to urge Laghi not to publish the Vatican chronology (*secrecy*). Hunthausen felt the chronology would "raise more questions than it could possibly hope to answer." He also feared that it "would generate a whole new round of publicity in a setting in which accusations and counter-accusations rather than the voices of reason would dominate and that, in the minds of many, it would ultimately reflect unfavorably on the Holy See…" Considering Hunthausen's own history of practicing and advocating openness (often against Rome's wishes), and considering, too, the strong case he makes against the use of secrecy in this text (secrecy smacks of the "pre-Vatican II Church") and in his address to the bishops (document 6, below), Hunthausen's remark here are a further sign of his ambivalence about this issue. In any case, one cannot categorically associate Hunthausen with openness and the Holy See with secrecy. (In the aftermath of the NCCB meeting, at least one commentator, a Hunthausen critic, pointed out that Hunthausen seemed comfortable with the bishops' decision to discuss his case in a closed session. Nonetheless, Hunthausen handed over his own texts to the press immediately thereafter.)

Before leaving the secrecy-openness issue, one further observation is in order. It is that Hunthausen follows his reference to "the Holy See" in the paragraph quoted above with a specific list of his conversational partners: Ratzinger, Laghi, Hickey and the Holy Father. This contrasts with the typically unspecified references to the Holy See that we have seen throughout the case. Though the list is not especially revealing in and of itself, it is a sign of the discussion forum – he is addressing bishops -- and of Hunthausen's readiness to get down to details (within the limits of *politeness*). Significant, too, is Hunthausen's reference to "a letter from Cardinal Ratzinger." This is almost certainly a reference to the 9.30.85 letter wherein Ratzinger shared the visitation findings with Hunthausen. Hunthausen has already shared this letter with his priests (and Wuerl mentioned it in his open letter to the priests). Its existence is now acknowledged in a still wider forum. In the commission report (see document 9, below) one finds further references to the letter, and with the release of the commission report comes release of the Ratzinger text as well. Thus, eventually Hunthausen achieves his original objective of having the letter made public -- and the Vatican itself takes the step to do so.

Tactically, the way Hunthausen proceeds to voice his complaints without getting personal is to heap blame on the chronology itself, and not on the chronology's author (from *ad hominem* to *ad rem*). Essentially this is the same approach Ratzinger and Laghi took in their letters presenting the visitation findings, when they described problems in the archdiocese but refused to directly connect the problems to a particular person (*saving face* for Hunthausen).

In Hunthausen's response to the Vatican chronology (not the *Laghi* chronology), we read: "the Chronology contains misleading things… disappointing things… inaccuracies," and so forth.

A significant portion of Hunthausen's *argumentation* goes to challenging the process used against him. Concerning the visitation, Hunthausen says, "If there were substantial complaints I was never told who made them or who substantiated them and on what basis." Only after the visitation was decided upon, was Hunthausen told "what *some* of those complaints were" (emphasis his). Hunthausen's irritation with the process is further signalled with his choice of a verb in this passage. He does not speak of the decision to *conduct* or *undertake* a visitation, but rather to "mount" a visitation, a word choice that echoes the common expression "to mount an attack." (This usage recurs in Hunthausen's address to the bishops.) Hunthausen maintains that in the period following the visitation, the provision of information to him continued to be inadequate. Thus, certain Vatican criticisms of Seattle were made known to him only through the Vatican chronology itself. Hunthausen also makes explicit his disapproval of the decision to divide power between the archbishop and the auxiliary bishop, and that ultimately he did not feel free to choose other than what the Vatican wanted him to choose. "That I 'agreed' to go along with these wishes is clear, too, although I did not do so with any sense of freedom since the consequences of my not agreeing to do so had been made clear to me on more than one occasion." (Hunthausen was on the receiving end of *coercive power*.) Indeed, in the course of his negotiations with Seattle, Hunthausen's frustration had been such that he had considered resigning his position.

A critical issue for Hunthausen in this presentation is making the case for his own integrity. The possibility of resigning was considered as the alternative to an unacceptable choice. The Vatican wanted Hunthausen to give Wuerl the powers but not to make Wuerl's possession of these powers public (*secrecy*). Hunthausen states here that he could not agree to such an arrangement – that it would amount to posing as the Archbishop of Seattle, pretending to have powers he did not in fact have. Hunthausen: "I made it clear that I would never carry out a public charade by pretending to be something I was not. I am just not constitutionally capable of that." Because Hunthausen believed he had made this stand on principle clear to Laghi, he was, in his own retelling of events, surprised that the Vatican later still had the expectation that he would give Wuerl the faculties. In Hunthausen's view, he had agreed to give Wuerl special responsibilities but not final decision-making power in the key areas. "It would later be suggested," Hunthausen said, "that I might have acted in bad faith. I did not."

Hunthausen also challenges the implication that he violated an earlier agreement by announcing Wuerl's faculties publicly (Laghi called this a "surprise announcement"). "The record will show… that I repeatedly made the point in my conversations and exchanges with Archbishop Laghi at Collegeville this past summer, that, in the then unlikely event that I would agree to accept the special faculties arrangement… I would have no choice but to make this matter known to all my priests and close collaborators since it would be absolutely essential for them to know to whom they were accountable…"

In making the case for the integrity of his own actions (*persuasive argumentation*), Hunthausen places his own personality and view of events in the forefront (*assertion of personal identity*). This makes Hunthausen's text a very different one from the chronology he is responding to, which strives for the appearance of impersonality and objectivity. Though Hunthausen has few options at this point in his exchange with the Holy See, the chosen strategy shows promise (and his own shrewdness?) because his personality is an attractive one (witness the strong loyalty shown to him within the archdiocese) and he already has a reputation for being principled (based on his public stand against nuclear weapons, among other things). In short, Hunthausen says here: I have only done what I thought right, according to my vision of how the Church should be. I am willing to accept the consequences as necessary.

Hunthausen implicitly invites the other bishops to identify with his cause and explicitly welcomes "some sort of review of all these matters" by the NCCB, "should that be the wish of the members." This is a *contentious* statement, which responds directly to the contentiousness of the Vatican chronology.

7.4 Document Number: 6
Hunthausen's 11.11.86 Address to the NCCB
Source: *The Progress*, 11/13/86, pp.11-13; *Origins*, 11/20/86, pp. 401-405

Whereas Hunthausen response to the Vatican chronology limits its consideration to the contents of that particular text, Hunthausen's address to his fellow bishops considers the conflict experience (the visitation and its aftermath) as a whole. The assembled bishops were given the opportunity to read Hunthausen's "address" to them, but he himself did not have the opportunity to read it aloud (which he knew in advance). Instead he made some brief oral remarks to the assembly (see section F., Intervening Developments, below). My analysis here is of the written text he supplied to the bishops.

7.4.1 Summary of Contents:
Introductory and closing remarks frame four main sections that make up the body of the text. Hunthausen's *introductory remarks* begin with an acknowledgement of his primary audience, the assembly of bishops, and of the relationship he has with them. Hunthausen expresses his distress at the thought that he may have brought "anguish" or "division" upon his "brother bishops," something he gladly would have spared them. But the controversial issues of the moment, he points out, "are not just issues that touch the life of the Church in Seattle: they are issues that touch the lives of each of our churches..." Following up on this thought, Hunthausen stresses that the matter at hand does not come down to "some sort of battle of wits between a maverick archbishop and the Holy See…" but that it is "an ecclesial matter with serious theological implications which touch very directly and profoundly on our individual role as bishops and on our corporate responsibility as members of the College of Bishops."

Hunthausen mentions the response to the Vatican chronology he has already released, but says he will not comment further on the chronology in the present context. He then names the "four main areas" he will address:

> 1) The process used in deciding to conduct the Visitation as well as the process followed in carrying it out.
> 2) The five areas of my ministry singled out by the Holy See as areas of serious concern.
> 3) The identification of the important issues which this entire matter has brought to light.
> 4) Some thoughts and suggestions regarding the future.

At one point in his prefatory comments Hunthausen pauses to put all of the recent events in context, reflecting on what the Church might learn from this experience.

> Most of you know that I am not a professional theologian. Many of you know far more about
> these matters than I do and can surely articulate them better. Nonetheless the experience that
> has been mine over these past years can perhaps serve as something of a laboratory for
> viewing, studying, and probing the issues in some way other than the purely theoretical. If that
> be so, then I honestly believe that this sad experience which has been the source of such pain
> and confusion for the Church of Seattle and beyond -- even to the point of causing serious
> scandal for many -- will not have been in vain, but will have been a new moment of life and
> growth.

Most of *section one* of the address presents an indictment of the Vatican's use of secrecy in the visitation process. Hunthausen criticizes the policy of secrecy on the grounds that "secrecy does not work in matters of this sort" and it "*should* not work." Hunthausen says he feels he compromised his own principles by agreeing to secretive methods. He also communicates his dismay that the Vatican use of secrecy put him at a disadvantage in the affair. Hunthausen laments never having received a "Bill of Particulars" -- that is, a formal, detailed summary -- of the Vatican concerns prior to the visitation, nor did he receive a copy of the visitation report Archbishop Hickey filed with the Vatican. In Hunthausen's view, the manner of proceeding, with "unwitnessed, private questionings" and "no opportunity for the subject of the questionings to face his accusers, or hear or to be informed of their allegations, or to defend himself" is not a "just" manner of proceeding. Moreover, "This kind of an approach seriously wounds the community of faith and trust that is the Church."

As final observations in section one, Hunthausen calls the Visitation process "badly flawed from the very start" and notes that "confusion and anger" in the local Church and elsewhere are the result. He also conveys his displeasure with the "punitive" dimensions of a Vatican action that was presented to him initially as "fraternal exchange of views."

Section two addresses the five areas of concern that led to the handing over of special faculties. Hunthausen broaches this topic with the help of "four headings for the purpose of clarity." Under the heading "matters of history" he lists specific problems identified through the Visitation process that have already been resolved. These include: "some confusion... with regard to the use of the so-called Internal Forum solution; the lack of a plan to employ degreed personnel in the Archdiocesan Tribunal; and the practice of one hospital of the Archdiocese permitting sterilization even for contraceptive purposes in some limited cases." According to Hunthausen, none of these problems continues to exist in the Archdiocese, nor have they for some years.

Under the heading "pastoral judgment" Hunthausen discusses criticisms of decisions he made in pastorally complex and sensitive matters. Calling pastoral judgment an "imprecise 'science'... even when carried out prayerfully under the guidance of the Holy Spirit and with every due regard for Church Tradition and Law," Hunthausen argues that mistakes and uncertainty are unavoidable in pastoral care. As examples, Hunthausen cites the conscientious effort he made to decide rightly in the questions of general absolution, the order of first reconciliation-first communion, and the use of the Cathedral church by the group Dignity.

Hunthausen's third category for the purpose of clarification bears the heading "ongoing concerns." In this area Hunthausen admits to having erred "on one or another occasion since coming to Seattle." He mentions two cases in which laicized priests served as lectors and eucharistic ministers in parishes, and another case in which the wife of an unlaicized priest was employed by the Archdiocese. Hunthausen characterizes this last case as an "oversight." In regard to the liturgical role of the laicized priests Hunthausen says that the practice was occurring long before he learned of it, and, in one of the instances, to have stopped it "would have caused *admiratio* of the most severe kind."

Under his fourth heading, "matters I do not understand," Hunthausen shares his perplexity at the negative assessment given to the Archdiocesan priestly formation program -- specifically, its admissions process. He observes that the process was reviewed and approved by the NCCB visitation team. Hunthausen also professes not to understand the criticism of the Archdiocesan program of continuing education for clergy, and he denies that he has tolerated practices of intercommunion.

Section three of Hunthausen's text focuses on "important issues which have been brought to light by the visitation and its processes." Hunthausen identifies three such issues. The first point he makes is that the present controversy is not a matter of "dissent" in the Church, and "I am not a dissenter..." More accurately, he says, what the controversy illuminates is the difficulty that teachers, pastors and servants of the Lord face as they strive to be both loving and truthful in their witness.

The second point Hunthausen makes in this section is that the controversy is also not a matter of "personal obduracy or obstinacy" on his part. Though Hunthausen admits to being "strong-willed," he assures the bishops that he has been "cooperative and obedient" throughout the affair. In a provocative aside, however, he notes that his understanding of the virtue of obedience has never allowed him "simply to acquiesce." "It has, rather," he declares, "prompted me to engage in a process of dialogue, one which, to the best of my ability, I have always carried out in a respectful, docile and faith-filled manner."

Hunthausen's final point in section three acknowledges that adverse publicity around the affair has caused confusion and scandal for many people. Hunthausen says that this fact grieves him, especially because he believes it could have been avoided. In his view, a more open and forthright manner of conducting the visitation would have better respected the people of the local Church, who have "come of age," and "deserve to be treated as adults."

Section four provides Hunthausen's "thoughts and suggestions regarding the future." Here Hunthausen invites the bishops to reflect on three "over-arching" issues. The first issue has to do with the mutual involvement of Church leaders. Hunthausen pursues this issue through two questions he puts to the bishops. The first is "How does a diocesan bishop who is himself the Vicar of Christ in his particular church, carry out his role with the degree of independence which this role implies while at the same time doing so in full union with and under the rightful authority of the Supreme Pontiff?" Hunthausen asserts that "very real practical questions" remain in this area. The second question is, what is the proper role of bishops' conferences in situations such as the present one? Hunthausen argues that the visitation should have been "carried out in close collaboration between the Holy See and this Conference."

The second over-arching issue Hunthausen wants the bishops to reflect on concerns "the role of legitimate diversity" in the Church. Hunthausen wonders what role bishops' conferences might play in establishing the legitimacy and limits of local ecclesial adaptations.

Hunthausen's third encompassing question places a challenge before the bishops. Church leaders, Hunthausen asserts, needs to be as eager to establish just structures inside the Church as they are promote them outside the Church.

Having offered these broad and far-reaching comments, Hunthausen brings his statement to a close with a personal appeal for help from the Conference in addressing the issues identified through the Apostolic Visitation. He calls the present power-sharing arrangement with Bishop Wuerl "unworkable" and voices his conviction that the governance of the Seattle Archdiocese needs to be returned to "normal" as quickly as possible. Hunthausen's final words propose that "the good of the Church is what is at stake here." He expresses his confidence in the ability of the bishops and of the Church itself to weather the difficulties before it.

7.4.2 Conflict Functionality of Hunthausen's 11.11.86 NCCB Address

Hunthausen pursues several strategies at once with this text. First, he *addresses multiple audiences* (the American bishops, the general public via the press, the people of his local Church, and the Holy See). Each of these audiences can help his case in a distinct way. Second, picking up where he left off in his response to the Vatican chronology, he challenges the validity of the overall visitation process and its conclusions (*persuasive argumentation*). Third, he recontextualizes the discussion of those issues, framing them within intraecclesial and extraecclesial perspectives that he perceives to be advantageous to his case (these frames are, respectively, the spirit of Vatican II and certain aspects of the American legal justice system). Fourth, he *asserts his own personality*, presenting himself as a man of integrity whose position has been compromised by a process that is not "just" (a highly provocative word choice, which Hunthausen underlines in the copy of the text he distributes). Fifth, Hunthausen raises the possibility that other bishops could be subjected to similar treatment if the present situation is not rectified. Sixth, Hunthausen suggests that the good of the Church as a whole is at stake in the handling of the case and that he himself is acting for the good of the Church (*associate oneself with the best interest of the Church*). Finally, Hunthausen makes an explicit appeal to the NCCB (*recruit allies*) to help Wuerl and Hunthausen address the matter with the Holy See. In the paragraphs that follow, I will succinctly characterize his application of these strategies.

Hunthausen indicates that his fellow American bishops are his primary audience by standing before them, naming them explicitly ("this assembly... this Conference") and supplying them with photocopies of his text. That Hunthausen is also concerned to convey his message to the local (Seattle), national and international press – and the audiences they serve – is indicated by his action of promptly handing over his text to them once the bishops had had a chance to discuss his case. When Hunthausen speaks directly to the bishops, his tone suggests familiarity (*fraternity*). "Most of you probably know me well enough to realize that I did not accept the invitation to make a presentation this afternoon because I personally relish speaking in a forum like this," he writes. But it was necessary to do so, because the issues under consideration are not peculiar to Hunthausen: they are "<u>our</u> issues" (the emphasis is Hunthausen's). Several times it becomes clear that Hunthausen is at pains to show the bishops he is not grandstanding of being unnecessarily resistant to the Vatican's wishes (*show deference to the order and mindset of the Church*). This is not, he declares, "some sort of battle of wits between a maverick Archbishop and the Holy See." Rather, the matter needs forthright discussion in this forum because it touches "very directly and profoundly on our individual role as bishops and on our corporate responsibilities as members of the College of Bishops."

That Hunthausen has a wider audience in mind as well is seen in the nontechnical language he employs. Church jargon and references to doctrines and documents appear rarely. (Admittedly, Hunthausen's style in general – and not just in this context – is to avoid rarefied terms when discussing Church matters. I attribute this to a self-professed lack of interest in the nuances of scholarly theology – "I am not a professional theologian," he says here – and to a fundamental predisposition on his part to speak as inclusively as possible.) Hunthausen focuses several of his arguments on issues sure to get a welcome hearing in an American (and, more-broadly, Western-democratic) setting. Among these are the Vatican's use of *secrecy* and its refusal to let Hunthausen confront the evidence and personal testimony against him. (For a discussion of contrasts between Roman Catholic and American (Roman) Catholic views on authority and governance, see Coriden 1999, O'Brien 1994 and Hellwig 1990.) Addressing as wide an audience as possible offers at least two potential benefits to Hunthausen's cause. One potential benefit is that persons around the country will be sympathetic to his position and pressure their own bishops to support him and challenge the Vatican. A second possible benefit is that outcry of any kind (even outcry that carries criticisms against Hunthausen) will work in Hunthausen's favor, simply by perpetuating a controversy that Rome has reason to want quieted as quickly as possible, in light of the Pope's approaching visit to the U.S., now just ten months away.

Though Hunthausen does not expressly address the Holy See with this text does not mean that he is not speaking to that audience. On the contrary, Hunthausen was fully aware that Archbishop Laghi would be present at the gathering and would read these same texts. More to the point, Hunthausen knows that ultimately only the Vatican has the power to change the situation as he wishes. Thus, near the end of his presentation we hear Hunthausen say: "For the good of the Church in Seattle and beyond, I am absolutely convinced that the matter of the governance of the Church of Seattle needs to be returned to normal as soon as humanly possible. I would even say *at once*." Here Hunthausen speaks most directly to the center, the party with the ultimate decision making power.

Hunthausen's challenge to the validity of the visitation process and its findings involves a series of assertions. He begins with an attack on the policy of *secrecy*. Though he allows that "in some extraordinary circumstances secrecy might be warranted, the presumption should nevertheless be against it because open disclosure and candor are far more consistent with respect for persons in a mature church." As negative developments emerging from the Vatican's practice of secrecy, Hunthausen cites: the absence of dialogue about whether a visitation was needed in the first place; the Vatican's failure to provide a "Bill of Particulars" in anticipation of the visitation; and "most devastating" of all, Rome's refusal to allow Hunthausen to see "the formal Visitation report including the testimony against [Hunthausen] and the appraisal made by Archbishop Hickey." For Hunthausen, "such unwitnessed, private questionings with no opportunity for the subject of the questionings to face his accusers, or hear or to be informed of their allegations, or to defend himself are not a just manner of proceeding. This kind of an approach seriously wounds the community of faith and trust that is the Church." By using the image of a "*shroud* of secrecy" (emphasis mine), Hunthausen suggests that the policy of secrecy is not merely unjust, it is deathly.

Two frames of reference (*persuasive argumentation*) are operative in Hunthausen's critique of the way the visitation was carried out. The first is an intraecclesial frame. In Hunthausen's view, the conduct of the visitation "seems extraordinarily inadequate given the kind of open Church we have become since the Second Vatican Council" (*ecclesiological God talk*). (Hunthausen invokes this same reference frame in section IV, where he discusses the relationship of local bishop to pope.) The second is an extraecclesial frame (*openness to the world*). Hunthausen grounds a number of his critiques of the visitation process in principles associated with the American legal justice system. (It is notable that he invokes these principles – and not those of the Church's own system of Canon Law -- as his reference frame.) Hunthausen sees the aforementioned proceeds as having, despite Vatican denials, the nature of a "trial" (employment of *legal power*) But to his dismay, "the rights of all concerned" have not been guaranteed. He himself has been denied the opportunity to know the charges against him, to face his accusers, and to hear the findings from his own trial. Only the nature of the punishment has been made clear to him. By making his arguments with reference to these two contexts of understanding (Vatican II and the American legal justice system), Hunthausen appeals to those who value those frames of understanding. Presumably, the American bishops would have some appreciation for both reference frames.

Hunthausen's challenge to the validity of the visitation process and its findings continues with a description of his view of the visitation findings themselves (section II). In short, Hunthausen claims that he has already addressed a number of the Vatican's concerns (subsection 1) and he is in the process of addressing others (subsection 3). Some problems are difficult matters of pastoral judgment (subsection 2), where the solution is not obvious and where charity to all those affected by the decisions must be carefully considered. Certain other matters Hunthausen professes not to understand (subsection 4). Taken together, the separate subsections of section II show Hunthausen justifying his own position by arguing that he has acted in good faith and he has acted to resolve problems known to him. Where he has failed, it has been due to the imprecise nature of pastoral judgment itself. Thus Hunthausen writes: "We all know that matters of pastoral judgment are always open to further understanding and that in such matters we never really get beyond the possibility of making a mistake no matter how hard we try to faithfully discern the Spirit" (*God talk*). This statement is a good example of how Hunthausen defends and advances his own position by employing several strategies at once. Here Hunthausen simultaneously minimizes the significance of his purported failure (characterizing it as a "mistake"), attests to his own conscientious effort and piety (he tried hard to faithfully discern the Spirit), and suggests that one can never comprehend pastoral situations in their fullness (they are "always open to further understanding").

It is remarkable how little Hunthausen concedes (*yields*) with this document. In section II as a whole, which treats the problem areas identified by the Vatican, Hunthausen gives hardly an inch. Not once does Hunthausen admit outright to having failed to carry out his responsibilities. The closest he comes is in his discussion of roles accorded to unlaicized priests within the archdiocese (subsection 3). Hunthausen says, "I believe I have erred in this matter on one or another occasion since coming to Seattle." But even this statement is qualified twice internally ("I believe… on one or another occasion") and is followed by a series of multi-layered qualifying statements:

> My doing so was never a purposeful defiance of Church regulations, however. In one case it involved an oversight with regard to the employment of a wife of an unlaicized priest; in two other cases it involved the well-accepted service as lector and Eucharistic Minister by a laicized priest, a practice that had been going on long before I learned of it and one which, to have discontinued it would have caused *admiratio* of the most severe kind. I am unaware of any cases beyond these.

In short, Hunthausen says that if in fact he did err, his intentions were still good, the number of instances was quite small, and for each instance there were relevant exculpatory factors (one problem was the result of "oversight," two were not obviously problems because they were in keeping with "well-accepted" practice – though presumably not well-accepted by the Vatican? – and one problem predated Hunthausen's arrival and would have created new problems by its discontinuance).

A similar example of Hunthausen's refusal to give ground appears in his discussion of his decision to allow the group Dignity (an organization of homosexual Catholics) to celebrate Mass in St. James Cathedral.

> I have subsequently been informed that it was an ill-conceived judgment. Perhaps it was. I am willing to stand corrected. But my decision does not differ in kind from the decision made by many bishops to allow local Dignity groups to celebrate Mass in or another church on a regular basis. Again, pastoral practice will now need to be looked at carefully in light of the most recent document from the Congregation for the Doctrine of the Faith, but I do not deem it fair to be placed under a judgment, even to the point of being deprived of significant pastoral responsibilities, because of the conclusion contained in a document that was not issued until some three years after my own conscientious, carefully studied judgment was made, a judgment, by the way, which I shared very openly with the Holy See in a timely fashion.

Again, Hunthausen does not make an outright admission of his own culpability. "Perhaps" it was an ill-conceived judgment, he says. And then comes a freestanding declaration (it is not of necessity related to the previous sentence) of his *willingness* to stand corrected – if at some point that should become necessary. And even if Hunthausen did make a poor decision, plenty of other bishops have done the same thing, he is being judged by a standard (expressed in the Congregation's 1986 Instruction) that postdates his action, and, again, his own action was the product of careful, conscientious discernment.

At the same time that Hunthausen refuses to budge on the Vatican's issues, he *opens up a whole set of new issues* (sign of *escalation*) of his own in this document. Some of these new issues he merely touches upon in the course of defending his own actions – as when he points out that certain resolutions to pastoral problems can themselves cause new problems. But others he develops with more extensive *argumentation*, as in his attack on the practice of secrecy in section I. Similarly, in section III, Hunthausen raises the question of how the standard of compassion (and the example of Jesus himself) applies in matters of pastoral leadership in general and in the present case in particular. Then he argues that one should not equate the virtue of obedience with mere acquiescence, and he makes a case for fostering dialogue in the Church and treating Church members as "adults" who share in the "ownership" of the Church. Thereafter, Hunthausen goes on to argue that much adverse publicity could have been avoided (*save face for the Church; associate self with best interest of Church*) if the Vatican had acted with more openness and forthrightness all along the way. (More on this later.) In section IV, Hunthausen raises still more new issues. First, he asks how a diocesan bishop is to go about independently exercising his role as Vicar of Christ in his particular church while remaining "in full union with and under the rightful Authority of the Supreme Pontiff." Then he asks whether the national conference of bishops should not have had some intervening or consultative role in the visitation process, and whether it should not in the future have some role in addressing "the role of legitimate diversity within a Church that is called to be one…" Finally, Hunthausen talks about the need to promote honest, just and loving relationships within the Church and not simply to direct exhortations outwardly, "toward the order of things *outside* the Church" (*openness to the world*).

More striking than any one argument in particular is simply the expansiveness of Hunthausen's argumentation. He *issues challenges on a multitude of fronts at once*. It is almost as though, on the Hunthausen side, no plausible argument is left untried in this forum with the bishops. The text creates an impression of Hunthausen venting accumulated frustration (near the end, Hunthausen says explicitly, "I guess a lot has built up within me during the past three and a half years") – and of his doing so on the occasion of his last stand, his last best chance in a conflict where the odds are against him.

This impression of Hunthausen heroically waging battle relates, too, no doubt, to his own self-presentation (*assertion of personal identity*) here. I have spoken previously of Hunthausen's tendency to stress his own commitment to act in good faith and according to principle. In the present text, his personality stands very much in the forefront. Despite humble professions of what he is not ("a maverick archbishop," a "professional theologian," a "dissenter"), and despite a tendency to describe his pastoral leadership as a matter of "striving" (to be "a teacher, a pastor, and a servant of the Lord and of the Church") rather than accomplishment (at best we can only *strive* to be servants of the Church!), the evidence of the text points demonstrates the combativeness of Hunthausen's personality while challenging Rome's combativeness. There is a decided *boldness* to Hunthausen's refusal to admit to failures of leadership. There is also boldness to his *recurrent association of immediate circumstances with a larger cause*. The conflict is not about specific pastoral problems, Hunthausen suggests, or about winning or losing. It is, rather, about making "the servant attitude of Jesus the most identifying mark of our own lives" (*God talk*), and about the relationship between individual bishops and the Holy Father, and about "the proper role of National Bodies of Bishops." Ultimately, Hunthausen says, it is about "the good of the Church" (*associate self with best interest of the Church*).

At least two advantages come to Hunthausen by claiming transcendent significance for the conflict developments at hand. One is that local and specific questions become minimized. Why should we worry about a few pastoral oversights when the real question is the state of our relationship to Jesus and the good of the Church? A second advantage is that Hunthausen thereby increases his own stature. He is no longer a bishop who is in trouble because he was not strict enough in his diocese. Instead he is an advocate in a great cause – one that is of relevance to all bishops and all Catholics.

Rhetorical flourishes at various points serve to heighten the effect of Hunthausen as crusader. Hunthausen's opening words in the text are a good example. (They are another good example, too, of his tendency to claim transcendent significance for the conflict.)

> Once before I had the privilege of addressing this assembly. It was at the time we came together in our common quest for peace in a nuclear world. Today I come before you again in the quest for peace, but for a different kind of peace: peace for the Archdiocese of Seattle, peace for the Church in this country, peace within this Conference, peace for the Church throughout the world, and my own personal peace with the Holy See.

This is elevated language. Hunthausen's use of parallel structure (signalled by the repeated use of "peace") and hyperbole (the question on the table is "peace for the Church throughout the world") make clear that he is addressing matters of consequence. His employment of the word "quest" (twice) deepens this impression. And with his use of pronouns (you, we, our), Hunthausen indicates his intention to enlist his fellow bishops in this same quest.

Nothing, of course, raises the stature of a protagonist like a good antagonist. In this text the antagonist is always just outside of view. We know from the beginning that whatever, or whoever, Hunthausen is up against is a threat to peace and is a source of "turmoil." In regard to that threat, Hunthausen expresses his own vulnerability in a disarmingly plainspoken way: "I wish it would all go away. How I wish that!" (It is good to keep in mind how different this sort of language use is from what we see in the Vatican communications from Ratzinger and Laghi. They themselves do not take the stage in their texts (*assert personal identity*). Moreover, Hunthausen himself, prior to the bishops' meeting, typically reserved this sort of linguistic self-presentation for communications to the people of his own archdiocese.)

Ironically, one of the ways Hunthausen sets up the protagonist-antagonist contrast early is by saying what sort of conflict this is *not*: "[T]his is not," he writes, "some sort of battle of wits between a maverick archbishop and the Holy See." Here Hunthausen conjures an image that we cannot simply erase from our minds because: (1) once it's there it's there; (2) despite Hunthausen's denial, it rings true to the conflict; and (3) the image of itself is a compelling one, with the lone cowboy figure taking on the diffuse and faceless bureaucratic entity (Hunthausen is not Reagan, but in a way he is!).

The enemy Hunthausen names is a wounding and unjust process (symbolically summed up as "the Visitation"), authorized and carried out ("mounted") by opaque agencies ("the Holy See," "the Apostolic Nunciature," "a Vatican official," "the Roman Curia," "the Congregation for the Doctrine of the Faith"). In this text, and to a lesser extent in Hunthausen's detailed response to the Vatican chronology (document 5), we find that the technique of refusing to name agents of the Holy See serves a strategic function that it did not in earlier documents (from Hunthausen and others). Whereas previously the emphasis seems to have been on maintaining secrecy as an expression of face-saving and of the hierarchy's standard operating procedure – keep the public out of the Church's internal affairs – here the technique serves Hunthausen's attack by taking on another dimension. It is easier to distrust and feel enmity toward one who is unknown, hidden, without a face. Hunthausen has argued strongly against the use of secrecy in this address. By repeatedly invoking the anonymous "descriptors" to name his antagonists, Hunthausen's own transparent humanity is cast in a more favorable light and the humanity of his opponents is called into question.

I have already Hunthausen's invitation to his audience to see this antagonist as a threat to us all: "they are really our issues," he writes in his introductory remarks (emphasis his). On a rhetorical level, we can only be grateful that he is willing to take up this fight on our behalf. A key to the success of this argument is Hunthausen's ability to generate the fear that any bishop, or any Catholic for that matter, could be subject to treatment similar to what he has suffered. (Notably, this fear of secretive and far-reaching Vatican power plays into longstanding historical fears of the papacy among Protestant Americans and more recent fears among those of a more secular viewpoint, who feel threatened by Vatican interventions in political affairs. In that sense, his message here also has the potential to find a receptive audience beyond the confines of the Catholic Church itself.) An example of Hunthausen's suggestion of shared vulnerability (susceptibility to punishment) appears in the discussion of his pastoral outreach to homosexual Catholics in the Archdiocese. "Each of us bishops," Hunthausen observes, is faced with the challenge of addressing such delicate matters. Noting that his own judgment was found lacking (with the loss of "significant pastoral responsibilities" as a consequence), he goes on to suggest that his decision did "not differ in kind from the decision made by many bishops" in similar circumstances (emphasis Hunthausen's). Hunthausen is still more explicit when he writes (in his closing remarks): "But it is not me I am concerned about. I am concerned about the Church. And I guess my realization that each of you shares that same concern just as deeply as I do has given me the courage to say more than I normally would in a situation like this."

Hunthausen does not limit his appeal to an invitation to make psychic identification with his cause. The conclusion of his address expressly formulates a call to action. The situation in Seattle, "as far as Bishop Wuerl's faculties are concerned" is "unworkable," he writes.

> [...] I would hope that this Conference would be willing to afford some positive assistance to address this issue with the Holy See. For the good of the Church in Seattle and beyond, I am absolutely convinced that the matter of the governance of the Church of Seattle needs to be returned to normal as soon as humanly

possible. I would even say *at once*."

Achieving that objective – which raises a question of *definition power*: who decides? -- will mark a significant advance, but by no means the only necessary advance in the great struggle that is already underway. Hunthausen's text closes with a rhetorical intensity that recalls his opening words.

> There are some major questions which will not go away no matter how much we might wish they would. They are questions which will severely test our mettle as a Conference of Bishops. But we have been tested before and we have almost always come through well. Amazingly well. And united, too. I firmly believe that the present moment will be no exception.
>
> A final word: my friends, we need not look upon this as a win / lose situation. I do not feel the need to win so that others will have to lose. Winning or losing is not what this is all about. The good of the Church is what is at stake here. Nothing less. We are all united in our commitment to that goal, and for that reason I have no doubt that we will find a way to address all the questions I have posed and others like them. And I have no doubt, either, that we will do so courageously – in a spirit that is truly and fully Catholic, with all that word implies: a spirit that is at the same time faithful to the Lord and His Gospel, loyal to our Holy Father, and true to the people of God whom we serve and who look to us now, perhaps, more than ever before, for guidance, inspiration, and leadership.

F. Intervening Developments (November 11-12, 1986)
Some time before the bishops' meeting Hunthausen had learned that he would have only a limited amount of time to address the bishops – in any case, not nearly enough to read the entire statement he had prepared. (As it turned out, he spoke for about two minutes, according to the 11.13.86 *Washington Post*.) In the week before the conference, a discussion ensued between Hunthausen and two friend-advisers, Fr. Michael G. Ryan and Archbishop Hurley (Anchorage, Alaska), about how best to use the time Hunthausen had available for oral remarks. Drawing on this input, Hunthausen decided upon a set of select remarks to share with the bishops at the beginning of the closed session on November 11.

This was a valuable opportunity for Hunthausen, since public speaking was one of his strengths. As an orator, Hunthausen possessed a low-key eloquence: he was persuasive in an understated way. In general, Hunthausen came across as a person internally at peace, as one who was nonthreatening and who had integrated his own values.

The *National Catholic Reporter* (11.21.86) account describes Hunthausen as "visibly tense" (cf. also Hurley's description in the 11.20.86 *Progress*) when he stood to address the bishops.

> He talked of his pain and of the hurt the episode was causing the church; he said he was personally embarrassed by the affair. Never did he have any intention of challenging papal authority, he said, adding he implied no ill will on anyone's part and saying it was understandable that differences in perception could occur regarding events which took place over several years.
>
> The first indication of the conference's sentiments followed Hunthausen's brief address. When the Seattle archbishop sat down… applause broke out throughout the chamber, a "sustained applause," according to one bishop.

(NB: Hunthausen's select remarks have not been published. A request to the NCCB also failed to turn up a transcript of the words that were actually spoken to the bishops.)

After Hunthausen spoke other bishops were given the opportunity to speak in turn, with each being allotted three minutes. The format for the discussion had been determined ahead of time (November 8-9) by the 48-member administrative board of the NCCB. The bishops were asked to focus their remarks not on the prior history of the visitation and disciplinary action but rather on the content of a statement draft that Conference President Malone had prepared (and the administrative board had approved) in advance. The statement had been prepared before the bishops had seen Hunthausen's texts. No copy of the draft statement is on the public record, but the (11.21.86) *National Catholic Reporter* revealed that the critical line under discussion in the subsequent debate was the following: "While we are not authorized to judge the facts of the case, it is clear that the process employed by the Holy See was in accord with the law of the church and was just and reasonable." After the bishops came to agreement about the final form of the statement, it would be issued to represent the bishops' collective view of the situation.

The session lasted four hours. Twenty-seven bishops spoke. Hunthausen was frequently given time to respond to questions or comments made by the other bishops (cf. *The New York Times*, 11.13.86). (Hunthausen also had another chance to speak, on the following morning, at the conclusion of all the debate. Cf. *The Progress*, 11.20.86.) The (11.21.86) *National Catholic Reporter* offers the fullest public accounting of what took place behind the closed doors.

> [...] Sentiments were divided, although most speakers offered Hunthausen significant fraternal support. "The real hurt in Seattle, the deep pain and divisions had come home, even if only in a direct way for a few hours," one bishop said of the meetings.
> Among the principal themes to emerge in the bishops' addresses were their desires to avoid being or appearing to be critical of the Vatican action, to be viewed in full accord with Rome, to address honestly any injustice that may have occurred, to pass to Rome the ever deepening distress of growing numbers of mainstream Catholics, including many priests, across the nation, and to be credible in the eyes of the public, especially the press.
> The dilemma the bishops faced, one said, was the need to address a perceived injustice without ending up pointing a finger at Rome.
> [Milwaukee Archbishop Rembert] Weakland was among the first to call for a change in the Malone letter. He said it lacked credibility in light of the Hunthausen documents.
> Seattle Auxiliary Donald Wuerl spoke early, calling for the bishops' support in making the situation work according to the Vatican's wishes.
> Cardinal Joseph Bernardin, speaking on behalf of "four cardinal ordinaries," offered his support for the Malone letter. He said it was essential that the conference offer Rome its support and also said unity was necessary so a climate of reconciliation could occur and the situation could move toward normalization.
> Washington Archbishop James Hickey, who conducted the Vatican apostolic visitation in Seattle, spoke about his personal involvement in the case, saying he did what was asked of him and carried out the visitation according to church procedures. Hickey said he had prepared the documents and knew them well, implying, in the eyes of several bishops, that there was definitely more to the story than was coming across in the Hunthausen documents. His remarks later moved Anchorage Archbishop Francis Hurley – a close personal friend of Hunthausen's and the man who served as his informal legal counsel – to speak as well. Hurley reminded the bishops that they were not gathered to discuss the specifics of the Vatican visitation. Then he said that, because Hickey had raised the subject, he felt free to reassure the body of bishops he, too, had seen many of the documents in the case and could attest to the correctness of Hunthausen's version.
> Minneapolis-St. Paul Archbishop John Roach made a strong appeal that the bishops change the Malone letter to reflect the sentiments of the entire conference. Anyone reading the letter in light of the Hunthausen documents would view the bishops as looking foolish, he said. His remarks drew loud applause.
> [....]
> New York Cardinal John O'Connor also spoke of the need to be one with Rome but added that the bishops also had to find a way to help Hunthausen resolve an unworkable situation.

By 5:30 p.m. the bishops had not yet reached agreement on the Malone statement and the session was adjourned, to be resumed the following morning. When the bishops met again the next morning, a new version of the Malone statement submitted to them had excised the phrase "just and reasonable" as a descriptor of the visitation process. It would be replaced in the final version by a declaration that "the process employed by the Holy See was in accord with general principles of church law and procedures."

F.f. Conflict Functionality of the Intervening Developments (November 11-12, 1986)
Having heard the reports of the center and periphery parties (the Vatican chronology and Hunthausen's two texts in answer), the question before the third party (the NCCB) is how to formulate its own reaction. The debate about which position to adopt takes place on the NCCB's own "territory," in the context of its own meeting in which its own leadership has set the agenda and parameters for debate. Both Laghi and Hunthausen have sought to win the outright support of the NCCB with their statements. In the discussion at hand, the individual bishops must decide how best to protect their own interests and, collectively, the interests of the conference, while carrying out their responsibilities on behalf of the Church universal.

Though the bishops mostly stay within the debate format set by the conference leadership in advance (note the exception of the Hickey-Wuerl exchange, wherein both refer to the history of the visitation), enough disagreement arises about the text of the Malone statement (Weakland and Roach are two who challenge its wording) to lead to its reformulation. Objections bring about removal of the phrase "just and reasonable" from the statement. Instead of an *ethical* value judgment (*legitimacy* standard) in the statement, the bishops offer the observation that the process was correct according to Church law (*legally legitimate*). This change considerably diminishes the expression of approval of the Vatican's handling of the case. To put it bluntly, the NCCB goes from saying the intervention was *just* to saying it was *not against any Church laws*.

It is unclear whether the papal pro-nuncio participated in this debate. (I have found no report of him speaking.) The most evident advocacy of the center party position in the debate comes from the apostolic visitator, Archbishop Hickey. Hickey defends his own conduct of the visitation (it was carried out according to Church procedures) and he *contests* the account offered in Hunthausen's texts, on the basis of his own knowledge. This provokes a response from Archbishop Hurley, who *aligns himself with the periphery party* by assertively defending Hunthausen's version of documents and events. Cardinal Bernardin and Bishop Wuerl stress the importance of supporting Rome (*center party alignment*). Cardinal O'Connor of New York does too, but he declares the need to support to Hunthausen at the same time.

Hunthausen himself speaks in defense of his own cause at times, but we lack a record of his exact comments. The *National Catholic Reporter*'s summary of his opening remarks shows him touching upon key themes he elaborates on in his two written texts. Judging by the summary, he is physically tense, *deferential*, apologetic and nonconfrontational (*courteous*) and he observes only good will (good intentions) on the part of all. This description is at odds with the more contentious stance Hunthausen adopts in his written texts (where we find vulnerability but also confrontation). If, based on their reading of his written statements, certain fellow bishops may have felt inclined to attack him or his positions verbally, his tense and deferential oral remarks might well have had a disarming effect, inviting a less-than-aggressive response from his fellow bishops. (Archbishop Hurley says as much in an interview in the 11.20.86 *Progress*: "[Hunthausen] speaks the truth… in a way that is very respectful of his audience. This was much appreciated by the bishops.")

In any case, none of the bishops seems eager to attack Hunthausen or the Vatican. This will be reflected in the Malone statement itself. This closed-door (*secret*) debate serves an effort to contain the conflict (prevent *escalation*), engage in *problem solving*, and *save face* for the Church (by managing the threat to *unity*). All of the American bishops have an incentive to preserve their own autonomy of action -- individually and as an episcopal conference -- which is symbolized in Hunthausen's predicament. But protecting their own freedom to move (including vertically within the hierarchy) requires not offending the Holy See, which has the power to grant and limit freedoms. It is a delicate balancing act, taking shape in words in Malone's statement on behalf of the conference.

7.5 Document Number: 7
Bishop Malone's Statement (11.12.86)
Source: *The Progress,* November 13, 1986, p. 11; Origins, November 20, 1986, pp. 400-401.

7.5.1 Summary of Contents:
Given the brevity of the Malone statement, I will quote it in its entirety.

In recent weeks all of us have felt much concern for those involved in the situation in Seattle. The pain of Archbishop Hunthausen and Bishop Wuerl, our brothers in the episcopacy, the abuse directed at the Holy Father and the Holy See, the dismay and confusion experienced by many good people – these things are deeply troubling.

Not only is there suffering in the church in Seattle, though: the controversy has spread via the media and in other ways and has affected Catholics throughout the country. It is unusual for the conference of bishops to address such a matter, but these are unusual circumstances.

The issues raised here touch on the relationship between the local churches and the universal pastor. Bishops exercise their office in communion with him and under his authority. On this occasion the bishops of the United States wish to affirm unreservedly their loyalty to and unity with the Holy Father.

The conference of bishops has no authority to intervene in the internal affairs of the diocese or in the unique relationship between the pope and individual bishops. By universal church law and the conference's norms, the conference is not able to review, much less judge, a case involving a diocesan bishop and the Holy See.

Based on experience, bishops are conscious that in such matters the Holy See proceeds carefully and charitably, employing procedures developed over many years to protect the rights of individuals and promote the common good of the church. With specific reference to Seattle, while we are not authorized to judge the facts of the case, I believe it is clear that the process employed by the Holy See was in accord with general principles of church law and procedures. The decision reached at the end of the process was made by proper church authorities. As such, it deserves our respect and confidence. Where there appear to have been misunderstandings at one point or another along the way, the need now is to look to the future, not to the past, and carry out the decision. The best assistance I or anyone can give is to offer precisely this counsel.

We could address the issues involved in this situation all week, but we would deceive ourselves if we thought that such discussions would solve all the problems, heal all the hurt. We need to do some additional things.

Is it paradoxically possible that what has happened in the Archdiocese of Seattle has given, and continues to provide, a vivid demonstration of the unity of the church, perhaps the best demonstration we have seen in many years? I am deeply convinced that the degree of pain which has been felt and enunciated in Seattle, but far beyond Seattle, really is the kind of pain that can only be felt by members of a family. At least that is how it feels to me.

If my analogy is correct, it suggests some of the directions in which we must go. There are certain things that a family must do when it wants to resolve a problem.

A family comes together. Each member expresses the pain, the anxiety, the doubts they feel. These things are listened to with respect and sympathized with, deeply and in the heart. Then support is expressed, for the persons as persons, and for the responsibilities they must bear. This we bishops have done together in these days. Archbishop Hunthausen and Bishop Wuerl have been given a job to do by the Holy See. We are prepared to offer any assistance judged helpful and appropriate by the parties involved.

A family also takes steps to see that, insofar as possible, a painful situation does not happen again. In our case that means working to find creative ways of presenting the church's teaching in the best light possible, but also seeking the mechanisms of responding when confusion or error occurs. We must be seen as committed to hearing and solving the problems.

There is at least one more thing a family of faith does when it is in difficulty, and that is pray. We of all people must not give short shrift to this. Let us bring our people together in prayer for the church in Seattle, so that what has happened may be an occasion of grace and growth, there and in the church universal.

7.5.2 Conflict Functionality of the 11.12.86 Malone Statement

Though Malone is the one who reads this text to the press, the statement itself shows an ambiguity of voice. It is not clear who is speaking in the text. (Nor is it clear *to whom* the speaker is speaking.) Is this Malone's statement or the bishops'? Alternations of usage within the text make it hard to know (e.g., we read "the bishops of the United States wish to affirm unreservedly…" but then later we encounter Malone saying, "I am deeply convinced…" and "at least that is how it feels to me."). As a reflection of this difficulty, the 11.12.86 *National Catholic News Service* report called it Bishop Malone's statement, whereas the 11.13.86 *New York Times* called it "the bishops' statement, read by… Malone." That this ambiguity is of some consequence is shown by an especially puzzling example of alternation in the grammatical presentation of person.

> Based on experience, bishops are conscious that in such matters the Holy See proceeds carefully and charitably, employing procedures developed over many years to protect the rights of individuals and promote the common good of the church. With specific reference to Seattle, while we are not authorized to judge the facts of the case, I believe it is clear that the process employed by the Holy See was in accord with general principles of church law and procedures. The decision reached at the end of the process was made by proper church authorities. As such, it deserves our respect and confidence. While there appear to have been misunderstandings at one point or another along the way, the need now is to look to the future, not the past, and carry out the decision. The best assistance I or anyone can give is precisely this counsel.

Here Malone begins by speaking of bishops ("bishops are conscious…") in the third person, but it is unclear to which bishops precisely he is referring (All bishops? Bishops in general? All American bishops? Some American bishops?). Then he shifts to the first person plural "we"("we are not authorized to judge the facts of the case"). Presumably here he speaks on behalf of the entire conference, but there is all the possibility that he means to include the general public with this usage (none of us, apart from the Rome and Seattle insiders, are in a position to judge --?). Then comes a shift, within the very same sentence, to the first-person singular ("I believe it is clear that the process…"). Here it is not the bishops who declare the process used to be "in accord with general principles of church law and procedures," but only Malone. Significantly, this passage, which is already toned down from an earlier version that declared the process used as "just and reasonable," is further qualified here with the expression "I believe." Thus, from draft to final statement the position has been watered down from a firm declaration by the entire conference that the process was just and reasonable to a *hesitant* declaration from *one* bishop that the process was *in accord with general principles of church law and procedures*.

The sentences that follow in the passage cited above mostly leave open the question of who is talking through the text. After offering us Malone's presentation of his own opinion, there follow three statements which cannot be attributed to any particular voice ("The decision reached… was made by proper church authorities. As such it deserves our respect and confidence. While there appear to have been misunderstandings… the need now is to look to the future, not the past, and carry out the decision.") Who is telling us this? Is it still Malone talking for himself, or has he shifted back to speaking on behalf of other bishops? Following these three statements comes another mixed message: "The best assistance I or anyone can give is to offer precisely this counsel." Malone's associates himself clearly enough with the counsel offered (though still only hypothetically: it is presented as an ideal possibility). But what are we to make of the reference to "anyone"? Suffice it to say that what we do not learn from these words is what exactly the position of members of the conference on this issue is.

The ambiguity of voice in this document is not a matter of haste or carelessness. Before its release the statement was reviewed line-by-line by the bishops. Strategically, the ambiguity of voice offers the advantage to the bishops of responding to the need to say something collectively without pinning any one bishop or group of bishops down to any particular set of positions. By this means, the conference is able to issue one statement that is acceptable to the majority of its membership.

But not only is the speaker in this text unclear, so too is the intended audience. The absence of a stated addressee and the release of the text as a press release point to the intention to reach the press and the general public. The opening sentence seems be a statement made on behalf of the bishops themselves, but also one directed to any and all who have a stake in the case's outcome: "In recent weeks *all of us* [emphasis mine] have felt much concern for those involved in the situation in Seattle." Malone (henceforth, I will refer to him as the text's producer, while keeping in mind the hidden participation of other bishops, as discussed above) is quick to express sympathy toward a number of parties within the Church: Hunthausen and Wuerl have suffered "pain;" the Holy Father and Holy See have been on the receiving end of "abuse;" "many good people" have faced "dismay and confusion;" Catholics in the Seattle Archdiocese have experienced "suffering;" and Catholics throughout the country have been "affected." These observations show Malone's readiness to identify with a variety of (afflicted) audiences within the Church. Strangely enough, there is no indication of who is causing all this misery (thus *saving face for the Church*).

Although Malone paints the matter at hand as an internal Church matter – albeit one that is relevant for the entire Church (he prays that this will be an occasion for growth within "the church universal") – he also uses language that shows openness to extraecclesial viewpoints as well (*openness to the world*). One example of this is his comment about procedures designed to "protect the rights of individuals and promote the common good" (of the church). The concept of protecting individual rights and promoting the common good is a keystone of American civil society. Whereas such language is also familiar within Catholic social teaching applicable at the time of the Hunthausen case (see, among numerous other writings, the papal encyclicals *Rerum Novarum* and *Pacem in Terris*, but also the U.S. bishops own pastoral letter, "Economic Justice for All," which was then in its final stage of production), the concept of individual rights, at least, is not an especially old tradition within the Church, and it is highly unusual to see this notion applied to papal-episcopal relations. Malone's choice to invoke these terms has an odd sound to it. One could almost rephrase his argument as follows: bishops don't need a union to protect their rights against the Holy See, because the Holy See always makes sure that individual rights and the common good are guaranteed within the Church. My only point here is to show that this language sounds more American than Catholic and appears directed to a broad American audience rather more than to Rome.

Other language in the statement seems to be explicitly meant for Rome. Thus the Pope's right to intervene in the local church is signalled by designating him "universal pastor" here. (NB: This usage echoes earlier communications from the Vatican. Cardinal Ratzinger prominently employed this same term to refer to the Pope in his 12.12.83 letter to Hunthausen announcing his receipt of the Hickey report, and the Pope used nearly the same formulation – "the successor of Peter has been constituted for the whole church as pastor" -- in his message presented to the U.S. bishops on 11.10.86. In the 11.7.86 issue of the *National Catholic Reporter*, the Vaticanologist Peter Hebblethwaite argued that the term is of recent origin in the Church and has come to be used "to mean that the pope can intervene anywhere, at any time, without consultation, thus usurping the pastoral function of the local bishops.")

The Malone statement declaration that the bishops exercise their office "in communion with [the Pope] and *under his authority*" (emphasis mine) also appears meant for the Vatican, as do the unreserved profession of "loyalty to and unity with the Holy Father" (*show deference to the order and mindset of the Church*) and the modest concession of the bishops' lack of authority to intervene in the case. In addition, the recommendation to look to the future (*minimize the appearance of conflict*) and carry out the decision also appears designed, in part, to please the Vatican. But beyond serving to reassure Rome, I assume these instances of language also are signals to overhearers that the bishops have no intention of instigating a rift with the Holy See.

At the same time, the bishops have something to offer Hunthausen as well. I have already mentioned their backing away from the description of the visitation process as "just and reasonable" and their acknowledgment of the pain he has suffered (he and quite a few others). Going further, they voice their willingness "to offer any assistance judged helpful and appropriate by the parties involved." (This, for Hunthausen, is a hopeful sign, since he made just such a request in his address to the bishops.) Moreover, they implicitly suggest that the handling of the visitation and post-visitation process was inadequate, with the statement that a family takes steps to see that "a painful situation does not happen again." "We must be seen as committed to hearing and solving the problems."

Apart from a desire to appease any audience in particular, however, the strongest impulse evident within this text appears to be a desire to *damp down the conflict (or the appearance thereof)* as much as possible. Several tactics work toward this end. First, we see the conciliatory acknowledgment of the suffering of all. Then there is the attempt to speak to all parties in their own language, in ways that I have detailed above. Next comes a (surprisingly quick) recommendation to move on to the future (the future orientation being fairly American in its own right). "We could address the issues involved in this situation all week," Malone writes, but then he asks, in essence, what would be the point? The important thing is to "look to the future, not the past." After this quick *shift of perspective*, Malone deftly manipulates language to make the conflict disappear. "Is it paradoxically possible," he asks, "that what has happened in the Archdiocese of Seattle has given, and continues to provide, a vivid demonstration of the unity of the church, perhaps the best demonstration we have seen in many years?" Here Malone substitutes a euphemistic erasure ("what has happened in the Archdiocese of Seattle") for a frank acknowledgment of conflict, but even this erasure is further erased by the assertion that what in fact is showing itself is "unity."

The linguistic sleight-of-hand continues with the employment of the extended metaphor that dominates the last part of the statement. A comforting image of family life is called forth, with the implication that the Church is a family. Families that want to resolve a problem come together, Malone declares. American-style "therapeutic culture" is well represented in the language that follows.

> Each member expresses the pain, the anxiety, the doubts they feel. These things are listened to with respect and sympathized with, deeply and in the heart. Then support is expressed, for the persons as persons, and for the responsibilities they must bear. This we bishops have done together in these days.

Neglected in the analogy, as it is thus far presented, is the fact that the whole family is not at the table. While the brother bishops commiserate and share their pain and anxiety, the patriarch – the Holy Father – is present to the discussion only in the form of an abstract statement. Also missing is a candid assessment of accountability. Who caused the pain that everyone is feeling so deeply? Though according to this image a highly meaningful conversation, marked by mutual vulnerability, has taken place, no change is the result. "Archbishop Hunthausen and Bishop Wuerl have been given a job to do by the Holy See." The bishops offer their assistance, but essentially Hunthausen and Wuerl are invited to make peace with the very arrangement that Hunthausen has come to the meeting to protest and has just called "unworkable." The family problem solving covers up the genuine disharmony that exists and pretends that a solution has been reached. The image of family as it is employed here also suggests that, in any case, the strength of the relational bond makes the tensions (conflict) irrelevant since they pose no threat to the bond (*fraternity; unity*).

In the next paragraph we find again a refusal to assign blame.

> A family also takes steps to see that, insofar as possible, a painful situation does not happen again. In our case, that means working to find creative ways of presenting the church's teaching in the best light possible, but also seeking mechanisms of responding when confusion or error occurs. We must be seen as committed to hearing and solving the problems.

In this passage, painful situations "happen" and confusion and error "occur" independently of any actors' actions. Thus do the bishops characterize their own responsibility not as a matter of stopping the infliction of pain, but of seeing that "a painful situation does not happen again." Surprising, too, is the emphasis on appearance. The bishops' role here is envisioned not as helping people to better understand church teaching, nor, still less, to change church teaching. It is, rather, "to find creative ways of presenting the church's teaching *in the best light possible*" (emphasis mine). This same disposition shows itself in the statement: "We must be *seen as* committed to hearing and solving the problems" (again, emphasis mine).

Malone rounds out the picture of family life with an image of the family at prayer. (In the American saying, "the family that prays together stays together.") The closing words recommend (to the whole Church "family" but also to the bishops themselves) prayer in regard to the current "difficulty" and hold out the possibility that the current "difficulty" may prove to be "an occasion of grace and of growth."

What gets lost in the Malone statement is not simply an articulation of the conflict issues and why these issues are of interest for the competing parties, but also a description of the concrete steps of conflict handling which have been taken and still need to be taken. From accounts that were leaked to the press, it quickly became apparent that the bishops had engaged in a rather heated exchange concerning the case. According to these reports, a number of significant concerns and questions were brought to the table in this process. But the Malone statement hides these exchanges (*secrecy*) and asserts that what is really important is holding fast to unity and harmony. Instead of a picture of ongoing conflict, the statement offers us ready-made resolution.

With this statement, the NCCB sends several messages at once. By professing loyalty to the

Holy Father and affirming their lack of authority to intervene, the bishops signal conformity (*deference*) to Rome's leadership. By acknowledging the pain felt in Seattle, refusing to decisively affirm Rome's action, and offering their assistance, the bishops indicate their intention to stand by Hunthausen as well. By avoiding the assignment of blame and arguing that the present conflict demonstrates the unity of the Church, the bishops proclaim to Church members and outside observers that the institution is unthreatened by the tensions at hand.

The NCCB debate of the Rome-Hunthausen case and the Malone statement that is its product do not resolve the conflict, but they do bring the conflict to the threshold of a new stage.

CHAPTER EIGHT

NARRATIVE AND ANALYSIS OF THE ROME-HUNTHAUSEN CONFLICT: THE
LATE STAGE (NOVEMBER 1986-APRIL 1989)

G. Intervening Developments (November 1986-February 1987)

The bishops came to final agreement on the Malone statement during their morning session on Wednesday, November 12, which lasted for more than an hour. At 10:15 a.m., Malone reopened the conference room to the press. Television cameras recorded Malone's reading of the statement and the standing ovation he received from his fellow bishops in response (*The New York Times*, 11.13.86).

Several bishops offered commentary afterwards. Malone said he saw the ovation as a sign of full support for the statement from the bishops. Cardinal O'Connor of New York said, "I think it's a very well-balanced statement. It shows the unity of the bishops, it shows the loyalty to the Holy See and it demonstrates our explicit recognition that the Holy See has acted very charitably and very justly." Juneau, Alaska Bishop Michael Kenny was blunt in expressing criticism of the statement, saying: "I am not satisfied. Archbishop Hunthausen was never given a chance to adequately respond to anonymous charges made against him, nor was he provided an opportunity to even correct problems he was said to have caused" (*Seattle Post-Intelligencer*, 11.13.86). Archbishop Pilarczyk of Cincinnati challenged those who would judge the handling of the case based on the "Anglo-Saxon system" of due process. Canon law, he said, was designed "for the protection of the individual, the protection of the Church, the protection of doctrine and the protection of the rights of the Holy See" (*The Washington Post*, 11.13.86). Bishop Wuerl, who, along with Hunthausen, had refused interview requests since September 4, described the discussion during the bishops' meeting as having been "open, fraternal, respectful" (*Seattle Post-Intelligencer*, 11.13.86).

On the same day that Malone issued his statement, Hunthausen issued a written response (*The Progress*, 11.20.86, *Origins*, 11.20.86). Hunthausen expressed his gratitude to Malone and to the Conference administrative board for the opportunity to speak. "I am hopeful," he continued, "that this documentation has clarified matters for my brother bishops and, indeed, that it will now do so for all our people who are trying to understand what is surely a very complex situation."

> Secondly, I want to say that I support the statement Bishop Malone issued this morning. Like any statement, it will probably not please everyone, but it is, in my judgment, a good statement, one that has emerged from a very honest exchange of many different points of view.
> It addresses the issues in a manner that respects our identity as a Conference of Bishops united with each other and with the Holy Father. It also indicated a genuine readiness on the part of the conference to offer any assistance judged helpful and appropriate by me and by the other parties involved. This is a very hopeful sign for me. It is the kind of assurance I was seeking when I accepted the invitation to make a presentation to the conference in the first place.

Hunthausen closed his statement by conveying his hope for healing and the resolution of any problems that still remained.

On November 13, Hunthausen returned to Seattle, where he was welcomed by 350 enthusiastic supporters at the airport. The following day, Hunthausen gave a press conference (cf. *The Seattle Times*, 11.15.86, *Seattle Post-Intelligencer*, 11.15.86, *The Progress*,

11.20.86), his first since the September 4 announcement of Wuerl's special faculties. At the briefing, Hunthausen's words suggested that the issues at hand were far from resolved. Hunthausen described himself as being "in the middle of a conflict that has the potential of causing a rift in the church" (with an accompanying qualification that working through tensions was "part and parcel of the Christian life"). The power-sharing arrangement continued to be, to his mind, "unworkable," and the source of inefficiency and confusion. Noting the bishops' conference's offer of assistance in the affair (and offering specific details of how the Malone statement had been reworked to omit the phrase "just and reasonable"), Hunthausen said that an appropriate type of assistance had not yet been decided upon, but that he would be discussing this further with other bishops and with the conference leadership. Especially troubling to Hunthausen was his perception of a media effort to portray the affair as "win or lose, me against the Vatican." And yet, he admitted that, while the words "apostolic visitation" are "very comforting words," the reality of having dealt with the visitation had been painful and made perhaps less effective through a shortcoming in the Holy See's understanding of American culture. "There are different approaches to making judgments in different cultures," he said.

Few public reactions to the recent developments in the Hunthausen case came forth from the Vatican, but those that did expressed satisfaction with the way the U.S. bishops had handled the matter. An Associated Press report (*Seattle Post-Intelligencer*, 11.14.86) quoted a Vatican official, who spoke on the condition of anonymity, as saying that "the U.S. bishops came out surprisingly strong on the side of the Holy See on the Hunthausen affair. They were on the right track." Another official, also unnamed, said there was a "general sense of relief and satisfaction" at the Vatican regarding the Malone statement, which he called "amicable and satisfactory."

The Pope's only public comment on the affair came on November 19 abroad the papal plane, en route to Bangladesh (cf. the 11.19.86 *Seattle Post-Intelligencer*; the 11.27.86 *Progress*). Asked about a possible rift between U.S. Catholics and the Vatican, the Pope replied, "Sometimes one creates divisions that do not exist" by "talking and writing." "Our task – that of myself and the bishops of the United States – is the same, the good of the church. It is our common ministry… The American Church is part of the universal church and still wants to be a part of the universal church." When asked specifically about the Hunthausen case, the Pope said, "I know only the statement by the (bishops' conference) president, and it was correct."

Further action in the case, however, was slow in coming. Four weeks after the bishops' conference meeting, newly elected president of the conference, Archbishop John May said there were reasons to hope "that the NCCB offer may be accepted to help work out a method of restoring peace and unity to the pastoral administration of the Seattle Archdiocese" (*The Progress*, 12.8.86). In Seattle, Hunthausen reiterated his willingness to go with Wuerl to Rome to discuss the situation, if Vatican officials would extend an invitation. "That has really been the intent we've had all along," Hunthausen said (*Seattle Post-Intelligencer*, 12.13.86). But Hunthausen acknowledged that even if the opportunity for such a trip were to develop, it could be "months away."

In the aftermath of the confrontation in Washington, Hunthausen had become a well-known figure in the culture at large and not simply in the Catholic community. For better or worse, Hunthausen would be chosen as one of *People* magazine's "25 Most Intriguing People of 1986." Hunthausen placed seventh on the list, after the Duchess of York, insider-trader Ivan Boesky, Dr. Seuss, entertainer Bette Midler, Lt. Colonel Oliver North and Nicaraguan

President Daniel Ortega.

Amid this period of waiting and newfound notoriety, came a different sort of unsettling development for Hunthausen. On December 10, he entered Providence Medical Center in Seattle for tests. Six days later Hunthausen underwent major prostatic surgery. The surgery successfully removed the tumor, which had spread in a microscopic amount into some of the lymph node tissues as well (cf. Archdiocesan news release, 12.16.86). After the surgery, Hunthausen's physicians said they expected Hunthausen to recover completely, and Maury Sheridan, director of the archdiocesan office of telecommunications, announced that Hunthausen would probably be hospitalized for 2 ½ weeks (*Seattle Post-Intelligencer*, 12.17.86). In fact, because his convalescence went smoothly, Hunthausen left the hospital sooner than expected, on Christmas Eve. During his hospital stay (on December 22), Hunthausen received a telegram from the Pope. It read: "I have been informed of your recent operation and I wish to assure you of my fraternal solicitude for your speedy recovery. I shall remembrance (sic) you in my prayers, especially as we celebrate the mystery of the incarnate word of God" (cf. *Seattle Post-Intelligencer*, 12.25.86).

Hunthausen returned to work in the middle of January, initially at less-than-full capacity. At the end of January, Archbishop Laghi granted an interview to the *New York Times*, which revisited certain points Hunthausen had made in his NCCB statements (see the 1.30.87 issue of the *Times*: the 90 minute interview took place at the Vatican Embassy in Washington), Laghi commented, with reference to the Hunthausen case, that Americans have a "complex of Watergate," which is reflected in an insistence on candor in judicial matters. "When something is behind the door, there is the impression that something is wrong." Laghi said that the Vatican believed more in the "principle of charity" and sensitivity to the need for privacy for those involved in an investigation. Application of this principle explained the Vatican's two-year silence concerning the case (broken by Laghi's release of the Vatican chronology in October of 1986). Issuance of the Vatican chronology, Laghi said, came at the urging of several influential American bishops, some of whom had complained that Hunthausen was being punished without a clear sense of the charges against him.

According to the *New York Times* interviewer (Joseph Berger), "Laghi seemed to acknowledge that the episode, if handled differently, might have had a less fractious outcome." Laghi was quoted as saying, "I am learning also." But in the same discussion Laghi observed that critics of the handling of the Hunthausen and (theologian Charles) Curran cases often focused on the Vatican's disciplinary procedures rather than on the doctrinal deviations that were at the heart of Rome's concern. "Our procedure, canon law procedure, does not match American procedure. But we cannot follow the procedure of a given country if we want to be a universal church."

In other remarks related to the Hunthausen case, Laghi said that the Vatican was well aware that many of the attacks on Hunthausen came from conservative groups, such as Catholics United for the Faith. Laghi resolutely denied that the Vatican had given these voices improper weight when making its assessments. Laghi also said that Hunthausen's stand on nuclear weapons had played no part in the case. Hunthausen offered no comment in response to the Laghi interview.

Less than two weeks later (February 9, 1987), Laghi issued an announcement (see document 8, below) that the Holy See had appointed an *ad hoc* commission of three American bishops to assess the situation in the Seattle Archdiocese. The two-sentence statement, which was relayed by a spokesman for Laghi in Washington, D.C., noted that Archbishop Hunthausen had expressed his concurrence. Background information provided by the nunciature along with the statement cited the offer of the NCCB to provide "any assistance judged helpful and appropriate by the parties involved," but referred, also, to the conference's observation that it had no power to intervene formally on Hunthausen's behalf. The spokesman for the nunciature who presented the statement to the press would not speculate on whether the committee's work could lead to the restoration of Hunthausen's power, but he said, "There is a wide scope of possible recommendations that could be made." He also observed that, while Pope John Paul II would have the final say in the matter, the input of the committee would be significant. "When they examine the situation, they will be in a better position than anyone to make a recommendation" (*The Wanderer*, 2.19.87).

In a telephone interview from Dallas, Laghi insisted that creation of the commission did not come in response to criticism of the Vatican's handling of the case. "This is just an assessment," he said (*Seattle Post-Intelligencer*, 2.10.87). "This was foreseen when he was given the auxiliary in January 1986. It's an internal helping, an assessment."

G.g. Conflict Functionality of the Intervening Developments (November 1986-February 1987)

After the NCCB meeting, all parties involved respond and offer interpretations of what has transpired. The first response is the standing ovation the bishops offer for their own statement, which Conference President Malone reads to the world at a televised press conference. The ovation provides symbolic "proof" of the conference's unity. But as the statement's contents show obliquely, and the press statements of individual bishops after the closed session show explicitly, the conference is more divided than it wants to let on. Juneau Bishop Michael Kenny's remarks are notably disputatious. Hunthausen's first reaction is haltingly pacific ("like any statement, it probably will not please everyone, but it is… a good statement"), but as soon as he arrives back in Seattle he restates his charge that the current situation is "unworkable" and he observes that the conflict "has the potential of causing a rift in the Church." Still more contentiously, he highlights the bishops' removal of the phrase "just and reasonable" from the Malone statement.

Other individual bishops offering early reactions defend the center party intervention in the local Church. Cardinal O'Connor disingenuously proclaims that the Malone statement explicitly recognizes that "the Holy See has acted very charitably and very justly" – exactly the conclusion the bishops had decided not to include in the statement. Archbishop Pilarczyk, for his part, challenges Hunthausen's "due process" argument and provides a defense of Church juridical procedures that is similar to what Laghi argues on other occasions (see, for example, Laghi's 1.30.87 New York Times interview). Church procedures, he argues, though distinct from the Anglo-Saxon procedures of legal justice, are fair and legitimate in their own right. Hence, we see that the immediate fallout from the NCCB debate is a willingness to take sides openly, as opposed to the more noncommittal statements that bishops issued before the debate.

Reactions coming from the Vatican show a uniform inclination to view the outcome positively: the press is invited to believe that the NCCB has sided with Rome and there is no reason for Rome to worry. Two officials who speak on the condition of anonymity pronounce the results satisfactory to Rome. Even the Pope, for the first and only time, makes specific reference to the affair. The Pope suggests that there is less to the conflict than some (apparently he means the media) would have us believe: "Sometimes one creates divisions that do not exist" (*minimize the appearance of conflict*). The Pope emphasizes that the American Church and world Church are unified, and that the American bishops and the Pope himself share a concern for "the good of the church" (*associate self with the best interest of the Church*). In his most direct reference to the Hunthausen case, the Pope offers a comment that is puzzling and even startling. What is puzzling is the Pope's declaration that the Malone statement is "correct." In what sense is it correct? Is it correct as a description of the NCCB's experience? (How would the Pope know?) Is it theologically correct? Is it functionally correct, staying within the bounds of what the conference should and should not say under the circumstances? The Pope does not elaborate. What is startling is his profession that Malone statement is all he knows about the case. Obviously this is not true. Part of the difficulty of making sense of the Pope's statements on this occasion may lie with the way the question was formulated and later reported in press accounts. But still, it is clear that the Pope is unready to talk publicly about a conflict that is the preoccupation of a large and influential national Church and three hundred of his fellow bishops. The Pope's strategy here is to keep silent and reserve the handling of the affair to a private forum (*secrecy*).

In an intriguing move in the other direction, however, the Pope's nuncio in America proves himself ready to be more forthcoming and open than he has shown himself to be up to this point. Though Archbishop Laghi offers no comment in the immediate aftermath of the NCCB debate, two months later he gives an interview to the *New York Times* that is more highly personal than any of his previous communications in the affair. There Laghi admits that Hunthausen case could have been handled better ("I am learning too"). This type of frankness is more akin to Hunthausen's usual style of first-person discourse and contrasts with the bureaucratic facelessness typical of Laghi's "official" statements. Perhaps Laghi, observing the effectiveness of Hunthausen's *assertion of personal identity*, seeks to counterbalance that by giving a more human face to the Vatican position? Most of Laghi's commentary in the interview responds to specific questions Hunthausen raised in his NCCB texts (*persuasive argumentation*), but Laghi does not initiate any new attacks.

This reluctance to further escalate the conflict is not limited to Laghi. After Hunthausen's ripostes immediately after the November meeting, he too settles into a period of nonconfrontational communication (which consists mostly in *silence* regarding the conflict), as do the American bishops in general. The period is one of stalemate, with all parties waiting to see how the Vatican will respond to the NCCB debate and the conference's offer to help find a more workable solution in Seattle.

Hunthausen's battle with cancer reminds all involved that Church politics is not everything. The Pope's telegram exemplifies a *personal form of fraternal solicitude*. Hunthausen's recovery allows the conflict handling to run its full course. Shortly after Hunthausen's return to work, Laghi announces that the Vatican has formed a three-man commission to assess the current situation in Seattle. With this announcement the Vatican signals its readiness to engage in a new form of *problem solving*. The announcement also serves as an implicit acknowledgment that the Vatican takes seriously Hunthausen's complaints and sees value in the NCCB's offer of assistance.

8.1 Document Number: 8
Laghi Announcement of Commission Appointment (2.9.87)
Source: *The Progress*, February 12, 1987.

8.1.1 Summary of Contents:
Here is the full text of the statement:

> The Holy See has appointed an *ad hoc* commission composed of Cardinals Joseph Bernardin and John O'Connor and Archbishop John Quinn to assess the current situation in the Archdiocese of Seattle. Archbishop Raymond Hunthausen has expressed his concurrence.

8.1.2 Conflict Functionality of the Laghi Announcement of Commission Appointment

Laghi's announcement marks a turning point in the conflict communication. It comes in the midst of a *stalemate* and signals the possibility of *de-escalation*. Laghi, however, avoids suggesting that the Vatican is committed to any particular course of action. Thus, the announcement is minimalistic: it is short and businesslike in tone.

In terms of content, the key items are the composition of the commission itself and the indication of Hunthausen's concurrence. Most observers at the time characterize the make-up of the commission as promising for Hunthausen. Quinn was considered to be rather progressive in Church matters, much in the way of Hunthausen. Bernardin was viewed as more of a moderate than a progressive, but nonetheless one who would have sympathy for Hunthausen. Only O'Connor was thought to be too strongly in Rome's camp to side with Hunthausen. The indication of Hunthausen's concurrence suggested that he, too, could imagine the commission's involvement as having favorable consequences.

Two word choices in particular stand out: "assess" and "situation." Both bespeak neutrality. "Assess" lacks the threatening finality of "judge," and "situation" sounds less worrisome than "conflict." But a conflict it was, and Hunthausen and his supporters were well aware that an assessment could bring unwanted outcomes. As proof of this, Hunthausen supporters needed only recall the statement of Archbishop Hickey's secretary, Fr. Maurice Fox, at the time of the visitation. Fr. Fox announced that Hickey "was not given any specific agenda or area of concern" but was rather given only a general mandate to "assess the situation" and report his findings back to the Holy See (*The Progress*, 11.3.83).

H. Intervening Developments (February-May 1987)

Following the announcement of the commission appointment, Hunthausen offered no comment and Archdiocesan spokesman Russ Scearce said, "We're not saying anything" (*Seattle Times*, 2.9.87). The timing of the announcement coincided with a gathering of most of the American bishops in Dallas, Texas for a workshop on medical ethics. Another topic of discussion at that gathering was the forthcoming visit of the Pope to the U.S., in September. It was not lost on observers that the bishops had incentive to bring the Seattle situation to a less volatile state prior to the Pope's arrival.

On February 10, Bernardin, O'Connor and Quinn issued a joint statement, saying that they had been notified of their appointment in a January 26 letter from Archbishop Laghi. The commission members noted that the formation of the commission was in keeping with a longstanding plan of the Vatican. The assessment "was envisioned by the Holy See and agreed to by Archbishop Hunthausen when the auxiliary, Bishop Wuerl, was appointed more than a year ago." The work of assessment was already underway. "We initiated our task in Dallas and will make our report to the Holy See when it has been completed." (The commission report, document 9, below, says that Hunthausen and Wuerl met with the commission in the presence of the pro-nuncio on the morning of February 10 in Dallas. Further meetings, without Laghi, took place between the commission and the Seattle bishops that same afternoon and evening. See also the 2.20.87 *National Catholic Reporter.*) The commission added in its press announcement that there would be "no further public statement" (*The Progress*, 2.12.87).

Taking the discussion of the case in a somewhat different direction, but only adding to the intrigue, was a 2.13.87 report that the Federal Bureau of Investigation had kept a file on Hunthausen and on another well-known "peace bishop," Thomas Gumbleton of Detroit (cf. the *National Catholic Reporter*, 2.13, 2.20 and 2.27.87). The *National Catholic Reporter* had filed a request for information from the FBI under the federal Freedom of Information Act and thereafter reported on the materials that had been released. Not everything in the bishops' files was made public. The majority (the great majority in Gumbleton's case, where only 26 pages were provided and 129 were held back) of items in the files were not released by the agency, for security and confidentiality reasons. According to the FBI declaration, the file on Hunthausen contained 10 pages in total, four of which were turned over for inspection. The four pages given over consisted of two newspaper articles on Hunthausen's activity of resistance to the use of nuclear weapons. The first was a 3.1.83 *Seattle Post-Intelligencer* article on a U.S.-Soviet cultural exchange in which Hunthausen was briefly mentioned. It attributed to Hunthausen a statement that nuclear weapons are immoral, even as a deterrent. The second was a 5.8.69 article in the *Montana Standard*. It concerned Catholic priests who were criticizing the installation of antiballistic missiles in Montana. Hunthausen was bishop of Helena, Montana at that time. An FBI statement said that the files on the two bishops were "cross-reference files," which are kept on individuals who are not necessarily under investigation but whose names appear in connection with other investigations. (A subsequent *National Catholic Reporter* article, 4.3.87, would reveal that U.S. Naval Intelligence also kept a file on Hunthausen. This file focused on Hunthausen's planned participation in a June, 1982 anti-nuclear submarine demonstration in Puget Sound and included a 6.8.82 article of the *Seattle Post-Intelligencer* describing Hunthausen's plans.)

Upon learning of the FBI's monitoring of his activity, Hunthausen said he was "surprised and concerned" that the FBI would feel compelled to "keep records on occasions or events when I simply exercise my right as a citizen to speak on public issues." In the context of Hunthausen's conflict with the Vatican, news of the FBI file furthered speculation that the Vatican action against Hunthausen was somehow related to Reagan administration displeasure with Hunthausen's peace activism. This theory had been previously voiced in a number of forums (cf., for example, Colman McCarthy's nationally syndicated column in the 11.18.86 *Seattle Times,* and Shelby Scates' column in the 9.7.86 *Seattle Post-Intelligencer*). The *Seattle Weekly*, in its 1.13.87 issue, framed the speculation this way:

> Conspiracy theorists note that the same Archbishop Laghi who implemented the pope's discipline is the Vatican's first-ever delegate to the U.S. [sic: actually, Laghi was the first to have the status of an ambassador; apostolic delegates had previously represented the Vatican in the U.S.], sent when the Reagan administration and the Vatican established formal diplomatic relations in 1984. They figure that reining in the tax-resisting archbishop was part of a quid pro quo for those formal ties. Laghi's statement that "at no time did the Holy See pursue with Archbishop Hunthausen the criticisms it received on controversial issues, e.g., nuclear weapons and the payment of taxes," is accordingly taken as evidence that the opposite must be true.

Was it possible that churchmen were "protesting too much" when they said that the visitation had nothing to do with Hunthausen's stand on nuclear arms and the payment of taxes? Throughout the conflict, the Vatican position on this issue remained consistent. On November 2, 1983 the apostolic visitator, Archbishop Hickey, said explicitly that the visitation had nothing to do with this issue. Then Laghi reaffirmed this in the Vatican chronology and in his *New York Times* interview, and Bishop Wuerl did so as well in 1987, when he was quoted as saying, "In none of the concerns listed at any point by the Holy See was the archbishop's political activity ever mentioned. Matters of Church teaching and practice were the only things indicated" (*Pittsburgh Catholic*, 6.19.87). (Perhaps most notably, the 9.30.85 Ratzinger letter makes no mention of Hunthausen's stand on nuclear weapons.)

In the absence of any conclusive proof for this "conspiracy theory," news of the FBI file on Hunthausen at least provided food for thought by supplying evidence of the government's interest in Hunthausen's activity. Still missing, however, was evidence that the Holy See would be willing to cut a deal to pressure one of its own bishops in exchange for favors from the U.S. government.

Another version of the conspiracy theory held that persons in the Seattle archdiocese who were unhappy with Hunthausen for political reasons sought to attack him on other grounds that were more telling for the Vatican: i.e., doctrinal and pastoral issues. Though its population was politically liberal in many respects, the Puget Sound area was also home to a number of key military bases (including the nuclear submarine base at Bangor, of course, but also including major installations such as the Ft. Lewis Army base and McChord Air Force base) and was a good example of the military-industrial economy at work, with military contractor Boeing being the most prominent local employer. Thus, any number of persons would have reason to be unhappy with Hunthausen's challenge to stop building and deploying weapons that were not only part and parcel of the nation's security strategy but also the source of paychecks to tens of thousands of local citizens. This theory may have been more plausible, and certainly was being discussed as the controversy continued, but again it seemed to result more from speculation than from hard evidence that emerged at the time.

Within days after meeting with the assessment commission in Dallas, Bishop Wuerl was in Rome, where he met privately with Pope John Paul II (*Seattle Post-Intelligencer*, 2.17.87). The fifteen-minute audience, in the Pope's study overlooking St. Peter's Square, came in the midst of a week Wuerl spent in Rome to carry out a study of the North American College. This task was in keeping with Wuerl's Vatican-assigned participation in an assessment of the state of American seminaries. Though many press accounts wondered whether the visit might have some special significance for the situation in Seattle, Vatican spokesman Joaquin Navarro-Valls called Wuerl's meeting with the Pope "routine." Wuerl declined comment.

In Seattle, Hunthausen's supporters continued their activism on his behalf. A favored activity was sending letters to influential members of the hierarchy. The Seattle-based groups Concerned Catholics and Catholic Network Northwest circulated lists of addresses for key American bishops, the pro-nuncio, and heads of Vatican congregations, along with suggestions of possible topics to be taken up in the letters. The same tactic had been and continued to be practiced by groups opposing Hunthausen as well. (This tactic for applying pressure on Church leaders is discussed in Reese 1996, 252-253 and Reese1989, 332-334. Many copies of letters sent to American bishops and Vatican officials, and the actual letters received in response, are contained in the Wasden Price collection.) On the national level, a Hyattsville, Maryland group called Catholics Speak Out lobbied for reinstatement of Hunthausen's powers. One of its tactics was to release a petition in a full-page advertisement in the 1.9.87 *National Catholic Reporter*. Critics of Hunthausen (prominent among them being Erven Park, editor of the newsletter, *The Catholic Truth*, and William Gaffney, president of the local chapter of *Catholics United for the Faith*), meanwhile, complained that thus far the visitation and presence of Bishop Wuerl had done little to correct abuses within the local Church (*Seattle Times*, 3.14.87).

Behind the scenes, the Vatican-appointed commission carried on with its work of assessment (See the commission report; the *Seattle Post-Intelligencer*, 3.9.87; *The Progress*, 3.12.87). On March 6-7, 1987 the commission interviewed a select group of archdiocesan leaders and Northwest bishops at St. Patrick's Seminary in Menlo Park, California. This group was comprised of eight bishops, seven members of the Archdiocesan Board of (Priest) Consultors and five members of the archdiocesan staff. The commission interviewed the invitees separately, for at least thirty minutes each. The bishops interviewed were Archbishop Levada (Portland, OR), Archbishop Power (retired, Portland, OR), Bishop Connolly (Baker, OR), Bishop Treinen (Boise, ID), Bishop Curtiss (Helena, MT), Bishop Murphy (Great Falls-Billings, MT), Bishop Schuster (retired, Great Falls-Billings, MT) and Bishop Skylstad (Yakima, WA). The priests interviewed, who held the status of priest consultor in the archdiocese, were Revs. Anthony Domandich, Richard Hayatsu, Joseph Kramis, James Mallahan, Theodore Marmo, Gerald Stanley and William Treacy. The archdiocesan staff members interviewed were Rev. Michael McDermott, archdiocesan director of administration; Rev. Michael G. Ryan, chancellor and vicar general; Rev. David Jaeger, director of seminarians; Patrick Sursely, associate director of administration; and Ned Dolejsi, director of faith and community development.

After the gathering, Revs. Stanley, Treacy and McDermott described their interview experience in positive terms. Fr. McDermott said the meetings were "very pleasant, helpful and hopeful." In McDermott's recounting, the commission members emphasized that they were making an assessment of Seattle "at this moment" and were not in any sense resuming the process of apostolic visitation. According to Mr. Sursely, the commission members left the impression that they did not foresee a need to make a personal visit to Seattle. Sursely noted that, while the interviewees had not been sworn to secrecy, they had agreed among themselves not to discuss specifics of their conversations with the commission in order to "respect the process and allow the commission the freedom needed to do its work."

Standing out by reason of his absence at the Menlo Park gathering was Bishop Wuerl, who was not asked to participate. (The reason is unclear.) But on March 12, Wuerl and Hunthausen met individually with the commission and the pro-nuncio in Chicago. (Again, none of the participants commented on the meeting.) Shortly thereafter, the members of the commission, together with several other American bishops, travelled to Rome for meetings (March 18-21) with the Pope and leaders of key Vatican congregations in preparation for the Pope's forthcoming U.S. visit (*Origins*, 4.2.87). The Hunthausen case was reportedly not on the agenda.

The commission report also tells us of subsequent consultations the commission pursued in the course of its assessment. On March 19, Archbishop Quinn interviewed Fr. William Lane. Lane was an archdiocesan consultor who was not present at the Menlo Park gathering. Then Quinn and Bernardin met with Archbishop Hickey on March 25 in Washington, D.C. On March 29, Quinn met with (Anchorage Archbishop) Hurley and on March 31 Quinn met with Hurley and Juneau bishop Kenny.

The assessment process for the two succeeding months (according to the commission report) was as follows:

> During the entire month of April and into the month of May, a number of visits and telephone conversations, as well as an exchange of letters with individuals who had previously been interviewed took place. In addition Archbishop Hunthausen met with the Commission in Chicago on April 8, 1987.

Since then the Commission has been in continuing contact with the Archbishop by telephone.

The commission also studied voluminous documentation, all of which was available to Archbishop Hunthausen and Bishop Wuerl.

Between the announcement of the commission's formation in February and the early part of April, little news came forth in the case. Then, on April 15 (in its issue dated 4.19.87), the *National Catholic Register* (a Catholic weekly that was a conservative alternative to the *National Catholic Reporter*) published a lead story declaring that, "according to highly placed sources," Wuerl was about to be reassigned to another diocese. Hunthausen's would be retired from office after a face-saving grace period in which his powers would be fully restored. Thereafter a new ordinary would be appointed "with an eye to calming hostilities between those who support Hunthausen and others who saw Wuerl's arrival as a welcome attempt at restoring order and direction" to the local Church.

The first official reaction (*Seattle Times*, 4.15.87) from the archdiocese came from public affairs director Russ Scearce. "It is a speculative story and we do not have a comment." He added, however, "This is not the kind of news we were hoping to receive during Holy Week." Increasing the plausibility of the *Register* report was the fact that Hunthausen had met with the commission the previous week, on April 8, in Chicago. Also, unnamed sources at the chancery described Hunthausen as appearing burdened of late and they noted that he had spent the weekend praying and consulting with trusted advisers. Archdiocesan Vicar General and Chancellor Michael G. Ryan immediately sent a letter to the priests of the archdiocese, which was released simultaneously to the press, that urged the priests to "disregard the *National Catholic Register* article, because not only is it speculative; it is incorrect (*Origins*, 4.30.87). The information that formed the basis of the article was apparently leaked to the reporter by an uninformed and irresponsible party in Rome or Washington, D.C...." Ryan went on to "assure" his readers that "the Archbishop has not been asked to retire or resign, nor are any 'deals' being made in that direction." Ryan also suggested that the story may have been intended as a sort of "trial balloon" to test acceptance among the U.S. bishops of a solution forcing Hunthausen's early retirement; or, conversely, it might have been meant to head off a commission proposal to restore Hunthausen's full authority (*Seattle Post-Intelligencer*, 4.17.87; *Seattle Weekly*, 5.5.87).

The reaction among Hunthausen supporters in the archdiocese was to organize quickly to voice their strong disapproval of the sort of resolution suggested by the *Register* article. In the first days after the story emerged, groups of priests, nuns and laypersons met separately within the archdiocese to formulate and express their concerns. According to Fr. David Jaeger, archdiocesan director of seminarians, many Hunthausen supporters had been kept silent in the recent past for fear that speaking out would only damage the prospects for a favorable outcome. But now in the face of a near-at-hand, possibly unacceptable outcome, many felt compelled to speak out forcibly. Jaeger himself offered some of the most contentious comments. He said, "This is a call for help. Do not let the Holy See do something that is going to do damage to the Catholic Church here and beyond. Stop them." Jaeger went on to say that "loyalty means more than consenting to something that is wrong" (*Seattle Post-Intelligencer*, 4.21.87).

On April 20, priests of the archdiocese gathered at St. Paul parish in Seattle to prepare a statement of support for Hunthausen (*The Progress*, 4.23.87; 4.30.87; *Origins*, 4.30.87). The statement affirmed the priests' conviction that Hunthausen was a "faithful and orthodox teacher of the Catholic faith" and it condemned the Vatican action against Hunthausen. Hunthausen, in the priests' view, had been "evaluated improperly, inadequately, and unjustly." The priests characterized the "remedies" applied to Hunthausen as having "all but been forced upon him through a form of moral persuasion based more on coercion than on evangelical obedience." The statement closed with a plea for the full reinstatement of Hunthausen's powers. (Eventually the statement would be signed by 150 of the 179 archdiocesan priests in active service at the time. It was published with the names of the priest signers in the 5.14.87 *Progress*.) On April 21, the archdiocesan Sisters' Council prepared a similar statement of support. The text from the sisters observed that "witnessing such scandalous actions against a highly respected prelate causes doubts and questions about the Catholic Church's commitment to living out its own principles and pronouncements about justice." The statement speculated that it might take "more than a generation" to overcome the confusion and divisions which had arisen because of the present arrangement. As in the priests' statement, the sisters (328 of approximately 500 active sisters signed it) called for full restoration of Hunthausen's powers.

The *Register* article proved to be by no means the final word of speculation about how the Hunthausen case would be resolved. The 4.24.87 edition of the *National Catholic Reporter* challenged the Register's information and declared that, in fact, an alternate kind of resolution was in the making. According to the *NC Reporter*'s own sources, the assessment commission had proposed a solution to Rome which had been accepted after the Pope had amended it. The agreed-upon solution involved no expectation that Hunthausen would retire early. Rather, the sticking point was the determination of the commission (and Rome) that a coadjutor archbishop be appointed to assist Hunthausen. While the coadjutor would have no special powers (these would be fully restored to Hunthausen), he would have the right of succession once Hunthausen did finally retire.

The *NC Reporter*'s sources said that

> Hunthausen was taken aback and would not agree to the proposed compromise during his meeting with Bernardin in Chicago. The commission members are irritated, even angered, by what they perceive to be Hunthausen's recalcitrance, the sources said. Though neither side is altogether happy with the compromise plan, sources said, it is the only way Hunthausen will be able to stay on as archbishop of Seattle. If he rejects the compromise, Rome will appoint an administrator and ask Hunthausen to step down, the sources said.

The 4.25.87 *New York Times*, citing "several Roman Catholic officials," also reported that a solution featuring the appointment of a coadjutor with right of succession was in the works. As in the *NC Reporter* version, Wuerl would be reassigned and Hunthausen's full powers would be restored. But, the *Times* pointed out, the plan for the coadjutor had "not been fully approved by the top Vatican officials." And, it was "unclear whether the plan was a harsher or more lenient measure against Archbishop Hunthausen than the ones taken against him in 1985 and 1986." The *Times* characterized the plan on the table as a "compromise." Whereas it would meet Hunthausen's goal of having his own power fully restored, the placement of a coadjutor would nonetheless provide a means for the Vatican to "maintain some control over the archdiocese." A new detail which cropped up in the *Times* account was word that Hunthausen was pressing for the right to decide whom the coadjutor would be, a request that the commission was not willing to grant.

On May 8, in an interview with the National Catholic News Service at the apostolic nunciature, Pro-Nuncio Laghi said he hoped the Seattle controversy would come to a conclusion soon (*The Progress*, 5.14.87). "I am the first one to hope there will be some reconciliation, but reconciliation without compromising" on principles, he said. Laghi stated that he expected the *ad hoc* commission to give its assessment soon and possibly make a recommendation. Implementation of the recommendation would depend on the approval of both Rome and Hunthausen.

Meanwhile, the atmosphere in Seattle was thick with expectation (*National Catholic Reporter*, 5.8.87). There appeared to be "no other issue, no other concern in the Catholic church save for resolution of the Archbishop Raymond Hunthausen affair."

> There is a feeling in western Washington that the end may be near. News reporters covering the story have cancelled scheduled trips out of town. A few from distant cities are prepared to fly into Seattle. Church people are staying close to home, too. They say they want to be here if and when something happens.

No account of the commission negotiations with Hunthausen has ever been issued by any of the direct participants. The most comprehensive record of the hidden proceedings comes from Briggs (1992, 337-341). As Briggs tells it, negotiations between Hunthausen and the commission broke down in the second half of April and first week of May. The solution proposed by the commission would restore full power to Hunthausen but would also require him to accept a coadjutor archbishop with right of succession. Moreover, it meant accepting the commission's report on the state of the archdiocese. But Hunthausen was reluctant to accept this solution because agreeing to a coadjutor would be a tacit admission that Seattle needed Rome's help to correct problems locally; and he disapproved, too, of the sharply critical tone of the preliminary draft of the commission report.

> Under the provisions spelled out by Cardinal Bernardin, the archbishop would have partial control over the selection of a coadjutor. The three names normally forwarded by Rome by the papal pro-nuncio, Archbishop Laghi, would be approved by the archbishop. That did not mean he would pick all three, only that he go along with whatever names made the final cut.
>
> ...[Hunthausen] forwarded to the commission three preferences of his own: Bishop Michael H. Kenny of Juneau, Archbishop Francis T. Hurley of Anchorage, and Bishop William S. Skylstad of Yakima. The commission scratched Bishop Kenny as too much a liberal in the Hunthausen mold. Archbishop Hurley was crossed off because, according to church protocol, the move to coadjutor would be considered a demotion for someone already an archbishop. That left Bishop Skylstad. After much jockeying, the commission agreed to submit two names, Bishop Skylstad, of the archbishop's choosing, and Bishop Thomas J. Murphy of Great Falls-Billings, Montana, a man the archbishop liked and respected but had some immediate qualms about placing in that role...
>
> The commission had also considered criticisms of its first evaluation and was busy revising it to rectify the tough-minded quality imparted to it by Cardinal O'Connor...
>
> [....]
>
> By the first days of May, the tension between the archbishop and the commission was at the breaking point. The archbishop remained adamant that his acceptance of a coadjutor was contingent on his choice of both nominees. The commission refused to back down from its offer. At this point, the four of them were wearing down each other's nerves daily during long, gruelling conference calls.
>
> [....]
>
> Though the settlement seemed rational, even generous, to [the commission] and the Vatican, it did not strike the archbishop that way. As the commission tried to seal the deal, an exasperated archbishop threatened to go over their heads by flying straight to Rome, only to have the Vatican put the kibosh on his plans. There would be no meeting with the pope or top Vatican officials, they informed him, without what amounted to a signed confession and a pledge to mend his ways.
>
> [....]
>
> Alarm was growing on both sides. But from the commission's perspective, the jittery impasse could not go on much longer. What resulted amounted to an ultimatum: accept the assignment of a coadjutor, agree to submit the names of Skylstad and Murphy, and go along with a final, revised assessment. He held out for the choice of both names. Without agreement, the settlement talks would break off. The consequences appeared dire. Archbishop Hunthausen would be forced by the Vatican to leave the archdiocese.

On May 4, all indications were that Archbishop Hunthausen would reject the package and, in effect, quit.

But on May 7, the archbishop "accepted that which he had nearly spurned." Briggs, citing the reports of persons close to Hunthausen, attributes this turnabout to Hunthausen's belief that he owed it to the Church of Seattle and to his loyal backers to stay on. More fundamentally, doing so was "God's will as he understood it." Briggs also notes the contribution of a "skilled lay intermediary" (unnamed), who played a crucial role in helping Hunthausen sort out the issues and make peace with the commission's proposal. "With the archbishop's acceptance in hand, the commission scheduled a trip to the Vatican to talk it over and nail down additional details."

The first official declaration that a decision in the case was imminent came on May 21 (cf. *National Catholic News Service* bulletin, 5.21.87). In a press conference at the Vatican, Cardinal Bernardin reported that the commission had met with Vatican officials (of the Congregation for the Doctrine of the Faith and the Congregation for Bishops – cf. the *National Catholic Reporter*, 6.5.87) and with Archbishop Laghi on May 19-20. An audience with the Pope took place on May 20. During these meetings, which Bernardin described as a "positive exchange," the commission delivered its assessment of the Seattle situation. Bernardin said: "We came over to present our report and in due time the Holy See will be making its recommendation. They are reflecting on it now. Our specific mandate was to assess the situation and present a recommendation, and that is what we did." Later that same day (May 21), the Pope agreed to the commission's recommended solution. The *National Catholic Reporter* (6.5.87) quoted him as saying to the commission: "It this is the way you want to do it, then this is the way we will do it." (Briggs 1992, 341 reports that Cardinal Ratzinger was more reluctant to endorse the plan.)

The commission's assessment report to the Vatican was dated May 20, 1987. The commission and pro-nuncio left Rome with instructions to implement the plan. Thereafter, the commission prepared a cover letter, dated May 25, 1987, to accompany the release of their report to the American bishops and to the press. Also included in the packet was a copy of the 9.30.85 letter from Cardinal Ratzinger to Hunthausen detailing the visitation conclusions, which the Vatican had authorized for release.

In the cover letter accompanying their report, the three bishops observed that on January 26, 1987 they had been appointed by the Holy See to "assess the current situation in the Archdiocese of Seattle" and that they had also been "invited to suggest a plan for resolving the difficulty." This task was now completed and "the Holy See has made its decision based substantially on the proposal we submitted." The letter then summarized the commission's main recommendations:

    (1) that full faculties be restored to Archbishop Hunthausen;
    (2) that he be given a Coadjutor to assist him in carrying out the provisions of the letter of the Congregation for the Doctrine of the Faith (enclosed);
    (3) that our Commission continue to assist him in fulfilling this responsibility during the course of the next year.

Hunthausen released the commission report at a 45-minute press conference in Seattle on May 27, 1987, his first formal meeting with reporters since November of 1986. Alongside Hunthausen at the press conference was newly appointed Coadjutor Archbishop, Thomas Murphy. (Murphy had been notified of his appointment on May 23.) Both bishops took reporters questions. Up to that time Murphy had been serving as bishop of Great Falls-Billings, Montana. (Hunthausen had met with Murphy in Great Falls on May 26.) Auxiliary Bishop Wuerl was not present at the news conference but did release a written statement. (Wuerl did conduct at least one individual interview on May 27, with the National Catholic News Service. See *Origins*, 6.4.87) Hunthausen and Murphy also released written statements at the press conference.

H.h. Conflict Functionality of the Intervening Developments (February-May 1987)
From the time of the commission appointment to the release of the commission report, the conflict handling activity of center, periphery and primary third party (the commission) stays mostly invisible. More easily observed is the activity of Hunthausen supporters and critics who are not part of the hierarchy. While the bishops attempt to hammer out a new accord in secret, other concerned parties pressure the decision makers to come to an agreement that is in keeping with their own interests.

Rome's appointment of the commission accomplishes several things at once. First, it pushes the parties beyond the impasse resulting from the NCCB debate by providing an alternate (once again *secretive*) avenue for conflict handling. Second, it places a new third party in the critical intermediary position of the conflict handling. The commission effectively displaces the NCCB itself, replacing it with a small body that symbolically represents the conference (Bernardin, O'Connor and Quinn are recognized leaders of the conference and recognized representatives of a cross-section of Church-political viewpoints). But now, instead of dealing with the entire conference, Rome is able to engage a much smaller group of its own choosing, according to a mission that Rome has determined. Third, it allows the pro-nuncio to take a *step back* (partially *withdraw*) from direct negotiations with Hunthausen. If the power-sharing arrangement with Wuerl was "unworkable," the same might be said of Hunthausen's bargaining with Laghi, following the misunderstanding about the faculties and their exchange of criticisms.

The decision to appoint the commission shows us that Rome agrees with the judgment that the current arrangement is Seattle is not working. (Wuerl's difficult relationship with the priests of the archdiocese is the strongest evidence of this.) If it had been working better – and if the public outcry had been less, Rome might simply have told the bishops and the local Church to learn to accept the decisions that had already been made. The commission appointment also signals Rome's intention to be sensitive to Hunthausen's preferences. Hunthausen could rightly perceive that Bernardin and especially Quinn would be sympathetic to his position, given their moderate (Church) politics and pastoral sensitivities (cf. the *Seattle Weekly*, 5.5.87). From the outside, the make-up of the commission hints of no intention by Rome to "crack down" on Hunthausen. One could almost argue the opposite. Given that, the Holy See's creation of the commission shows a *flexibility* on the part of Rome and a genuine interest in *problem solving*, and it suggests that Rome's primary need in the conflict is not simply to demonstrate its power to make Hunthausen submit to centralized control.

For Hunthausen, the establishment of the assessment commission is a promising sign but not unequivocally so. Though the composition of the commission could be more threatening, the commission's reason to be comes from Rome, and ultimately the commission will submit its recommendation to Rome and seek Rome's stamp of approval. Moreover, with the introduction of the commission, the conflict negotiations now return officially to a private forum, where Hunthausen's success in pursuing his own objectives has been mixed. Hunthausen offers no public comment about the commission itself.

The apostolic commission has the least to lose in the conflict handling. While a successful resolution brings enhanced prospects for future remuneration (more influence in Rome, perhaps a cardinal's hat for Quinn), failure can likely be blamed on intransigence from Hunthausen, and at worst probably brings only a loss of prestige and influence. For Hunthausen, the optimal outcome is a complete restoration of authority, with no threats to that in sight (other bishops who might potentially encroach upon his power). Less palatable options are regaining power, but with conditions (as in the appointment of a coadjutor with right of succession) or leaving office, either through resignation or forced retirement. Hunthausen must consider not only the consequences to his own person if he leaves office, but also to the local Church (turmoil, probably, but also freer reign for Rome to impose its own style of pastoral leadership locally and the likely removal of Hunthausen friends from leadership posts). For Rome, the most desirable outcome is to have Hunthausen accept, in appearance and in fact, Rome's vision for the future of the local Church. But since Hunthausen seems not to share that vision on the level of specifics of governance, the Holy See faces a choice between making Hunthausen back down and backing down itself. By making Hunthausen back down, it "wins" the administrative conformity issue and shows that it is in charge, but it loses the public relations battle with a large sector of the Church (including the target archdiocese) and likely stirs further unrest and confrontation. By backing down itself, Rome admits that it is not all-powerful and must retreat in a confrontation with one of its own bishops, but it comes out better on the public relations front and avoids further controversy in this corner of the Church.

Once the commission's work is underway, both the Vatican and Hunthausen remain tight-lipped in public. Archbishop Laghi meets with Hunthausen, Wuerl and the commission on at least two occasions early on, but most of the commission's work involves exchanges with Hunthausen, Wuerl and other parties. The practical challenge for the commission is as follows. To appease the Vatican it needs to find a mechanism for addressing the pastoral problems (a means for monitoring and correcting abuses) in Seattle, while quieting the public outcry there and elsewhere. To appease Hunthausen it needs to restore his power and remove Wuerl (not necessarily because Hunthausen has personal difficulties with Wuerl, but because Wuerl is unavoidably linked in people's minds to the unwanted Vatican intervention).

In the course of seeking a new arrangement agreeable to both parties, certain questions are more easily resolved than others. Apparently, there is no disagreement about moving Wuerl (even Wuerl himself later admits that the situation were "unworkable" once his faculties became known – see section I, subsequent developments). There also seems to be little disagreement about the restoration of full decision-making power to Hunthausen. Hunthausen insists on this, and it appears the Vatican is open to the possibility. The sticking point is how Rome – at a minimum symbolically, but preferably in effective practical ways as well – will maintain its own control over the local Church while exiting the conflict gracefully.

The commission's coadjutor plan offers a creative resolution to this difficulty. It offers to Hunthausen the restoration of his power (no special faculties are involved) and the removal of Wuerl. To Rome it offers a means for establishing tighter control over the archdiocese in the future: by appointing someone of its own choosing, by having that person in office alongside Hunthausen, and by having that person inherit the position of ordinary once Hunthausen retires. It also offers to Rome the face-saving advantage of replacing one "helper" bishop with another (who has the potential to be more easily accepted). Thus, Rome shows it has not beaten a complete retreat: it retains control.

For Hunthausen, there are several problems with the coadjutor solution. First, as a matter of appearances, a coadjutor appointment is worse than an auxiliary appointment, since auxiliaries normally come as a reward to a bishop, but a coadjutor appointment often signals leadership trouble in a diocese. Second, a coadjutor has right of succession, which gives the appointment long-term implications. Third, Hunthausen has just had a bad experience with an assistant bishop, one in which the arrangement turned out to be other than expected. Could the same situation recur? Finally, and perhaps most crucial of all: Who will the person be? If Hunthausen must, for the Vatican, have a bishop serve alongside him, Hunthausen wants the right to decide who he is. The most difficult questions in Hunthausen's negotiations with the commission appear to concern whether it is necessary for another bishop to come to Seattle, and if so, whether Hunthausen will be able to guarantee for himself that it will be someone he finds compatible.

The Briggs account gives us a glimpse of the exchange of arguments (*persuasive argumentation*) that occurs behind the scenes. A key tactic the commission employs is to give Hunthausen freedom of choice within a predetermined range. Hence, he is allowed to give input into the selection of a coadjutor by forwarding names and "approving" the final selection of names to be sent to Rome. But the impact of Hunthausen's contribution is minimalized, since two of the three names he proposes (Hurley and Kenny) are rejected before submission to Rome and the final name (Skylstad) is rejected in Rome. Though Hunthausen agrees to submit Murphy's name, he does so only under (*social*) *pressure* and after first *resisting*.

The hidden negotiations reproduce the pattern of earlier conflict developments. *Contention* by both parties (Hunthausen's resistance, the commission's insistence) escalates the conflict until a *stalemate* is reached. The stalemate is broken when one party (Hunthausen) *yields*. *Settlement* (agreement) follows. A difference, however, is that, following the more open conflict handling of the NCCB debate, Rome yielded to break the stalemate. Here, however, in much more private negotiations, Hunthausen yields.

The commission is not inflexible. According to Briggs, it meets Hunthausen's request (*yields*) by toning down the language (*face saving*) of the assessment report somewhat (though obviously not to Hunthausen's satisfaction, since he later criticizes the report). And while Murphy is not one of the choices that Hunthausen himself advances for coadjutor, his naming shows willingness by the commission to find someone reasonably acceptable to Hunthausen. On the other hand, in the face of resistance from Hunthausen, the commission shows it can also stand firm, and increase the pressure on Hunthausen as necessary. Eventually Hunthausen is left with a take-it-or-leave-it offer: accept the submission of the two names and the commission's assessment or be prepared to step down.

When Hunthausen expresses the intention (*threat*) to fly to Rome to deal directly with the Holy See, it becomes clear that Rome is ready to back up the decision-making authority of the commission. Rome refuses to grant permission for Hunthausen to come unless he meets certain conditions (in effect: gives in completely) first. This is a pronounced example of *territorial control* by the Vatican. The doctrinal or legal basis for the Holy See's *refusal to grant* to a fellow bishop *access* to the Pope and the Vatican bureaucracy is unknown. (Note on the question of territorial control. It is striking that the commission never visits Seattle during its assessment. The assessment information gathering and negotiations take place almost exclusively on what might be described as *neutral territory*: that is, not in Seattle, but not in

Rome either.)

The key to Hunthausen's decision to yield appears to be his perception that no better outcome can be obtained otherwise. Since he does not have the option of bypassing the commission's authority with an appeal to Rome, his only options are to further escalate the conflict by taking his complaints to the press (likely consequence: removal from office and chaos in the local Church), step down without protest (likely consequence: chaos in the local Church), or give in and make the best of the commission solution (likely consequence: personal dissatisfaction but the possibility of returning conditions to normal in the archdiocese in the near future). Hunthausen chooses to submit rather than rejuvenate the conflict.

The seal of secrecy put on the conflict negotiations between Hunthausen and the commission proves to be not inviolable. The April 15 story in the *National Catholic Register* (declaring that Wuerl would leave and Hunthausen would be retired after a face-saving period of restoration of power) shows that some person familiar with the negotiations was willing to go to the press to influence public discussion of the case. On behalf of the archdiocese, Fr. Michael G. Ryan denies the story. He also suggests that the story may have been put forth as a "trial balloon," to see how American bishops would react to the prospect of Hunthausen retiring early or, alternatively, to try to raise protest against the possibility that Hunthausen's powers would be fully restored. This concept of the leak as a "trial balloon" is plausible, but we lack evidence to ascertain the specific intention(s) behind the leak.

The *Register* leak does not prove to be the last. Quickly, in answer, news stories with inside information appear in the April 24 *National Catholic Reporter* and the April 25 *New York Times*. Again, the source of the leaks is unknown, but there is little room for doubt that the leaks constitute intentional efforts to influence the public debate by controlling the flow of information. One more notable example of this is the apparently autonomous action on the part of the *National Catholic Reporter* to inquire about and then report on the FBI's surveillance of Hunthausen's peace activism. The NC *Reporter* never made a secret of its support for Hunthausen, and this sidelight investigation and report appears to be an attempt to generate support for him by winning him sympathy. Probably, too, it is the product of a genuine curiosity about possible ties between the Vatican and the Reagan White House.

The public debate fueled by the news media places a continuous pressure on the conflict handling. So, too, do letter-writing campaigns to members of the hierarchy carried out by Hunthausen supporters and opponents. And finally, there is the impending pastoral visit of the Pope: at the start of May it is only four months ahead. It is not surprising that the conflict negotiations come down to an ultimatum.

By agreeing to the commission's proposal, Hunthausen accepts a *compromise*. Though he does not get everything he wants, and he remains frustrated, he nonetheless finds himself in a significantly improved position at the end of May, 1987: he has the final word in his archdiocese again, and he has an assistant bishop in place who is more familiar to Hunthausen and more likely to be effective than his predecessor. The commission has reason to be pleased, or at least relieved, that agreement has been reached. It has achieved its most important objective of getting an agreement in timely fashion that avoids further escalation of the conflict and that offers face-saving for both sides. The Vatican, too, has reason to be satisfied. Though it is doubtful that Hunthausen's pastoral vision is significantly more "Roman" than it was prior to the conflict (the opposite may even be true), it has at least established greater control over the archdiocese and has sent a strong signal of its expectations to the American Church. Most importantly of late, it has removed itself from a conflict that was quickly becoming more costly than it was worth.

With the press conference announcing implementation of the commission solution, the principal parties share with the public the details of the plan they have worked out in private.

8.2 Document Number: 9
Assessment Commission Report (5.20.87)
Source: *The Progress*, 5/28/87, pp. 3-4; *Origins*, 6/4/87, pp. 39-41.

8.2.1 Summary of Contents:
The document is divided into four numbered sections. No title appears on the versions of the document published in *The Progress* or *Origins*, but a copy of the document distributed to the chancery staff of the Seattle Archdiocese (Wasden Price collection) shows the following title: "Report to the Holy See Presented by Commission Appointed by the Holy See To Assess the Current Situation in the Archdiocese of Seattle." No introductory remarks precede the first section. Concluding remarks appear in section IV. The section titles are as follows: I. The history; II. The assessment; III. Proposal for resolving the problem and concluding remarks.

Section I., "The history," begins with a statement of the commission's appointment and mandate. The commission was appointed by the Holy See, through a letter of the Apostolic Pro-Nuncio, "to assess the current situation in the Archdiocese of Seattle." The rest of the section describes the history of the commission's activity. It consists mostly of a list of interviews conducted, each of which identifies the principal participants and date of the interview. The final two paragraphs of the section note that telephone conversations, letters, and "voluminous documentation" also served as information sources for the commission.

Section II, "The assessment," declares that, in the absence of a mandate regarding the *procedure* for conducting the assessment, the commission has adopted informal methods in order to arrive at what it believes to be a "common sense judgment." As a "context" for its approach, the commission has chosen two documents, "both known to Archbishop Hunthausen, to the Holy See and to everyone concerned," these being a summary of Archbishop Hickey's interview with Hunthausen, dated 8 November 1983, and Cardinal Ratzinger's letter to Hunthausen, dated 30 September 1985. Section II also contains an explicit statement of the commission's procedural decision to base its conclusions "only on documents seen by Archbishop Hunthausen and on discussions with persons designated by him or consulted with his knowledge and concurrence." The remainder of this section lists, in numbered subsections, the nine "judgments" unanimously decided upon by the commission. The judgments:

1) Archbishop Hunthausen has taken "laudable steps" to carry out "certain of the provisions" in the 9/30/85 Ratzinger letter.
2) In spite of these steps, confusion still exists among some in the Archdiocese about certain "clear" magisterial teaching, and some teachings have been "modified arbitrarily" by archdiocesan leaders.
3) The Archdiocese "suffers an inadequacy in communications" which may be interfering with reception of the Archbishop's articulations of magisterial teaching.
4) Though the Archbishop, who is well known for his compassion, "seems generally to balance compassion with the law," some in the archdiocese neglect Church law "under the

aegis of compassion."

5) In sum, though the Archbishop himself may be firm in his teachings and practices, "he is *perceived* as generating or at least accepting a climate of permissiveness."

6) One could supply examples of all of the observations above, but the Commission has decided not to because "it is the overall attitudinal 'climate' or psychological and ecclesiological orientation of the Archdiocese which is the ultimate key to the situation. No substantive changes will perdure until this climate or orientation changes." This climate has remained unchanged since the Visitation and Ratzinger's letter.

7) The Commission finds Ratzinger's 9.30.85 letter "reasonably clear in both specifics and intent." The Commission speculates that the Ratzinger letter did not provide an "exhaustive" list of "concrete points for correction" because he too was more concerned with broader perspectives or attitudes that inform specific decisions about practice. Ratzinger's preference was to write to Hunthausen "as bishop to bishop."

8) The Commission concludes that the Ratzinger letter should stand as "the primary guide" for future action. The Commission has, in a separate forum, provided Hunthausen with specific examples of problems in need of correction and will supply more if necessary.

9) Bishop Wuerl merits "highest praise" for his dedication in carrying out his responsibilities in such difficult circumstances.

Section III, "Proposal for resolving the problem and concluding remarks," begins with a statement that the proposal was developed "in consultation with the Holy See taking into account both the concerns of Archbishop Hunthausen as well as those of the Holy See." It then declares that one point of near unanimity among persons interviewed by the Commission was that the present arrangement of "divided authority" was "not effective and should be changed."

The Commission report then identifies five "essential elements" of its proposal. I reproduce the list below, retaining its exact wording.

> 1) The Auxiliary Bishop should be transferred to another See.
> 2) The Archbishop should recover his faculties as diocesan bishop.
> 3) A Coadjutor Archbishop should be appointed to Seattle.
> 4) The Holy See should establish target dates for the completion of the tasks referred to in the letter of the Congregation for the Doctrine of the Faith.
> 5) The Commission should be mandated for a period to be determined by the Holy See, to assist in the accomplishment of these tasks.

The final paragraphs of the Commission report assert the report represents the "best, most honest and unprejudiced judgment" of the commission members, who unanimously agreed on the findings therein. The Commission also pledges future assistance to the Holy See in carrying out elements of the report, however that may be deemed necessary.

No steps taken by the Holy See or the present Commission were, in the Commission's view, intended to be "punitive, regardless of perceptions to the contrary." Throughout its own involvement, the Commission has sought to keep before its eyes "the need for charity and compassion, the need for fairness and openness, the need to reach decisions and to make recommendations." It has also been mindful of the Second Vatican Council's perspective on the role of a bishop, wherein he is understood to be both one who exercises power in his own right in caring for his flock (he is not simply the Pope's vicar), and one who is a member of the College of Bishops under its Head, the Pope. But since the first century, it has occasionally been necessary for the Pope to intervene in local situations for the good of the

Church. "If the Church, spread through many cultures and existing on all continents is to remain one and maintain its identity, the Pope must make decisions which must be binding on the whole body of the Church."

The Commission document supports this last point with a quote from the well-known Jesuit theologian Karl Rahner, which emphasizes the papacy's place in "the binding content of our faith." The quotation proceeds to observe that "the Church cannot be a debating society: it must be able to make decisions binding on all within it. Such a demand cannot be *a priori* contrary to man's dignity if... he is indeed a social being. And then a supreme point at which all reflections and democratic discussions are turned into universally binding decisions cannot be without meaning."

The final paragraph of the report offers the hope and prayer of the Commission members that humility, obedience, charity and peace will prevail in the acceptance of the Holy See's decision. The signatures of the three Commission members appear at the end of the report.

8.2.2 Conflict Functionality of the 5.20.87 Assessment Commission Report

The assessment report tells the public, and fellow bishops in particular, what process the commission has followed in making its evaluation of Seattle, what conclusions it has drawn, and what recommendations it makes for the future. Its primary purpose appears to be one of *legitimation*: of the commission itself, and of the commission's process and conclusions. Beyond this, it seeks to persuade all involved of the efficacy of the recommendations. The text saves face for both Rome and Hunthausen, sparing both parties direct criticism but not indirect criticism.

In order to sell the agreement, the report establishes the legitimacy of the commission and the assessment process it has employed. The first words of the report tell us that the commission was "appointed" and given a "mandate" by the Holy See (*deference to the order and mindset of the Church*). Official notification of this appointment took place through the bureaucratic apparatus of the Church (the communication of the pro-nuncio, prot. n. 317/87/2). The remainder of section I and much of section II offer a rationale (*persuasive argumentation*) for the chosen assessment procedure and a description of how this was carried out. Legitimation takes several forms in these sections. Section I suggests that the assessment process was extensive in time, carefully documented and varied in its information sources (not only in the people consulted but also in the forms of information: visits, telephone conversations, letters, documentation; see also section III's comment that "we listened to many voices and weighed many views"). Section II suggests that the means of making the assessment were acceptable to the conflict parties themselves. Thus, the commission explains how it interpreted and carried out the mandate given it by the Vatican in a manner that was open to Hunthausen's concerns as well (*fraternity*): the commission would speak only with Hunthausen, Wuerl and persons designated by Hunthausen; the commission would refer only to documents known by Hunthausen, the Holy See and everyone concerned; and the assessment's conclusions would be based only on these personal and documentary sources. A further legitimation of the commission's process is the minor aside that "shared prayer" would be an element in the assessment procedure (*God talk*). In section III, we have an additional attestation in the same vein as the mention of prayer. After setting forth the heart of its assessment and proposals, the three bishops declare: "By signing this document, each Commission member testifies that it represents his best, most honest and unprejudiced judgment..." In other words, the bishops are willing to assert their own personal integrity (*personal identity*) as one more guarantor of the report's legitimacy. On the whole, however, the commission members play down their own personal identities in this report. The commission typically refers to itself in the third person (as "the Commission") or in the first person plural and their individual identities are distinguished only in the report of who met with whom when. They also stress the unanimity of their judgments (*fraternity*). These tactics of self-presentation minimize the reminders that human fallibility and personal biases are a factor in the assessment process.

Strikingly, the commission report states explicitly that the commission understood its assignment to be to conduct an "assessment," not an "Apostolic Visitation." One has to wonder at the significance of this distinction. (I pointed out is section 4.8.2, above, that the word "assess" was used by Archbishop Hickey's secretary to describe the visitation process.) What exactly is the difference between an assessment and a visitation, since the Vatican seems to have been at pains to present the visitation as a rather detached form of looking into the archdiocese? One key difference appears to rest in the matter of whether the archdiocese actually receives a personal visit from the official enquirer. The commission, according to its own report, never visited Seattle. All personal meetings took place elsewhere.

The commission's rationale for its manner of proceeding takes an interesting turn in section II, when the following connection is made.

> It [the commission] was asked to provide an *assessment* of the "current situation" in the Archdiocese of Seattle. In common sense terms, it seemed quite clear that the Holy See was looking for a common sense judgment, and this is all the Commission attempts to provide here.

One wonders how the second proposition "quite clear(ly)" follows from the first. In the first sentence, the commission highlights the words "assessment" and "current situation." According to the commission, this common-sensically leads to the conclusion that a "common sense" judgment is sought. The connection between the two sentences is puzzling, as is the meaning of common sense in this context. What sort of reference frame is implied by "common sense" here? Does this mean doing away with all technical, theological arguments (like those in the 9.30.85 Ratzinger letter)? We might translate passage as: We heard the Vatican telling us to resolve the conflict as quickly and efficiently as possible, not to go over old ground or to engage in theoretical reflection. So that is what we have tried to do.

In the remainder of the report are three key components. The first (completing section II) is the statement of the commission's "judgment," expressed in nine numbered points. The second (in section III) is the statement of the commission's proposals. And the third (completing section III and the document itself) is a set of concluding remarks which serve as a guide for interpreting the document. Some comments are in order about how these messages are packaged for public consumption. Essentially, the legitimation work of the first third of the document should place the reader in a position to accept the findings and proposals contained in the middle third. Lingering questions about whether the conflict is being validly resolved by the present means are taken up in the last third of the document.

The nine numbered points in section II, declaring the "unanimous judgment of the Commission," are the findings uncovered by the commission's work of assessment. Of chief importance in these points is that the commission offers no direct criticism of Hunthausen or the Vatican (*courtesy*). Hunthausen, for his part, is given the benefit of the doubt in regard to his carrying out of the visitation instructions received from Cardinal Ratzinger, his readiness to balance the prescripts of compassion and the law, and his personal firmness as a leader. And yet, at the same time, doubts about his leadership are *sustained* by this report. Praise and exculpatory comments in regard to Hunthausen's leadership are invariably qualified. Almost every sentence appears to carry a double meaning. To illustrate, I will reproduce a portion of the passage and insert indications of constructions that appear to show favor (indicated with an H+) or cast doubt (H-) on Hunthausen's leadership. In some cases, a given construction may bear positive and negative implications at the same time (H+, H-).

1) Archbishop Hunthausen has taken laudable steps (H+) to carry out certain (H-) of the provisions of the letter of the Congregation for the Doctrine of the Faith.

2) In spite of such steps, certain clear teachings of the Magisterium seem to be confused (H-) in the minds of some, and certain practices mandated by the Holy See seem to be modified arbitrarily (H-) by some pastors and other persons charged with responsibility for Archdiocesan activities (H+, H-).

3) Archbishop Hunthausen himself observed that the Archdiocese suffers an inadequacy in communications (H-). It seems possible, therefore, that certain ambiguities exist because not everyone is adequately familiar (H-) with the Archbishop's policies (H+) or with his articulations of magisterial teaching.

4) At the same time, the Archbishop attributes great value to *compassion*. His own practice of compassion has become almost legendary (H+). While the Archbishop himself, however, seems (H-) generally (H-) to balance compassion with the law (H+), and asserts unconditionally his own commitment to formal Church teaching (H+), it seems that some who admire his compassion may not give similar weight to the place and demands of law (H-), bending it in important matters under the aegis of compassion (H-).

5) In sum, no matter how personally firm (H+) in his teachings and practices the Archbishop himself may (H-) be, without intending it (H+), he is perceived (H+, H-) as generating (H-) or at least accepting (H-) a climate (H-) of permissiveness (H-) within which some feel themselves free to design their own policies and practices (H-).

What I have tried to show with my marking of this passage is that while the report never offers outright criticism of Hunthausen, his portrayal here is loaded with implied criticism. A persistent ambivalence is seen in the fact that all praise for Hunthausen is qualified. Hence, Hunthausen has taken "laudable steps" to carry out Ratzinger's provisions, but (unfortunately) he has only done this in regard to "certain" of those provisions. And while Hunthausen himself seems to have a clear grasp of Magisterial teaching and a real commitment to it, he has, the document suggests, failed to inculcate this same attitude in the people of his local Church. And though Hunthausen himself is admirably (legendarily!) compassionate, while still managing to balance compassion with the law, some of his followers have taken advantage of the freedom entrusted to them.

Repeatedly the criticism is deflected away from Hunthausen himself to his archdiocese, but the implication (but only the implication) always surfaces that Hunthausen himself bears significant responsibility for having allowed these conditions to develop locally. Even criticisms of the archdiocese are relentlessly qualified, usually with the word "seems." Magisterial teachings "seem to be confused in the minds of some" and certain practices "seem to be modified arbitrarily." "It seems possible that ambiguities exist," the report tells us – a remarkably tentative assertion of ambiguity! And so on. Through this strategy the commission avoids being tied to particularities in its "unanimous judgment." The report points in the general direction of the problem, but not to specific persons or groups or problems. By this means, Hunthausen and his local Church are allowed to *save face*.

Saving face for the Vatican consists primarily in another strategy. A basic source of face saving for the Vatican has to do with the fact that the Holy See is mostly out of view in this document. The focus is on Hunthausen, not Rome. Hunthausen's volatile charges against Rome – that the decision to undertake the visitation was presented to him as a *fait accompli*; that secrecy does and should not work; that the process was unjust because Hunthausen was not given a chance to see the charges or his accusers; etc. -- are taken up here only obliquely. Hunthausen's more contentious word choices are not repeated in this report (e.g., secrecy, unjust). Nor are the Vatican's (e.g., Laghi's suggestion that the Holy See found Hunthausen lacking the necessary "firmness). The main points at which the report speaks (directly) to the Vatican's handling of the affair are in numbered subpoints 6-8 of section II (the 'unanimous judgment" passage); in section III, when the commission says that interviewees found the divided authority arrangement "not effective;" and again in section III, when the commission denies that any Vatican actions were intended to be punitive. In each case the report offers a defense of the Vatican's conduct.

Section II, subpoint 6, addresses the charge (placed in the mouth of persons the commission interviewed, not Hunthausen himself) that Hunthausen had been "unfairly asked to correct aberrations without being told what they were..." In answer to this the commission says that real issue is the "climate" of pastoral practice in Seattle. Thus does the commission reaffirm a central argument of Ratzinger's 9.30.85 letter to Hunthausen. For that reason, the report continues (in subpoint 7), it would not be sufficient to supply a list of concrete examples. Nonetheless, if examples are necessary, some have already been provided to Hunthausen by Ratzinger's letter (cf. subpoint 7), some have been provided by the commission itself, and the commission is prepared to offer more as needed (subpoint 8).

Left unanswered (as it was in the Ratzinger letter) is the question of how Hunthausen is to go about changing the archdiocesan "climate." What *is* clear, however, is that this is one of the more damning issues in the report for Hunthausen. According to the commission, the problematic "psychological and ecclesiological orientation" of the archdiocese "seems [*seems*!] to have remained substantially unchanged since the time of the Apostolic Visitation and the letter of the Congregation for the Doctrine of the Faith." Hunthausen is immediately given an out from this from this charge – this is "in no way to suggest a lack of sincerity or the presence of malicious resistance" on Hunthausen's part – but again we find that a denial can be an effective way, rhetorically, to make a charge that one purportedly is not making.

As for Ratzinger, the commission finds that his letter is "reasonably clear in both specifics and intent," a statement that constitutes an endorsement but less than a ringing endorsement. While admittedly Ratzinger "made no effort to provide an exhaustive list of concrete points for correction," this is understandable, the commission finds, because he was speaking to Hunthausen as "bishop to bishop, as between those who share one Lord, one faith, one baptism, one Church." It is unclear why speaking bishop-to-bishop brings supercession of the need for specifics, but in terms of the discursive strategy of this report it answers the charge of insufficient detail in Ratzinger's letter.

Perhaps the most negative statement that focuses on the Vatican's actions occurs at the beginning of section III, where the commission report tells us: "Virtually all persons interviewed by the Commission agreed that the present arrangement of divided authority... was not effective and should be changed." In other words, the Vatican instituted an arrangement of power sharing that all agreed did not work. But the report does not put it so bluntly. The arrangement itself exists, here, independently of agency: the Vatican is not named as the entity establishing the arrangement. And since it does not work, the commission concludes, someone, somewhere would do well to change it. Significantly, the report makes no attempt here to explain why the arrangement was not effective. It simply notes it in passing, disassociates the situation from Vatican action and moves on.

One more instance of the commission presenting Vatican decisions in a less than critical light comes in section III, where the report declares: "Thoroughly aware of the steps taken by the Holy See up to this point, the Commission is convinced that no steps were intended as punitive, regardless of perceptions to the contrary." It is curious that (after asserting full knowledge of the history of the Vatican's actions, and thereby its own legitimacy as judge) the commission wants to make this argument. In public discussion of the case there was little disagreement about the fact of punishment itself. Hunthausen, his supporters *and* his opponents generally saw the Vatican's taking of power from Hunthausen as a kind of punishment. Even the undersecretary for the Congregation for Bishops had called the action "disciplinary." The issue was not whether disciplinary action had been taken but whether such action was appropriate. So why does the commission want to insist that "no steps were intended as punitive," and this "regardless of perceptions to the contrary"(!)? Is there something embarrassing in the idea that the primacy would punish a local ordinary? Or does this sticking point have something to do with the Vatican claim that Hunthausen *agreed* to give the faculties? In any case, it seems a moot point in light of Hunthausen's obvious unreadiness to have this power-sharing arrangement posed on him. Notice that the commission says that no steps were "intended" as punitive. Is this to say that the intention was some higher motive (such as pursuing unity through a more efficacious form of collegiality – i.e., redistributing powers to those who are best able to dispose them) and the punishment was an unintended consequence? This question cannot be answered on the basis of the text, but what is apparent is that the commission wants to rhetorically disassociate the Vatican from the unpleasant practice of dealing out punishment.

Thus far I have gone to some lengths to describe how this report "sells" the commission's own involvement and its findings, a persuasive effort that has been infused with an emphasis on saving face for Rome and for Hunthausen. Remarkably, however, there is no attempt to sell or even explain the five specific proposals themselves (i.e.: transfer Wuerl; restore the faculties; appoint a coadjutor; establish target dates; have the commission continue to assist). The report gives almost no context to illuminate why these specific recommendations are set forth. A minor exception applies in the case of the first and second recommendations, which seem directly related to the observation that the arrangement of divided authority has been found ineffective. But all in all, we have no rationale supplied to us for why these changes and not others should be implemented. Most especially, we are left to wonder about the rationale for appointing a coadjutor archbishop. Certainly the commission has reasons for this, reasons which have been shared with Hunthausen and the Holy See, but for whatever reason, this rationale is not shared with the public in the report. Another question surrounds the fourth recommendation ("The Holy See should establish target dates for the completion of the tasks referred to in the letter of the Congregation for the Doctrine of the Faith"). If the expectation is that Hunthausen will change the "overall attitudinal 'climate'" of the archdiocese, how is his success or failure to be measured? There are more questions that can be raised, but of immediate significance for our analysis here is the silence kept here in regard to the thinking that informs the recommendations themselves. Since the overall orientation of this document appears to be to put an end to the conflict, it may well be that the decision to leave out the rationale for the recommendations was based on the sense that including the rationale would open up new issue fronts in the affair, an unwelcome prospect.

The portion of the document that follows the statement of recommendations and closes the document itself takes the form of a theological reflection on the office of bishop and the place of the primacy as the "supreme point" of decision making in the Church (*ecclesiological God talk; expert power; persuasive argumentation*). Here the document places the entire conflict in context, answering past arguments (specifically, certain arguments Hunthausen made in his NCCB address) and foreclosing future arguments at the same time. The reflection begins with a nod to Hunthausen's authority and the authority of individual bishops. Citing the Vatican II document *Lumen Gentium* (itself an acknowledgment of Hunthausen's preferred ecclesiological starting point), the report affirms what Hunthausen says in section IV of his NCCB address: that local bishops possess authority in their own right: they are not merely vicars of the Roman Pontiff. As a strategy of argumentation, there are clear advantages to beginning with the viewpoint and strongest argument that one wishes to refute, as the commission does here. And indeed refutation – or, to put it more mildly, counterbalancing of the argument – is what follows. "At the same time," the report continues, "… No bishop is an independent agent, standing in isolation. As a member of the College of Bishops, he exercises his office only in communion with and obedience to the Head of the College of Bishops, the Pope, the Successor of Peter and Bishop of Rome." The concept of obedience finds reiteration in the succeeding sentence, which notes that every bishop promises obedience to the Pope in his ordination (i.e., obedience is inseparable from the office of bishop itself).

We recall that in his address to the NCCB, Hunthausen argued that obedience should involve more than a simple acquiescence, and rightfully includes dialogue. The final paragraphs of the commission report (excluding the very last) answer this argument. The components to the response are the following propositions: (1) Tradition justifies such interventions by the primacy: the Pope has intervened in local churches since the first century. (2) This power to intervene is necessary to maintain the unity and identity of the Church. (3) The papacy "belongs to the binding content of our faith itself." In other words, the papacy's role within the Church is divinely sanctioned, permanent and of fundamental importance. (4) Democratic discussions have their place in the Church but there needs to be an end point for debates. It is meaningful to have a means for turning democratic discussions into binding decisions. (5) The papacy's power to make universally binding decisions poses no threat to the dignity of the human person, who is rightfully acknowledged to be a social being. The gist of these arguments for accepting the commission's recommendations is that doing so is in keeping with what the Church is (a hierarchical, divinely-sanctioned unity) and how it has always conducted itself (since the first century A.D.), and what it must do for its own good ("We are and we shall remain also in the future the *Roman* Catholic Church). Hunthausen's desire to keep arguing is uncalled for ("the Church cannot be a debating society") because it is not consistent with the Church's identity, its traditional practice and its concern for its own well being (it is *not* in the *best interest of the Church*).

While making this response, the commission quotes extensively from a theological work by Karl Rahner. This instance of manifest intertextuality is striking for two reasons. First, Rahner is an academic theologian writing expressly in that capacity. No other such sources have been cited in the case documents analyzed thus far. Theological writings produced by the hierarchy (in the form of Conciliar documents, papal teachings, curial instructions, bishops' pastoral letters) have been invoked, but no works of academic theologians. One can imagine why this has not been done in the past. Such works by definition lack the authority of teaching issued by the Church hierarchy (thus, they are not the best source for "proving" a point), and, contemporaneous with the Hunthausen case, certain theologians were in the process of being taken to task by the Vatican (most prominently, Charles Curran and Leonardo Boff). Hence, the works of academic theologians were doubly suspect.

The second reason the commission report's citation of Rahner is striking is that the reference is highly intraecclesial. Rahner is well known among theologically educated Church insiders (i.e., the target audience of bishops), but the name would mean little to the general public. The choice to quote him in particular marks something of a departure from the commission report's overall approach, which seems to be to use straightforward, nontechnical language to persuade as broad an audience as possible to accept the conflict resolution here proposed.

So what is the Rahner passage doing here, then? It may be primarily a choice of convenience. The passage says what the bishops want to say, and there is always value in showing that outside authorities hold the same view as oneself. The commission is busy making the point that Hunthausen cannot simply go his own way as a bishop, he has to answer to Rome, and Rahner makes this point succinctly in this particular book. One need attribute only minimal significance to the fact that Rahner *per se* is chosen (as opposed to some other theologian or theological source). In any case, Rahner is a safe choice as far as the conflict parties are concerned. Rahner can be characterized as a forward-thinking theologian (acceptable to Hunthausen) who was not subject to Vatican suspicion (acceptable to the Vatican).

Two other references to external texts – to the transcript of the 11.8.83 Hickey-Hunthausen interview and the 9.30.85 Ratzinger letter -- stand out in this report. These are the documents known to all parties which have served the commission's assessment process. The commission puts forth one of these documents, the 9.30.85 Ratzinger letter, as a guide for future pastoral action in the Seattle archdiocese. Use of the letter in this way is a cornerstone of the commission's proposal for addressing the situation in Seattle. This letter, which Hunthausen was not originally allowed to share with the public, has undergone a process of progressive revelation to the public (first through rewriting by Laghi, then by Hunthausen's sharing of the letter with his priests, then by Wuerl's mention of the letter in his own letter to priests, then by Hunthausen's mention of the letter obliquely in his response to the Vatican chronology, and finally by the commission report's provision of the letter itself in accompaniment to the commission report). What are we to make of this progressive unveiling? Does it constitute a minor success for Hunthausen, who wanted the letter released in the first place? This is hard to say. Since the letter was not especially favorable toward Hunthausen to begin with (it was less favorable, in fact, than the Laghi rewrite), it does not seem to benefit Hunthausen by polishing his image. Moreover, at this late date it may not even amount to a concession, since it is not clear that Hunthausen still desires its release. Seen from another angle, the Vatican's publication of the letter further chips away at the wall of secrecy, which has been one of Hunthausen's priorities. The handling of the Ratzinger letter runs as a thread through the conflict as a whole. The fact that references to it recur and that it finds an ongoing functional relevance make it one of the keys to comprehending the total conflict.

The Hickey-Hunthausen interview is the second key reference document the commission makes use of in its assessment. Like the Hickey visitation report to the Vatican, the Hickey-Hunthausen interview transcript has never been made public. It is interesting that Hunthausen never criticizes the Vatican's use of secrecy in regard to this document and that he never presses to have this transcript made public (nor does he release his own copy), especially since the quality of his responses to questions raised by the Vatican is a conflict issue. There are some reasons we can imagine for Hunthausen's not being interested in doing so. For one thing, he already knows its contents, so the secret is not being kept from him. Another reason may be that he agreed to the use of secrecy in this interview ahead of time: so perhaps it is simply a question of keeping his word. A further reason could be a desire to protect the identities of persons mentioned in the interview. The most likely reason, however (and this does not rule out the relevance of the other reasons), for not releasing the transcript or excerpts thereof is simply that, for whatever reason, doing so would not, on balance, help his cause. It is probable that the contents of such a long interview session would prove to be a mixed bag. Apparently benign things said in private conversation may look very different when one considers the prospect of their widespread public distribution. We should note, too, that Hunthausen had no opportunity to edit the interview transcript. He was simply presented with a word-for-word transcript that he was asked to sign as an indication of accuracy. Thus, he was not offered the opportunity to rework his comments for a target audience.

I have sought to illustrate the apostolic commission's attempt to usher in the end of the Rome-Hunthausen conflict by means of its evaluation and report. The report itself answers a number of questions raised by the conflict exchanges, proposes a new arrangement in Seattle, and markets a vision of resolution that, the commission hopes, will be acceptable to the American bishops and the public at large. The success of the document in achieving these ends depends on public reception of the report and the cooperation of the direct participants in the affair.

I. Subsequent Developments (May 1987-April 1989)

At the May 27 news conference (*Seattle Times*, 5.28.87; *Seattle Post-Intelligencer*, 5.28.87) with Murphy, Hunthausen appeared, for the most part, positively disposed to the settlement and at ease with his new coadjutor. Of the agreement he said, "I am so hopeful, so desirous of making it work. I just think it has tremendous potential. Calling Murphy "a friend and a trusted co-worker," Hunthausen said, "I have assurance that Archbishop Murphy comes without special faculties. I think you know that I could not and would not accept such an arrangement."

When Murphy was asked about his own understanding of his role, he answered, "Archbishop Hunthausen is my archbishop just as he is the (archbishop) of the others in the faith community of Western Washington. I really am looking forward to the experience of sharing this responsibility with a person I respect…" Does Murphy represent "the long arm of the Vatican?" Hunthausen was asked. Hunthausen patted Murphy on the back and turned the question over to him. Murphy replied: "I am here primarily because of a process where I was one of the people Archbishop Hunthausen felt he could work with and share ministerial responsibilities that are his in this archdiocese."

But despite the apparent satisfaction and good rapport between Hunthausen and Murphy, it was also evident from one of the written statements Hunthausen distributed that he had mixed feelings about the settlement that had been reached. Whereas Hunthausen's general press statement offered up only a minor indication of dissatisfaction and a lingering combativeness ("It is only honest for me to acknowledge that that [the commission and I] have not always agreed on every aspect of the work they have done – even some important aspects…"), his letter to priests of the archdiocese, which was also released to the press, was more explicitly contentious. There Hunthausen wrote, "I want you to know that, while I am not in agreement with a number of important aspects of the assessment and am therefore not prepared to endorse it, I have nonetheless come to the point of accepting the Commission's proposed resolution to our situation."

Even the letter to the priests, however, was essentially conciliatory. "For better or worse," Hunthausen wrote, "we are at this particular moment in our history. While there are many thoughts and hopes in my heart at this time, my prayer is simple: that we will be able to see this new moment as a graced moment; a moment in which we are challenged as a Church to become all we strive and profess to be and more…"

In his general statement to the press, Hunthausen began by thanking the Pope for Murphy's appointment. He then said he saw this as an "opportunity for us to move forward together as a Church after a long and very difficult period of struggle and uncertainty." Hunthausen praised Murphy for his energetic and committed service to the Church; the assessment commission for their dedication to the good of the Church while carrying out their difficult assignment; and Bishop Wuerl for giving himself generously to his episcopal duties, which were made all the more demanding by the circumstances. The remainder of the statement offered words of thanks and spiritual encouragement to the people of the archdiocese.

Murphy's statement called his appointment as Coadjutor Archbishop "a great honor." Murphy said, "I have responded to this request of the Holy Father in a spirit of prayer and hope that I may be of help and service to the Church of Seattle." Murphy went on to say that he looked forward to his assignment but that it would be difficult to leave the Church of Eastern Montana, which he had grown to love. Murphy pledged his "respect, loyalty and commitment to Pope John Paul II and the Holy See" and he also pledged his "support and service to Archbishop Hunthausen and the Archdiocese of Seattle."

Wuerl's statement called Murphy's appointment "a welcome sign of the resolution of the difficulty and tension that has developed in this local church." Wuerl described Murphy as "an energetic, gifted, prayerful and articulate bishop" and he expressed his hope that Murphy's talents and gifts would "work to the healing and benefit" of the archdiocese. Wuerl noted that his own new assignment had not yet been specified but that he was grateful for the occasion to reflect on his own ministry in Western Washington. Most especially, he was grateful for the warmth of welcome and depth of kindness that had been shown to him by the people of the archdiocese during his period of service. Wuerl also extended his appreciation to Archbishop Hunthausen: "During the time we worked together, even though the situation was difficult, he was always considerate and kind."

Cardinal Bernardin of the assessment commission also released a statement of his own on May 27 (cf. *National Catholic Reporter*, 6.5.87), saying, "I am very pleased with the resolution proposed by our commission and accepted by the Holy See.

> I believe we have addressed the concerns of both the Holy See and Archbishop Hunthausen with sensitivity to the persons involved and to the needs of the universal and local church.
> I know that many join me in prayer and good wishes for Archbishop Hunthausen, Archbishop-elect Murphy, Bishop Wuerl and the priests and people of the Archdiocese of Seattle. Those of us on the commission remain ready to assist in every way possible, confident that everyone involved is eager to move forward in truth, peace, unity and love.

Bernardin's final sentence clearly relates to the intention for the commission to continue in existence ("for a period to be determined by the Holy See") to aid Hunthausen and Murphy in carrying out the provisions of the 9.30.85 Ratzinger letter summarizing the visitation conclusions.

More generally, the first reactions to the settlement were typically expressions of satisfaction tinged with uncertainty. Interestingly, this was true of both supporters and critics of Hunthausen. Both sides seemed to struggle to discern what the full implications of the new arrangement were, while finding reason to be optimistic. Sister Chauncey Boyle, president of the 700-member archdiocesan Sisters' Council, said, "My reaction is really mixed. This is sort of the best we could get" (*Seattle Times*, 5.27.87). Some were puzzled by the decision to send a coadjutor archbishop who would not have special faculties, since coadjutors normally were appointed with possession of such faculties. Erven Park, an outspoken Hunthausen critic, said that restoring Hunthausen's power while appointing a coadjutor amounted to "a contradiction in terms." Hunthausen himself repeatedly resisted attempts to characterize the resolution as a matter of winning or losing. "That spirit comes out of a spirit of competition, and that's not where we are here."

The response to Murphy himself was, for the most part, positive. The two main local newspapers and the archdiocesan newspaper all reported that Murphy had made a good first impression on the priests of the archdiocese at a large gathering on May 29 (*Seattle Post-Intelligencer*, 5.30.87; *Seattle Times*, 5.30.87; *The Progress*, 6.4.87). From his first moments in Seattle, Murphy had shown his talent for defusing troublesome questions with humor. When asked what might have possessed him to step into the Seattle mess, he attributed it to "the Gaelic spirit of adventure" (*Seattle Weekly*, 6.9.87). And at his first gathering with the priests, Hunthausen told of a young relative who asked him what it meant to be named "co-agitator." Early accounts noted, too, that Murphy had a knack for Church politics. During Murphy's years of service as a young priest in Chicago, he had "gained a reputation as a conciliator amid the ecclesial infighting rampant under the late Cardinal John Cody" (*National Catholic Reporter*, 6.19.87).

After the first flurry of news reports about the implementation of the commission recommendation in Seattle came a more extended period of reflection on what the developments meant. This discussion was carried on in the Catholic press, primarily, and among Catholic theologians. Contrary to Hunthausen's wishes, many observers were inclined to speak in terms of political victory and defeat. University of Notre Dame theologian Fr. Richard McBrien said, "On balance, Hunthausen is the victor. The bottom line is that he has full episcopal authority restored. It shows once again that the pope is much more a political realist than some of his right-wing supporters... and if people and especially the bishops confront him, the pope does back off, and he has backed off" (*National Catholic Reporter*, 6.5.87). Though not normally one to agree with McBrien, *Wanderer* editor A. J. Matt expressed the same view. "In the political sense, it certainly is a victory (for Hunthausen)," Matt said. "Whether it is a moral or spiritual victory, I would have serious reservations." James Hitchcock, a historian at St. Louis University, however, cautioned against overstating the extent to which the outcome favored Hunthausen. Not only did the commission report present "very strong criticism of Archbishop Hunthausen's governance;" it also established "target dates" that indicated an expectation of "measurable results." "There is already a mechanism in place," Hitchcock said, "whereby if the results don't come, then Hunthausen can be made to move aside" (*Seattle Times*, 5.30.87). Fr. Andrew Greeley of the National Opinion Research Center in Chicago called the settlement "a typical Cardinal Bernardin solution – one with which everyone can live, but with which no one is completely happy." Father Richard Hynes, president of the National Federation of Priests' Councils, described the settlement as a healthy "exercise of the collaborative process."

More of Hunthausen's thoughts and feelings about the outcome and the process that led to it emerged in a May 28 interview with *The Progress*, which was publicly circulated in the June 4 issue. The central point in Hunthausen's message was the need to move forward. "I think we are at the point where a decision has been made, and so there is nothing to be served by going back and saying, 'I wish that.... I think that....' I just don't think that is what we need to do or want to do."

> Archbishop Hunthausen said the commission's report and solution were "obviously the result of a great deal of prayer. We have all been praying and I believe the prayers are answered.
>
> "As they describe this church, it is not the church that I know," he said. "I don't view the ministry as they have viewed it; but they have come to this position by a process" which was open and honest.
>
> The archbishop said that the process was a "constant dialogue. It was a discussion of pros and cons. They legitimately examined my wish list and honestly told me what was viable and what was not, and ultimately we got to this point."
>
> "I am confident that this is what God wants and it will work for the best," the archbishop continued. "My own wish and will doesn't always identify with what God wants, and I think one has to be open to finding out what God wants."
>
> [....] I am grateful that I was given the opportunity, and the freedom and the privilege to say what I felt about these developments as I went," he said. "To try and keep these those from being from being the center of public attention and the center of public debate... that's a hard thing."
>
> "I guess in all this, one of the real tensions has been how to bring forth the reality of who we are and the truth of this church without giving the impression that we were setting ourselves up in opposition to our superiors," Archbishop Hunthausen said.
>
> "That is a very, very fancy balancing act."
>
> Questioning judgments made by church leaders, even when invited to do so, he said, can give some the impression of disloyalty and disobedience.
>
> "If you give that impression, then you also run the risk of scandalizing some of the faithful," he said.
>
> "I don't think there were ever instances of loyalty or disobedience," he added, "but if it is perceived that way, you run the risk of really alienating some people."
>
> "That's been the tension," he said. "It's been extremely difficult."
>
> Archbishop Hunthausen also emphasized that he has "never, never had the slightest question about my loyalty to the Holy Father or his right to act in this (local) church."
>
> While questions about parts of the four-year process remain, the local church has its agenda for the next year: addressing the concerns in the Ratzinger letter with the assistance of the commission members.
>
> "Obviously, this has touched the church well beyond Seattle, which means that it hit a sensitive nerve.... It says something about the way we view how the church ought to function," he said.
>
> Archbishop Hunthausen said he would rather leave the lingering questions to theologians and historians to wrestle with. "We have to move forward or we will destroy ourselves."

On June 7, Bishop Wuerl celebrated his farewell Mass at Holy Rosary Church in West Seattle, the parish where he had been in residence. Wuerl's new assignment was not yet known. After the Mass, Wuerl said he felt no bitterness and was "glad it's over. I'm glad it's settled" (*Seattle Post-Intelligencer*, 6.8.87). One week later, on July 13, a formal service of welcome to Archbishop Murphy was celebrated at St. James Cathedral. In what was perhaps a Freudian slip of the liturgical variety, Fr. John Pinette, one of the masters of ceremonies, absent-mindedly handed the crozier to Archbishop Murphy at the end of the service. Murphy laughed, shook his head, and handed the crozier to Hunthausen.

A press conference followed three days later (July 16). Hunthausen and Murphy answered questions and said they would soon be meeting with the assessment commission in Chicago (*Seattle Post-Intelligencer*, 7.16.87). They said the Chicago meeting would be their first opportunity to seek clarification and guidance from the commission since the settlement had been reached. Hunthausen and Murphy were jovial and appeared to quite at ease with one another. At one point Hunthausen was asked if events in Seattle had shed light on what had been called a tension between the "Roman Catholic" and the "American Catholic" views of their church, Hunthausen sighed deeply. "I appreciate your question," he said. "It's a question I ask myself very, very often. I'm not sure I've found the answer" (*Seattle Times*, 7.16.87).

Back in his home diocese of Pittsburgh, Bishop Wuerl broke his extended silence regarding the Seattle controversy. In an interview with the diocesan newspaper, *Pittsburgh Catholic* (6.19.87), Wuerl said that certain "myths" had developed during his time in Seattle. In sum, these mistaken notions were "that he had arrived in Seattle with 'special faculties,' that there ever was a secret agreement unknown to Archbishop Hunthausen, that his appointment was an 'injustice' to the archbishop, and that Vatican decisions were designed to discourage the archbishop's well-known anti-nuclear arms activities."

Wuerl noted that he and Hunthausen had always enjoyed a good relationship personally, but that the assignment had been a difficult one. "I'm physically and psychologically tired," he said. Though his parish visits were as positive as his exchanges with Hunthausen, Wuerl admitted that some in the archdiocese had been less than welcoming, and some had shown him outright animosity. (The 4.30.87 *Seattle Post-Intelligencer* reported that Wuerl had received death threats during his time in Seattle. In its 6.9.87 editorial on the occasion of Wuerl's departure, the same newspaper noted that Wuerl had even drawn fire from Hunthausen opponents, "who expected Wuerl to champion their cause to drive Hunthausen out.") A daily toll was taken by the fact that, "My very presence was an implied criticism. Some of them had difficulty with that," Wuerl told the Pittsburgh paper, "yet others tried very hard to keep the focus on issues and not the person. I said to a gathering of all priests and chancery staff that I don't think I was ever seen as an individual human being but more as a symbol of the visitation."

Wuerl observed that addressing the issues identified by the Vatican became impossible amid the controversy around his role. "From the time the faculties were granted in August (1986) until last week, the public furor over all this became so intense it was impossible to address the issues." Wuerl said that he had maintained his silence during the controversy because "my hope was to effect some healing in Seattle rather than add to the tension and division."

Sustaining Wuerl was the sense that the Church is bigger than "human misunderstandings," which are, in any case, "a natural part of life." "What is important is not that there are misunderstandings, but the manner in which you resolve them. That should always be done with patience, understanding and, above all, love." Bishop Wuerl was appointed ordinary of his home diocese, Pittsburgh, on February 12, 1988. (The apostolic visitator, Washington Archbishop James Hickey, was elevated to cardinal on June 28 of that same year.)

Starting on July 16, 1987 in Chicago, Hunthausen and Murphy met with the assessment commission quarterly to discuss their progress in addressing the concerns identified in the Ratzinger letter. The next meeting took place on November 10, 1987 in Washington, D. C. The third meeting was on February 26, 1988 in Seattle. Archbishop Quinn did not participate in this meeting. He was on a leave-of-absence at this time (*Seattle Post-Intelligencer*, 2.26.88). Cardinal Bernardin offered a few remarks to the press during the Seattle meeting. Murphy and Hunthausen appeared to be working well together, he said: "things are going quite well. The situation has been very tranquil." Bernardin said he intended to make no formal statements in connection with the quarterly meetings that had been agreed upon by Hunthausen, Murphy and the commission. Bernardin also reiterated that "the only purpose of this commission is to assist Archbishop Hunthausen as diocesan bishop and Archbishop Murphy as his assistant in fulfilling the requests of the Holy See. There is no hidden agenda here" (*The Progress*, 5.3.87). Two subsequent meetings occurred between the Seattle Archbishops and the commission (dates unknown. Apparently the last meeting took place during an extraordinary synod of bishops in Rome, March 1989: cf. *Seattle Post-Intelligencer*, 3.15.89).

The exchanges between Hunthausen, Murphy and the commission concluded with Hunthausen's filing of a set of formal responses to the concerns identified through the visitation and post-visitation process. The Holy See accepted these responses (*National Catholic Reporter*, 4/21/89).

The completion of the work of the apostolic commission was made public through an announcement of the papal pro-nuncio in Washington, D.C. and an announcement by Hunthausen in Seattle on the same day (*The Progress*, 4.13.89; see also the inter-office memorandum from Hunthausen to "Central Agency Employees," dated 4.11.89, in the Wasden Price collection.) The statement from the nunciature reads:

> Archbishop Pio Laghi, Apostolic Pro-Nuncio, announced today, April 11, 1989, that the work of the Apostolic Commission chaired by Joseph Cardinal Bernardin is completed and its mandate has been terminated in relationship to the Archdiocese of Seattle.
> Archbishop Raymond G. Hunthausen has indicated that he, along with Coadjutor Archbishop Thomas J. Murphy, will continue to address the issues which have been of concern to the Church in the Archdiocese of Seattle by implementing the changes in the pastoral care of the Archdiocese which have already been initiated.

Hunthausen thanked Laghi and the commission, and put the conflict experience in a positive light.

> I am grateful for the announcement by Archbishop Laghi of the closure of the work of the Apostolic Commission. I am also grateful to the members of the Apostolic Commission, Joseph Cardinal Bernardin, John Cardinal O'Connor and Archbishop John Quinn, for their pastoral assistance.
> Both Archbishop Murphy and I acknowledge the trial the Church here has faced over the past several years, yet we are also able to view the whole experience as a time of grace, a grace which, with the Lord's help, will enable us to offer our leadership to the Church in Western Washington in the years ahead with renewed dedication and commitment to the Gospel and the Universal Church under our Holy Father, Pope John Paul II. We ask for your prayers as we continue to meet the challenges of being a Roman Catholic community of faith here in Western Washington.

In somewhat less formal language, Hunthausen said at a press conference, "I rejoice in the fact that the apostolic visitation is over… We're going to have a party" (*Seattle Post-Intelligencer*, 4.13.89). When asked what changes had been wrought by the prolonged review, Hunthausen said, "I'm not sure the ministry has changed. In those areas especially, we have deliberately examined what as archdiocese… we should be doing. We have reissued the guidelines, but if you look you will see there have been no substantive changes." Hunthausen observed that violations which had taken place in the archdiocese had been limited to isolated instances. "Generally speaking, we have not been in violation. This has been a very limited thing." Hunthausen also shared the view that Seattle's pastoral policies were not notably different from those of other dioceses. "I'm not able to say precisely why we were singled out…" he said. Hunthausen indicated that he would continue to "redirect" his income tax and be active in the anti-nuclear arms movement. The years of visitation and assessment, he said, had not compromised his ministry.

From beginning to end, the process of active intervention by the Holy See in the Archdiocese of Seattle lasted five-and-a-half years. Archbishop Hunthausen retired from office on his seventieth birthday, August 21, 1991, some two years after the conflict had run its course. That same year, Archbishop Laghi, who had served as pro-nuncio in the U.S. until 1990, was made a cardinal.

I.i. Conflict Functionality of the Subsequent Developments (May 1987-April 1989)

The release of the commission report and announcement of Murphy's appointment as coadjutor archbishop of Seattle marks the beginning of the end of the Rome-Hunthausen conflict. The announced agreement proves to be a lasting one, with no further escalations of consequence occurring beyond this point. The tensions between center and periphery never disappear entirely. At the time of the announcement itself, Hunthausen expresses his disagreement with certain aspects of the commission report, and even at the end of the commission's oversight, almost two years after the implementation of the new arrangement, Hunthausen continues to profess bewilderment about the Vatican's intervention. But for the most part, from the time of the agreement announcement forward, Hunthausen downplays his dissatisfaction, and couches any disgruntlement in abundant expressions of cooperativeness and hopefulness.

When Hunthausen presents the commission report and his new coadjutor archbishop to the press, he shows that he has not lost all taste for *contention*. Though he publicly welcomes Murphy with open arms, he puts in writing at the same time his opposition to important aspects of the commission report. This is a surprisingly provocative declaration, since it contradicts the public display of acceptance of the plan and resolution for the conflict. But Hunthausen buries his provocation in a show of loyalty and obedience (*deference to the order and mindset of the Church*), and indeed, the announcement ushers in a new period of *graciousness* (*courtesy*) all around. Hunthausen thanks the Holy Father and praises Murphy, the commission and Wuerl. Wuerl praises Murphy and thanks the people of the archdiocese. Bernardin offers his prayer and good wishes to Hunthausen, Murphy, Wuerl and the people of Seattle, and he expresses his confidence that "everyone involved is eager to move forward in truth, peace, unity and love." Significantly, Hunthausen's prickly comment prompts no response from the commission, the pro-nuncio or Rome: as a result, no escalation occurs.

Similarly, in April of 1989, when the pro-nuncio announces the completion of the assessment commission's work of evaluation of Hunthausen's ministry, Hunthausen gives the impression that center and periphery still do not see eye-to-eye. When asked what changes had resulted from the extended Vatican intervention, Hunthausen responds by saying that "there have been no substantive changes," except for in isolated instances. "Generally speaking, we have not been in violation." One can imagine that these remarks were received with some irritation in Rome and at the nunciature in Washington. But again, no retort comes from the center and no rise in conflict tension materializes in consequence. These comments suggest that, even at the apparent end of the conflict handling process, Hunthausen is not fully reconciled to the visitation and its conclusions.

Nonetheless, it is not to be denied that, once the commission plan is announced and he has voiced his immediate reservations, Hunthausen works determinedly to quiet the conflict (*minimize the appearance of conflict*) and put it behind him and the archdiocese. As part of the resolution plan, Hunthausen accepts the continued monitoring of his ministry by the commission (*surveillance*; or as Bernardin euphemistically puts it: "the commission remain(s) ready to *assist* [emphasis mine] in every way possible"). Apart from his comments in April of 1989, Hunthausen rarely ever speaks of the visitation experience again – in any case, not in detail and not in public. His *silence* is matched by other direct participants. Once it is over, it is over for Laghi, Hickey, Wuerl, the assessment commission, and above all for the key players in Rome, who almost never spoke about the case in public anyway, even when it was in the fullness of intensity.

As before, Hunthausen's meetings with the commission (they are now joined by Murphy in place of Wuerl) take place in private (*secrecy*). Though the commission report recommends that the commission stay in its role of assistance role for a year, its service continues for almost two full years. No public record accounts for the content of the meetings or the reason for their extended continuance. The *bureaucratic act of closure* of the assessment process – Hunthausen's filing of formal responses to the Vatican's concerns – is also not open to public scrutiny, at the time or thereafter.

Implementation of the commission plan brings about a restoration of Hunthausen's power in the local Church (*territorial control*). No longer is there someone who can overrule him within the archdiocese. Over time, Murphy succeeds in the archdiocese (effectively contributes) in a way that Wuerl was unable to. Whereas Wuerl was widely seen to be "symbol of the visitation," as Wuerl himself put it, Murphy receives the benefit of the doubt from many in the archdiocese. Wuerl's strong ties to Rome and his rather formal personal style fueled suspicions, Murphy's prior period of service in the Northwest and his casual style and quick wit work to undermine suspicions. Most critical to Murphy's acceptance is the basic fact that his presence does not come at the cost of Hunthausen's own power to lead.

As the conflict experience recedes, the Holy See *remunerates* several who have served the center party cause. Pope John Paul II rewards for his efforts in a difficult assignment with an appointment as ordinary of his home diocese, Pittsburgh. The Pope makes Archbishop Hickey and Laghi cardinals. Archbishop Quinn retires without having been made a cardinal, as, of course, does Hunthausen. Upon Hunthausen's retirement, Archbishop Murphy succeeds him in office in Seattle, according to plan. Murphy dies in office of cancer in 1997, without having been promoted further.

CHAPTER NINE

INTEGRATED ANALYSIS OF COPING STRATEGIES
APPLIED IN THE ROME-HUNTHAUSEN CASE

9.1 Review of the Expected Findings

The question that guides the present investigation is, *what coping strategies are observable in center-periphery conflict discourse?* After having summarized the case and having analyzed the strategic functionality of selected documents and other case developments, I am now prepared to put an answer to that question.

The expectations I formulated (chapter 3) were the following:

> **General Stance Toward Conflict Handling:** All members of the hierarchy participating in center-periphery conflict will strive to save the face of and enhance the power of the Church organization and themselves.

> **Perspective on the Use of Power:** All members of the hierarchy participating in center-periphery conflict will strive for (the appearance of) legitimacy in their employments of power.

> **Operative Strategies:**
> 1. Show deference to the existing structural order and mindset of the Church
> 2. Associate one's own efforts with the best interest of the Church
> 3. Minimize the appearance of conflict
> 4. Show fraternity
> 5. Practice courtesy
> 6. Employ secrecy
> 7. Recruit allies

I anticipated that the above-named strategies would be embraced by all members of the hierarchy participating in the conflict, but that they would be embraced in more or less enthusiastic ways depending on one's position in the hierarchy and the circumstances of the conflict. In this chapter I will compare my expected findings with the data from the case, a process that includes the identification of strategies that were not anticipated. I will then integrate the findings in a summary table for the conflict as a whole and will consider the findings in light of the conflict theory material presented in chapter four. Finally, I will conduct two forms of validational control of my findings: first, by means of an analysis of certain documents that have been set aside for comparative purposes; and then by comparing my own view of the conflict with another provided by a conflict insider (Fr. Michael G. Ryan).

9.2 Confirmation / Disconfirmation of Expected Approaches to Conflict Handling

I will now reconsider the expectations in light of the data presented in the case narrative chapters (6-8). For each expectation, I will declare whether it was confirmed or disconfirmed, or both, and in what ways.

9.2.1 General Stance toward Conflict Handling:

Save the face of and enhance the power of the Church organization and oneself. By formulating the expectation in this way, my intention was to point to the intermingling of concern for oneself and for the Church organization that marks the Church hierarchy, a concern that translates into efforts to save face (for oneself and the organization) and grow in power (personally and organizationally). The data from the case confirms that members of the hierarchy pursue each of these four distinct interests in conflict situations and that they are indeed intermingled in practice. It remains difficult to say, however, which of these four converging priorities (saving face for self, saving face for the Church, enhancing one's own power, enhancing the Church's power) is predominant for a given party at a given time. Making such distinctions is complicated by the fact that saving face itself can be a form of power enhancement. My inclination is to continue to see these priorities as interrelated and often simultaneously applied. But at the same time I must acknowledge that the problem of sorting out these interconnected interests is only slightly clarified by the present study.

Before considering evidence of how this stance is operative in practice, it is worth our while to consider a few things we *never* see in the empirical example. For one, in the entire five-and-a-half year period, we never see a single bishop criticize the Church institution itself, nor do we ever see one bishop criticize another outright. For another, we never see a bishop make a *convincing* admission of his own error or sin. In the rare instances when such admissions (of shortcomings but not of sin) appear at all, they are consistently minimized by qualifying and justifying language that contextualizes them and even turns them into attractive forms of "humility."

Instead, what we *do* see is that all parties use euphemisms and indirect language to downplay the negative appearance of the conflict and to save face for themselves and their opponents. The Vatican says it is "visiting" Hunthausen rather than investigating him and tries to keep the entire business as discrete as possible. The curial officials stay out of sight and manage the affair as an impersonal, bureaucratic problem-solving exercise. (The key to their power is their hiddenness, their role of organizational oversight and their ability to have access to the Pope while denying access to others.) The papal nuncio and visitator seek the practical implementation of Vatican preferences by presenting themselves as fraternal intermediaries. (The key to these intermediaries ability to stay in power is their effectiveness in carrying out Rome's – the Pope's – bidding effectively: that is, without alienating Hunthausen, they need to make him fall in line.) Hunthausen continually walks a tightrope. He tries to preserve his own power and autonomy (the right to stay in office and govern his diocese in the way he judges best), which depends on staying in Rome's good graces. His strategic solution is to resist the Vatican intervention in private while politely cooperating in public.

For a time, these converging approaches save face for the Church leadership, allowing it to continue to give the appearance of moving ahead harmoniously according to its vision of unity. Harmony suggests effectiveness, and effectiveness is a sign of power and a magnet for power. By refusing to criticize one another, the participant bishops preserve their own power through reinforcement of the closed, autonomous and self-protective culture of the hierarchy. At the same time, they guard individual possibilities of favor and advancement. But eventually a breakdown occurs when the periphery party realizes there is not a one-to-one correspondence between his own power and that of the Church. Hunthausen is forced to choose between running his archdiocese Rome's way – which implies keeping power and losing power at the same time – or trying to run the archdiocese according to his own vision and running the risk of removal from office.

Faced with this pressure, Hunthausen tries to achieve both ends, of staying in office and maintaining as much leadership autonomy as possible. This requires pushing Rome back (going public with his case), but not so hard that retaliation results (he stays polite and continues to profess loyalty). When Hunthausen begins to resist Rome's course of action, the papal pro-nuncio's position (appearance) is threatened, because he is the one responsible for generating compliance on a practical level. The Holy See's face is also threatened because the resistance sends a signal to all observers that Roman orders do not automatically meet with compliance on the periphery (not just in the pews, but even in the hierarchy itself). Once Hunthausen's resistance comes into the open, the equation for face saving changes. Rome is left to choose between various ways of looking good and / or being powerful. By forcing compliance from Hunthausen, Rome looks good to those who want a strong central leadership and who distrust peripheral diversity; but at the same time it looks bad to those who favor peripheral freedom and a more tolerant style. By giving in to Hunthausen, Rome looks good to those freedom-tolerance partisans, but looks weak to those who want strict uniformity and control in the Church. So long as no conflict was apparent, Rome had the luxury of having most people believe whatever they wanted to believe about relations between Rome and the local Church.

Rome, like Hunthausen tries a balancing act. After a brief outburst of open conflict (marked by Hunthausen's announcement of Wuerl's faculties, the Vatican chronology, the NCCB debate), Rome makes the concession of establishing the assessment commission. The point of this act is to show some degree of flexibility while angling, once again, for a solution in a closed forum.

In the end, it is hard to say who comes out ahead. Hunthausen comes out looking like a man of principle to reform-minded members within the Church and to many outside the Church. But his possibilities for exercising greater power within the hierarchy itself are negated. The hierarchy ends up looking heavy-handed without clearly having its own way. It cannot be counted as a public relations success for the Vatican, but perhaps it sent the signal that Rome wanted to send and has had the desired effect of bolstering centralized control in the long run. The Church itself shows itself to be internally divided, which is the reality.

In general, we can observe that center-periphery conflict appears to change the dynamics of intrahierarchical discourse by straining the link between the identity of the individual bishop and the identity of the hierarchy and the Church itself. When all is well, a bishop should have no problem seeing his own well being as one with the hierarchical culture and institutional culture that has already amply rewarded him with his prestigious office. But center-periphery conflict drives a wedge between the personal and collective identity. For the local bishop, who may find himself (as Hunthausen does) unhappily constrained by his superiors, personal power may no longer be closely associated with institutional deference. The dilemma for the periphery party is knowing how far to continue in support of the existing Church culture, knowing that one's own position and power may or may not be enhanced by doing so. This will surely involve questions of personal principle and one's understanding of the nature of the Church. The dilemma for the center party is different. Being the higher power party, it has, on the one hand, nothing to lose by reinforcing the current Church order and by continuing to identify oneself fully with that order. It also has reason to want to retain conformity within the hierarchy. On the other hand, however, refusing to share power more widely may lead to a loss of face for the Church and perhaps even to severe structural tensions that could eventually jeopardize the hierarchy's privileged position of power.

At the beginning of this section I pointed out the difficulty of knowing when a bishop is acting primarily to secure personal advantages and when he is acting more selflessly for the sake of some greater good ("the good of the Church," for example). To illustrate the difficulty, let us recall the evidence provided by two key documents from the Rome-

Hunthausen conflict, Ratzinger's 9.30.85 letter to Hunthausen and Hunthausen's address to the NCCB. The Ratzinger letter is, on the surface, much concerned with the well being of the Church and little concerned with Ratzinger himself. But one can make a pretty good case that Ratzinger wants to save face for himself (he hides his individual involvement in the decision to impose discipline) *and* for the Church (he writes privately to Hunthausen and he presents arguments directed to the good of the Church, as he understands it). One can also show rather easily that Ratzinger desires to enhance the power of the Church by maintaining order within the hierarchical ranks and clarity and discipline within the organization as a whole. Given Ratzinger's high position within the Church, there are obvious advantages to him (in terms of his own possession of power) if the Church's success and his own vision for that success go hand in hand. But at what point, if any, does Ratzinger put his own ambition ahead of the well being of the Church? Is a disinclination to speak in the first-person a sign that he is humbly carrying out his duty or is it a way of protecting and applying his own power?

To take another example, consider Hunthausen's address to the NCCB. Here Hunthausen takes a very different approach from the Ratzinger letter. Hunthausen consistently foregrounds his own identity, and through this approach he invites the other American bishops to see the business at hand as a human business, one that has touched him and has the potential to affect them profoundly as well. Hunthausen also professes to be desirous of what is best for the Church. But what are we to make of his words and actions? Is he a prophet, putting his own office and reputation on the line for the sake of a better future for the Church? Or is he embracing the prophetic role as a means of raising his own profile?

It may be possible in future studies to characterize bishops with the terms realism and idealism (see also the discussion of worldly-type and spiritual-type Church leaders in section 2.4.3.1). If the realist values ideals for their service to the acquisition of power, then the idealist values power for its service of ideals. The pure realist places a premium on his own power and any institutions that guarantee his power. The pure idealist values power (his own or an institution's) only to the extent that it contributes to the realization of his ideals. (In this scheme, face saving can serve either idealistic or realistic ends.) The realist and idealist are ideal types. Bishops will inevitably show degrees of both qualities. The most the present study reveals in this matter is the tension between realism and idealism that seems to be present in all bishops' conflict handling. It does not provide us with a decisive way of ascertaining which bishops are more realistic and which more idealistic, since hidden components of internal motivation complicate the discernment.

9.2.2 Perspective on the Use of Power:
All members of the hierarchy participating in center-periphery conflict will strive for (the appearance of) legitimacy in their employments of power. My expectation was that applications of power in center-periphery conflict participants would reflect an overriding concern with having one's own / the Church's use of power look good (legal, just, charitable). As a normative organization, the Church is limited in its ability to command compliance (it lacks the apparatus to coerce its membership by physical force), and the Church's stated ideals (regarding justice and charity, for example) further restrict Church leaders ability to apply certain kinds of (raw) power. Church leaders, however, remain likely to encounter situations in which they will want to generate compliance over and against the natural inclinations of the Church membership. I presupposed that in such situations Church leaders would favor power employments strong enough to work but legitimate enough to go unchallenged. I also anticipated that the degree of rawness of the power applied would increase in the face of resistance from the other party. My confrontation of the data largely

confirmed these expectations, but applications of raw power showed up earlier and more often than expected.

There is in the case no tidy pattern of center-periphery cooperation giving way gradually to heavier and more coercive employments of power in the face of resistance over the course of the case. Instead we see an up-and-down pattern, wherein less coercive means are followed by more coercive means when the less coercive means have failed, but thereafter we often see what appear to be more cooperative exchanges (less coercive exchanges again) for a time. To illustrate, let us consider some of the more coercive and less coercive actions taken by both parties. Four conflict moves show the center at its most coercive: the visitation, the placement of an auxiliary with special powers, the distribution of the Vatican chronology and the appointment of a coadjutor with right of succession. Legitimation for the visitation was provided by the Holy See's expression of concern for the local Church, its right under canon law to conduct a visitation, and Hunthausen's agreement to the process. Legitimation for the appointment of Wuerl came again from the Holy See's legal right and Hunthausen's agreement to the appointment. Note, however, that the justification for (legitimation of) the release of the chronology is of a rather different quality. Legitimizing this harsh criticism of Hunthausen's leadership is not only the Vatican's legal prerogative but also, as Laghi characterized it, Hunthausen's provocative behavior. (Here legitimation is also indictment.) Finally, in the case of the coadjutor appointment, legitimation was provided by the show of good will contained in the commission's involvement and, again, by Rome's legal right to decide.

The center at its least coercive would seem to be those moments when the Vatican most fully concedes the legitimacy of Hunthausen's viewpoints and leadership autonomy. Since so much of Rome's conflict negotiating takes place in private, it is hard to know when and if such moments take place. But perhaps the best example of Rome apparently showing a willingness to take seriously the periphery position is in its creation of the (mostly) independent commission and its willingness to accept the commission's recommendation (although, admittedly, the commission proposal is not fully acceptable to Hunthausen). Perhaps, too, the previsitation exchanges between the Holy See and Hunthausen were also noncoercive, but this is speculation since they were hidden from view.

As for Hunthausen, his employment of coercion is rather subtler, since he is the lower power party. He has at least five options for coercing Rome, either by acting directly himself or employing surrogates. He can: (1) resist Rome's will in a low-key way through argumentation, delay, putting up a false appearance, etc.; (2) resign, or threaten to; (3) reveal secret information, or threaten to; (4) criticize Rome; or (5) generate social pressure that makes Rome's position untenable. Hunthausen appears to be at his most coercive at three points: when he reveals Wuerl's faculties (thus he resists, reveals and invites criticism of Rome all at once), when he expands the conflict debate at the NCCB meeting, and when he resists the commission's recommendations and proposes resigning during the commission negotiations. Hunthausen offer's rhetorical legitimation for announcing Wuerl's faculties, associating the act with his official accountability to the people he serves (leads). The need to act on principle again serves as the primary legitimation when Hunthausen expands the NCCB debate to include a range of issues not yet considered and when he proposes resigning.

Hunthausen is at his least coercive when he takes to heart the Vatican's concerns without reacting defensively or resistantly in response. From what we see, he is at his most agreeable prior to the visitation and, secondarily, after the visitation but prior to the communication of faculties to Wuerl.

If we see these less- and more-coercive applications of power by both parties in the context of the conflict as a whole, we see that the Vatican pattern is one of heavy tactic followed by retreat (spread out over the five years of conflict), whereas Hunthausen's is one of persistent resistance with three main attempts to force the Vatican's hand in the most intense (nine month) period of the conflict. As a visual aid, I provide the following chart of conciliatory and coercive gestures by both parties over time.

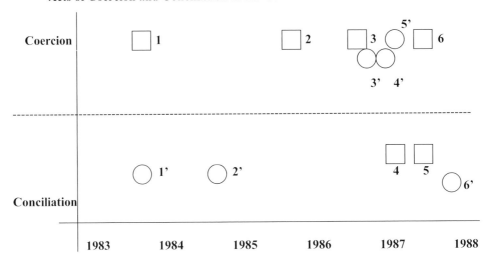

Acts of Coercion and Conciliation in the Conflict

Key
Center:
- ☐ 1 Visitation (coercive)
- 2 Appointment of auxiliary with intention for special faculties (coercive)
- 3 Vatican chronology (coercive)
- 4 Creation of assessment commission (conciliatory)
- 5 Acceptance of commission's recommendations (conciliatory)
- 6 Appointment of coadjutor archbishop with right of succession (coercive)

Periphery:
- ◯ 1' Hunthausen cooperates with visitation process (conciliatory)
- 2' Hunthausen cooperates after visitation (conciliatory)
- 3' Hunthausen reveals Wuerl faculties (coercive)
- 4' Hunthausen argues case before NCCB (coercive)
- 5' Hunthausen resists commission recommendations and proposes resigning(coercive)
- 6' Hunthausen accepts implementation of commission plan

FIGURE 9.1
(Note: With this figure I do not attempt to distinguish between levels of intensity within the coercion or conciliation areas.)

One of the surprises from the case is that Rome employs a rather heavy tactic – a visitation -- quite early in the conflict handling. This challenges the expectation that more coercive kinds of intervention will only show up after less coercive means have failed, since prior to this we do not see lighter tactics failing. Consequently, we are left to suppose that either the expectation is wrong or there was more contentious conflict negotiation going on behind the scenes prior to the announcement of the visitation itself than we have access to. We cannot know for certain (this discussion continues in the conflict-theory analysis, later in the chapter), but it is worth noting that the visitation apparently catches Hunthausen off guard, which suggests that, in his own understanding as well, there is a gap between the use of such a drastic means and his perception of the quality of his exchanges with Rome before the visitation.

Invariably, the parties to the conflict try to put a good face on their employments of power. For a further discussion of some of the techniques used for doing so, see section 9.2.2.1, which follows.

In order to further break down the use of power in the conflict, let us now return to the typology from Vaillancourt (1980), which we considered in chapter two. Vaillancourt identifies three types of "raw" power employed by members of the Church hierarchy to coordinate and control the Church (ecological power, remunerative power and coercive power) and five types of normative power put to the same end (social power, legal power, traditional power, expert power and charismatic power). Here below I present an overview of how each of these types of power was applied in the Rome-Hunthausen conflict. A summary table precedes a detailed discussion with examples.

Applications of Types of Power in the Rome-Hunthausen Conflict

	Center Party (The Vatican)	Periphery Party (Hunthausen / Seattle)
1. Ecological Power	Rome exercises various forms of territorial control: A. Conducting visitation B. Denying Hunthausen access to Visitation report. C. Appointing Roman insider as auxiliary bishop with special faculties. D. Limiting Hunthausen's access to the Vatican decision makers and site of decision-making. E. Making a rhetorical case for the Pope's jurisdiction at the Nov. 1986 NCCB meeting. F. Appointing coadjutor archbishop with right of succession. G. Placing apostolic commission in ongoing assessment role. H. Pope's pastoral visit to U.S., 1988.	A. Hunthausen exercises territorial control by maintaining strong support within the Seattle archdiocese (the support of his priests, in particular, was crucial) and signalling his wariness of Roman (interventionist) initiatives.
2. Remunerative Power	A. Hickey, and to a lesser extent Ratzinger, remunerates Hunthausen publicly with praise. B. After reassigning Wuerl out of Seattle, Rome appoints him	Applies only in the minimal sense of Hunthausen's public shows of good will toward Rome.

	ordinary of his home diocese, Pittsburgh. C. John Paul II elevates visitor Hickey to cardinal. D. The Pope makes Laghi a cardinal.	
3. Coercive Power	A. Rome conducts the visitation. B. Rome sends an auxiliary bishop not of Hunthausen's choosing. C. Rome takes faculties from Hunthausen and gives them to Wuerl. D. Rome appoints a coadjutor archbishop not of Hunthausen's choosing and gives him the right of succession. E. Rome keeps Hunthausen under assessment for almost two years after the agreement announcement.	A. Hunthausen holds out the possibility of escalating the public, through public disclosure, further confrontations, his own resignation, etc. – all actions that could make the Holy See look bad. B. Hunthausen resists Vatican initiatives in public and private. C. Hunthausen holds out the possibility (threat) of resignation.
4. Social Power	A. Rome pressures Hunthausen to behave loyally and faithfully (by not challenging Rome). B. Rome pressures the NCCB executive committee to endorse Laghi's chronology. C. Rome releases Vatican chronology, which paints Hunthausen as a weak leader and recalcitrant. D. Laghi reminds NCCB of his own role in appointing almost 100 conference members. E. The Pope's address to the NCCB reminds the bishops of their duty of loyalty.	A. Hunthausen takes his case to the news media as a means of pressuring the Vatican, playing on American cultural biases in favor of open and democratic decision making. B. Hunthausen presses his fellow U.S. bishops to empathize with and support his case, playing on shared cultural viewpoints and shared vulnerabilities to Vatican action.
5. Legal Power	A. Rome undertakes the visitation. B. Rome assigns an auxiliary bishop with special faculties. C. Rome appoints a coadjutor archbishop with right of succession.	A. Hunthausen attacks the Church's application of legal power on the basis of American civil legal standards calling for the right of the accused to confront his accusers and the charges against him.
6. Traditional Power	A. Ratzinger holds out a vision of singularity and uniformity of tradition, with the hierarchy, and Rome above all, as the guardians thereof.	A. Hunthausen proposes a more pluriform ("People of God") vision of tradition, rooted in Vatican II notions of reform and lay empowerment. He makes a case for discernment of the promptings of the Holy Spirit when making pastoral judgment. B. Hunthausen positions himself as a man of the people, minimalizing the use of linguistic signals of hierarchical authority.
7. Expert Power	A. Ratzinger acts as an expert on Church affairs and doctrine in his 9.30.85 letter to Hunthausen. B. The Pope employs expert power in his Nov. 1986 message to the U.S. bishops.	A. Hunthausen acts as an expert on conditions in the local church when defending his pastoral leadership decisions.
8. Charismatic Power	NA	A. Hunthausen courts the people

		of his own diocese in person and in writing. B. Hunthausen makes a passionate appeal to the U.S. bishops in person and in writing, drawing on his reputation as an advocate for peace. C. Hunthausen appeals to a wide (in particular, American) audience through statements he releases to the press.

TABLE 9.2

9.2.2.1 Applications of Raw Power

Ecological power, especially in the form of *territorial control*, was the most commonly employed type of raw power in the Rome-Hunthausen conflict. It is interesting that neither party enjoyed much success at establishing control over the territory controlled by the other. Hunthausen never made significant inroads at the Vatican: he appeared to gain few, if any, allies or advocates there; showed little awareness of how to manipulate the Vatican bureaucracy; and was physically present there only at the time of Wuerl's ordination, which amounted to a symbolic concession within the conflict. He was also denied the opportunity to go to Rome to carry out the late-stage conflict handling directly with the Pope and top Vatican officials. On the other hand, Rome had equally little success making its case and asserting control in Seattle. Though of course the Holy See demonstrated and maintained its juridical power of governance over the archdiocese, it failed to garner anywhere near the level of popular support for its position that Hunthausen enjoyed within the archdiocese. During the course of the conflict, the constituency which favored Rome over Hunthausen did not appear to grow any larger than it had been prior to the visitation. Most crucially, Hunthausen maintained strong, vociferous support among his priests. This made it difficult for the Holy See to generate a feeling among the people in the pews that Hunthausen was somehow a danger to the faith. The fact that Hunthausen enjoyed such consistent support in the archdiocese made it highly risky for Rome to act upon its juridical right to control the local church. Before the end of the conflict, Rome was forced to make a partial retreat from its intervention as a result.

The most crucial intermediate territory between Rome and Seattle proved to be the forum of negotiation provided by the American bishops' conference. Without being able to anticipate support from his fellow bishops, and then actually gaining it, Hunthausen surely would have been chastened in his struggle. Whereas bishops positioned at the Vatican have the reassurance of working alongside the Pope and many other bishops who hold key offices within the hierarchy, a local bishop is more or less alone as a member of the hierarchy within his own diocese. This amounts to a physical and psychological isolation which can only be counteracted periodically and with some effort. The obvious outlets for contact and alliance-formation with other bishops lie in the regional and national bishops' conferences. There a bishop has the opportunity to commiserate about the unique burdens, challenges and possibilities of his office. Through contact with his fellow American bishops, Hunthausen was able to gain advice and personal support for his conflict handling, and awareness that the pastoral problems in his own diocese were not unique within the American Church. Having the benefit of this input made the thought of continuing to defend his position against Rome conceivable.

Rome attempted to establish control over the NCCB response to the conflict issues in several ways. Most especially, it sought to do so through hidden negotiations and procedural manipulations, as in the effort to gain an NCCB endorsement for Laghi's chronology. Rome finally did manage to gain more control over the NCCB's participation in the affair by selecting out the three members who served on the apostolic commission. With this act, Rome took the body as a whole out of the discussion and replaced it with a much smaller entity that it might have more influence over.

The NCCB leadership (as embodied in the executive committee and administrative board) demonstrated a form of territorial control of its own by sticking to its preference for neutrality and by setting up terms for the debate of the Hunthausen case which kept the discussion within prescribed limits.

Hunthausen enjoyed strong support among individual bishops of the NCCB, and Rome had strong supporters of its own. On the whole, the NCCB's stance of neutrality worked in Hunthausen's favor because it kept Rome from isolating Hunthausen. Moreover, the NCCB's refusal to criticize Hunthausen, much like the show of support by his own priests, sent a signal to Catholics at large that Hunthausen's leadership was not necessarily out of line with mainstream (and even official) Catholic thinking. In strategic terms, fending off the Holy See's attempt to control the intermediate territory represented by the NCCB ultimately was a key to his retention of power in his own archdiocese.

Remunerative power was employed most obviously in the affair in the later appointments of Bishop Wuerl as ordinary of his home diocese of Pittsburgh and promotion of Archbishops Hickey and Laghi to cardinal. These appointments are rewards for faithful service, with the handling of the Hunthausen affair being but one component of that. It is more difficult to say whether Rome remunerated Hunthausen as a conflict strategy, or vice-versa. By loosely interpreting the concept of remuneration, one might argue that mutual remuneration was shown between these parties in the form of praise, signs of favor and acts of compliance. Thus, perhaps Rome rewarded Hunthausen for his public show of docility and politeness by agreeing to provide a rewritten version of the 9.30.85 Ratzinger letter and by allowing Hunthausen to give Wuerl faculties himself (though this did not work out according to the Vatican's plan). And perhaps, in some sense, Hunthausen rewarded signs of forbearance by Rome with continued obeisance. But it is probably more accurate to understand these actions as applications of social power, since they seem to be more reflective of conditioned politeness and a strategic effort to ingratiate oneself with the other party than anything else.

Although applications of **coercive power** in the conflict were much more apparent coming from the center party, the periphery party also applied such power, and to a greater extent than I expected. Rome applied coercive power rather transparently by undertaking the visitation, by appointing an auxiliary bishop who was unknown to Hunthausen, by redistributing key powers from Hunthausen to Wuerl, by appointing a coadjutor archbishop with right of succession who was not of Hunthausen's choosing, and by holding out the threat of removing Hunthausen from office.

I would call the undertaking of the visitation itself an employment of coercive power because, though Rome prefers to paint the visitation process as a neutral inquiry, it is in fact a rather drastic step, which automatically casts a shadow over a bishop's leadership. In other words, visitation in and of itself amounts to "denouncement," which Vaillancourt declares to be a form of coercion. The counter-argument may be made that, if a local bishop cooperates in keeping a visitation out of public view, no shadow is cast over his leadership. But the visitation of the diocese of Bishop Walter Sullivan (Richmond, Virginia), which came close in time to the Seattle visitation, does not bear this view out. Even with Sullivan's cooperation, the visitation of Richmond could not stay completely hidden. And though the specific nature of the Vatican's doubts about Sullivan never surfaced in a highly public way, the fact that his leadership had been called into question became well known. (For further discussion of Sullivan and the relevance of his case to the Hunthausen case, see section 9.6.4.4, but also Granfield 1987, Briggs 1992, Tom Fox' editorial in the 11.21.86 *National Catholic Reporter*, and the 11.10.86 issue of *Sojourners* magazine.)

It is also possible to see Rome's appointment of Wuerl as auxiliary bishop, as opposed to a local or at least known candidate, as an application of coercive power. Though it is not known which names Hunthausen advanced as his own preferences for filling the position, it is at least known that Wuerl was not one of the names because Hunthausen had to inquire about who Wuerl was at the time of his naming. (He remembered Wuerl but vaguely from an earlier meeting.) As for the mandated redistribution of power from Hunthausen to Wuerl, this is a blatant act of (legal) coercion. This change was made against Hunthausen's will and by virtue of the Vatican's possession of greater power.

The imposition of a coadjutor archbishop with right of succession amounts to a further application of coercive power by the Holy See. Symbolically, the appointment of a coadjutor normally suggests that something is wrong in a diocese. Whereas an auxiliary is normally seen to be an assistant to help meet the growing pastoral and administrative needs in a diocese (the bishop of a vibrant and growing diocese is seen to be rewarded with the appointment of one or more auxiliaries), a coadjutor often comes as a remedy for specific problems that have arisen, often due to some incapacity or negligence on the part of the ordinary. Though in this case the coadjutor improved Hunthausen's situation in one respect (he possessed no special faculties), the stigma of the need for a coadjutor remained. Moreover, unlike the auxiliary appointment, the coadjutor appointment came with a right of succession clause. Thus, the Vatican asserted its power to declare future control over the life of the Archdiocese.

Finally, the ever-present threat of imposing additional sanctions – most especially, the possibility of removing Hunthausen from office or of publicly humiliating him in some other way – served as another form of coercive power, though it came to be voiced in only the subtlest ways (the most suggestive language is in Ratzinger's 9.30.85 letter and Laghi's chronology).

On the periphery party side, though Hunthausen was less well positioned to apply coercive power, he managed to do so in three ways: by forcing the Vatican, against its wishes, to address the conflict issues in the open; by raising the prospect of his own resignation, with the likely result of heightened fractiousness in the Church; and by delaying resolution of the affair, thereby opening up the possibility of controversy clouding the Pope's imminent pastoral visit. By forcing the conflict discussion into the open, Hunthausen played away from the Vatican's advantage in closed bureaucratic struggles. Hunthausen applied this strategy repeatedly, if selectively, pushing for public disclosure of the visitation, of the visitation findings and of Wuerl's possession of faculties. Tactically, Hunthausen succeeded in pushing the conflict into the open by arguing this point with Rome, by taking advantage of news leaks (from unknown sources), by moving unilaterally to reveal information to the news media, by employing his own archdiocesan communications resources, by sharing information with his own priests and key archdiocesan insiders, and by taking his case to the NCCB. At the same time, Hunthausen expanded the scope of the debate, which drew more and more participants into the discussion: no longer was the debate about conditions in his diocese, it was about secrecy and fairness and the role of individual bishops and the role of conferences of bishops. Once the issues were in circulation, Rome had the choice of either speaking to them or of appearing to be stonewalling. Either response held possibilities for intensifying the dispute.

Another way Hunthausen was also able to force degrees of acquiescence from Rome was by consistently working to maintain his own level of support in the local Church, while holding out an offer to resign at the same time. (According to Hunthausen's own report -- cf. his response to the Vatican chronology – he voiced his readiness to resign soon after the visitation process began.) Strategically, the offer to resign functioned simultaneously as a demonstration of devotion to the Church and as an implicit threat. It showed Hunthausen's desire to put the well being of the Church ahead of his own office. Concurrently, it invited consideration of an unwelcome scenario: the popular bishop stepping down and the local church erupting angrily in response. With this approach, Hunthausen was able to confront Rome with a hard choice, with neither outcome being optimal.

In a similarly indirect but nonetheless effective application of pressure, Hunthausen delayed resolution of the conflict past a point beyond which Rome was comfortable. At the time of the NCCB meeting, the Pope's forthcoming pastoral visit was but ten months away. Such trips were a critical tool of the Pope's pastoral outreach. It would not do to have the event marred by controversy. Though Hunthausen simply presented himself as declaring his own position and responding to charges made in the Vatican chronology, the effect of his pressing his case was that the controversy remained unresolved after the NCCB meeting, since he himself had shown no inclination to accept the status quo. The longer that the matter remained unresolved, the greater the time pressure on Rome proved to be.

Summary of the Use of Raw Power
Drawing on these findings, we can make a few general observations about the employment of raw power in this case of center-periphery conflict. To begin, the center party had greater opportunity to employ raw power and did so more often in practice. Rome held more cards and played more cards. This was as expected. What was not expected was that the periphery party would be able to force concessions from the center party as effectively as it did. Having been rather familiar with the case beforehand, I was nonetheless surprised to see, after detailed study, how often Rome was made to go in a direction it did not want to go. Consider: Against its wishes, the Holy See was induced to (1) publicly announce the visitation; (2) publicly announce the visitation findings (if only in summary form); (3) break with its own politeness norms; (4) debate the conflict issues in public; (5) withdraw Wuerl; and (6) restore Hunthausen's faculties. Though to some extent achieving these concessions was the product of effective use of more normative kinds of power (exercising forms of social influence that leave significant room for personal choice), beneath the surface (on both sides) lay a willingness to play hardball as necessary. By going public with the news of Wuerl's faculties and then opening up a full-scale defense of his position at the NCCB gathering, Hunthausen forced Rome's hand. Hunthausen put his own office on the line and confronted Rome with a choice: either take further action against him and bear the consequences (likely a public relations fiasco), or make concessions and perhaps

thereby win his renewed cooperation. What gave this challenge its rawness was the fact that Hunthausen did not leave Rome to make the choice it wanted to make: i.e., have the current power sharing arrangement work without friction and public complaint.

The expectation that all parties would be inclined to demonstrate the legitimacy of their uses of power was confirmed. Throughout the conflict one finds an effort to cloak the use of raw power in "normative" language and recognizable politeness conventions. This question and this finding stand central in this research project.

Though the Holy See made Hunthausen do things against his will, it did so while by applying legally sanctioned powers and by going to great lengths to portray its own actions as reasonable, for the good of the Church and accepted by Hunthausen. Prominent examples of the effort to put a rational (and well-meaning) framework on uses of raw power were Ratzinger's letter presenting the visitation findings and Laghi's chronology. The effort to secure Hunthausen's agreement can be seen in the pro-nuncio's asking Hunthausen if he would be willing to receive a visitation (it was not necessary to have Hunthausen's permission to intervene), in the center party's persistent commitment to respectful language, and in its willingness to make certain concessions (Hunthausen was provided with a visitation findings report to make public; he was also permitted to think about Wuerl's possession of powers in language of his own choosing – though this flexibility later backfired on the Vatican when Hunthausen interpreted the agreed-to language to mean that Wuerl did not have final say in any area). Later, after Hunthausen announced Wuerl's possession of faculties, the Vatican cried foul (in Laghi's chronology), saying that Hunthausen had failed to hand over the "agreed-to" faculties and suggesting that he had broken another implicit agreement by issuing his "surprise" announcement.

Hunthausen also made a point of putting a normative sheen on his more "raw" applications of power. After having put the Vatican in a bind by going his own way (resisting giving Wuerl faculties, and then publicly announcing the faculties once they were given), Hunthausen stressed that both actions were the product of prior discussions where, supposedly, common understanding had been reached. Thus the failure to give over the faculties in a timely matter was the result of miscommunication. And the Vatican, Hunthausen said, should not have been surprised by his announcement of Wuerl's faculties because he had made it clear to Rome that he would need to publicly reveal such powers were they to be given. Hunthausen also consistently respected the prevailing politeness conventions (with a few exceptions) and underscored his deference to Roman authority.

9.2.2.2 Applications of Normative Power
It was often difficult to tell within the conflict precisely when one party was effectively *forcing* another to a particular action and when more room for *real choice* was being allowed – this because so much emphasis was placed by both sides on having the conflict appear to be a reasonable and amicable exchange within the episcopal brotherhood. But the Rome-Hunthausen case shows that raw power can serve both the center and periphery parties as necessary. Let us now consider how various kinds of normative power were employed by the principal participants in the conflict.

Social power was applied pervasively in the conflict. Rome applied social power by playing on Hunthausen's sense of loyalty, duty and commitment to the good of the Church. A common way to pressure Hunthausen to keep his social obligations was to praise and thank him for having acted in accord with these standing responsibilities and ties.

(Ratzinger in his 12.12.83 letter to Hunthausen: "I want to express to you my sincere thanks for your own complete cooperation in this understandably difficult project...") This tactic served as a reminder and exhortation to him to persist in the docility and conformity to the prevailing Church order he had already shown. Notably, this form of social pressure was applied primarily in public and in the early stages of the conflict, before the conflict handling became openly antagonistic. Ratzinger's private letter to Hunthausen detailing the visitation findings (9.30.85) makes only minimal attempts to establish camaraderie, leaving us to conclude that praise and flattery are more meant as a show for the public (as in the Laghi rewrite of Ratzinger's letter) than for Hunthausen himself.

Placing Wuerl in a power-sharing arrangement with Hunthausen was as a further application of social power. Through this act, the Holy See forced Hunthausen to cooperate closely with someone who, at the very least, reminded Hunthausen of the Roman point of view. Even if Wuerl himself had no intention of watching over Hunthausen in a suspicious or critical way, Hunthausen himself could not have avoided the feeling that he was being monitored -- by a fellow bishop, with strong ties to Rome, who now was fully on the inside of the Seattle archdiocesan operation.

Once Hunthausen began to act independently of the Vatican's wishes – that is, once he announced Wuerl's possession of faculties – public praise for him from Rome ceased. The Vatican chronology, contrarily, applies a new form of social pressure – the threat of exclusion -- by criticizing Hunthausen and attempting to shame him into renewed conformity. The most stinging charges in the Vatican chronology were that Hunthausen was judged to lack the firmness necessary to govern the archdiocese and correct its longstanding problems, that his own response to the situation had been inadequate, and that of late he had failed to carry out Vatican directives and had begun to go his own way in the handling of the matter.

Rome (Laghi) sought an NCCB endorsement of Laghi's chronology. Thus social pressure was applied to the NCCB executive committee as a means of applying pressure to Hunthausen. (Ratzinger and Gantin increased the social pressure by communicating their displeasure that no endorsement was forthcoming.) This effort succeeded only minimally, since the NCCB ended up releasing the document but only with a neutral statement in accompaniment, not with an endorsement.

During the November 1986 NCCB meeting, Rome applied social power through the public messages of Pope John Paul II and Archbishop Laghi. Laghi's brief address to the bishops reminded them of his own role in appointing nearly one hundred of the conference members present in the room. Unavoidably, this suggested a debt owed and the power of Laghi's office which would continue into the future. The Pope's message offered a reminder of his own power. It was less nakedly political than Laghi's remark, offering instead a theological reflection on the Pope's traditional authority to preside over the bishops, who owe their fidelity to him.

When it became clear, in the aftermath of the NCCB meeting, that Hunthausen was not going to back down and that the NCCB was willing to stand behind Hunthausen (without making a big show of doing so), the Vatican options for applying social pressure diminished considerably. Hunthausen had support from the priests and people of Seattle, support from many of his fellow bishops and support from many in the news media. With Laghi and Hunthausen at loggerheads, the pro-nuncio was no longer in a position to persuade Hunthausen individually in private negotiation. Thus, the most obvious options left were either to have Vatican operatives or the Pope himself more directly involved, or to call upon a third party that might have more possibility of bringing Hunthausen back in line. Rome decided to pursue the latter option and the assessment commission was formed.

The commission became Rome's new channel for directing social pressure in the Hunthausen case. Formation of the commission, and in particular its conciliatory makeup suggested that the Vatican was willing to pursue Hunthausen's renewed cooperation through concessions. From this point on, until the time of the disbanding of the commission, social pressure was applied through the behind-the-scenes, directly personal persuasion of the commission members. The key to the agreement appeared to be to allow both Hunthausen and Rome to save face.

Hunthausen was not simply on the receiving end of social power; he also applied it himself in his exchanges with the Vatican. Hunthausen's strategy early on (up until his announcement of Wuerl's faculties) was simply to demonstrate, particularly in public, his own faithful, deferential and polite compliance with Vatican wishes. By so doing he placed limits on the sort of action the Vatican could take against him. So long as Hunthausen kept up the appearance of a good and faithful bishop, the burden of showing reason to challenge him would remain with Rome. So long as Hunthausen did not show signs of dissension, the average churchgoer would have no reason to fear him as a dangerous rebel and would be willing to give him the benefit of the doubt. A circumstantial factor enhancing the effectiveness of this strategy was the Vatican's own delay in processing the visitation findings. The result of this was that Hunthausen was able to show himself to be cooperative and nonthreatening for a very long time (almost two full years), at little cost to himself, since no changes had yet been implemented in the archdiocese.

Even after Rome finally did take action, Hunthausen maintained the posture of respectful cooperativeness in public. When the break in public politeness finally came, it came from the Rome side first, by means of the Vatican chronology. Apparently, what piqued Laghi's anger (barely disguised in the chronology) was the difficulty of dealing with a Hunthausen who, as Laghi saw it, was significantly more resistant in private than he showed himself to be in public. (Laghi accuses Hunthausen of responding inadequately to issues Rome had brought to his attention, failing to give the "agreed-to" faculties to Wuerl, and issuing a "surprise" announcement of Wuerl's faculties.)

Because Hunthausen had been publicly cooperative for so long, and because the Vatican side had been the first to break with the policy of mutual graciousness, Hunthausen was able to gain newfound stature as a victim, which increased the social pressure on the Holy See. Many are put off by the thought that an innocent victim is being attacked. The key to this perception of victimization working in his favor was that Hunthausen came across as an attractive underdog, a heroic figure people who heroically stood alone against long odds, not an anathema whose victimization might appeal to baser instincts. Hunthausen's reputation for integrity and a willingness to take a moral, and even prophetic, stand had already been established. (Charisma was a factor here. More on this shortly.) By going on the attack, Rome achieved the unintended consequence of enhancing Hunthausen's stature as an opponent. Hunthausen appealed to many in the United States, both inside and outside the Church, who saw the Roman Catholic bureaucracy as tending to overstep its bounds to try to control areas of life it had no right to control. By issuing the first attack, moreover, Rome gave Hunthausen license to counterattack, under cover of simply defending his own reputation and situation.

During the NCCB meeting Hunthausen placed social pressure on Rome by gathering support from other American bishops. By building support within the NCCB, Hunthausen made Rome's task much more formidable. This effort greatly increased the number of persons directly involved in the conflict and, consequently, increased the scale of damages to be incurred by Rome in the event of failure. For Rome, the risk of failure became that dissent would manifest itself nationally rather than just in Seattle.

Hunthausen cultivated sympathy from his fellow American bishops by drawing on existing personal bonds (based on personal friendship and shared theological / political views); by making arguments favorable to his own position that other bishops would identify with (the right to due process; the need for bishops to be granted leeway in making pastoral judgments in their own dioceses; etc.); and by playing on the fear that what had happened to Hunthausen could happen to any local bishop.

Through his arguments Hunthausen was able to point out that the matter at hand was not simply a matter of one kind of loyalty – that of an individual bishop to the Holy See – but that other questions of conscientious fidelity were also at stake in the matter. Hunthausen never denied that bishops had an obligation to the Holy See. He conceded this fully. But with varying degrees of explicitness, he pointed out that bishops also have a duty to be faithful to their own conscience, to the people they serve (who might also be in agreement with key Hunthausen positions), and to one another. The result of taking this approach was that Hunthausen gave his fellow bishops the opportunity to be *for* something (e.g., the right to due process, or autonomy for bishops), as opposed to being simply *against* the action of Rome.

Another way that Hunthausen put social pressure on Rome during the course of the NCCB meeting was by opening up a wide-ranging series of charges against Rome. Hunthausen, in effect, complicated the matter as a whole. It was not, as the Vatican chronology would have it, a rather straightforward matter of Hunthausen failing to govern his particular church properly and then dragging his heels against corrective interventions. It was instead a convoluted business of values in contestation – secrecy vs. openness, control vs. freedom, clarity in Church teaching vs. compassion in pastoral discernments. By injecting all of these questions into the discussion at the height of public attention to the affair, Hunthausen in effect clouded the air and hindered Rome's ability to wrap the debate up quickly. At the same time, he drew to his side a wide variety of complainants against Rome. By opening up so many issues he gave a foothold to any number of parties who might have reason to be unhappy with Rome. And finally, Hunthausen, by illustrating the complexity of it all, further reinforced his own defensive position. Given how involved it all was, who could blame Hunthausen if he struggled with pastoral judgments and chose to err on the side of compassion?

Ultimately, perhaps the greatest pressure was put on Rome by virtue of the fact that these discussions took place more or less in the open. Though the oral debates were closed to the press, the public had the benefit of statements issued by all sides (Laghi's chronology, Hunthausen's responses, the Malone NCCB statement), and many bishops also offered commentary outside of the closed sessions. For an intrachurch conflict, the exchanges were quite public and highly charged. The controversy reached the point of drawing front-page attention in the *New York Times*. What had been a highly private business now generated a public uproar: certainly that is not too strong a word to describe the discursive volatility manifest at the bishops' gathering and in the Seattle Archdiocese both during the time of the meeting and shortly thereafter.

After the NCCB meeting ran its course, the conflict entered a period of stalemate. Neither party showed an inclination to escalate the conflict further, but neither was anxious to give ground on its position either. No resolution had been achieved during the meeting, and contrary to its own intention to have put further pressure on Hunthausen to cooperate, Rome found itself under increased pressure to make amends to Hunthausen. Time became the critical factor, a state of affairs that played in Hunthausen's favor. Within less than a year the Pope would be visiting a cross-section of America in a pastoral visit. The more that time passed without a resolution acceptable to Hunthausen supporters, the more that the Pope faced the prospect of public protests during his American visit. Rather than being a demonstration of effective territorial oversight, a much-protested visit would show that the universal pastor (like his local counterpart Hunthausen) did not have control over the people under his governance. The task for Hunthausen became simply to do nothing. Having no authority to change the problematic arrangement in his archdiocese, he could only wait until Rome decided to take action to address this threat to the appearance of the Church.

Legal power is a second type of normative power applied in the conflict. Rome applied legal power in the conflict by making use of its right, recognized in canon law, to survey and control local dioceses. The primary means chosen were the *ad limina* visit, the apostolic visitation process, the appointment of an auxiliary bishop with special faculties, the appointment of a coadjutor archbishop with right of succession, and the ongoing interventions of the apostolic pro-nuncio. All of the above-named powers to act are entrusted to the Holy See to be exercised in regard to particular churches. They are not powers which can be applied in the other direction: that is, a local bishop cannot conduct a visitation of Rome, appoint Roman officials, etc. Rome also applied legal power through the act of interpretation. Cardinal Ratzinger's letter to Hunthausen with the visitation findings is perhaps the best example. Here Ratzinger explained to Hunthausen which specific teachings – some articulated in canon law, some in other Church documents -- needed *binding* application in the local church (in other words, which Church rules needed enforcing). Notably, some of the directives that Ratzinger called on Hunthausen to enforce were rules that his own congregation had established (cf. his references to the 1975 instruction *Inter Insigniores* and the 1976 *Declaration on Sexual Ethics*). Thus Ratzinger demonstrated the Holy See's and his own congregation's power to not only interpret and enforce Church guidelines, but also to make them in the first place.

Hunthausen's options for applying legal power over and against the opposing party were limited. The Holy See possessed superior legal power in every respect. But Hunthausen challenged Rome by suggesting that having laws on the books (i.e., within the Code of Canon Law) does not guarantee the correct interpretation and application of such. Thus he pointed to the "misunderstanding" that had arisen between himself and Rome regarding the correct "interpretation of the precise nature and extent of Bishop Wuerl's special faculties" as articulated in canon 403.2 in the Code of Canon Law (cf. Hunthausen's response to the Vatican chronology). In the same line, though in a much more general sense, Hunthausen argued (in his NCCB address) that even showing "every due regard for Church Tradition and Law" does not rule out "the possibility of making a mistake" in pastoral judgments. Essentially, by making these points, Hunthausen created room to maneuver in relation to the existing legal structure. This approach did not work so much to put pressure on Rome as it did to take pressure off of Hunthausen. It allowed him to suggest that his own actions, while perhaps not strictly in accord with Rome's preferences, were nonetheless within the bounds of the existing Church laws.

Hunthausen also raised a challenge of a more fundamental kind. Put simply, he argued that certain existing laws of the Church, at least insofar as they were applied in the Seattle case, stood in questionable relationship to other crucial values. At least two examples of this form of critique appear in Hunthausen's address to the NCCB. There Hunthausen argued that the Vatican's failure to provide Hunthausen in advance with reasons for the visitation and its subsequent refusal to allow him to see the Hickey report was not just. "I must state emphatically… that such unwitnessed, private questionings with no opportunity for the subject of the questionings to face his accusers, or hear or to be informed of their allegations, or to defend himself are not a *just* manner of proceeding. This kind of an approach seriously wounds the community of faith and trust that is the Church." Here Hunthausen criticizes the Vatican's handling of the case with reference to principles that would have been applied in a trial conducted within the Anglo-Saxon legal justice system, but he also relates the concept of justice to the Church's concern for its own well-being. Later in the same address, Hunthausen asserts that "the very concept of special faculties – at least of the sort and extent we are dealing with here – is already on somewhat shaky ground from a theological point of view." In other words, the redistribution of faculties may have been legal in a technical sense but, as with the visitation process, within the framework of other essential values it may be seen to be questionable and even illegitimate.

Ultimately, however, applications of legal power did not prove decisive in the conflict. Though Rome employed legal power in substantial ways and Hunthausen had little legal power of resistance, and though Rome could have continued to take increasingly strong legal measures against Hunthausen, it chose not to do so. My sense is that social pressure not to take further action kept Rome from taking further legal action against Hunthausen. Rome could have forced Hunthausen's further cooperation or removal from office, but the cost would have been more unwelcome publicity, more dissent and less-than-clear possibilities for resolving the conflict thereafter. For this reason, Rome, after the NCCB debate, limited its legal activity to implementation of a new agreement that was minimally acceptable to Hunthausen himself (the appointment of Murphy as coadjutor archbishop with right of succession but no special faculties).

Traditional power will unavoidably suffuse any case of center-periphery conflict. The Church itself and the offices of Pope and bishop are incomprehensible apart from long-applicable concepts of Church authority and how such authority becomes manifest in practice in recognizable ways. The key to this issue is discerning which elements of Church tradition are called forth to serve the conflict handling in the present.

A good place to start in the Rome-Hunthausen conflict is to compare the parties' views of the responsibility of the hierarchy to Church tradition (as expressed in the Church's teaching and practice). Perhaps the sharpest contrast can be found between the visions articulated in Ratzinger's 9.30.85 letter and Hunthausen's address to the NCCB. Ratzinger's perspective is that Church teaching, as contained in specific documents which can be named, clearly and dependably establishes norms for Church practice. The role of the magisterium is to work out and declare such teachings. Local bishops have a secondary role in contributing to the making of such teaching, but more primarily their task on behalf of the Church is to see that this teaching is implemented and adhered to in the life of the local church. This is a top-down, governance-based view of the activity of the Church. (Ratzinger's letter to Hunthausen favors verbs such as correct, overrule, inculcate, and engender, all of which imply one-way transactions between a bishop and his people.) Hunthausen, on the other hand, shows much more of a tendency to work from the bottom up. As an example, Hunthausen points out that the human encounter precedes the emergence of Church teaching on the encounter. "[T]he matter of ministry to homosexuals… recently called forth an *Instruction* from the Congregation for the Doctrine of the Faith," Hunthausen noted. The lived experience comes first, but even when clear teaching is made available, that by itself does not eliminate gray areas of pastoral discernment. Hunthausen also states that the faithful themselves, and not simply the members of the hierarchy, have the capability and responsibility "of dealing maturely with problems where they exist." These same (lay) people share in the "ownership" of the Church as a birthright of their baptism.

Another contrast lies between Ratzinger's portrayal of Church teaching as internally consistent and fully sufficient in its current form – when properly understood, clearly taught and conscientiously administered – and Hunthausen's conception of the same as a "vital and living tradition." Whereas Ratzinger's letter associates Church teaching primarily with its encoding in curial documents and canon law, Hunthausen invokes the "Gospel message of Jesus proclaimed throughout the ages and in our own time in ways that reflect both its enduring significance as well as its perennial relevance." Practically speaking, the difference here is that Ratzinger points to specific documents which spell out particular solutions to particular contemporary problems, whereas Hunthausen argues for the validity of an approach that centers on ongoing and highly personal interpretation of Scripture itself. With Ratzinger's approach one can find the answer to a pastoral problem by looking it up. With Hunthausen's it is more a matter of faithfully discerning the foundational texts and the promptings of the Holy Spirit – a process wherein the answers and the requisite accountability remain hidden within oneself, and the possibility of making a mistake" is never ruled out.

Within the context of the conflict, these contrasting ecclesiologies served to position Ratzinger and Hunthausen oppositionally. Ratzinger proposed to Hunthausen in a private forum that the identified concerns be managed quietly in a technical way by elite technicians. Only a small highly trained minority within the Church would be familiar with the documents Ratzinger cites (bishops, some clerics, some religious, some lay professionals, academics, intellectuals) and fewer among these would be in a position to enforce the directives therein (bishops and, to a lesser extent clerics and others). Hunthausen had, in Rome's view, shown a reluctance to implement strict forms of top-down control in his archdiocese (where control rests with a small minority). Ratzinger's earliest attempts to gain Hunthausen's cooperation in doing this were undertaken within the very operative mode from which he desires Hunthausen to operate. Hunthausen, who had chosen to undertake his leadership, generally speaking, according to a populist stance, resisted Ratzinger's effort (which is supported by the pro-nuncio) to keep the discussion under wraps. From the time of the proposal of the visitation itself, Hunthausen attempted to bring others into the discussion, first within the hierarchy (he consults with NCCB President Roach) and his own inner circle of advisers, but very shortly thereafter the public at large (he argued with the pro-nuncio for the need to publicize the forthcoming visitation process). Eventually it became clear that Hunthausen would not be driven to operate according to the clerical mode. Only then did the Vatican proceed to make its case with the public. But this was not in fact an example of the Holy See (represented by Laghi and his chronology) suddenly embracing a more populist view and mode of operation. The public appeal, when it came, was made primarily to other members of the hierarchy. The public involvement was welcomed insofar as it put pressure on Hunthausen. But strikingly, at no point did the Vatican attempt to involve the people of Seattle or the American people in a serious discussion of the pastoral issues themselves, which purportedly were the crux of the entire affair. Whereas Hunthausen, according to his populist ecclesiology argued that the people of the Church "deserve to be treated as adults" and are "capable of dealing maturely with problems where they exist," the main Vatican effort to take its case to the public (the Vatican chronology) focused on Hunthausen's ostensible intransigence rather than on the pastoral concerns.

The advocacy of clerical and populist mindsets are both longstanding traditions within the greater (total, integrated composite) tradition of the Church. In that sense, both Rome and Hunthausen drew on tradition, albeit competing strands, to bolster their own position within the conflict. Strategically, Hunthausen gained more by his employment of traditional power within the conflict than did Rome. Though Rome retained its overwhelming advantage in bureaucratic power, Hunthausen secured enough support from "among the people" to offset the advantage and secure his own position.

Expert power was employed strategically in the Rome-Hunthausen conflict, but not with decisive consequences. Its most prominent application appeared in Ratzinger's letter to Hunthausen detailing the visitation findings. There Ratzinger presented himself as an expert on the teaching of the Church. Implicit throughout the letter is an assertion of his own superiority in this regard over and against Hunthausen. Ratzinger leaves no room for discussion of the points he raises. Having clarified the issues for Hunthausen, he turns over to Hunthausen responsibility to implement the clarifications.

Hunthausen employs expert power in a contrasting and, in some sense, internally contradictory way. He positions himself as the anti-expert or, put more positively, as the people's expert. In a nutshell, his message is, I may not be an expert on these technical questions but I do know the people I serve. The internal contradiction in this stance lies in the simultaneous desire to offer himself as a man of the people (thus, as one among them) while at the same time implicitly suggesting that he has a superior knowledge of what is operative in ordinary people's lives (particularly within his own archdiocese) – superior, at a minimum, to the knowledge thereof that Ratzinger possesses. There are links here to Hunthausen's employment of a populist ecclesiology (see the discussion of traditional power above) and his effective use of charismatic power (see discussion that follows). Hunthausen's self-presentation as a people's expert (himself being one of the people who knows the people very well) comes out most clearly in his address to the NCCB. "Most of you know that I am not a professional theologian," Hunthausen writes. "Many of you know far more about these matters than I do and can surely articulate them better." This disclaimer serves Hunthausen in two ways at this point. First, it sends a signal that he is not "putting on airs." Thus his fellow bishops need not feel threatened. Second, it excuses him from losing the arguments of the present day on technical grounds. How can a simple diocesan bishop be expected to compete in theological debates against the theological firepower of the Vatican itself? Finally, it sets up what comes next: Hunthausen shifts the focus away from "theoretical" questions entirely to the more pertinent matter of personal suffering. "Nonetheless," Hunthausen continues,

> The experience that has been mine over these past years can perhaps serve as something of a laboratory for viewing, studying and probing the issues in some way other than the purely theoretical. If that be so, then I honestly believe that this sad experience which has been the source of such pain and confusion for the Church of Seattle and beyond – even to the point of causing serious scandal for many – will not have been in vain, but will have been a path to a new moment of life and growth.

In effect, Hunthausen raises a rhetorical question here – what is theory (i.e., the involved matter of the visitation issues currently under consideration) compared with the lived experience of human suffering? The suggestion is that the Vatican is attempting to get the questions right on paper but is failing to attend to the human dimension and costs of the actions being pursued.

Hunthausen's strategy plays to his advantage within the series of communications that is underway between the two parties. To this point the Vatican communications to the public have been minimal and largely impersonal. Archbishop Hickey had offered but a few remarks to the press. Ratzinger allowed one brief letter (of 12.12.83) to Hunthausen (acknowledging receipt of the Hickey materials) to be published, but not the critical 9.30.85 letter. Laghi made available his own letter revealing the visitation findings but the text is impersonal in a conscientiously polite and formal way. Laghi's next widely distributed statement in the affair was the Vatican chronology, which is a diatribe against Hunthausen. In contrast, Hunthausen all along structured personal appeals and injected his own personality into his communications. What makes his NCCB address effective is that he does not simply profess to know how the people feel, but that more than that, he shows that he himself experiences the same kinds of feelings and vulnerability. Hunthausen's expertise is the product not of external analysis but of relating-to and suffering-with. Along these lines, Hunthausen stakes a cautious claim to knowing well what his fellow bishops are thinking and feeling. "[W]e all struggle to teach in a manner that is both faithful and compelling; and we all strive in our own lives not only to find the right words to call our people to service but to make the servant attitude of Jesus the most identifying mark of our lives."

One key difference between Ratzinger and Hunthausen's applications of expert power is that, whereas Ratzinger applies expert power in a direct way to Hunthausen himself, Hunthausen, at least in the dimensions of the conflict that we are able to observe, applies (anti-)expert (populist) arguments to win the support of third parties, but he shows little inclination to try to win over Roman representatives themselves with this approach. In other words, he does not attempt to feel Rome's pain or identify with Rome's struggles in the same way he does with other parties. It would be interesting to see if use of such a strategy is any more apparent in Hunthausen's private correspondence with Rome, especially that which took place before the appointment of Bishop Wuerl.

Others playing important roles in the Rome-Hunthausen conflict tended to present themselves as experts on the conflict itself more than anything else. This was true both of Laghi's report of the visitation findings and his chronology and of the assessment commission's report. This is not surprising, since both of these parties were carrying out rather clearly defined roles, which limited the scope of the attention they were to give.

As in the case of his employment of traditional power, Hunthausen's populist instincts in his employment of expert power proved advantageous in his conflict with Rome. With little chance of winning arguments over Church teaching or policy with Rome, Hunthausen showed that he could make use of other forms of expertise to advance his own position.

Charismatic power proved to be crucial to the unfolding of the conflict. Hunthausen demonstrated charismatic power and employed it to great effect as the conflict handling came increasingly into the open. The overall strategy of the center party, however, mostly excluded attempts to employ charismatic power. The obvious candidate to effectively employ charismatic power oppositionally to Hunthausen was Pope John Paul II, but the Pope never introduced his own personality into the conflict. This left only Roman curial officials who, as a matter of standard practice, operate off stage rather than on it, and Vatican representatives with the status of high-ranking functionary (diplomat, spokesperson, temporary intermediary), who also were expected to do their work unobtrusively. Thus on the center party side there was no one to serve as a charismatic challenger to the charismatic Hunthausen. Moreover, doing so would not have been in keeping with Rome's intention to manage this particular affair quietly and efficiently behind the scenes. As a result, Hunthausen's personality was seen to be pitted against a secretive and conspiratorial bureaucracy rather than against other, equally legitimate leaders of the Church who also sweated and suffered and tried to do their best on behalf of the community. Instead of Hunthausen versus another bishop of human appeal, it became Hunthausen versus the establishment, Hunthausen versus unnecessary restrictions on freedom, Hunthausen versus a distant force of control that had little grasp of local realities, Hunthausen against "Rome."

Hunthausen's successful projection of charismatic power transpired in personal encounters. Though not the most eloquent of orators, he was skilful at reaching his audience by means of a down-to-earth style and a peaceful manner that reinforced his own reputation for integrity. Hunthausen came across as a calm and peaceful person who had integrated his own values. But the conflict with Rome was only partially transacted through personal encounters, and one wonders whether Hunthausen's particular type of charisma was effective with Vatican representatives. Hunthausen could persuade people in a very direct way in Seattle, and he could persuade his fellow American bishops in their semi-annual meetings. But his contact with Roman officials was much more limited, and in any case it seems not to have been very effective with that particular audience, since Hunthausen did not get far in his behind-the-scenes negotiations with the Holy See. Indeed, Hunthausen's responses in these private forums were found lacking. What ultimately made Hunthausen's charisma a tremendous asset was his ability to communicate it across time and space to those who *were* more susceptible to its appeal: that is, to those who were essentially the stakes in the conflict itself, the Catholics in the pews. Because Hunthausen enjoyed great popularity in his own archdiocese and elsewhere, other bishops were inclined to listen to him, and so was Rome.

One lingering question from the discussion of charismatic power is why the Pope's own well-known charismatic resources (cf. Melady 1999) were never put into play. Given the Pope's flair for dramatic self-presentation and the strong loyalty he has commanded among American Catholics (though, admittedly, he has more than a few against him as well), his active participation in the foreground of the conflict would have put considerable pressure on Hunthausen to back off of his own role as busy, public protagonist. Instead, the Pope chose to inject himself into the affair in a public and personal way on only four occasions: he ordained Wuerl in Rome; he indirectly touched on the conflict issues in his November, 1986 written message to the NCCB; he voiced to the press his support for Malone's statement on the conflict; and he sent a telegram to Hunthausen when Hunthausen was recovering from his cancer surgery (December, 1986). None of these occasions offered served to raise the profile of his participation in the controversy in any significant way.

Presumably the Pope weighed for himself the potential costs and benefits of taking a more active, public role in the affair. Some of these potential costs and benefits we can imagine for ourselves. Potential costs would include: (1) drawing still more media attention to a conflict that the Vatican preferred to keep offstage; (2) sending the signal that the conflict was more serious than the Vatican wanted it to appear to be; (3) offering for public consumption the unsightly fare of two successors to the apostles in opposition to one another; and (4) having the Pope appear to be heavy-handed in his use of power rather than above the fray of internal squabbles. The greatest potential benefit would be that the conflict would be more quickly and efficiently resolved because neither Hunthausen nor other American bishops would be likely to challenge the Holy Father himself. Whatever his own reasons, the Pope remained remarkably hidden during the handling of a conflict that was highly public and highly controversy, and his own charisma played only a limited and obscured role.

Summary of the Use of Normative Power
Of the five types of normative power named above (social power, legal power, traditional power, expert power and charismatic power), all five are employed by both parties in prominent ways except for charismatic power. In my view, the Vatican did not put a premium on employing charismatic power, though it could have chosen to do so. Applications of power in the conflict were necessarily linked to operative ecclesiological conceptions of the given type of power. Thus, on the Vatican side there was a prevailing emphasis on the unicity and self-sufficiency of tradition (Church teaching and practice) as encoded in Church law and guaranteed through monitored conformity of thought and practice. The use of social power involved calling on Hunthausen's feeling of loyalty to the Church (a loyalty which could be verified through his conformity to the Vatican's wishes and his overt posture of deference to Vatican authority) and playing on his fear of exclusion. The Vatican applied legal power in the form of specific legal mechanisms (visitation, power of appointment) and operated within the traditional hierarchical mode of secrecy to ensure his compliance. To a lesser extent, the Vatican tried to convince Hunthausen to cooperate by supplying him with expert reasoning for doing so (Ratzinger's report of the visitation findings).

Hunthausen, for his part, operated according to a different ecclesiological perspective. His more populist view held that Church tradition was marked by a plurality of understandings, by diversity, change ("renewal") and ambiguity. Thus, his employment of traditional power was to highlight, as others had before him (reformers in particular), that flexibility, open discussion and even change were real options for the Church. Hunthausen appeared to be little interested in legal power (more precisely, in legal enforcement) – perhaps because he did not enjoy much beyond the bounds of his own archdiocese and it offered little leverage in his conflict with Rome. But he did employ legal power through his act of legal argumentation and interpretation. This was primarily a defensive move. Similarly, as a "man of the people," Hunthausen showed little inclination to set himself apart as an "expert" in the affair – except in the paradoxical sense of being the people's expert, the one who is on the journey with them and knows them and their suffering. This subtle application of (anti-)expert power converged with Hunthausen's deployment of his own charisma – he took advantage of the growing perception that he was a heroic figure – to apply a form of social power that was itself from the bottom up. Since Hunthausen lacked resources to press Rome from above, as he himself was being pressed, he opted instinctively, and astutely in terms of strategy, to press Rome from the bottom. Hunthausen held popularity within his own local church. As the conflict continued, Hunthausen strengthened this local support while gaining a vociferous following nationally. By positioning himself as a lonely figure standing on principle, Hunthausen grew in stature within and without the Church. At the same time, Hunthausen avoided violating the politeness conventions of the hierarchy and constantly reaffirmed his loyalty to Rome. (That is, he constantly honored Rome's ecclesiological perspective while managing to remain somewhat detached from it.) Since Rome was unable or unwilling to condemn Hunthausen according to any obvious and inexcusable violation of Church policy, and since it was under increasing time pressure to end the conflict, it was left with no better option than giving in to key Hunthausen demands and retreating from certain of its own decisions.

Perhaps the most significant difference in the applications of normative power between the center and periphery party was that, while Rome preferred in public to depersonalize its own self-presentation and use of power, Hunthausen chose in public to maximally personalize his own self-presentation and use of power. On the Rome side, the personalities of individual advocates were not allowed to emerge in public and there was great pressure put on Hunthausen to allow the conflict handling to take place out of public view. The emphasis was on the logic of the existing organizational machinery, which should be allowed to have its way: the Roman curia (distant, anonymous) would determine the nature of the problems; canon law and designated Church teachings (both inanimate) would declare the parameters of permissible solutions; and clarification, as necessary might be sought by having quiet recourse again to the Holy See's expert representatives (the pro-nuncio, curial officials). Especially notable here is the great distant which exists between the Vatican city state -- where decisions regarding punishments are made -- and the local See – where the effects of such decisions were felt. This isolation and the hiddenness of the decision making process kept the Roman officials who issued the negative judgments from having to personally come into contact and work with those who were judged (Hunthausen, first and foremost).

Hunthausen, while pursuing his own interests within the conflict, seemed to grasp instinctively that Rome's preference for hiding from view and acting with bureaucratic anonymity was a public relations disadvantage in his own local church, but also nationally. Few myths are more powerful within the American psyche than that of the lone, principled figure standing up against monolithic vested interests (the establishment, the bureaucracy) which seek to limit personal freedom. Ronald Reagan, who served as President through the greater part of the Hunthausen affair, made supremely effective political use of this mythic appeal – positioning himself as the cowboy outsider who would face down the corruption of Washington and its mass of restrictive regulations. Hunthausen, at the opposite pole from Reagan on many (but not all) political questions, nonetheless had something in common with the public relations posturing of Reagan. Hunthausen said he was not some sort of "maverick archbishop" (the cowboy lore imagery is reminiscent of Reagan), but in a way he was, and in that same way many Americans would approve. Like Reagan, Hunthausen took an individual stand arguing for local control and personal freedoms (in matters of spiritual and pastoral discernment) over and against a distant, controlling bureaucracy.

This is not to suggest that Hunthausen relished his confrontational role with Rome. By all accounts, it disturbed him. But when Hunthausen was pushed too far, the decision to assert himself seemed to come naturally. He did not hesitate to take a stand on principle and to assert his own personality on behalf of his cause. In this regard, perhaps he had been well prepared for this confrontation by his years of anti-nuclear arms activism. There he had often taken a stand publicly. Hunthausen's style – underplaying his bishop status, while arguing his position in a nonconfrontational, but calmly self-assured way – had served him well in those debates. Hunthausen would have been aware of his own effectiveness in such exchanges.

One can imagine, too, that Hunthausen was battle-hardened from his participation in the nuclear weapons controversies. The public-forum weapons debate featured high levels of contestation, anxiety and mutual distrust between opposing groups. By participating in those debates, Hunthausen exposed himself to the sort of stressful political infighting that later came – in much more intense form – in his conflict with Rome. Either Hunthausen was by nature one who could take a beating or he was toughened up by earlier political battles: in any case, his ability to tolerate criticisms directed against him and to persevere for years in an unlikely cause was one of the keys to his coming out of his conflict with Rome as well as he did.

The outcomes of these contrasting strategies – Rome's anonymous maneuvers versus Hunthausen's highly personal assertions -- varied according to the playing field. If the matter was handled out of public view, Rome tended to gain ground. But when Hunthausen brought matters into the open, Rome was put on the defensive. To be more specific, up until September, 1986, Rome had forced Hunthausen to yield: thus, he was left to accept a visitation of his archdiocese, the imposition of an outsider bishop, and the loss of certain of his own powers of leadership. None of these steps were discussed publicly before they were taken. But once Hunthausen took his case into the open with the announcement of the faculties, the momentum shifted in his favor. Thereafter, Rome was induced to abandon its own preferred appearance of harmony within the leadership, to discuss the case in public, to defend its own actions, and eventually to retreat from the earlier punitive action. If these general patterns hold true, then why, according to the rationale I have just advanced, did Hunthausen succeed to the extent he did, since the decisive stage of conflict handling (Hunthausen's meetings with the assessment commission) took place behind closed doors? I see two reasons for this. First of all, Hunthausen's public forays had greatly increased public pressure on the Vatican to let Hunthausen off the hook. Secondly, the commission membership, on the surface would appear to have been relatively sympathetic to Hunthausen, being comprised of two of three members who stood on the moderate to liberal end of American Church politics (Quinn and Bernardin; I would place Hunthausen on the liberal end). It is important to recall, too, that Hunthausen did not get all that he wanted through the closed-door negotiations with the commission. He declared the report itself to be unsatisfactory in its descriptions; Hunthausen was not thrilled to be receiving a coadjutor archbishop instead of an auxiliary; and he was not allowed to have his own first choice for helper bishop appointed.

Before leaving this consideration of the employment of normative power in the conflict, it is worth noting that the coordinated application of various types of normative power – on both sides – had something of a raw effectiveness. By this I mean that employing several types of normative power at once in coordinated fashion can have a combined effect whereby the opposing party is more or less forced to take action it does not wish to take. One can make a case that Rome won as many, and perhaps more, concessions from

Hunthausen by applying a combination of social, legal, traditional and expert pressure on Hunthausen (all forms of normative power) as it did by applying (legitimate) resources of coercive power directly (i.e., invoking its canonical right to intervene in his administration). I have already observed that Rome had much more success imposing its will on Hunthausen behind the scenes than it did in the open. The key to keeping the discussion out of public view was not coercive power – Rome did not require it of Hunthausen with threat of sanction – but social and traditional power. Implicitly, Rome's message was: Let's keep it among ourselves, within the episcopal fraternity (social power), because that is how it has always been done in the Church (traditional power). Though ostensibly, Hunthausen remained free to accept or reject these normative pressures, there came a point at which apparent choice became not much of a choice at all. Going the other way, Hunthausen did not gain ground in his exchanges with the Vatican by refusing to grant Rome access to the archdiocese or publicly supporting rebellion. He did it instead by making use of his own charisma and communicative effectiveness to galvanize support among the media, the American public, and especially the American bishops, the achievement of which pressed Rome into an ever-tighter corner for decision-making. After the NCCB meeting an impasse was reached because, though further options for forcing the other party remained, the costs became prohibitively high for doing so. In light of the unappetizing potentialities of escalation, de-escalation became a much more desirable option.

Having reflected at some length on the question of normative versus raw applications of power in the affair, let us now consider the appearance or non-appearance of specific anticipated strategies.

9.2.3 Coping Strategy 1: Show deference to the existing structural order and mindset of the Church

My presupposition was that members of the hierarchy would draw on existing organizational structures and defer to existing organizational norms in center-periphery conflict situations. I expected that they would be careful for the appearance of the Church and would want to demonstrate their own trustworthiness as institutional guardians, which they would do through conservative pronouncements and behaviors and shows of respect for the hierarchical order. Analysis of the Rome-Hunthausen conflict confirms these expectations, but we see too that numerous challenges to the established order arise, and that the order itself is in flux.

The case narrative and analysis above (chapters 6-8) gives us a glimpse of the conflict handling styles of at least eleven bishops. Across the board, the bishops consistently (even during periods of high conflict intensity) use traditional ecclesiastical terms, speak reverently of the Church and its traditions, address one another politely, and only reluctantly take action or speak in ways that directly challenge prevailing norms in the Church. The use of such tactics was anticipated. (See section 3.5.3.)

At the same time, however, the Hunthausen affair shows that bishops may feel personal, internal tensions (visible in their words and actions) around questions of institutional deference. The requirement of deference at times stands at odds with personal beliefs or principles that invite bishops to challenge the status quo. This tension is highly evident in the case of Hunthausen himself, but it is also clearly present in a more diffuse way, in the American bishops' conference's approach to the conflict.

The Vatican's clash with Hunthausen demonstrates that the Church's structural order and mindset is something in contested transition. Though none of the bishops involved show an inclination to challenge the existing order and mindset in radical ways, even the more conservative-sounding pronouncements within the case offer signs that the Church does not simply stand still in time. A notable example is Ratzinger's 9.30.85 letter to Hunthausen, which, for all its emphasis on the surety of the teaching of the Magisterium, nonetheless admits the legitimacy of the concept of "renewal" in Church thinking (presuming, of course, that Ratzinger is not saying this solely to gain a more receptive hearing from Hunthausen). The fact that there may be competing concepts of how renewal should be understood and implemented (Ratzinger's view versus Hunthausen's) simply reinforces the point that there is not a fixed unanimity of thought and practice in the Church organization and that arrangements within the Church are the product of ongoing negotiation.

Indeed, to take this point further, we see that well developed but contrasting ecclesiologies emerge in the course of the conflict. On the one hand we have Ratzinger's presentation of the Church as an essentially complete and impersonal entity, whose aspects are consistently designated with the definite article: "the Church's clear teaching about the indissolubility of a sacramental marriage;" "the nature and mission of the Church;" "the meaning of the Church;" the Church's integral faith concerning Christ;" "the clear vision of the human person which is at the heart of the Gospel message;" etc. On the other hand, we have Hunthausen's tendency to speak in relational terms of the Church as a collectivity of persons: "Our people have 'come of age' and they deserve to be treated as adults. They are capable of dealing maturely with problems where they exist and they take seriously the 'ownership' of the Church that is their birthright as baptized members of the Body of Christ." Though both of these ecclesiological visions are traditional within the Church, they do not sit together easily, and the predominance of one over the other bears significant implications for the future of the Church.

At times in this case, Hunthausen challenges Church procedural practices outright – as in regard to the visitation process, the use of secrecy, the role of bishops' conferences -- but we should note that he almost always does this with an eye toward face saving for the Church and with a marked ambivalence. The emphasis on face saving shows itself in his refusal to name names and assign personal blame and the consistent stance of reverence he adopts toward the Church itself. Hunthausen's ambivalence can be seen in the reluctance with which he openly challenges Rome (his resistance to Rome takes shape behind the scenes long before it does so in public) and in his own continued adherence to norms that he purportedly is challenging (though he voices opposition to the use of secrecy, he employs the same himself). In other words, even in the rare instances in which Hunthausen challenges the dominant Church culture, he does so in Church-familiar ways.

9.2.4 Coping Strategy 2: Associate own efforts with the best interest of the Church
This is a fairly obvious strategy to employ. I anticipated that all participants in center-periphery conflict would be likely to use this strategy, but perhaps according to different views of the Church's interest. This expectation is born out in the Rome-Hunthausen conflict. Ratzinger, Laghi, Hunthausen, Malone and the assessment commission members all apply this strategy explicitly in the course of public statements and argumentation, with contrasts arising in their articulation of which course of action is in keeping with the best interest of the Church.

The expected tactics for carrying out the strategy – drawing attention to the Church, doing so in positive ways, and explicitly associating oneself with the Church's best interest – can all be found in the case history. Of greater interest is the case's revelation of the various forms, depending on the actor, that associative posturing can take. These relate to conceptions concerning the type of organization that the Church is. Ratzinger presents himself as a rational guardian of (expert on) the deposit of faith (the truth). The well being of the Church consists in keeping this truth from being tainted by error, and passing it on successfully into the future (Church as mission). Laghi positions himself as a facilitator of the organizational machinery (Church as bureaucracy). Like Ratzinger, he tends to background his own personality in his writing, but unlike Ratzinger, his focus goes to relational politics as well (Church as clan and political-economic market). The good of the Church within his orientation is achieved by having the Church leadership in sync and the processes of decision-making and implementation well oiled. Hunthausen acts on behalf of the good of the Church as a populist spokesperson (Church as mission and market). The good of the Church is inseparable from the good of the Church's people. Hunthausen represents the people in the pews (who deserve to be treated as adults) and his fellow diocesan bishops (who deserve autonomy in their own local churches). Malone and the members of the assessment commission are like Laghi in associating their own efforts and the good of the Church with the maintenance of intraecclesial harmony (Church as clan). They position themselves as servants of unity.

In the course of the conflict, the question of how most properly to understand the best interest of the Church stands central and is a source of much tension.

9.2.5 Coping Strategy 3: Minimize the appearance of conflict

My expectation was that members of the hierarchy would be strongly inclined to minimize the appearance of conflict among themselves, first by hiding such conflicts and then, when necessary, by putting the best face possible on aspects of the conflict that come into the open. I also anticipated that the center party would have a stronger incentive to minimize the appearance of conflict (because it is the greater beneficiary of the appearance of harmony and unity) and that minimization of the conflict on the periphery side would come more from a desire to prove its loyalty. These expectations were only partly confirmed by my confrontation of the Hunthausen case data. Though the Holy See, Hunthausen and key third parties of bishops do show a predisposition to keep conflict handling hidden and to minimize the seriousness of those aspects of the conflict that come into the open, there are also surprisingly numerous moves (by center and periphery both) to uncover the conflict for the sake of advantage.

We see the Vatican's preference to minimize the appearance of conflict in its initial intention to keep the conflict entirely hidden from view: it seeks to conduct the visitation in secret and to make the report to Hunthausen of its findings in secret. When Hunthausen insists on having a report of the visitation findings that he can make public, Rome commissions Laghi to write a revised version of the Ratzinger letter that has a softer tone than its source. After escalation of the conflict leads the center and periphery parties to criticize one another publicly, we see a swift resumption of secret negotiations and silence and / or polite public pronouncements thereafter.

From the periphery party, as expected (see section 3.5.3), we see a much more ambivalent approach to minimizing the appearance of conflict. Though Hunthausen consistently shows a reluctance to appear at odds with Rome, and with the Holy Father in particular, he shows an equal disinclination to be disadvantaged by conflict negotiations that are hidden. Thus, while Hunthausen cooperates with the Vatican intention to keep the visitation secret (*cooperative behavior* can serve as a tactic to minimize the appearance of conflict), he also (reportedly) argues against this decision in private. Then, once the visitation announcement is made, Hunthausen speaks of the process euphemistically, making it seem more benign than it is. While waiting the better part of two years for the Vatican's report on the visitation avoids public comment on the matter altogether. Hunthausen's announcement of Wuerl's faculties shows his ambivalence in a microcosm. Hunthausen reveals a controversial conflict development that Rome does not want revealed, but he does so in determinedly neutral language. Later, after responding contentiously to Laghi's contentious chronology, Hunthausen returns to the practice of conflict engagement in private and silence in public.

Throughout the conflict, the press serves as a strategic outlet for both parties. Unilateral distributions of information to the news media play a critical role in the affair on multiple occasions. Among the key examples of this are the news leak forcing Hickey and Hunthausen to announce the visitation, Hunthausen's revelation of Wuerl's faculties (against Rome's wishes), Laghi's circulation of the Vatican chronology (against Hunthausen's wishes) and the news leaks that precedes the release of the commission report. On one more occasion, Hunthausen presses the Vatican to make public a document (the 9.30.85 Ratzinger letter) it does not wish to make public. Though Hunthausen proves to be much more ready to take his case to the public through the press than does Rome, Rome also shows a willingness to reveal aspects of the conflict to the news media when it is advantageous to do so.

Perhaps most surprising in the case, in light of my expectations, is that both sides reach the point of publicly attacking one another. Rome suggests that Hunthausen lacks firmness as a leader; Hunthausen suggests that Rome uses methods that are unjust and do a disservice to the people of the Church. Admittedly, it takes at least three years before it gets to this point, but this does show that, with time and pressure, the proclivity to minimize the appearance of center-periphery conflict can dissipate. We should not overlook the potential strategic advantages to each side that come from revealing the conflict. By taking his message to the public, Hunthausen garners sympathy as a courageous underdog. Rome, for its part, gains the opportunity to paint Hunthausen as one who is wilful and a threat to Church unity.

9.2.6 Coping Strategy 4: Show fraternity
Before confronting the data of the Rome-Hunthausen case, I anticipated that participants in center-periphery conflict would be both empowered and restricted by the bond(s) of episcopal fraternity, and that all participants would explicitly and implicitly invoke the concept. I expected that the center party would do so as a way of keeping control over the periphery and that the periphery would do so to retain the privileges that follow from loyalty and to avoid punishments.

We find all of these expectations confirmed in the Rome-Hunthausen case. This empirical example shows the bond of fraternity to be quite strong within the hierarchy. It also shows us that bishops are strongly inclined to preserve the strength of the bond in appearance and in fact. Finally, the evidence of the case suggests that, while outside pressures can significantly influence the course of intrahierarchical conflict handling, the ultimate key to resolution of the conflict lies within the fraternity. *Resolution depends on what the bishops (and first and foremost the bishop of Rome) decide and not on what anyone else decides.*

During the Hunthausen affair we find many occasions where the concept of episcopal

273

fraternity is invoked explicitly. When Archbishop Hickey announces his forthcoming visit to Seattle, he says that he comes "as a brother bishop… to offer appropriate fraternal assistance and support." In public, Hickey shows only graciousness to Hunthausen, and Hunthausen shows the same to Hickey. Archbishop Laghi, in his 11.14.85 letter to Hunthausen, repeats this description of Hickey's role: "It was the Visitor's role to speak with you as a brother bishop… and to offer you appropriate fraternal assistance and report." The purpose of such statements appears to be to reassure Hunthausen and the public that the business at hand is well intentioned (families look out for their own), but they also serve as a subtle justification for conducting the business behind closed doors (families keep their squabbles to themselves).

In the course of the conflict, the setting where the concept of episcopal fraternity gets its most thoroughgoing treatment is at the November 1986 gathering of the American bishops, where invocation of the concept appears mandatory. The pro-nuncio's remarks begin with a greeting to "Bishop Malone, my dear brother bishops and friends," but any suggestion of equality within the episcopal family is quickly dashed by Laghi's suggestion that he has been instrumental in the appointment of one-third of the bishops in the room. On the whole, Laghi's reference to fraternity seems perfunctory. Decidedly more than perfunctory is the Pope's embrace of the concept in his written address to the bishops. The Pope begins with a greeting comparable to Laghi's ("To my dear brother bishops in the United States of America"), but then repeatedly reintroduces the concept of fraternity and explores its theological implications. Thus, he says, "I wish to assure you of my fraternal solidarity with you…" and proceeds to explore what such solidarity entails. What it clearly does not entail in his presentation is independence or equality in regard to the papacy. The role of the Pope is "to confirm the bishops in their apostolic faith and ministry" and "to preside in love." "It is an awareness of my own role in the church, and especially in regard to her unity and universality," the Pope writes, "that has prompted me to do everything possible to confirm my brother bishops throughout the world in their own collegial ministry." There is nothing surprising in the content of the Pope's message here. Church teaching is consistent on the point that the Pope is unique among bishop: he is not simply one among many bishops, he is first among them as leader of the Church. In essence, he reminds his brother bishops that he is more father than brother. When the Pope reminds his brother bishops of ways he has been of "service" to them, he highlights undertakings that, from another angle, can be seen to be acts of surveillance: the apostolic visitation of American seminaries, the formation of the Pontifical Commission for Religious Life, and the Pope's own forthcoming pastoral visit to the U.S. In short, the strategy of showing fraternity cannot be understood without reference to papal fatherhood.

In Hunthausen's address to the American bishops, he too draws on the fraternity concept. Hunthausen clearly has something to gain if his fellow bishops turn to him as a brother. "I want to tell you that I am particularly distressed about any anguish or even division that may have come about among you, my brother bishops," Hunthausen writes. Hunthausen's use of the term "brother bishops," in the context of an extended, passionate plea, comes as a reminder that family members have special responsibilities to one another. In contrast with the Hickey and Laghi invocations of the concept, which are rather detached and impersonal, Hunthausen infuses his employment of the brotherhood concept with feeling. Of Bishop Wuerl he writes: "He is my brother and my friend and my heart aches for him when I consider the ordeal he has had to suffer…" With Hunthausen, the emphasis stays on the personal dimensions of the bond.

In certain respects, Bishop Malone's 11.12.86 statement on behalf of the NCCB is similar to Hunthausen's NCCB address in its tendency to personalize and associate feelings with the concept of episcopal fraternity. There Hunthausen and Wuerl are referred to as "our brothers in the episcopacy" and Malone develops an extended, and somewhat sentimental, metaphor of a family coming together in a time of difficulty. Malone's concern is with a "kind of pain that can only be felt by members of a family." This statement shows a longing to make peace as quickly as possible. Hence the reminder that bishops are family and therefore ought to be able to put their differences behind them. The idea of fraternity carries a serious pressure for harmony.

Taken together, the examples above show that the notion of episcopal fraternity is a commonplace within the discourse of the hierarchy and that *invocation of the concept* can serve strategic purposes. But we also see fraternity practiced *nondiscursively* in the case.

We see it in the presumption in favor of keeping the bishops' business among themselves (private meetings, private correspondence, private debates) and in the formal instruments of collaborative reflection and decision making (ad limina visits, the relationship between ordinary and assistant bishops, national and regional episcopal conferences. We also see it in the form of (purportedly) cooperative pastoral interventions (the visitation, the appointment of auxiliary and coadjutor, the NCCB's role of mediation, the ad hoc commission's assessment) and in more personal one-to-one or small group exchanges (as in Hurley and Roach's roles advising Hunthausen and in the hidden negotiations concerning the NCCB endorsement for the Vatican chronology). Common to all of these experiences is an operative sense that only bishops can solve bishops' problems and that a sharp line of demarcation exists between those who belong to the brotherhood and those who do not. What this implies for handling of the conflict is that the ultimate key to resolution lies within the fraternity of bishops and is not external to it. The alliances within are what matters. Hunthausen survives his conflict with the Vatican and ultimately achieves certain key objectives largely because he secures critical support from the national episcopal conference -- active support from some members and support in the form of neutrality from the conference as a whole. This support keeps the Vatican from taking further action against Hunthausen. Another key to Hunthausen's effectiveness is that, though he tests the limits of the fraternal rules, he never goes so far as to break them until Rome itself does so. Hunthausen, even under extreme duress never once openly and directly criticizes another bishop, and his most critical language comes only when the pro-nuncio himself has abandoned the politeness standard.

The Vatican could, of course, have acted unilaterally at any point to remove Hunthausen or discipline him in another way, but the fact that it does not suggests that good relations with national episcopal conferences are very important to the Holy See. When push comes to shove, the Pope shows a willingness to accept and implement a solution not his own making – one that comes from the assessment commission, which has listened to Hunthausen at least well enough to find a solution he can live with.

9.2.7 Coping Strategy 5: Practice Courtesy
Prior to systematically analyzing the Rome-Hunthausen case data, my expectation was that bishops would show a high degree of courtesy toward one another in center-periphery conflict, and that this would be one means for defending or advancing one's own position within the conflict. This expectation was abundantly confirmed by the Hunthausen case, but the empirical evidence from the case raised questions as well as answering them.

From the time the pro-nuncio approaches Hunthausen to the time of the release of the Vatican chronology, politeness reigns in both parties' approach to conflict handling. Prior to the release of the chronology, both parties – without obvious deviation – show courtesy toward one another, going to significant lengths to be respectful, to not criticize the other, and often to praise the other. The Vatican chronology instantiates a breach in this policy of politeness on the center party side, an act that is quickly followed by a retaliatory breach of politeness from the periphery party side (contained in Hunthausen's NCCB messages). The expressions of impoliteness on both sides are quickly contained after this outburst. After the 1986 NCCB meeting, courtesy again becomes the norm, though the quality of the courtesy changes. Rather than offering public statements laced with words of deference and praise, the parties adopt a more negative form of politeness, wherein the two sides limit contact and keep silent about the conflict as much as possible, thereby voicing no criticism of the other (and concomitantly avoiding the obligation to use terms of deference and praise in regard to the other). Once the commission releases its report, Hunthausen briefly resumes public discussion of the conflict, offering a few statements that can be considered contentious and somewhat discourteous, but thereafter he adopts a more or less permanent silence in regard to the conflict and its history. Rome also adopts a policy of silence about the affair after the NCCB debate, with normally only terse, official statements breaking the (ultimately permanent) silence.

Regarding the strategic employment of courtesy in the Rome-Hunthausen conflict, a few conclusions can be drawn. First, both the center and periphery parties by their conduct show that courtesy – often in an exaggerated form -- is the norm in intrahierarchical relations. Both the center and periphery parties put a premium on saving face for the other: at a minimum by refusing to criticize the other or show the other in a negative light; and more actively by publicly praising and expressing solidarity with the other member(s) of the hierarchy. Apparently, maintaining this picture of mutual respect and harmony is one of the unwritten rules of the hierarchy. Thus, in more than five years of (varying degrees of) tense exchange, only a handful of obviously discourteous remarks surface publicly in the Rome-Hunthausen conflict, and even these remarks come amid a flurry of face-saving statements. On the surface, the episcopal culture is one of *invincible graciousness*.

Nonetheless – and this is my second conclusion about courtesy drawn from the Rome-Hunthausen case -- for all its strength, the culture of graciousness does in fact break down under great stress. Frustration with the other party appears to be the immediate cause of the breakdown. Frustrated with Hunthausen's public announcement of Wuerl's faculties and the resulting storm of protest, Laghi issues the face-threatening Vatican chronology. In response, Hunthausen issues his own highly charged statements to the NCCB. Two observations are in order concerning this breakdown: (1) the break with courtesy comes initially from the center party side; and (2) Laghi's is the more directly personal attack. By being the first to break with courtesy, the center party gives Hunthausen an opportunity to depart from courtesy – an opportunity that, in my view, he would not have had otherwise (without likely suffering the consequence of removal from office). Since the Vatican fires first, Hunthausen can, briefly at least, get away with firing defensively in response. But even in responding defensively, Hunthausen apparently does not see advantage to be gained by blaming any other member of the hierarchy, especially since, across the board, his opponents are more powerfully positioned within the hierarchy than he. Instead, Hunthausen avoids gaining particular enemies and does his best to maintain an appearance of faithful service within the fold, while stoking a fire of public discontent about the way he has been treated. Thus courteousness can be a means of contention.

A third conclusion we can draw concerning strategic applications of courtesy in the conflict is that, after the outburst of contentious exchange between the parties, order is quickly restored and politeness rules once again. The inclination to mutual courtesy appears to be a standard that it is so firmly engrained in intrahierarchical relations that it can be breached only under the most volatile of conditions, and even then only for a brief time.

The fourth conclusion I would offer concerning the strategic employment of courtesy in the case is that the Pope, at least so long as he stays in the background, is *untouchable* by other members of the hierarchy. Whereas Hunthausen shows a willingness, when pressed , to challenge – in a very indirect way – the decisions or actions of other members of the hierarchy, he speaks only deferentially of the Pope throughout the entire affair, generally invoking his name in relation to the conflict only when necessary. And that is true of all bishops involved in the controversy from beginning to end. Though the question of the Pope's involvement is crucial from beginning to end in the conflict – he has the ultimate authority to determine Hunthausen's fate, after all – no bishop ever once publicly and directly raises the question of the Pope's involvement in the affair or his view of it, and certainly no one ever implies anything approaching criticism of the Pope. Perhaps if the Pope had publicly involved himself in the affair, he might have exposed himself to criticism (at least of the indirect kind). But in this case he does not become publicly involved and is spoken of only with reverence.

9.2.8 Coping Strategy 6: Employ secrecy

My expectation concerning the strategic use of secrecy in center-periphery conflict was that both parties would employ secrecy to protect the appearance of the Church and to guard their own leadership autonomy. I presupposed that bishops would respect conventional domains of secrecy and would respect conditions of secrecy around conflict handling so long as doing so would not significantly disadvantage them. I also speculated that the periphery party would likely be the first to forgo or resist secrecy since it is the party less likely to be advantaged by secrecy. How far the center or periphery would go in turning its back on secrecy was unclear to me.

The evidence from the Rome-Hunthausen case confirms the expectation that the hierarchy's commitment to secrecy in conflict handling is strong but not unconditional. There are obvious instances of both sides breaking with secrecy, as in Hunthausen's announcement of Wuerl's faculties and Laghi's issuance of the Vatican chronology. What is not clear is which side first breaks with secrecy. (We do not know who leaked the news of the visitation.) Notable is Hunthausen's open criticism of the use of secrecy and own ambivalent practice thereof.

Certain factors complicate the analysis of secrecy employments in the conflict. One complication is the difficulty of distinguishing between secrecy employed as a matter of habit and secrecy applied deliberatively for strategic gain. Another complication involves distinguishing between silence and secrecy. Silence may look like secrecy but be simply a reflection of a party's lack of information or lack of desire to speak. Silence may also be more a matter of politeness than of hiding something for direct gain. Finally, it may simply be a matter of human limits and / or administrative efficiency. Organizational leaders cannot possibly share all available and potentially relevant information with organizational members and other interested parties. This would create functional gridlock. In other words, not sharing all information is not automatically equivalent to keeping secrets. As much as possible, I have tried to keep my focus on acts of hiding that appear to be clearly strategic in terms of the conflict handling itself.

One should also note that there are layers of secrecy which apply. As far as possible, I distinguish here between secrecy practiced jointly by the Vatican and Hunthausen (and other members of the hierarchy) in relation to the public and these parties' own strategic keeping of secrets from one another. While Rome kept secrets from Hunthausen which can be enumerated, the evidence is less clear about which kinds of secrets Hunthausen kept from the Vatican, since Hunthausen protested specific uses of secrecy but the Vatican did not.

To sum up the strategic use of secrecy in the Rome-Hunthausen case, I offer the following observations. First, all parties (center, periphery, third) use secrecy with regularity, but their use also shows that adherence to secrecy is not an inviolable norm of intrahierarchical relations. Secrecy appears to be a normal mode of operation for discussing delicate matters within the hierarchy – an approach reinforced by social pressure within the hierarchy and by habit. The Hunthausen case begins and ends in secrecy and is suffused with secrecy throughout. But significant resistance to secrecy and the abandonment of secrecy crop up within the case as well. Breaks from secrecy come in the form of news leaks, joint center-periphery party announcements (of the visitation, Wuerl's appointment, implementation of the commission plan), unilateral press announcements (Hunthausen's announcement of Wuerl's possession of faculties), the release of relevant documents (the Laghi and Ratzinger letters summarizing the visitation findings, the Vatican chronology, Hunthausen's NCCB statements, etc), and other interviews and comments shared with the press.

Rome evidently is much more committed to adhering to secrecy than Hunthausen. Hunthausen presses for a public announcement of the visitation, but the Holy See refuses this request, giving in only after the news leak made it unavoidable. In the same vein, the Holy See denies Hunthausen's request to make the 9.30.85 Ratzinger letter public and also refuses his request to view the Hickey report. The Vatican's own clearest, most significant (unilateral) break from secrecy is the issuance of the Vatican chronology. This step comes under duress: Rome is obviously frustrated by Hunthausen's unilateral move to reveal Wuerl's possession of faculties and the public criticism of Rome that emerges as a result.

Hunthausen, for his part, expressly objects to secrecy on principle – highlighting modern expectations of transparent leadership in his NCCB address – but in practice he maintains a posture of adherence to Vatican secrecy wishes up to the point at which, apparently, he feels he has been pushed too far by Rome (i.e., when he must give up the faculties). As with Rome, Hunthausen's most significant departures from secrecy comes under duress. The two texts he supplies to the NCCB are also circulated within the period of highest tension in the conflict, once the door to a more free discussion has been thrown open by Hunthausen's announcement and the Vatican chronology. While Hunthausen appears, all along the way, to share as much information as he feels he can with the people of his archdiocese, it is clear that he feels significantly constrained in what he is permitted to share.

This period of fairly open discussion in the conflict is short-lived, lasting less than three months within a conflict of five-and-a-half years (September-November, 1986). For the remainder of the conflict (and for the years preceding and succeeding the conflict as well) we must speak of secret negotiations and only minimal presentations of the information that has been gathered.

Third party participants in the conflict consistently keep secrecy as well. Bishop Wuerl keeps quiet the fact that he is to have special responsibilities in Seattle and he also refuses to reveal details of his personal meetings in Rome. The NCCB keeps its debate of the case and other relevant negotiations out of view of the press. The assessment commission offers its views only in its final report: all transactions prior to that are conducted in secret.

The use of secrecy in the conflict serves the parties in the following ways. By keeping secrets from Hunthausen, Rome prevents him from interfering with certain courses of action it chooses to pursue. Thus, Hunthausen is not presented with the possibility of a visitation until that decision has already been made; he is denied access to the visitation report, and is thereby kept from contesting its conclusions; and he is left to wait the better part of two years to learn what the Vatican concludes from the visitation. Secrecy also serves Rome, so long as Hunthausen remains complicit, by saving the appearance of the Church and its hierarchy. As long as the conflict is out of sight, there is no conflict as far as most of the Church and most of the public at large is concerned.

Secrecy serves Hunthausen in different ways. Most importantly, it keeps him out of trouble with Rome. By conforming to secrecy expectations, Hunthausen does not make waves and does not give Rome reason to be less happy with him than it already is. Secrecy also serves Hunthausen by saving face for him. If secrecy keeps Rome's heavy-handed use of its own power from view, it also keeps any deficiencies in Hunthausen's leadership from view, as well as the fact that the Vatican is unhappy with him. Secrecy, in short, allows Hunthausen to selectively determine his self-presentation to the public. Thirdly, secrecy is also, as with the Vatican, a guarantor of his own autonomy. Secrecy enables him to take decisions without interference, relative to his conflict with Rome but also in regard to day-to-day affairs in his own archdiocese.

I have already noted that the most prominent departures from secrecy in the conflict occur during the period of greatest tension in the affair. (The departures themselves contribute to the escalation of tension.) To nuance that observation a bit, I would add that disclosure apparently is applied when secrecy seems not to be working. Hunthausen goes to the press when he finds himself in an intolerable situation and he has little left to lose. (The legitimacy of Hunthausen's point that the news would of necessity come forth anyway must be conceded. Can the Vatican truly have imagined otherwise?) On the Vatican side, it no longer works to manage Hunthausen in private once he himself takes the case to the public. Only a public response will suffice if the Vatican hopes to regain its grip on the affair. At that time, secrecy offers little hope of success, so disclosure is applied.

An interesting feature of the use of secrecy in the affair is how it comes to need justification for its application. The practice of justifying one's own use of secrecy starts with Hunthausen's announcement of Wuerl's faculties. In the course of that announcement, Hunthausen provides a rationale for not sharing his full awareness of Wuerl's responsibilities at the time of the appointment. "The importance of making Bishop Wuerl's transition to the archdiocese as smooth as possible and of assuring him of the best possible climate for beginning this ministry among us seemed to outweigh any possible good that might have been realized by giving a full public acknowledgment of all the specifications surrounding his appointment as auxiliary bishop," Hunthausen writes. This justification for using secrecy exemplifies a recurring phenomenon. Both the center and periphery parties typically justify their employment of secrecy by saying it is on behalf of another. Here Hunthausen says secrecy was practiced for Wuerl's benefit. In the Vatican chronology, Laghi writes the visitation publicity was minimized to avoid fostering criticism of Hunthausen. Laghi also says in the chronology that data from the visitation interviews was not released to Hunthausen because confidentiality for those who provided the information needed to be respected. Still later, in his response to the Vatican chronology, Hunthausen declares that he asked Laghi not to distribute the chronology because it would generate publicity that would reflect unfavorably on the Holy See. Notably, such justifying statements only occur during the brief period when the use of secrecy itself is under discussion (i.e., around the time of the NCCB gathering) by the principal parties. Before and after this period, the use of secrecy was normally undertaken without explanation or comment.

9.2.9 Coping Strategy 7: Recruit allies

My expectation was that both center and periphery would try to recruit fellow bishops as allies in the conflict once a lack of self-sufficiency became apparent in the conflict handling. I supposed that the most powerful and influential members of the hierarchy (the Pope, officials of the Roman curia, leaders of episcopal conferences) would be most in demand as allies. I also presumed that conflict participants would seek support from outside the hierarchy as a means of pressuring the opposing party.

These expectations were largely confirmed, but one surprise from the Rome-Hunthausen conflict is how hard the Vatican works to gain the cooperation of the American bishops' conference, given that the Pope himself could simply resolve the conflict unilaterally, by personal fiat.

Both the center and periphery parties address multiple audiences with the hope of winning allies, but the target audiences vary as do the means used to reach the audiences. On both sides, the initial efforts go to recruiting the support of fellow bishops directly (through personal meetings and phone calls). As the conflict expands, both Rome and Hunthausen take their case to the media as a way of winning support from other members of the hierarchy and from the public at large (which can in turn put pressure on bishops to take one side or the other.

At the beginning of the conflict, Rome (Ratzinger) focuses primarily on reaching Hunthausen and perhaps insiders who have influence with Hunthausen to get him to cooperate with its intervention in the archdiocese. This contact is undertaken in the form of private correspondence, personal visits with Hunthausen in Rome (ad limina visits), and communications via the papal pro-nuncio. Ratzinger's 9.30.85 letter to Hunthausen does not appear directed to a wide audience, given its highly technical ecclesiastical language. But it is cautiously written, suggesting that Ratzinger foresees its possible release to a broader audience and prepares for this possibility. (Perhaps he does this as a matter of habit?) Laghi's redraft of the Ratzinger letter, given the circumstances of its production and evidence in the text itself, is clearly intended for a wide intraecclesial and (to a lesser extent) extraecclesial audience. Hunthausen is also a target audience of this communication. The key to reaching Hunthausen in this case is not in offering him the information he already has, but in presenting the material for public consumption in such a way that Hunthausen's further cooperation is enlisted.

To successfully defend his own position in his conflict with Rome, Hunthausen must address Rome. He does so by means of personal visits and correspondence and through the mediation of the papal pro-nuncio. Hunthausen's principle message is to reassure Rome he is a trustworthy bishop and that he should be allowed to govern his diocese without exceptional forms of involvement by Rome. A less direct but nonetheless crucial way Hunthausen sends messages to Rome is by demonstrating his support in his own archdiocese and in the United States. (Hunthausen's handling of the news media is instrumental in this effort.) Hunthausen's indirect message to Rome by way of this show of the support he commands is to serve notice that he is effective in his own way and that many will be upset if he is perceived as being mistreated. Demonstrations of strength also contribute to his ability to recruit allies.

All along the way Hunthausen speaks to the people of his own archdiocese (especially through the archdiocesan newspaper), expressly for the purpose of keeping them informed, but also as a shepherd caring for his flock. Through his pastoral messages he both offers support to his people amid the confusion and difficulty of the conflict and builds support for his own position. A key group within this local audience are the priests of the archdiocese. The stalwart support the local priests show Hunthausen significantly limits the Vatican's ability to paint him as a renegade and act against him on that basis. Hunthausen communicates with his priests directly, through periodic meetings and letters, and indirectly, through presbyteral council meetings and *The Progress*.

As the conflict progresses, Hunthausen increasingly turns his attention to convincing the other American bishops to support him. Hunthausen forges alliances with individual bishops (such as Archbishop Hurley), consults with others (e.g., Archbishop Roach), lobbies other small groups of bishops (e.g.: the members of the NCCB executive committee, prior to release of Laghi's chronology; the assessment commission members; and the bishops of the Northwest region), and communicates with the entire body of American bishops both orally and in writing. Particularly notable is Hunthausen's handling of his auxiliary and, later, coadjutor bishops. By successfully establishing bonds with both of these fellow bishops serving within his archdiocese, Hunthausen avoids the serious problems that could arise by having a powerful opponent under his own roof. This is crucial in Wuerl's case. Though Hunthausen may have had theological differences with Wuerl and had reason to be suspicious of his presence given the circumstances of his appointment, Hunthausen saves face for himself before the Vatican and his fellow bishops by treating Wuerl well. Indeed, Hunthausen comes to be Wuerl's most visible supporter in Seattle. In retrospect, there was no reason for Hunthausen to oppose Wuerl outright because there were countless others who were ready to protest his presence in Seattle. In the case of Archbishop Murphy, Hunthausen had less to fear from him because he was a known quantity (a fellow bishop of the same region, and not a Roman insider like Wuerl), and there was no expectation of him having special powers. Nonetheless, the positive personal relationship that emerges between Hunthausen and Murphy was an important factor contributing to the ultimate resolution of the conflict.

9.3 Coping Strategies Encountered That Were Not Expected
My confrontation of the data of the case reveals at least two, and likely more, coping strategies that play a significant role in the conflict handling that I did not expect to find. I will now introduce these strategies and describe aspects of their application in the case.

9.3.1 Coping Strategy 8: Argue persuasively

In one sense, it is hardly surprising that highly educated people would apply rational argumentation to sort through conflict issues and to persuade others. Perhaps the fact that this seemed a bit too obvious kept me from including this among my initial expectations of strategies applied. (Pruitt and Rubin cite persuasive argumentation as a potential strategy of contention in their theory of conflict handling. See section 4.2.3) What is striking in the Rome-Hunthausen case is how little persuasive argumentation between the principal parties takes place in public. The most obvious places where it does are in Laghi's chronology, Hunthausen's NCCB statements and the commission report, but all of these texts seem more concerned with winning over the opinions of third party text consumers (other bishops especially, and the public at large) than with persuading the opposing party.

Most attempts by center and periphery to persuade one another occur in places where the public is not invited – in one-to-one discussions and private letters and phone calls. As an example, Ratzinger's 9.30.85 letter to Hunthausen seems to make a real effort to rationally persuade Hunthausen. Ratzinger grants the legitimacy of Hunthausen's principles – implementing the renewal called for at Vatican II, for example – but then challenges Hunthausen to see the difference between lesser and fuller concepts of what that renewal entails. Contrast this with Laghi's chronology, which shows no obvious rhetorical attempt to win Hunthausen himself over, but does seek to persuade the American bishops and other American Catholics. Similarly, Hunthausen's NCCB addresses are directed more to his fellow bishops and to the American public than to Rome, and the commission report is meant at least as much for the bishops and the public as for Hunthausen himself. One can argue that participants in center-periphery conflict prefer to conduct their open-ended, rational debates out of sight (so as not to awaken unrest among the faithful), but in the Hunthausen affair it seems to have been a constant frustration of Hunthausen's that his own viewpoints are not accepted as legitimate by Rome.

The range of techniques available for purposes of persuasion is vast (see, for example, the survey in Kennedy 1980). Thus I am not in a position to catalogue the rhetorical tactics that might serve to carry out a strategy of persuasive argumentation. But the following are tactics that appeared functional within the handling of the Rome-Hunthausen conflict at various times.

Ingratiation: By this technique, one shows favor to win concessions from the other (often through praise or flattery). It would seem to be most effective when received as a genuine expression of good will. In conflict situations, it may be hard for antagonistic parties to apply this tactic directly in regard to one another, due to the undermining effect of mutual suspicion. In the public dimensions of the Rome-Hunthausen case, it seemed to be directed primarily toward third parties that might be recruited as supporters or allies. The best example is probably Hunthausen repeated expression of affection and respect for his fellow bishops and the people of his archdiocese.

Demonization: This tactic involves casting serious aspersions on the other and the other's intentions. Obviously, given all that I have said thus far, no bishop is likely to demonize another in any overt way (that is, in any way he can be held accountable for). But we see at least a mild version of this tactic when Rome suggests that Hunthausen is infirm and intransigent, and when Hunthausen proposes that Rome has acted unjustly and brought about unnecessary suffering.

Definition power: The right to decide which words apply and what they mean is a classic question in power struggles (cf. Alinsky 1971). In the Rome-Hunthausen case, both parties attempt to claim the high ground in disputes about what the rightful interests and aspirations of the Church are. This clash is abundantly evident when one places Ratzinger's 9.30.85 letter to Hunthausen alongside Hunthausen's address to the NCCB. These two texts advance sharply contrasting views of what the Church is and should be about.

Perspective Shift: Related to the tension around words and their meaning is the contestation over the conceptual frameworks that apply to a given question. Whereas Rome (Ratzinger) tries to frame the discussion of Hunthausen's leadership within one particular set of strictly intraecclesial perspectives (the perspectives of the "human sciences" are excluded), Hunthausen invites his audience to (re)consider the same question according to the perspective of the Church "come of age" in the world. Hunthausen also seeks a perspective shift when he asks his hearers to evaluate the "justice" of Church procedures according to the standards of civil law. In a more fleeting example, Bishop Malone proposes in his NCCB statement that we look to the future and not the past.

Simplification / Complexification: One can argue that matters are simpler or more complex than they seem. Ratzinger's emphasis on clarity (he argues that Hunthausen can consult and transmit Church teachings that are straightforward and definitive) stands at odds with Hunthausen's position that pastoral leadership involves subtle discernments and the weighing of multiple priorities. The simplicity argument puts pressure on Hunthausen to take the specific action that Rome wants. The complexity argument enables Hunthausen to excuse himself from committing to some particular course. In ecclesiological-organizational perspective, simplicity arguments are especially helpful for top-down control, whereas the acknowledgment of complexity preserves room for local autonomy.

God talk: Bishops use explicitly Catholic forms of God talk all the time. I use the term God talk here as a catchall for explicit references to God and the Church. Such references may be matters of habit (as in epistolary salutations), of pious show (I have identified "pious interjections" in this research), of heartfelt belief, or of painstaking theological reflection. The prime strategic potential of God talk would seem to be its demonstration of full socialization on the part of bishops (bishops show that they belong) and its provision of the vocabulary that one needs to carry out business (apply power) in the Church. Though the Church enjoys similarities with other organizations, its terminology (and the religious ideology it expresses) is one area that is highly idiosyncratic. One cannot manage the Church without speaking this language. In the Rome-Hunthausen conflict, a highly contested word such as "renewal" must be understood against a backdrop of Church history and teaching. Both Hunthausen and Ratzinger attempted to place this particular word in their own preferred interpretive context. The fact that neither won this argument definitively says as much about the case, and the state of the Church, as anything else.

All of the tactics I have just described -- some of which (e.g., God talk) might better be described as substrategies, or strategies in their own right – contributed to party employments of persuasive argumentation in the Rome-Hunthausen conflict, with God talk being especially significant.

9.3.2 Coping Strategy 9: Assert personal identity

Given my general expectation that participants in center-periphery conflict would tend to minimize the appearance of conflict and emphasize communal harmony, I did not anticipate that there would be much readiness to strategically emphasize one's own personal identity in such conflicts. But in the Rome-Hunthausen conflict the periphery party asserts this strategy consistently and the center party (Laghi, in late-stage news interviews) asserts it occasionally as well. Given this finding, it remains puzzling that the Pope refuses to inject his own personality into the public dimensions of the conflict handling.

In general, one can draw a sharp contrast between the center party's tendency to erase signs of personal identity in its public communications and the periphery party's persistent accentuation of personal identity in such communications. Whenever possible in the affair, the Vatican conducts its conflict transactions in private. When this is not possible (because of news leaks or pressure from Hunthausen), Rome minimizes traces of personal identity in other ways. The key players in Rome keep out of sight (invocations of the Pope's name come mostly in the form of pious injunctions; Ratzinger's involvement is obscured behind the release of Laghi's summary of the visitation findings; Gantin stays in the shadows throughout). Center party self-references typically speak of "the Holy See" rather than of distinct persons. Hunthausen, on the other hand, consistently speaks in the first person and highlights the human, personally felt dimensions of the conflict at hand. By emphasizing his own humanity, beliefs, principles, suffering and struggles, Hunthausen positions himself to relate to others on this same level (something the Vatican almost never attempts to do) and he takes full advantage of his own notable charisma.

The first public statement issued in regard to the affair, Hickey and Hunthausen's joint announcement of the forthcoming visitation, shows that this difference of approach manifests itself from the beginning. Whereas Hickey offers almost no personal remarks in favor of a description of his function, Hunthausen writes: "I welcome Archbishop Hickey's visit... my faith tells me that this renewal in the church is the work of the Holy Spirit... I am convinced that our efforts in this archdiocese are in keeping with the spirit and intent of the Council... I believe it will help bring into focus both our strength and our weaknesses... I ask your prayers for the continued guidance of the Holy Spirit..."

After Hickey concludes his visit to Seattle, he effectively withdraws from public involvement in the conflict altogether. When Ratzinger reports to Hunthausen what Rome has learned from the visitation, he uses, even in the context of a private letter, formal, bureaucratic language that disassociates the findings from his individual person. Laghi's redraft of the Ratzinger letter has a warmer tone and is phrased in more personal terms ("I commend you, Archbishop Hunthausen, for your loyal cooperation and kindness during the Apostolic Visitation..."), but it distinguishes Laghi's personal identity only slightly more than Ratzinger distinguished his own. It is simply more "diplomatic" than the Ratzinger letter, which is not surprising considering its intended public release.

When releasing the Laghi letter, Hunthausen demonstrates his inclination to assert his identity in the affair by releasing a letter of his own in the *Progress* (11.26.85 issue). There Hunthausen shows his preferred I-you stance in regard to the people of the archdiocese ("I am writing in order to share with you a very important letter I have just received from the Apostolic Pro-Nuncio...") and he reminds his fellow "Friends of Christ" that they are "a family" and are together on "a journey." "I take courage for the future and look forward to the journey we will continue together," Hunthausen writes. The contour of identity that

Hunthausen illuminates is that of pastor of the local Church. The I-profession is the basis for establishing relationship. It is a form of self-presentation that he maintains in local communications throughout the conflict.

At times, personal acknowledgments of his own suffering (to the point of suggesting his own victimization) invite sympathy and support for Hunthausen. But Hunthausen also presents himself as a man of principle (of integrity, of "good faith") and as an "ordinary guy," as in his declaration that he is not a "theologian." This last example shows how one can make claims for oneself implicitly by stating the opposite (Hunthausen says he is no maverick either).

Bishop Wuerl finds himself in the interesting position in the conflict of having to thrust off an identity that is consistently forced upon him: that of the Roman infiltrator in Seattle, the living "symbol of the visitation." Hence Wuerl, by training a good Church company man, and therefore self-effacing, finds himself having to assert his own identity to fend off an identity that is imposed from without.

By humanizing his own position, in contrast with the faceless Vatican foe, Hunthausen is able to generate broad sympathy for his cause. This proves to be one of the most important keys to periphery party effectiveness in the conflict.

9.3.3 Other Strategies of Note

Though the following strategies are not given the fullness of consideration provided to the nine strategies above – I did not identify them early enough in the research process to discern their presence on a micro-level in texts – they deserve mention (and more careful attention in the future, in other studies) for the contributions they appear to have made to the conflict handling.

Manipulations of the Church bureaucracy serve strategic purposes in the Rome-Hunthausen case. The attempt to **establish procedural control** is one strategy along this line. Though the periphery party was not in a position to decisively determine what bureaucratic procedures affected him and how, he often was able to have some influence over procedures that, in many cases, were set up according to the circumstances at hand. Both the visitation and assessment commission processes were ad hoc efforts, and the NCCB's handling of the Hunthausen case was also a matter of constructing a process along the way. Gaining control over specific aspects of process can be a source of advantage. We see applications of this strategy in the wrangling over the release of the Vatican chronology (Laghi sought an NCCB endorsement and Hunthausen opposed this, in the context of an administrative board meeting) and in the discussion determining the format of the NCCB debate. Though Hunthausen had no control whatsoever over bureaucratic processes unfolding at the Vatican, he showed more facility with processes closer to home, as in his exchanges with the assessment commission.

Avoidance is another strategy that appears to be operative in the Rome-Hunthausen conflict. The extended time frame of the conflict seems to have something to do with the application of this strategy, which involves "taking one's sweet time" or providing the clues and letting the other party put them together to draw its own conclusions. Avoidance allows a party to deal out its blows slowly, over time, or to delay the receipt of blows. It might be seen a form of what Pruitt and Rubin refer to as "gamesmanship" (section 4.2.3). The Vatican seems to employ this strategy when it makes Hunthausen wait almost two years to hear the results of the visitation, and again, when it keeps the assessment commission in place for an equal length of time. Conceivably, Hunthausen, too, uses the strategy. Did he ignore Rome's pastoral leadership concerns in the years prior to the visitation? Once Wuerl was in place, did he stop asking Rome questions about what Wuerl's role was intended to be, for fear of what he might find?

One more strategy worth considering is the strategy of **revealing**. Revealing is the opposite of hiding (employing secrecy). In this study I have chosen to treat revealing as a matter of forgoing or overturning secrecy requirements or expectations about minimizing the appearance of conflict, but revealing may well need to be handled as a strategy in its own right. Tactics of revealing, which have been amply considered in the course of this research, include unilaterally sharing information with the press (through official statements or news leaks) and sending up "trial balloons" (i.e., provisional statements to test reactions). As a strategy, revealing always has reference to some expectation about secrecy. Not all sharing of information qualifies. Its power lies in the fact that the information in question is not yet publicly available and someone may have reason not to want it available. In the Rome-Hunthausen conflict, news leaks (the sources of which always remained hidden) often served to put pressure on one or the other party.

Finally, we should ask ourselves what role, if any, **threats** may have played in the conflict handling. Pruitt and Rubin identify threats as a contentious tactic. In my commentary on the Rome-Hunthausen case, I have more than once speculated that an implicit threat may be contained in one bishop's message to another. Given politeness requirements, we should not expect to see bishops threatening one another outright. But in the Rome-Hunthausen conflict , it seems clear that Rome held the prospect (threat) of further punishment over Hunthausen's head and he used the offer (threat) to resign as a tool to gain leverage against his opponent.

Summary
The following table offers a capsule summary of coping strategies and related tactics encountered in the case, as compared with prior expectations.

Strategies and Tactics Encountered in the Rome-Hunthausen Case
Newly uncovered tactics (as compared with the expectations expressed in section 3.5.3 and table 3.3) are highlighted below in **bold** *print. The information summarized in the "Notable Findings, Surprises" column consists entirely of unanticipated findings, as does all information related to strategies 8-10 C.*

Strategy	Tactics	Notable Findings, Surprises
1. Show deference to the structural order and mindset of the Church	Refraining from criticism of Church thought and practice and of its leaders; using euphemisms to describe problems in the Church; invoking familiar ecclesiastical terminology (jargon, official titles, theological words) and thought (Church doctrines); praising the Church and its leaders; obeying one's superiors.	1. Some bishops showed an internal, personal tension produced by the requirement of deference and held principles that might have lead them in another direction. 2. The structural order appeared to be in flux and the struggle for its future was phrased in ecclesiological terms.
2. Associate one's own efforts with the best interest of the Church	Making frequent reference to the Church; refraining from criticizing the Church (through silence, the use of euphemisms, indirect language, etc.); expressly linking oneself to the effort to achieve recognized goals of the Church.	1. The case reveals various forms of associative posturing, which depend on the view of the Church and the view of its best interest that the bishop proposes.
3. Minimize the appearance of	Conducting conflict negotiations in secret; refusing to publicly acknowledge the existence, relevance	1. Both the center and periphery parties chose to resist or forgo the

conflict	and / or importance of conflict (silence, denial); using euphemisms to improve the appearance of one's relations with other parties, understate the gravity of the problems, or overstate the degree of harmony or prospects for resolution. // **Behaving cooperatively.**	strategy of minimizing the appearance of conflict more often than expected.
4. Show fraternity	Referring to other bishops as "brother bishops" in public; invoking the concept of episcopal fraternity (and related concepts such as bondedness, collegiality, etc.); showing a heightened level of graciousness and deference toward other bishops (in comparison with what is shown toward those who do not belong to the hierarchy); showing what appears to be genuine kinds of trust and friendship toward other bishops; conducting substantial intrahierarchical exchanges in private; symbolically drawing distinctions (through attire, use of technical language, liturgical action, closed meetings, etc.) between the knowledge and experience of the bishops and the knowledge and experience of others; indicating (one bishop to another) what the limits of acceptable thought or action are. // **Employing formal instruments of collaborative reflection and decision making (ad limina visits, cooperation between the ordinary and helper bishops, episcopal conferences, etc.). Engaging in cooperative pastoral interventions (visitation, appointment of helper bishop, ad hoc roles of mediation and assessment).**	1. The resolution of center-periphery conflicts appeared to depend on what the fraternity of bishops (and not anyone else) decided. 2. The notion of episcopal fraternity in the case is incomprehensible without reference to the Pope's one-of-a-kind role as "Holy Father." 3. Support from the national episcopal conference was crucial to the bargaining effectiveness of the periphery party.
5. Practice courtesy	Matter-of-course (defensive) courtesy: avoiding criticism of the Church and Church leaders; using honorary titles; showing respect for and carrying out the wishes of superiors; honoring formality rules; and using euphemisms and other forms of indirect language to give a positive appearance to problematic situations; diminishing oneself. Tactics seeking advantage: using praise, shows of common feeling, etc. to create a climate of goodwill, thereby inducing concessions or cooperation; demonstrating politeness to give a good appearance (of reasonableness, charity) to outsiders; using euphemisms, indirect language, etc. to reduce conflict tensions. // **Limiting contacts and communications with the opposing party in order to avoid confrontation.**	1. A culture of *invincible graciousness* applied within the episcopal fraternity. 2. The courtesy that bishops showed one another in public was commonly exaggerated. 3. The practice of courtesy broke down under great stress (when frustrations mounted). 4. The break from courtesy came first from the center party. 5. The center party's break from courtesy appeared to give permission to the periphery, who responded (forcibly but less directly) in kind. 6. In the Rome-Hunthausen case, order was quickly restored after the breach in civility. 7. On no occasion did the Pope come in for criticism from other bishops. In the present case, he proved *untouchable.*
6. Employ secrecy	Refusing to acknowledge that a conflict exists; minimizing even insider access to the conflict handling; keeping the conflict handling out of sight (by keeping silent about it and limiting its handling to private meetings, private correspondence, phone calls); hiding the identity of conflict participants (through silence or linguistic techniques that hide agency); lying; limiting press contacts (refusing	1. Secrecy served the center party by allowing it to pursue a chosen course of action with limited interference. 2. Secrecy served the periphery party by showing cooperation with the center's preferences, by preserving a certain amount of

	interviews, offering minimal press conferences, providing little information in writing); and archiving sensitive documents.	autonomy for the periphery, and by saving face by hiding possible deficiencies. 3. Secrecy itself became an issue in the conflict and the use of secrecy required justification.
7. Recruit allies	Consulting with and drawing on the support of friends within the hierarchy; looking for agreeable intermediary contacts within the hierarchy who are well positioned to influence a targeted party; using persuasive argumentation to win potential allies; appealing for support by going directly to the people (of one's own diocese, the broader Church); appealing for support through the news media. // **Demonstrating own strength as an attraction for others**.	1. The center party worked harder than expected to gain the national bishops' conference as an ally. 2. Retaining solid support from his priests was a key to Hunthausen's effectiveness in the conflict handling. 3. Maintaining good relations with his auxiliary (Wuerl) and, later, coadjutor (Murphy) also contributed to his strength in relation to Rome.
8. **Argue persuasively**	Presenting rational arguments; ingratiation; demonization; definition power; simplification / complexification; God talk.	1. Most of the direct attempts of the center and periphery parties to persuade one another with rational arguments seem to have taken place in private. Arguments shared in public tended to be targeted at third parties.
9. **Assert personal identity**	Speaking in the first person; sharing information about oneself, including principles, feelings, vulnerabilities, etc.; creating various kinds of public personae (man of the people, man of principle, victim, etc.) for oneself; using I-statements as a basis for establishing relationship with others; humanizing one's own position to throw negative contrast on impersonal foe; countering identities others want to impose.	1. The center party consistently avoided assertions of personal identity, while the periphery consistently adopted the strategy (to advantage). 2. The Pope's decision not to insert his own personality into the affair remains a mystery.
10. **Other strategies:** A. **Establish procedural control** B. **Avoidance** C. **Revealing** D. **Threats**	A. Establish procedural control: determine or influence relevant bureaucratic procedures. B. Avoidance: delay; deal out blows slowly. C. Revealing: news statements; news leaks; trial balloons. D. Threats: suggesting (implicitly, probably) that one is prepared to take punitive action against the other if concessions are not made.	A. Though the periphery had no control over bureaucratic processes carried out at the Vatican, he had more opportunity to control ad hoc procedures (as in the assessment commission process) closer to home. B. The center avoided supplying the periphery with the results of the visitation and later extended the period of the assessment commission's functioning. C. News statements and leaks frequently put pressure on one party or the other in the conflict. D. The Vatican implicitly threatened to take further action against Hunthausen; he offered threatened to resign.

TABLE 9.3

9.4 Integrated Summary of Coping Strategies Applied

In the foregoing sections I have identified nine main coping strategies I have found to be applied in the Rome-Hunthausen case. As a first step toward seeing the interrelationship of these strategies within the whole of the conflict, I provide the following table, indicating which party applies which strategies at which point in the conflict.

Coping Strategies Applied in the Rome-Hunthausen Case

Key for Strategy Applications:
+ = evidence of application of the strategy
O = no evidence of application of the strategy
A = ambiguous
R = resistance to or rejection of the strategy

Key for Conflict Document and Development Period Identification:
Early Stage
A'. Developments prior to Hunthausen's reception of 9.30.85 Ratzinger letter
1. Ratzinger, Letter to Hunthausen with Visitation findings, dated September 30, 1985
B. Intervening developments
2. Laghi, Letter to Hunthausen with Visitation findings, dated November 14, 1985
C. Intervening Developments
Middle Stage
3. Hunthausen, Public announcement of Wuerl's faculties, released September 4, 1986
D. Intervening developments
4. Laghi, Vatican Chronology, released October 24, 1986
E. Intervening Developments
5. Hunthausen, Response to Vatican Chronology, released November 12, 1986
6. Hunthausen, Address to NCCB, released November 12, 1986
F. Intervening Developments
7. Malone, Statement at NCCB meeting, released November 12, 1986
G. Intervening developments
8. Laghi, Announcement of Commission appointment, released February 9, 1987
Late Stage
H. Intervening developments
9. Commission, Assessment Report, released May 27, 1987
I. Developments subsequent to release of commission report

Key for Party Identification:
c. Center party
p. Periphery party
t. third party

THE CONFLICT OVER TIME: DEVELOPMENTS AND DOCUMENTS

	Early Stage						Middle Stage						Late Stage				
STRATEGIES	A'	1/c	B	2/c	C	3/p	D	4/c	E	5/p	6/p	F	7/t	G	8/c	H	9/t	I
General Stance: Save face and enhance power for self and for Church	c+ p+ tA	+	c+ p+ tO	+	c+ p+ t+	+	c+ p+ t+	+	c+ p+ t+	+	+	c+ p+ t+	+	c+ p+ t+	+	c+ p+ t+	+	c+ p+ t+
Perspective on Power: Strive for the appearance of legitimacy	c+ p+ t+	+	c+ p+ tO	+	c+ p+ t+	+	c+ p+ t+	+	c+ p+ t+	+	+	c+ p+ t+	+	c+ p+ t+	+	c+ p+ t+	+	c+ p+ t+
1. Show deference to order and mindset of Church	c+ p+ tA	+	c+ p+ tO	+	c+ p+ t+	+	c+ p+ t+	+	c+ p+ t+	+	+	cO p+ t+	+	c+ p+ t+	+	c+ p+ t+	+	c+ p+ t+
2. Associate own efforts with best interest of Church	c+ p+ tA	+	cO pO tO	+	c+ p+ t+	+	c+ p+ t+	+	c+ p+ t+	+	+	cO p+ t+	+	c+ p+ t+	O	cA pO t+	+	c+ p+ t+
3. Minimize the appearance of conflict	c+ p+ tA	+	c+ p+ tO	+	c+ p+ t+	A	c+ pR t+	R	cA pR t+	R	R	cA pR tR	+	c+ pA tA	+	c+ p+ t+	+	c+ pA t+
4. Show fraternity	c+ p+ t+	+	cA pA tO	+	c+ p+ t+	A	cO p+ t+	O	c+ p+ t+	+	+	cA p+ t+	+	c+ p+ t+	A	cA pA tA	+	c+ p+ t+
5. Practice courtesy	c+ p+ tA	+	cO pO tO	+	c+ p+ t+	A	c+ p+ t+	R	c+ p+ t+	A	A	cO p+ t+	+	c+ pA tA	+	c+ p+ t+	+	c+ pA t+
6. Employ secrecy	c+ p+/R t+	+	c+ p+ tO	+	c+ p+ t+	+/R	c+ p+ t+	+	c+ p+ t+	+/R	+/R	c+ p+ t+	+	c+ p+ t+	+	c+ p+ t+	+	c+ p+ t+
7. Recruit allies	c+ p+ tO	O	cO pO tO	+	cO pO tO	+	c+ p+ t+	+	c+ p+ t+	+	+	c+ p+ t+	+	c+ p+ t+	A	c+ p+ tO	+	c+ p+ tO
8. Argue persuasively	cA pA tA	+	cA pA tO	A	cA p+ tA	+	c+ p+ tA	+	c+ p+ t+	+	+	cA p+ t+	+	c+ p+ t+	A	c+ pA tA	+	cO p+ t+
9. Assert personal identity	cO p+ tA	O	cO pO tO	O	cO p+ tA	O	cO p+ t+	+	cO p+ tO	+	+	cA p+ t+	O	c+ p+ t+	O	c+ pO tO	O	cO p+ t+

TABLE 9.4

The table provides us with a glimpse of the conflict in its entirety. Some reflections based on this overview are in order. I will now offer a generalization concerning the application of each strategy and the interrelationship of strategies within the conflict as a whole.

9.4.1 The Identified Coping Strategies Seen Separately over Time

Each row in the table summarizes the use of a given strategy over the duration of the conflict. Before considering how the strategies interrelate, I will offer a few more observations about the individual strategies, based on the tabular presentation.

General stance toward conflict handling: Save the face of and enhance the power of the Church organization and oneself.

This stance is honored by all parties in all stages of the conflict.

Perspective on the use of power: Conflict participants will strive for (the appearance of) legitimacy in employments of power.

All parties in all stages of the conflict strive to have their use of power appear legitimate.

Show deference to the existing structural order and mindset of the Church

The table shows my finding that this strategy was applied by the center, periphery and third parties throughout their involvement in the conflict. I find evidence of this sort of institutional and ideological deference in all of the chosen documents and in all of the surrounding developments -- with one possible exception. The exception is in the brief period between the Hunthausen's presentation of his statements to the NCCB and the subsequent release of the Malone statement, less than one day later. Because I find no trace of center party activity during this time, I mark this O. Nonetheless, I am by no means under the impression that the Vatican abandons the strategy of deference during this time.

Though on one level it seems self-evident that members of the hierarchy, even in conflict situations, will show deference toward their own Church (i.e., toward prevailing currents of its thought and practice), the table is helpful for showing that close examination of an empirical example bears this out. Within the data of the case one can find evidence of challenges to an opposing party's decision making and even to its ecclesiology, but challenges are always issued from within recognizable existing parameters of Church thought and practice. Perhaps the closest we come to that is Hunthausen's suggestion that the Church's practice of apostolic visitations should be reformed in light of more just procedures which can be identified outside the Church (in Anglo-Saxon civil courts of law). But of course Hunthausen does not make his point nearly so bluntly, and the suggestion itself comes within a presentation that is exceedingly deferential toward the Church as institution and tradition.

When we consider that the table summarizes the public activity of more than a dozen members of the hierarchy over a five-and-a-half year period, it is a striking testimony to the commitment to deference toward the Church shown by members of the hierarchy. Though the experience of conflict puts pressure on the participants' attitudes toward the Church, Hunthausen, the most pressed of all, pronounces himself ready to resign sooner than bring harm to the Church. We find no evidence of resistance to or rejection of the strategy.

Associate one's own efforts with the best interest of the Church

All parties employ this strategy during all phases of the conflict. Certain positions in the table are marked O, indicating there is no evidence of application of the strategy. This is true of Laghi's (minimalistic) announcement of the commission appointment, where the absence of the strategy may be a function of the text's brevity. Discourse samples from the center and periphery parties regarding the visitation are lacking between Hunthausen's receipt of the 9.30.85 Ratzinger letter and the 11.14.85 Laghi redraft of the same. Also much of the conflict handling that took place during the November 1986 NCCB meeting is obscure; the activity of center and periphery parties both is largely hidden in the interim period between Laghi's announcement of the commission appointment and the release of the commission report.

Judging by the fact that it was so commonly applied -- by all parties, in all stages of the conflict – this party appears to be a standard feature of intrahierarchical conflict handling.

Minimize the appearance of conflict

This strategy is not applied nearly as consistently as the strategy of showing deference toward the Church. From the table we can see that early in the conflict there was a shared commitment between all involved to minimize the appearance of conflict. Not only was the conflict handling itself kept largely from view, but also all public statements emphasized a prevailing harmony within the hierarchy. Public revelation of the existing tensions came from the periphery party side (with Hunthausen's announcement of Wuerl's possession of faculties and his subsequent elaborations in other statements), but it was quickly answered by the center party (in Laghi's chronology). By making clear its displeasure with Hunthausen, the Holy See reveals a dimension of the conflict previously kept from view. The willingness to forgo the policy of minimizing the appearance of conflict lasts only a short time, crystalizing in the Vatican chronology and Hunthausen's statements to the NCCB. Thereafter the commitment to hiding the conflict resumes – permanently, essentially, with a few provocative comments (from Hunthausen, primarily) serving as exceptions. Third parties show little inclination to call attention to the existence of conflict or reveal more about the conflict than has already been revealed. A prominent exception is isolated commentary after the conclusion of the NCCB debates, wherein certain bishops who had participated note their displeasure with Hunthausen's treatment.

Some positions are marked ambiguous. Document 3 (Hunthausen's announcement of Wuerl's faculties) is an ambiguous example of minimizing the appearance of conflict, because, though the announcement brings a key conflict issue into the open, it does so in neutral language. The statement does not acknowledge conflict per se, nor does it criticize the Holy See. More directly revealing, and serving to heighten tensions further, are the other letters and interview Hunthausen makes public at the same time. I also mark as ambiguous two periods of center party activity. The first period is between the release of the Vatican chronology and the NCCB meeting two weeks later. During this time the Vatican refrains from public comment on the affair (normally a tactic for minimizing the appearance of conflict), but also lobbies for support among the American bishops, thereby drawing more participants into the conflict. In the one-day period between Hunthausen's NCCB presentation and the release of the Malone statement, it is unclear how exactly the Vatican is active in the affair. So I mark this ambiguous.

Note that the deviations from the strategy of minimizing the appearance of conflict appear in the middle stage of the conflict, wherein the conflict most sharply escalates and reaches its widest participation and intensity.

One finds much resistance to minimizing the appearance of conflict in the middle (high intensity) stage of conflict, and this resistance comes from all sides (first, second and third parties). This suggests that minimizing the appearance of conflict is not an inviolable rule and that all parties involved may find advantage in bringing aspects of a conflict into the open, especially when tensions run high.

Show fraternity

Demonstrations of fraternal relationship come forth from all parties to the conflict, but the modality of fraternity varies. Beyond a habitual tendency to keep their business within the family (fraternal clannishness), the bishops participating in the conflict also show, especially early on, a tendency to play up the notion of episcopal fraternity in public. Thus in the early stage we find repeated invocations of the term "brother bishops" and testimony of a readiness to provide "fraternal" assistance. Later in the conflict, as tensions mount, these showy, public attestations to the brotherly bond came forth less frequently, being replaced by the more clannish type of fraternal behavior: the bishops close ranks to resolve the conflict out of the sight of outsiders. Harder to detect are instances where bonds more personal than official play a strategic role in the affair (Hurley's support of Hunthausen is an example). The table above accounts for strategic use of the fraternal relationship (draws on the fraternal bond) in various forms, but accounts only for the activity of the center and periphery parties. Demonstrations of fraternity by third parties are not accounted for here.

The center party stresses its fraternal relationship with Hunthausen in the early stage of the conflict, but then drops its public display of fraternal good will (early in the middle stage) with the release of the Vatican chronology. After the NCCB meeting come two months of limited communication between the center and periphery parties. Once the apostolic commission is appointed, this threesome becomes the fraternal stand-in for the center party. But beyond this, the Vatican does not make further use of the strategy of demonstrating its fraternity with Hunthausen. (The Pope does make a point of stressing his brotherly relationship to all American bishops during his message to the NCCB, November 1986.) In many instances it is unclear whether the center party shows fraternity. The ambiguity comes from the fact that the conflict handling is out of sight or the message is mixed. The Vatican shows a very strong inclination to preserve the clannish aspects of intrahierarchical relations, repeatedly demonstrating a preference for keeping sensitive matters contained within the episcopal family. The Holy See argues its case publicly in the affair only when forced to. But its effort to handle the conflict within the confines of the hierarchy itself is a constant throughout. On the Vatican side it is unknown where and when more personal kinds of ties are a factor in the conflict handling. A possible example of this sort of outreach may be the Pope's (December 1986) telegram to Hunthausen, shortly after Hunthausen's cancer surgery.

For Hunthausen, acting fraternally is normally a matter of cooperating and professing his loyalty to the Holy Father. He applies this strategy through all stages of the conflict, with the major exception of the (uncooperative) protests he registers at the NCCB meeting and some minor exceptions in the late stage of the conflict. Hunthausen shows his willingness to participate in the more exclusive aspects of the fraternal relationship with his fellow bishops during all stages of the conflict, but he also shows, on several occasions a resistance to proceedings which offers limited access to those who are not part of the hierarchy. More personal draws on the fraternal bond appear to be a key form of support for Hunthausen in all three stages of the crisis. Hunthausen consults with NCCB President Roach in 1983, and later receives support and advice from his friend Archbishop Hurley of Anchorage.

Third parties tend to verbally highlight the relationship of episcopal fraternity (as Wuerl and Malone do) as much as or more than the center and periphery parties. The third parties show haste to have the principals reconciled.

Practice courtesy

All parties to the conflict practice courtesy in all stages of the conflict, but one also finds breaches of courtesy during the height of conflict tensions (the middle stage), as in the Vatican chronology (the most discourteous document in the case because it directly criticizes Hunthausen) and Hunthausen's two statements to the NCCB (which criticizes the Holy See without assigning personal blame). In the early stage of the conflict, the practice of courtesy is exaggerated by all parties, center, periphery and third. After the breakdown in courtesy in the middle stage between the center and periphery parties, these parties resume their show of graciousness, but then in the form of polite silence and without hyperbole. Third parties employ exaggerated forms of courtesy not only in the early stage, but in the middle stage (cf. Malone's statement) and in the late stage as well (cf. Wuerl's words of parting and Murphy's statement upon his appointment as coadjutor).

In the table I mark Hunthausen's statements to the NCCB as ambiguous in regard to courtesy. The ambiguity rests in the fact that, while highly contentious, the documents also contain professions of loyalty to the Holy See and respect for the nunciature, and direct criticisms of other members of the hierarchy are absent. Hunthausen's announcement of Wuerl's faculties is marked ambiguous because, while the language of the statement is polite enough, the act of releasing the text may be construed as discourteous because it goes against Rome's wishes. Some third parties statements following the NCCB debate can also be considered discourteous toward Rome. Since these are mixed in among courteous statements coming from other bishops, I mark this position ambiguous. Certain other positions are marked ambiguous because the conflict handling is hidden at that point.

Employ secrecy

One may be surprised to find that I have marked every position on the table as positive in regard to applications of secrecy. Indeed, it is striking how pervasively secrecy is employed within the Rome-Hunthausen conflict handling. The degree of secrecy varies, but it is inevitably operative on some level. In the earliest phase of the conflict, prior to the visitation itself, there is no public discussion of the Holy See's concern with the situation in Seattle (by either the center or periphery party), though according to the Vatican chronology, this concern has been operative since 1978. When the decision to undertake a visitation is made, Hunthausen resists the plan to keep the visitation secret, but he does so in secret (he is complicit in the secrecy). Though the visitation is publicly announced, it is nonetheless conducted in secretive fashion and its results are largely kept secret (even from Hunthausen himself). Hunthausen shows a readiness to challenge the policy of secrecy (see column 3/p-row 6, column 5/p-row 6, column 6/p-row 6), and gain strategic advantage in the conflict by means of his challenge, but every time he reveals information (as in the announcement of Wuerl's faculties) he keeps information secret at the same time (e.g., Hunthausen repeatedly keeps the details of the conflict handling itself out of the public eye). The debates about the affair at the November 1986 NCCB meeting – which explicitly consider the matter of secrecy – are not open to the public. Hence, we have no record of what the other American bishops have to say about the use of secrecy. The Pope's feelings about and level of involvement in the conflict are almost entirely hidden from view from start to finish. The involvement of Vatican officials is also hidden. The assessment commission's meetings are also private, with no public record of their contents. Though news leaks and press statements occasionally break through the secrecy somewhat, they hardly make a dent in the overall embrace of secrecy, which is steadfastly maintained by all parties. In the years since the conflict, documents revelatory of the inside of the conflict handling have yet to be released for public inspection.

Recruit allies

There appear to be two phases in the periphery and center parties' attempts to recruit fellow bishops as allies. In the first phase, the parties seek out individual allies behind the scenes. The Vatican recruits Hickey as visitator and later seeks support from the NCCB executive board and from Cardinal Bernardin. Hunthausen also quietly consults with, first, Archbishop Roach and, then, Archbishop Hurley. And Hunthausen, too, attempts to sway the NCCB executive board in the question of the endorsement for Laghi's chronology. In the second phase of ally recruitment, the Vatican and Hunthausen make broader, more public appeals for support from fellow bishops, with both taking their case to the American bishops' conference as a whole (prior to and during the November 1986 NCCB meeting). In the late stage of the conflict, after the appointment of the assessment commission, the key party to be persuaded is the commission itself. Both Hunthausen and Laghi have access to the commission and have opportunities to make their view of matters known.

Argue persuasively
Rarely in the case do we find examples in the open of either the center or periphery party trying to convince the other with rational arguments. Presumably such exchanges, when they do arise, take place out of sight of the public. (The 9.30.85 Ratzinger letter is a good example. There Ratzinger attempts to enlist Hunthausen's cooperation with a rationalistic presentation of ecclesiological positions. Typically, both parties reserve their persuasive arguments for third parties, such as other bishops, the press, American Catholics. While Hunthausen presents many rational arguments in his NCCB statements, I would propose that he directly targets the American bishops there, and the Holy See only indirectly.

Center and periphery party attempts to rationally persuade third parties are often undertaken in public, at least during the middle stage of the conflict, when more of the conflict management comes into the open. The best example from the center party is the Vatican chronology (which seeks to gain the support of the bishops and secondarily of the press and the American public). Hunthausen, for his part, consistently strives to persuade others of the reasonableness of his position, starting with the people of his own archdiocese (early stage) and later with the American bishop and American (press and) public.

The commission report is the most prominent example of a third party using rational arguments strategically in the conflict. The primary addressees in this case were the American bishops and the American (press and) public. In its report, the commission sought to show that it was reasonable in its methods and conclusions.

On the table I normally marked as ambiguous those occasions on which the conflict handling was out of sight. I marked with an O the documents and periods where there was reason to believe that an emphasis on persuasive argumentation had been bypassed in favor of another strategy (applications of coercion or social pressure, for example, or a refusal to communicate about the conflict at all).

Assert personal identity
In the conflict this is primarily a periphery party strategy. Hunthausen uses the strategy from start to finish. Most representatives of the Holy See (Ratzinger, Gantin, Hickey) avoid this approach altogether, though the pro-nuncio, Archbishop Laghi, asserts his own identity somewhat in public in the middle and late stages of the conflict, after the conflict has reached its most heated and public level (e.g., he grants interviews to the *New York Times* and National Catholic News Service that show the more informal side of his personality). In contrast with Hunthausen's self-presentation, which constructively builds on his personal qualities to establish the very core of his strength in relation to the position of the Vatican,

Laghi's assertions of personal identity appear to be more of an attempt to counter the advantage Hunthausen had gained through use of this strategy.

An interesting assertion of personal identity from a third party is Bishop Wuerl's effort to overcome the perception that he represents the visitation and a Roman infiltration of Seattle's affairs. Wuerl directly challenges such perceptions once the conflict issues came into the open and also in the immediate aftermath of the commission's settlement (i.e., during the middle and late stages of the conflict). Certain other bishops also show a willingness to assert themselves individually immediately following the NCCB debate. Bishop Kenny of Juneau, Alaska, for example, offers a straightforward criticism of the Malone statement and thereby stands apart from the collegial show of unity. More typically, however, third parties playing a direct role in the conflict handling keep a low profile. Bishop Malone's NCCB statement has more "we" than "I" in it, and the apostolic commission communicates not as three individual bishops but as one unit with no internal distinctions. An unwritten rule for representing the Holy See during the conflict appears to be: do not call attention to oneself any more than is strictly necessary.

9.4.2 Comparative Observations of the Use of Strategies

A look at the table lets us comparatively assess employments of each of the strategies by all three parties in all three stages of the conflict. A summary of my findings from this comparative assessment appears below.

Strategy Applications by Party (at Some Point) in Each Stage of Involvement

A. Strategies Applied by the Center Party in All Three Stages: Strategies 1-8. I find no evidence of the center party applying strategy 9 (assert personal identity) in the early stage. Certain strategies are practiced by the center party less consistently (and are even resisted or rejected at times) during the middle, highest intensity stage of the conflict. We find resistance or nonpractice of strategies 3 (minimize the appearance of conflict), 4 (show fraternity), 5 (practice courtesy) and 6 (employ secrecy) during the middle stage.

B. Strategies Applied by the Periphery Party in All Three Stages: All strategies with the exception of 3 (minimize the appearance of conflict). The periphery party shows little inclination to minimize the appearance of conflict during the middle stage.

C. Strategies Applied by Third Parties in the All Three Stages: Strategies 1-6. The main representative of third party activity in the early stage is Wuerl. There is no clear evidence of Wuerl applying strategies 7 (recruit allies), 8 (argue persuasively) or 9 (assert personal identity) in the early stage.

D. Strategies Applied by All Parties (First, Second, Third) in All Three Stages: Strategies 1 (show deference to the order and mindset of the Church), 2 (associate own efforts with best interest of Church), 4 (show fraternity), 5 (practice courtesy), 6 (employ secrecy). Of these strategies, 1 was applied most consistently and 6 was abandoned most frequently.

Unbroken Commitments to Strategy Use

E. Strategies Applied by the Center Party in an Unbroken Way (used in all stages with no evidence of intentionally forgoing use of the strategy in any stage of involvement in the conflict)**:** Strategies 1 (show deference to the order and mindset of the Church), 2 (associate own efforts with the best interest of the Church), 4 (show fraternity), 7 (recruit allies), 8 (argue persuasively).

F. Strategies Applied by the Periphery Party in an Unbroken Way: Strategies 1 (show deference to the order and mindset of the Church), 2 (associate own efforts with the best interest of the Church), 4(show fraternity), 7(recruit allies), 8 (argue persuasively, 9 (assert personal identity).

G. Strategies Applied by Third Parties in an Unbroken Way: Strategies 1 (show deference to the order and mindset of the Church), 2 (associate own efforts with best interest of the Church), 4 (show fraternity), 5 (practice courtesy), 6 (employ secrecy).

H. Strategies Applied by All Parties in an Unbroken Way: Strategies 1 (show deference to the order and mindset of the Church), 2 (associate own efforts with the best interest of the Church), 4 (show fraternity).

<u>Notable Departures from Strategy Use</u>
I. Notable Departures from Strategy Use by the Center Party: There are significant departures from strategies 3 (minimize the appearance of conflict), 5 (practice courtesy) and 6 (employ secrecy) in the middle stage. Shows of fraternity – strategy 4 -- are less explicit in the late stage.

J. Notable Departures from Strategy Use by the Periphery Party: The periphery party noticeably departs from the use of strategies 3 (minimize the appearance of conflict) and 6 (employ secrecy) in the middle stage. Shows of courtesy are less effusive and more guarded in the middle and late stages.

K. Notable Departures from Strategy Use by Third Parties: Certain members of the hierarchy choose not to minimize the appearance of the conflict (strategy 3) in the immediate aftermath of the NCCB debate.

Can the Observations Be Integrated?
Attempts to read the table **vertically** have not yielded findings that jump out at the reader, but one finding worth noting is that center and periphery party uses and abandonments of strategies tend to correlate. In other words, the parties appear to use and abandon strategies (such as courtesy and adherence to secrecy rules) in conjunction. This may stem from the fact that most of the identified strategies function as general rules for practice (and hence are normally applied by both). When one party breaks the rule seeking advantage, the other may feel it has permission to do the same.

Configuring findings A-K, above, together suggests that intensification of the conflict invites both parties to abandon of the ordinary rules of engagement (deference, courtesy, secrecy) in favor of strategies that offer alternative routes to advantage (such as recruiting allies or asserting personal identity.

9.5 Assessment of the Applied Coping Strategies in the Light of Conflict Theory
To take our effort to integrate our findings a step further, let us now reintroduce Pruitt and Rubin's theory of conflict handling (see chapter four) as an evaluative framework. With the help of that theory we can describe the Rome-Hunthausen conflict in the following way:

9.5.1 Sources of the Rome-Hunthausen Conflict

Pruitt and Rubin conceive of conflict as "perceived divergence of interest." Conflict arises when one party's pursuit of its own interest is perceived to be incompatible with another party's pursuit of its interest. In Pruitt and Rubin's terminology, *interests* ("people's feelings about what is basically desirable") translate into *aspirations* (directed actions) toward *goals* that are in keeping with one's interests. At the same time, a party will have minimum *standards* of achievement that are acceptable in regard to its interests.

In the Rome-Hunthausen case, we can express the apparent interests at stake most simply as follows: Rome's interest (the center's interest) lies in seeing Hunthausen govern Seattle Rome's way; Hunthausen's interest (the periphery's interest) lies in governing Seattle his way without alienating Rome. To simplify even further, the center has an interest in control and the periphery has an interest in autonomy.

Rome's interest in controlling the local Church involves ensuring that the thought and practice operative in the local Church are in accord with the "official" thought and practice of the Church universal. Thus, conformity from the people and from the bishop is sought, with the local bishop occupying a crucial intermediate position between Rome and the people. In the Hunthausen case, Rome sets as its goal the achievement of greater conformity and tighter control in Seattle by means of applied pressure on Hunthausen (aspiration).

Hunthausen, however, does not equate his own best interest or that of his archdiocese with a clampdown on thought and practice. From his earliest statements in regard to the visitation (see his statement in the 10.27.83 *Progress*, chapter six, section A), Hunthausen defends and praises the state of the local Church ("I am convinced that our efforts here in this archdiocese are in keeping with the spirit and intent of the Council"). Repeatedly, his ecclesiological emphasis is on renewal, the guidance of the Holy Spirit, and the need to treat Church members as adults – concepts that suggest an openness to change and a preference for freedom and flexibility.

The central incompatibility in the conflict is the clash between the center party's attempt to control the periphery and the periphery party's attempt to allow for freedom and flexibility in its pastoral activity and style of governance. Rome and Hunthausen perceive that their respective interests in freedom and control stand in tension.

Pruitt and Rubin hold that three elements need to converge for conflict to develop: (1) Party's level of aspiration, (2) Party's perception of Other's level of aspiration, and (3) the apparent lack of integrative alternatives. In the Rome-Hunthausen case, Rome's level of aspiration is apparently high. The Vatican engages Hunthausen over the course of years and employs heavy tactics (visitation, redirection of faculties) to achieve its objectives. Hunthausen also shows his own level of aspiration to be high, by resisting Vatican initiatives in private and ultimately taking his case to his fellow bishops and the public at large. Both parties, observing the actions of the other, have good reason to believe that the other's level of aspiration is high (the other's commitment to own position is determined).

Pruitt and Rubin observe that other factors can contribute to raising a party's level of aspiration, including: own past achievements, perception of own strength, normative justification, invidious comparisons and the formation of struggle groups. Rome's level of aspiration was likely raised by its awareness that local bishops normally conformed to Rome's wishes (past achievement), by its assurance that it held an overwhelming advantage in ecclesiastical power, and by its normative conviction that bringing the local churches in line with Rome is the right thing to do (a position best expressed in the 9.30.85 Ratzinger letter). Hunthausen's level of aspiration, on the other hand, was likely raised by his success at maintaining a cooperative relationship with Rome in the past, by his perception of the support he commanded in his own local church, by his conviction that he was doing what was right for his people, by his awareness that the identified problems in his own diocese were also taking place in many other dioceses (invidious comparison), and, over time, by the formation of struggle groups in defense of his cause.

In the early and middle stages of the conflict, one finds the parties unable to recognize "integrative alternatives," that is, alternatives that would satisfy the aspirations of both sides. There is, first of all, little agreement between the two sides about the seriousness of the problems in Seattle. Hunthausen repeatedly emphasizes the positive conditions to be found in Seattle, while minimizing or arguing away several cited examples of shortcomings, and in only the most limited sense does he concede a need to tighten the reins of governance in Seattle. Rome, however, shows a clear determination to establish stricter control over Church communications (especially in the teaching of doctrine) and Church practice in Seattle, and the Holy See betrays a lack of trust in Hunthausen to establish this stricter control. In short, Rome wants Hunthausen to do what Hunthausen is not inclined to do, and both sides feel (ethically, theologically) justified in their position. Rome's lack of trust in Hunthausen (embodied in the visitation and ordered redistribution of power to Wuerl) invites Hunthausen's lack of trust in response.

What makes the situation so difficult is Hunthausen's own personal centrality relative to Rome's goal of establishing greater pastoral and doctrinal conformity in Seattle. Though of course Rome could remove him at any time, this would likely be self-defeating, given Hunthausen's popularity locally. (It would possibly lead to more pronounced kinds of "problematic" behavior in the local Church.) Thus, the ideal for Rome is to have Hunthausen himself make the desired changes. Hunthausen, for his part, appears to be trapped between a number of personal principles that are difficult to reconcile in the context of affair: he wants to be true to his own experience of the local Church and his own belief about what is best for it, but he also wants to be loyal to Rome. As the conflict progresses, his loyalty to Rome undergoes serious tests when power is taken away from him. Hunthausen's ideal solution would be to honor his own experience and beliefs while pleasing Rome: but how to do this?

Thus far in this section I have spoken of the parties' interests and goals in rather simple terms and I have spoken of "Rome" as a univocal entity. These are oversimplifications, which are partially corrected (but only partially) by the table below. The table provides a glimpse of various participants' interests, standards and goals. I take as a given (but do not mark on the table) the fact that all parties have an interest in enhancing the appearance and power of the Church universal.

Orientations of Party Interest

PARTY	INTEREST	STANDARD	GOAL
Pope John Paul II	1. Maintain papal control over local churches 2. Promote the appearance of the papacy	1. Do not make pastoral situation worse in Seattle 2. Do not damage the appearance of the papacy by intervening in Seattle	1. Establish greater pastoral discipline in Seattle 2. Look good (strong but compassionate) when intervening in Seattle
Cardinal Ratzinger	1. Serve the Pope's interests 2. Maintain own power and prestige (operational forms: access to Pope, control over Church bureaucracy, denied access to others, theological expertise)	1. Resolve the Seattle situation without making the Pope look bad. 2. Resolve Seattle situation without damaging own power and prestige (do not diminish viability of operational forms of power)	1. Resolve the Seattle situation in a way that makes the Pope look good. 2. Resolve Seattle situation in such a way that own power and prestige are enhanced (accentuate the effectiveness of personal operational forms of power)
Cardinal Gantin	1. Serve the Pope's interests 2. Maintain own power and prestige (operational forms: access to Pope, control over Church bureaucracy, denied access to others, control over bishop appointments)	1. Participate in handling of Seattle situation without making the Pope look bad. 2. Help manage Seattle situation without damaging own power and prestige (do not diminish viability of operational forms of power)	1. Contribute to resolution of the Seattle situation that makes the Pope look good. 2. Resolve Seattle situation in such a way that own power and prestige are enhanced (accentuate the effectiveness of personal operational forms of power)
Archbishop Laghi	1. Serve the Pope's interests 2. Maintain own power and prestige (operational forms: access to Pope, control over bishop appointments in U.S., diplomatic-intermediary role)	1. Resolve the Seattle situation without making the Pope look bad. 2. Resolve Seattle situation without damaging own power and prestige (do not diminish viability of operational forms of power)	1. Resolve the Seattle situation in a way that makes the Pope look good. 2. Resolve Seattle situation in such a way that own power and prestige are enhanced (accentuate the effectiveness of personal operational forms of power)
Archbishop Hickey	1. Serve the Pope's interests 2. Maintain own power and prestige (operational forms: status as a leading U.S. bishop, access to Pope, control over own archdiocese	1. Conduct visitation without making the papacy look bad (heavy-handed, petty). 2. Conduct visitation without damaging own power and prestige (by reducing own access to papacy or status within American Church)	1. Conduct visitation in a way that makes the papacy look good (showing papacy to be strong, fair, compassionate) 2. Conduct visitation in a way that enhances own power and prestige (showing self to be efficient, effective and able to accomplish task without making unnecessary waves
Archbishop Hunthausen	1. Maintain own power and prestige (operational forms: control over Seattle archdiocese, status as	1. Avoid diminishing own power and prestige (e.g., by appearing not to have control over own	1. Handle conflict in a way that maintains own power and prestige (i.e., by demonstrating

	prophetic/justice-peace bishop) 2. Maintain positive relationship with the Holy See	archdiocese; by seeming not to act according to own principles) 2. Avoid damaging relationship with Holy See (e.g., by offending Pope, nuncio or curial officials; by appearing rebellious; by appearing ineffective as an ordinary)	effectiveness as an ordinary while remaining faithful to justice-peace and renewal principles) 2. Handle conflict in a way that enhances relationship with the Holy See (by demonstrating effective discipline in Seattle and personal loyalty to Rome)
Auxiliary Bishop Wuerl	1. Please Rome 2. Establish self as capable bishop	1. Do not disappoint Rome (by creating more problems than already exist in Seattle) 2. Demonstrate personal competence, even if Seattle situation does not improve	1. Effectively serve Rome by establishing good relationship with Hunthausen while bolstering discipline in Seattle 2. Demonstrate personal competence by playing key role in improving Seattle conditions
NCCB	1. Maintain good relations with Rome 2. Promote own status and autonomy as an episcopal conference 3. Protect freedoms of individual bishops (principle of subsidiarity)	1. Demonstrate loyalty to Rome 2. Avoid losing status or autonomy as an episcopal conference (e.g., by offending Rome or by giving control of local matters over to Rome unnecessarily during handling of Hunthausen case) 3. Do not diminish freedom of individual bishops (by failing to defend Hunthausen)	1. Enhance relations with Rome by intervening to support resolution of Hunthausen case in a way that Rome approves (get Hunthausen back in line, in time for papal pastoral visit to U.S.). 2. Improve status and autonomy as an episcopal conference by introducing self into conflict handling and coming up with a better solution than Rome (without offending Rome by doing so) 3. Defend Hunthausen in such a way that subsidiarity is affirmed with Rome's approval
Assessment Commission	1. Satisfy Rome in the business at hand 2. Guard own careers within hierarchy 3. Protect autonomy of national episcopal conference of individual bishops	1. Generate solution to conflict that Rome can live with (minimal conditions: reduced disharmony in U.S. Church and Seattle archdiocese; Hunthausen returned to docility or removed; no appearance of abandoning principle of pastoral discipline) 2. Don't show incompetence by intensifying already volatile conflict 3. Don't lose ground for the national conference or individual bishops by seeming eager to promote	1. Generate solution to conflict that pleases Rome (by restoring peace in U.S. Church and in Seattle in particular; by bringing Hunthausen into line in such a way that he actively supports efforts to tighten discipline; by creating impression that Rome has won the conflict but in a fair and compassionate way). 2. Show selves to be loyal and effective servants of Rome who know how to speak the language of American Catholics 3. Enhance autonomy of

		independence from Rome	national conference and individual bishops by showing how papacy is best served by guaranteeing such autonomy
Coadjutor Archbishop Murphy	1.Please Rome 2. Please Hunthausen 3. Distinguish self (own identity) as a bishop	1. Keep further controversy from arising 2. Give no public perception of being at odds with Hunthausen 3. Do not appear overly tied to Rome's or Hunthausen's perspectives	1. Increase level of pastoral discipline in Seattle without raising further controversy 2. Demonstrate empathy with his pastoral approach 3. Show that one can creatively integrate the Rome and Hunthausen approaches to pastoral leadership

TABLE 9.5

The table above is *realistic*, in that it focuses only on the question of power – personal power and power of office. As such it does not take into account the complicating factor posed by personally held, idealistic hesitations about power. One thing the table makes clear is that, for bishops, power is a matter of properly distributing one's loyalties. One eye must always be on the papacy, and the other must attend to the specific constituency one serves as leader.

9.5.2 Choices of Strategy

Pruitt and Rubin point to two main concepts that help us to understand why parties act as they do in the face of conflict (see section 4.2.2). These concepts are mutual concern (Are the parties concerned for the other's outcome as well as their own?) and feasibility (Is a course of action likely to succeed?).

In the Rome-Hunthausen conflict, it is fair to say that the two parties show high levels of concern for one another's outcomes. The best evidence for this is the persistent attention to face saving on both sides. Neither party wants to "win" the conflict at the expense of embarrassing the other. Apparently this disposition is operative genuinely (on the level of personal feeling) and instrumentally (for the sake of advantage). By virtue of their membership in the hierarchy, bishops have much in common (identity, responsibilities, burdens) and they enjoy opportunities for personal bonding. At the same time, in their role of leadership, they are conditioned to an ideology of charity. These factors can work to induce a genuinely felt common concern. On a more instrumental level, fostering good relations with other bishops, and especially with powerful bishops in Rome, is important for guarding one's own professional privileges and prestige.

Though it is very difficult for an outsider to know when mutual concern is present (and still harder to know how "genuine" it is), we see potential signs of concern for the other in the use of politeness (refusing to criticize, employing euphemisms, keeping silence about embarrassing matters) and in acts of deference (Hunthausen accepts the visitation, Rome provides Hunthausen with an alternative to the 9.30.85 Ratzinger letter) and kindness (Hunthausen shows a gracious welcome to Wuerl, the Pope sends Hunthausen a telegram at the time of his cancer surgery).

Feasibility is a second matter fundamental to strategic choice in conflict. On a global level in the Rome-Hunthausen conflict, there are clear limits of feasibility that apply to certain courses of action. Though feasibility is, again, a question of perception, and the principals' perceptions are not fully accessible to outsiders, we can at least say that certain desirable outcomes must have appeared highly unlikely to the conflict participants. Rome, for example, must have known that Hunthausen was not going to become a bishop entirely different from the bishop he was. Telling him to be a law-and-order bishop would not make him one. Thus it became necessary to determine how far Hunthausen could be pushed to reform the archdiocese according to Rome's wishes, as weighed against the consequences of removing Hunthausen altogether. The experiments with assistant bishops appear to be an attempt to strike a balance that achieves the best possible result. Hunthausen, on the other hand, must have soon realized that Rome was not going to intervene as drastically as it had and then simply walk away and admit to a mistake. If the purpose of the intervention in the first place was, as many speculated, to send a message to local churches everywhere (and especially in America) that Rome would not tolerate local pastoral experimentation, backing off entirely would send precisely the opposite message. It would give the impression that the center did not and could not control the periphery. So feasibility, for Hunthausen, was limited by Rome's need to save face for itself.

Levels of concern and perceptions about feasibility inform actual conflict choices. Pruitt and Rubin characterize conflict activity with five key descriptors of strategy: **contending** involves trying to prevail without regard to the other party's aspirations; **problem solving** is a matter of trying to satisfy the aspirations of self and other; **yielding** entails lowering one's own aspirations in favor of the other's aspirations; **inaction** involves temporarily stepping back from attempts to resolve the controversy; and **withdrawal** amounts to a permanent withdrawal from the conflict handling process. In the figure that follows, I offer my own general assessment of when these strategies were applied by the center and periphery parties. The figure does not account for all applications of the (general) strategies, but rather, those that in my view are most pertinent. The applications of the various strategies are presented in chronological order.

Chronological Presentation of General Coping Strategies Applied

Key:
C = Contending
Y = Yielding
P = Problem Solving
I = Inaction
W = Withdrawal

	Rome	Hunthausen
Early Stage: 1978-Sept. 1986	C/P: Proposes visitation	Y/P: Agrees to visitation C: Requests bill of particulars and public announcement of visitation
	C : Refuses request for bill of particulars and for public announcement Y/C: Agrees to make public announcement of visitation (reluctantly, following news leak) but maintains as much secrecy as possible	Y: Accepts visitation process that is largely secretive
	C: Withholds visitation conclusions from periphery for 22 months	I: Hunthausen stays in a conflict holding pattern while Rome processes visitation report
	C/P: Delivers unfavorable visitation report (Ratzinger letter)	C/P: Requests public disclosure of Ratzinger letter
	C: Refuses to grant permission to disclose Ratzinger letter	C/P: Insists on having visitation report to release to public
	Y/P: Provides Laghi redraft of Ratzinger letter	C/P: Presents Laghi statement of findings in advantageous light
	C/P: Proposes appointment of auxiliary bishop (outsider with special faculties)	C: Challenges the intention for the auxiliary to have special faculties
	Y/P: Gives in to Hunthausen's request to grant faculties to Wuerl his own way	Y/P: Agrees to cooperate with Wuerl appointment P: Hunthausen works with Wuerl to address Rome's pastoral concerns in Seattle C?/P?: Hunthausen grants Wuerl substantial authority in Seattle but not faculties
		Y: Hunthausen grants Wuerl faculties
	C/P: Rome declares its intention for Hunthausen to give Wuerl faculties	
Middle Stage: Sept. 1986-Nov. 1986	C: Produces Vatican chronology C: Angles for NCCB endorsement of	C: Issues press release announcing Wuerl's possession of faculties C: Begins public relations campaign to explain own position

304

	chronology	C: Works against release of chronology and provision of NCCB endorsement of chronology C: Prepares statements (response to Vatican chronology and more general address) to argue case before NCCB
	C: At NCCB meeting, Laghi reminds bishop of his critical role in U.S. bishop appointments C: The Pope's message to the bishops reminds them, in ecclesiological language, of the importance of following his lead	C: Hunthausen argues his case before the NCCB
	C: Vatican officials paint the NCCB debate outcome as favorable to the Holy See	C: Hunthausen points to positive outcomes from the NCCB debate I: Hunthausen waits to see what the Vatican's next move will be (keeping silence)
Late Stage: Nov. 1986- April 1989	Y/P: Laghi announces appointment of assessment commission I: Laghi and other officials of the Holy See step back from direct involvement in conflict handling while commission conducts its assessment	
		P: Hunthausen (and Wuerl) meet with commission to discuss resolution options C: Hunthausen resists coadjutor idea; offers to resign C: Hunthausen presses for choice of who coadjutor will be C: Hunthausen challenges conclusions drawn in commission report P/Y: Hunthausen agrees to commission's proposal for resolution
	P: Pope agrees to accept commission recommendation	
		P/C: Hunthausen publicly accepts commission plan and Murphy appointment, while expressing reservations about the commission report
	P/C: Vatican keeps commission in place to monitor Seattle for almost two years	
		P/C: Hunthausen acknowledges end of commission oversight, acknowledging reservations one last time before maintaining a more or less permanent silence about the affair

FIGURE 9.6

The figure helps us to see that, whereas contending is mixed in with the use of a variety of other strategies (excluding withdrawal, which never shows up) in the early and late stages, it stands almost alone as the preferred strategy in the middle stage. The middle stage is the period of highest conflict intensity. Note that instances of yielding usher in new stages in the conflict: by Hunthausen (granting Wuerl faculties, which marks the beginning of the middle stage) and by Rome (announcing the commission appointment, which signals the beginning of the late stage.

9.5.3 Escalation

As noted, the middle stage is the stage of contention. Clear signs of yielding and problem solving are lacking during this relatively brief but intense period. Tensions between center and periphery reach their height. Hunthausen, while giving in to Rome's wishes by granting faculties to Wuerl, nonetheless displeases Rome by announcing this publicly. Rome then releases the highly critical Vatican chronology. Thereafter, both parties search aggressively for bishop allies and public support.

Pruitt and Rubin equate contention with conflict escalation, identifying five transformations that occur during escalation (see section 4.2.3, above): (1) heavy tactics replace gentle tactics; (2) the conflict issues proliferate and parties commit increased resources to the struggle; (3) specific issues give way to general issues and there is a deterioration of relationship between the parties; (4) the emphasis shifts from doing well to winning to hurting the other; (5) the number of conflict participants increases. Most of these signs of escalation are readily visible in the Rome-Hunthausen conflict, especially in the middle stage.

Pruitt and Rubin note that the likelihood of escalation is reduced when conflict-limiting norms and institutions are present, when there is fear of escalation, when significant bonds join the antagonists, and when relevant other parties oppose the conflict. Several of these conditions applied in the Rome-Hunthausen case and perhaps contributed to the tapering off of escalation and the emergence of the stalemate and settlement stages. Certainly the Church knows norms, or unwritten rules of conflict, that discourage bishops from openly waging conflict with one another. As an institution, however, the Church lacks stated policies for conflict handling and established structures (bodies) of mediation that could serve the management of center-periphery conflict. In the Rome-Hunthausen case the parties appear to make up the rules for conflict handling as they go along, with the basic rule being that the *center decides*. Fear of escalation seems to have been an important factor preventing further escalation of the conflict. By the time of the conclusion of the NCCB debate, certain consequences of escalation are apparent to all concerned, with potential costs to center (disruption of the Pope's pastoral visit, damaged prestige), periphery (removal from office, retraction of the process of "renewal" underway) and the Church organization (harms to appearance, disunity). The bonds existing between the center and periphery parties seem not to have been personal so much as official and Church-cultural, with religious belief and membership in the hierarchy being held in common. The "fraternal" relationship between parties appears not so much to have served as a limit on expressing disagreement privately, but more as a restriction on transparent conflict handling that threatens the appearance of the Church "family." The center and periphery parties' ties to fellow bishops – especially the American bishops' conference – also seems to have been a factor limiting the escalation of the conflict. At least in the short run, these bishops had little to gain by seeing the conflict continue. The unrest the case was generating in the pews did not make the bishops' own tasks of leadership in their own dioceses any easier, and those bishops who would be hosting the Pope in their own local churches in the coming year had an additional reason to want to see the conflict resolved quickly. Moreover, the readiness of the conference to be of "assistance" in the case offers a practical limit to the escalation, providing a new route to an "integrative alternative" that had not yet been pursued.

Let us now pause to consider the specific types of transformations related to contention that can be viewed in the conflict.

Signs of Escalation in the Rome-Hunthausen Conflict

1. **Light to Heavy**. The most obvious example of this occurs when center and periphery challenge one another in public: open criticism of the other party replaces more polite and hidden attempts to exercise influence. But both parties apply heavy tactics at other times as well. The Vatican's use of heavy tactics in the early stage (visitation, Wuerl appointment) is striking. Why are such heavy tactics used so early on? And Hunthausen appears to have a standing offer (threat?) to resign on the table during all stages of the conflict.

2. **Small to Large**. The most pronounced proliferation of issues takes place during the NCCB debates. Hunthausen is the main instigator, bringing issues such as secrecy, the relationship individual bishops to Holy Father, the role of national episcopal conferences, the place of pastoral discretion in bishop's power of governance, the right of Church goers to be involved in pastoral discernment, and the justice of ecclesiastical procedures into the discussion. Perhaps the best example of the center and periphery parties committing increasing resources in order to prevail is their enhanced effort to recruit allies and supporters and their investment of personal prestige in the conflict handling.

3. **Specific to General**. Specific issues give way to general issues as the discussion moves from the consideration of specific pastoral problems and solutions in Seattle (as summarized in the Ratzinger letter and, presumably, the Hickey report) to more global questions of how the Church should be governed. Along the way, there is evidence of a deteriorating relationship between center and periphery as positive forms of courtesy are abandoned.

4. **Doing Well to Winning to Hurting the Other**. Ambiguous. Despite Hunthausen's declarations that the point is not about winning or losing, it is clear that both center and periphery act on the basis of strong convictions and desire to prevail over the position, if not the person, of the other. Much more doubtful is whether either party gets to the point of wanting to "hurt" the other. I see little evidence for making this claim.

5. **Few to Many**. The number of participants increases. Both direct participants (third parties of bishops) become involved (Wuerl, Hurley, Malone, other bishops, the commission) as well as the media and general public.

BOX 9.7

One of the challenging tasks of discernment in the case involves identifying when *problem solving* takes place, as opposed to *contention* disguised as problem solving. In the chronological table of strategies applied (above), I identify some acts as examples of two strategies at once, to indicate this ambiguity. A related but different challenge for discernment involves deciding when *yielding* is an end in and of itself (one yields on principle, or one yields because no real alternative exists) and when yielding is more strategic in nature: that is, when the concession is made for the sake of showing good faith or winning future concessions. If we refer back to figure 9.6, we see that instances of yielding that were apparently unavoidable (as when Hunthausen grants Wuerl faculties against his will) are marked with a simple "Y" symbol and more ambiguous or apparently strategic instances with a "Y/P" symbol. From the table we see that most of the identifiable acts of yielding (Y or Y/P) take place in the early stage, with a few more in the late stage and none in the middle stage. The table also conveys a sense of the importance of acts of yielding to the shape of the conflict as a whole. Hunthausen's unwilled yielding marks a crossing over into the heaviest phase of escalation, and the Vatican's willingness to yield by creating a new vehicle for problem solving (the commission) ushers in the stage of settlement.

I find only a few occasions of party *inaction* during the conflict. Mostly this is a matter of Hunthausen's waiting for Vatican action (while Rome processes the visitation findings and while Rome decides what to do after the NCCB clash). But I also find a form of inaction on Rome's part when it makes room for the ad hoc commission to take the lead in the conflict handling. I do not assume that the center and periphery parties in fact stopped all their efforts to manage the conflict during these periods, but the evidence does seem to show that each stepped back from a more active, interventionist approach during these times.

9.5.4 Stalemate and Settlement
The table carries forth my preference for understanding the conflict in terms of three distinct stages (see section 5.2.1.5, above): roughly, an *early stage* of gradually rising conflict intensity, wherein the parties feel one another out and employ a variety of conflict handling approaches (problem solving / contending / yielding / inaction); a *middle stage*, wherein the conflict intensity rises dramatically and contention is the norm; and a *late stage*, when a new approach toward settlement is adopted and the level of conflict intensity diminishes considerably.

Though I have chosen not to do so (since the period is brief and its conflict handling is not very transparent), one might also mark off a fourth stage, *stalemate*. Following the airing of views at the NCCB committee, both parties show a disinclination to escalate the conflict further (cf. section 4.2.3, above), but steps toward agreement are also not apparent. Pruitt and Rubin cite four major reasons for the development of a stalemate: the failure of contentious tactics, the exhaustion of necessary resources, the loss of social support and unacceptable costs. Of these possible reasons, the failure of contentious tactics and the prospect of unacceptable costs seem to apply to both parties in the Rome-Hunthausen case, and the loss of social support appears to have been an influence on Rome's decision not to press Hunthausen further. The contentious tactics failed in the sense that neither party achieved its own goals outright by means of the increasing escalation, and potential for unacceptable costs presented itself in the possibility of Hunthausen's loss of leadership power altogether and public relations damage for the Holy See.

Pruitt and Rubin observe that *third parties* often play a role in conflict *settlement*, though it is not automatic that third party participants will enhance rather than hinder opportunities for settlement. In the Rome-Hunthausen conflict we see a variety of third party participants. The key third parties from within the hierarchy are Wuerl, the NCCB, the assessment commission and Murphy. The roles of Wuerl and Murphy need to be distinguished from the roles played by the NCCB and the commission. Whereas Wuerl and Murphy act in some sense as bridges between the general ecclesiological interests of the center and periphery parties (concretely addressing the source issues on a day-to-day basis over time), the involvement of the NCCB and the commission, functionally speaking, is of limited duration and focused on the conflict handling itself (rather than the source issues). Wuerl's introduction as a third party becomes a source of conflict in and of itself (because he is perceived as too closely aligned with the center), and eventually he is removed from Seattle for that reason. The NCCB's main role is as a sounding board whereby the conflict issues may be aired publicly. By signalling a significant level of conference support for Hunthausen, the NCCB puts pressure on Rome to look for an alternative solution for Seattle. The assessment commission completes the difficult assignment of finding specific proposals that would achieve Hunthausen's cooperation and save face for Rome. Murphy, finally, serves as the linchpin of future harmony. His successful working relationship with Hunthausen and his acceptability to Rome allows the resolution to succeed over time.

Of the three *models of conflict escalation* that Pruitt and Rubin identify (aggressor-defender, conflict spiral, structural change), the conflict spiral and structural change models appear most directly applicable. It is insufficient to characterize Hunthausen as merely reacting or defending himself against the actions undertaken by Rome, as in the aggressor-defender model. Hunthausen shows a quality of self-certainty and a willingness to assert himself (contend) from the beginning. As for the structural change model, perhaps the most noticeable structural changes are on the psychological level. Hunthausen / Seattle comes to perceive itself to be beset by an unfriendly, intrusive Rome; Rome comes to perceive Hunthausen to be uncooperative as well as not firm enough. There are also changes that take place in the perception of what the conflict is ultimately about -- from specific pastoral leadership questions to control-vs.-freedom, for example. Beyond the matter of perception, however, one can also identify structural changes in the practice of the conflict handling itself, as when the assessment commission is introduced. The conflict spiral model, on the other hand is helpful for showing how specific conflict moves lead to specific responses, in escalating fashion. Thus do we see the escalation that occurs when Hunthausen is forced to give over the faculties to Wuerl. Hunthausen reveals the faculties (to Rome's irritation), Laghi produces the Vatican chronology in response, Hunthausen answers the chronology, and so forth.

The outcome to the conflict may be termed a *compromise*. Both center and periphery lower their aspirations in order to come to agreement. Rome accepts the need to backtrack on its earlier appointment of Wuerl and its decision to transfer power away from Hunthausen. Hunthausen accepts the imposition of a coadjutor archbishop who is acceptable but not necessarily of his choosing. In many respects, it is surprising that Hunthausen comes out as well as he does, given his significant disadvantage in formal kinds of organizational power.

On the other hand, it is not at all clear that Hunthausen's position has won in the long run. If Rome's purpose was to "send a message" through its intervention in Seattle, it appears to have succeeded. Regardless of how Hunthausen himself emerged, the fact is there have been almost no bishops willing to openly stand against the Vatican in the years since the Hunthausen case (the French bishop Gaillot and the Zambian bishop Milingo have been exceptions, but both have been disciplined and all but removed from the public scene). More important is the question of whether the *Church* has won as a result of the handling of the Rome-Hunthausen case. Was the goal of joining people more closely to one another and to God furthered through these events? I will return to this question when I present my conclusions in chapter ten.

9.5.5 Reconsideration of the Conflict Theory Framework

Pruitt and Rubin's descriptive theory of social conflict has served our purposes by supplying sensitizing concepts that have helped orient our consideration of the Rome-Hunthausen conflict. Of particular value has been their discussion how assessments of interest (one's own and the other party's) and feasibility play into decisions about strategic choice. Just as important has been their highlighting of levels of mutual concern as a factor in strategic choice. More specifically, their perspective has advanced this research by calling attention to four strategies of contention that have been found to be relevant to center-periphery conflict handling (ingratiation, gamesmanship, persuasive argumentation and threats). At a later stage in this research, during and after confrontation of the case materials, Pruitt and Rubin's theory has helped us to think about the variety of conflict events as an integrated whole, with attention going to the transitions through conflict stages and the outcomes ultimately achieved.

Having observed that Pruitt and Rubin's theory has served us well in many respects, the limits of the theory for our purposes must be noted as well. Pruitt and Rubin's concern with social conflict in general carries us only so far in understanding the specific dynamics of Church center-periphery conflict. One of the more important presuppositions and findings of this research is that organizational and societal pressures play a huge role in shaping conflict choices. Pruitt and Rubin (1986, 187) acknowledge that, in their attempt to provide a general theory of conflict that transcends levels and arenas of society, they run the risk of ignoring "real differences between conflict arenas." With this general theory, one is able to reach the point of identifying the basic class of five strategic options, but one is not able to proceed to say what specific forms those strategies are likely to take under what conditions. In short, the social-psychological theory of Pruitt and Rubin needs to be complemented by organizational-societal theories of conflict handling, such as the one I am pursuing here, which give us a more specific idea of strategic choice in context.

9.6 Ascertaining the Validity of the Above-Named Findings from the Rome-Hunthausen Case

Thus far in chapter nine I have offered a preliminary description and analysis of the coping strategies I have found to be applied in the Rome-Hunthausen conflict. The question remains, however, whether these findings can be taken to be accurate reflections of what actually transpired in the case. Though I have tried at every step along the way to present the evidence and logic leading to the conclusions drawn, I believe there is nonetheless value in imposing two confirmatory / disconfirmatory tests to the findings. The first, whose results are presented in the section that follows, is a control of the findings from the closely read selected documents. The other is a more global test of validity, drawing on an interview with a case informant (section 9.7 and following).

It must be acknowledged that these are only two among a number of different types of confirmatory tests that might be conducted. While there is no general agreement among researchers about how the validity of findings can be ascertained with great confidence (cf. Miles and Huberman 1994, 262), I want as much as possible to guarantee the correctness of my analysis. That is what I attempt to accomplish with the two tests named above, while admitting that certain other kinds of tests (for representativeness of the case, researcher effects, spurious relationships, etc.) are not conducted. These two tests in particular are chosen because of priority concerns to see that 1) my selection of documents has not skewed the findings (since many of my findings are based on the concentrated reading of limited number of documents), and 2) my overall reading of the case has not wildly differed from the view of actual participants.

9.6.1 Use of Control Documents

It is possible that the results described above may have been skewed through a nonrepresentative selection of documents. Though I have attempted to avoid this problem by choosing documents for analysis that have already been described as critical to the case by external observers (i.e., the composite source), and that represent the discursive contributions of a variety of participants in all of the stages of the conflict, it is nonetheless possible that the chosen documents are not reflective of the conflict handling strategies applied in the case as a whole. As a check on this possibility, therefore, I have reserved a set of documents for comparative purposes. This set of eight documents, representing the contributions of center, periphery and third parties across all three stages of the conflict, can help us to determine whether the findings from the earlier set of selected documents show up elsewhere in the conflict data. (For a description of the control document selection process, see section 5.8.1, above.) Here below one finds a list of the selected control documents. The numbering of the documents picks up where the list of documents originally selected leaves off. Hence, the first number here is 10.

Documents Selected for Control Analysis

10. Ratzinger, Letter to Hunthausen announcing Vatican reception of Visitation Report, dated December 12, 1983 (*The Progress,* 26 Jan. 1984)

11. Hunthausen, Press Statement welcoming Wuerl as Auxiliary Bishop of Seattle, December 3, 1985 (*The Progress*, 5 Dec. 1985)

12. Wuerl, Press Statement regarding his appointment as Auxiliary Bishop, December 3, 1985 (*The Progress,* 5 Dec. 1985)

13. Hunthausen, Press Statement offering first response to Vatican Chronology, released October 27, 1986 (*The Progress*, 30 Oct. 1986; *Origins,* 6 Nov. 1986)

14. Bishop Nicholas Walsh (Bishop Emeritus of Yakima, Washington and former Auxiliary Bishop of Seattle), Newspaper column recounting his decision to make a recent trip to Rome to offer assistance in Hunthausen case, published November 20, 1986 *(The Progress,* 20 Nov. 1986)

15. Hunthausen, Statement accepting Commission Report, released May 27, 1987 (*The Progress*, 28 May 1987)

16. Wuerl, Press Statement re. his reassignment, released May 27, 1986 *(The Progress,* 28 May 1987)

17. Laghi, Announcement of completion of work of assessment commission, released April 11, 1989.

BOX 9.8

In order to carry out this process of ascertaining validity, I prepared a statement of positive expectations (presented below). The positive expectations declare what I have consistently found in the documents previously analyzed and what I anticipated finding in other documents from the case. Following the statement of expectations, I offer a table summarizing the presence or absence of the specified strategy in each of the control documents and a written assessment of the new findings. Besides generating a set of positive expectations, I also produced a set of negative expectations (a search for negative evidence). These expectations concern applications of conflict strategies that *must not* appear if my findings are to be considered valid. Again, a table summarizes the absence or presence of evidence of such a strategy being applied, followed by a written reflection on the findings.

9.6.2 Application of Positive Expectations to the Control Documents
Based on the analysis of the Rome-Hunthausen case as presented thus far, I have come to expect that the following coping strategies will be applied in center-periphery conflict, and in the Rome-Hunthausen case in particular.

Positive Expectations
1. All parties (Center, Periphery, Third) will always (in every stage of the conflict) show **deference to the order and mindset of the Church**.
2. All parties will consistently **associate their own efforts with the best interest of the Church**.
3. All parties will show a tendency to **minimize the appearance of conflict**, except for in periods of unusually high tension.
4. All parties will **show fraternity** toward one another, but the quality of fraternity may be more a matter of closed in-fighting than public bonhomie during periods of highest tension.

5. All parties will **practice courtesy** consistently, with exceptions only during periods of highest tension.
6. All parties will employ **secrecy** in some form during every stage of the conflict.
7. The center party will make little effort to **recruit allies** in the early stage, but more in the middle and late stages. The periphery party will attempt to recruit allies in all three stages.
8. All parties will employ **persuasive argumentation** on occasion, but such argumentation between the direct participants in the conflict will be shared privately. Public presentation of persuasive argumentation will be directed to non-direct participants in the conflict.
9. The center party will show very little readiness to **assert personal identity** during the conflict handling. The periphery party will show more readiness to do so.

Confirmation / Disconfirmation of Positive Expectations in the Control Documents

Key:
+ = expectation confirmed by the document
O = expectation disconfirmed by the document
A = it is ambiguous whether the expectation is confirmed by the document
NA = expectation is not applicable to party in question

Expectations	Doc. 10	Doc. 11	Doc. 12	Doc. 13	Doc. 14	Doc. 15	Doc. 16	Doc. 17
1.	+	+	+	+	+	+	+	+
2.	+	+	+	+	+	+	+	+
3.	+	+	+	+	+	+	+	+
4.	+	+	+	+	+	+	+	+
5.	+	+	+	+	+	+	+	+
6.	+	+	+	+	+	+	+	+
7.	A	+	NA	+	NA	+	NA	+
8.	+	+	+	A	+	+	+	+
9.	+	+	NA	+	NA	+	NA	+

TABLE 9.9A

9.6.2.1 Commentary
Six of the eight control documents (documents 11, 12, 14, 15, 16 and 17) offered evidence that confirmed each of the nine positive expectations. No documents showed evidence that clearly disconfirmed the expectations. Two documents stood in ambiguous relationship to one or more of the expectations.

Of the six documents which confirmed all expectations, two were produced by Hunthausen, two by Wuerl, one by Laghi, and one by Bishop Nicholas Walsh, retired auxiliary bishop of Seattle. Document 11, Hunthausen's statement welcoming Wuerl as auxiliary bishop, is most notable for its emphasis on fraternal good feeling, its heightened expressions of courtesy and its complete neglect of the presence of conflict. Document 12, Wuerl's press statement acknowledging his appointment as auxiliary bishop is highly polite and deferential in its tone, as is document 16, his press statement acknowledging his reassignment elsewhere. Since Wuerl is a third party, expectations 7 and 9 do not apply to these documents. Document 14, Bishop Walsh's account of his trip to see the Pope, is an interesting example of a third party interjecting himself discursively into the conflict handling. The text confirms all expectations except for the two that do not apply to third party contributions. Document 15, Hunthausen's statement accepting the commission report, is somewhat surprising in its inclusion of a criticism of the commission report (Hunthausen says he is "not in agreement with a number of important aspects" of the report and is "therefore not prepared to endorse it"), but, as has consistently been his approach, Hunthausen refuses to criticize any member of the hierarchy directly and he does not depart from his stance of deference. Document 17, Laghi's announcement of the completion of the work of the commission, is a minimalistic statement much like his announcement of the commission's formation. It is short and businesslike.

Two documents (10 and 13) confirmed all expectations but one. Document 10, Ratzinger's letter to Hunthausen announcing reception of the visitation report, is ambiguous in regard to expectation 7. Though there is no clear evidence that Ratzinger attempts to recruit allies through this statement, he does provide it to Hunthausen with approval for its public release, which makes it a potential vehicle for seeking public support. Document 13, Hunthausen's first press statement commenting on the Vatican chronology is ambiguous in regard to expectation 8. Though Hunthausen appears primarily to be addressing the public here, he signals his intention to introduce counter-arguments and he previews some of those arguments here. One can see this as a persuasive foray directed toward the Holy See.

In short, the positive expectations were confirmed across the selection of control documents, with the exception of two instances of ambiguity.

9.6.3 Application of Negative Expectations to the Control Documents
Based on my analysis of the Rome-Hunthausen case thus far, I have come to expect that the following phenomena *will not* be observable in the eight control documents.

Negative Expectations
1. An explicit attack on the order and mindset of the Church.
2. A profession of disinterest in what is best for the Church.
3. A statement highlighting the fact that conflict is taking place prior to Hunthausen's announcement of Wuerl's possession of faculties.
4. A personal attack on a fellow bishop or an attack on the notion of episcopal fraternity.
5. An insult directed from one member of the hierarchy to another.
6. A written communication meant for the public that reveals in comprehensive detail an intrahierarchical exchange that took place in private.
7. A refusal to address influential other parties during the period of open conflict (middle stage).
8. An example of the center or periphery party directly engaging the other in persuasive argumentation in a document intended for public release.
9. A strategic assertion of personal identity coming from the center party prior to the November 1986 NCCB meeting.

Confirmation / Disconfirmation of Negative Expectations in the Control Documents

Key:
+ = negative expectation confirmed
O = negative expectation disconfirmed
A = unclear whether negative expectation is confirmed or disconfirmed
NA = not applicable to document

Negative Expectation	Doc. 10	Doc. 11	Doc. 12	Doc. 13	Doc. 14	Doc. 15	Doc. 16	Doc. 17
1.	+	+	+	+	+	+	+	+
2.	+	+	+	+	+	+	+	+
3.	+	+	+	+	+	+	+	+
4.	+	+	+	+	+	+	+	+
5.	+	+	+	+	+	+	+	+
6.	+	+	+	+	+	+	+	+
7.	+	+	+	+	+	+	+	+
8.	+	+	NA	A	NA	+	NA	+
9.	+	NA	NA	NA	NA	NA	NA	+

TABLE 9.9B

9.6.3.1 Commentary

A glance at the table shows that none of the nine negative expectations were clearly disconfirmed by evidence in any of the documents. The one instance of ambiguity concerned negative expectation 8 (one will not find the center or periphery party directly engaging the other in persuasive argumentation in a document intended for public release) in document 13, Hunthausen's press release offering his first response to the Vatican chronology. In this document it does appear that Hunthausen engages in a bit of persuasive argumentation which can be seen to be as much intended for the center party as for any third parties.

A number of positions on the table are marked not-applicable. These can be accounted for by the fact that negative expectation 8 does not apply to third parties and negative expectation 9 does not apply to periphery or third parties.

The most significant conclusion that we can draw from this confrontation of the control documents with the negative expectations is that we find here no evidence which in and of itself radically undermines the perspective of center-periphery conflict handling already advanced in this research. But it is necessary to keep in mind that the absence of strong forms of evidence to the contrary of expectations is no guarantee that the expectations themselves are correct.

Perhaps the most interesting finding from the application of negative expectations to the control documents was the ambiguity which arose concerning Hunthausen's initial response to the Vatican chronology (document 13). There, contrary to the (negative) expectation, Hunthausen appeared to engage in a limited form of persuasive argumentation which was directed toward the center party (though surely, and perhaps primarily, toward other parties as well). One will recall that when I expressed a related expectation in positive form (positive expectation 8, in section 9.6.2, above) the finding was also ambiguous in regard to this document. Thus, we have reason to look especially closely at our understanding of how the strategy of persuasive argumentation was applied in the conflict. It appears to be less than straightforward, given the results of validation attempted with the control documents.

9.7 Use of the Fr. Ryan Interview for Validation Purposes

Thus far I have applied one form of validation technique (the use of control documents) in search of confirmation or disconfirmation of my findings from the Rome-Hunthausen case. I will now apply another form of validation technique, drawing on an interview conducted with a key participant in the conflict, Very Rev. Michael G. Ryan. Fr. Ryan served as Hunthausen's chief collaborator and adviser during the conflict, in a formal capacity as Vicar General and Chancellor of the Seattle Archdiocese and in an informal capacity as friend. In a late stage of the research process I asked Fr. Ryan to sit for an extended interview to discuss the case. Fr. Ryan granted my request and the interview took place in two sessions (on Friday, May 11, and Friday, May 18, 2001), each lasting two hours, with both taking place in the rectory of St. James Cathedral, Seattle.

My purpose in conducting the interview was threefold. First, I wanted to hear him tell his own version of the conflict history. Thus I started by presenting him with an open-ended question (see appendix vi) and asked him to recount the story of the case from beginning to end. Once Fr. Ryan had constructed a case narrative based on his own recollections, I then raised certain informational questions in need of clarification which had emerged from my own research. Finally, I asked Fr. Ryan to assess the credibility of a number of statements which articulated key findings of my own at that point concerning the case (a direct attempt at validation).

What follows is a presentation of material from the interview. I begin by presenting new information about the case garnered from the interview. Thereafter, I discuss statements from the interview (empirical referents or opinions) which, variously, appear to confirm and / or disconfirm my findings from the case. In particular, my focus goes to the use of coping strategies in the case.

A few things need to be kept in mind while processing the findings from the Ryan interview. First, Ryan, probably more than any person besides Hunthausen himself, was informed about and committed to the periphery party position in the Rome-Hunthausen conflict. In that sense, his recollections and opinions are highly illuminating but also partisan. To my mind that does not detract from their value, but it is a factor to be considered when evaluating the comments. Secondly, one of my tasks in interviewing Ryan was to gain access to how Hunthausen himself saw the conflict and his own role in it. (Hunthausen himself refused my interview request.) Though Ryan often served as Hunthausen's ghost writer and appears to have been his closest adviser, again, we must keep in mind that he stands a step removed from any number of critical negotiations (and private, personal decision making processes) that Hunthausen and others experienced first-hand. Finally, I asked Fr. Ryan about the case some twelve years after it ran its course and eighteen years after it began. His recollections, as he himself admitted more than once, are subject to limits of memory.

9.7.1 New Information from the Fr. Ryan Interview

Beyond providing insight into Fr. Ryan's own perspective on the Rome-Hunthausen conflict, my two-session interview with him also yielded information I had not yet encountered in my own survey of the public record of the affair. Before discussing how Fr. Ryan's observations affirmed or challenged my own conclusions about the case, I want first to share some pieces of information emerging from the interview that were new to me. I will summarize these findings in chronological order and in more or less "digital" fashion. As much as possible, the statements below represent Fr. Ryan's descriptions of what actually happened. I have tried to exclude his opinions about or interpretations of what happened. But obviously, the "objective" occurrences have been translated through the subjectivity of his perception and subsequent communication to (through) me.

1. According to Ryan, Hunthausen first became aware that the Vatican was receiving letters of complaint concerning his leadership sometime during the tenure of Archbishop Jean Jadot as Apostolic Delegate to the U.S. When Jadot discussed this matter with Hunthausen, Hunthausen invited him to come to Seattle to see for himself how the Church was operating. Jadot pronounced himself amenable to this idea, but the visit did not transpire before he was withdrawn as Apostolic Delegate.

2. Fr. Ryan also cited one other, pre-visitation exchange of correspondence with the Holy See. It concerned Hunthausen's granting of an imprimatur to Philip Keane's book, *Sexual Morality: A Catholic Perspective*. Rome asked Hunthausen to withdraw the imprimatur, which he eventually did. Ryan recalled, however, that the Congregation for the Doctrine of the Faith had been somewhat impatient with Hunthausen's request to consult first with Keane's superior (the Superior General of the Sulpicians). As Ryan remembers, Hunthausen had earlier been told by the American Sulpician Provincial that the matter was already being handled between the Sulpician Superior General and the Holy See. Hunthausen therefore thought it possible that there had been a misunderstanding (or even that letters might have crossed in the mail) and for that reason, along with his own vision of subsidiarity and collegiality, he politely requested permission to consult again with Keane's Superior.

3. Archbishop Hunthausen first learned of the Vatican's interest in conducting a visitation at a May 1983 meeting of the NCCB, which focused on the bishops' peace pastoral. The possibility of conducting the visitation was broached by the papal pro-nuncio, Archbishop Laghi, during a coffee break, in what was "an extremely informal situation" and "rather rushed moment."

4. After Archbishop Roach (then President of the NCCB) recommended to Hunthausen that he request a "bill of particulars" to specify the concerns prompting the visitation, Hunthausen wrote to Archbishop Hickey shortly after his appointment as visitator to request the same. Hickey wrote Hunthausen back in the latter part of August (his response was delayed by illness) to say that such a legalistic approach was not necessary, since this was a matter between brother bishops.

5. Ryan offered a breakdown of those within the archdiocese who complained about Hunthausen's leadership. He named the following persons or groups: (1) Erven Park, publisher of *The Catholic Truth*; (2) readers and affiliates of the *Wanderer World Forum*; (3) persons who had had more standing in the archdiocese during the administration of Hunthausen's predecessor as Ordinary, Archbishop Connolly, who now felt themselves to be marginalized; (4) persons who disagreed with Hunthausen's stance on the nuclear arms question; (5) persons who would have preferred to see Hunthausen take a more prominent anti-abortion stance; (6) persons who complained about ministerial or teaching roles undertaken by laicised priests; (7) persons who were concerned about instances of liturgical experimentation within the archdiocese; (8) Gary Bullert, author of *The Hunthausen File*; Bullert disagreed strongly with Hunthausen's nuclear arms stance and also felt that he had been wrongly removed from archdiocesan teaching positions.

6. When Archbishop Hickey conducted the visitation, he was accompanied not only by Fr. William Coyle (whom I mentioned in my account), but also by another priest, Fr. Lorenzo Albacete. Hickey had also intended to bring Fr. William Levada (currently Archbishop of San Francisco), but Levada was unable to come.

7. Fr. Ryan took Archbishop Hickey to the airport after his work in Seattle was completed. During that trip, Hickey encouraged Ryan to see how important his own role was in the affair and to draw on his Roman training (Ryan had been a seminarian in Rome) to help Hunthausen meet Rome's expectations.

8. Sometime in the aftermath of the visitation, but prior to Wuerl's appointment, Archbishop Laghi suggested to Hunthausen that he find another bishop to serve as a private sounding board – someone he might speak with confidentially and ask for advice. Laghi suggested a few names, one of which was Archbishop Francis Hurley of Anchorage, Alaska. Hunthausen took this suggestion and asked Hurley, who was his friend, to serve in this capacity. Hurley agreed, and from that point forward served as an important adviser to Hunthausen during the conflict.

9. More than one option for the placement of a helper bishop in Seattle was discussed with Hunthausen in the aftermath of the visitation. The first proposal from Rome came sometime in 1984. The Holy See raised the possibility of sending a coadjutor archbishop to Seattle. Ryan reported that Hunthausen was unhappy with this suggestion, since he was led to believe he would receive an auxiliary bishop. The next possibility discussed was the appointment of an auxiliary bishop. When it became clear that Rome wanted to appoint an auxiliary from outside the archdiocese. Hunthausen said that he could accept this arrangement if he were also allowed to receive an auxiliary who came from within the archdiocese (thus, Seattle would receive two auxiliaries). Rome eventually decided it wanted to appoint one auxiliary (from without) who would have special faculties.

10. Hunthausen learned of the plan to appoint Wuerl by means of a phone call from Archbishop Laghi in the summer of 1985.

11. Ryan observed that, many times during his exchanges with the Vatican, Hunthausen offered to resign his office. But the response from the pro-nuncio was also to say that the Holy Father did not want Hunthausen to resign. Ryan said that Hunthausen's willingness to resign and the Vatican's resistance to this option was "one of the motifs" running through much of the affair.

12. When Hunthausen conveyed his acceptance of the special faculties arrangement in a December 2, 1985 letter to the pro-nuncio, inclusion of the key words of qualification in the letter (cited by Hunthausen in his November 1986 NCCB address) came at the suggestion of Archbishop Hurley. Ryan quoted the key passage:

It is further my understanding that this arrangement is being adopted in place of the first one proposed to me in the letter of July 9, 1985, whereby Fr. Wuerl would have been empowered with special faculties in accord with the provisions of canon 403, paragraph 2. Therefore, since the empowerment comes by way of delegation from me, it is my understanding that it will not impinge on my ultimate authority as ordinary of the archdiocese. [The second sentence here comes from Hurley.]

Five days later, the pro-nuncio wrote in response:

You are correct in noting that the special faculties empowering Fr. Wuerl to oversee the five listed areas are to be granted by you. While this does not lessen your authority as a local bishop, it is understood that this action is being undertaken at the specific instruction of the Holy See.

13. Communications between the Vatican and Hunthausen were normally passed on through the pro-nuncio. Letters authored in Rome were sent to the pro-nuncio in a diplomatic pouch, who then passed them on to Seattle through the U.S. mail in envelopes marked strictly personal and confidential.

14. Laghi often downplayed his own role as intermediary. "I am only a conduit," he would say to Hunthausen.

15. When Cardinal Gantin sent his response to Hunthausen confirming that Wuerl was to have final say in the designated areas of decision-making, he asked Hunthausen to put in writing to Wuerl his granting of these faculties. Hunthausen then wrote Gantin back to say that as of August 1 (1986) he would convey the faculties. In that letter, Hunthausen explained to Gantin that he had not been dissembling or delaying: he simply had been acting according to the understanding he had from the beginning. Hunthausen carried out Gantin's instructions in a July 28 letter to Wuerl.

16. The matter of disclosing Wuerl's faculties became a point of contention between Hunthausen and Laghi. Hunthausen wanted to disclose the faculties, but Laghi did not want him to do so. Fr. Ryan recalled that there were several phone conversations about this matter between Hunthausen and Laghi. Ryan assumed there were also written exchanges between the two concerning that matter, but he could find no record of such exchanges in his own file. Laghi eventually granted Hunthausen permission to make the disclosure, presumably (Ryan's presumption) motivated by his fear that Hunthausen might resign otherwise.

17. On August 31, 1986, Hunthausen and Wuerl met. Ryan did not specify the exact topic of their meeting. Shortly thereafter, Hunthausen met with his staff. One task taken up in the meeting with the staff was the drafting of a letter to the priests of the archdiocese, which was dated September 3, 1986. At that meeting, Hunthausen also shared with his staff the contents of a letter he had drafted to Wuerl (dated September 4, 1986), expressing his desire to make the new arrangement work.

18. Ryan noted that with the conveyance of faculties, Hunthausen made a change in Wuerl's role within the administration. Whereas before, Wuerl had served as an unofficial "moderator of the curia" – whereby all department heads reported to Hunthausen through Wuerl (but Wuerl had final say in no particular area) – in the new arrangement (effective September 4, 1986), Wuerl did have final say in the specified areas, but no longer served as an intermediary between Hunthausen and all the department heads. Department heads in areas not specified could report to Hunthausen without Wuerl's mediation.

19. In anticipation of Hunthausen's chance to address the American bishops at the November 1986 NCCB meeting, Fr. Ryan tried to obtain press credentials to be in some of the meetings at the conference, but this request was refused.

20. When Hunthausen saw Ryan after the bishops had debated his case, Hunthausen mentioned that (then retired) Cardinal John Dearden of Detroit had spoken especially strongly in his defense.

21. In Fr. Ryan's view, Cardinal Bernardin of Chicago – who had been brought into conversations about the Seattle situation prior to the NCCB meeting (his advice was sought; he gave his opinion) – was the person most influential in bringing about the three-person assessment commission approach.

22. Responding to the decision to appoint an apostolic commission, Hunthausen wrote to Archbishop Laghi, in letter dated February 6, 1987: "I welcome this step. It is my strong hope that the results of the assessment made by the commission will provide the Holy See with a firm basis for returning the governance of the Archdiocese to normal in the near future."

23. In a letter to Bernardin, dated February 17, 1987, Hunthausen thanked Bernardin for his willingness to take on the commission assignment and expressed Hunthausen's hopes for resolution. The same letter made reference to a meeting Hunthausen had with Bernardin in Dallas. The letter also made a suggestion to the commission which originated with Fr. Ryan. Ryan had suggested that it would be profitable for the commission to meet with the archdiocesan Board of Consultors. The commission took up this suggestion and met with the consultors (as well as with the Northwest bishops and archdiocesan officials) on March 6-7 at St. Patrick Seminary, Menlo Park, California.

24. In Fr. Ryan's perception, Hunthausen consulted most closely with the following persons during the period of the visitation controversy and its resolution: Bishop Wuerl, Archbishop Hurley, Fr. Ryan, Fr. Michael McDermott (Director of Administration), Mr. Russ Scearce (Public Affairs Director), and on occasion, Fr. David Jaeger (Director of Seminarians).

25. Hunthausen frequently had Ryan draft statements, after close consultation between the two. At times, others (typically from the above-named inner circle) were asked to comment on the prepared draft. The comments sometimes led to changes in the final draft. Ms. Marilyn Maddeford was normally the secretary who prepared the letterhead copy for distribution.

26. Hunthausen often communicated directly in writing to the priests of the archdiocese (by letter) and chancery department heads (by memorandum). Hunthausen also met in person with the department heads, with the presbyteral council, and (less frequently) with all priests of the archdiocese. Hunthausen also met in person regularly with the Archdiocesan Pastoral Council and the Archdiocesan Finance Council.

27. Ryan identified the archdiocesan newspaper, *The Progress*, as the most efficient way Hunthausen had of reaching many Catholics within the archdiocese. On occasion, copies of *The Progress* were distributed to all Catholic households within the archdiocese. Ryan was not aware of any way that the Vatican newspaper *L'Osservatore Romano* played a significant role in the way that the conflict unfolded.

9.7.2 Confirmations / Disconfirmations of My Findings by the Ryan Interview

I will now consider each of my own findings from the case, as articulated in sections 9.1-9.6.3.1 above, in light of the observations offered by Fr. Ryan in my interview with him. In regard to each of my own findings, I will consider how Fr. Ryan's provision of information and commentary tends to confirm or disconfirm my own findings.

1. Show deference to the existing structural order and mindset of the Church.

In my interview with him, Fr. Ryan stressed that it was never Hunthausen's intention to act out of any sort of disloyalty to the Church or to the Holy Father. ("He's a unifier. He never wanted himself to be perceived as at odds with the Pope, or our local church with Rome.") Though Ryan readily conceded that Hunthausen found himself in tension with positions taken by, or roles played by Cardinal Ratzinger, Archbishop Laghi and Archbishop Hickey (but not with these persons themselves), he emphasized that, according to the pro-nuncio, the Pope did not want Hunthausen to resign. Ryan shared two anecdotes which illustrated the persistence of positive personal feeling between Hunthausen and John Paul II. The first recalled that the Pope had sent Hunthausen a telegram (an unusual move) wishing him well during the time of his hospitalization for cancer surgery. The second anecdote originated with Hunthausen himself. On the occasion of a party for his eightieth birthday, Hunthausen recounted how he had been in Rome with other bishops for a meeting with the Pope in 1988. As the bishops exited the room from one of the sessions, the Pope came up to Hunthausen, put his arm around him and said, "I'm very glad you came." Ryan retold this story because, in his words, "this would be partly what the Archbishop would want to have known."

Ryan acknowledged that Hunthausen did resist certain courses of action that representatives of the Holy See wanted to pursue, but he characterized Hunthausen's resistance as "never… in the sense of do-or-die. Always the resistance was, 'This was not our understanding' and he would try to keep the conversation going in terms of a dialogue." According to Ryan, Hunthausen strongly associated stances he took with a vision of Church he acquired at the Second Vatican Council, which began less than two months after Hunthausen was made bishop.

The Ryan interview confirmed my impression that Hunthausen ordinarily went through "proper channels," conducting critical negotiations with other members of the hierarchy who had authority in the given area. Hunthausen made a point of keeping his fellow bishops of the Northwest region informed. Disagreements with representatives of the Holy See were normally pursued out of sight. Concerning Hunthausen's relationship with the pro-nuncio, Ryan observed that, though they were "sources of frustration to each other," their discourse toward one another remained "cordial." Keeping up the appearance of the Church was a priority for Hunthausen and other bishops. Ryan described the statement the NCCB issued on the Seattle situation as sounding "exactly like you would have expected… 'We support the Holy See' and 'We're concerned for our brother.' It was even-handed but it was certainly not saying, 'We feel Archbishop Hunthausen has been wronged and we are going to take his case.' Nothing of the sort. They wouldn't do that. But they, I would have to say, privately must have felt that there was a very serious problem that needed decisive and immediate action and advocacy."

2. Associate one's own efforts with the best interest of the Church
Certain observations offered by Fr. Ryan affirmed my perception that Hunthausen was inclined to justify his own positions by relating them to the well-being of the Church – and that this notion of well-being was associated in Hunthausen's discourse with currents emerging from the Second Vatican Council, particularly the Council's focus on the "people of God." Thus, Ryan noted that Hunthausen based his resistance to keeping the visitation secret on the grounds that such a policy was "unfair to the people of God."

At one point, Ryan mentioned that Hunthausen had invited then-apostolic delegate Jadot to Seattle to assess the state of the local Church for himself (in response to complaints that had been communicated). Ryan paraphrased the argument Hunthausen had used to propose this idea to Jadot. "I would love it if you would come out to Seattle and spend some time in the diocese and absorb whatever you can. Talk to people, listen to people, see how we operate. Because I have nothing to hide. The Church is strong. It's vital, it's growing." By telling this anecdote, Ryan suggests that, in his view, Hunthausen associated his own pastoral efforts with successes that could be measured (with positive outcomes) in terms of Church strength, Church vitality and Church growth, and that the people of the Church were the ones to offer evidence for these successes. In other words, Hunthausen saw the best interest of the Church in terms of the experience of the people in the pews, and he saw himself as contributing positively toward that end.

3. Minimize the appearance of conflict

Several pieces of information offered by Fr. Ryan confirmed my observation that members of the hierarchy participating in the conflict showed a strong tendency to minimize the appearance of the conflict. Ryan observed that the Vatican's request to conduct a visitation was brought to Hunthausen's attention in a "rather rushed moment" and "very informal situation" – during a coffee break from a May 1983 meeting of the NCCB. The choice of moment and setting in which the pro-nuncio broached the possibility of a visitation suggested that the Holy See (or the pro-nuncio himself) did not want Hunthausen to consider the question to be a matter of great consequence. Nor, at that time, did Laghi give Hunthausen any indication of what, specifically, the Vatican's concerns were.

When Hunthausen later sought to receive a "bill of particulars" from Archbishop Hickey, who was appointed visitator in July, Hickey responded that a bill of particulars was not necessary because the visitation was not a legal matter, it was a matter among friends. According to Ryan,

> Hickey said he was simply coming out as a brother bishop to find out what was going on. The Holy See had some concerns, Hickey said, and some people had complained. Hickey wanted to hear Hunthausen's response. Hickey also made clear that he wanted to keep the visitation as quiet and unobtrusive as possible.

Fr. Ryan's impression was that Hickey's insistence on secrecy was rooted in instructions he had received from the Holy See to keep the matter secret. When word of the imminent visitation was leaked to the press, Hickey and Hunthausen jointly agreed to make a public statement in order to (in Ryan's words) "put as good a face as possible" on the situation.

As another example of the Vatican's tendency to keep the conflict exchanges under wraps, one can point to the Holy See's refusal to allow Hunthausen to release the 9.30.85 Ratzinger letter, with its summary of the visitation findings. When I asked Ryan why Hunthausen was not permitted to release the letter, he replied:

> My feeling about it all along is that they wanted things quiet. It's just their preferred way of doing things. And that was true from the beginning with regard to the Visitation itself, it was true with regard to the letter, and it was true, later, of the special faculties. The whole notion of disclosing these kinds of things... that people have a right to know these things, is not in their vocabulary.

But it was not just Rome that tended to minimize the appearance of conflict. Ryan's reflections bear out the judgment that Hunthausen himself was disposed to minimize the appearance of conflict. Ryan observed that

> Hunthausen was never one to say that he was right and others were wrong but instead would say, "I thought I knew what being a bishop was all about." At worst, Ryan observed, he would express "a certain

disillusionment" that the direction being taken seemed at odds with what he had learned at the Council.

It is telling, too, that Hunthausen's general inclination was to comply with the requests for secrecy, even when he himself opposed the idea (the disclosure of Wuerl's faculties and his text submissions to the NCCB being the most prominent exceptions). See also Hunthausen's assertion of positive relations with the Holy Father, even as recently as 2001 (cf. Ryan's story above about Pope John Paul II's greeting to Hunthausen during a 1988 visit to Rome). We also have Ryan's statement that Hunthausen "never wanted to be perceived as at odds with the Pope, or our local Church with Rome."

This commitment to maintaining the appearance of harmony did not lessen the fact that serious disagreements were being argued out behind the scenes. Ryan confirms the impression given by the public record of the case that Hunthausen pushed hard in his private negotiations to learn the precise reasons for the visitation, to learn the specific information resulting from the visitation, to have his own choice of auxiliary bishop, to have certain matters made public, and to determine the nature of the authority an auxiliary (and later coadjutor) would have. Ryan also makes clear that he was not always happy with the way his case was handled by his center-party counterparts and the decisions that were handed down over his objections. Tensions arose at times, according to Ryan, in Hunthausen's negotiations with Laghi, Hickey, Ratzinger and Gantin.

Ryan also offered further evidence for a hierarchy-wide commitment to minimizing the appearance of conflict when he observed that the NCCB did not and would not under ordinary circumstances make a statement that showed itself to be standing in opposition to Rome or to a brother bishop. During the crucial debate about Hunthausen's case, not only was the press denied access, but so too was Ryan himself, who served as Hunthausen's right-hand man. Certain things are for the hierarchy's eyes only.

When I invited Fr. Ryan to use a pre-established scale (the selection of available answers being: 5, very believable; 4, somewhat believable; 3, uncertain; 2, not believable; 1, absurd) to characterize the following statements, he answered as follows. His answers are in italics.

The Catholic hierarchy normally tries hard to avoid conflict within its ranks. -- *Five.*
    This principle applied during the Rome-Hunthausen case. -- *Five.*

When conflict within the hierarchy does arise, the natural tendency is for members of the hierarchy to keep it out of public view. -- *Five.*
    This principle applied during the Rome-Hunthausen case. -- *Five.*

When conflict within the hierarchy exists and is in public view, the natural tendency of members of the hierarchy is to minimize the appearance of conflict and downplay its significance. -- *Five.*
    This principle applied during the Rome-Hunthausen case. -- *Five.*

4. Show fraternity

During the interview, Fr. Ryan emphasized how Hunthausen felt strongly connected to his fellow bishops. Twice, Ryan explicitly invoked the concept of episcopal fraternity to characterize Hunthausen's relationship with (or vision of his relationship with) his fellow bishops. As Ryan saw it, Hunthausen interpreted Vatican concerns within the context of his awareness that other bishops faced similar challenges. "He talked to his brother bishops a lot. They all had people who were writing letters to Rome. They all had struggles within their own ministry that presented them with pastoral decisions that were not easy to come by." Along this same line, Ryan observed that Hunthausen was careful to keep his fellow bishops of the Northwest region informed of developments in his case, and he honored the concept of "collegiality" in his relationship with bishops in general (as exemplified in his consultation of NCCB President Roach and his request to consult with Philip Keane's superior in the matter of revocation of the imprimatur Hunthausen had granted Keane's book).

At the same time, however, Ryan makes clear that fraternity can be more a matter of show than of a deeply felt, familial or affectionate bond. Thus, Ryan expresses an obvious wariness in regard to Archbishop Hickey's profession, in the period prior to the visitation, that he was simply coming out as a "brother bishop" to find out what the situation was in Seattle. The implication in Ryan's phrasing is that there was clearly something at hand that was more troubling than Hickey wanted to make it sound. Ryan also hinted at his distrust of occasional euphemistic employments of the concept of brotherhood in regard to the NCCB statement on Hunthausen's case. Though I have already quoted this in a prior section, I will reintroduce it here because I find it to be a telling remark.

> Fr. Ryan noted that the NCCB went on record with a public statement about the affair that "sounded exactly like you would have expected. It must be on the public record. 'We support the Holy See' and 'We're concerned for our brother.' It was even-handed but it was certainly not saying, 'We feel Archbishop Hunthausen has been wronged and we are going to take his case.' Nothing of the sort. They wouldn't do that. But they, I would have to say, privately must have felt that there was a very serious problem that needed decisive and immediate action and advocacy.

On the whole, Ryan's commentary on the case gives the impression that bishop-to-bishop inquiries, consultations, negotiations and alliances were at the heart of the Rome-Seattle conflict handling. It also shows that fraternity can be expressed in superficial as well as substantial ways and can be conducted in public (rarely, as in the semi-public exchanges of the November 1986 NCCB meeting) or in private (much more commonly, as in most of Hunthausen's individual consultations with other bishops).

One interesting bit of information emerging from the Ryan interview is that the suggestion for Hunthausen to find one bishop in particular to consort with privately came from Archbishop Laghi. Ryan praised this suggestion by Laghi, implying that it proved to be especially helpful to Hunthausen over time. Laghi's having made this suggestion offers evidence that he saw genuine possibilities for more substantial kinds of mutual – fraternal or collegial – support among bishops and that he, at the time he made the suggestion (1984?), felt himself inclined to be supportive in this way toward Hunthausen (through the act of making the suggestion).

In response to my inquiry, Fr. Ryan characterized as "very believable" the statement that professions of unity, loyalty and episcopal collegiality are ordinarily features of intrahierarchical conflict handling

5. Practice courtesy
Fr. Ryan's comments offered confirmation of my finding that showing courtesy was a priority in the handling of the Rome-Hunthausen conflict, and that often the use of politeness put a harmonious façade before substantial tensions. The strongest evidence for this was Ryan's report of Hunthausen's relationship with various opposing parties in the conflict. Concerning Hunthausen's relationship with Cardinal Ratzinger, Hunthausen recalled that there were "tensions," "disagreements," and "seldom a meeting of minds"

between the two, but their exchanges were "always cordial." Ryan also acknowledged that Hunthausen experienced tension in his exchanges with Cardinal Gantin (of the Congregation for Bishops), specifically in regard to the multiple proposals of helper bishop options that were advanced, but that, again, the exchanges between the two were "always cordial." Similarly, though Ryan admits that Archbishops Laghi and Hunthausen were "sources of frustration to each other" (even "deep" frustration), he observes that "it was always a cordial discourse" between the two.

I have already noted Fr. Ryan's comment on the NCCB's statement concerning Hunthausen's case. Ryan signalled his awareness of a discrepancy between the bishops' conference's neutral public statement (in Ryan's words: "We support the Holy See" and "We're concerned for our brother") and the reality of private discussions that were much more heated ("they, I would have to say, privately must have felt that there was a very serious problem that needed decisive and immediate action and advocacy").

Near the end of my interview with him, I asked Fr. Ryan to characterize the credibility of the following statements concerning the employment of courtesy in intrahierarchical conflict in general and in the Rome-Hunthausen case in particular. Again, I invited him to use the following scale of responses: 1 = very believable; 2 = somewhat believable; 3 = uncertain; 2 = not believable; 1 = absurd. Ryan's replies follow my questions.

When conflict exists between members of the hierarchy, a premium is placed on saving the face of all those involved. -- "Five."

This principle applied during the Rome-Hunthausen case. -- "Five."

6. Employ secrecy

The Ryan interview confirmed a number of my own perceptions concerning the use of secrecy in the Rome-Hunthausen conflict. It confirmed my overall sense that secrecy was a key strategy used to defend or advance one's own position within the conflict, and that this strategy was employed more heavily, but not exclusively, by the center party side. It also makes clear that the Vatican's use of secrecy at several points placed Hunthausen at a disadvantage. In response, he resisted not only the use of secrecy on those particular occasions, but also argued against the use of secrecy in general.

Ryan identified the following occasions when the Vatican's use of (or preference for) secrecy either limited Hunthausen's access to information he desired or otherwise placed him at a disadvantage:

(1) Laghi approached Hunthausen about the Vatican's interest in conducting a visitation, but offered no specific accounting of the concerns prompting this request.

(2) Hickey insisted on keeping the visitation itself quiet. (Ryan had the impression that Hickey's insistence on secrecy was rooted in instructions he had received from the Vatican.)

(3) The Holy See supplied only minimal information in response to Hunthausen's inquiries about how the visitation and his prior request for an auxiliary bishop were proceeding.

(4) The Holy See did not allow Hunthausen to make the 9.30.85 Ratzinger letter, with its report of visitation findings, public at the time Hunthausen received it.

(5) Laghi opposed Hunthausen's intention to make Wuerl's faculties public.

(6) Fr. Ryan was denied access (admission credentials) to the NCCB's executive session debate of the Hunthausen case.

Ryan also identified one occasion when Hunthausen urged the non-disclosure of information on the Holy See: when Hunthausen tried to persuade Laghi not to release the Vatican chronology. According to Ryan, Hunthausen argued against its release on the grounds that it was inaccurate and would not help anything. Ryan's own description of this event does not associate it with the notion of keeping something (Laghi's understandings) secret. He characterizes it instead as a matter of Laghi putting his own "spin" on the telling of developments thus far and Hunthausen's need to avoid having this misleading narrative released. When Laghi went ahead and released the document, Hunthausen responded by releasing his own documents, which, as Ryan saw it, served to "clarify, nuance and even correct" the Laghi account.

In the picture that Ryan paints, Hunthausen was philosophically opposed to the use of secrecy because it was not in the interest of the people of God. Ryan noted that for Hunthausen the emphasis on secrecy was both "ill advised, out of keeping with the American ethos, and unfair to the people of God." (Ryan: Hunthausen argued that we should trust the people -- they were mature enough to deal with [relevant information].) This standpoint, in Ryan's view, was diametrically opposed to the Vatican's consistent preference to use secrecy, and the Vatican's philosophical position that its use was justified. In response to my question about why the Vatican wanted to keep the 9.30.85 letter out of public view, Ryan replied (I have quoted this passage once before) that this decision was but one in keeping with the Vatican's overriding policy of secrecy.

> My feeling about it all along is that they wanted things quiet. It's just their preferred way of doing things. And that was true from the beginning with regard to the Visitation itself, it was true with regard to the letter, and it was true, later, of the special faculties. The whole notion of disclosing these kinds of things... that people have a right to know these things, is not in their vocabulary.

Ryan also shared the view that news disclosures (breaks with secrecy) played an important role in the conflict management. He mentioned the following specific instances of one party or another breaking with secrecy:
(1) The news leak concerning the visitation itself. According to Ryan, the leak originated in Washington, D.C. (out of the office of the papal nunciature or of Archbishop Hickey). He insists that the "two or three" persons in Seattle (Hunthausen, Ryan and…?) who were aware of the plans for a visitation did not leak the news to the press. Ryan:

> All I know is, in this See, secrecy was the word simply because the Archbishop, even though he thought it was a bad idea, had agreed to go along with it, and being a man of his word that's exactly what he did. And it's what the two or three of us who were aware of it did.

(2) In July of 1986, the *National Catholic Register* published an article which said that Wuerl had been in Rome and he was going to get special powers. "Floods of phone calls" came into the Archdiocese after this article was published. This response, Ryan said, was a factor in Hunthausen's later insistence about disclosing Wuerl's possession of special faculties to the priests. In response to the article, Bishop Wuerl, according to Ryan, "indicated that he knew nothing about it."
(3) Hunthausen's disclosure of Wuerl's faculties, in September of 1986. According to Ryan, Hunthausen wanted to make word of Wuerl's possession of faculties public, but Laghi insisted that Hunthausen not tell anyone about the faculties. In Ryan's recollection, Hunthausen said in response that he needed to do one of two things. He needed either to disclose the arrangement ("I'm not going to pretend to be what I am not" was his typical way of expressing it") or to resign. These were put forth, Ryan said, "not as a tactic but as

a matter of conscience." Laghi, eager that Hunthausen not resign, eventually agreed that he could make a public announcement of the arrangement. Ryan recalls that there were several phone conversations between Hunthausen and Laghi around this time and that permission may have been granted over the phone. (Ryan noted too that this particular disclosure was "the thing more than anything else that really touched off the firestorm" of public controversy.)

At the time I interviewed Fr. Ryan, my focus was on the Vatican's use of secrecy and Hunthausen's resistance to that practice. Thus, I asked him to assess the credibility of the following two propositions, using a given scale (5 = very believable, 4 = somewhat believable, 3 = uncertain, 2 = not believable, 1 = absurd). Here are the statements and Ryan's responses:

Secrecy was an essential tool the Vatican employed in its management of the conflict. – "Five."

One technique Archbishop Hunthausen used to gain leverage in his conflict with the Vatican was to resist Vatican preferences for silence and secrecy. -- "Four. It was less a question of resisting and more an attempt to convince them it wasn't a good idea."

Had I conducted the interview at a later stage of the research, I would have probed more deeply into Hunthausen's complicity in the Vatican's use of secrecy and his own independent employment of secrecy, as a means of defending or advancing his own position. Based on the interview material that is available to me, which I have just summarized, I find little inclination on Ryan's part to see Hunthausen's own use of secrecy as willed or conscientiously strategic, and much more of an inclination to see Hunthausen as avoiding secrecy in practice and opposing the use of secrecy on principle. This more neutral or "innocent" reading of Hunthausen's motives and actions offers counterpoint (i.e., some level of disconfirmation) to my own more "suspicious" view, which sees Hunthausen as operating according to an awareness that the practice of secrecy and resistance to secrecy, depending on the circumstances, offer distinct strategic advantages for conflict handling.

7. Recruit allies

The interview with Fr. Ryan confirmed my impression that both the center and periphery parties sought out strategic alliances with other parties as part of their conflict handling.

Ryan reaffirmed what Hunthausen said in his NCCB address, that Hunthausen had consulted very early on with NCCB President John Roach, who suggested that Hunthausen request what Roach termed a "bill of particulars" justifying the visitation. (Ryan tells us that Hunthausen called Roach a second time after having waited some time to hear back from Archbishop Hickey in answer to his request). Ryan also spoke of the key role of Archbishop Hurley, who served as an adviser to Hunthausen for much of the duration of the conflict and provided the specific language that placed conditions on Hunthausen's acceptance of an auxiliary bishop with special faculties. Neither of these consultations could, according to Ryan's report, be considered unusual, since Hunthausen "talked to his brother bishops a lot," but they do show his readiness to turn to friendly fellow bishops for support. Another bishop Hunthausen consulted with along the line was Cardinal Bernardin. Ryan did not supply many details of the manner our precise outcome of this consultation, but he does make clear that, in his view, Bernardin played a pivotal role in bringing about the formation of the assessment commission and the shape of its recommended resolution. Ryan also shared his supposition that Bernardin was regularly in communication with a key Hunthausen supporter in the media world, editor Tom Fox of the *National Catholic*

Reporter. But Ryan could not state with certainty the existence of such a relationship.

The Ryan interview does not leaves us so much with a picture of Hunthausen courting allies as it does a picture of seeking advice privately from fellow bishops, especially at critical moments. Ryan has much to say about people rallying around Hunthausen. Among the examples Ryan mentions: Hunthausen received a letter of support from Bishop Walter Sullivan; vocal support at the NCCB meeting from Cardinal Dearden; and much support from his own priests and local entities such as Concerned Catholics. He has little to say about Hunthausen recruiting persons (members of the hierarchy or otherwise) who offered possible strategic support for his cause.

8. Argue persuasively
The Ryan interview offers evidence that competing rationalities were at work in the Rome-Hunthausen. Put simply, the implication emerging from Ryan's commentary is that Hunthausen's people-based rationality stood in opposition to Rome's control-based rationality. Ryan described Hunthausen's response to the 9.30.85 Ratzinger letter as follows.

> "He felt that many of the things were based on serious misunderstanding and misinterpretation. And there is some very high-flown language in this letter that you would have to wonder, What in the world does it mean?" Fr. Ryan cited an example from the letter: "'Incorrect notions of the Church's mission and nature, as well as flawed understandings of the dignity of the human person leading to false Christologies.' Pretty heady stuff!"

The suggestion here, and elsewhere in the Ryan interview is that the Vatican's findings from the visitation tended to focus on positions that could perhaps be justified intellectually but that lacked relationship to human experience (particularly the experience of persons within the local Church). As an example, Ryan cited Ratzinger's criticism of the archdiocese's use of questionnaires in its pastoral planning process. Ryan:

> The questionnaires asked about the beliefs people held. The Holy See interpreted this to be an effort to gain "theological consensus by counting noses." But Ryan recalls that the Archbishop understood the function of the questionnaires differently. "How do we *teach* the people, how do we really effectively catechize or evangelize if we don't know where people are in their understanding. And if they don't seem to be very well informed about what the Trinity means or the two natures of Christ or you name it -- if their Christology is flawed or their ecclesiology is one-sided -- we'd better know that so that we know how to teach, how to catechize." The Vatican held that the questionnaires gave people the impression they were helping to establish what doctrine is. Ryan remembers that this issue came up more than once. "I think it shows clearly how poorly the American way is understood in that culture, in the Vatican culture."

Ryan noted that Hunthausen himself tended to receive things at "the human level" in his own thinking and observed more than once that it was Hunthausen's view that the hierarchy needed to trust the people of the Church (i.e., those not of the hierarchy) and entrust responsibility to them.

Ryan points to the following examples of Hunthausen attempting to win over his center party counterparts in private negotiations. (I list them in the order that Ryan mentioned them. Note that many of Hunthausen's assertions and proposals reflect his preferred ecclesiological model of openness.)
1) Hunthausen tried to persuade Hickey to supply a bill of particulars enumerating the Vatican concerns prompting the visitation. Hickey refused.
2) Hunthausen tried to persuade Hickey to publicly announce the visitation. Hickey refused at first, but then agreed after the news leak.

3) Hunthausen presented his view of the state of the archdiocese in a lengthy interview with Hickey during the visitation.

4) Hunthausen carried out a limited number of individual exchanges with Laghi and Ratzinger during the extended period when Hunthausen waited to learn the visitation results.

5) Hunthausen tried to persuade apostolic delegate Jadot the come to Seattle to assess conditions for himself (in the pre-visitation years).

6) Hunthausen proposed to the Congregation for the Doctrine of the Faith that he first consult with Philip Keane's superior before withdrawing the imprimatur for Keane's book.

7) Hunthausen argued against several options for the appointment of a helper bishop. He was opposed to the appointment of someone from outside the archdiocese, he opposed having a coadjutor, and he opposed the concept of special faculties.

8) Hunthausen made the case to Laghi that he needed to disclose Wuerl's faculties. Laghi resisted, but Hunthausen prevailed on this point.

9) Hunthausen argued against Laghi's intention to release the Vatican chronology.

10) Hunthausen presented his view of the visitation / post-visitation controversy to his fellow American bishops at the November 1986 NCCB gathering.

11) Hunthausen suggested to the assessment commission, in a letter to Bernardin, that they interview the Seattle Board of Consultors to gain insight into conditions in the archdiocese. The commission agreed to do so.

Ryan also cites instances when representatives of the Holy See attempted to persuade Hunthausen to take a particular course of action:

1) Laghi requested Hunthausen's cooperation in the carrying out of a visitation, in part by suggesting that the visitation was not a matter to be worried about. Hunthausen agreed.

2) Hickey pressed Hunthausen to keep the imminent visitation secret. Hunthausen agreed reluctantly. Hickey also suggested that the visitation itself was not something serious enough for Hunthausen to become exercised about.

3) Ratzinger's 9.30.85 letter presenting the visitation findings sought to bring Hunthausen around to a particular view of what needed to be accomplished in the local Church.

4) The Congregation for the Doctrine of the Faith requested that Hunthausen withdraw his imprimatur of the Philip Keane book.

5) Laghi attempted to persuade Hunthausen to accept various forms of helper bishop arrangements.

6) Laghi argued against Hunthausen's intention to disclose Wuerl's faculties. Hunthausen did not accept these arguments.

The Ryan interview bears out my view that most attempts by the center and periphery parties to persuade one another took place in closed forums.

9. Assert personal identity

The Ryan interview challenged my views about the assertion of personal identity in the Rome-Hunthausen case in one way in particular. My view has been that Hunthausen asserted his own identity publicly in strategic fashion throughout the affair, but that representatives of the center party did so minimally. More specifically, I have been struck by Pope John Paul II's absence from the observable dimensions of the conflict handling. Ryan countered my perception that the Pope refused to become directly or personally involved in the affair by telling two anecdotes of the Pope's having reached out to Hunthausen in a personal way. I recount these two stories, as Ryan told them, below.

In December of 1986 Archbishop Hunthausen had surgery for prostate cancer, which had been recently diagnosed. "He received a telegram from the Holy Father, expressing his concern and his prayers for him.

327

It was very difficult to tell whether it was authentic because I suppose anyone could have done that, so I called the Nunciature and asked if they could verify that indeed a telegram had been sent from the Holy Father to Archbishop Hunthausen. They said, 'Absolutely impossible. The Holy Father never would send a telegram directly to anybody. It would come through us.' But shortly thereafter they called me back and said, 'The Holy Father *did* send a telegram directly to Archbishop Hunthausen.' Which is an interesting little piece. He obviously was aware of all the goings-on, and he certainly had a personal concern and a regard for the Archbishop, so much so that he departed from the usual protocol – the normal way of doing things."

When I asked Fr. Ryan whether he recalled any instance where the Pope had weighed in on the conflict itself in any public and specific way, he gave the following response. (This is the second story.)

"No, I think that at a pastoral, personal level – witness the telegram, for instance – he did. It's interesting. You need to hear this little story maybe, because this would be partly what the Archbishop would want to have known. The other night (May of 2001) at a party we had for Archbishop Hunthausen's eightieth birthday, I thought it was very vintage Hunthausen that the story he chose to tell his friends at the end of Mass -- he didn't give the homily at the Mass, he just spoke at the end -- was a story recalling how in 1988, I think it was, the Pope called all the archbishops of the country to Rome for a meeting. During an early session they were given a chance to share their hopes and concerns. The Pope met with them and listened to them in a formalized setting, which is typical of those Roman meetings. At the end of the session they crowded into the aisle as the Pope was walking out. And [Hunthausen] told us how the Pope came over to him, put his arm around his shoulder and said, 'I'm very glad you came.'

"Hunthausen's a unifier. He never wanted himself to be perceived as at odds with the Pope, or our local Church with Rome. And I think he wanted the people in that room (at the party the other night) to be reminded of our communion with the larger Church. I tell that story to you because I think it is vintage Hunthausen. He could have told other stories but he chose to tell that one.

"So, to answer your question, No, I don't think the Pope did weigh in any public way. It's probably not the normal way of doing things. I mean, think about some of the things that have happened over the years, the theologians who have been silenced, for instance. These things always seem to get played out on a different (lower) level and are handled by those cardinals whose role it is. Maybe the Pope preserved his right to let the thing play out on a legal level, while he did the pastoral thing. That's my guess."

It was clear to me that the question of the Pope's involvement in the affair was a sensitive point for Fr. Ryan. Both of the stories he told were new to me at the time. Admittedly, only one of the incidents described took place during the extended period of high conflict between Rome and Seattle. My impression was that Fr. Ryan had two objectives in telling these stories. One was to argue against the notion that the Pope was somehow unconcerned with the affair. The other was to guard Hunthausen's reputation (by making the case that Hunthausen was both loyal – yesterday and today – and enjoyed a good relationship with the Holy Father).

Ryan, as Hunthausen himself consistently was in his public statements, was decidedly less guarded in his comments about other high-ranking Church officials. While he did not openly criticize these other persons, he did not hesitate to give the impression that Hunthausen did not see eye-to-eye with these persons and the agendas they advanced. But not once did Ryan make room for the suggestion that Hunthausen and the Pope were not on good terms.

9.7.3 An Additional Coping Strategy?: Shifting Ground (Gamesmanship)
One of the more interesting observations offered by Fr. Ryan in the interview was that the Holy See adopted a strategy of "shifting ground" in its dealings with Seattle. Ryan used this phrase four times in the interview, and he attributed the origin of his own use of the phrase to Archbishop Hunthausen. In Ryan's recollection, Hunthausen was frustrated at having to give over the faculties to Wuerl after having long believed that that was not going to be necessary.

Ryan: "The Archbishop would say sometimes, 'We always seem to be standing on new ground – shifting ground.'"

Later Ryan used this same phrase in reference Hunthausen's being surprised on two other occasions, both having to do with proposed solutions involving bishop appointments in Seattle. Ryan:

First, he was to be given an auxiliary of his own choosing, then a coadjutor, then two auxiliaries (one from Seattle and one from somewhere else), then an auxiliary with special faculties, and finally at the very end a coadjutor without special faculties! I may have the order a little confused here – I don't think so -- but the point is made: the ground was constantly shifting.

And again:

When the proposal came to send Bishop Thomas Murphy [of Great Falls-Billings, Montana] to Seattle, Hunthausen expected it, based on previous discussions. What he did not expect was the stated intention that Murphy should serve in Seattle as Coadjutor Archbishop [with right of succession]. "That was a big surprise. It was not anticipated, but worked through. It was yet another question of the kind of shifting ground that characterized so much of the entire saga.

On another occasion, once more in regard to Wuerl's faculties, Ryan invoked the concept of shifting ground and then extended the metaphor by association with another image. Ryan compared the shifting ground experience to a chess game. "It was a kind of chess game – that's how I remember it. A chess game with frequently changing rules."

The fact that Ryan repeatedly invoked the concept of shifting ground suggests to me that it is a key to his understanding of how Rome dealt with Seattle in the conflict. The question remains whether this concept can illuminate our own understanding of the conflict. One reason for thinking that it might is that Pruitt and Rubin, as I have already noted, identify something similar in their own conflict theory. There among the strategies of contention one finds "gamesmanship." Gamesmanship involves fostering a state of upset or unrest in the other party as a means of reducing their resistance to yielding. Surprise is an important element in the strategy – surprise which results in the other party becoming flustered or feeling off balance or uncertain how to proceed.

If one simply looks at the effects of the Vatican's conflict handling, and how this was perceived on the Seattle side, it is easy to find reason to believe that the center party employed gamesmanship as a means of obtaining its own objectives within the conflict. The Vatican's approach over time was indeed constantly changing – the Vatican representatives changed (Ratzinger, Laghi, Hickey, Gantin, the assessment commission), as did the legal means (visitation, power of appointment, assessment) and proposals for the kind of episcopal appointment (coadjutor, two auxiliaries, one auxiliary with faculties, coadjutor with no faculties) – and secrecy and delay compounded the uncertainty on the periphery party side.
Hunthausen rarely seemed to know what to expect or when to expect it. But the question remains to what extent this approach was calculated by the Vatican and how much it was the result of Rome's disorganization and own uncertainty about how to proceed. At one point in the interview, Fr. Ryan mentioned that Laghi and Ratzinger did not seem to speak with one voice in their dealings with Seattle. As I understood it, Ryan was not suggesting that they were consciously working at cross purposes but simply that, for whatever reason, their communications were not always entirely in synch. It strikes me that to some degree Rome's conflict handling approach, which led Hunthausen (apparently) and Ryan to feel that the ground was constantly shifting, can be attributed to organizational inefficiency (the delay in

processing the Hickey visitation findings), a pre-given culture of secrecy (thus, applied as a general rule rather than as a specifically chosen means for keeping Hunthausen off balance), and poor internal communications between the Holy See's representatives. But I have no difficulty imagining as well, given the perspectives and findings of this study, that more intentional forms of gamesmanship were applied for advantage.

Another interesting question, if we turn Ryan's comment around, is whether Hunthausen employed gamesmanship as a means of defending his position or gaining advantage. One might well make a case that he did. For example, was Hunthausen practicing gamesmanship by giving the Vatican the impression of cooperating with the Vatican's objectives while in fact resisting or doing little to realize those objectives? (Hunthausen himself said at the time of the disbanding of the commission that little had changed in Seattle's overall ministerial approach as a result of the visitation process.) Or did Hunthausen practice gamesmanship by wilfully misunderstanding the Vatican's intention for Wuerl to have final say in the key areas from the time of his appointment to Seattle? I do not have evidence that Hunthausen was employing gamesmanship in these instances, but I cannot say definitively that he did not employ such a strategy on these or other occasions.

Though I find Ryan's observation intriguing, I will leave my own investigation off with these comments I have just offered.

9.7.4 Summary of Findings from the Ryan Interview

Beyond providing numerous pieces of information I had not previously encountered, the interview with Fr. Ryan brought new perspective to my view of how the conflict handling in the Rome-Hunthausen case was carried out. On certain points Ryan confirmed views I already held. On others he offered no support or challenged my views. The strongest confirmation from Ryan came for my belief that secrecy was a key strategy whereby Rome maintained its advantage of power in the conflict. Ryan also offered strong confirmation of my beliefs that bishops are strongly disposed to show courtesy toward one another in their open exchanges and that intrahierarchical disharmony is to be kept out of sight as much as possible. On an informational level, Ryan also offered support for my view that the concept of episcopal fraternity and a variety of forms of the same in practice are highly relevant to intrahierarchical conflict handling. In a more indirect way, the material from the Ryan interview offered support for my views that participants in center-periphery conflict will show deference to the order and mindset of the Church, associate their own efforts with the best interest of the Church, recruit influential allies, strive to make their applications of power look legitimate, and use persuasive argumentation.

Ryan challenged my own view of the conflict handling in three key ways. First, he was much more ready to attribute the cause of the visitation to some hidden arrangement between Rome and the Reagan government that resulted from Hunthausen's controversial stance on nuclear weapons. Ryan cited three reasons for believing this to be true: (1) the visitation came very close in time to the American government's granting of diplomatic status to the Holy See (in January of 1984); (2) a visitation of another "peace" bishop, Bishop Walter Sullivan of Richmond, Virginia, took place at approximately the same time as the Seattle visitation (though in a much quieter, less publicized fashion); and (3) the Holy See's representatives in the Hunthausen case seemed to "protest too much" when denying that the Seattle visitation had anything to do with Hunthausen's position on the nuclear arms question.

If Ryan is correct in his view, then my own findings here suffer from some serious deficiencies, because then the conflict would have been about something very different than what I have believed it to be about. Moreover, there would have been a crucial participant involved (one or more representatives of the U.S. government) that I have failed to identify. Were this the case, I do not believe that my findings here would be entirely undermined (whatever their ultimate motives, I think it is clear that the bishops participating in the Rome-Seattle conflict used secrecy, politeness, etc. in strategic fashion), but obviously my overall picture of the conflict would be less correct than I believe it to be. Regarding Ryan's theory, I can only say that I have not found enough evidence in my own investigation to establish its credibility. The only additional piece of information that I have come across that might fit in with this theory concerns the revelation of the FBI and U.S. Naval Intelligence files on Hunthausen's anti-nuclear activity. But this surveillance activity does not surprise me and seems not, in and of itself, to increase the likelihood of there having been some sort of cooperation / conspiracy between Rome and Washington. Perhaps someday further evidence will give us an entirely new picture of the Hunthausen case. But in my view the evidence presently available suggests that Rome was indeed concerned with pastoral issues and maintaining its control over local churches. Involvement by the U.S. government in the affair is only speculative at this point.

A second way Ryan challenged my own findings concerning the case was in his commentary on the Pope's involvement in the conflict. While I was struck by the fact of the Pope's non-involvement, Ryan painted a picture of the Pope being involved on the pastoral (and feeling) level. Thus did Ryan tell two stories of Pope John Paul II reaching out to Hunthausen during the conflict years, once in the form of a telegram wishing him well (at the time of Hunthausen's cancer surgery) and once with the gesture of putting his arm around Hunthausen and saying he was glad Hunthausen came to a particular meeting of bishops in Rome (in 1988). I must say that even after hearing these two anecdotes I remain mystified by the Pope's choice not to intervene in a more prominent way in the affair. John Paul never offered his opinion in any clear way in public, a fact that puzzles me considering the publicity which came to surround the case. Moreover, I am left to wonder what collegiality or fraternity means when the head of the college of bishops does not sit down for an extended conversation with a local ordinary in such a tense and consequential situation. I offer this judgment in passing by way of introduction to my view that Ryan in the interview seemed to want to protect the appearance of the Pope's participation, much in the way he did Hunthausen's. Ryan was much more willing to be critical of other participants' approaches to the conflict handling, but Hunthausen and the Holy Father were both spared from criticism.

A third way Ryan challenged my view of the conflict was, as I have just suggested, in his presentation of Hunthausen's involvement. Ryan portrays Hunthausen much less suspiciously than I do here. As I said, he offers no criticism of Hunthausen and, across the board, emphasizes Hunthausen's integrity, lack of ambition and commitment to the Church. In response to this, I will say that I find reason to take Ryan's viewpoint seriously. The other side of saying that Ryan was too close to Hunthausen to be unbiased is to say that, by being closer than anyone else, he may have had the best and most accurate view of all. I myself have only a paper trail as evidence of the level of Hunthausen's humility and guilelessness. And while I find value in not rushing to embrace a person's public image (Hunthausen as prophet; Hunthausen as simple and honest Vatican II bishop), I recognize that never parting from suspicion can be socially corrosive and can result in the distortion of the truth. Ryan's inclination to see nobility in Hunthausen's motives offers a useful counterpoint to my own inclination in this research to see a more or less calculated will to power at work (a human trait that we all share) in the activity of all conflict participants.

CHAPTER TEN

CONCLUSION AND EVALUATION

10.1 Conclusions About Center-Periphery Conflict Handling Derived from the Rome-Hunthausen Case

Near the beginning of this investigation, I posed the following question: *What coping strategies are observable in center-periphery conflict?* Having intensively studied the Rome-Hunthausen case its breadth and depth, and to the level of minute detail – I will now summarize my answer to that question. Here below I state the most pertinent findings. Thereafter I formulate a series of propositions, based on the findings, that I believe have the possibility of applying generally to cases of center-periphery conflict. These propositions might well serve as hypotheses for future studies. In the final section of this chapter I evaluate the total research project.

10.1.1 Summary of Findings and Statement of Propositions

General Stance toward Conflict Handling: All members of the hierarchy participating in the Rome-Hunthausen conflict sought to save face for the Church organization and for themselves. They also sought to enhance the Church's possession of power and their own possession of power. Participants appeared to want to pursue all four priorities simultaneously, and much of the time (particularly during periods of lower conflict intensity) the priorities seemed compatible. As the conflict intensified, however, it apparently became more difficult to know what face saving (for self and for the Church) and power enhancement (for self and for the Church) required. Finding themselves in opposition to one or more other bishops seemed to complicate bishops' discernments about what was in the best interest of the Church organization and in their own best interest. As a result we saw signs of ambivalence regarding how to proceed from both the center and periphery parties. Rome tried first to enlist Hunthausen's compliance through pressure applied in private, then through public challenges, and finally it backed off of punitive steps it had taken earlier. Hunthausen continually walked a fine line between local autonomy and conformity to Rome's wishes. His ambivalence was seen most starkly in his varying approach to the matter of secrecy. The discourse of both the center and periphery parties shows a calculative attitude at work, wherein an attempt was made to reconcile personal and organizational interests.

> **Proposition 1:** Center-periphery conflict complicates participant bishops' discernments about what is in their own best interest and what is in the Church's best interest. Participants will need to reaffirm or reformulate the balance they have struck between the priorities of saving face for self and the Church and enhancing power for self and the Church.

In this research one sees a number of strategies, identified from the actual practice of center-periphery conflict, that bishops employ in their effort to negotiate the tension between these priorities.

Use of Power: All members of the hierarchy participating in the conflict strove for (the appearance of) legitimacy in their employments of power. In the context of the center-periphery conflict, the center placed on early emphasis on gaining the periphery's agreement for its interventions (in the form of the visitation and auxiliary bishop with special powers). In the face of resistance from the periphery, the center fell back on legitimation grounded in its responsibility to the good of the Church and its legal right to intervene.

Hunthausen, for his part, tended to legitimate his actions by arguing that he had acted "in good faith" (that is, ethically and in accord with Church norms, including legal norms). He also justified his actions with reference to an ecclesiological perspective shift (his actions were "right" according to worldly perspectives that a Church come of age must recognize).

In general, bishops showed a preference for having their actions appear virtuous and, short of that, legal in ecclesiastical and civil terms.

Though the center party enjoyed a great advantage in almost every form of ecclesiastical power in the Rome-Hunthausen case, it had serious difficulty achieving its will in Seattle. Though Rome employed several rather heavy inducements (forms of raw power) to enjoin Hunthausen's cooperation (e.g.: *legal-coercive* interventions such as the visitation and appointment of a bishop with special faculties; applications of *social pressure* to conform; *ecological power* in its entrance of Hunthausen's archdiocese while denying him access to the Vatican decision-making center) these were not enough to gain his cooperation on key points (such as acceptance of the loss of faculties to an auxiliary). Hunthausen, though on the surface seemingly disadvantaged in his possession of power, managed to hold out surprisingly well in his conflict with the Vatican, even forcing a significant retreat by Rome (in the form of the reassignment of Wuerl and restoration of Hunthausen's faculties).

The basis of Hunthausen's success in achieving a compromise appears to lie with his consistent maintenance of a posture of deference and loyalty – toward the Holy See (and Holy Father in particular) and the Church, while waging his resistance quietly (in behind-the-scenes negotiations) and in publicly defensible ways (when he did go on the attack in public against the Vatican, it only came after he himself had been publicly attacked by the pro-nuncio; and the case he argued on that occasion was one that the American bishops and American Catholics in general could sympathize with). In essence, Hunthausen, through his consistently respectful language and actions (with some minor exceptions) provided Rome with no grounds for automatic removal. At the same time, he drew on his great popularity in his own archdiocese and among liberal-progressive Catholics around the country, who admired his stands on principle (something accentuated and communicated through his personal charisma).

Surprisingly, while Hunthausen often drew effectively on his own charisma, the Pope offered only a minimal projection of his own personality (and well-known charisma) into the affair. After Hunthausen argued his case at the November 1986 NCCB meeting, the negotiations reached an impasse. Rome was forced to choose between an unpopular departure from office by Hunthausen (via resignation or removal) – and a likely public backlash during the Pope's papal visit in 1987 – or some loss of face for itself in the short time by retreating from the hard line it had taken against Hunthausen. Rome decided to retreat, while imposing lesser sanctions that allowed it to save face somewhat (by asserting its own power even in retreat). In general, the use of power did not appear to follow an orderly progression (increase) in the heaviness of tactics. Some of Rome's most heavy-handed interventions (the visitation, the imposition of an auxiliary bishop with special faculties) came fairly early in the conflict, after little build-up (in public at least). Hunthausen's use of contentious tactics appeared to escalate in accord with rising feelings of frustration, desperation and the sense that he had little left to lose.

Proposition 2: Bishops participating in center-periphery conflict will strive to have their employments of power appear legitimate.

Proposition 3: Critical to a periphery bishop's ability to survive a conflict with the center is his ability to offer resistance without giving the appearance of disloyalty.

Specific Coping Strategies Employed:
1. Shows of deference to the existing structural order and mindset of the Church: The evidence of the Rome-Hunthausen case shows this to be a cardinal rule of intrahierarchical discourse. Nowhere in the case do we find any outright abandonments of this principle in practice. All bishops made it a point not to criticize the Church itself and consistently showed deference to other Church leaders (especially in the form of obedience to superiors). Use of this strategy served to reassure fellow bishops and Church members at large that one was loyally committed to the Church and not a threat to harmony or unity.

At the same time, it is clear that the structural order and mindset were under contestation in the case. Hunthausen pushed for local autonomy and for a vision of Church that, while not external to the (pluriform) total Church tradition, was not in a dominant position within the Church organization. The rule of engagement appears to be that bishops may argue for their own vision for Church thought and practice so long as they employ familiar concepts and terminologies exclusively when doing so. We saw this rule applied in the Rome-Hunthausen case when Hunthausen argued for "renewal" as justified by the Second Vatican Council. Ratzinger, for his part, took a different approach, arguing for pastoral reforms in Seattle according to norms expressed in an array of ecclesiastical instructions (papal, congregational, conciliar).

Proposition 4: Bishops participating in center-periphery conflict will show deference to the order and mindset of the Church. Though they may challenge the Church's prevailing thought and practice, they will do so only in terms that are familiar from Church tradition and Church culture and Church socialization.

2. Association of one's own efforts with the best interest of the Church. This strategy is in some sense an extension of the previous strategy. No Church leader wants to show himself to be a danger to the Church: rather, he will want to appear to have its best interests at heart. This was consistently evident in the Rome-Hunthausen case. All bishop participants signalled with their words, often quite explicitly, that they were acting for the good of the Church. (Though discussions about the nature of that interest were often avoided out of fear of conflict.) As with the strategy of showing deference, we see in the conflict that differing words and actions were adopted as expressions of this concern for the Church's interest. Center party representatives tended to focus on the need for control within the Church and the adequate presentation of doctrine. Hunthausen associated his own efforts with the well being of the people of the Church.

Proposition 5: Bishops participating in center-periphery conflict will associate their own efforts with the best interest of the Church.

3. Minimization of the appearance of conflict. The bishop participants in the Rome-Hunthausen conflict consistently sought to minimize the appearance of conflict, but briefly abandoned this strategy (by making press statements, leaking news, offering implicit and implicit criticisms of opponents, and acknowledging the fact of conflict itself) during the most tense phase of the conflict. Once a stalemate was reached in the conflict handling, members of the hierarchy participating resumed the effort to minimize the appearance of conflict.

Proposition 6: Bishops participating in center-periphery conflict will minimize the appearance of conflict but may briefly abandon this strategy for the sake of advantage.

4. Shows of fraternity. Bishop participants in the Rome-Hunthausen conflict drew upon their fraternal relationship by calling upon one another for support (Hunthausen turned to Roach and Hurley, and later appealed to the NCCB as a whole; the Vatican employed Hickey as visitator, and later called Bernardin, O'Connor and Quinn to serve on the assessment commission; etc.). This draw on fraternal relationship served both the center and periphery parties well, but Hunthausen gained the most in the conflict by convincing the American bishops to signal support for his position. All bishop participants showed a clannish tendency to keep intrahierarchical disputes within the confines of the hierarchy. This tendency served the center more than the periphery. Hunthausen gained greater leverage over Rome when the conflict came more fully into the open. The concept of episcopal fraternity was frequently invoked -- by all parties -- apparently as a reminder of obligations (as when the Pope reminded the American bishops, in his message to them, of their accountability to Rome) or as a signal of one's own belonging and loyalty (as in many of Hunthausen's pronouncements).

Proposition 7: Bishops participating in center-periphery conflict will show fraternity by saving face for one another, by keeping the hierarchy's business within the hierarchy and by emphasizing the concept of episcopal fraternity.

5. Practice of courtesy. All bishop participants showed an almost invincible commitment to graciousness toward one another in public. Tactically, this involved employing praise, addressing one another respectfully, avoiding direct criticisms or assignments of blame and maintaining silence about sensitive matters. Only briefly, at the point of greatest intensity of conflict, did the center and periphery parties in the Rome-Hunthausen conflict forgo shows of courtesy toward one another. In general, this compact of courtesy served center and periphery bishops equally well, since it maintained the appearance of strength (through unity) in the hierarchy. In the Rome-Hunthausen case it appeared that the opportunity to abandon courtesy was increased by proximity to the center (and the greater possession of organizational power). Hunthausen did not appear free to make statements critical of Rome's approach until Rome (Laghi, in the Vatican chronology) had openly criticized him (and then in harsher and more personal attacks than Hunthausen would voice).

Proposition 8: Bishops participating in center-periphery conflict will show courtesy toward one another in public almost without exception. When a breach in courtesy comes, it will likely come first from the center party.

6. Employment of secrecy. All bishop participants in the Rome-Hunthausen conflict practiced secrecy. The greatest information divide resulting from the use of secrecy lay between those within the hierarchy and those without. Those outside the hierarchy almost always had less access to information relevant to the conflict than those within the hierarchy. Secrecy served to downplay the seriousness of the conflict, thereby preserving the appearance of unity within the hierarchy. Secrecy also served to keep those not of the hierarchy out of the conflict negotiations. Rome took the lead in maintaining this policy of secrecy over and against the public (in its containment of the visitation findings, for example). Hunthausen alternately complied with and resisted this policy (thus, he participated in private meetings and exchanges of correspondence and reserved information for himself, but he also revealed Wuerl's possession of faculties).

Within the hierarchy itself, there was also an information divide resulting from the use of secrecy. Rome used secrecy against Hunthausen, repeatedly placing him at a disadvantage by not supplying information he requested (the Hickey visitation report being the most prominent example). Hunthausen fought this disadvantage during the middle stage of the conflict by repeatedly bringing conflict issues into the open and by making secrecy itself an issue (at the November 1986 NCCB meeting). By denying information to Hunthausen and excluding him from discussions that would affect his fate, the Vatican kept tight control over what the pertinent issues were and what the practical consequences should be. Through his resistance, Hunthausen introduced his own voice into the decision making process and also the voices of an interested public that was positioned to put social pressure on the negotiating bishops.

While adherence to secrecy was, to a high degree, a matter of standard practice in the conflict handling, so too were breaks from secrecy. Both the center and periphery parties, on at least one occasion, released information against the wishes of the other. Another significant form of departure from secrecy were news leaks, which shaped the conflict on several occasions. The source of the news leaks was in every instance unclear. One learning from this study was that the use of secrecy created rifts within the hierarchy (between center and periphery) and stood in problematic relationship with cultural expectations about transparency. Whereas Hunthausen made this point explicitly, he apparently felt constricted enough by his role as a bishop that he could never make a clean break from the use of secrecy himself. He remained complicit in its use (though ambivalently) during the conflict and beyond.

> **Proposition 9:** Bishops participating in center-periphery conflict will show a basic preference for conducting their conflict negotiations in secret, but they will break with secrecy when there is an apparent advantage to doing so.

> **Proposition 10:** The center party will benefit more from secrecy than the periphery party and will show a greater commitment to secrecy than the periphery.

7. Recruitment of allies. Center and periphery attempts to recruit fellow bishops as allies increased as the conflict increased in intensity. Certain individual bishops were approached early on (Rome brought on Hickey as visitator, Hunthausen consulted with Roach and Hurley), but the main attempt to enlist support from fellow bishops took place prior to and during the November 1986 NCCB meeting (during the discussions about the Vatican chronology's release and the NCCB debate itself). Hunthausen, being the lower power party, was more in need of third party support and he pursued it more actively, turning not only to fellow bishops but also to the public at large. The NCCB's decision to stand by him (without challenging Rome) was crucial to Hunthausen's emerging as well as he did from the conflict. Many bishops may have felt pressured to support Hunthausen in light of the widespread popular support for his cause. The Vatican, for its part, made only a minimal attempt to win public support to its side during the affair – or perhaps its attempts were simply ineffective, by virtue of seeming heavy-handed (no public relations campaign laid the groundwork for the use of heavy tactics such as the visitation and release of criticisms in the Vatican chronology).

Proposition 11: The lower power party in center-periphery conflict (likely the periphery party) will have a greater need of bishop allies and will make a more concerted effort to recruit them.

Proposition 12: While fellow bishops are the most important allies to have in center-periphery conflict, popular support from outside the hierarchy can also have a strategic impact on the conflict handling.

8. Use of persuasive argumentation. It was difficult to evaluate the use of persuasive argumentation in the Rome-Hunthausen conflict because the most crucial conversations between the principal parties were carried out in private. Most of the available evidence shows the parties' employment of rhetoric to win public support, with attempts to convince one another having been already carried out in another, hidden, forum. But presumably the argumentation that did come into view (employing rhetorical tactics such as ingratiation, demonization, simplification / complexification, perspective shifts and God talk) was somewhat reflective of the exchanges that took place in private.

The chief difference between the argumentation advanced by Rome and by Hunthausen may well have been the discrepant ecclesiological visions at hand. What Rome saw as Hunthausen's main weakness, his flexible and tolerant leadership style (his lack of "firmness"), was in Hunthausen's view a necessary and valuable component of Church leadership. Hunthausen presented himself as treating Church members as adults, making room for participation and tolerating the unavoidable failures that accompany participation as an acceptable cost. Hunthausen also showed a higher comfort level with intraecclesial diversity. The Vatican position (expressed most concisely by Ratzinger), however, saw in this approach of toleration a threat to the full realization of the Church's own ideals. Toleration might make Hunthausen popular in his own archdiocese, but it could also interfere with those same people's ability to face up to the difficult challenges that God has placed before them. In simple terms, Hunthausen's ecclesiology of forgiveness and charity clashed with the Roman emphasis on the demands of the cross. Both are central and fully orthodox perspectives within Christian theology: they are theologically inseparable but not always easily reconciled.

> **Proposition 13:** Bishops participating in center-periphery conflict will make their primary attempt to win over other bishops through persuasive argumentation in private. Persuasive argumentation in public will be directed mainly to third parties.

9. Assertion of personal identity. Among the bishop participants in the Rome-Hunthausen conflict, only Hunthausen regularly asserted his own personal identity in public as a means of managing the conflict. Vatican representatives rarely drew attention to their individuality in public as a conflict coping strategy. The strategy proved to be a great source of strength for Hunthausen, humanizing his position and winning much support for his cause. Foregrounding one's own personality appeared to be a major taboo on the center party side, but in the late stage of the conflict there were signs that the pro-nuncio attempted the strategy as well, to counter Hunthausen's effective use of the approach. Third party bishop negotiators (NCCB leaders, the commission) consistently kept a low profile during their involvement in the conflict.

The key to Hunthausen's success with the strategy lay in highlighting his charismatic personality and reputation for integrity, and establishing a link between his conflict positions and these qualities. Also critical was the fact that he personalized his position (humanized it) without giving the appearance of grandstanding or willful disloyalty. His individualized stance came to be associated with integrity and a commitment to principle and not with putting himself above the best interest of the Church.

The Vatican's disinclination to highlight individual personalities appeared to be related to overriding commitment to managing the conflict out of public view (and perhaps to limit the opponent's access to the conflictual partner). The most visible representative of the Vatican position was pro-nuncio Laghi. Curial officials and the Pope stayed almost entirely off the record. It is unclear why the Pope chose not to interject his own personality into the affair in any direct and public way, given his proven ability to assert his own personality effectively in public.

> **Proposition 14:** Center party bishops in center-periphery conflict will show little inclination to assert their own identity in the course of the conflict handling. Periphery party bishops will enjoy more freedom to assert their own personality and will have more incentive to do so.

10.2 Generalizability of the Findings to Other Cases of Center-Periphery Conflict

How transferable are theses findings? Without making actual comparisons to other cases of center-periphery conflict, it is difficult to know for sure, but observations about the prospects for generalization – and the limits thereof -- are offered below.

In this study I have striven to lay the groundwork for future comparisons (as, for example, with the aforementioned Alfrink case). I started with a review of theoretical materials to shed light on the phenomenon of center-periphery conflict (chapters 2-5) and referred back to that material repeatedly in the course of the investigation. Thus one may speak of an ongoing engagement of empirical findings with existing theory, and a basis for theoretical generalization.

Beyond that, I have adopted a "thick description" approach in my presentation of the case findings, showing how I have built toward conclusions from the ground up. I have moved in my analysis from the level of individual documents to the level of the constructed case narrative to the extraction of conclusions, explaining my own methodological steps and presenting the relevant data (or citing a consultable source) all along the way.

Moreover, I have consistently tried to give a three-dimensional picture of case developments themselves, supplying enough data so that multiple potential influences on the case handling (personal factors, organizational factors, societal factors) could be identified and considered. This three-dimensionality favors the possibility of making cross-case comparisons fruitfully. (Relevant similarities and differences can be more easily identified.)

Finally, I would point out that this case description does not simply confront us with a picture of conflict coping behavior of two bishops (the Pope and the local bishop) over a brief time, but with multiple samples of discursive coping from more than a dozen bishops (of multiple nationalities) over a five-and-a-half year period. In that respect, I believe it provides a good glimpse of widely prevailing discursive preferences within the hierarchy of the contemporary Church and, again, a good foundation for theoretical generalization.

On this basis, I advance the fourteen propositions articulated above as fruitful possibilities to inform future studies of center-periphery conflict.

10.3 Relevance of the Findings

The following observations about the potential practical and practical theological relevance of the research findings are normative and speculative in nature.

The Church is an organization that seeks to forge unity from diversity. The tension between central control and local (peripheral) autonomy is a reflection of the effort to cull oneness from plurality. Conflict between Rome and the local Church (or between the Pope and a local bishop) is a phenomenon that can, from various angles, be understood as an inherent characteristic of the Church, as the product of societal-historical conjuncture, or as the challenge inevitably faced by any large-scale centralized and bureaucratized multinational.

This research demonstrates that one may coherently read center-periphery conflict (and arguably intrahierarchical conflict in general, given the findings' multiple groundedness in the Church's belief system, culture, socialization, etc.) in terms of the hierarchy's desire to protect the appearance and preserve the power of the Church organization and of the hierarchy itself, in the course of its quest for unity. The study does not conclude that these are the only motivations compelling bishops in their leadership of the Church – normative-ideological motivations remain highly relevant -- but simply that these motivations apply, and are instrumental to greater extent than members of the hierarchy let on. Thus the study offers a necessary amendment to the hierarchy's own descriptions of what takes place and is at stake in such conflicts.

Within the Church organization a taboo around conflict applies, apparently rooted in the perception that conflict is incompatible with the preferred state of charity and unified harmony. Because conflict is not supposed to arise, especially within the hierarchy, which symbolizes Church unity, bishops show themselves to be unhelpfully constricted when dealing with the conflicts that inevitably occur within their ranks. In the absence of Church teachings that openly value conflicts (acknowledging them as unavoidable in organizations of all kinds and useful when managed well), and lacking structures and guidelines for handling conflicts productively, bishops "cope" by avoiding conflict with one another (placing a premium on deference to rank and shows of courtesy) and minimizing its appearance when it develops (downplaying its significance, hiding it, etc.). They seek to contain the conflict handling within the bounds of the episcopal brotherhood, often by means of secrecy. (The real arguments occur out of public view.) By default, bishops' efforts at conflict problem solving depend on improvisation. The findings from this research point to the urgent need for a Church teaching about conflict that does justice to modern realities (such as expectations about transparency and wide participation) and relevant normative, ecclesiological and practical concerns.

Within the prevailing approach to conflict handling (one of the contributions of this research is to clarify what that approach is), the hierarchy – the center party in particular -- shows a reluctance to invite Church constituents (Catholics at large) into the discussion as full-fledged participants. When the broader public *does* participate, it is often the result of either having forced itself into the conversation (through letter writing, activism, media barrages – compare the recent crisis around the question of pedophilia in the US Church) or as the consequence of one party's attempt to apply social pressure to the another. By the exclusion of the Church public from the conflict discussion, the bishops deny Catholics the opportunity to speak to issues that concern them directly and thereby underserve the process of determining what is truly in their interest. Without knowing and addressing the real interests of the people they lead, bishops undermine their own authority and hinder the possibility of attaining authentic unity. This is not to overlook practical limits that apply (chaos would be the result of everyone speaking at once), nor is it to suggest that the strategies currently applied for the resolution of center-periphery conflicts are in and of themselves wrong. Showing deference and courtesy, minimizing the appearance of conflict – these and the other strategies all can be helpful if used in the right way. The problem in the current state of affairs, however, is that the strategies appear to be chosen unthinkingly and applied (often) in the absence of communal consent and ecclesiological, ethical and practical reference frames that offer explicit justification for their use. To take the highly charged example of secrecy: secrecy can be used to harm, but it can also serve to protect the vulnerable. The key is knowing when it is proper to use secrecy, given the Church's identity and mission, its ethical standards, and the practical limits on secrecy's effectiveness. The ongoing challenge of discernment about the appropriate use of conflict handling strategies, recognized in the course of this study and in the light of its findings, is an appropriate object of (future) reflection for the Church and for the normative science that is practical theology.

10.4 Evaluation of the Total Research Project
The present study of center-periphery conflict has a number of strengths and weaknesses that can be identified. In the following section I provide my own perspective on this matter, assessing first certain weaknesses I recognize in my work.

One weakness I perceive is that I have reduced my analysis to a focus on manipulations of power (through the use of language) for the sake of strategic advantage. This gives the impression that I perceive only selfish (power-hungry) motives at work in the actors I have studied. This type of analysis makes no room, really, for consideration of altruistic impulses and for the participants' own professions that God is somehow present to the conflict handling. Nor does it account for more tortured kinds of wrestling with questions about power and ideals (of the sort that the novelist Graham Greene described so well) that bishops may experience internally. The result of this approach is a two-dimensional depiction of the participants' exchange: we see a shadow drama about power and not much else. Acknowledging this deficiency, I will confess nonetheless to feeling justified in adopting this approach. My reasons for having proceeded with this type of analysis are that one simply cannot account for everything, a choice must be made; and to my mind, attention to how power is manipulated in intrahierarchical conflict is a topic worthy of consideration that has been neglected. This does not mean that there is nothing but the pursuit of power at work in these conflicts, but rather that the way power is employed is crucial and is, without question, a legitimate focal point. By at least offering some clarification to the power question, I believe myself to be making a contribution to a later, fuller portrait of center-periphery conflict dynamics that takes into account other dimensions of the conflict handling as well.

Another weakness in this work is a certain unbalanced quality in the treatment of the participant parties. It was unavoidable, given my own circumstances, that I would gain more insight into the periphery party position than into the center party position. Most of the research was conducted in Seattle and most of the publications I had available for consultation originated in Seattle or elsewhere in the United States. Knowing ahead of time that I would not have the opportunity to travel to Rome for interviews or other kinds of research gathering – and since Hunthausen himself refused an interview request early on – I decided to establish as much balance in the data gathering as I could by giving most of my attention to the documents released publicly by both sides. This seemed to me to offer something of a level playing field, since both Hunthausen and Vatican representatives had the opportunity, realized in practice, to release texts that served to make their views known. In a perfect world, I would have gained access to the principals on both sides for interviews and would have been able to compare private documents with public documents. But in this real world I have had to settle for piecing together, as best I could, the inside story based on the pieces of evidence that turned up in the open in the places where I could get to them. I feel the need to add, too, however, that Rome's general orientation against transparency in its bureaucratic affairs makes it harder for researchers like myself to tell the Roman side of the story completely.

As a means to overcome problems of lack of access – to hidden dimensions of the conflict handling, for example – I employed in this research a method that is designed to help one read between the lines of textual interchange. Critical discourse analysis, while offering valuable techniques for perception, clearly has functional limits. One such limit is the subjectivity of interpretation that applies when one describes the social function of a given text. To put it bluntly, texts production and text consumption are highly ambiguous processes. A text producer may write a certain way with a clear strategic intention, but he or she may also do so out of habit or carelessness or with an entirely unexpected intention in mind. On the consumption side, interpretations of a text vary according to the reader, time and setting of consumption, and so forth. My basic approach to addressing this difficulty has been to introduce the actual contents of the text, describe the context of its production / consumption (while identifying key sources of information), and allow the reader to judge for herself or himself the quality of the conclusions. My expectation is not necessarily that the reader agree with my interpretation, but that he or she easily see how I arrived at that interpretation and why.

As an analytical tool for gaining insight into the Rome-Hunthausen conflict handling, I have drawn on a particular perspective on conflict handling, that of Pruitt and Rubin (1986). One advantage of their approach for my own work is the attention they give to the perceptions and consequent decision making of individual actors. This has worked well with my own inclination to view the conflict participants as individual actors (decision makers, text producers, text consumers), but there are obvious drawbacks to such an approach – in my own work and that of Pruitt and Rubin. For example, the question of how group participation (on a small scale) tends to influence individual choice is neglected. Also not incorporated into the conflict model is a means for theoretically relating conflict events to more usual, tranquil patterns of group or organizational life. The theory also leaves the potential long-term (post-conflict) effects of the use of particular conflict strategies unexplored.

To my regret, certain strategies of interest did not come up for systematic examination because they were recognized too late in the research process. These include the strategies of establishing procedural control, avoidance, revealing and threats. These strategies are worthy of future examination.

The main strengths I see in the present study are that, first, it relates -- systematically and with attention to documentary detail -- an important story of intrachurch conflict that has not yet been told in that fashion. (As a case in point, a recently released 144-page history of the Catholic Archdiocese of Seattle – published by the archdiocese itself – offers only a three-sentence description of the entire conflict. Cf. Taylor 2000.) Simply for the sake of the historical record, the chronological account of the case presented here makes a contribution by consolidating dates, information sources, descriptions of events and document references that are not yet available in any other single source.

Secondly, this study makes a contribution as a social scientific work by providing a theoretically- and empirically-grounded introduction to how members of the hierarchy use language and actions to further their own interests and the interests of the Church organization in conflict situations. Studies of intrahierarchical conflict handling are lacking and the provision thereof has value for the organization and outsiders as well.

Finally, I believe that this work ultimately raises questions – difficult questions about what the Church is called to be, and who will lead it, and how – that I believe the Church must confront if it is to reach its own goals. I hope that this effort will help to gain for those questions a more sustained hearing.

10. 5 Afterword

When I set out to investigate the Hunthausen case five years ago, I had a simpler and more naïve view of the affair than I do now that I have completed this study. My intention was to write about how the bishops involved used language to resolve the conflict. I was primarily interested in the specific techniques bishops would use to dance around conflict issues I was sure they would be queasy about (in public). What I was less conscious of was that whenever I would be writing these reflections I would be writing about power, and that it would be impossible to avoid confronting this question head on.

My previous awareness of the case had told me that people either loved Hunthausen as a progressive leader of the Church or were frustrated with him because he was (reputedly) so lax in his leadership. One or two more subtle writings I encountered early on speculated about Hunthausen's level of political astuteness: was he as mild and peaceable (and naïve) as he seemed, or was this the preferred front of a canny infighter?

Though I have my own answer to that last question – that he was an idealist who was smart enough to realize the situation he was in, and pragmatic enough to do what he had to to survive (for himself but also for the sake of the ideals) – it seems to me to overlook an important point. Ultimately there is something tragic about Hunthausen, not so much for what he himself experiences in the case, but for the troubling constriction of leadership that his case exemplifies.

One of the main points I make in my study of the case is that, while arguing for an "open Church" – for transparency and broad participation in the leadership of the Church – Hunthausen himself remained complicit, off and on, in the restrictive practices of silence and secrecy that he himself argued against. I believe this proved to be the case because Hunthausen was so strongly socialized to do so (thus, it was to a degree a matter of unconscious habit), and because ultimately he realized that he could not say what he wanted to say and change what he wanted to change and still remain in the hierarchy. I cannot help but feel that on some level Hunthausen knew all too well that the self-protective mechanisms of the hierarchical culture – which are fully operative when Church conflicts of interest arise – pose a danger to the credibility of the hierarchy and to the viability of the Church. One need only look as far as the recent crisis around the issue of pedophilia to recognize the calamity that comes when bishops put the appearance of the Church and of the hierarchy ahead of the open and honest acknowledgment of real problems. My sense is that Hunthausen felt himself to be, to some extent, trapped within structures that he could not see a way to change and that he felt frustrated as a result. I do not imagine him to be alone among bishops in feeling this way.

APPENDIX 1: CHRONOLOGY OF THE ROME-HUNTHAUSEN CASE

1983

5.83   Archbishop Pio Laghi, Papal Pro-Nuncio to the United States, informs Seattle Archbishop Raymond Hunthausen, at a meeting of U.S. bishops in Chicago, that the Vatican wants to conduct a Visitation of Seattle. Hunthausen agrees.

7.6.83   The Vatican names Washington, D.C. Archbishop James Hickey Apostolic Visitator.

9.83   Seattle Auxiliary Bishop Nicholas Walsh resigns for health reasons.

9.15-16.83   Hunthausen and Hickey, in Chicago, discuss how Visitation will be conducted.

9.22.83   Hunthausen in Rome for ad limina visit.

10.4.83   Date of letter (never released publicly) from Cardinal Ratzinger, Prefect of the Congregation for the Doctrine of the Faith, to Hunthausen concerning forthcoming Visitation.

10.26.83   Hunthausen and Hickey announce the impending Visitation of Seattle.

11.2-8.83   Visitation of Seattle. Archbishop Hickey, accompanied by two assistants, interviews more than seventy priests, Religious, and lay people, including Hunthausen and members of his staff.

12.12.83   Date of letter from Ratzinger to Hunthausen acknowledging the Vatican's reception of Hickey's Visitation report.

1984

3.14.84   Date of Hunthausen letter (never released publicly) to Ratzinger responding to issues raised by Visitation report.

7.6.84   Hunthausen installs Fr. Michael G. Ryan, archdiocesan chancellor, as vicar general of the archdiocese as well. Hunthausen also names Fr. Michael McDermott director of administration.

1985

9.11.85   Date of Hunthausen letter to Laghi discussing possible appointment of helper bishop in Seattle.

9.30.85   Date of Ratzinger letter (released publicly 5.87) to Hunthausen concluding the Visitation and outlining its findings.

10.9-10.85   Hunthausen and Laghi meet at Apostolic Nunciature in Washington, D.C. to discuss findings from Visitation and follow-up action.

11.14.85   Date of Laghi letter to Hunthausen announcing conclusion of Visitation and outlining its findings.

11.25.85   Date of Laghi letter (never made public) sent separately to Hunthausen and Wuerl in which Laghi reportedly thanked Hunthausen for agreeing to welcome new auxiliary bishop.

11.27.85   Hunthausen releases Laghi letter announcing conclusion of Visitation.

12.2.85   Date of Hunthausen letter to Laghi discussing appointment of Auxiliary Bishop Wuerl and matter of special faculties.

12.3.85   Laghi announces Vatican appointment of Donald Wuerl to serve as Auxiliary Bishop of Seattle.

1986

1.6.86   Pope John Paul II ordains Wuerl auxiliary bishop in Rome.

1.7.86   The Pope meets with Hunthausen and Wuerl in Rome.

1.23.86   Prior to Wuerl's arrival in Seattle, Hunthausen meets with priests of Archdiocese and reads Ratzinger letter of 9.30.85 to them. (Hunthausen had shared the contents of the same letter with the archdiocesan presbyteral council in late 1985.)

1.26.86   Wuerl arrives in Seattle.

3.86   Hunthausen and Wuerl reach impasse in their power-sharing arrangement and discover they have different understandings of what the arrangement entails. Both write to Laghi for clarification.

4.29.86   Date of internal archdiocesan report (prepared by Wuerl, Fr. Michael G. Ryan and Fr. Michael McDermott) meant to be a first step toward designing a process to address the concerns of the visitation. The report was requested by Hunthausen and it was submitted to him. Later in the same year, in September, Hunthausen would distribute the report more widely among archdiocesan leaders.

6.86   Hunthausen and Wuerl meet with Laghi at the National Conference of Catholic Bishops (NCCB) meeting in Collegeville, Minnesota. Laghi confirms that Hunthausen was to have given Wuerl final authority in the specified areas.

6.26.86   Pope John Paul II meets with Wuerl and Bishop John Marshall of Burlington, Vermont at the Vatican to discuss their work in the ongoing study of U.S. seminaries.

7.1.86   Hunthausen receives letter from Cardinal Gantin, prefect of the Congregation for Bishops, reaffirming that the Vatican's intention was for Hunthausen to have given final authority to Wuerl in the specified areas.

7.27.86   *National Catholic Register* article, citing Vatican sources, says Wuerl will be assuming a "heavier share of real authority" in Seattle.

7.28.86   Date of Hunthausen letter to Wuerl (never released to the public) officially granting the special faculties, effective August 1, 1986.

8.1.86   Wuerl's special faculties take effect.

9.3.86   Hunthausen makes public announcement of Wuerl's possession of special faculties and releases a chronology of the Visitation and subsequent events.

9.11.86   Seattle Archdiocesan newspaper, *The Progress*, features Hunthausen open letter concerning changes in the Archdiocese and an interview with Hunthausen and Wuerl.

9.12.86   Hunthausen and Wuerl meet with 250 priests of archdiocese for five hours to discuss recent developments and give priests opportunity to voice reactions.

9.18.86   Hunthausen and Wuerl meet with archdiocesan presbyteral council at St. Edward's Hall, Seattle. Others present included members of the Archbishop's staff (Dennis O'Leary, Olivia Zapata, Fr. Michael McDermott) and archdiocesan public relations director Russ Scearce.

9.19.86   Date of Wuerl letter to priests of Archdiocese discussing current situation.

9.22.86   Region XII bishops (Northwestern U.S.), meeting in Portland, Oregon, issue statement expressing support for Hunthausen and Wuerl.

9.26.86	Hunthausen and Wuerl meet with priests of Archdiocese, Archdiocesan Pastoral Council, Archdiocesan Finance Council, and chancery department directors at St. Thomas Center, Bothell, Washington.
9.29.86	Date of Hunthausen memorandum to "Designated Leaders in the Archdiocese of Seattle," which introduces the April 29, 1986 report prepared by Wuerl, Fr. Michael G. Ryan and Fr. Michael J. McDermott. Hunthausen had appointed this committee of three to review the 9.30.8 Ratzinger letter and to begin developing a strategy for addressing its concerns in the Archdiocese.
10.16.86	*The Progress* publishes Hunthausen letter to people of Archdiocese concerning recent developments. The letter, dated 10.14.86, was also mailed to all registered Catholics in the archdiocese.
10.23.86	Archbishop Hickey (Apostolic Visitator) meets privately with Pope John Paul II in Rome. NCCB executive committee (Members: NCCB President James Malone, NCCB Vice President John May, Cardinal Bernard Law of Boston, Auxiliary Bishop Eugene Marino of Washington, D.C., and Bishop John McGann of Rockville Centre. It is not known if all participated) discuss options for releasing the (Vatican) chronology prepared by Archbishop Laghi in a conference call. Laghi had shown his chronology to Hunthausen prior to this date.
10.24.86	Laghi provides "A Chronology of Recent Events in the Archdiocese of Seattle" to the U.S. bishops in anticipation of the imminent NCCB meeting.
10.27.86	NCCB President James Malone (Archbishop of Youngstown, Ohio) releases the Vatican chronology to the press at the request of the Vatican and authorization of the Holy See. Hunthausen releases statement in response to Vatican Chronology.
11.5.86	NCCB confirms that Pope John Paul II will visit eight cities during nine-day U.S. trip in September, 1987.
11.10.86	NCCB fall meeting (five days) begins in Washington, D.C. The Rome-Hunthausen case is on the agenda.
11.11.86	At the NCCB meeting, the bishops meet in closed executive session to discuss the Seattle situation. Hunthausen addresses the body briefly. Four texts frame the debate that follows: (1) the full text of Hunthausen's address to the bishops; (2) Hunthausen's written response to the Vatican Chronology; (3) the Vatican Chronology; and (4) a draft of a statement from NCCB President James Malone (Bishop of Youngstown, Ohio) which he proposes to release publicly as the NCCB's commentary on the Seattle situation.
11.12.86	The bishops as the NCCB meeting gather again in closed session in the morning to continue discussion of the Rome-Hunthausen case. Later in the day Hunthausen's address to the bishops and his response to the Vatican Chronology are released to the press along with the final version of Bishop Malone's statement.
11.13.86	NCCB meeting concludes.
12.16.86	Hunthausen has surgery to remove cancerous prostate gland. He is released from the hospital on 12.24.86.

1987

1.26.87	Date of Laghi letter to three bishops – Cardinal John O'Connor of New York, Cardinal Joseph Bernardin of Chicago and Archbishop John Quinn of San Francisco -- appointing them to an ad hoc commission to assess the Seattle situation.
2.9.87	Laghi issues brief written statement (in Washington, D.C., through the NCCB), announcing formation of ad hoc assessment commission.

2.10.87	Commission members meet with Hunthausen and Wuerl in Dallas, Texas. The pro-nuncio is present for the morning but not the afternoon and evening sessions.
2.13.87	The *National Catholic Reporter* reveals that the FBI has kept a file on Hunthausen and on another "peace bishop," Thomas Gumbleton of Detroit.
2.16.87	Wuerl meets privately with the Pope at the Vatican. Wuerl's visit to Rome is occasioned by his work on the seminary study committee.
3.6-7.87	Commission hears testimony of eight bishops of the Northwestern U.S., five archdiocesan officials and seven priests belonging to Seattle's board of consultors at a meeting in Menlo Park, California.
3.12.87	Commission, together with pro-nuncio, meets with Hunthausen and Wuerl individually in Chicago.
3.18-21.87	Commission members in Rome as part of delegation of American cardinals and bishops preparing for Pope's forthcoming trip to U.S.
3.25.87	Commission members Bernardin and Quinn meet with (visitator) Hickey in Washington, D.C.
3.29.87	Quinn meets with Archbishop Francis Hurley of Anchorage, Alaska.
3.31.87	Quinn meets with Hurley and with Bishop Michael Kenny of Juneau, Alaska.
4.8.87	Hunthausen meets with Bernardin in Chicago.
4.20.87	Priests of Archdiocese meet in Seattle and many sign statement of support for Hunthausen.
5.7.87	Hunthausen informs commission he is willing to accept its proposed resolution of Seattle situation.
5.19-20.87	Commission members and Laghi meet with Pope and other Curial officials (including Congregation for Bishops) in Rome to discuss the proposed resolution the commission has worked out with Hunthausen. The commission's assessment report is dated 5.20.87.
5.23.87	Thomas Murphy, Bishop of Great Falls-Billings, Montana is notified of Holy See's desire to appoint him Coadjutor Archbishop of Seattle.
5.25.87	Date of commission report cover letter, addressed to U.S. bishops.
5.26.87	Hunthausen with Bishop Thomas Murphy in Great Falls, Montana.
5.27.87	Commission releases its report, together with a cover letter and a copy of Cardinal Ratzinger's 9.30.85 letter to Hunthausen. Hunthausen holds press conference to discuss the report and introduce newly appointed Coadjutor Archbishop, Thomas Murphy.
6.13.87	Archdiocesan service of welcome for Murphy in Seattle.
6.15.87	Hunthausen and Murphy hold press conference in Seattle.
7.16.87	Assessment commission meets with Hunthausen and Murphy in Chicago.
9.10-19.87	Pope John Paul II visits eight U.S. cities.
11.10.87	Assessment commission meets with Hunthausen and Murphy in Washington, D.C.
1988	
2.12.88	Donald Wuerl appointed bishop of Pittsburgh, his home diocese.

2.26.88	Assessment commission meets with Hunthausen and Murphy in Seattle. (Archbishop Quinn was not present because of a leave of absence.)
6.28.88	Washington, D.C. Archbishop James Hickey elevated to Cardinal.
10.88	Final meeting between apostolic commission and Hunthausen, Murphy.
11.29.88- 12.6.88	Hunthausen and Murphy in Rome for ad limina visit. (Because of a scheduling conflict, the Seattle archbishops travelled with the bishops of Region VII, instead of with their fellow Region XII bishops, who had gone to Rome in August.)

1989

| 4.11.89 | Laghi announces that the commission's oversight of conditions in the Archdiocese of Seattle is ended. |

APPENDIX II: FIELD OF DOCUMENTS IDENTIFIED
AND DISTRIBUTION ACCORDING TO PRODUCER AND STAGE

Field of Document of Document Possibilities

A. Significant Documents From the Case As Identified by the Composite Source

Document	Identified in: Briggs	Reese	Granfield
Early Stage			
1. Hickey, Visitation Report (never made public)	x	x	
2. Ratzinger, Letter to Hunthausen with Visitation findings, dated September 30, 1985 (released by assessment commission on May 27, 1987)	x	x	
3. Laghi, Letter to Hunthausen with Visitation findings, dated November 14, 1985	x	x	x
4. Hunthausen, Letter to Laghi re. giving over faculties, dated December 2, 1985 (never made public)	x		
5. Laghi, Announcement of Wuerl's appointment, released December 3, 1985	x		
6. Gantin, Letter to Hunthausen re. Wuerl's faculties, (date of letter unknown; received by Hunthausen on July 1, 1986)	x		
Middle Stage			
7. Hunthausen, Public announcement of Wuerl's faculties, released September 3, 1986	x	x	x
8. Wuerl, Letter to priests of Archdiocese, dated September 19, 1986	x		
9. Laghi, Vatican Chronology, released October 24, 1986	x	x	x
10. Hunthausen, Response to Vatican Chronology, released November 12, 1986	x	x	x
11. Hunthausen, Address to NCCB, released November 12, 1986	x	x	x
12. Malone, Statement at NCCB meeting, released November 12, 1986	x		x
13. Laghi, Announcement of Commission appointment, released February 9, 1987	x		x
Late Stage			
14. Laghi, Announcement, Vatican accepts Commission Report, released May 27, 1987			x
15. Commission, Assessment Report, released May 27, 1987	x	x	x
16. Hunthausen, Announcement of Murphy's appointment, released May 27, 1987	x		
17. Hunthausen, Statement accepting Commission Report, Released May 27, 1987	x		

B. Documents Identified by Other Sources

Document	Source
Early Stage	
1. Hunthausen, Open Letter to Seattle Catholics announcing Visitation, dated October 26, 1983	*The Progress* (27 Oct. 1983), *Origins* (10 Nov. 1983)
2. Ratzinger, Letter to Hunthausen announcing Vatican reception of Visitation Report, dated December 12, 1983	*The Progress* (26 Jan. 1984)
3. Hunthausen, Statement accompanying release of	*The Progress* (26 Jan. 1984)

Ratzinger letter of December 12, 1983. Undated,
Published in *The Progress* on January 26, 1984.

4. Hunthausen, Letter to Ratzinger re. Visitation
findings, dated March 14, 1984 (never made public)

Ratzinger Letter (30 Sept. 1985)

5. Hunthausen, Letter to Pro-Nuncio re. appointment
of auxiliary bishop, dated September 11, 1985
(never made public)

Vatican Chronology

6. Hunthausen, Open Letter to Seattle Catholics
accompanying release of Nov. 14, 1985 Laghi Letter.
Hunthausen's open letter appears in Nov. 26, 1985
issue of *The Progress*.

The Progress (26 Nov. 1985)

7. Hunthausen, Press Statement re. Wuerl's appointment
as Auxiliary Bishop of Seattle, December 3, 1985

The Progress (5 Dec. 1985)

8. Wuerl, Press Statement re. his appointment as
Auxiliary Bishop, December 3, 1985

The Progress (5 Dec. 1985)

9. Laghi, Letter to Hunthausen confirming that
Hunthausen was to have given Wuerl special
faculties, dated July 1, 1986 (never made public)

Hunthausen Letter (9 Sept. 1986)

Middle Stage

10. Hunthausen, Letter to priests of Archdiocese re.
Wuerl's special faculties, dated September 3, 1986

Fr. Michael G. Ryan provided copy

11. Hunthausen, Open letter to Seattle Catholics re.
Wuerl's special faculties, released
September 11, 1986

The Progress (11 Sept. 1986)

12. Public Affairs Office of the Seattle Archdiocese,
Chronology of the Visitation, released
September 11, 1986

The Progress (11 Sept. 1986),
Origins (18 Sept. 1986)

13. Wuerl, Letter to priests of Archdiocese re. power-
sharing arrangement, dated September 19, 1986

The Progress (25 Sept. 1986),
Origins (9 Oct. 1986)

14. Hunthausen, Letter to chancery staff re. leadership
of archdiocese, dated September 22, 1986

Wasden Price collection

15. Bishops of Region XII (Northwestern U.S.),
Statement on Seattle situation,
Released September 22, 1986

The Progress (25 Sept. 1986)

16. Hunthausen, Open Letter to Seattle Catholics re.
recent events in Archdiocese,
released October 16, 1986

The Progress (16 Oct.1986),
Origins (6 Nov. 1986)

17. Hunthausen, Press Statement offering first response to
Vatican Chronology, released October 27, 1986

The Progress (30 Oct. 1986)
Origins (6 Nov. 1986)

18. Hunthausen, Press Statement in Response to Malone
Statement of November 12, 1986,
released November 12, 1986

The Progress (20 Nov. 1986)

19. Bishop Nicholas Walsh (Bishop Emeritus of Yakima,
Washington and former Auxiliary Bishop of Seattle),
Newspaper article recounting his decision to make a
recent trip to Rome to offer assistance in Hunthausen
case, published November 20, 1986

The Progress (20 Nov. 1986)

20. Laghi, Letters to O'Connor, Bernardin and Quinn
appointing them to ad hoc Commission,
dated January 26, 1987 (never made public)

The Progress (12 February 1987)

Late Stage

21. Commission, Letter to U.S. Bishops accompanying
its assessment report, dated May 25, 1987

The Progress (28 May 1987)

22. Murphy, Press Statement re. his appointment as
Coadjutor Archbishop of Seattle,
released May 27, 1986

The Progress (28 May 1987)

23. Wuerl, Press Statement re. his reassignment,
released May 27, 1986

The Progress (28 May 1987)

24. Bernardin, Press Statement re. resolution of Seattle
situation, released May 27, 1986.

National Catholic Reporter (5 June 1987)

25. Laghi, Announcement of completion of work of assessment commission, released April 11, 1989.
26. Hunthausen, statement acknowledging completion of work of assessment commission, released April 11, 1989.

Archdiocese of Seattle, Inter-office memorandum (11 April 1989), Wasden Price collection
Archdiocese of Seattle, Inter-office memorandum (11 April 1989), Wasden Price collection

Distribution of Documents According to Producer and Conflict Stage when Produced
Letter-number combinations below refer to lists A and B above.

	Early Stage	**Middle Stage**	**Late Stage**
Center Party	**A2**, **A3**, A5, *A6*, B2, *B9*	**A9**, **A13**, *B20*	A14, B25
Periphery Party	*A4*, B1, B3, *B4*, *B5*, B6, B7	**A7**, **A10**, **A11**, B10, B11, B12, B14, B16, B17, B18	A16, A17, B26
Third Party	*A1*, B8	A8, **A12**, B13, B15, B19	**A15**, B21, B22, B23, 24

Key: **Bold** = Document selected for comprehensive analysis
Underline = Document selected for control analysis
Italics = Document not available to public

APPENDIX III: TEXTS OF PRIMARY DOCUMENTS SELECTED FOR ANALYSIS

Document Number: 1
Document Title: Ratzinger Letter (9.30.85) Summarizing Visitation Findings
Source: *Origins*, 6/4/87, p. 41; *The Progress*, 5/28/87, p. 5.

Your Excellency,

I am writing to bring to a close the Apostolic Visitation process, which was assisted by the visit of Archbishop James Hickey of Washington, D.C., to the Archdiocese of Seattle from November 2-8, 1983.

Prior to that visit, both significant criticism and considerable praise had been directed toward your own pastoral ministry and that of your collaborators in Seattle. To quote from this Congregation's own October 4, 1983 letter to you, "It was precisely because it did not want to give uncritical acceptance to the published and private criticisms made about the Archdiocese of Seattle, that the Holy See has undertaken this project." Toward that end, the Visitor conferred with at least sixty-seven members of the clergy, religious and laity. In addition, he examined many pertinent documents, statements issued by the Archdiocese, and letters. Principally, though, Archbishop Hickey spent some four to five hours of intense discussion with you. That interview, taped and transcribed, was later reviewed by you and approved. Archbishop Hickey, with a model sense of cooperation and collegial concern, filed a lengthy and exhaustively documented report with this Congregation, and with that his involvement with the Apostolic Visitation process ended.

After a careful review of the entire body of testimony and of other materials as well, this Congregation is now in a position to make the following observations, which we hope will be received by you in the spirit in which they are offered and will be of assistance to you as Archbishop of Seattle.

1. There are many indications that you have striven with heart and mind to be a good bishop of the Church, eager to implement the renewal called for in the decrees of the Vatican Council. You have worked zealously to bring into existence the various consultative bodies promoted by the Council and mandated by the recently revised Code of Canon Law. Numerous people spoke of your laudable and conscientious efforts to involve the laity in the work of the Church and you have sought diligently to be open and accessible to your people. You have been repeatedly described as a man of gospel values, sensitive to the needs of the suffering and the aggrieved. Your concern for justice and peace is well known. Time and time again you have given clear evidence of your loyalty to the Church and you devotion and obedience to the Holy Father.

2. It is also true that you and those who assist you have suffered from exaggerated criticism and routine misunderstanding. Our observations are based neither on the complaints of your more strident critics nor on publications that are obviously biased. Nor do we wish to encourage extremist groups who are wholly lacking in a spirit of cooperation and seek to destroy or suppress whatever is not to their liking. It is our intention, rather, to support what you have done to promote the renewal of the Church in Seattle and to point out, at the same time, areas which we consider are in need of correction and improvement.

3. It is with this background of your own commitment to the real service of the Lord and the authentic renewal of his people that this Congregation wishes to outline these problems and to enlist your cooperation in resolving them.

4. It appears that there has been a rather widespread practice of admitting divorced persons to a subsequent Church marriage without prior review by your Tribunal or even after they have received a negative sentence. Catholics have been advised that after divorce and civil remarriage they may return to the Sacraments. Such a practice lacks foundation in the Church's clear teaching about the indissolubility of a sacramental marriage after consummation, and in sound jurisprudence. A clear presentation, then of the sacramentality and indisssolubility of Christian marriage should be made to all your people. Every effort must be made to avoid written materials which equivocate regarding the essential properties of marriage and which may encourage the divorced to attempt a second marriage without the Tribunal's declaration of nullity. At the same time, steps need to be taken to ensure that your Metropolitan Tribunal, both in its constitution and practice, conforms with all the prescriptions of the revised Code of the Church's public law.

5. A number of other basic doctrinal problems can be identified. While it is impossible to judge how widespread they are, and although they may seem to be abstract, they too often have had real implications and concrete effects in the day-to-day life of the Church in Seattle.

a. It is important that clear and firm guidance be offered to those in the Archdiocese who seem reluctant to accept the Magisterium as capable of giving definitive direction in matters of faith and morals.

b. It is important that the nature and mission of the Church be taught in their entirety. The Church should be understood as more than a merely social entity, governed chiefly by psychological, sociological and political processes. When it is viewed this way, its institutional or visible dimension is placed in opposition to its divine origin, mission and authority. Such a view misunderstands the meaning of the Church and destroys all prospects of the authentic renewal for which Vatican II so clearly called.

c. Incorrect notions of the Church's mission and nature, as well as flawed understandings of the dignity of the human person, can frequently be traced to faulty Christologies. It is imperative that every effort be made to ensure that the Church's integral faith concerning Christ be handed on: his divinity, his humanity, his salvific mission, his inseparable union with and Lordship over the Church.

d. Vigorous efforts must be made to engender in priests, religious and laity a correct appreciation of the sacramental structure of the Church, especially as it provides for sacred ministry in the Sacrament of Holy Orders. An effective seminary program needs to be established which inculcates in candidates for the priesthood an understanding of the sacraments as the Lord's gifts to His Church. While efforts to encourage the laity to fulfill their apostolate and assume their proper roles in the Church should continue, the unique ministry and office of the Bishop, as well as that of priests who assist him, must never be obscured.

e. A critical re-examination of policies and programs of the Archdiocese should be conducted to ensure that they are based on the clear vision of the human person which is at the heart of the Gospel message. An anthropology which is dominated by the tentative conclusions of the human sciences could well undermine many pastoral initiatives, however well intentioned.

f. There is a need to correct misunderstandings concerning the role which conscience plays in making moral decisions. In particular, it is necessary to highlight the valid claim on the Catholic conscience which is made by the authoritative teaching of the Church.

In all these areas it is vitally important to consult with competent, faithful theologians, clergy and religious to determine how best to proclaim the Church's entire deposit of faith in our changing times.

When guided by an authentic theological method such efforts are not only not in conflict with the teaching of the Church, they are a faithful response of her constant call to vindicate the rights of the poor.

It is also important that the faith be imparted in such a way which is sensitive to the suffering and the powerless.

No bishop should hesitate to overrule advisers who propose opinions at variance with the authentic teaching of the Holy See. At the same time, he must seek ways to hand on that teaching convincingly.

6. As per your letter of March 14, 1984, we realize that you have taken steps to correct the practice of contraceptive sterilization which had been followed in local Catholic hospitals. Such procedures are clearly and explicitly forbidden in all Catholic institutions. The clear moral teaching contained in this Congregation's 1976 Declaration on Sexual Ethics, as well as the teaching found in the documents of the U.S. Bishops' Conference must be maintained in an effective manner.

7. In matters of pastoral practice, first Confession should precede first Communion. This decision, which terminates any authorized experimentation, was incorporated in c. 914 of the revised Code. Accordingly, the sequence of first Confession prior to first Communion is not optional, nor can a custom to the contrary be established.

8. Similarly, the use of general Absolution must be strictly limited to the conditions listed in the relevant documents of the Holy See and in particular in c. 961 par. 1. The fact that many penitents would naturally congregate at times of great feasts, Christmas and Easter for example, would not of itself constitute the necessary condition that they would be deprived of the grace of the sacrament for a long time if general absolution were not given. Responsible supervision on the part of the office for Liturgy is indicated.

9. Likewise, the attention of the clergy and faithful should be drawn to the fact that non-Catholic Christians may be admitted occasionally to communion in the Catholic Church under specific conditions as listed in c. 844 par. 4, and in the related documents of the Holy See on this question. Catholics, however, are permitted in some cases to receive the Eucharist in non-Catholic churches, but only in those whose sacraments are recognized by the Catholic Church, as is clear from c. 844, par. 2.

The Catholic Church believes the Eucharist to be a sign of unity already achieved. Routine intercommunion on the occasion of weddings or funerals, wherever it is the practice, should be recognized as clearly abusive and an impediment to genuine ecumenism.

10. Efforts to encourage full and lively participation in the sacred liturgy should be fostered. However, practices which are not in accord with the Roman Sacramentary and the related directives of the Holy See should be eliminated. The appointment of a carefully trained priest to aid in the supervision of sacramental and liturgy discipline is indicated here as well.

11. Concern for priests who have left the ministry is obviously a duty of a bishop, but he must always be aware of the Church's discipline. Laicized priests are excluded from performing certain roles, as amply described in their rescripts of laicization. The status of priests who have left the ministry but who have not been laicized must be recognized as much more irregular, and they can hardly be employed formally or informally by the Church in any way. The same applies for their civilly married wives.

12. It has been noted that in 1976 and in 1979, the Archdiocese of Seattle devised questionnaires to obtain information useful for the formation and conduct of Archdiocesan programs. Some, unfortunately, understood these questionnaires to be a kind of voting process on doctrinal or moral teachings. The questionnaire did reveal certain deficient doctrinal understandings and the results point to the need for a more careful and extensive

catechesis both for children and adults.

13. With regard to the role of women in the Church, the teaching of the Church regarding their God-given dignity and importance should be given full weight. The current fierce politicization of this issue must not impede the Church's efforts to vindicate the rights of all. The exclusion of women from Sacred Orders was dealt with at length in this Congregation's 1975 Instruction, *Inter Insigniores* and should be explained unambiguously.

14. A final question of pastoral practice pertains to ministry to homosexual men and women. The Archdiocese should withdraw all support from any group which does not unequivocally accept the teaching of the Magisterium concerning the intrinsic evil of homosexual activity. This teaching has been set forth in this Congregation's *Declaration on Sexual Ethics* and more recently in the document, *Educational Guidance in Human Love*, issued by the Congregation for Catholic Education in 1983. The ill-advised welcome of a pro-homosexual group to your cathedral, as well as events subsequent to the Apostolic Visitation, have served to make the Church's position appear to be ambiguous on this delicate but important issue. A compassionate ministry to homosexual persons must be developed that has as its clear goal the promotion of a chaste life-style. Particular care is to be exercised by any who represent the Archdiocese, to explain clearly the position of the Church on this question.

In bringing all the above points to your attention, it has been our purpose to assist you as effectively as possible in your offices as Archbishop of Seattle. We commend you for your kindness and patience during the Apostolic Visit and during the many months needed by the Holy See for careful review and appropriate action.

May the Holy Spirit of Christ be with you and with His people whom you serve.

With my own best wishes, I am

Sincerely yours in the Lord,

Joseph Cardinal Ratzinger
Prefect

[For text of document 2, see appendix iv, below.]

Document Number: 3
Document Title: Hunthausen Press Statement Announcing Wuerl Special Faculties
Source: *Origins* 9/18/86, pp. 250-251.

I am aware that for quite some time speculation has taken place, both in printed form and in less formal ways, regarding the roles and responsibilities of Bishop Donald Wuerl. His appointment here shortly after the formal conclusion of the apostolic visitation made it inevitable that people would wonder whether, in appointing him as my auxiliary, the Holy See had intended for him to have some specific additional responsibilities with reference to the findings and conclusions of the visitation. As a matter of fact, it did; but at the time of his appointment both Bishop Wuerl and I, along with the apostolic pro-nuncio, judged it best to make no public announcement to that effect. The importance of making Bishop Wuerl's transition to the archdiocese as smooth as possible and of assuring him of the best possible climate for beginning this ministry among us seemed to outweigh any possible good that might have been realized by giving a full public acknowledgement of all the specifications surrounding his appointment as auxiliary bishop.

However, at the time of his appointment, I did not understand the nature and extent of Bishop Wuerl's role. After considerable discussion with the Holy See, it was confirmed that it was the understanding of the Holy See in December 1985 when appointing Bishop Wuerl that he not only assist me by assuming a general oversight for these five areas (identified in the apostolic visitation), but that he actually be delegated by me to have complete and final decision-making power over them. The clarification of this decision took lace in June at the Collegeville (Minn.) meeting of bishops, where I met with the apostolic pro-nuncio. It was subsequently confirmed to me in a letter dated July 1, 1986.

Once I received this clarification, I not only took steps to carry out the wishes of the Holy See, but also arrived at the conclusion that it was important for me to share these matters with my close collaborators in the ministry and administration of the archdiocese.

Document Number: 4
Document Title: The Vatican Chronology
Source: *The Progress*, 10/30/86, pp. 2-4; *Origins*, 11/6/86, pp.362-364.

A CHRONOLOGY OF RECENT EVENTS IN THE ARCHDIOCESE OF SEATTLE

1) **Decision for an Apostolic Visitation of Seattle**

   a) For the past several years, at least since 1978, the Holy See, through the then Apostolic Delegation, has corresponded with Archbishop Hunthausen on matters related to pastoral practices and the presentation of the church's teachings. Through this exchange the Holy See sought the assistance of the Archbishop of Seattle in responding to the high volume of complaints that were sent to Rome by priests, Religious and faithful in the archdiocese. The Holy See's interest in this matter reflected its responsibility for the well-being of the Universal Church, as outlined in the "Constitution on the Church" of the Second Vatican Council. It should be stressed that at no time did the Holy See pursue with Archbishop Hunthausen the criticisms it received on controversial issues, e.g., nuclear weapons and the payment of taxes. The concerns were strictly and solely of a doctrinal and pastoral nature.

   b) The archbishop agreed that there were abuses in a number of cases and that corrective action was needed. In fairness to Archbishop Hunthausen, he did address some of the problems brought to his attention by the Holy See.

   c) Substantial complaints nevertheless continued. But, the decision to inquire further was primarily provoked by the documented responses of the archbishop himself. Moreover, in expressing their fraternal concern for Archbishop Hunthausen and the church in Seattle, certain bishops suggested that there was a need to "clear the air." Prominent among their recommendations was the appointment of a brother bishop to visit Archbishop Hunthausen and the church in Seattle in order to gather factual information on behalf of the Holy See. Accordingly, on July 6, 1983, the Most Reverend James A. Hickey, Archbishop of Washington, was named Apostolic Visitator.

2) **Preparation of the Apostolic Visitation:**

   a) From the beginning the priorities of the Holy See were two-fold: 1) to promote the building up of the church in Seattle in harmony with the Universal Church and 2) to protect the good name of Archbishop Hunthausen. Consequently, it was determined that publicity would be kept to a minimum, so as to avoid fostering criticism of the archbishop. Furthermore, it was the firm intention of the Holy See that any action required would come only after fully informing Archbishop Hunthausen and making every effort to secure his agreement and support.

   b) Before Archbishop Hickey began the Apostolic Visitation, he consulted with Archbishop Hunthausen both in a long telephone conversation and in a day-and-a-half meeting in Chicago. Both the procedure and the various doctrinal and pastoral aspects were reviewed in detail. Many of those who had lodged complaints against Archbishop Hunthausen had sent him copies of their letters to the Holy See and / or spoke to him personally. Archbishop Hickey discussed these persons with Archbishop Hunthausen and asked for an evaluation of the authenticity of their remarks and their reliability. The visitator also asked Archbishop Hunthausen's help in drawing up a list of persons to be questioned. Archbishop Hickey stressed his desire to gain a balanced view of the archdiocesan situation, the positive as well as the negative.

   c) Archbishop Hunthausen insisted that a public announcement be made about the visitation. Once this was done, the statements of Archbishop Hickey were designed to offer support and advice to Archbishop Hunthausen in accord with the initial and constant wish of the Holy See.

3) **The Visitation:**

   a) Information was gathered from the following sources:

   1) Public documents such as archdiocesan policy statements on matters dealing with church teaching and discipline.

   2) The testimony given by those on the list prepared in advance. This was done through consultation with Archbishop Hunthausen and Reverend Michael G. Ryan, vicar general of the Archdiocese of Seattle, so that a cross section of the priests, Religious and laity in the archdiocese would be represented. In all, this included 70 individuals, nearly one half of whom were priests of the archdiocese.

   3) The testimony of the archbishop himself, a written copy of which he reviewed and signed. It should be noted that the visitator spent 13 hours in conversation with Archbishop Hunthausen. Every effort was made to assess the credibility of the persons who had complained to the Holy See.

   b) Throughout the investigation a number of allegations were judged as insufficiently based in fact or as corrected by an adequate response of Archbishop Hunthausen. However, after careful attention was given to the facts verified by the three sources of information noted above, five areas of concern remained: the tribunal, liturgy, clergy formation, priests leaving the ministry or who are laicized, moral issues in health care institutions and ministry to homosexuals. The testimony of "unfriendly" witnesses added little to the data on which the criticism of the Holy See was based.

In more specific terms the problems included the following:

- The Tribunal – the misunderstanding and systematic misapplication of the so-called internal forum solution, and the lack of a plan to employ degreed personnel in the Tribunal.
- The Liturgy – the widespread use of general absolution on a regular basis and the practice of First Communion before First Confession; repeated instances of intercommunion, e.g., permitting non-Catholics to receive communion at Catholic Masses and Catholics in Protestant services.
- Health Care – the continued inadequate response in both teaching and practice to the directives of the Holy See and the National Conference of Catholic Bishops regarding contraceptive sterilization in Catholic hospitals.
- Homosexuals – the need to develop a ministry to homosexuals that is at once unequivocally based on the teachings of the Magisterium, rather than on erroneous doctrines, and which avoids affiliations with groups promoting doctrines contrary to the church's teachings.
- Inactive Priests – the employment of those who have left the active ministry and / or who have been laicized, in teaching positions and for the service in the liturgy contrary to the directives of the Holy See and the rescripts of laicization.
- Clergy Formation – because of concern regarding the admissions practices for candidates for the priesthood and because of concern and questions surrounding the continuing formation of the clergy, efforts must be taken to ensure that the continuing education of priests be done in ways that emphasize the bonds of the local church with the Universal Church, and which are firmly rooted in sound theology, especially in these areas: Christology, Anthropology, the Role of the Magisterium, the Nature of the Church and Priesthood and Moral Theology.

c) After hearing a preliminary report on the visitation, Archbishop Hunthausen concluded that the Holy See judged him to be an effective bishop in many respects. At the same time, Archbishop Hunthausen understood that the Holy See considered him lacking the necessary firmness to govern the archdiocese. The archbishop would dissent from such a judgment, but stated in a letter to the pronuncio (Sept. 11, 1985) that "if it (the judgment) has been made, then I can perhaps begin to understand why the Holy See might reason that the only workable solution to this matter is the appointment of a man to assist me whose principal responsibilities will be to supply or 'fill in' in those areas where it is thought that I am lacking."

4) The Decisions after the Visitation:

a) On Oct. 9 and 10, 1985, the results of the visitation were again shared with Archbishop Hunthausen in extensive consultation with the Apostolic Nunciature. It should be noted that the actual raw data from the interviews were not released to him given the confidentiality assured to those who provided the information. However, the specific areas of concern to the Holy See were reviewed in detail and the archbishop was given the possibility to offer a response and seek clarification. In large numbers he did not dispute the facts. Rather, it was his interpretation of the importance of these matters and the inadequacy of his response that were the principal concerns.

b) Before his request for an auxiliary was granted, consideration was given to a number of ways that another bishop could be of assistance in addressing the five problem areas, e.g., the appointment of a co-adjutor with full power, the temporary appointment of an administrator, the appointment of an auxiliary with special faculties from the Holy See. In considering the alternative, the Holy See gave careful attention to the effects that any decision would have on the church and the Archbishop of Seattle.

c) The Code of Canon Law (canon 403:2) does contemplate cases when the Holy See grants special faculties. However, upon the recommendation of members of the hierarchy in the United States, it was agreed that Archbishop Hunthausen, after accepting the auxiliary, would himself give Bishop Wuerl responsibility over the areas of particular concern to the Holy See. This compromise, which the archbishop formally accepted in a letter dated Dec. 2, 1985, was not to lessen the significance of those special faculties. Rather, it allowed the archbishop to follow a procedure analogous or similar to that used by other diocesan bishops, who share authority with auxiliaries in areas or over a territory. Simultaneously, the Archbishop of Seattle did acknowledge that the Holy See could reserve to itself, in an uncontested way, the right to adopt such measures as may subsequently become necessary. At no time did the Holy See require Archbishop Hunthausen to make a public announcement that he had agreed to surrender any episcopal duties. This was never contemplated.

d) For more than six months after the arrival of Bishop Wuerl, the agreed-to faculties were not given. When this was brought to the attention of Archbishop Hunthausen, he stated that, in his original understanding, he agreed that the auxiliary would supervise or manage these areas of concern as he, the archbishop, determined. This could be attributed to a misunderstanding or misinterpretation on his part. The pronuncio, therefore, reminded him of the sequence of events that led to the compromise. The faculties, which were originally to be given by Rome, would be given instead by him as archbishop, but with the same effect. The Archbishop of

Seattle then petitioned the Holy See for an authoritative clarification.

e) When this was given, the Archbishop of Seattle granted the faculties and made the announcement that they were mandated by Rome. In fact, a more precise description would have been that this was the agreement reached between Archbishop Hunthausen and the Holy See after much discussion and effort to support him. Regretfully, the surprise announcement made by Archbishop Hunthausen after granting the faculties was interpreted as portraying this whole process as a one-sided affair.

f) The efforts made by the Holy See after the visitation were designed to address and strengthen those areas that were found wanting, and at the same time, to respect and recognize the position of the archbishop. Meeting these goals required the corresponding cooperation of the Holy See, of the man who was selected and accepted as auxiliary, and of the Archbishop of Seattle.

October 24, 1986

Document Number: 5
Document Title: Hunthausen's Detailed Response to the Vatican Chronology
Source: *The Progress*, 11/13/86, pp. 15-16; *Origins*, 11/20/86, pp. 406-408.

Your Eminence / Your Excellency:

Because of necessary time restrictions limiting my presentation about the Apostolic Visitation of the Archdiocese of Seattle and related matters, I have decided it will be best for me to convey to you in printed form my response to the "Chronology of Recent Events in the Archdiocese of Seattle," released on October 24, 1986, by the Apostolic Nunciature.

As you know, I chose to make a generic response at the time the Chronology was released. My respect for Archbishop Laghi and for the position that is his made it difficult for me to do otherwise. I was convinced that a point-by-point response at that time would only have escalated an already tense situation and that it would cause further confusion for our people. Also, I had been offered by Bishop Malone, our President, the opportunity to present a further response at this meeting.

I hesitate to burden you with further reading material at this time. I do so only because I think the record demands it and because, from my perspective at least, what follows will shed light on an extremely complex situation.

I want to say, too, that it frankly embarrasses me to be engaging in this form of exchange of information. I have the greatest respect and admiration for Archbishop Laghi and appreciate his time and efforts to resolve this matter. I trust you will understand, then, that the matters which I will set forth herein are in no sense an attack upon his person or his integrity. That our recollections and interpretations differ in some important respects should not be so surprising when one considers that we are both attempting to present in capsule form a very long and complicated series of events.

In the first place, it is probably important for you to know that, after I first read the Chronology, I asked Archbishop Laghi not to publish it because I felt it would raise more questions than it could possibly hope to answer. I feared it would generate a whole new round of publicity in a setting in which accusations and counter-accusations rather than the voices of reason would dominate and that, in the minds of many, it would ultimately reflect unfavorably on the Holy See, the very thing both Archbishop Laghi and I had striven to avoid all during this time.

From the very outset of these events, which now go back some three-and-one-half years, I have been concerned about adverse publicity for the Holy See. I expressed this concern in my earliest correspondence and in all my correspondence with the Holy See, with Cardinal Ratzinger, Archbishop Laghi, Archbishop Hickey, and even with the Holy Father himself. It was always my deepest desire and my strongly expressed wish that, whatever steps might be taken to address certain concerns in Seattle, that they be taken in a way that would strengthen and cement our relationship with the Holy See, and not in any sense detract from it.

As far as the Chronology itself is concerned, let me say that I believe it either attempts to do too much (i.e., to tell the whole story in too brief a space), or to do too little (by that I mean that it doesn't really get to some of the deep, underlying problems which are at stake here).

As to particulars which are set forth in the Chronology, I must say that I find that the Chronology contains some misleading things, some things that were quite new to me, some rather disappointing things and some very real inaccuracies. I will address each of these four headings in sequence.

1) **The Chronology contains some misleading things:**

For example: reference is made early on to "substantial complaints" against my teaching or with regard to certain pastoral practices in the Archdiocese of Seattle. My observation is that if there were substantial complaints I was never told who made them or who substantiated them and on what basis. Nor was I told till considerably after the Visitation was decided upon and announced to me, (and then in only the most generic manner) what *some* of those complaints were.

The Chronology goes on to indicate that certain responses I myself gave to inquiries were primary among the causes that led to the decision to mount a Visitation. That may be so. But I would have to state clearly (and our files certainly bear this out) that if certain responses I provided to inquiries made by the Holy See – some of them as far back as 1978 – were viewed as unsatisfactory, then I must ask why I was never informed of this fat as the time I made those responses. Why, instead, was I politely and routinely thanked for the information I provided only to hear nothing further at all until the major decision was made that only an Apostolic Visitation could set matters straight in Seattle. So, for anyone to review that correspondence now and suggest that it was the cause of the Visitation troubles me greatly.

Another misleading point: the Chronology states that at the time I announced the granting of special faculties to Bishop Wuerl I indicated that they were "mandated by the Rome" when, in fact, a more precise description would have been that this was the "agreement" reached between the Holy See and myself. As a matter of fact, in my letter to our priests and people, I made no reference to a "mandate from Rome." I spoke only of carrying out "the wishes of the Holy See," which was manifestly what was at stake here. That I "agreed" to go along with those wishes is clear, too, although I did not do so with any sense of freedom since the consequences of my not agreeing to do so had been made clear to me on more than one occasion.

2) The Chronology contained some new learnings:

From the Chronology, I learned for the first time that the problem with our formation program for seminarians (we have no seminary in Seattle) had to do with the admissions practices followed by the Archdiocese. That was news to me. I had never before been told that. I also learned that the rather all-encompassing theological concerns (embracing such things as the relationship of the local Church to the Universal Church, the teaching of Christology and of a sound anthropology, the role of the Magisterium, the nature f the Church, of priesthood and moral theology) were apparently all concerns that related to the programs followed in the Archdiocese for the Continuing Education of our priests. I do not find this particularly enlightening since our priests are certainly orthodox on these matters and our education programs employ the same personnel and deal with the same themes as those of dozens of other dioceses in this country, but I do find it revealing to discover that this was the context for all those serious theological concerns which I first learned of last year at this time in a letter from Cardinal Ratzinger.

Whatever the case, it would have been helpful to have had this information during this past year when painstaking efforts were being made to understand the precise nature of Cardinal Ratzinger's concerns so that we could address them in a conscientious and responsible manner.

I would also have to say that it came as a surprise to me that I had been judged by the Holy See to lack the necessary firmness to govern the Archdiocese of Seattle. I had, of course, wondered out loud whether this might indeed have been the case. I had even speculated bout it openly in a letter to Archbishop Laghi, but while I had learned from him that I enjoyed no credibility whatever in Rome, I had never been told until the publication of the Chronology that the judgment has been made that I lacked the necessary firmness to govern my Archdiocese.

3) The Chronology contained some disappointing things:

I found very disappointing the intimation that in dealing with Bishop Wuerl and, specifically with regard to his special faculties, I did not carry out my promises, that I exhibited a certain intransigence, or even that I acted in bad faith. This is simply not true. The misunderstanding that came to light regarding the nature and extent of Bishop Wuerl's faculties was a genuine one. Indeed – and I don't say this in any sense to be self-serving or contentious – it is difficult for me to believe how anyone who was present to the conversations and who saw the correspondence could interpret it any way other than the way I did. From the start of the Visitation and all during the long process that took place with regard to the appointment of an Auxiliary Bishop, I had made certain things abundantly clear. Among them was the fact that I would gladly resign the Archdiocese should that be the wish of the Holy See or, of course, of the Holy Father himself.

Secondly, I made it clear that I would never carry out a public charade by pretending to be something I was not. I am just not constitutionally capable of that. In other words, if significant or substantial powers were to be taken away from me (and here it goes without saying that if final decision-making authority for critically important areas of Archdiocesan life and governance were to be taken from me), I would choose to resign rather than to stay on and pose as the Archbishop of Seattle when, in fact, I would scarcely be that except, perhaps, in some vague, legalistic, and rather meaningless sense. My thinking in this regard, incidentally, had nothing to do with any need I had to hold on to power. It had to do with my need for personal authenticity and my willingness to get out of the way entirely if it was perceived that I was the source of some grave problems in my Archdiocese. I always presented these convictions to Archbishop Laghi as matters of conscience for that is what they were. With him I tried to discern as best I could what was for the good of the Church.

In a crucial letter dated December 2, 1985, which I wrote to Archbishop Laghi, I agreed to give substantive authority without, however, relinquishing my ultimate authority. These are the words I used: "(this arrangement) will not impinge upon my ultimate authority as Ordinary of the archdiocese." I went on to quote the code of Canon Law to make the matter unmistakably clear. Archbishop Laghi's response stated: "While this does not lessen your authority as the local Bishop, it is understood that this action is being taken at the specific instruction of the Holy See." For this reason, it troubles me greatly not only that a great misunderstanding could have later ensued, one that in the end I was informed was mine, but also that it would later be suggested publicly that I might have acted in bad faith. I did not.

Perhaps it is at this point that I need to say a word about why in the end – this past July, to be exact – after the Holy See had given its decisive interpretation of the precise nature and extent of Bishop Wuerl's special faculties, I agreed to accept the arrangement, preferring the course of resignation to what would amount to pretending to be what, in fact, I was not. In the end, my very reluctant decision to remain as the Archbishop of Seattle was made on the basis of what several trusted brother bishops and close advisers convinced me would be for the ultimate good of the Church in the Archdiocese of Seattle.

4) The Chronology also contains some very real inaccuracies:

The Chronology speaks of my "insistence" that a public announcement be made at the time the Apostolic Visitation was undertaken. A more accurate statement would have referred to my earnest desire, expressed to Cardinal Ratzinger, Archbishop Laghi, and Archbishop Hickey that, if the Visitation did indeed have to take place, I would like it to do so in as open and positive and constructive a spirit as possible. I took this position because I honestly recognize the value in my own life of careful, objective evaluation, and because I felt that our priests and people were mature enough to deal with such a process, particularly if they understood and supported it – even welcomed it – as a step toward answering some of my more vocal critics and toward improving certain aspects of a Church which is *semper reformanda*. In addition, I repeatedly expressed my fear that to undertake a Visitation under the cloak of secrecy would be a mistake for at least two reasons: first, it would smack of a method of operating that was more characteristic of the pre-Vatican II Church than of the post-, and, second, it was clear to me that no amount f effort to maintain the curtain of secrecy would ever succeed, and that the embarrassment which would follow any disclosure by "leak" would be far greater than that which might accompany an open and honest disclosure from the start.

I made these points clear from the beginning, and I brought them personally to Cardinal Ratzinger during my 1983 *Ad Limina* visit. I even offered to personally and publicly invite him or his designees to come to the Archdiocese so that the onus for the Visitation would be on my shoulders. But my invitation and my point of view were not accepted. Secrecy was to be the rule, and I adhered to it.

As matters turned out, when the inevitable leak did come, it came not from Seattle but from the East Coast. Archbishop Hickey called to tell me about it and to say that, after consultation with Archbishop Laghi, he had decided that we needed to issue a news release that would be given out simultaneously in Washington, D.C., and Seattle. This is what, in fact, took place.

A second inaccuracy: the Chronology makes reference to my "surprise announcement" at the time I granted the Special Faculties to Bishop Wuerl, the implication being that I did something that was outside or contrary to prior agreement or understanding between myself and the Pro-Nuncio. The record will show, however, that I repeatedly made the point in my conversations and exchanges with Archbishop Laghi at Collegeville this past summer, that, in the then unlikely event that I would agree to accept the special faculties arrangement according to the manner in which they were being understood by the Holy See, I would have no choice but to make this matter known to all my priests and close collaborators since it would be absolutely essential for them to know to whom they were accountable and from whom they would receive orders and directives. I never left the slightest doubt about this matter since I knew that to have acted in any other way would have resulted in a chaotic situation with regard to the governance of the Archdiocese.

For this reason I am simply unable to understand how my subsequent announcement about the Special Faculties could have been the source of surprise for anyone who had been party to our conversations, or how it could be stated in the chronology that my actions had never "been contemplated." I also find it difficult to understand how anyone could ever have believed that keeping the Special Faculties a secret could possibly have worked in the first place. If nothing else, the early history of the Visitation to which I have just referred should have clearly indicated otherwise.

To the best of my ability, I have reflected on the contents of the Chronology and presented my understanding of events. Since there seems to be such a divergence of opinion between my understanding and interpretation and that set forth in the Chronology, I would certainly welcome some sort of review of all these matters should that be the wish of the members of the Conference.

In my oral presentation during the Executive Session, I will attempt to address these and other matters from a different perspective than that demanded by a response of this sort.

I am grateful to you for taking the time to read this rather tedious exposition. I sincerely hope that you have found it helpful.

With warm and personal regards, I am

Fraternally in Christ,

Raymond G. Hunthausen
Archbishop of Seattle

Document Number: 6
Document Title: Hunthausen's Address to the NCCB
Source: *The Progress*, 11/13/86, pp.11-13; *Origins*, 11/20/86, pp. 401-405

My Friends in Christ,

Once before I had the privilege of addressing this assembly. It was at the time we came together in our common quest for peace in a nuclear world. Today I come before you again in a quest for peace, but for a different kind of peace: peace for the Archdiocese of Seattle, peace for the Church in this country, peace within this Conference, peace for the Church throughout the world, and my own personal peace with the Holy See.

I want to tell you right at the outset that I am personally very distressed by all the turmoil that has come about in our Church because of what has transpired in Seattle. I wish it would all go away. How I wish that! And I want to tell you also that I am particularly distressed about any anguish or even division that may have come about among you, my brother bishops. If I could have done anything in good conscience to spare you this moment I would have.

Most of you probably know me well enough to realize that I do not accept the invitation to make a presentation this afternoon because I personally relish speaking in a forum like this. I accepted it only because I believe with all my heart, as I have from the very beginning, that in many respects the issues of the Seattle Visitation are not just issues that touch the life of the Church in Seattle: they are issues that touch the lives of each of our churches in one way or another to a greater or lesser degree. For that reason they are really our issues. In what I have to say I will try to show you why I believe this to be so.

In making this presentation, I have a number of hopes that will become clear as I proceed. One underlying hope is that you will come to understand that the Apostolic Visitation of the church of Seattle and its aftermath is not simply my own personal struggle, nor is it, as some have suggested, some sort of battle of wits between a maverick Archbishop and the Holy See. Those who suggest this do not really know me or my attitude toward the Church I love and try to serve. It is my hope that you will see the Apostolic Visitation of the church of Seattle as an ecclesial matter with serious theological implications which touch very directly and profoundly on our individual role as bishops and on our corporate responsibilities as members of the College of Bishops.

And let me acknowledge at the start that it is surely not mine to presume to lecture the members of this body on such subjects. Most of you know that I am not a professional theologian. Many of you know far more about these matters than I do and can surely articulate them better. Nonetheless the experience that has been mine over the past years can perhaps serve as something of a laboratory for viewing, studying, and probing the issues in some way other than the purely theoretical. If that be so, then I honestly believe that this sad experience which has been the source of such pain and confusion for the Church of Seattle and beyond – even to the point of causing serious scandal for some – will not have been in vain, but will have been a path to a new moment of life and growth.

You have already received in printed form my somewhat detailed response to the Chronology released by the Apostolic Nunciature. I put that response together in a respectful spirit – in the hope that it would answer some of the questions the Chronology may have raised in your minds. Obviously, it raised some in my own mind, but I suppose it should be expected that there would be differing perspectives in a matter such as this. In what follows I will refrain from making any further commentary on the Chronology itself and concentrate, rather, on four main areas:

1) The process used in deciding to conduct the Visitation as well as the process followed in carrying it out.

2) The five areas of my ministry singled out by the Holy See as areas of serious concern.

3) The identification of the important issues which this entire matter has brought to light.

4) Some thoughts and suggestions regarding the future.

I. First, the Visitation and its process. In my printed response I have already made reference to the Visitation Process and to my dissatisfaction with the manner in which the decision was made to undertake an Apostolic Visitation in the first place. I also alluded to the manner in which the Visitation was conducted and followed up on. Please know that my reference here is not a personal one with regard to Archbishop Hickey who carried out his duties as Visitator in a gracious and gentlemanly manner. My reference has to do with processes, not persons.

My printed remarks allude to the matter of secrecy that was intended to surround the Visitation. I need to tell you that in agreeing to that, I feel I compromised my principles as a Bishop committed to the deep and powerful reality that we are all the Church and that we can only live out our common call as members of the Body of Christ if we do so in a manner that respects the rightful role of each member of that Body, from child to mature and committed adult. I would hope that, in the future, if the weighty decision is made to undertake an Apostolic Visitation for the good of the Church, at least two lessons will have been drawn from this aspect of the Seattle experience: 1) that secrecy does not work in matters of this sort, and 2) that secrecy should not work. I realize that that is a value judgment. But it is a very considered one. And even though I acknowledge that in some extraordinary circumstances secrecy might be warranted, the presumption should nevertheless be against it because open disclosure and candor are far more consistent with respect for persons in a mature Church.

And secrecy in situations like this has further inimical effects: secrecy is responsible for the fact that there was a total absence of dialogue with me as to whether a Visitation was needed in the first place, and, if so, why and according to what specific ground rules. I was simply informed of the fact and given no opportunity whatever to object or even to respond. In other words, I was presented with a fait accompli.

Yet another consequence of secrecy has to do with the concerns which prompted the decision to undertake a Visitation in the first place. On the good advice of then President of this Conference, I asked at the very beginning for a Bill of Particulars specifying the reasons for mounting the Apostolic Visitation and the concerns to be talked over between Archbishop Hickey and any persons he might choose to interview. I was never given such a list. Rather I was told that it was not necessary because what was to take place was in no sense in the nature of a "trial," that the Visitor himself was in no sense a "judge," and that what was involved was nothing more than a thorough and fraternal exchange of views and information.

In place of a Bill of Particulars, I was formally questioned by Archbishop Hickey about a range of issues touching on matters both doctrinal and disciplinary, several of which were clearly based on simple misunderstandings or miscommunications of facts, others of which had already been dealt with in what I had been led to believe was a satisfactory manner, and one or two of which admittedly needed further attention on my part. It is important to remember, however, that all of this took place several months after the decision had *already been taken* to mount a full-scale Apostolic Visitation. From my point of view, had the kind of exchanges I had with Archbishop Hickey been allowed to take place before that decision had been made, a great deal of harm could have been avoided and the demands of justice would have been better served.

The shroud of secrecy spread even further – to what I have to regard as one of the most devastating points of all. I have never been allowed to see the formal Visitation report including the testimony against me and the appraisal made by Archbishop Hickey. All the witnesses were placed under secrecy, not just guaranteed confidentiality. And, of course, once that stricture was made, it had to be respected. I must state emphatically, however, that such unwitnessed, private questionings with no opportunity for the subject of the questionings to face his accusers, or hear or to be informed of their allegations, or to defend himself are not a just manner of proceeding. This kind of approach seriously wounds the community of faith and trust that is the Church. The allegations, findings, judgments and conclusions made during the Visitation must surely be contained in a formal report, yet no matter how many times I have asked, I have never been allowed to see that report. Instead, I have been left with some generalities and a few particulars received in subsequent letters from the Holy See, conversations with the Pro-Nuncio and, later, from comments appended to the Special Faculties I was directed to give to Bishop Wuerl. To this I would have to add that each time a conversation has taken place, or a letter or document issued, I seem to have learned something new, something which, I presume, must have appeared in the Visitation Report in one form or another, but which I was prevented from seeing for reasons still unknown to me. In my printed response to the Chronology I have already alluded to some very recent learnings, so I will not dwell on them any further at this point.

My brothers, I hope that I have reported enough o make clear why I feel that the Visitation was so badly flawed from the very start, not, as I have said, due to bad faith on anyone's part but due to a process that seems extraordinarily inadequate given the kind of open Church we have become since the Second Vatican Council.

Before I proceed any further, there is still one more note that needs to be added here. It has to do with the assurance I was given from the very beginning that nothing punitive was envisioned by the Visitation, only a fraternal exchange of views for the purpose of gaining better information and understanding. Nonetheless, the action taken as a result of the Visitation could hardly be interpreted as anything other than punitive and, indeed, a recent public statement issued by a Vatican official in this regard made specific reference to the fact that the action taken as a result of the Visitation was meant to be "disciplinary." If this be the case, and I have no doubt whatsoever that it is, I have to wonder why certain formal Church processes were not followed, processes that would have better guaranteed the rights of all concerned. I have to wonder, too, why this change of attitude and intent was not communicated to me much more directly.

Perhaps from all I have said, you will now begin to understand the level of confusion and anger that exists among the priests of the Archdiocese as well as among all the ranks of the faithful. That this confusion and anger should have heated up and even ignited to the point that it has spread to many areas of our country at this moment is not surprising to me. Nor, perhaps will it be to you. But it is surely distressing because, as I have maintained from the very first, it need not have happened this way.

II. Let me now pass on to those five areas of concern which finally became enshrined in the Special Faculties I was directed to give to Bishop Wuerl. I will deal with these concerns under four headings for the purpose of clarity, but you should understand that some of them overlap a bit, especially that of "pastoral judgment," something that was involved in nearly every case. The four headings under which I will deal with the concerns are these: 1) matters of history (i.e., matters already addressed); 2) matters of pastoral judgment; 3) ongoing concerns; 4) matters I do not understand.

Let me begin with those that are **matters of history**. Under that heading I would include the issue of some confusion that existed at one time in the Archdiocese with regard to the use of the so-called Internal Forum solution; the lack of a plan to employ degreed personnel in the Archdiocesan Tribunal; and the practice of one hospital of the Archdiocese permitting sterilization even for contraceptive purposes in some limited cases. For the record, the teaching of the Church in this matter was never under question, only a long-standing pastoral practice at one hospital, a practice that pre-dated my arrival in Seattle.) I can honestly say that none of the above listed problems exists in the Archdiocese of Seattle today. They haven't for some years now.

Others of the concerns come under the heading of **pastoral judgment**, something I scarcely need to tell you that every pastor comes to recognize early on in his ministry as a rather imprecise "science" at best, even when carried out prayerfully under the guidance of the Holy Spirit and with every due regard for Church Tradition and Law. We all know well that matters of pastoral judgment are always open to further understanding and that in such matter we never really get beyond the possibility of making a mistake no matter how hard we try to faithfully discern the Spirit. Among such pastoral judgments for which I have not only been called to task but deprived of my Episcopal responsibilities are the allowing of general absolution when the crowds of the faithful are so very large, the numbers of available confessors so very small, and the opportunity for providing suitable opportunities for the worthy celebration of the Sacrament of Reconciliation for each of these people so demonstrably distant that general absolution seemed a prudent decision for the pastor on the spot to make.

Another is the practice of preparing children for First Communion before undertaking the formal, structured catechesis for First Confession – a practice we have for some time been studying in light of the Revised Code of Canon Law and in dialogue with many other dioceses and archdioceses. Now that directives are clear, I am committed to implementing them in fidelity to Church Law, but this will have to be done in a pastorally sensitive manner.

Still another area has to do with the matter of ministry to homosexuals, something that has recently called forth an *Instruction* from the Congregation for the Doctrine of the Faith for the benefit of the entire Church. From this, I would have to gather that the Church in Seattle is not alone in the sincere efforts it is making to deal with the delicate matter of how best to minister faithfully and lovingly to these members of our flock. Each of us Bishops is faced with the same question and each of us, I suppose, on the basis of careful and prayerful discernment, has arrived at a pastoral judgment in this regard. That it will now be guided and influenced by the most recent Instruction from the Congregation for the Doctrine of the Faith I have no doubt, but I am equally confident that, although Church teaching is abundantly clear on the matter of the specific immorality of homosexual acts, and I have always made it plain that I stand in full accord with that teaching, Church practice with regard to the best way to minister to these members is nowhere near as clear and, I suppose, never will be. Again, we find ourselves in the oftentimes gray area which we call "pastoral discretion."

In this context, I should make mention of my decision back in 1983 to allow the members of the Dignity group to celebrate Mass in our Cathedral church. My public statement at the time reaffirmed Church teaching and described my decision as a pastoral judgment. I have subssequently been informed that it was an ill-conceived judgment. Perhaps it was. I am willing to stand corrected. But my decision does not differ *in kind* from the decision made by many bishops to allow local Dignity groups to celebrate Mass in one or another church on a regular basis. Again, pastoral practice will now need to be looked at carefully in light of the most recent document from the Congregation for the Doctrine of the Faith, but I do not deem it fair to be placed under a judgment, even to the point of being deprived of significant pastoral responsibilities, because of the conclusion contained in a document that was not issued until some three years after my own conscientious, carefully studied pastoral judgment was made, a judgment, by the way, which I shared with the Holy See in a timely fashion.

Under the heading of ongoing concern I would mention the employment in teaching positions and for service in the liturgy of priests who have left the active ministry and / or who have been laicized. I believe I have erred in this matter on one or another occasions since coming to Seattle. My doing so was never a purposeful defiance of Church regulations, however. In one case it involved an oversight with regard to the employment of an unlaicized priest; in two other cases it involved the well-accepted service as lector and Eucharistic Minister by a laicized priest, a practice that had been going on long before I learned of it and one which, to have discontinued it would have caused *admiratio* of the most severe kind. I am unaware of any cases beyond these.

Under the heading of matters I do not understand I would have to list that of the admissions process we use for accepting candidates for the priesthood. The process we use was carefully reviewed and approved by an NCCB Visitation Team and, as I understand it, has become something of a model for many other dioceses in this country. Under this heading I would also include the whole question of continuing education for clergy, something I already dealt with in my response to the Chronology. Lastly, I would also list here the inaccurate statement that I have permitted non-Catholics to receive Communion at our Masses or, conversely, for Catholics to receive Communion at Protestant services. Our diocesan regulations governing communicatio in Sacris are clear and unequivocal. It is, of course, impossible for me to oversee the pastoral implementation of those regulations in any but the most global fashion. But I can assure you that when abuses have been brought to my attention I have promptly and appropriately dealt with them, as the records will show.

III. I have spent considerable time addressing the concerns singled out by the Holy See. Now I believe I have come to the point in this presentation where I can more clearly move toward delineating for you some other very important issues which have been brought to light by the Visitation and its process.

As I do so, however, let me first say a word or two about what is certainly not at issue here.

1) First of all, we are not dealing with a matter of dissent in the Church. The news media have sounded this theme and I suppose I can understand why, given other currents presently flowing in the Church. But I am not a dissenter from the Church's teaching. I hold with the Magisterium conscientiously and I make every effort – personal and professional – to deepen my understanding of the teaching of the Church so that I willl be able to present it to my people as the vital and living tradition it is – the very Gospel message of Jesus proclaimed throughout the ages and in our own time in ways that reflect both its enduring significance as well as its perennial relevance.

What I am is what each of us in this room is – or, perhaps I should say, what I *strive* to be is what each of us in this room *strives* to be: a teacher, a pastor, and a servant of the Lord and of the Church. I think we all struggle to teach in a manner that is both faithful and compelling: and we all strive in our own lives not only to find the right words to call our people to service but to make the servant attitude of Jesus the most identifying mark of our own lives. But I suppose there is on greater challenge given to us than the one to be good pastors. The Lord himself must have grappled with this challenge as He reached out with love and compassion to those weak in faith as well as to those involved in sin. Never did He compromise the truth He had come to reveal, but neither did He fail to extend to all He encountered the warm and compassionate embrace of a loving God. That's the challenge I face day after day in my ministry to the Church in Seattle, and I know it is the struggle of each of us in this room. I would never even for a moment maintain that I have always succeeded in carrying it out, or deny that I have made many mistakes along the way. But I have never stopped trying and, please God, I never will.

2) Another important point about what this matter most surely is not: it is not a case of personal obduracy or obstinacy on my part. I suppose I am a strong-willed person (my priests would probably bear me out on that!) but I have always striven to be a loyal son of the Church and a faithful member of the College of Bishops. From the very start, I have always made it clear to the Holy Father and to everyone I have dealt with in the Roman Curia that I would happily resign if my doing so would help this situation, and that I would *sooner* resign than bring dishonor to our Church in any way. The voluminous correspondence between me and the Holy See these past three years will make it clear that my attitude has always been a cooperative and obedient one. But my understanding of the virtue of obedience, coupled with my role as a Bishop with responsibility not only for my own Archdiocese but with shared responsibility within the Episcopal College for the entire Church – my understanding of the virtue of obedience has never allowed me simply to acquiesce. It has, rather, prompted me to engage in a process of dialogue, one which, to the best of my ability, I have always carried out in a respectful, docile and faith-filled manner.

3) Perhaps I also need to acknowledge the extremely widespread publicity which has surrounded this entire case, to the point of causing confusion and serious scandal for many of our people. I am grieved by this, and I think it could have been otherwise. I have already told you that, and why. Our people have "come of age" and they deserve to be treated as adults. They are capable of dealing maturely with problems where they exist and they take seriously the "ownership" of the Church that is their birthright as baptized members of the Body of Christ.

In view of this, I honestly believe that the current waves of adverse publicity could have been avoided had the decision regarding the Visitation, the process followed in the Visitation, and all that has ensued since been dealt with more openly and forthrightly. Had this happened, I know that the people in our Archdiocese who have been so badly hurt, scandalized, and even outraged by these events would have found themselves in a far different place. Much adverse publicity could have been avoided from the very start and the same outcomes intended by the Holy See could have been achieved; namely the careful evaluation of my stewardship, my ministry as Archbishop of Seattle, something which I would have warmly and enthusiastically welcomed, as I am certain each of us here would.

IV. Having tried to set forth those matters which, in my judgment, have most assuredly not been at stake in this whole case, may I attempt to conclude this overly-long presentation by suggesting some of those which most certainly are involved in it? I will list them only briefly because they are, it seems to me, the sort of things that need to be addressed carefully and systematically by this Conference.

1) The first has to do with a relationship: the absolutely essential and life-giving relationship that exists between an individual bishop and the Holy Father himself (and, I would have to add, to those who assist him in the day-to-day administration of the Church.) The Second Vatican Council addressed this relationship in depth from a scriptural and theological perspective, one that gave great hope to all of us, I think – certainly to me, a bishop who got his first "on-the-job training" during the Council itself. Subsequently, this relationship has been dealt with in documents such as *De Episcoporum Muneribus* and, most recently, by the Revised Code of Canon Law. But very real practical questions remain, and those better equipped than I am need to address them. The most obvious way of putting the question, to my way of thinking at least, is simply this: how does a diocesan bishop who is himself the Vicar of Christ in his particular church, carry out his role with the degree of independence which this role implies while at the same time doing so in full union with and under the rightful authority of the Supreme Pontiff? I do not meant to suggest for a moment that we are dealing here with polarities but they are surely values that sometimes find themselves in tension.

And, secondly, what is the proper role of National Bodies of Bishops such as this one, mandated by the documents of the Council, yet variously interpreted as being anywhere from essential to collegial Church governance to merely useful in carrying out certain forms of non-binding consultation? This question has far-reaching implications, to be sure, but it has particular relevance to the whole matter of the decision to undertake the Visitation of the church of Seattle and to how such a Visitation ought to have been carried out. I am firmly of the opinion that it ought to have been carried out in close collaboration between the Holy See and this Conference. I am further of the mind that this Conference should have been the very agency for carrying out the Visitation. That is why, from the very beginning, I chose to keep the leadership of this Conference apprised of each major development as it unfolded, and why I am gratified that the moment has finally arrived for it to be dealt with by the entire active membership of this Conference. I believe that this will ultimately be of benefit to the whole Church.

2) I believe, too, that it is the proper role of a Conference such as this to address the issue of the legitimacy as well as the limits of local adaptations which are truly reflective of a particular Church., its history, traditions, and lifestyle, not to mention its special characteristics and problems. You hardly need me to remind you of the role of legitimate diversity within a Church that is called to be one—one in itself, one among the local churches, and one with the See of Peter. We all know this. I mention it here because I believe it has applicability with regard to our own Apostolic Visitation and to the reasons which prompted it in the first place.

3) My third over-arching concern has to do with another question which touches on us as a Conference. Following the lead of our Holy Father who has repeatedly sounded the call for peace, not for peace at any price but peace with justice, we have all labored hard these past many years, under some very able leadership and thanks to the incredibly generous and gifted contributions of our members, to speak out publicly and forcefully on some of the most delicate, complex and compelling moral and societal issues of our times. Our work this week is only one case in point. We have often paid a price for speaking out honestly and without concern for our own selfish interests. It is clear that each of us here has a deep and passionate concern for a more just and Christian social and economic order, and that each one of us is committed to doing all he can to bring about his order. I think our record is impressive, even if incomplete. At the same time, our ongoing commitment cannot only be toward the order of things outside the Church. It must embrace as well the very Church we are trying to become. Our people expect this of us. They will listen to us even more attentively, I think, if they see mirrored in our own honest relationships and just treatments of one another the same kind of loving and just relationships to which we are calling them. I make this observation not in an accusatory fashion. Indeed, I must first speak these words of challenge to myself and acknowledge innumerable ways in which I fail in this respect.

I have mentioned three rather over-arching issues that I feel we must deal with. I would now like to mention a concern that applies only to the Church of Seattle. It is this: I need some help, some direction in coming to understand just how we in Seattle – bishops, priests and people working together – are to address the issues identified by the Apostolic Visitation, and to satisfy the concerns of the Holy See, in a situation and according to a methodology that I, quite frankly, have to acknowledge as being all but impossible, even to the point of being unworkable. I honestly do not know the answer to that question, but I must state it. And I must go even further, especially in this setting, and say that with all due respect for the provisions of Church Law, I believe that the very concept of special faculties – at least of the sort and extent we are dealing with here – is already on somewhat shaky ground from a theological point of view. Given the present situation in Seattle, however, the theological problem seems an academic luxury in the fact of the pressing practical problems that are involved.

I have talked overly long and I apologize for that. I guess a lot has built up within me during the past three and a half years in which these events have taken place. But it is not me I am concerned about. I am concerned about the Church. And I guess my realization that each of you shares the same concern just as deeply as I do has given me the courage to say more than I normally would in a situation like this. Thank you for letting me.

At this point, I suppose, it is likely that the question on the minds of many of you is "What does he want us to do, anyway?" Let me attempt to answer that by reminding you that there are really three sets of issues here. First, there is the question of my ministry, my stewardship over the Church entrusted to me. I have been found wanting in some ways. Seriously wanting, it appears. And even though I object to the methods that were used to arrive at this conclusion, I have to take to heart the need to I have to be evaluated, and I accept the fact that I must work very hard with my priests and people, and as conscientiously as possible, in order to address and correct any areas in which I have been found wanting. I am committed with all my heart to doing this.

The second set of issues has to do with what surely seems to be an unworkable situation as far as Bishop Wuerl's special faculties are concerned. And the problem here has nothing to do with Bishop Wuerl personally. He is my brother and my friend and my heart aches for him when I consider the ordeal he has had to suffer during this past years. But in view of the situation in which we find ourselves, I would hope that this Conference would be willing to afford some positive assistance in helping bishop Wuerl and me to address this issue with the Holy See. For the good of the Church in Seattle and beyond, I am absolutely convinced that the matter of the governance of the Church of Seattle needs to be returned to normal as soon as humanly possible. I would even say at once.

The third set of concerns are those I labelled "over-arching" toward the end of this presentation. There are some major questions which will not go away now matter how much we might wish they would. They are questions which will severely test our mettle as a Conference of Bishops. But we have been tested before and we have almost always come through well. Amazingly well. And united, too. I firmly believe that the present moment will be no exception.

A final word: my friends, we need not look upon this as a win / lose situation. I do not feel the need to win so that others will have to lose. Winning or losing is not what this is all about. The good of the Church is what is at stake here. Nothing less. We are all untie in our commitment to that goal, and for that reason I have no doubt that we will find a way to address all the questions I have posed and others like them. And I have no doubt, either, that we ill do so courageously – in a sprit that is truly and fully Catholic, with all that word implies: a spirit that is at the same time faithful to the Lord and His Gospel, loyal to our Holy Father, and true to the people of God whom we serve and who look to us now, perhaps, more than ever before, for guidance, inspiration, and leadership.

Document Number: 7
Document Title: Bishop Malone's Statement
Source: *The Progress*, November 13, 1986, p. 11; *Origins*, November 20, 1986, pp. 400-401.

In recent weeks all of us have felt much concern for those involved in the situation in Seattle. The pain of Archbishop Hunthausen and Bishop Wuerl, our brothers in the episcopacy, the abuse directed at the Holy Father and the Holy See, the dismay and confusion experienced by many good people – these things are deeply troubling.

Not only is there suffering in the church in Seattle, though: the controversy has spread via the media and in other ways and has affected Catholics throughout the country. It is unusual for the conference of bishops to address such a matter, but these are unusual circumstances.

The issues raised here touch on the relationship between the local churches and the universal pastor. Bishops exercise their office in communion him and under his authority. On this occasion the bishops of the United States wish to affirm unreservedly their loyalty to and unity with the Holy Father.

The conference of bishops has no authority to intervene in the internal affairs of the diocese or in the unique relationship between the pope and individual bishops. By universal church law and the conference's norms, the conference is not able to review, much less judge, a case involving a diocesan bishop and the Holy See.

Based on experience, bishops are conscious that in such matters the Holy See proceeds carefully and charitably, employing procedures developed over many years to protect the rights of individuals and promote the common good of the church. With specific reference to Seattle, while we are not authorized to judge the facts of the case, I believe it is clear that the process employed by the Holy See was in accord with general principles of church law and procedures. The decision reached at the end of the process was made by proper church authorities. As such, it deserves our respect and confidence. Where there appear to have been misunderstandings at one point or another along the way, the need now is to look to the future, not to the past, and carry out the decision. The best assistance I or anyone can give is to offer precisely this counsel.

We could address the issues involved in this situation all week, but we would deceive ourselves if we thought that such discussions would solve all the problems, heal all the hurt. We need to do some additional things.

Is it paradoxically possible that what has happened in the Archdiocese of Seattle has given, and continues to provide, a vivid demonstration of the unity of the church, perhaps the best demonstration we have seen in many years? I am deeply convinced that the degree of pain which has been felt and enunciated in Seattle, but far beyond Seattle, really is the kind of pain that can only be felt by members of a family. At least that is how it feels to me.

If my analogy is correct, it suggests some of the directions in which we must go. There are certain things that a family must do when it wants to resolve a problem.

A family comes together. Each member expresses the pain, the anxiety, the doubts they feel. These things are listened to with respect and sympathized with, deeply and in the heart. Then support is expressed, for the persons as persons, and for the responsibilities they must bear. This we bishops have done together in these days. Archbishop Hunthausen and Bishop Wuerl have been given a job to do by the Holy See. We are prepared to offer any assistance judged helpful and appropriate by the parties involved.

A family also takes steps to see that, insofar as possible, a painful situation does not happen again. In our case that means working to find creative ways of presenting the church's teaching in the best light possible, but also seeking the mechanisms of responding when confusion or error occurs. We must be seen as committed to hearing and solving the problems.

There is at least one more thing a family of faith does when it is in difficulty, and that is pray. We of all people must not give short shrift to this. Let us bring our people together in prayer for the church in Seattle, so that what has happened may be an occasion of grace and growth, there and in the church universal.

Document Number: 8
Document Title: Laghi Announcement of Commission Appointment
Source: *The Progress*, February 12, 1987.

The Holy See has appointed an ad hoc commission composed of Cardinals Joseph Bernardin and John O'Connor and Archbishop John Quinn to assess the current situation in the Archdiocese of Seattle. Archbishop Raymond Hunthausen has expressed his concurrence.

Document Number: 9
Document Title: Assessment Commission Report
Source: *The Progress*, 5/28/87, pp. 3-4; *Origins*, 6/4/87, pp. 39-41; Archdiocese of Seattle photocopy, Wasden Price collection.

Report to the Holy See Presented by the Commission Appointed by the Holy See to Assess the Current Situation in the Archdiocese of Seattle

I. The history

The Commission appointed by the Holy See to assess the current situation in the Archdiocese of Seattle was officially notified of its mandate in a letter from the Apostolic Pro-Nuncio, Archbishop Pio Laghi, dated January 26, 1987 (prot. n. 317/87/2). In pursuit of its task the Commission conducted the following interviews:

1) On February 10, 1987, the Commission met with Archbishop Hunthausen and Bishop Wuerl in Dallas, Texas. The entire morning was spent with them together in the presence of the Pro-Nuncio. In the afternoon, the Commission met separately with Archbishop Hunthausen and Bishop Wuerl. The Pro-Nuncio was not present at these meetings, which occupied the entire afternoon and early evening.

2) On March 6 and 7, 1987, the Commission met at Menlo Park in the Archdiocese of San Francisco with eight bishops of the ecclesiastical provinces of Seattle and Portland, with eight priest consultors of the Archdiocese of Seattle and with four staff members of the Archdiocese of Seattle. All these individuals were suggested by Archbishop Hunthausen.

3) On March 12, the Commission, together with the Pro-Nuncio, met individually with Archbishop Hunthausen and Bishop Wuerl in Chicago.

4) Subsequent to the above-mentioned sessions, individual members of the Commission met with the following persons:

A) On March 19, Archbishop Quinn met with Father William Lane, an Archdiocesan Consultor attending a continuing education program in Rome.

B) On March 25, Cardinal Bernardin and Archbishop Quinn interviewed Archbishop James Hickey, who had been the Apostolic Visitator to the Archdiocese of Seattle, in Washington, D.C.

C) On March 29 and 31, Archbishop Quinn met with Archbishop Francis Hurley of

Anchorage, Alaska, and on March 31 he met with Bishop Michael Kenny of Juneau and again with Archbishop Francis Hurley.

During the entire month of April and into the month of May a number of visits and telephone conversations, as well as an exchange of letters with individuals who had previously been interviewed took place. In addition, Archbishop Hunthausen met with the Commission in Chicago April 8, 1987. Since then the Commission has been in continuing contact with the Archbishop by telephone.

The Commission also studied voluminous documentation, all of which was available to Archbishop Hunthausen and Bishop Wuerl.

II. The assessment

The Commission was given no mandate on the procedure to be followed in carrying out its task. The Commission, therefore, decided that while its task was official, its procedure would be informal and would consist largely of informal discussions with bishops, priests and lay persons designated by Archbishop Hunthausen, informal discussions with Archbishop Hunthausen and with Bishop Wuerl, and informal discussions and shared prayer by the members of the Commission.

The Commission further decided that the primary context for its approach would be two documents, both known to Archbishop Hunthausen, to the Holy See and to everyone concerned.

1) The summary of the Archbishop Hickey-Archbishop Hunthausen interview of November 8, 1983, signed jointly by Archbishop Hickey and Archbishop Hunthausen as a fair and accurate summary.

2) The letter of the Congregation for the Doctrine of the Faith signed by the Prefect, Cardinal Joseph Ratzinger, September 30, 1985 (prot. no. 102/79), bringing to a close the Apostolic Visitation process and listing fourteen specific observations, eleven of them raising questions or making recommendations and issuing directives and guidelines for corrective action where required.

The Commission further agreed internally that it would base its conclusions only on documents seen by Archbishop Hunthausen and on discussions with persons designated by him or consulted with his knowledge and concurrence. Each person interviewed was free to share with Archbishop Hunthausen everything discussed with the Commission and the Archbishop was free to seek any such information from any person interviewed by the Commission.

Finally, and of critical importance to the integrity of the process and the merit of the conclusions, is the fact that the Commission decided that it had been asked neither to prove nor to disprove anything whatsoever. It interpreted its task as the mandate to make an assessment. The Commission was not asked to carry out an Apostolic Visitation. It was asked to provide an assessment of the "current situation" in the Archdiocese of Seattle. In common sense terms, it seemed quite clear that the Holy See was looking for a common-sense judgment, and this is all the Commission attempts to provide here.

The following, then, is the unanimous judgment of the Commission:

1) Archbishop Hunthausen has taken laudable steps to carry out certain of the provisions of the letter of the Congregation for the Doctrine of the Faith.

2) In spite of such steps, certain clear teachings of the Magisterium seem to be confused in the minds of some, and certain practices mandated by the Holy See seem to be modified arbitrarily by some pastors and other persons charged with responsibility for Archdiocesan activities.

3) Archbishop Hunthausen himself observed that the Archdiocese suffers an inadequacy in communications. It seems possible, therefore, that certain ambiguities exist because not everyone is adequately familiar with the Archbishop's policies or with his articulations of Magisterial teaching.

4) At the same time, the Archbishop attributes great value to *compassion*. His own practice of compassion has become almost legendary. While the Archbishop himself, however, seems generally to balance compassion with the law and asserts unconditionally his own commitment to formal Church teaching, it seems that some who admire his compassion may not give similar weight to the place and demands of law, bending it in important matters under the aegis of compassion.

5) In sum, no matter how personally firm in his teachings and practice the Archbishop himself may be, without intending it he is *perceived* as generating, or at least accepting, a climate of permissiveness within which some feel free to design their own policies and practices.

6) It would not be difficult to illustrate each of the above observations with concrete examples. It is tempting to do this, particularly since a number of persons interviewed informed the Commission that they felt the Archbishop had been unfairly asked to correct aberrations without being told what they were, that is, without being given an extensive list of concrete matters of teaching or practice requiring correction.

The Commission understands this allegation, but disagrees with its implications. The reason is that, more than individual items which might need correction, it is the overall attitudinal "climate" or psychological and ecclesiological orientation of the Archdiocese which is the ultimate key to the situation.

No substantive changes will perdure until this climate or orientation changes. And this climate or orientation seems to have remained substantially unchanged since the time of the Apostolic Visitation and the letter of the Congregation for the Doctrine of the Faith. This is in no way to suggest a lack of sincerity or the presence of malicious resistance to recommendations and directives of the Holy See. It is to suggest, however, that the correction of individual aberrations, laudable though this be, is not sufficient.

7) The Commission believes that the letter of the Congregation for the Doctrine of the Faith is reasonably clear in both specifics and intent. Cardinal Ratzinger made no effort to provide an exhaustive list of concrete points for correction, very probably, the Commission believes, for the reasons cited in no. 6 above. He prefers, rather, to speak of "imperfect notions of the Church's mission and nature," or "faulty Christologies" or the "role of conscience." Hence, while providing certain concrete examples, he is speaking as bishop, as between those who share one Lord, one faith, one baptism, one Church.

8) It is the conclusion of the Commission, therefore, that the letter of the Congregation for the Doctrine of the Faith should remain in place as the primary guide for the direction in which the Church in Seattle must move beyond the point it has already reached. Despite its conviction that a listing of individual points does not go to the heart of the problem, the Commission has orally provided the Archbishop with a number of specific examples and is prepared to discuss these and others with him if so desired.

9) In submitting this assessment we express highest praise for Bishop Wuerl and his dedicated efforts to carry out his special responsibilities in the Archdiocese of Seattle despite exceedingly difficult circumstances beyond his control.

III. Proposal for Resolving the Problem and Concluding Remarks

The proposal for resolving the problem in the Archdiocese of Seattle was devised by the Commission in consultation with the Holy See, taking into account both the concerns of Archbishop Hunthausen as well as those of the Holy See.

Virtually all persons interviewed by the Commission agreed that the present arrangement of divided authority (i.e. an auxiliary bishop with special faculties) was not effective and should be changed.

Hence, the proposal of the Commission contains these essential elements:

1) The auxiliary bishop should be transferred to another See.

2) The Archbishop should recover his faculties as diocesan bishop.

3) A Coadjutor Archbishop should be appointed.

4) The Holy See should establish target dates for the completion of the tasks referred to in the letter of the Congregation for the Doctrine of the Faith.

5) The Commission should be mandated, for a period to be determined by the Holy See, to assist in carrying out whichever of its elements the Holy See approves and directs.

Thoroughly aware of the steps taken by the Holy See up to this point, the Commission is convinced that no steps were intended as punitive, regardless of perceptions to the contrary. The same must be said of the proposal set forth above.

In the fulfillment of our task, we listened to many voices and weighed many views. We recognize that some of those interviewed may not agree with our interpretation of their statements. Nevertheless, throughout we kept before our eyes some very basic considerations: the need for charity and compassion, the need for fairness and openness, the need to reach decisions and to make recommendations to the best of our ability. But we also kept in mind the nature of the bishop's role in the Church.

Hence we acknowledge the teaching of the Second Vatican Council, according to which: "The pastoral charge, that is, the permanent and daily care of the flock, is entrusted to (bishops) fully; nor are they to be regarded as vicars of the Roman pontiff; for they exercise the power which they possess in their own right" (*Lumen Gentium*, 27).

At the same time, the Council also teaches that every bishop, by reason of his episcopal ordination, is a member of the College of Bishops. He is not an independent agent standing in isolation. As a member of the College of Bishops, he exercises his office only in communion with and obedience to the Head of the College of Bishops, the Pope, the Successor of Peter and Bishop of Rome. Indeed, every bishop in his ordination publicly declares his promise to fulfill his ministry in obedience to Peter and his successors.

From the first century to this, it has been the role of the Bishop of Rome to intervene in local, regional or national situations when required by the greater good of the Church, as attested by the earliest documents of Christian history. If the Church, spread through many cultures and existing on all continents, is to remain one and maintain its identity, the Pope must make decisions which must be binding on the whole body of the Church.

In this connection we cite the words of Karl Rahner:

"We are and we shall remain also in the future the *Roman* Catholic Church....

"The papacy belongs to the binding content of our faith itself, in its proper place within the hierarchy of truths and in our own Christian life. This holds absolutely....

"We can insist that the Church is not a secular reality, but has a quite different nature. But the Church cannot be a debating society: It must be able to make decisions binding on all within it. Such a demand cannot be *a priori* contrary to man's dignity if -- as people today are never tired of impressing upon us -- he is indeed a social being. And then a supreme point at which all reflections and democratic discussions are turned into universally binding decisions cannot be without meaning' (Karl Rahner, SJ, *The Shape of the Church to Come*, Part 2, c. 2).

With this in mind the Commission continues to hope and pray that all will walk together the Gospel path of humility, obedience, charity and peace in accepting the decision of the Holy See.

Joseph Cardinal Bernardin
Archbishop of Chicago

John Cardinal O'Connor
Archbishop of New York

Archbishop John R. Quinn
Archbishop of San Francisco

APPENDIX IV: SAMPLE DISCOURSE ANALYSIS OF DOCUMENT

Text: Laghi letter to Hunthausen reporting visitation findings

November 14, 1985

Most Reverend Raymond G. Hunthausen

Archbishop of Seattle

910 Marion Street

Seattle, WA 98104

Honorary title (courtesy)

Dear Archbishop Hunthausen,

1.   With this letter I write to inform you that the Apostolic Visitation requested by the Holy See, and conducted by Archbishop James A. Hickey of Washington, has been concluded and is considered closed.

Visitation: euphemism (courtesy; minimize the appearance of conflict)

Hickey: recruited ally; fraternity

2.   Prior to that Visitation, both significant criticism and praise had been directed toward your pastoral ministry in Seattle. The Holy See considered it necessary to evaluate certain allegations and also to explore in a wider and more positive fashion your pastoral service in the Archdiocese. Toward that end, the Visitator conferred with more than seventy members of the clergy, religious and laity. In addition, he examined many pertinent documents, statements issued by the Archdiocese and letters. Most importantly, while in Seattle, Archbishop Hickey spent some four or five hours to exchange views with yourself, reviewing the allegations and seeking a deeper insight into your governance of the Archdiocese. This had been preceded by mutual discussions held in Chicago on September 15-16, 1983. It was the Visitator's role to speak to you as a brother bishop, to observe the situation at firsthand, to obtain necessary facts and to analyze them for the Holy See, and to offer you appropriate fraternal assistance and support.

Criticism: legitimizes intervention

"Holy See" hides identity (secrecy)

Wide-ranging consultation: legitimizes action

Consultation with Hunthausen: legitimation

Earlier discussions: further legitimation

Brother bishop (fraternity; minimize the appearance of conflict)

Fraternal assistance: show fraternity; minimize the appearance of conflict

3.   After a careful review of the entire body of testimony and, in

Careful review: legitimation

373

particular, on the basis of your own extensive testimony of November 8, 1983, I bring to your attention the following observations.

Observations: euphemism (courtesy; minimize appearance of conflict)

4.   1. There are many indications that you have striven with heart and mind to be a dedicated bishop of the Church, eager to implement the renewal called for in the Documents of the Second Vatican Council. The record is clear that you have worked zealously to bring into existence the various consultative bodies promoted by the Council and mandated by the recently promulgated Code of Canon Law. You have devoted much time and attention to bodies such as the Council of Priests and the Archdiocesan Pastoral Council, seeking to enable them to function effectively.

Praise: courtesy

Renewal: code word (persuasion: associate self with best interest of Church)

You have worked zealously: praise (courtesy)

Praise: courtesy

5.   Numerous witnesses spoke of your laudable and conscientious efforts to involve the laity actively in the work of the church. You have set up processes of dialogue with priests, religious and laity, and you have sought most diligently to be open and accessible to your people. You have been described repeatedly as a man of Gospel values, sensitive to the needs of the suffering and aggrieved. Your apostolic zeal and your concern for peace and justice are well-known. Time and again you have given clear evidence of your loyalty to the Church and your devotion and obedience to our Holy Father.

Praise: courtesy

Praise: courtesy

Praise: courtesy

Praise: courtesy

Praise: courtesy

Praise: courtesy

6.   2. You have given much time to fostering the morale of your priests and religious, meeting with them and encouraging them to participate in a renewal of Church life. Efforts have been made to develop local lay leadership and to deepen the life of prayer for the people entrusted to your care. Your own special skills as a homilist and speaker have played a significant role toward that renewal.

Praise: courtesy

Praise: courtesy

7.   3. At the same time, you and your collaborators have suffered from exaggerated and mean-spirited criticism. These observations are based neither on the testimony of strident critics, nor on obviously

Empathy: fraternity; persuasion

Attestation to fairness: legitimation; persuasion

biased publications. Nor are they offered to encourage in any way extreme groups seeking to undermine the authority of a local bishop. Rather, they are designed to support you in your efforts toward Church renewal and to offer, where necessary, certain guidance and advice.

> Intervention is designed to support you: associate self with best interest of Church

8. 4. Against this basic background of an apostolate conscientiously conducted, I wish to express the following concerns, asking at the same time your assistance in addressing them in a way that will contribute to the spiritual well-being of the Archdiocese of Seattle.

> Conscientiously conducted: courtesy; persuasion

> Concerns: euphemism (courtesy; minimize the appearance of conflict)

> Contribute to the well being of archdiocese: associate self with best interest of Church

9. a. The need to bring into clear focus – working together with priests, religious and theologians – certain teachings of the Church and their implications for the pastoral practice of the Archdiocese. These include the role of the conscience in making moral decisions; the role of the Magisterium in giving definitive guidance in matters of faith and morals; the nature and mission of the Church, together with its sacramental and hierarchical structure; an anthropology which provides an authentic understanding of the dignity of the human person; and a Christology which correctly reflects our Catholic faith concerning Christ's divinity, His humanity, His salvific mission, and His inseparable union with the Church.

> The need: indirect expression avoids appearance of blaming Hunthausen (courtesy; minimize the appearance of conflict)

> Definitive guidance: control, surveillance

> Authentic understanding: depends on expert power

> Correctly reflects our Catholic faith: expert power; associate self with best interest of Church

10. b. In particular, the need to present more clearly the Church's teaching concerning the permanence and indissolubility of marriage and to ensure that the Archdiocesan Tribunal, both its constitution and practice, conforms with all the prescriptions of the revised Code of Canon Law.

> The need: indirect language avoids blaming of Hunthausen (courtesy)

> The Church's teaching: tradition as singular

> Tribunal, Canon Law: legal power

11. c. Greater vigilance in upholding the Church's teaching, especially with regard to contraceptive sterilization and homosexuality.

> Greater vigilance: avoids blame (courtesy), highlights need for control

12. d. The need to ensure that pastoral practice regarding the

> The need-indirect language (courtesy)

liturgical and sacramental ministry of the Archdiocese is in accord with the Church's universal norms, especially in the celebration of the Eucharist. This includes, for instance, routine intercommunion on the occasion of weddings or funerals. Such a need also involves the Sacrament of Reconciliation, mentioning particularly the proper sequence of first confession / first communion and regulations regarding general absolution.

> The Church's universal norms: tradition as singular

13.   e. The need to review the ongoing education of the clergy and the selection and formation of candidates for the priesthood, and to be clear that laicized priests are excluded from certain roles in accord with the rescripts of laicization.

> The need-indirect language (courtesy)

> Topic of leadership gatekeeping: monitoring, control

14.   In conclusion, I commend you, Archbishop Hunthausen, for your loyal cooperation and kindness during the Apostolic Visitation and during the many months of study needed by the Holy See for a careful review and an appropriate reaction. Even as I offer these observations, I am aware of your continuous efforts to promote genuine growth and renewal in the Archdiocese of Seattle. The Church is grateful for what you have accomplished and I am confident that you will be able to address effectively the concerns expressed in this letter. You can rely on my assistance and support.

> I commend you: praise (courtesy; minize the appearance of conflict)

> Many months needed: legitimation of delay

> Holy See: hides identity of evaluators (secrecy)

> Praise: courtesy; persuasion

> Concerns: euphemism (courtesy)

> My assistance and support: fraternity; courtesy

15.   Asking God's many blessings on you and your people, I am

Sincerely yours in Christ,

> God talk-pious interjection

Archbishop Pio Laghi

Apostolic Pro-Nuncio

APPENDIX V: ANALYTIC SUMMARY TABLES

Observable Strategies: Early Developments, A. (From 1978 to 9.30.85 Ratzinger Letter)

	Strategies	Tactics	Objectives
Center	1. Show **deference** to the structural order and mindset of the **Church** 2. **Associate** one's own efforts with the best interest of the **Church** 3. **Minimize** the appearance of **conflict** 4. **Show fraternity** 5. **Practice courtesy** 6. **Employ secrecy** 7. **Recruit allies** 8. **Argue persuasively** 9. **Assert** personal **identity**	1. a. Vatican employs canonically recognized instruments of control and surveillance (ad limina, visitation); b. Vatican shows preference for bishop-to-bishop problem solving 2. a. Hickey says he comes to assist the Holy Father and support Hunthausen in his ministry 3. a. Holy See confines discussion of issues to private meetings and correspondence; b. euphemism "visitation" paints over negative quality of intervention; c. Hickey says he goes to Seattle to offer "fraternal assistance and support;" 12.12.83 Ratzinger letter thanks Hunthausen for his cooperation 4. a. Pro-nuncio acts as go-between; Laghi approaches Hunthausen about visitation in informal way; b. visitation intention posed as a request; c. Vatican appoints fellow U.S. bishop as visitator; d. Hickey explicitly stresses concept of fraternity when arriving in and leaving Seattle 5. a. Hickey uses euphemisms to save face for Hunthausen; b. Hickey praises Hunthausen 6. a. private meetings; b. private correspondence; c. Hickey defends use of secrecy; d. visitation interviews were conducted with interviews in private; e. Hunthausen was not allowed to see visitation report 7. a. Vatican enlists Hickey to serve as visitator 8. **Ambiguous**: a. Did Hunthausen try to persuade Hunthausen to cooperate in its private exchanges with him, 1978-83, and if so, how? b. Hickey argues legitimacy of use of secrecy to press 9. **NA** (no evidence)	Bring Hunthausen to correct the perceived problems in the local Church. Maintain a low profile for the intervention.
Periphery	1. **Deference-Church** 2. **Associate-Church** 3. **Minimize-conflict** 4. **Show fraternity** 5. **Practice courtesy** 6. **Employ secrecy** 7. **Recruit allies** 8. **Argue persuasively** 9. **Assert identity**	1. a. Hunthausen accepts Vatican monitoring (ad limina, visitation); b. Hunthausen says publicly that he welcomes Hickey's visit 2. a. conceptualized with reference to "renewal," Vatican II, and guidance of the Holy Spirit 3. a. Hunthausen confines disagreement discussions to closed forums; b. Hunthausen's public statements downplay the contentious dimension of the visitation process 4. a. Hunthausen consults NCCB Pres. Roach; b. Hunthausen welcomes Hickey to Seattle 5. a. Hunthausen welcomes Hickey into his archdiocese (hospitality) 6. a. Hunthausen does not reveal details of his exchanges with the Vatican which took place prior to the visitation; b. Hunthausen cooperates with Vatican wish for secrecy (though, by his own account, he argued against its use, i.e. he **resisted**) 7. a. Hunthausen turns to Roach for help; b. Hunthausen addresses people of Seattle	Cooperate with Holy See while minimizing own loss of power and prestige.

		archdiocese in open letter in *Progress* 8. **Ambiguous**. a. Hunthausen denies wrongdoing 9. a. Hunthausen's press statement announcing visitation uses the first person repeatedly and associates the ministerial situation with Hunthausen himself ("my faith tells me that…")	
Third	1. **Deference-Church** 2. **Associate-Church** 3. **Minimize-conflict** 4. **Show fraternity** 5. **Practice courtesy** 6. **Employ secrecy** 7. **Recruit allies** 8. **Argue persuasively** 9. **Assert identity**	1. **Ambiguous**: third party involvement is mostly hidden. 2. **Ambiguous**: third party involvement is mostly hidden. 3. **Ambiguous**: Roach advises Hunthausen to request a bill of particulars (likely leading to escalation), but he, like Hunthausen, keeps the affair quiet 4. a. Roach advises Hunthausen 5. **Ambiguous**: third party involvement is mostly hidden. 6. a. Roach cooperates with secrecy surrounding visitation 7. **NA** (no evidence) 8. **Ambiguous**: Roach argues in favor of bill of particulars? 9. **Ambiguous**: third party involvement is mostly hidden.	Offer support to friend Hunthausen.

Analytic Summary, Document 1 (9.30.85 Ratzinger letter to Hunthausen):

	Overview	Indications in Document
I. Analysis of Text Construction		
1. Production	The Holy See is the principal and Ratzinger is the author. Influence of others on production is unknown. Earlier draft in German? One-to-one correspondence, intended to be private (secret), but possibility of public consumption is not ruled out in production phase.	Sign of production is seal of the congregation on original, with administrative file no. 102/79. Only Ratzinger's signature appears. Technical language is sign of Hunthausen as intended audience , but balanced content and polite tone suggest possibility of public consumption is considered.
2. Distribution	Postal courier, Ratzinger to Hunthausen (via Laghi?). Hunthausen shared with Seattle insiders. An edited version of the letter's contents would appear in the 11.14.85 Laghi letter. Hunthausen shared the Ratzinger letter with priests of archdiocese. Assessment commission had the Ratzinger letter to read and they eventually released it with their report.	Photocopies of the letter distributed to the press in May, 1987 show the congregational seal and Ratzinger's signature, but the gravity of these signs is lost with photocopying. The version of the letter printed in *The Progress* retains the signature but not the seal. Many newspaper accounts carry neither and offer only abridged accounts of the letter. Broadcast reports carry even more abbreviated accounts.
3. Consumption	Consumption, as best I can discern, took place in the following order: 1. Ratzinger and the Congregation for the Doctrine of the Faith; 2. other Vatican insiders; 3. Laghi and Hunthausen; 4. insiders in the Laghi	Letter is addressed formally to Hunthausen alone. When the letter was released in Seattle on 5.27.87, members of the press received photocopied packets which included: Hunthausen cover letter,

	and Hunthausen offices; 5. priests of the Seattle Archdiocese; 6. assessment commission; 7. U.S. bishops; 8. news media.	Hunthausen statement, Murphy statement, commission cover letter, commission report, Ratzinger letter. Newspapers then reproduced these documents according to their own priorities.
4. Text Type	Business letter with aspects of a personal letter and formal report.	Formal stationery, seal and use of official form of address indicate that it is a business letter. Ratzinger's reference to previous meetings with Hunthausen, his words of praise and expressed intention to be of assistance personalize the communication. List of observations is typical of a formal report.
5. Diction	Formal, polite, church-bureaucratic. Certain words appear heavily laden with strategic intentionality. Other word choices maintain secrecy.	"Your Excellency" greeting establishes formal tone and elevated diction carries throughout ("A critical reexamination of policies and programs of the Archdiocese should be conducted…"). Politeness is seen in praise ("There are many indications that you have striven with heart and mind to be a good bishop…") and euphemisms ("visit/visitation instead of investigation; "assist you" instead of "correct you."). Examples of church-bureaucratic language are ample: Apostolic Visitation, Congregation, Vatican Council, Canon Law, etc. Key strategic words include: "renewal" (suggests Vatican has affinity with Hunthausen's desire to lead in the spirit of Vatican II), "extremist" (appears to be a response to Hunthausen's charge that "reactionary elements" and the Church are opposed to his ministry), and "clear and firm" (Ratzinger repeatedly suggests that problems in Seattle have to do with a failure to provide clear and firm guidance to the faithful: too many matters are left ambiguous). Words which maintain secrecy include: "Holy See," "this Congregation," and nonspecific use of "we."
6. Usage	Ratzinger repeatedly obscures agency and causality. First- and second-person comments appear early on but give way to depersonalizing third-person. The relational modality is one of exhortation and expected fulfilment: Ratzinger tells Hunthausen what he should (must) do, a manifestation of normative power.	Obscured agency and causality: "Catholics have been advised that after divorce and civil marriage, they may in conscience return to the Sacraments." (Passive voice hides agency.) Third-person depersonalizing: "this Congregation is now in a position to make the following observation." Relational modality: "Vigorous efforts must be

		made to engender in priests, religious and laity, a correct appreciation of the sacramental structure of the Church."
7. Substructures of the Text	Greeting,, introduction, numbered report of findings, salutation.	The main substructure is the list of observations that makes up the heart of the document. This section makes up most of the letter and produces a feeling that the text is essentially bureaucratic in function.
8. Intertextuality	References to previous correspondence between Congregation and Hunthausen, and to visitation report place this letter in context. Citations of magisterial documents signals the specific Church teachings (and forms of authority) Hunthausen needs to acknowledge and apply locally. A citation of questionnaires produced in the Seattle Archdiocese serves as a counter-example of how confusion can be spread.	Mention of Congregation's 10.4.83 letter to Hunthausen, Hunthausen's 3.14.84 letter to Congregation, and Hickey visitation report suggest formational history of issues currently being discussed. Magisterial documents cited: decrees of the Vatican Council; recently revised Code of Canon Law; CDF's 1976 *Declaration on Sexual Ethics*; documents of U.S. bishops' conference; the Roman Sacramentary; CDF 1975 Instruction, *Inter Insigniores*; Congregation for Catholic Education's 1983 document, *Educational Guidance in Human Love*. All of these documents are meant to provide Hunthausen with clear reference points (limits) for pastoral decision making. When documents produced by the Seattle Archdiocese are mentioned (questionnaires developed by the Seattle Archdiocese in 1976 and 1979), they are cited as examples of pastoral outreach which can be confusing to the faithful.
II. Coping Strategies in Evidence	**Tactics**	**Indications in Document**
1. Show deference to the structural order and mindset of the Church	Ratzinger uses formal Church titles, invokes own authority as curial official, engages in processing of Church disciplinary procedure (visitation), cites official sources of Church teaching, and makes arguments based on his perception of the proper function of the Church.	Titles: "Your Excellency," "this Congregation," "Prefect." Ratzinger signals his own authority when he says that he himself is closing the visitation process." Engagement in process of visitation is in keeping with Code of Canon Law. Ratzinger's citation of Church teaching draws heavily on formal instruction, most of which is the product of the Roman Curia. He does not cite Scripture, classics of spirituality or teachings produced within the local Church (with the exception of one non-specific reference to documents produced by the U.S. bishops). The overall thrust of Ratzinger's argument focuses on a vision of the Church that Hunthausen and his archdiocese are

		failing to realize.
2. Associate one's own efforts with the best interest of the Church	Ratzinger offers a vision of "the Church" as a singular, definitive entity which thrives on correct and clear doctrine and practice. He presents himself as a teacher and defender of correct doctrine.	Example: "With regard to the role of women in the Church, the teaching of the Church regarding their God-given dignity and importance should be given full weight… The exclusion of women from Sacred Orders was dealt with at length in this Congregation's 1975 Instruction, *Inter Insigniores…*"
3. Minimize the appearance of conflict	Privacy and indirect language are the primary tactics used to minimize the appearance of conflict.	Ratzinger writes Hunthausen privately and individually and then refuses his request to make the letter public. Ratzinger brings the "observations" to Hunthausen's attention, but never once directly blames Hunthausen for abuses taking place.
4. Show fraternity	This strategy is employed but not with great emphasis. Ratzinger frames this letter as an offer of assistance and an expression of well-meant concern. (Notably, however, explicit references to the episcopal fraternity and episcopal collegiality are absent.)	"It is our intention, rather, to support what you have done to promote the renewal of the Church in Seattle and to point out, at the same time, areas which we consider are in need of correction and improvement."
5. Practice courtesy	The use of the honorary title "Your Excellency" and the invocation of the Holy Spirit of Christ at the end are standard forms of courtesy we would expect to find in formal, episcopal correspondence. Other forms of courtesy in the letter are praise for Hunthausen and a refusal to criticize him directly.	"You have been repeatedly described as a man of Gospel values, sensitive to the needs of the suffering and the aggrieved." "It is important that the nature and mission of the Church be taught in their entirety."
6. Employ secrecy	The letter is addressed to Hunthausen alone. The Holy See (presumably Ratzinger) refused permission to make the letter public. Other examples of private correspondence are mentioned in the letter (these have never been made public). The use of the terms "Holy See" and "this Congregation" hides various actors' identities. Hickey report, cited here, was never made available (even to Hunthausen). Ratzinger offers no details about who participated in the process of evaluating the Hickey report and how.	Ratzinger mentions two previous letters exchanged between Rome and Seattle (see Intertextuality section above). "'It was precisely because it did not want to give uncritical acceptance to the published and private criticisms made about the Archdiocese of Seattle, that the Holy See… has undertaken this project." "… this Congregation is now in a position to make the following observations…" "Archbishop Hickey… filed a lengthy and exhaustively documented report with this Congregation…"
7. Recruit allies	**NA.** This appears to be a letter meant for Hunthausen alone, thought the possibility of wider distribution appears to be foreseen, given the cautious character of its expression.	**NA.**
8. Argue persuasively	Ratzinger holds that the visitation was a rational process, the	Ratzinger cites reasons for undertaking the visitation

		(criticisms made against Hunthausen). He stresses the careful process of evidence collection and the fact that "obviously biased" and "extremist" accounts were recognized as such thus: it was an objective evaluation). One can also read the section praising Hunthausen as a demonstration of Ratzinger's ability to see both sides. Ratzinger's extended section identifying the problems shows his organizational ability, his eye for detail, and his knowledge of Church teaching – all of which lend gravity to his argument. Ratzinger provides various kinds of evidence for his conclusions and he backs up his own opinions with citations of Church documents. He also repeatedly makes distinctions between concepts that are apparently only partially grasped (in Seattle) and the fullness of understanding that must ultimately prevail.
	conclusions are rational, and that it would be rational for Hunthausen to respond in the recommended fashion.	
9. Assert personal identity	**NA.** Ratzinger submerges his own identity. The use of the first person does not reveal much of his own identity: more commonly, self-references are to "this Congregation."	"To quote from this Congregation's own October 4, 1983, letter to you…" "this Congregation is now in a position to make the following observations…"
III. Overall Coping Strategy	**Explanation**	**Indications in Document**
a. Contending	This document reflects the fact that the Holy See unilaterally made a decision to conduct the visitation (I consider Hunthausen's agreement to have been a formality that did not represent a real choice) and carry it out on its own terms. The Congregation for the Doctrine of the Faith determined what the relevant findings were and presented these to Hunthausen in the form of "problems" for him to resolve. There is no invitation to discuss further whether the issues were accurately identified and indeed constituted problems.	Though Ratzinger consistently avoids language that criticizes Hunthausen himself, the letter offers a thoroughgoing critique of the pastoral ministry taking place under his guidance. Criticism (appearing in 21 paragraphs) heavily outweighs praise (appearing in 4 paragraphs). Ratzinger is at pains to show the critique is justified: "the Visitor conferred with at least sixty-seven members of the clergy, religious and laity" and filed "a lengthy and exhaustively documented report." The congregation itself made a "careful review of the entire body of testimony." These statements pre-empt possible Hunthausen arguments that he was evaluated unfairly. Another contentious tactic Ratzinger employs is repeatedly drawing distinctions between truths or doctrines that are only partially grasped and those that are fully and properly understood. He repeatedly suggests that Hunthausen has failed to bring people to a full

		understanding of Church teaching (with the implication that Hunthausen himself may be falling short in his own understandings.	

Observable Strategies: Intervening Developments, B. (October, November 1985)

	Strategies	Tactics	Objectives
Center	1. Show **deference** to the structural order and mindset of the **Church** 2. **Associate** one's own efforts with the best interest of the **Church** 3. **Minimize** the appearance of **conflict** 4. **Show fraternity** 5. **Practice courtesy** 6. **Employ secrecy** 7. **Recruit allies** 8. **Argue persuasively** 9. **Assert** personal **identity**	1. a. Center exercises own decision making power; b. by partially agreeing to Hunthausen's request, shows respect for his office as bishop 2. **NA** (no evidence) 3. a. CDF refuses Hunthausen's request to make Ratzinger letter public 4. **Ambiguous**. Activity is mostly hidden, but the exchanges between Ratzinger, Hunthausen and Laghi show a preference for keeping the business within the episcopal fraternity (CDF gives in to Hunthausen's request for publishable letter; Laghi produces new letter at request of CDF) 5. **NA** (no evidence) 6. a. Rome does not allow Hunthausen to release Ratzinger letter; b. Rome does not allow Hunthausen to read Hickey report; c. Laghi functions as gatekeeper 7. **NA** (lack of evidence) 8. **Ambiguous**. Discussion of letter for public distribution likely involved persuasive argumentation 9. **NA** (no evidence)	To maintain a low profile for the affair as a whole and to ensure Hunthausen's continued cooperation.
Periphery	1. **Deference-Church** 2. **Associate-Church** 3. **Minimize conflict** 4. **Show fraternity** 5. **Practice courtesy** 6. **Employ secrecy** 7. **Recruit allies** 8. **Argue persuasively**	1. a. Hunthausen defers to decision of superior in the hierarchy 2. **Ambiguous** 3. a. Hunthausen carries out dialogue with Vatican in private; b. Hunthausen respects Vatican wishes about not publishing Ratzinger letter 4. a. Hunthausen carries	To learn what the visitation findings are and to reveal them without further alienating Rome.

| | 9. **Assert identity** | on dialogue in private with Laghi
5. a. Hunthausen respects Vatican wishes
6. a. Hunthausen engages in private dialogue with Vatican representatives; b. Hunthausen cooperates with Vatican intention to keep Ratzinger letter secret. c. [**Resist**] Hunthausen presses to make Ratzinger letter public.
7. **NA**
8. a. Hunthausen argues to be provided with some document he can release publicly | |
| Third | 1. **deference-Church**
2. **Associate-Church**
3. **Minimize conflict**
4. **Show fraternity**
5. **Practice courtesy**
6. **Employ secrecy**
7. **Recruit allies**
8. **Argue persuasively**
9. **Assert identity** | No third party activity accounted for. | NA |

Analytic Summary, Document 2 (11.14.85 Laghi letter to Hunthausen):

	Overview	Indications in Document
I. Analysis of Text Construction		
1. Production	The Holy See is the principal and Laghi is the author. It is unknown if others besides Ratzinger directly influenced the content of the letter. The letter was written in response to Hunthausen's request to make the 9.30.85 Ratzinger letter public. That request was refused, but this letter was supplied in its place.	That the Ratzinger letter is a source for this letter becomes clear by comparing the wording and information of the two letters. The Laghi letter follows the organization and wording of the Ratzinger letter closely.
2. Distribution	Laghi passed on a copy to Hunthausen (presumably to Ratzinger also, at the same time or in advance). Hunthausen released the letter to the press.	Hunthausen published the letter in the November 28, 1985 issue of *The Progress*.
3. Consumption	An influence on consumption for many would be the sense of curiosity and expectation concerning what the visitation issues were for the Vatican.	There is a reference to "the many months of study needed by the Holy See for a careful review and appropriate reaction."

4. Text Type	Personalized business letter meant for public consumption.	Marks of a business letter present here include the formal heading, greeting and words of closure. The body of the letter consists primarily of a brief report of the visitation findings in elevated but not technical language.
5. Diction	Several instances of rewording soften the tone of the Laghi letter, as compared with the Ratzinger letter. The word choices are also less formal and technical. The word "renewal" gets notably heavy use.	One example of rewording softening the tone is Laghi´s use of "concerns" in the place of "problems." Another is Laghi´s choice to address Hunthausen as "Archbishop Hunthausen" rather than "Your Excellency" (for Americans, the latter is an unusual and exceptionally formal usage). Much of the technical vocabulary from the Ratzinger letter drops away altogether (e.g., Latin names of curial documents) to be replaced by general, summary descriptors for Church thought and practice. The word "renewal," which has already cropped up in earlier texts (from Hunthausen and Ratzinger) and which appears to be a site of ideological contestation, appears 5 times here. Ratzinger's emphasis on clarity also reappears here.
6. Usage	Laghi hides agency by providing no concrete referent for his term "the Holy See." Laghi praises Hunthausen directly in the second person, but then switches to indirect constructions that lack defining subjects and verbs when he lists the identified concerns.	"The Holy See considered it necessary to evaluate certain allegations": Who, precisely, was involved in the decision? Example from the list of concerns: "Greater vigilance in upholding the Church's teaching, especially with regard to contraceptive sterilization and homosexuality." The nominalization employed here hides Hunthausen's relationship to the problem and the specific nature of the problem.
7. Substructures of the Text	Standard forms of epistolary greeting and closure, brief history of visitation process, report of conclusions (in the form of a numbered list).	There is a significant change in the proportionality of parts, in comparison with the Ratzinger letter. This letter divides into even thirds: preliminary comments (review of visitation process), praise for Hunthausen, concerns re. archdiocese. Thus, whereas the Ratzinger letter read primarily as a highly detailed description of problems, this comes across as a more collaborative and friendly text.
8. Intertextuality	Laghi makes explicit reference to the texts that the Visitator examined; the Documents of the Second Vatican Council; and the Code of Canon Law. Notably absent are references to previous correspondence, to specific curial	"There are many indications that you have striven with heart and mind to be a dedicated bishop of the Church, eager to implement the renewal called for in the Documents of the Second Vatican Council."

	instructions, and to the 1976 and 1979 Archdiocesan questionnaires, all of which appeared in the Ratzinger letter. In a hidden way, of course, the letter also refers directly to and depends on the Ratzinger letter.	
II. Coping Strategies in Evidence	**Tactics**	**Indications in Document**
1. Show **deference** to the structural order and mindset of the **Church**	Laghi shows deference first by carrying out his assignment of composing the new letter. He shows his respect for Ratzinger's higher position in the Church hierarchy by adhering closely to the compositional structure that Ratzinger has established. The new material that Laghi adds is primarily praise for Hunthausen. The material that he subtracts implies Hunthausen's criticism of Hunthausen's leadership. By making these changes, Laghi precludes opportunities for outsiders to see a bishop (and intrahierarchical relations) of the Church put in a less than favorable light.	Note that Laghi himself does not "close" the visitation (as Ratzinger does) but he "informs" Hunthausen of its closure, thus signalling that, within the hierarchy it is not his place to make this decision. Another example of deference to hierarchical structure: "It was the Visitator's role to speak to you as a brother bishop… to obtain necessary facts and to analyze them for the Holy See." Example of respecting Hunthausen's office and presenting Church intrahierarchical relations positively: "The Church is grateful for what you have accomplished and I am confident that you will be able to address effectively the concerns expressed in this letter."
2. Associate one's own efforts with the best interest of the Church	Near the end of the letter, Laghi allows himself to speak on behalf of "the Church."	"The Church is grateful for what you have accomplished and I am confident that you will be able to address effectively the concerns expressed in this letter."
3. Minimize the appearance of conflict	The letter as a whole, by its very existence and by the way it re-presents the contents of the Ratzinger letter, provides strong evidence of the Holy See's desire to minimize the appearance of conflict. Ratzinger's more critical letter is replaced by a much milder version which can be distributed publicly.	Added paragraph of praise (not appearing in Ratzinger letter): "You have given much time to fostering the morale of your priests and religious, meeting with them and encouraging them to participate in the renewal of the Church…. Your own special skills as a homilist and speaker have played a significant role toward that renewal."
4. Show fraternity	This is more strongly in evidence than in the Ratzinger letter. Laghi describes Hickey's involvement as an act of "fraternal assistance and support," a phrase that does not appear in the Ratzinger letter. Laghi also praises Hunthausen for his loyalty and cooperation and offers his own future assistance.	In contrast with the Ratzinger letter, which praised Hunthausen for his "kindness and patience" during the visitation, Laghi speaks of his "loyalty and cooperation." Laghi then says, "You can rely on my assistance and support." In Ratzinger's letter he mentions only the assistance he and his congregation have offered up to this point ("In bringing all the above points to your attention, it has been our purpose to assist you as effectively as possible…"). Ratzinger makes no explicit offer of future assistance.

5. Practice courtesy	Many politeness tactics are repeated from the Ratzinger letter (especially the indirect language which avoids blaming Hunthausen outright for the problematic conditions in his archdiocese). What is new is the omission of the detailed description of problems and the increased amount of praise.	What were "problems" in the Ratzinger letter become "concerns" here.
6. Employ secrecy	Laghi hides the same things that the Ratzinger letter does (Who does "the Holy See" refer to exactly? What was in the visitation report?) and more (the involvement of the Congregation for the Doctrine of the Faith, the existence of the Ratzinger letter and the specific contents of the letter).	Compare this sentence from the Laghi letter – "Greater vigilance in upholding the Church's teaching, especially with regard to… homosexuality" – with the following from Ratzinger: "The Archdiocese should withdraw all support from any group which does not unequivocally accept the teaching of the Magisterium concerning the intrinsic evil of homosexual activity." Laghi keeps inflammatory language from public view.
7. Recruit allies	Though the letter is addressed to Hunthausen, it shows clear evidence of being written for a more general readership, with fellow bishops being likely consumers.	Technical terms and references to congregational documents disappear: they are not inviting or of interest to the general public. The removal of critical passages and addition of laudatory passages suggests that Laghi wants not to offend Hunthausen supporters and fellow bishops.
8. Argue persuasively	**Ambiguous**. The organization and content are mostly taken over from Ratzinger. Laghi is more concerned to placate Hunthausen than persuade him.	Placation: See the added passages of praise, e.g., "You have given much time to fostering the morale of your priests and religious…"
9. Assert personal identity	**NA**. Laghi's self-presentation is warmer and more prominent than what we find in the Ratzinger letter, but his personal identity is only minimally revealed.	Warmer tone to self-presentation: "Even as I offer these observations, I am aware of your continuous efforts to promote genuine growth and renewal…"
III. Overall Coping Strategy	**Explanation**	**Indications in Document**
a. Yielding	By ordering the production and distribution of this letter, the Vatican gives in to Hunthausen's request to have something he can make public regarding the outcome of the visitation. It is only a partial concession because Hunthausen had asked to make the Ratzinger letter public. This amounts to a notable but not dramatic concession of the center party to the periphery party.	The document itself (its availability for distribution) is the indication.

Observable Strategies: Intervening Developments, C. (November 1985-September 1986)

	Strategies	Tactics	Objectives
Center	1. Show **deference** to the structural order and mindset of the **Church** 2. **Associate** one's own efforts with the best interest of the **Church** 3. **Minimize** the appearance of **conflict** 4. **Show fraternity** 5. **Practice courtesy** 6. **Employ secrecy** 7. **Recruit allies** 8. **Argue persuasively** 9. **Assert** personal **identity**	1. a. center applies own powers of appointment and governance 2. a. Pope's letter installing Wuerl speaks of good of Church 3. a. Holy See keeps exchanges regarding special powers hidden 4. a. Pope, Wuerl and Hunthausen pose for picture together in Rome; b. they also meet privately; c. Pope's letter installing Wuerl speaks of brother bishops, unity 5. a. Pope's letter is gracious 6. a. Vatican does not disclose intention for Wuerl to have special faculties 7. **NA** (no evidence) 8. Ambiguous. Though textual evidence is lacking, it is apparent that the pronuncio attempted to persuade Hunthausen to accept bishop with special powers 9. **NA** (no evidence)	Transfer power from Hunthausen to Wuerl without raising further controversy.
Periphery	1. **Deference-Church** 2. **Associate-Church** 3. **Minimize conflict** 4. **Show fraternity** 5. **Practice courtesy** 6. **Employ secrecy** 7. **Recruit allies** 8. **Argue persuasively** 9. **Assert identity**	1. a. Hunthausen thanks pro-nuncio and Holy See publicly for having supported his ministry; b. Hunthausen expresses gratitude and joy for Wuerl appointment; c. praises Wuerl 2. a. Hunthausen says he accepts presentation of concerns in spirit in which they were offered 4. a. Hunthausen says concerns were presented to him in a "fraternal and constructive spirit" 5. a. Hunthausen thanks Laghi for letter and thanks Laghi and Holy See for support 6. a. Hunthausen does not disclose existence of Ratzinger letter when releasing Laghi letter; b. Hunthausen does not mention intention for Wuerl to have unusual degree of oversight; c. [Sign of **resistance**] Hunthausen reads Ratzinger letter to priests of the Archdiocese 7. **NA** (no evidence) 8. a. Hunthausen assesses contents of letter (noting concerns and affirmations); b. defends self, saying he has already taken action; c. pledges to deal with all concerns; d. calls for cooperation 9. a. Hunthausen admits limitations; b. makes personal appeal for support	Maintain appearance of cooperation with Rome. Surrender as little power as possible to Wuerl.
Third	1. **Deference-Church** 2. **Associate-Church** 3. **Minimize**	1. a. Wuerl expresses joy at appointment; b. Wuerl praises Hunthausen and Seattle Archdiocese; c. Wuerl thanks Holy Father 2. a. Wuerl uses imagery of service in Christ's vineyard 3. a. Wuerl does not mention visitation	Wuerl: Present self as humble servant of Church.

388

| | conflict 4. **Show fraternity** 5. **Practice courtesy** 6. **Employ secrecy** 7. **Recruit allies** 8. **Argue persuasively** 9. **Assert identity** | 4. a. Wuerl speaks of serving "distinguished archbishop" 5. a. Wuerl responds enthusiastically and gratefully to news of his appointment 6. a. Wuerl does not acknowledge special nature of his assignment 7. **NA** (no evidence) 8. **Ambiguous**. a. Wuerl argues with Hunthausen about faculties he is supposed to have. 9. **Ambiguous**: Wuerl speaks in first person but in conventionally self-effacing way. | |

Analytic Summary, Document 3 (9.3.86 Hunthausen Press Statement Announcing Wuerl's Special Faculties):

	Overview	Indications in Document
I. Analysis of Text Construction		
1. Production	Hunthausen is the principal. Hunthausen's vicar general, Fr. Michael G. Ryan was probably the author, and Hunthausen's secretary, Marilyn Maddeford, was probably the animator. The text was produced and released to the press in Seattle.	Hunthausen releases the document to the press in his own name and writes in the first person. (Fr. Ryan indicated in a private interview that he typically wrote Hunthausen's statements and that Ms. Maddeford normally prepared the typed version. After producing a first draft, Ryan would give the text to Hunthausen, who might choose to solicit input from other advisers as well.)
2. Distribution	Normally, a final draft press release was passed on from Hunthausen / Ryan to Archdiocesan Public Affairs Director Russ Scearce, who would then share it with the press. Archdiocesan statements were also normally published in *The Progress*. (The *Progress* editor at the time was Bill Dodds.)	In this case, the statement was released to the press by the archdiocesan public affairs office. This statement was not published in *The Progress*. Instead, Hunthausen published a similar but more detailed statement there. Various newspapers reprinted the full text of the statement as did *Origins* (9.18.86).
3. Consumption	The target audience that is mentioned are Hunthausen's "close collaborators" in archdiocesan ministry and administration, but obviously the text was distributed to a much wider audience than this. Consumption of the statement took place in various formats including those of: the original news release, newspaper articles, radio and TV broadcast reports, later magazine and journal versions. Notably, accompanying the statement in many forms of distribution was a "Chronology of Events Related to	*Origins* published both the first statement and the accompanying chronology from Seattle under the heading, 'Archbishop Hunthausen Statement: Authority of Seattle's Auxiliary Bishop." In *The Progress* (9.11.86), a subsequent more detailed version of the original statement appears addressed to "Dear Friends in Christ," and is accompanied by the Seattle chronology.

	Apostolic Visitation and Appointment of Auxiliary Bishop Donald W. Wuerl…" issued by the archdiocesan public affairs office. It is likely that reading this supplementary document would have colored one's reading of the Hunthausen statement (though how exactly it would have influenced this reading is hard to say).	
4. Text Type	Press announcement. Chronological narrative.	No explicit addressee is indicated, which is common for a press release, but Hunthausen does express a general need to make this news known, and in particular to his collaborators in ministry and administration. Hunthausen states that earlier he did not feel a full public acknowledgment of Wuerl's faculties was called for, but now he felt the need to "share these matters with my close collaborators in the ministry and administration of the archdiocese." Chronological narrative: Hunthausen tells the story of his understanding of Wuerl's role in Seattle, from the fall of 1985 to September of 1986.
5. Diction	Hunthausen repeatedly refers to "the Holy See" but does not say whom he means with this term. Hunthausen also suggests the inadequacy of the word "assist" to describe Wuerl's role in Seattle: Wuerl is obviously in place to do more than assist. Hunthausen's diction is nonconfrontational. He presents himself as one who passively receives "understanding" and "clarification."	There are four uses of "the Holy See." Hunthausen chooses the pronoun "it" to refer to this antecedent, which draws out the sense that the Holy See is some sort of faceless, impersonal entity. "Assist" brings an echo of both the Ratzinger and Laghi visitation findings letters, both of which emphasized the Vatican's desire to provide Hunthausen with assistance. "Once I received this clarification, I… took steps to carry out the wishes of the Holy See."
6. Usage	Hunthausen writes in the first person. Apart from announcing Wuerl's faculties, this also offers a self-presentation (and justification) of Hunthausen's actions thus far. Hunthausen's usage also hides (or reveals that he does not know) aspects of process insofar as the Holy See is involved.	Six of the nine sentences contain a first-person pronoun. "…I did not understand the nature and extent of Bishop Wuerl's role." Process involving the Holy See: "After considerable discussion with the Holy See, it was confirmed that it was the understanding of the Holy See…"
7. Substructures of the Text	There is a *fact* (Wuerl's possession of powers) presented in the middle of a *story* (how we got to this point from the time of Wuerl's appointment).	The fact: Wuerl has "complete and final decision-making power" in the designated areas. The story: There was a discussion; Hunthausen misunderstood; now he understands.
8. Intertextuality	The only document explicitly named is a July 1, 1986 letter which confirmed that Hunthausen was to delegate final-decision making	"It was subsequently confirmed to me in a letter dated July 1, 1986."

	power in the five areas to Wuerl. A more oblique reference to other texts is Hunthausen's mention of speculation about Wuerl's role which had taken place "in printed form." His mention of the formal conclusion of the visitation brings to mind the 9.30.85 Ratzinger letter.	
II. Coping Strategies in Evidence	**Tactics**	**Indications in Document**
1. Show deference to the structural order and mindset of the Church	Hunthausen adopts a tone of humble submission and acceptance of his subordinate position within the hierarchy. Hunthausen does not contest the legitimacy of the process.	Submission: "Once I received this clarification, I… took steps to carry out the wishes of the Holy See."
2. Associate one's own efforts with the best interest of the Church	Hunthausen indicates that his silence regarding Wuerl's role was precipitated by a concern for the successfulness of Wuerl's ministry. Hunthausen's concluding sentence also suggests that the present disclosure is undertaken for the success of his own ministry and that of his collaborators.	"assuring Wuerl of the best possible climate for beginning this ministry among us…" "I… also arrived at the conclusion that it was important for me to share these matters with my close collaborators in the ministry…"
3. Minimize the appearance of conflict	**Ambiguous**. Hunthausen expresses no anger or disappointment here concerning the delegation of faculties to Wuerl. Hunthausen also admits that he had not made his earlier understanding of Wuerl's special responsibility known out of a desire to minimize friction in the transition. On the other hand, by making this announcement, he brings the conflict into the open.	"The importance of making Bishop Wuerl's transition to the archdiocese as smooth as possible and of assuring him of the best possible climate for beginning this ministry among us seemed to outweigh any possible good that might have been realized by giving a full public acknowledgment…"
4. Show fraternity	**Ambiguous**. Hunthausen provides an example of collegial (possibly fraternal) decision making. His expressed desire to have given Wuerl a smooth start in Seattle can be considered and act of fraternity.	Decision making: "Bishop Wuerl and I, along with the apostolic pro-nuncio, judged it best to make no public announcement…" Smooth start: "The importance of making Bishop Wuerl's transition… as smooth as possible…"
5. Practice courtesy	**Ambiguous**. The usual, exaggerated forms of courtesy are absent, but Hunthausen offers no criticism of the other parties or the process.	NA.
6. Employ secrecy	Hunthausen indicates that he practiced secrecy himself in regard to Wuerl's role. He also uses the term "the Holy See" to avoid naming specific agents. But here Hunthausen also **resists** secrecy by bringing the business into the open.	"at the time of his appointment both Bishop Wuerl and I, along with the apostolic pro-nuncio, judged it best to make no public announcement to that effect…" "After considerable discussion with the Holy See, it was confirmed that it was the understanding of the Holy See…"
7. Recruit allies	By revealing his own loss of power, Hunthausen makes an implicit plea for help.	"Once I received this clarification, I… arrived at the conclusion that it was important for me to share these matters…"

8. Argue persuasively	Hunthausen offers a brief explanation and justification for his actions.	"The importance of making Bishop Wuerl's transition... as smooth as possible... seemed to outweigh any possible good that might have been realized by giving a full public acknowledgment.
9. Assert personal identity	NA. Though Hunthausen gives his account in the first person, he seems mostly concerned to pass on the basic information (and not to highlight aspects of his own identity for the sake of advantage)	NA.
III. Overall Coping Strategy	**Explanation**	**Indications in Document**
a. Contending	This is a subtle form of contending. Hunthausen makes a show of humbly submitting while undertaking an act sure to displease the Vatican (forcing the discussion into the open).	"Once I received this clarification, I not only took steps to carry out the wishes of the Holy See, but also arrived at the conclusion that it was important for me to share these matters..."

Observable Strategies: Intervening Developments, D. (September-October 1986)

	Strategies	**Tactics**	**Objectives**

Center	1. Show **deference** to the structural order and mindset of the **Church** 2. **Associate** one's own efforts with the best interest of the **Church** 3. **Minimize** the appearance of **conflict** 4. **Show fraternity** 5. **Practice courtesy** 6. **Employ secrecy** 7. **Recruit allies** 8. **Argue persuasively** 9. **Assert** personal **identity**	1. a. Laghi works through structure of episcopal conference to release his chronology 2. a. Laghi, in press comments, speaks of need to keep Church energies in a straight line 3. a. Laghi discussions with NCCB and Hunthausen are held in private; b. Vatican officials request endorsement for chronology, NCCB distribution, in private; 4. a. Laghi, Holy See work in cooperation with NCCB; b. Laghi shows Hunthausen the chronology before he releases it; c. see the complicated sequence leading to NCCB release of the Vatican chronology: Laghi calls Rome; Laghi calls Bernardin; Bernardin calls Malone; Malone calls Laghi; Malone calls 2nd executive committee meeting 5. a. Laghi shows Hunthausen the chronology before releasing it publicly 6. a. Holy See conducts its negotiations with NCCB and with Hunthausen re. chronology in secret; b. **[Leak]** Vatican official Costalunga says taking power from Hunthausen was disciplinary and not necessarily permanent; c. **[Leak]** Vatican spokesman Navarro-Valls says Vatican action was regular in accord with canon law and perhaps reversible 7. a. NCCB seeks to bring NCCB (via its executive committee) on board as an ally; b. Laghi calls on Bernardin after failing to gain NCCB endorsement for chronology 8. a. Laghi argues for NCCB endorsement of Chronology 9. **NA** (no evidence)	To formulate a public response to the outcry that arose in conjunction with Hunthausen's announcement of Wuerl's faculties.
Periphery	1. **Deference-Church** 2. **Associate-Church** 3. **Minimize conflict** 4. **Show fraternity** 5. **Practice courtesy** 6. **Employ secrecy** 7. **Recruit allies** 8. **Argue persuasively** 9. **Personal identity**	1. a. Hunthausen (& Wuerl) interview is highly respectful of Church; b. so too are Hunthausen's letters to local Catholics ("I feel honored and deeply privileged to be able to serve this Church") 2. a. Hunthausen, in interview, says he acted in good faith; b. in letter to Catholics, Hunthausen says he is "firmly committed" to witnessing to the Gospel 3. **Resist**: Though Hunthausen consistently employs measured language when doing so, he makes a clear and concerted effort to bring the conflict issues (and his view thereof) into the open via various statements. 4. a. Hunthausen emphasizes his solidarity with Wuerl; b. Hunthausen stresses that he acted in good faith (i.e., not intentionally against Rome's wishes); c. Hunthausen participates in NCCB negotiations re. Vatican chronology 5. a. Hunthausen interview shows courtesy toward Wuerl and Rome; b. Hunthausen letters show courtesy toward Wuerl and Rome 6. a. Hunthausen engages in secret negotiations re. release of Vatican chronology; b. Hunthausen asks Laghi not to release Vatican chronology; c. Sign of **resistance**: Hunthausen's PR campaign is a concerted	To show that Hunthausen has acted in good faith and to shore up his personal support within the Seattle Archdiocese.

		effort to tell his side of the story and to reveal past developments that put his past and current decisions in a favorable light 7. a. Hunthausen's interview explains his position and answer questions for people of his own archdiocese (shoring up support); b. Hunthausen's letters to local Catholics explain his position and explicitly ask for help ("I cannot do it alone"); c. Hunthausen's negotiations with NCCB almost certainly involve a search for allies 8. a. Hunthausen interview offers persuasive argumentation; b. so too do his letters to local Catholics; c. see also the behind-the-scenes NCCB negotiations, where Hunthausen gave reasons to Laghi not to release his chronology (would distract NCCB; would cause further division) 9. a. Strong assertions of personal identity by Hunthausen appear in the interview; b. and in the letters to local Catholics also ("I feel it is important for me to tell you that…").	
Third	1. **Deference-Church** 2. **Associate-Church** 3. **Minimize conflict** 4. **Show fraternity** 5. **Practice courtesy** 6. **Employ secrecy** 7. **Recruit allies** 8. **Argue persuasively** 9. **Personal identity**	1. a. Wuerl in interview refuses to call the visitation process "unjust;" b. Wuerl, in his letter to priests, quotes Vatican's praise of Hunthausen's leadership; c. Wuerl considers visit / consultation in Rome; d. NCCB exec. committee abides by Vatican request for conference to release Vatican chronology; e. Cardinal Bernardin restarts NCCB discussion at Laghi request. 2. a. Wuerl in interview: "I think it's important for the good of the church… to always say this is not an injustice" 3. a. Wuerl, in interview, stresses the existing unity in the Church and says that while a painful situation has developed, it is not the product of an unjust process (i.e., he refuses to assign blame); b. Wuerl in his letter to priests: "It is clear to me that the person of the archbishop and the sincerity of his ministry were never challenged, much less attacked;" c. [Counterpoint] Wuerl acknowledges the dispute that took place among the priests; d. Statements of individual bishops (Walsh, Power, Law) are tight-lipped about the conflict; e. NCCB negotiations, struggles take place in secret 4. a. Wuerl refuses to criticize Hunthausen or Vatican; b. NCCB exec. committee consults with Laghi and with Hunthausen; c. Cardinal Bernardin intervenes with NCCB exec. committee at request of Laghi 5. a. Wuerl, in his letter to priests, cites Vatican's praise of Hunthausen 6. a. NCCB executive committee conducts discussion of release of Vatican chronology in secret 7. a. Much lobbying takes place in NCCB executive commitment regarding endorsement	Wuerl: To defend the Vatican against attack while showing loyalty to Hunthausen. NCCB Executive Committee: To respond to the Vatican's wishes without taking a stand against Hunthausen. Individual bishop commentators: To respond to questions about the affair and perhaps signal a view without committing oneself to a specific position.

		/ release of Vatican chronology.
		8. **Ambiguous**. Possible evidence for: Wuerl argues against the idea that the visitation was an unjust process; b. the NCCB exec. committee argues for the need to maintain neutrality
		9. a. Wuerl steps forward by himself to challenge priests who would call the visitation unjust (Wuerl's letter to priests)

Analytic Summary, Document 4 (The Vatican Chronology, 10.24.86)

	Overview	Indications in Document
I. Analysis of Text Construction		
1. Production	The Holy See is the principal; Laghi is the author. The influence of others on the text (Ratzinger? Gantin?) is unknown. The document was produced (probably in Washington, D.C.) amid the controversy which followed Hunthausen's announcement of Wuerl's faculties.	A signal of the impetus leading to production: "Regretfully, the surprise announcement made by Archbishop Hunthausen after granting the faculties was interpreted as portraying this whole process as a one-sided affair."
2. Distribution	Laghi prepared the document and released it, with an authorization from Rome, for distribution to the U.S. bishops and the press through then NCCB President James Malone (Bishop of Youngstown, Ohio). A neutrally-phrased Malone cover letter accompanied the letter's distribution. (The 10.31.86 *National Catholic Reporter* offers a detailed discussion of the behind-the-scenes negotiations regarding the chronology's distribution. Many persons gave input in this matter including Hunthausen, Ratzinger, Gantin and members of the NCCB executive committee.) Hunthausen asked Laghi not to publish the Chronology.	The report, dated 10.24.86, appeared in newspapers on 10.28. It appeared in the 10.30 issue of *The Progress* and in the 10.31 issue of the *National Catholic Reporter*. Hunthausen, in his response to the Chronology: "after I first read the Chronology, I asked Archbishop Laghi not to publish it because I felt it would raise more questions than it could possibly hope to answer…"
3. Consumption	The NCCB executive committee and Hunthausen were able to preview the document before its distribution to the NCCB. Cardinals Ratzinger and Gantin in Rome also had the opportunity to preview the document. Thereafter the American bishops were the next known consumers, followed immediately by members of the press and then, thereafter (via newspapers and other publications) the public. The primary intended consumers appear to be the American bishops, given	The text is constructed with multiple layers of units and sub-units, most of which are assigned numbers or letters. This construction makes the text easily consumable for readers, gives the impression of rationality, and allows easy citation of the various points in future discussions.

	the direct distribution to them and the structuring of arguments toward winning support for the Vatican position and the public at large (note the limited use of technical language).	
4. Text Type	A chronology. This is a much more argumentative chronology than the one issued by the Seattle Archdiocese accompanying Hunthausen's announcement of Wuerl's possession of faculties.	The title: "A Chronology of Recent Events in the Archdiocese of Seattle." The narrative moves forward in time from 1978, with date indications along the way, up to the date of the issuance of the chronology itself (October 24, 1986).
5. Diction	Though much of the diction is measured (polite, euphemistic), we see significant breaks from graciousness. Laghi contests a word choice which he attributes to Hunthausen (the granting of faculties were "mandated" by Rome) – inaccurately, as it turns out, since Hunthausen did not use the term in his press announcement.	Laghi drops the euphemism "visitation" in favor of "investigation" at one point. Hunthausen's "firmness" as leader of the archdiocese is called in into question, as is adequacy of his response to Vatican concerns. "[Hunthausen] granted the faculties and made the announcement that they were mandated by Rome. In fact, a more precise description would have been that this was the agreement reached by Archbishop Hunthausen and the Holy See…"
6. Usage	Gives appearance of objectivity (almost entirely in third person, excludes self-references from Laghi: at one point Laghi refers to himself in the third person as "the pronuncio."). No center party participants are named, apart from the visitator, Hickey. There are numerous agentless, passive-voice constructions. Hunthausen's opposition is a bureaucratic fog ("The Holy See").	"Substantiated complaints nevertheless continued. But, the decision to inquire further was primarily provoked by the documented responses of the archbishop himself." "It should be stressed that at no time did the Holy See pursue with Archbishop Hunthausen the criticisms it received on controversial issues, e.g., nuclear weapons and the payment of taxes."
7. Substructures of the Text	The chronology is divided into four sections, each of which stands in time and topical relation to the apostolic visitation. These subdivisions make the case that the visitation was undertaken for good reason, was conducted thoroughly and with the cooperation of Hunthausen himself, and has fairly resulted in the current outcomes.	The numbered section titles: 1) Decision for an Apostolic Visitation of Seattle. 2) Preparation of the Apostolic Visitation. 3) The Visitation. 4) The Decisions after the Visitation.
8. Intertextuality	It is interesting that the Laghi issues a chronology just seven weeks after Seattle issued its own, but the two are functionally dissimilar. The Seattle chronology appears to be little more than a fact sheet for the press, whereas the Vatican chronology is a complex piece of argumentation. Nonetheless, one can imagine that Laghi's choice of	A sample of explicit references to other texts contained within the Vatican chronology: "the Holy See sought the assistance of the Archbishop of Seattle in responding to the high volume of complaints that were sent to Rome by priests, Religious and faithful…" "The Holy See's interest in this matter reflected its responsibility for

	text type was prompted by the prior example. This text makes explicit reference to multiple other texts. Almost always the references to other texts are part of a strategy of justification of the Vatican's handling of the affair. Thus, there are references to complaints sent to Rome; to troubling "documented responses" of the archbishop; to the documentation that served as evidence on which the visitation conclusions were based; to the archbishop's interview text, which he "reviewed and signed" (attesting to its accuracy); to a 9.11.58 from Hunthausen to the pro-nuncio which acknowledged the Vatican doubts about Hunthausen's leadership; and to other correspondence and documentation. Across the board the intertextual references work to undermine Hunthausen's position. References to official Church documents (Vatican II's "Constitution on the Church" – i.e., Lumen Gentium; blanket references to directives of the Holy See and NCCB, and the "teachings of the Magisterium;" the Code of Canon Law) serve the same purpose.	the well-being of the Universal Church, as outlined in the "Constitution on the Church" of the Second Vatican Council. "the decision to inquire further was primarily provoked by the documented responses of the archbishop himself…" "Many of those who had lodged complaints against Archbishop Hunthausen had sent him copies of their letters to the Holy See…" "Information was gathered from the following sources: 1) public documents such as archdiocesan policy statements… 2) The testimony given by those on the list prepared in advance… 3) The testimony of the archbishop himself, a written copy of which he reviewed and signed…" "The Code of Canon Law (canon 403.2) does contemplate cases when the Holy See grants special faculties…"
II. Coping Strategies in Evidence	**Tactics**	**Indications in Document**
1. Show deference to the structural order and mindset of the Church	Laghi refers to teaching of Vatican II. He refers to Vatican's prerogative to appoint a visitator. He emphasizes the many steps taken to consult with and respect the office of the local bishop. He notes Church standards that apply to the pastoral practices in question. He calls attention to Holy See's power of episcopal appointment. He refers to Canon Law.	The Vatican II teaching cited is the "Constitution on the Church" (*Lumen Gentium*). Visitator appointment: "on July 6, 1983, the Most Reverend James A. Hickey… was named Apostolic Visitator." Consultation / respect: "since 1978, the Holy See… has corresponded with Archbishop Hunthausen on matters…" Church standards that apply: See the presentation of the six areas of concern. Power of appointment: see extended discussion in section 4. Canon Law: reference is to canon 403.2, in section 4.
2. Associate one's own efforts with the best interest of the Church	Laghi makes this point explicitly in the text.	"The Holy See's interest in this matter reflected it responsibility for the well-being of the Universal Church." "From the beginning the priorities of the Holy See were two-fold: 1) to promote the building up of the church in Seattle in harmony with the Universal Church and 2) to

		protect the good name of Archbishop Hunthausen."
3. Minimize the appearance of conflict	**Resistance**. The text brings the Vatican's side of the controversy into the open. The text contains numerous explicit and implicit criticisms of Hunthausen's handling of the affair and of his leadership ability.	"Archbishop Hunthausen understood that the Holy See considered him lacking the firmness necessary to govern the archdiocese" "For more than six months after the arrival of Bishop Wuerl, the agreed-to faculties were not given."
4. Show fraternity	**NA** (no evidence).	**NA**.
5. Practice courtesy	**Resistance**. Laghi questions Hunthausen's firmness as a leader and his cooperativeness.	"the Holy See considered him lacking the firmness necessary" "it was his [Hunthausen's] interpretation of the importance of these matters and the inadequacy of his response that were the principal concern"
6. Employ secrecy	Though this document brings information and certain of Laghi's views into the open, it also conceals the identity of those involved in Rome and keeps secret the great majority of the contents of previous discussions between Laghi and Hunthausen	Laghi begins by telling us that the conversation between the Apostolic Nunciature (Delegation) has been taking place since 1978, but this brief accounting is the first report from the nunciature regarding those exchanges. Laghi quotes from Hunthausen's letter of Sept. 11, 1985, but we have no idea of the remainder of the letter's contents.
7. Recruit allies	Laghi's statement makes a case (to fellow bishops in particular) that the Vatican has been thorough and fair in its dealings with Hunthausen, that it has legitimate concerns, and that its current frustrations have much to result from Hunthausen's failure to cooperate fully. Laghi also points out that "other bishops" were the ones who suggested the need for a visitation.	"the Holy See sought the assistance of the Archbishop of Seattle in responding to the high volume of complaints" "The archbishop agreed that there were abuses in a number of cases…" "Substantial complaints nevertheless continued…" After the visitation, "five areas of concern remained" "For more than six months… the agreed-to faculties were not given" "Regretfully, the surprise announcement… was interpreted as portraying this whole process as a one-sided affair."
8. Argue persuasively	The entire text argues the pro-nuncio's position. There is an appeal to common standards, both ecclesiastical (Church teaching, Canon Law) and ethical (fairness, thoroughness, reasonableness, the importance of living up to one's word, etc.) On the one hand, the text strives for a feeling of rationality and objectivity (the first person is avoided; it moves from "facts" to analysis to conclusions). On the other hand, the language at certain points is passionately critical.	Appeal to standards: The Holy See's involvement "reflected its responsibility for the well-being of the Universal Church, as outlined in the Constitution of the Church'" "It was the firm intention of the Holy See that any action required would come only after fully informing Archbishop Hunthausen and making every effort to secure his agreement and support." Critical language: "the Holy See considered him lacking the firmness necessary to govern the

			archdiocese…"
9. Assert personal identity	**NA**. Laghi downplays his own identity in this document. It is not issued in his name and in the contents of the text he refers to himself as "the pro-nuncio."		**NA**.
III. Overall Coping Strategy	**Explanation**		**Indications in Document**
Contending	In response to a wave of negative publicity, Laghi prepares a document to tell Rome's side of the story. He also attempts to gain an NCCB endorsement for his version, an effort that fails.		The criticisms of Hunthausen are the strongest indications of its contentious intent. Note, too, that the document was released against Hunthausen's wishes.

Observable Strategies: Intervening Developments, E. (October-November, 1986)

	Strategies	Tactics	Objectives
Center	1. Show **deference** to the structural order and mindset of the **Church** 2. **Associate** one's own efforts with the best interest of the **Church** 3. **Minimize** the appearance of **conflict** 4. **Show fraternity** 5. **Practice courtesy** 6. **Employ secrecy** 7. **Recruit allies** 8. **Argue persuasively** 9. **Assert** personal **identity**	1. a. Pope's message to NCCB reflects on the mystery of the Church and the responsibilities of leadership 2. a. Pope describes own role as a matter of promoting the universality of the Church, protecting legitimate variety, guaranteeing Catholic unity, etc. 3. **Ambiguous**. a. Laghi's message to NCCB does not mention conflict; b. Pope's message to NCCB does not mention conflict; but c. Rome shows a willingness to have the case be debated in the wider context of the NCCB. 4. a. Pope speaks of ecclesial communion among bishops, referring to "collegitas effectiva et affectiva" 5. a. Pope offers no criticism of Hunthausen; b. Pope addresses American bishops respectfully 6. a. Pope keeps his personal assessment of the affair hidden, speaking of applicable issues only in general terms; b. Laghi participates in closed executive session of NCCB meeting. 7. a. Pope and Laghi appear to be recruiting the conference as a whole 8. a. Pope's address offers doctrinal arguments for his own intervention and the bishops' responsibility to be loyal 9. **NA**. Laghi's assertion of his own identity with his comment about his role in bishop appointments is fairly minor. Mostly he withdraws from public assertion of his person. The Pope's involvement is also impersonal.	To establish symbolic (territorial) control over the NCCB meeting and remind the bishops of their duty to be loyal to the Holy See.
Periphery	1. **Deference-Church** 2. **Associate-Church** 3. **Minimize-conflict** 4. **Show**	1. a. Hunthausen explicitly declares his "respect for Archbishop Laghi and for the office he holds" and his "personal loyalty" to the Pope 2. a. Hunthausen: "let us do all we can to preserve the bond of unity that is ours as faithful members of the church" 3. **Resistance**: a. Hunthausen acknowledges the reality of the conflict and brings discussion of its issues into the open: "Let us help break the cycle	To profess loyalty to Rome while offering a first challenge to the Vatican chronology.

	fraternity 5. **Practice courtesy** 6. **Employ secrecy** 7. **Recruit allies** 8. **Argue persuasively** 9. **Personal identity**	of tension that now exists… to rise above any contentious spirit;" Hunthausen's mixed feelings are shown by his argument for rising above contentious spirit, coupled with his preparation of two contentious statements for distribution to NCCB. 4. a. Hunthausen refers to his respect for Laghi, his loyalty to the Holy Father and his intention to speak to his fellow bishops at their forthcoming meeting 5. a. Hunthausen refuses to criticize Laghi or Pope; b. Hunthausen expressly affirms his bondedness to them 6. a. Hunthausen hides his experience and feelings in his first response to Vatican chronology 7. a. Hunthausen prepares texts to persuade NCCB 8. a. Hunthausen uses complexity argument to challenge the Vatican chronology (Laghi oversimplifies: it is all more complex than that) 9. a. Hunthausen speaks in the first person here but he does not foreground his personality nearly as much as in some other statements	
Third	1. **Deference-Church** 2. **Associate-Church** 3. **Minimize-conflict** 4. **Show fraternity** 5. **Practice courtesy** 6. **Employ secrecy** 7. **Recruit allies** 8. **Argue persuasively** 9. **Personal identity**	1. a. Malone shows strong inclination to protect Church's favored appearance of unity; b. NCCB agenda grants speaking time to pro-nuncio, who offers his own comments and message from Pope 2. a. Malone speaks of need to address "developing estrangement" between Church in the U.S. and the Holy See 3. a. Meeting opening address shows hurry to resolve the conflict (wants no discussion of "past" issues); b. NCCB meeting agenda shows interest in limiting the debate. 4. a. Malone says purpose is "to offer fraternal support to Archbishop Hunthausen and Bishop Wuerl" and refers to "the collegial spirit which unites us with one another and with the Holy Father" 5. a. Malone shows respect toward Hunthausen and Holy See 6. a. Malone gives no indication of all the preliminary conversations that have shaped the current agenda for the meeting 7. a. NCCB discussion is focused on generating support for one position or the other. 8. a. Malone points out two sides of center-periphery Church control question and argues that the two of necessity go together ("We cannot exist alone. We are a communio. We are a church.") 9. **NA** (No evidence).	NCCB Executive Committee: To use control of bishops' meeting agenda to prevent the debate from becoming too divisive.

Analytic Summary, Document 5 (Hunthausen's 11.11.86 Response to Vatican Chronology)

	Overview	Indications in Document
I. Analysis of Text Construction		
1. Production	Hunthausen is the principal. Hunthausen's Vicar General, Fr. Michael G. Ryan was the author. Hunthausen secretary Marilyn Maddeford was (I believe) the animator.	Hunthausen's status as principal is affirmed by his signature at the bottom of the text, by his use of the first person, and by the contents, which are only coherent if read as the testimony of Hunthausen himself. Indications of the involvement in Fr. Ryan and Ms. Maddeford in the production process are not self-evident within the final text products distributed through the media (unless one is able to identify particular elements of Fr. Ryan's writing style).
2. Distribution	Hunthausen prepared a written copy of the text, which was then distributed through the NCCB leadership to all of the bishops present at the Nov. 1986 NCCB meeting shortly prior to Hunthausen's oral address to the body. After the two sessions of debate of his case (Nov. 11 and 12), Hunthausen's text was released to the press (on Nov. 12), along with the written copy of Hunthausen's address to the bishops and the Malone statement. Further distribution took place through various media outlets.	In what is, I presume, an early copy of the text prepared for distribution as a press release, one finds the archdiocesan letterhead, the date November 11, 1986 and a space for Hunthausen's signature (but no signature) at the bottom. There is a reference to the fact that this response was distributed to Hunthausen's fellow bishops in Hunthausen's NCCB address (see doc. 6). The NCCB released the text to the press on 11.12.86. The full text of Hunthausen's response to the Vatican chronology was published in the 11.13.86 *Progress* (with a reproduction of Hunthausen's signature) and in the 11.20.86 *Origins*. Only excerpts from the text were shared in an 11.12.86 National Catholic News Service report and in the 11.13.86 newspaper accounts of the *New York Times*, *Seattle Times* and *Seattle Post-Intelligencer*.
3. Consumption	Bishops present at the NCCB meeting consumed the text simultaneously, reading individually (facsimiles of) the letter-report that Hunthausen supplied. Their interpretation would be influenced by his oral remarks, which offered a partisan frame of reference and influenced by the tension of the imminent debate. The press got its first look at the text at the conclusion of the NCCB debate of the Hunthausen case and in the immediate aftermath of hearing Malone's statement wrapping up the	Cues for consumption: Letter format, but the contents show it to be a formal report and it is released in a formal, communal setting. Thus, Hunthausen apparently wanted to invite a personal response to a rather serious matter of official business. Hunthausen leads with a series of pre-emptive remarks, which appear designed to soothe potential points of irritation ahead of time: "I hesitate to burden you with further reading material at this time.... I want to say, too, that it

	debate. The press' reading of the Hunthausen text was likely influenced by comments from other bishops about the debates that had taken place and the presence of the accompanying texts (the Hunthausen address, the Malone statement) which served as a context (together with the Vatican chronology). Other consumers were dependent on second- and third-hand reports from individuals, and on newspaper and broadcast news reports. (And later, magazine accounts.)	frankly embarrasses me to be engaging in this form of exchange of information…. I trust you will understand, then, that the matters which I will set forth herein are in no sense an attack upon his person [Laghi] or his integrity…" Along these same lines, Hunthausen says that he has long been concerned about the prospect of negative publicity for the Holy See resulting from the visitation and subsequent events.
4. Text Type	An *open letter* that functions rhetorically as an argumentative point-by-point *response* and a general *apologia*.	Hunthausen opens the letter with the greeting, "Your Eminence / Your Excellency" and he closes it with the salutation, "Fraternally in Christ" and his signature. All four of the internal section titles refer to the Vatican chronology, indicating Hunthausen's concern to respond directly to the contents of the chronology (which his own contents do). As an example of Hunthausen's intention to offer an apologia that goes beyond the chronology itself, see comments such as: "It was always my deepest desire and my strongly expressed wish that, whatever steps might be taken… they be taken in a way that would strengthen and cement our relationship with the Holy See…"
5. Diction	The diction is largely non-technical and plainspoken, which reflects Hunthausen's usual style but also an interest in reaching a wide audience. Hunthausen contests certain word choices of the Vatican chronology ("mandate;" "insistence;" "surprise announcement") as a part of an attempt to claim the high ground in the argument. Hunthausen also uses less guarded language here: thus he speaks of the Vatican "mounting" a visitation (echoes mounting an attack), uses critical terms such as "misleading" and "disappointing," and he straightforwardly uses the words "tense" and "confusion" to acknowledge the difficulties of the conflict situation.	Example of non-technical, plainspoken language: "I want to say, too, that it frankly embarrasses me to be engaging in this form of exchange of information." Contestation of word choices: "I made no reference to a 'mandate from Rome.'" "The Chronology speaks of my 'insistence'… A more accurate statement would have referred to my earnest desire…" "The Chronology makes reference to my 'surprise announcement'…" Less-guarded language: "The Chronology contained some misleading things…" "a point-by-point response at that time would only have escalated an already tense situation…"
6. Usage	Hunthausen's use of the first person contributes to his highly personal style. Active voice gives the text clarity. Hunthausen is selectively clear about agency, but there is significantly more naming of names	First person: "after I first read the Chronology, I asked Archbishop Laghi not to publish it…" Naming: "I expressed this concern in my earliest correspondence and in all my conversations with the

	than we have seen previously (Hickey, Laghi, Ratzinger and "the Holy Father" are named on one or more occasions). Shifts between past and present tense: Hunthausen describes and criticizes past developments and declares present bewilderment, disappointment. Grammatically, Hunthausen makes the Chronology the antagonist. He challenges persons only indirectly.	Holy See, with Cardinal Ratzinger, Archbishop Laghi, Archbishop Hickey, and even with the Holy Father himself." Obscured agency: "response I provided to inquiries made by the Holy See… were viewed as unsatisfactory…" Use of tense: "So, for anyone to review that correspondence now and to suggest that it was the cause of the Visitation troubles me greatly." Chronology as antagonist: "As far as the Chronology itself is concerned,… it either attempts to do too much… or to do too little…"
7. Substructures of the Text	The text has the ordinary subdivisions of a letter (address / greeting; body; conclusion / salutation). It also contains four easily distinguishable topical sections, each of which has a numbered title referring to a particular problem with the Vatican chronology. Prior to the first numbered section, one finds a rather personal preamble addressed directly to the bishops themselves in the second person.	Greeting: "Your Eminence / Your Excellency:" Titles of topical sections: 1) The Chronology contains some misleading things; 2) The Chronology contained some new learnings; 3) The Chronology contained some disappointing things; 4) The Chronology also contains some very real inaccuracies. Sample from personal preamble: "I hesitate to burden you with further reading material at this time. I do so only because I think the record demands it…"
8. Intertextuality	In an immediate sense, the reason to be for this text is to respond to another, the Vatican chronology. Throughout this letter, Hunthausen cites and cross-examines Laghi's chronology. Other explicit references to other texts focus on correspondence and public statements pertinent to the conflict handling itself – not to official Church documents, teachings, laws, etc.	Opening reference to Chronology: "I have decided it will be best for me to convey to you in printed form my response to the "Chronology of Recent Events in the Archdiocese of Seattle…" Other texts cited: general references to correspondence with the Holy See; Hunthausen's letter to Laghi, dated Dec. 2, 1985; one mention of the Code of Canon Law; the news release announcing the visitation; Hunthausen's announcement of Wuerl's possession of faculties; Hunthausen's address to the NCCB.
II. Coping Strategies in Evidence	**Tactics**	**Indications in Document**
1. Show deference to the structural order and mindset of the Church	Hunthausen professes his respect for the pro-nuncio. Hunthausen apologizes to the NCCB for burdening them. He says he is embarrassed to be engaging in the present exchange. He expresses his loyalty to the Holy See and his concern for its public appearance.	Respect: "My respect for Archbishop Laghi and the position that is his…" Apology: "I hesitate to burden you with further reading material at this time…" Embarrassment: "it frankly embarrasses me to be engaging in this form of exchange of information"

		"I feared it would ultimately… reflect unfavorably on the Holy See"
2. Associate one's own efforts with the best interest of the Church	Hunthausen explicitly states his concern for the Church.	"It was always my deepest desire… [that the steps taken would] strengthen and cement our relationship with the Holy See"
3. Minimize the appearance of conflict	**Resistance**. Hunthausen provides this argumentation not only to the bishops, but also to the press.	"The record will show… that, in the then unlikely event that I would agree to accept the special faculties arrangement… I would have no choice but to make this matter known…"
4. Show fraternity	Hunthausen takes his case directly to his fellow American bishops. He asks for their support and invites a review by the members of the Conference.	"I would certainly welcome some sort of review of all these matters should that be the wish of the members of the Conference."
5. Practice courtesy	**Ambiguous**. Hunthausen's language avoids personalizing the attack (he attacks the chronology and not Laghi) and he professes to want to save face for the Holy See, but his language is also highly critical.	Re. Laghi: "the matters… herein are in no sense an attack on his person or integrity…" But Hunthausen says the chronology contains "misleading things… disappointing things… inaccuracies"
6. Employ secrecy	Hunthausen keeps much information from previous exchanges secret, but he also **resists** the use of secrecy by taking his case to the bishops and the public.	"The Chronology speaks of my 'insistence' that a public announcement be made at the time the Apostolic Visitation was undertaken. A more accurate statement would have referred to my earnest desire… that, if the Visitation did indeed have to take place, I would like it to do so in as open and positive and constructive a spirit as possible"
7. Recruit allies	Hunthausen invites his fellow bishops and the public to understand his predicament and take up his cause.	"To the best of my ability, I have reflected on the contents of the Chronology and presented my understanding of events. Since there seems to be such a divergence of opinion… I would certainly welcome some sort of review of all these matters should that be the wish of the members of the Conference."
8. Argue persuasively	Hunthausen attacks the contents of the chronology on the grounds that some things were misleading, some were new to him, some things were disappointing and some were inaccurate.	"As far as the Chronology itself is concerned, let me say that I believe it either attempts to do too much (i.e., to tell the whole story in too brief a space) or too do too little (by that I mean that it doesn't really get to some of the deep, underlying problems which are at stake here).
9. Assert personal identity	This is a highly personal plea. Hunthausen tells his story in terms of his own recollections and experience, in stark contrast with the impersonal approach of the Vatican chronology.	"In the first place, it is probably important for you to know that, after I first read the Chronology, I asked Archbishop Laghi not to publish it because I felt it would raise more questions than it could possibly

		hope to answer."
III. Overall Coping Strategy	**Explanation**	**Indications in Document**
Contending	Hunthausen aggressively pursues the support of his fellow bishops and of the public.	Hunthausen's profession of being embarrassed to be involved in such an exchange of information is a good indicator of this document's likelihood to fuel controversy.

Analytic Summary, Document 6 (Hunthausen's 11.11.86 Address to the NCCB)

	Overview	**Indications in Document**
I. Analysis of Text Construction		
1. Production	Hunthausen is the principal, Fr. Michael G. Ryan the ghost writer and the animator was likely Hunthausen's secretary Ms. Marilyn Maddeford. Hunthausen was offered the opportunity to address the US bishops, but later learned that he would only have a few minutes for oral remarks. Thus this text reads as if it were meant to be read aloud, but in fact it was consumed in a collective silent reading. This text was produced in conjunction with another text, Hunthausen's response to the Vatican chronology.	The intent to read the speech aloud is indicated by the opening words: "Once before I had the privilege of addressing this assembly… Today I come before you again…" Reference to the Vatican Chronology: "You have already received in printed form my somewhat detailed response to the Chronology released by the Apostolic Nunciature…. I will refrain from making any further commentary on the Chronology itself and concentrate, rather, on four main areas…"
2. Distribution	Hunthausen distributed photocopies of this text, with the cooperation of the NCCB leadership, to his fellow bishops during the closed executive session of the NCCB (Nov. 11). The next day the text was released to the press along with Hunthausen's response to the Vatican chronology and the Malone statement on behalf of the conference.	The distribution pattern is essentially the same as that of Hunthausen's response to the Vatican chronology (see doc. 5, above), since the two were distributed together.
3. Consumption	The U.S. bishops were the first persons, apart from people close to Hunthausen himself, who had the opportunity to read the document. Though the document was written to be read aloud, the bishops consumed it by reading silently during a limited amount of time set aside for this at the beginning of the closed executive session. They read this document side-by-side with Hunthausen's response to the Vatican chronology and an early draft of the Malone statement that would be finalized and released the next day. The press first read it immediately after the press conference where Malone read his (final draft) statement for television	Archbishop Hurley of Anchorage commented (*The Progress*, 11.20.86) that Hunthausen's "respectful" way of communicating his views to the NCCB "was much appreciated by the bishops." Hurley reported that there was loud applause after Hunthausen spoke, but not a standing ovation. "That reflected the delicacy we all felt in the situation," he said.

	cameras. (The Malone statement was greeted with rousing applause from the bishops.)	
4. Text Type	An orational apologia. This is a formal, self-justifying speech that adopts a rather familiar, personal tone. The emphasis is on persuading other bishops to identify with Hunthausen's difficulty and his cause. The argumentation here supplements the arguments in his response to the Vatican chronology. Here he takes on the topic of the affair as a whole, giving his perspective on it all.	Hunthausen signals the text type with this opening words: "My Friends in Christ, Once before I had the privilege of addressing this assembly…" Hunthausen quickly invites empathy for his position by first empathizing with the other bishops: "And I want to tell you also that I am personally distressed about any anguish or even division that may have come about among you, my brother bishops."
5. Diction	An important technique of Hunthausen's argumentation is his presentation of dichotomous word sets, which allows him to contrast concepts in tension to advantage. Hunthausen's word choices are mostly polite but certain selections are heated, direct and confrontational, acknowledging the fact of conflict and emphasizing his own sense of having been treated unjustly. "Vatican II" appears to be a code word for Hunthausen (for a view of Church that emphasizes freedom, transparency and participatory leadership). "The Holy Spirit" also has the status of a code word (guaranteeing the orthodoxy of those who are allowed to be free).	Dichotomous word sets: Hunthausen associates himself with a desire for peace over turmoil and openness over secrecy. He makes a case for the place of pastoral judgment alongside the directives of Canon Law. And he discusses the built-in tension between the offices of Pope and local ordinary. Breaks from politeness: "fait accompli," "mounting / mount" a visitation, "shroud of secrecy;" "such.. are not a *just* manner of proceeding;" "the Visitation was so badly flawed from the very start;" "punitive… disciplinary;" "confusion and anger… have heated up and even ignited;" "in a situation and according to a methodology that I, quite frankly, have to acknowledge as being all but impossible, even to the point of being unworkable." Code words: "a process that seems extraordinarily inadequate given the kind of open Church we have become since the Second Vatican Council…;" "me, a bishop who got his first 'on-the-job training' during the Council itself;" "pastoral judgment, something…every pastor comes to recognize rather early on in his ministry as a rather imprecise 'science' at best, even when carried out prayerfully under the guidance of the Holy Spirit…. We never really get beyond the possibility of making a mistake no matter how hard we try to discern the Spirit."
6. Usage	First-person account, foregrounds self. Hunthausen avoids personal attacks: instead he challenges the visitation process and the judgments made (omitting agency). He blends	First person: "In making this presentation, I have a number of hopes that will become clear as I proceed." Avoiding personal attacks: "my

	first-person-singular and second-person-plural references into first-person-plural references (establishment of connection on the grammatical level). Use of the past tense primarily depicts the flawed handling of the visitation and subsequent steps. The present tense focuses on the current impasse. The future tense (employed least of all) expresses positive expectations for overcoming the problems at hand.	dissatisfaction with the manner in which the decision was made to undertake an Apostolic Visitation." Toward the first-person plural: "Most of you probably know me well enough to realize that I did not accept the invitation to make a presentation this afternoon because I personally relish speaking in a forum like this. I accepted it only because I believe… they are really *our* issues…" Past: "the shroud of secrecy spread even further…" Present: "I am grieved by this [widespread publicity], and I think it could have been otherwise." Future: "I have no doubt that we will find a way to address all the questions I have posed and others like them."
7. Substructures of the Text	Introductory comments with focus on the other bishops and Hunthausen himself. Then comes the body of the address, which is divided into four numbered sections that organize Hunthausen's complaint and (concluding) hopes for the future. Sections II, III and IV are also further divided into numbered subpoints.	Introduction: Hunthausen notes that he and the other bishops have worked together successfully in the past. He apologizes for burdening them with this matter, but he expresses his view that it is an important matter and addressing it can serve the Church. The four sections making up the body of the text: 1) "The process used in deciding to conduct the Visitation as well as the process followed in carrying it out. 2) The five areas of my ministry singled out by the Holy See as areas of serious concern. 3) "The identification of the important issues which this entire matter has brought to light." 4) "Some thoughts and suggestions regarding the future."
8. Intertextuality	Hunthausen refers directly to the Vatican chronology and his response to the same but says he will refrain from offering any further commentary on the chronology itself (thus, it is present to and absent from this text). Nonetheless, Hunthausen does make reference to his response, as in his treatment of the matter of secrecy. Hunthausen mentions the Hickey visitation report and complains that he has never been allowed to see it. Apart from the references to the chronology and his response to the chronology, there is no other text that is a recurrent reference point (explicitly cited). Instead we have references to a	Reference to chronology response: "You have already received in printed form my somewhat detailed response to the Chronology…. I will refrain from making any further commentary on the Chronology…. My printed remarks [the chronology response] allude to the matter of… secrecy…" Hunthausen also mentions: subsequent letters from the Holy See, conversations with the Pro-Nuncio, "comments appended to the Special Faculties I was directed to give to Bishop Wuerl," "a recent public statement issued by a Vatican official," the CDF's instruction on ministry to homosexuals, the Gospel message of Jesus, the Vatican II

II. Coping Strategies in Evidence	Tactics	Indications in Document
	range of Church textual authorities (Biblical, legal, magisterial…).	document *De Episcoporum Muneribus*, the Revised Code of Canon Law.
II. Coping Strategies in Evidence	**Tactics**	**Indications in Document**
1. Show deference to the structural order and mindset of the Church	Hunthausen expresses respect for Church, the Holy See and fellow bishops.	Respect for Church: "Those who suggest this do not really know me or my attitude toward the Church I love and try to serve." Respect for Holy See: "the absolutely essential relationship that exists between an individual bishop and the Holy Father" Respect for fellow bishops: "I am particularly distressed about any anguish or even division that may have come about among you, my brother bishops."
2. Associate one's own efforts with the best interest of the Church	Hunthausen repeatedly claims that he has the best interest of the Church in mind (which he associates with the teachings of Vatican II)	"What I am is each of us in this room is… a teacher, a pastor, and a servant of the Lord and of the Church" "a process that seems extraordinarily inadequate given the kind of open Church we have become since the Second Vatican Council"
3. Minimize the appearance of conflict	**Resistance**. Hunthausen acknowledges the fact of conflict and brings the discussion of several conflict issues into the open for the first time, including the legitimacy of the visitation process, the use of secrecy, and the question of collegiality.	Acknowledges conflict: "I am personally very distressed by all the turmoil that has come about" Legitimacy of visitation process: see discussion is section I. Use of secrecy: section I. Collegiality: section IV.
4. Show fraternity	Hunthausen invites fellow bishops to empathize, and repeatedly mentions their bond as bishops.	"Each of us bishops is faced with the same question and each of us, I suppose, on the basis of careful and prayerful discernment, has arrived at a pastoral judgment in this regard." "They are questions which will severely test our mettle as a Conference of Bishops. But we have been tested before…"
5. Practice courtesy	**Ambiguity**. Hunthausen refuses to engage in personal attacks, but he goes so far as to question the justness of the visitation process.	Avoiding personal attacks: "Please know that my reference here is not a personal one with regard to Archbishop Hickey who carried out his duties as Visitator in a gracious and gentlemanly manner. My reference has to do with processes, not with persons." Justness of process: "such unwitnessed, private questionings with no opportunity for the subject of the questioning to face his accusers… [is] not a just manner of proceeding"

6. Employ secrecy	First distribution of document is in a closed forum. Hunthausen selectively reveals information (revealing some, hiding some), but he also [**resistance**] attacks the use of secrecy.	Hides: Hunthausen refers to visitation process and previous exchanges with Vatican, but these experiences remain mostly opaque in his descriptions. Hides / reveals: Hunthausen mentions his "voluminous correspondence" with the Holy See over the last three years, but the contents of these exchanges remains hidden. Resistance to secrecy: "that secrecy does not work in matters of this sort, and… *should* not work"
7. Recruit allies	Hunthausen puts his appeal to his fellow bishops in personal terms. He justifies the positions he has taken. He points to the vulnerability of his fellow bishops that the case illustrates. And he makes an explicit request for help.	Personal terms: " I am particularly distressed about any anguish or even division that may have come about among you, my brother bishops…" Justification: A linchpin of his case is his claim that the process used was not just. Shared vulnerability: "the issues of the Seattle Visitation are not just issues that touch the life of the Church in Seattle: they are issues that touch the lives of each of our churches…" Request for help: "I would hope that this Conference would be willing to afford some positive assistance…"
8. Argue persuasively	Hunthausen structures his argument around an attack on the visitation process, an attack on its findings, a consideration of relevant ecclesiological / pastoral / theological issues and an appeal for empathy and support.	The Visitation process: considered in section I. The visitation findings: considered in section II. The theological issues: sections III and IV. The appeals for support: throughout the text, but most especially in the introductory and concluding remarks.
9. Assert personal identity	The strategy is strongly present in the document. Hunthausen speaks in the first person, on a feeling level, about his own experience and experiences shared with his fellow bishops.	"Today I come before you again in the quest for peace…" "I need to tell you that in agreeing to that I feel I compromised my principles as a Bishop"
III. Overall Coping Strategy	**Explanation**	**Indications in Document**
Contending	The address reads as an extended, alternately attacking and pleading, challenge to the Vatican's position. It is Hunthausen's all-out attempt to win support for his cause from his fellow bishops and from the public.	"This kind of an approach seriously wounds the community of faith and trust that is the Church."

Observable Strategies: Intervening Developments, F. (November 11-12, 1986)

	Strategies	Tactics	Objectives
Center	1. Show **deference** to the structural order and mindset of the **Church** 2. **Associate** one's own efforts with the best interest of the **Church** 3. **Minimize** the appearance of **conflict** 4. **Show fraternity** 5. **Practice courtesy** 6. **Employ secrecy** 7. **Recruit allies** 8. **Argue persuasively** 9. Assert **personal identity**	1. **NA** (no evidence). 2. **NA** (no evidence). 3. **Ambiguous**. Closed forum discussion is one means of minimizing appearance of conflict. 4. **Ambiguous**. Laghi is present during floor debate, a sign of fraternity, but his contributions are unknown. 5. **NA** (no evidence). 6. Floor debate is secret. 7. Attempt to win allies is underway during floor debate. 8. **Ambiguous.** Hickey argues for the legitimacy of the visitation process and suggests that there is more to the case than Hunthausen tells. 9. **Ambiguous**. Hickey calls attention to own role. Laghi's contributions are unknown.	Objective is ambiguous. There is little observable center party movement during this period.
Periphery	1. **Deference-Church** 2. **Associate-Church** 3. **Minimize-conflict** 4. **Show fraternity** 5. **Practice courtesy** 6. **Employ secrecy** 7. **Recruit allies** 8. **Argue persuasively** 9. **Assert Identity**	1. a. Hunthausen stays within prescribed limits and format for addressing NCCB; b. Hunthausen states explicitly in his oral remarks that he never had any intention of challenging papal authority 2. a. Hunthausen, in his oral remarks, shares his concern of the hurt caused to the Church by the affair 3. **Resistance**. Hunthausen brings his complaints to a much wider audience (all US bishops and national press) 4. a. Hunthausen pleads his cause before his fellow bishops 5. a. Hunthausen implied no ill will on anyone's part (oral remarks) 6. a. Hunthausen addresses bishops in closed executive session 7. a. Hunthausen's plea is a request for support from his fellow bishops 8. a. Hunthausen argues that he is not being rebellious and that it is understandable that differences of perception have arisen 9. a. Hunthausen speaks of his own pain and embarrassment (oral remarks)	To reassure his fellow American bishops that he has no rebellious intentions.
Third	1. **Deference-**	1. a. Wuerl calls for support in making	NCCB: To send three

410

Church 2. **Associate-Church** 3. **Minimize conflict** 4. **Show fraternity** 5. **Practice courtesy** 6. **Employ secrecy** 7. **Recruit allies** 8. **Argue persuasively** 9. **Personal identity**	Seattle situation work according to Vatican wishes; b. Bernardin says it is essential that the conference offer Rome its support; c. O'Connor says the conference needs to be one with Rome 2. Bishops declare the need to be faithful to Rome and Hunthausen and to address the specific challenges to the Church posed by the situation. 3. **Resistance**: a. the NCCB acknowledges the fact of conflict, debates its issues; b. individual bishops make some of contents of debate known to the press. 4. a. Bishops take up the matter in the fraternal body which is the NCCB; b. the NCR reports that "most speakers offered Hunthausen significant fraternal support;" c. Wuerl calls on bishops' support to make Seattle situation work; d. Bernardin stresses unity in the conference; e. O'Connor speaks of need to help Hunthausen 5. a. Bishops offer applause in response to Hunthausen's oral remarks 6. a. Bishops consider the case in closed executive session; b. Hunthausen's oral remarks are not made public, nor are the remarks of the other bishops 7. a. Hurley and Hickey recruit support for Hunthausen's position. 8. a. Weakland argues Malone statement should be changed; b. Bernardin argues for unity; c. Hickey argues legitimacy of his own role; d. Hurley argues that Hunthausen's version of events is correct; e. O'Connor argues for need to support Rome and Hunthausen 9. a. Several bishops take individual stands during the NCCB debate.	signals to the outside world: The bishops are loyal to Rome, they support Hunthausen, and they are internally unified as a conference.

Analytic Summary, Document 7 (Bishop Malone's Statement, 11.12.86)

	Overview	Indications in Document
I. Analysis of Text Construction		
1. Production	Malone drafts early version of statement, which is submitted to fellow bishops at the beginning of the debate of the Hunthausen case. The statement is revised after the NCCB gives its input. The NCCB approves the revised version.	No version of the first draft was available for comparison. Press accounts (and Hunthausen himself) later reported that the phrase "just and reasonable," to describe the visitation process, was excised from the text. One sign of the individual-collective tension of production appears in the uneasy mix if first-person-plural and first-person-singular statements.
2. Distribution	The text was distributed to the press simultaneous with a televised press conference, wherein Malone read	None.

	the statement aloud. Upon completion of the reading, Malone's words were greeted with loud applause from the bishops.	
3. Consumption	The bishops received their own copies first hand, and were privy to the context of production. Most others received the text through broadcast or printed (newspaper) reports.	Newspaper presentations placed the statement in the middle of other articles and statements from the affair.
4. Text Type	A reassuring press release. (It calls to mind a corporate chairman putting stockholders' minds at ease.)	Malone delivers the message himself: "In recent weeks all of us have felt much concern for those involved in the situation in Seattle…. Based on experience, bishops are conscious that in such matters the Holy See proceeds carefully and charitably…. While there appear to have been misunderstandings at one point or another along the way, the need now is to look to the future, not the past…"
5. Diction	Malone downplays the fact of division with euphemisms, upbeat words and images of family. He talks of pain suffered but does not assign culpability.	Euphemisms: "situation" in place of "conflict;" "dismay and confusion" instead of anger, bitterness, etc.; "misunderstandings" instead of something more sinister; "an occasion of grace and growth." Family: "the degree of pain which has been felt and enunciated in Seattle, but far beyond Seattle, really is the kind of pain that can only be felt by members of a family." Who is responsible?: "The pain of Archbishop Hunthausen and Bishop Wuerl… the abuse directed at the Holy Father and the Holy See, the dismay and confusion experienced by many good people – these things are deeply troubling."
6. Usage	The point of view shifts make it unclear who is speaking. A euphemistic erasure turns the conflict into an experience of "unity."	Point of view: "In recent weeks all of us…" "On this occasion the bishops of the United States wish to affirm unreservedly their loyalty…" "while we are not authorized to judge the facts of the case…" "At least that is how it feels to me" Euphemistic erasure: "Is it paradoxically possible, that what has happened in the Archdiocese of Seattle has given, and continues to provide, a vivid demonstration of the unity of the church…?"
7. Substructures of the Text	There are no obvious markers internally dividing the text (numbers, subheadings, etc.). Topically, Malone moves from a	The family metaphor: the pain felt in Seattle and beyond "is the kind of pain that can only be felt by members of a family… There are

	brief acknowledgment of the difficult "situation" to a statement that the NCCB has no authority to intervene to a statement of confidence in the Holy See and, finally, to the extended metaphor of family. This last is can be considered a distinct, interesting substructure because it is highly developed and makes up a full one-third of the statement. In effect, the metaphor allows Malone to talk around the conflict in a comforting way without grappling with the issues or assigning blame.	certain things a family must do when it wants to resolve a problem (comes together, shares feelings, listens, show respect and sympathy, express support, see that painful situation does not recur, pray) "This we bishops have done together in these days."
8. Intertextuality	Malone does not refer to specific texts but does refer to Church law and NCCB rules. He also makes reference to "the church's teachings," which the bishops have the responsibility to present. Implicitly, this text has obvious reference to the Vatican chronology and the two texts Hunthausen submitted to the NCCB.	"By universal church law and the conference's norms, the conference is not able to review, much less judge, a case involving a diocesan bishop and the Holy See."
II. Coping Strategies in Evidence	**Tactics**	**Indications in Document**
1. Show deference to the structural order and mindset of the Church	Malone affirms bishops' loyalty to Holy Father.	Loyalty: "On this occasion the bishops of the United States wish to affirm unreservedly their loyalty to and unity with the Holy Father."
2. Associate one's own efforts with the best interest of the Church	Malone asserts bishops' interest in well-being of local and universal Church.	"Let us bring our people together in prayer for the church in Seattle, so that what has happened may be an occasion of grace and of growth, there and in the church universal."
3. Minimize the appearance of conflict	The statement hurries past the fact of conflict to the restored unity. Malone suggests that the conflict itself is a sign of unity.	"The need now is to look to the future, not to the past…" "Is it paradoxically possible that what has happened… has given, and continues to provide, a vivid demonstration of the unity of the church…?"
4. Show fraternity	Malone expresses concern for bishops of Seattle and Holy See. The statement also reflects on the familial relationship of bishops.	"The pain of Archbishop Hunthausen and Bishop Wuerl, our brothers in the episcopacy, the abuse directed at the Holy Father and the Holy See, the dismay and confusion experienced by many good people – these things are deeply troubling. Family: "A family comes together…. This we bishops have done…"
5. Practice courtesy	The statement declares sympathy for all involved and attempts to save face for both center and periphery.	"the kind of pain that can only be felt by members of a family"
6. Employ secrecy	The statement discloses little of the contents of the debate that has shaped the statement.	"These things are listened to with respect… Then support is expressed… This we bishops have

		done together in these days."
7. Recruit allies	The statement advocates showing support for both of the parties to the conflict.	"A family also takes steps to see that, insofar as possible, a painful situation does not happen again. In our case, that means working to find creative ways of presenting the church's teaching… but also seeking mechanisms of responding when confusion or error occurs"
8. Argue persuasively	The text recommends faithfulness to Rome, sympathy and support for Hunthausen, and a quick resolution to the conflict.	"The decision reached at the end of the process was made by proper church authorities. As such, it deserves our respect and confidence." "We are prepared to offer any assistance judged helpful and appropriate by the parties involved."
9. Assert personal identity	**NA**. Ultimately this is a collective expression, not a statement from Malone himself.	**NA**.
III. Overall Coping Strategy	**Explanation**	**Indications in Document**
Problem solving	The statement signals a willingness to take Hunthausen's complaints seriously and to stand by him. But it also acknowledges the untenability of a direct challenge to Rome and the need to demonstrate loyalty to the Holy See. The NCCB tries to smooth over the conflict, but also offers to be of further assistance if the principal parties so desire. The statement also recommends prayer.	"We are prepared to offer any assistance judged helpful by the parties involved."

Observable Strategies: Intervening Developments, G. (November 1986-February 1987)

	Strategies	**Tactics**	**Objectives**

414

Center	1. Show **deference** to the structural order and mindset of the **Church** 2. **Associate** one's own efforts with the best interest of the **Church** 3. **Minimize** the appearance of **conflict** 4. **Show fraternity** 5. **Practice courtesy** 6. **Employ secrecy** 7. **Recruit allies** 8. **Argue persuasively** 9. Assert **personal identity**	1. a. Pope's interview comments on the universal Church; b. Laghi defends secrecy and canon law procedures 2. a. Pope, in interview, says he and the U.S. bishops are both concerned for the "good of the church" 3. a. Vatican official calls the Malone statement "amicable and satisfactory;" b. The Pope tells reporters, "Sometimes one creates divisions that do not exist" 4. a. Pope emphasizes his unity with U.S. bishops; b. Pope's telegram to Hunthausen expresses his "fraternal solicitude; c. Vatican appoints commission of 3 American bishops to work with Hunthausen and "assess the situation" 5. a. Pope refuses to criticize anyone in interview; b. Pope sends supportive telegram to Hunthausen when he undergoes cancer surgery. 6. a. Pope in interview refuses to discuss specifics of case or share his own view; b. Vatican's decision making process during these 2+ months is hidden; c. Laghi defends the use of secrecy in his NY Times interview 7. Continuing to clarify and defend its position serves as a tactic in support of the recruitment of more bishop allies to the Vatican side. 8. a. Two Vatican officials both put their own "spin" on the NCCB debate outcome; b. Pope argues that conflict is less than the media makes it out to be; c. Laghi defends secrecy and offers responses to several of the specific charges made by Hunthausen 9. a. Laghi interview exposes him to questions and includes his own view of events and admission of fallibility	To put the best possible spin (media-distributed interpretation) on the outcome of the NCCB debate and to privately formulate a new plan for resolving the conflict.
Periphery	1. **Deference-Church** 2. **Associate-Church** 3. **Minimize conflict** 4. **Show fraternity** 5. **Practice courtesy** 6. **Employ secrecy** 7. **Recruit allies** 8. **Argue persuasively** 9. **Personal Identity**	1. a. Hunthausen's response to Malone statement says he supports the statement; he also refers to unity with Holy Father; b. 2. a. Hunthausen expresses concern about the possibility of a "rift in the church" 3. **Ambiguous**. a. Hunthausen's response to Malone statement has conciliatory tone; b. **[resistance]** Back in Seattle, Hunthausen says he is "in the middle of a conflict that has the potential of causing a rift in the church;" c. **[resistance]** Hunthausen offers details of how the "just and reasonable" description was dropped; d. **[resistance]** Hunthausen unmasks the euphemism "apostolic visitation;" e. Hunthausen maintains silence about the conflict after Nov. 14 4. a. Hunthausen says the Malone statement "emerged from a very honest exchange of many different points of view" among "brother bishops" and "respects our identity	To assert (one more time) the need for a new arrangement in Seattle (facilitated, preferably, with the help of the NCCB) and to refrain from further contentious acts until the Vatican's next step is clear.

		as a Conference… united with each other and with the Holy Father"; b. In his response to the Malone statement and in Seattle, Hunthausen draws attention to the NCCB's offer of assistance; c. Hunthausen speaks of possibility of Rome trip 5. **Ambiguous**. a. Hunthausen praises Malone statement; b. Hunthausen, in Seattle, resists characterizing conflict as matter of winning or losing (desire for face saving for both sides); c. **[resistance]** Hunthausen implies that the Vatican lost on the "just and reasonable" question; d. **[resistance]** In Seattle, Hunthausen criticizes the visitation process once again 6. a. Hunthausen does not reveal much specific information from NCCB debate; b. after Nov. 14 Hunthausen keeps silence about the affair 7. a. Hunthausen continues to plead his case. 8. a. In Seattle, Hunthausen argues that the case is still unresolved and still unworkable 9. a. In his response to the Malone statement, Hunthausen expresses his hopefulness; b. Back in Seattle, he expresses his hopefulness but also his feelings of dissatisfaction and pain	
Third	1. **Deference-Church** 2. **Associate-Church** 3. **Minimize conflict** 4. **Show fraternity** 5. **Practice courtesy** 6. **Employ secrecy** 7. **Recruit allies** 8. **Argue persuasively** 9. **Personal identity**	1. a. O'Connor speaks of loyalty to Holy See; b. Pilarczyk defends canon law; c. Wuerl praises the tenor of the NCCB debate 2. a. Pilarczyk defends canon law, which he says is designed for the good of the Church 3. **Ambiguous**. a. O'Connor emphasizes the unity of the bishops with the Holy See; b. Wuerl describes NCCB debate as fraternal and respectful; c. **[resistance]** Kenny criticizes the way the case has been handled 4. a. O'Connor says the Malone statement shows the unity of bishops and their loyalty to the Holy See; b. Wuerl describes the NCCB debate as "fraternal" 5. **Ambiguous**. a. O'Connor, Pilarczyk and Wuerl offer no criticism of Holy See or of Hunthausen; b. **[resistance]** Kenny criticizes Rome's handling of the case (without naming Rome outright) 6. a. None of the bishops offer much about the debate that took place 7. a. Various bishops take public stances in favor of supporting either Hunthausen or Rome. 8. a. O'Connor argues that the Holy See acted charitably and justly; b. Kenny argues that the Vatican treated Hunthausen unfairly; c. Pilarczyk argues that canon law procedures should not be judged by civil law principles 9. a. Kenny sticks his neck out by criticizing the Vatican's treatment of Hunthausen	Individual bishops: to signal whether they align themselves more closely with the center or periphery positions.

Analytic Summary, Document 8 (Laghi Announcement of Commission Appointment, 2.9.87)

	Overview	Indications in Document
I. Analysis of Text Construction		
1. Production	The Holy See is the principal. The Apostolic Nunciature releases the text. Laghi, presumably, is the author.	A National Catholic News Service article encapsulating the text of the statement in the 2.12.87 *Progress* attributes the statement to Laghi, but the text itself reads, "*The Holy See* has appointed an ad hoc commission…" (emphasis mine). Laghi does not refer to himself in the text.
2. Distribution	The Apostolic Nunciature hands the text over to the NCCB for release. Carl Eifert, information officer for the NCCB, refers questions about the statement to Laghi, who is at a bishops meeting in Dallas at the time.	None, but see the 2.9.87 *Seattle Times*, the 2.10.87 *Seattle Post-Intelligencer*, the 2.12.87 *Progress* and 2.9.87 archdiocesan inter-office memo in the Wasden Price collection.
3. Consumption	Seattle Archdiocese "Central Agency Managers" receive an inter-office memo 2.9.87 with a text of the statement, which cites the Apostolic Nunciature as the source of the statement. The statement is widely distributed through the Catholic and secular press. Laghi offers some comments in a telephone interview with the NY Times from Dallas, which provide some context for interpretation. Some background / interpretive material, provided by the nunciature, accompanies the press statement.	Laghi in his telephone interview with the *NY Times*: "This is just an assessment." The background material accompanying the press statement notes that the formation of the commission relates to the NCCB's Nov. 1987 offer of assistance in the case (cf. *Seattle Post-Intelligencer*, 2.10.87).
4. Text Type	Press release.	The impersonal style and use of the third person (the "Holy See" is the subject of the first sentence, as seen here, are standard in press releases. The text is formal in tone and businesslike in its two declarations.
5. Diction	Two key word choices: "assess" and "situation." "Assess" makes room for a variety of approaches and outcomes. "Situation" downplays the difficulty of the conflict.	"The Holy See has appointed an ad hoc commission … to assess the current situation in the Archdiocese of Seattle."
6. Usage	Both statements are in the present perfect tense. Laghi reports on (just) completed actions. There is no room for discussion or debate.	"The Holy See has appointed…. Archbishop Raymond Hunthausen has expressed his concurrence."
7. Substructures of the Text	There is one sentence to represent each party to the conflict. The Holy See acts, and Hunthausen accepts the action.	"The Holy See has appointed an ad hoc commission…. Archbishop Raymond Hunthausen has expressed his concurrence."
8. Intertextuality	There are no explicit references to other texts in the statement, but the	See the 2.10.87 *Seattle Post-Intelligencer* for a description of the

	accompanying background material refers explicitly to the Malone statement offer of assistance by the NCCB. The word "situation" implicitly refers to the NCCB statement, where Malone prominently employs the same word.	contents of the background material provided by the apostolic nunciature.
II. Coping Strategies in Evidence	**Tactics**	**Indications in Document**
1. Show deference to the structural order and mindset of the Church	Laghi acknowledges (the statement takes for granted) the Holy See's right to create the commission.	"The Holy See has appointed an ad hoc commission composed of Cardinals… and Archbishop…"
2. Associate one's own efforts with the best interest of the Church	**NA** (no evidence).	**NA**.
3. Minimize the appearance of conflict	The statement makes no mention of conflict or of controversial issues. The conflict is declared a "situation."	"to assess the current situation in the Archdiocese of Seattle."
4. Show fraternity	**Ambiguous**. Creation of the commission establishes a new avenue of fraternal engagement. Mention of Hunthausen's concurrence is a sign of a fraternal approach.	"Archbishop Raymond Hunthausen has expressed his concurrence."
5. Practice courtesy	Mention of Hunthausen's concurrence is a minor demonstration of courtesy.	"Archbishop Raymond Hunthausen has expressed his concurrence."
6. Employ secrecy	The statement hides the logic for choosing to establish a commission – and why these three bishops in particular?	The brevity of the statement is the chief indication of how little it tells.
7. Recruit allies	**Ambiguous**. At the very least, the statement signals the Holy See's effort to take seriously the NCCB debate and its outcomes.	Background material provided with the statement made reference to the NCCB's offer of assistance.
8. Argue persuasively	**Ambiguous**. The mention of Hunthausen's concurrence gives the impression that the Vatican is treading lightly.	"Archbishop Raymond Hunthausen has expressed his concurrence."
9. Assert personal identity	**NA** (no evidence).	**NA**.
III. Overall Coping Strategy	**Explanation**	**Indications in Document**
Yielding	This statement signals the Vatican's intention to look for a new route to resolution. It amounts to a concession in that symbolically and practically it accepts Hunthausen's recommendation and the NCCB's offer for other (American) bishops to be involved.	One needs to refer back to the NCCB debate (to the Hunthausen and Malone statements) to see the significance of this statement.

Observable Strategies: Intervening Developments, H. (February-May 1987)

	Strategies	Tactics	Objectives
Center	1. Show **deference** to the structural order and mindset of the **Church** 2. **Associate** one's own efforts with the best interest of the **Church** 3. **Minimize** the appearance of **conflict** 4. **Show fraternity** 5. **Practice courtesy** 6. **Employ secrecy** 7. **Recruit allies** 8. **Argue persuasively** 9. Assert **personal identity**	1. a. Laghi, in NC News Service interview, indicates that implementation of a resolution proposed by the commission will depend on the approval of Rome and Hunthausen. 2. **Ambiguous**. a. Laghi: "I am the first one to hope their will be some reconciliation." 3. a. Center party keeps conflict handling and commentary out of sight during this period. 4. **Ambiguous**. a. Vatican trusts commission of 3 fellow bishops to come up with a solution. b. Laghi says that a solution will depend on the agreement of all parties. 5. a. Rome voices no criticism of Hunthausen during these months. 6. a. Rome makes no report of progress of commission negotiations. 7. a. Appointing these three American bishops may be a subtle form of recruitment (to do Rome's bidding) 8. a. The commission tries to persuade Hunthausen (and later the Pope) to accept its proposed resolution (in private) 9. a. Laghi NC News Service interview	Maintain silence and trust in appointed third party (assessment commission) to come up with acceptable resolution.
Periphery	1. **Deference-Church** 2. **Associate-Church** 3. **Minimize conflict** 4. **Show fraternity** 5. **Practice courtesy** 6. **Employ secrecy** 7. **Recruit allies** 8. **Argue persuasively** 9. **Personal Identity**	1. a. Hunthausen's silence is a sign of deference to Rome and submission to the process Rome has initiated. b. **[Resist]** Hunthausen resists the commission's proposal and threatens to go over its head to Rome. 2. **NA** (no evidence). 3. a. Hunthausen maintains silence and does not reveal his conflict with the commission. 4. **Ambiguous**. a. Hunthausen cooperates with the assessment commission: private negotiations 5. a. Hunthausen shows politeness by refraining from voicing criticism 6. a. Commission negotiations are in secret 7. a. The number of those publicly supporting Hunthausen grows. It is unclear how active he is behind the scenes to promote this. 8. **Ambiguous**. a. Hunthausen argues with the commission for the right to determine who the coadjutor will be; b. he also argues for changes in the commission assessment report 9. **NA** (no evidence).	Maintain silence and pursue advantageous outcome in secret negotiations with assessment commission.

| Third | 1. **Deference-Church** 2. **Associate-Church** 3. **Minimize conflict** 4. **Show fraternity** 5. **Practice courtesy** 6. **Employ secrecy** 7. **Recruit allies** 8. **Argue persuasively** 9. **Personal identity** | 1. a. Commission accepts Holy See's appointment & says it will report to Pope when done; b. Wuerl reports to Pope on progress of seminary evaluation; c. third party bishops respect the privacy of the process 2. a. Commission says it will do the work and report to the Holy See when done. 3. a. Wuerl and NW bishops cooperate with commission in maintaining privacy of conflict negotiation 4. **Ambiguous**. a. Commission negotiates directly with Hunthausen and Wuerl and also seeks counsel of NW bishops 5. a. Third party bishops refrain from public criticisms of process and avoid speaking publicly about conflict issues; b. commission does not voice complaints about Hunthausen's resistance in public 6. a. Commission carries out its process in secret: discussions and structure of assessment itself are not revealed while it is underway; b. **[resistance]** Certain insiders (who?) leak information to NC *Register* and NC *Reporter* 7. **NA** (no evidence). 8. **Ambiguous**. a. Commission seeks to bring Hunthausen around to its plan for resolution (coadjutor appointment) 9. **NA** (no evidence). | Commission: Develop plan acceptable to both Hunthausen and Rome. Wuerl: Keep low profile. Northwest bishops: Share opinion about Hunthausen's case with commission (in private exchange).

Third parties not of the hierarchy: Seattle priests: Push for restoration of Hunthausen's power by publicly declaring support for him. Other Seattle activists: Support or criticize Hunthausen privately to other bishops or Rome and publicly to the press. National Catholic Reporter: Support Hunthausen (request and report existence of FBI file) |

Analytic Summary, Document 9 (Assessment Commission Report, 5.20.87)

	Overview	Indications in Document
I. Analysis of Text Construction		
1. Production	After the commission finishes its initial work of assessment, Laghi refers to it as the "Bernardin commission," suggesting an unofficial or official role as chair (and lead writer?) of the group. Briggs 1992 says the harder edge of Hunthausen criticism in the document originates mostly with O'Connor. The commission, after two months of consultation with Hunthausen, Wuerl and others, prepares a draft assessment report, which Hunthausen rejects in April 1987. Hunthausen reluctantly accepts a rewritten (toned-own) version in May. The report offers a rather detailed description of the steps laying the groundwork for composition of the report, including references to persons and documentation consulted.	The text itself does not distinguish between the contributions of the three commission members to the actual writing of the report. It does cite documents and persons contributing information during the assessment process (sections I-III). See Briggs 1992 for details of production process. See Laghi announcement of conclusion of commission's work, 4.11.89 for reference to Bernardin's chairmanship of commission. Various issues of *the National Catholic Reporter* from April-May, 1987 also offer clues about the production process.

2. Distribution	Before it was released to the public, the report was shown to Hunthausen, to the Pope, to members of key congregations in Rome (and undoubtedly to Laghi, though I have no record of this). The report was mailed individually to the U.S. bishops prior to its distribution to the press.	The accompanying cover letter (dated May 25, 1987) to bishops is one sign of an intended distribution route. The text was released to the press on May 27. Hunthausen issues copies of the report at a press conference with Murphy on the 27th.
3. Consumption	Conflict insiders first consume the report in the context of directly personal conflict negotiations (Hunthausen with the commission; the commission with Vatican officials and the Pope). The American bishops receive their own copies in the mail, accompanied by a cover letter and a copy of the Ratzinger letter (two documents that provide interpretive context). Reporters receive the first copies of the report and Ratzinger letter at a press conference. The public at large first reads about it in newspaper and electronic broadcast accounts. The commission, with its argumentation in the report, strives to create an impression among readers that the commission has judged the situation carefully and fairly.	
4. Text Type	A formal report from an appointed commission to its organizational superior.	Title: "Report to the Holy See Presented by Commission Appointed by the Holy See To Assess the Current Situation in the Archdiocese of Seattle."
5. Diction	There is an emphasis on neutrality and fair-mindedness, as signalled by noncritical word choices such as "assess" and "situation." The language is consistently formal and impersonal. For the most part, however, the report avoids highly technical (intraecclesial) terminology and professes a "common sense" orientation (accessible to all). The discussion of certain words ("firm," "punitive") is under contestation. Ecclesiological language at the end appears to be directed toward bishops in particular.	Neutrality: "The Commission appointed by the Holy See to assess the current situation in the Archdiocese of Seattle was officially notified of its mandate in a letter..." Formal, impersonal language: "The proposal for resolving the problem in the Archdiocese of Seattle was devised by the Commission in consultation with the Holy See taking into account both the concerns of Archbishop Hunthausen as well as those of the Holy See." Use of nontechnical language: "it seemed quite clear that the Holy See was looking for a common sense judgment, and this is all the Commission attempts to provide here." Contested words: (1) "In sum, no matter how personally firm in his teachings and practices the Archbishop himself may be, without

		intending it, he is *perceived* as generating or at least accepting a climate of permissiveness…" (2) "the Commission is convinced that no steps were intended as punitive, regardless of perceptions to the contrary." Ecclesiological language: "The papacy belongs to the binding content of our faith itself, in its proper place within the hierarchy of truths and in our won Christian life."
6. Usage	The commission's habit of referring to itself in the third person (and not distinguishing between the contributions of individual members of the commission) gives an impression of impersonality, detachment and objectivity. The use of the (first person plural) pronoun "we" in section III adds an accent of personal conviction the conclusion of the report, but again the report does not distinguish between the three commission members. The first two sections are primarily descriptive, the final section couches exhortations in descriptions.	Impersonality / detachment / objectivity: "In common sense terms, it seemed quite clear that the Holy See was looking for a common sense judgment, and this is all the Commission attempts to provide here." First person plural: "In the fulfillment of our task, we listened to many voices and weighed many views. We recognize that some of those interviewed may not agree with our interpretations of their statements. Nevertheless…" Exhortation as description: "Hence the proposal of the Commission contains these essential elements: 1) the Auxiliary Bishop should be transferred to another See; 2) the Archbishop should recover his faculties as diocesan bishop…"
7. Substructures of the Text	There are three subsections to the report that are marked with Roman numerals and titles. The first section is a description of the commission's activity. The second is a rationale for how the commission reached its conclusions. And the third declares their proposal. A theological reflection closes out the third section and the report as a whole.	Section titles: I. The history; II. The assessment; III. Proposal for resolving the problem and concluding remarks. The theological reflection considers the relationship between the Bishop of Rome and the other bishops of the Church.
8. Intertextuality	The commission traces its own mandate to a letter of empowerment from the pro-nuncio. There are references to the conversations and documentation that inform the commission's recommendations in the section I "history." Two key documents that are cited as reference texts are the summary of the Hickey-Hunthausen interview and the 9.30.85 Ratzinger letter. An allusion to documents not seen by Hunthausen indirectly points to other texts. As theological reference documents, the commission invokes Lumen Gentium and a work of	Mandate: "The Commission… was officially notified of its mandate in a letter from the Apostolic Pro-Nuncio, dated January 26, 1987 (prot. n. 317/87/2)." Meeting references: There are multiple dates given (section I.) for meetings that took place between the commission and Hunthausen / Wuerl / other bishops and / or priests. Documentation reference: "The Commission also studied voluminous documentation, all of which was available to Archbishop Hunthausen and Bishop Wuerl."

		theologian Karl Rahner.	The references to the interview summary and Ratzinger letter appear early in section II. Allusion to documents not seen by Hunthausen: "The Commission further decided that the primary context for its approach would be two documents both known to Archbishop Hunthausen, to the Holy See and to everyone concerned…. The Commission further agreed internally that it would base its conclusions only on documents seen by Archbishop Hunthausen." The Lumen Gentium passage quoted (chapter 27) acknowledges that bishops are not merely vicars of the Roman pontiff: they exercise power in their own right. The Rahner quotation comes from his *The Shape of the Church to Come.*
II. Coping Strategies in Evidence	**Tactics**	**Indications in Document**
1. Show deference to the structural order and mindset of the Church	The commission refers to its appointment and mandate from the Holy See. It refers to the various forms of Church authority (the Congregation for the Doctrine of the Faith, Church teaching, Church law…)	"The Commission appointed by the Holy See to assess the current situation in the Archdiocese of Seattle was officially notified of its mandate in a letter from the Apostolic Pro-Nuncio…" "It is the conclusion of the Commission… that the letter of the Congregation for the Doctrine of the Faith should remain in place as the primary guide…" "Hence we acknowledge the teaching of the Second Vatican Council"
2. Associate one's own efforts with the best interest of the Church	The Commission declares its concern for the Holy See and for Hunthausen	"The proposal for resolving the problem in the Archdiocese of Seattle was devised by the Commission in consultation with the Holy See taking into account both the concerns of Archbishop Hunthausen as well as those of the Holy See."
3. Minimize the appearance of conflict	The document is designed to close down the conflict debate. Thus the issues discussed are already resolved within the context of the document.	"Hence, the proposal of the Commission contains these essential elements: 1) The Auxiliary Bishop should be transferred to another See. 2) The Archbishop should recover his faculties…"
4. Show fraternity	The Commission emphasizes its effort to hear concerns on both sides.	"The Commission further decided that the primary context for its approach would be two documents, both known to Archbishop Hunthausen , to the Holy See, and to everyone concerned."

5. Practice courtesy	There are no direct criticisms of Hunthausen or of the Holy See. There is praise for Hunthausen, but it is mixed at best.	"Archbishop Hunthausen has taken laudable steps to carry out certain of the provisions of the letter of the Congregation for the Doctrine of the Faith."
6. Employ secrecy	The report does not explain how it came up with the coadjutor solution.	"A Coadjutor Archbishop should be appointed."
7. Recruit allies	The Commission seeks the support of other bishops for its plan for resolution.	"With this in mind the Commission continues to hope and pray that all will walk together the Gospel path of humility, obedience, charity and peace in accepting the decision of the Holy See."
8. Argue persuasively	Much argumentation legitimates the Commission's own process and decision-making rationale.	"We listened to many voices and weighed many views"
9. Assert personal identity	**NA**. The commission identity is a collective one, exclusively.	**NA**.
III. Overall Coping Strategy	**Explanation**	**Indications in Document**
Problem solving	The Commission proposes a give-and-take solution. Hunthausen's power is to be restored and Wuerl removed. But a coadjutor with right of succession will be appointed and the commission will stay on in a role of oversight.	"In the fulfillment of our task, we listened to many voices and weighed many views…. We kept before our eyes… the need for charity and compassion, the need for fairness and openness, the need to reach decisions and make recommendations…"

Observable Strategies: Intervening Developments, I. (May 1987-April 1989)

	Strategies	**Tactics**	**Objectives**

Center	1. Show **deference** to the structural order and mindset of the **Church** 2. **Associate** one's own efforts with the best interest of the **Church** 3. **Minimize** the appearance of **conflict** 4. **Show fraternity** 5. **Practice courtesy** 6. **Employ secrecy** 7. **Recruit allies** 8. **Argue persuasively** 9. **Assert** personal **identity**	1. a. Laghi announcement of termination of commission recalls Vatican's power to form and dissolve the commission; 2. a. Laghi statement of completion of commission's work notes that Hunthausen and Murphy will continue to address the "issues which have been of concern to the Church" 3. a. Laghi statement makes no mention of past or present tensions; b. brevity and businesslike style reopens the conflict discussion only minimally 4. a. Laghi refers to cooperative efforts of commission, Hunthausen, Murphy and Holy See 5. a. Laghi's statement is polite in the sense that no criticisms are voiced and no unpleasant subjects are raised; but it lacks expressions of praise or thanks. 6. a. The Vatican is secretive about the ongoing negotiations between Hunthausen, Murphy and the commission from beginning to end 7. a. The Vatican continues to have an interest to see that the commission aligns itself with Rome's interest in the course of the negotiations with Hunthausen. 8. **NA** (no evidence). 9. **NA** (no evidence).	To take the conflict off the public agenda permanently.
Periphery	1. **Deference-Church** 2. **Associate-Church** 3. **Minimize-conflict** 4. **Show fraternity** 5. **Practice courtesy** 6. **Employ secrecy** 7. **Recruit allies** 8. **Argue persuasively** 9. **Assert Identity**	1. a. Hunthausen accepts the proposal of the apostolic commission; b. Hunthausen says commission report was obviously the result of prayer; c. Hunthausen says he is confident this is what God wants 2. a. Hunthausen resists characterizations that speak of winning or losing by either side; b. Hunthausen emphasizes the need to move forward; c. Hunthausen's statement at the time of the commission's termination speaks of "renewed dedication and commitment to the Gospel and the Universal Church" 3. **Ambiguous**. a. Hunthausen speaks positively about the commission solution; b. Hunthausen says he is not prepared to endorse commission report; c. Hunthausen says it is not a matter of winning or losing; d. Hunthausen speaks of the need to move forward, beyond conflict 4. a. Hunthausen accepts proposal of fellow bishops; b. Hunthausen welcomes Murphy to Seattle; c. Hunthausen praises Wuerl; d. Hunthausen thanks Pope for Murphy appointment; Hunthausen praises commission. 5. **Ambiguous**. a. Hunthausen welcomes Murphy; b. Hunthausen thanks Pope for Murphy appointment; c. Hunthausen says he is not prepared to endorse commission report; d. at end of commission's service, Hunthausen thanks them for their pastoral assistance; e. at end of commission's work, Hunthausen says little has changed in ministerial situation of archdiocese	To conclude the Vatican intervention in Seattle once and for all, while signalling a refusal to capitulate entirely.

		6. a. the commission negotiations remain a secret affair 7. a. the process of trying to "win over" the commission continues so long as the commission stays in existence 8. a. Hunthausen argues that commission report is dissatisfying in some important respects but that it is time to move on; b. at end of commission's service, Hunthausen argues that little changed ministerially in the archdiocese 9. a. Hunthausen's initial responses to commission resolution convey his (mixed) feelings: relief, resignation, hope, dissatisfaction; b. Hunthausen's comments at the time of the disbanding of the commission show his lingering combativeness.	
Third	1. **Deference-Church** 2. **Associate-Church** 3. **Minimize-conflict** 4. **Show fraternity** 5. **Practice courtesy** 6. **Employ secrecy** 7. **Recruit allies** 8. **Argue persuasively** 9. **Assert identity**	1. a. Murphy agrees to appointment; b. Murphy pledges his loyalty to Holy See; c. Bernardin says he believes commission has addressed needs of local and universal Church 2. a. Murphy says he hopes to be of help and service to Church of Seattle; b. Bernardin says he believes commission has addressed needs of local and universal Church 3. a. Wuerl statement calls Murphy's appointment a welcome sign of the resolution of the difficulty and tension that has developed;" b. Bernardin statement suggests concerns of all sides have been addressed 4. a. Wuerl thanks Hunthausen and people of Seattle; b. Wuerl praises Murphy; c. Bernardin wishes Murphy and Wuerl well; d. Wuerl says he had a good relationship with Hunthausen personally; e. Murphy continues private meetings with Hunthausen and commission for almost two years 5. a. Murphy calls his appointment "a great honor;" b. Wuerl praises Murphy and thanks Hunthausen; c. Bernardin extends prayers and good wishes for Murphy, Wuerl and people of Seattle. 6. a. Commission continues to meet with Murphy and Hunthausen privately for almost two years. 7. **NA** (no evidence). 8. a. Bernardin argues that commission has addressed the concerns of all sides; b. Wuerl challenges "myths" that developed during his time in Seattle 9. a. Murphy uses his sense of humor to ease his transition in Seattle; b. Wuerl offers a forthcoming interview to the Pittsburgh diocesan newspaper, challenging mistaken notions about himself and his role in Seattle	Murphy: To show himself to be a trustworthy coadjutor (to the people of Seattle in particular, but also to Rome). Wuerl: to exit Seattle gracefully. The commission: to complete the period of oversight without further controversy.

APPENDIX VI: OPEN-ENDED INTERVIEW QUESTION POSED TO FR. RYAN

At the beginning of the interview, I posed the following question to Fr. Ryan:

> In November of 1983, Washington, D.C. Archbishop James Hickey conducted an Apostolic Visitation of Seattle on behalf of the Holy See. This occurrence gained much media attention, as did events subsequent the Visitation, including the appointment of Donald Wuerl as auxiliary bishop with (as was later made public) special faculties, Archbishop Hunthausen's address to the National Conference of Catholic Bishops in November of 1986, and the appointment of a three-man commission of bishops, in 1987, to assess what had become a highly problematic situation.

> During the period described above, you served as both Chancellor and Vicar General of the Archdiocese. In these roles you worked closely with Archbishop Hunthausen and had the opportunity to observe up-close the unfolding of the events I mention above and any number of other related occurrences. Could you please now share with me your recollections of the Visitation and the controversies that followed?

Fr. Ryan's response to this question took approximately three hours.

CONFLICTEN BINNEN DE KATHOLIEKE HIËRARCHIE:
EEN STUDIE NAAR STRATEGIEËN IN HET HANTEREN VAN DE KWESTIE HUNTHAUSEN, MET BIJZONDERE AANDACHT VOOR DISCURSIEVE STRATEGIEËN.

Overzicht

De uitdrukking "centrum-perifeer conflict" kan gebruikt worden om conflicten binnen de Rooms-Katholieke hiërarchie te beschrijven, die de structurele spanning tussen het centrale gezag van Rome en het lokale leiderschap van de Kerk aan het licht brengen. Hoewel er sinds het tweede Vaticaans Concilie een aantal van dergelijke conflicten tot ontwikkeling is gekomen, door de media kritisch onderzocht werden en onderwerp waren van theologische studie, is er verrassend weinig systematisch analytische aandacht geweest voor de strategieën om zulke conflicten te kunnen hanteren. De voorliggende kwalitatieve studie is er op gericht om in deze lacune te voorzien en wel door middel van een literatuurverkenning, gevolgd door een zorgvuldig, empirisch onderzoek van een recent voorbeeld van een dergelijk "centrum-perifeer conflict", nl. de kwestie Rome-Hunthausen. Richting aan het onderzoek gaf de centrale vraag: "Welke strategieën zijn waarneembaar in de taal van het centrum-perifeer conflict?". Hieronder vindt men een samenvatting van de Hunthausen-casus, gevolgd door een beschrijving van de onderzoeksmethodologie, de bevindingen, de conclusies en de relevantie van dit onderzoek.

Samenvatting van de Hunthausen-kwestie

In 1983, informeerde de pauselijke pro-nuntius in de Verenigde Staten, aartsbisschop Pio Laghi, de aartsbisschop van Seattle, Raymond Hunthausen, dat het Vaticaan een apostolische visitatie wenste door te voeren in het aartsbisdom van Seattle. Hunthausen beloofde medewerking aan de visitatie zonder het doel van het bezoek precies te kennen. Daarop volgende mediaverslagen speculeerden over de redenen, met name zich richtend op Hunthausens reputatie als een linkse, tolerante kerkleider, en als een tegenstander van de Amerikaanse nucleaire wapenopbouw die geen blad voor zijn mond nam. Commentatoren veronderstelden dat één of beide van deze aspecten van Hunthausens leiderschap tot ongenoegen had(den) geleid in Rome.

In september 1985 informeerde kardinaal Ratzinger Hunthausen over de resultaten van zijn onderzoek. Uitgaande van de uitkomsten, verwachtte Rome van Hunthausen in elk geval tweeërlei: dat Hunthausen adequater toezicht zou houden op bepaalde, welomschreven gebieden van het pastoraat in zijn aartsbisdom en dat hij daartoe de hulp zou accepteren van een hulpbisschop met specifieke bevoegdheden. (De kernwapens werden niet expliciet genoemd.) Kort daarna accepteerde Hunthausen de benoeming van Donald Wuerl als hulpbisschop van Seattle. Tijdens diens eerste acht maanden in Seattle, werd niet publiekelijk bekend gemaakt dat hem specifieke bevoegdheden door het Vaticaan verleend waren. Hunthausen maakte dit feit in september 1986 bekend, waarbij hij aangaf niet volledig begrepen te hebben hoever de macht van Wuerl reikte toen deze door het Vaticaan werd benoemd. Hunthausens bekendmaking was het begin van een periode van grote onrust alsmede van acties en publiciteit in de lokale en nationale Kerk, met als hoogtepunt de verhitte debatten gedurende de bijeenkomst van de Bisschoppenconferentie (National Conference of Catholic Bishops – NCCB) in november 1986. Gedurende de NCCB, presenteerde Hunthausen zijn lezing van de zaak in een voordracht die sterk afweek van een eerder feitenoverzicht van de apostolische pro-nuntius. Dertien weken na de NCCB maakte de pro-nuntius bekend dat de Heilige Stoel een apostolische commissie had aangewezen van drie Amerikaanse bisschoppen (Bernardin, O`Connor en Quinn) om de situatie in Seattle te beoordelen. Na vier maanden van onderhandelen met Hunthausen en de Heilige Stoel, kwam de commissie eind mei 1987 met zijn beoordeling naar buiten. Meteen werd het voorstel van de commissie in alle openheid doorgevoerd: hulpbisschop Wuerl werd overgeplaatst, weg uit Seattle, en Thomas Murphy, toentertijd bisschop van Great Falls-Billings, Montana, werd benoemd tot coadjutor aartsbisschop van Seattle (zonder speciale bevoegdheden, maar met het recht van opvolging). Hunthausen aanvaardde deze nieuwe regeling met enige aarzeling. Bovengenoemde commissie bleef periodiek ontmoetingen hebben met Hunthausen en Murphy, tot april 1989. Op dat ogenblik eindigde de gerichte interventie van het Vaticaan in Seattle.

Methodologie

Hoewel dit onderzoek geen expliciet theologische reflectie biedt, speelt het zich af binnen de theoretische kaders van de praktische theologie, opgevat als een empirisch georiënteerd interdisciplinair veld (in sterke mate steunend op sociale wetenschappen) en gericht op de bestudering van de kerkelijke praktijk. Hieronder wordt hoofdstuksgewijs de onderzoeksgang beschreven die geleid heeft tot de bevindingen en conclusies van deze studie.

Hoofdstuk 1 van dit proefschrift introduceert het probleem van steeds weer optredende "centrum-periferie conflicten" – hierna CPC te noemen – in de Kerk en het ontbreken van systematische studies van dit verschijnsel. Het levert de aanzet tot het onderhavige onderzoek, presenteert de leidende vraagstelling en resumeert de gekozen onderzoeksbenadering om deze vraag te beantwoorden.

Hoofdstukken 2 en 3 bieden tezamen een overzicht van de concepten, ontleend aan relevante literatuur, die dienen om de teksten van het gekozen, concrete voorbeeld van een CPC, nl. de Hunthausen-kwestie, opmerkzaam aan een analytische lectuur te kunnen onderwerpen.
Hoofdstuk 2 plaatst het CPC in een organisatorische context. Het geeft aandacht aan:
- de potentiële deelnemers en hun hiërarchische rollen in een CPC;
- het type organisatie (bureaucratie – clan – politiek economische markt – missie) dat de Kerk is;
- de overkoepelende, non-operationele doelstelling van de Kerk (het bijeenbrengen van alle mensen bij God);
- specifieke, operationele doelstellingen van de Kerk (het laten groeien en goed leiden van de Kerk, liefdadigheid organiseren, erop toezien dat interne verschillen de eenheid voeden, verkondigen van de boodschap, vieren van de sacramenten, noden lenigen, groeien in heiligheid);
- de menselijke en materiële hulpmiddelen die de Kerk daartoe ter beschikking heeft;
- en de middelen voor coördinatie en sturing, beschikbaar aan kerkelijke leiders (acht types van bisschoppelijke machtsuitoefening worden besproken: afgeleide macht, beloningsmacht, dwang, verder: sociale, wettelijke, traditionele, deskundigheids- en charismatische macht).
De reflectie op elk van deze aspecten van het kerkelijk institutionele leven, loopt uit op een beschouwing hoe het betreffende aspect doorgaans speelt in het hanteren van een CPC.

Hoofdstuk 3 plaatst een CPC in een maatschappelijke context. Omdat een CPC plaatsvindt binnen de kerkelijke organisatie in de moderne wereld, is het noodzakelijk de kwaliteit van de kerkelijke betrokkenheid bij die wereld in ogenschouw te nemen. De Kerk wordt opgevat als een open systeem dat de omgeving beïnvloedt maar ook door die omgeving beïnvloed wordt. Kernvragen in dit hoofdstuk zijn de positiebepalingen van de top met betrekking tot de betrokkenheid bij de wereld (met speciale aandacht voor de leer van Vaticaan II) en met betrekking tot de situatie van de moderniteit (zoals uiteengezet in het werk van A. Giddens). Beide spelen naar verwachting steeds in de afwikkeling van een CPC. Aan het einde van dit hoofdstuk wordt samengevat wat men mag verwachten met betrekking tot het hanteren van het CPC (inclusief de benoeming van zeven mogelijke strategieën); daarmee is richting gegeven aan de aansluitende lectuur van de casus.

Hoofdstuk 4 biedt een conflicttheoretisch kader ter bestudering en analyse van de casus. Het doel van dit hoofdstuk (dat steunt op het werk van D. Pruitt en J. Rubin) is het scheppen van een referentiekader ter analyse van het Rome-Hunthausen conflict *als conflict*. De gekozen theorie dient dit doel door beschrijvende en verklarende duidingen te leveren van karakteristieke elementen van interpersoonlijke conflicthantering, met speciale aandacht voor vragen als het belang der partijen, de waarneming van andermans belangen en de haalbaarheid van bepaalde acties, alsmede de strategieën die toegepast worden indien partijen onderling een belangverschil constateren. Behulpzaam in de theorie was ook het verband tussen strategieën en het stadium, waarin het conflict verkeert. In hoofdstuk 9 wordt de conflicttheorie geraadpleegd in een poging specifieke bijzonderheden van het conflict tussen Rome en Hunthausen te belichten.

Hoofdstuk 5 geeft een gedetailleerd overzicht van de methodologie die gebruikt werd in de confrontatie met de "case data". Het bespreekt de afbakening van de casus, de constructie van het relaas van de casus, en hoe het case-materiaal (in het bijzonder de documenten die door de bisschoppen geproduceerd zijn) onderzocht is met de techniek van de zogeheten "critical discourse analysis" (N. Fairclough). Dit hoofdstuk legt tevens uit hoe al hetgeen uit de documenten naar voren komt, in verband is gebracht met begrippen van conflictstrategieën.. Het eindigt met een bespreking van validatietechnieken die toegepast werden zodra de onderzoeksbevindingen provisorisch geformuleerd waren.

Hoofdstukken 6 t/m 8 vertellen het verhaal van het conflict tussen Rome en Hunthausen, steunend op de documenten die door de conflictanten zijn geproduceerd alsmede op de geschreven verslagen van waarnemers, die buiten het conflict stonden. De behandeling van een negental kerndocumenten vormt de ruggengraat van deze hoofdstukken. Elk document is geanalyseerd naar zijn strategische 'functionaliteit' binnen het conflict. Eveneens geanalyseerd (met een alternatieve methode) zijn de daaraan voorafgaande, de interveniërende en de daaropvolgende ontwikkelingen, die ons toestaan om de conflictactiviteiten te zien als een geïntegreerd geheel.

Hoofdstuk 9 integreert de analyse van de gevonden hanteringstrategieën die in een geleidelijke opbouw in de hoofdstukken 6 t/m 8 is gepresenteerd. Om te beginnen worden de bevindingen uit het empirische voorbeeld geresumeerd en worden deze vergeleken met de verwachtingen die op basis van de literatuurstudie waren geformuleerd. Vervolgens worden deze bevindingen in verband gebracht met het theoretische model van conflicthantering. Hoofdstuk 9 sluit af met een verslag van de resultaten van twee validaties. De eerste betrof een controle op het niveau van de documenten. De tweede was een controle op het gehele relaas van en de centrale gebeurtenissen in deze kwestie; deze controle werd doorgevoerd via een interview met een conflictinsider (de eerwaarde Michael G Ryan, de vicaris generaal van aartsbisschop Hunthausen).

Hoofdstuk 10 ten slotte formuleert de uiteindelijke conclusies en evalueert het onderzoeks-project.

Conclusies en relevantie

De conclusies geven een uiteindelijk beeld van de kwestie Rome-Hunthausen. De daarmee verbonden stellingen verduidelijken dat aspecten van de casus vermoedelijk veralgemeniseer-baar zijn naar andere CPC's. Deze stellingen kunnen als hypothesen in andere, soortgelijke kwesties getoetst worden.

Algemene positiebepaling ten aanzien van conflicthantering:
Alle leden in de hiërarchie betrokken bij de kwestie Rome-Hunthausen waren erop uit het gezicht te redden van de kerkelijke organisatie en van zichzelf. Zij streefden naar de machtshandhaving van zichzelf alsmede van de Kerk.

Gebruik van macht:
Alle leden van de betrokken hiërarchie streefden naar de (schijn van) legitimatie van hun machtsgebruik. Hoewel de centrale partij (Rome) een groot voordeel genoot in nagenoeg alle vormen van kerkelijke macht in de kwestie Rome-Hunthausen, had ze toch de grootste moeite om haar wil door te zetten in Seattle. De basis van Hunthausens succes (de perifere partij) lijkt te liggen in zijn consistent vasthouden aan een houding van achting en loyaliteit – naar de Heilige Stoel (de Heilige Vader in het bijzonder) en de Kerk – terwijl hij tegenstand bood (in onderhandelingen achter de schermen), stilletjes en op een voor het publiek aanvaardbare manier.

Toegepaste hanteringstrategieën:
1. **Toont hoogachting voor de bestaande structurele orde en het gedachtegoed van de Kerk:** Alle betrokken bisschoppen zien erop toe de Kerk niet te bekritiseren en volmondig trouw te betuigen aan andere kerkleiders. Nergens in de casus vinden we een enige substantiële afwijking van deze praktijk.
2. **Het eigen streven in verband brengen met positieve belangen van de Kerk:** Alle betrokken bisschoppen lieten blijken, vaak in uitdrukkelijke bewoordingen, dat ze ter wille van de Kerk handelden. Vertegenwoordigers van het centrum (Rome) waren geneigd dit kerkelijk belang te formuleren in termen van het noodzakelijke toezicht op en de juiste vertolking van de kerkelijke leer, terwijl Hunthausen het belang van de Kerk (en zichzelf) in verband bracht met het welzijn van het kerkvolk.
3. **Minimaliseert de zichtbaarheid van het conflict:** De betrokken bisschoppen in het conflict Rome-Hunthausen zochten gedurende het gehele conflict en consequent naar wegen om het conflict naar buiten toe te minimaliseren (omvang, relevantie, betekenis); slechts in de spannendste fase van het conflict werd deze strategie – en dan nog slechts kort – verlaten.
4. **Toont broederschap:** De bisschoppen die deel hadden aan het conflict tussen Rome en Hunthausen spraken elkaar aan op hun broederlijke relatie door bij elkaar een beroep op bijstand te doen. Alle bisschoppen vertoonden de clan-achtige neiging om ruzies in hun geledingen ook binnen die perken te houden. Het (kerkelijk) idee van 'bisschoppelijke broederschap' werd regelmatig aangehaald, door alle partijen, om de betrokkenen aan hun verplichtingen te herinneren of als een teken van de eigen binding en loyaliteit.

5. **Hoffelijkheid:** Alle bisschoppen die deel hadden aan het conflict toonden een bijna niet kapot te krijgen toewijding aan beminnelijkheid jegens elkaar, zeker publiekelijk. Tactisch gesproken betekende dit: elkaar prijzen, elkaar respectvol bejegenen, rechtstreekse kritiek of verwijten vermijden, en zwijgen over gevoelige zaken. Slechts kort, toen het conflict het hevigst was, lieten zowel de centrale als de perifere partijen in het conflict tussen Rome en Hunthausen dit vertoon van hoffelijkheid naar elkaar achterwege.

6. **Geheimhouding:** Alle bisschoppen die deel hadden aan het conflict tussen Rome en Hunthausen brachten geheimhouding in praktijk. Het belangrijkste verschil in informatie ten gevolge van deze geheimhouding, lag tussen degenen binnen de hiërarchie en degenen die erbuiten stonden. Geheimhouding diende om de ernst van het conflict te minimaliseren, zodat de schijn van eenheid binnen de top bewaard bleef. Geheimhouding diende ook om degenen die buiten de hiërarchie staan buiten de conflictonderhandelingen te houden. Binnen de top gebruikte Rome geheimhouding tegen Hunthausen; door hem de gevraagde informatie te onthouden werd hij regelmatig in een nadelige positie geplaatst. Hunthausen vocht terug door (gedurende het middelste stadium van het conflict) zaken in de openbaarheid te brengen en de geheimhouding zelf tot kwestie te maken, maar meestal hield hij zichzelf wel aan het gebruik van geheimhouding in de hiërarchie. Terwijl vasthouden aan geheimhouding tot op grote hoogte een standaard manier van doen was in het hanteren van het conflict, was het verbreken van geheimhouding dat ook (meestal om daar voordeel uit te halen), net als het lekken van nieuws.

7. **Medestanders winnen:** Pogingen van het centrum en van de periferie om collega bisschoppen als medestanders te winnen namen gelijk met het oplopen van het conflict toe. De belangrijkste poging om steun te verwerven onder collega bisschoppen vond plaats voor en tijdens de nationale bisschoppenconferentie (NCCB) van november 1986. Hunthausen had als minder machtige partij meer behoefte aan de steun van een derde en zocht er daarom ook actiever naar dan Rome. Het uiteindelijke besluit van de NCCB om achter Hunthausen te gaan staan (zonder Rome te schofferen) was cruciaal voor Hunthausens succes om het conflict redelijk goed te doorstaan.

8. **Gebruik van overtuigende argumentatie:** Het was lastig een oordeel vellen over de pogingen van de belangrijkste partijen om elkaar rechtstreeks te overtuigen met behulp van steekhoudende argumenten omdat het merendeel van de meest relevante gesprekken zich aan het gezicht onttrok. Voor zover dergelijke argumentaties wèl waarneembaar waren, laten de meeste ervan zien dat de partijen hun welsprekendheid aanwendden om *publieke* steun te verwerven. Letten we op de waarneembare uitwisselingen tussen de voornaamste betrokkenen, dan blijkt echter dat het belangrijkste verschil tussen de argumentatie van Rome en Hunthausen van doen heeft met uiteenlopende ecclesiologische visies, waarbij Hunthausen de klemtoon legt op de volwassenheid van de kerkleden en op hun wettige autonomie, terwijl Rome geconcentreerd is op de behoefte om kerkelijke praktijken en locale vertolkingen van de kerkelijk leer te controleren.

9. **Persoonlijke identiteit poneren:** Onder alle bisschoppen die deel hadden aan het conflict tussen Rome en Hunthausen bracht alleen Hunthausen bij tijd en wijle zijn persoon(lijke identiteit) in het openbaar naar voren als een van de middelen het conflict aan te kunnen. De vertegenwoordigers van het Vaticaan vestigden slechts zelden openlijk en bij wijze van conflictbeheersing de aandacht op hun persoon(lijke identiteit). Deze manier van doen bleek voor Hunthausen een bron van kracht: ze vermenselijkte zijn positie en schiep aanhangers van zijn standpunt. De eigen persoon(lijkheid) op de voorgrond plaatsen leek een klein taboe aan de kant van de

centrale partij, en zolang ze in het conflict gemoeid waren, waren de bisschoppen van de derde partij die de onderhandelingen voerden eveneens geneigd een laag profiel te kiezen. De meest zichtbare vertegenwoordiger aan Vaticaanse zijde was de pronuntius Laghi. Curiefunctionarissen en de paus bleven bijna volledig buiten beeld. Het is onduidelijk waarom de paus ervoor koos met zijn persoon(lijkheid) niet op een directe en openlijke manier tussenbeide te komen in het conflict, gegeven zijn evidente vermogen zijn eigen persoon(lijkheid) doeltreffend in het openbaar naar voren te brengen..

Algemene stellingen:

Stelling 1: CPC maakt het voor de betrokken bisschoppen moeilijk te onderscheiden wat in het belang is van henzelf en wat in het belang van de Kerk. De participanten zullen het evenwicht moeten herbevestigen of herformuleren dat ze gevonden hebben tussen de prioriteiten van het voorkomen van gezichtsverlies voor henzelf en de Kerk enerzijds, en het versterken van de macht voor henzelf en de Kerk anderzijds.

Stelling 2: Bisschoppen die deelhebben aan een CPC zullen ernaar streven dat hun machtsuitoefening legitiem lijkt.

Stelling 3: Van beslissend belang voor een perifere bisschop om een conflict met het centrum te kunnen overleven is zijn vermogen om weerstand te bieden zonder de schijn op zich te laden dat hij disloyaal is. De perifere partij moet gedurig zijn loyaliteit belijden alsmede gehoorzaamheid aan het centrum tonen en elke woord of handeling zien te vermijden dat/die rechtstreeks het gezag van het centrum zou aantasten.

Stelling 4: Bisschoppen, gewikkeld in een CPC, zullen respect betuigen aan de voorschriften en het gedachtegoed van de Kerk. Hoewel ze het heersende denken en handelen van de Kerk ter discussie mogen stellen, kunnen ze dat alleen zodanig doen dat het past binnen de traditie, de cultuur en de socialisatie van de Kerk.

Stelling 5: Bisschoppen, gewikkeld in een CPC, zullen hun eigen inspanningen in verband brengen met het belang van de Kerk, maar wat men in concreto ziet als de beste bijdrage aan het belang van de Kerk, kan botsen en zelf een bron van conflict worden.

Stelling 6: Bisschoppen, gewikkeld in een CPC, zullen de zichtbaarheid van het conflict minimaliseren, maar kunnen ter wille van het voordeel deze strategie even terzijde laten.

Stelling 7: Bisschoppen, gewikkeld in een CPC, zullen broederschap aan de dag leggen door gezichtsverlies bij elkaar te voorkomen, door zaken van de hiërarchie in die geledingen te houden en door de idee van bisschoppelijke broederschap te benadrukken.

Stelling 8: Bisschoppen, gewikkeld in een CPC, zullen in het openbaar en vrijwel zonder uitzondering wellevendheid jegens elkaar tonen. Wanneer deze regel doorbroken wordt, gebeurt dat meestal door de centrale partij.

Stelling 9: Bisschoppen, gewikkeld in een CPC, vertonen een standaard voorkeur om hun onderhandelingen over het conflict in het geheim te voeren, tenzij er een duidelijk voordeel is om dat niet te doen.

Stelling 10: De partij van het centrum heeft meer voordeel bij geheimhouding dan de perifere partij en zal dus vaker vasthouden aan geheimhouding dan de periferie.

Stelling 11: De onderliggende partij – vanuit machtsoogpunt – in CPC, meestal de perifere partij, heeft meer behoefte aan bisschoppelijke bondgenoten en zal een gerichtere poging doen deze ook te werven.

Stelling 12: Hoewel collega bisschoppen de belangrijkste medestanders zijn in een CPC, kan ook de steun van buiten de hiërarchie strategische invloed hebben op het aankunnen van het conflict.

Stelling 13: Bisschoppen, gewikkeld in een CPC, zullen allereerst trachten andere bisschoppen in de privé sfeer over te halen met overtuigende argumentatie. Overtuigende argumentatie die openlijk wordt ingezet, zal voornamelijk gericht zijn op derde partijen.

Stelling 14: Bisschoppen van de centrale partij zullen in de loop van een CPC weinig geneigd zijn hun persoon(lijkheid) in te brengen om het conflict aan te kunnen.. Bisschoppen van de perifere partij, zullen meer vrijheid genieten om hun eigen persoon(lijkheid) naar voren te schuiven en hebben ook meer motivatie om dat te doen.

Relevantie:

Onderstaande opmerkingen over de praktische en praktisch theologische relevantie van het onderzoek zijn normatief en speculatief van aard.

De Kerk is een organisatie die poogt uit diversiteit eenheid te smeden. De spanning tussen centrale beheersing of controle en lokale (perifere) autonomie is een weerspiegeling van de krachtsinspanning veelheid tot eenheid te verzamelen. Strijd tussen Rome en de plaatselijke Kerk (of tussen de paus en de plaatselijke bisschop) is dan ook een verschijnsel dat, vanuit verschillende invalshoeken, opgevat kan worden als een onvermijdelijke kenmerk van de Kerk, als de uitkomst van een maatschappelijk-historische conjunctuur of als de onvermijdelijke uitdaging die elke grootschalige, gecentraliseerde en gebureaucratiseerde multinational onder ogen moet zien.

Het onderzoek laat zien dat men zonder problemen een conflict tussen centrum en periferie (en op goede gronden conflicten binnen de top überhaupt, gegeven de uitkomst van de veelzijdige verworteling in het geloofssysteem, de cultuur , de socialisatie etc. van de Kerk) kan uitleggen in termen van de wens van de top het aanzien en de macht van de kerkelijke organisatie en van de hiërarchie zelf te bewaren met het oog op het streven naar eenheid. De studie trekt niet de conclusie dat dit de enige motieven zijn die de bisschoppen bewegen in hun kerkelijk leiderschap – normatief-ideologische beweegredenen blijven buitengewoon ter zake doend – , maar stelt slechts dat deze (andere) motieven in de praktijk voorkomen en op een grotere schaal werkzaam zijn dan leden van de hiërarchie toegeven. Op die manier biedt de studie een noodzakelijke aanvulling op de eigen beschrijving door de top van wat er plaatsvindt en op het spel staat in zulke conflicten.

Er heerst binnen de kerkelijke organisatie een taboe op conflicten, kennelijk gebaseerd op de idee dat ruzie onverenigbaar is met de wenselijke situatie van liefde en eensgezindheid. Omdat conflicten geacht worden niet te rijzen, in het bijzonder niet binnen de top die de eenheid van de Kerk symboliseert, blijken bisschoppen in een onhandige klem te raken wanner ze toch van doen krijgen met conflicten die in hun geledingen onvermijdelijk voorkomen.Bij gebrek aan een kerkelijk leer die conflicten klip en klaar op hun waarde schat (toegevend dat ze in geen enkele organisatie ontlopen kunnen worden en nuttig zijn indien ze goed geleid worden) en bij ontstentenis van structuren en richtlijnen om conflicten productief aan te pakken, 'behelpen' bisschoppen zich met onderlinge conflictmijding (terwijl ontzag voor posities en blijken van hoffelijkheid beloond worden) en het minimaliseren van de zichtbaarheid indien het conflict opbloeit (geringschatten van zijn betekenis, het verbergen etc.). Ze streven ernaar de omgang met het conflict binnen de perken van bisschoppelijke broederschap te houden, meestal met behulp van geheimhouding. (De werkelijke onenigheden zijn voor het grote publiek onzichtbaar.) Door dat tekort komen de pogingen van bisschoppen conflicten het hoofd te bieden af te hangen improvisatie. De uitkomsten van dit onderzoek wijzen op de dringende behoefte aan een kerkelijke leer omtrent conflicten, die recht doet aan de moderne werkelijkheid (zoals de wens van doorzichtigheid en brede deelname) en aan ter zake doende normatieve, ecclesiologische en praktische bekommernissen.

Volgens de heersende manier om met conflicten om te gaan (een van de bijdragen van dit onderzoek is opheldering te verschaffen wat die manier is) vertoont de top – in het bijzonder de centrale partij – weerzin om het kerkelijk draagvlak (katholieken in het algemeen) uit te nodigen om als volwaardige deelnemers mee te praten. Als het brede publiek al meedoet, dan komt dat vaak ofwel doordat het met kracht binnendringt in de discussie (door het schrijven van brieven, door acties, door een stortvloed van media-aandacht – vergelijk de jongste crisis in de Amerikaanse Kerk rond pedofilie) ofwel dankzij de poging van de eigen partij sociale druk op de ander uit te oefenen. Door het katholieke publiek buiten de discussies over conflicten te plaatsen, ontnemen de bisschoppen katholieken de gelegenheid zich uit te spreken over kwesties die hen direct aangaan en dienen zo het proces waarin bepaald kan worden wat werkelijk in hun belang is in het geheel niet. Zonder kennis van en tegemoet te komen aan de werkelijke belangen van de mensen die ze leiden, ondermijnen bisschoppen hun eigen gezag en vormen ze een hinderpaal voor de mogelijkheid waarachtige eenheid te bereiken. Hiermee wordt niet voorbij gezien aan de praktische beperkingen die in acht genomen moeten worden (als allen tegelijk zouden spreken, is chaos het resultaat) en evenmin wordt beweerd dat de huidige strategieën die aangewend worden ter oplossing van centrum-periferie conflicten in en uit zichzelf fout zijn. Hoogachting en hoffelijkheid aan de dag leggen, de zichtbaarheid van het conflict minimaliseren – deze en de andere strategieën kunnen stuk voor stuk behulpzaam zijn als ze op de juiste manier worden aangewend. Het probleem op dit moment is echter dat de strategieën onnadenkend gekozen lijken te worden en (vaak) toegepast worden los van gemeenschappelijke overeenstemming en los van ecclesiologische, ethische en praktische referentiekaders die nadrukkelijk een rechtvaardiging voor hun gebruik bieden. Om het zwaarwegende voorbeeld van de geheimhouding te nemen: geheimhouding kan gebruikt worden om te schaden, maar ook dienen om de kwetsbare te beschermen. Het komt erop aan te weten wanneer het juist is geheimhouding te gebruiken, gegeven de identiteit en opdracht van de Kerk, gegeven ook haar ethische standaarden, en de praktische beperkingen die met de doeltreffendheid van geheimhouding zijn gegeven. De voortdurende uitdaging een scherp oog te krijgen voor het passende gebruik van strategieën om conflicten aan te kunnen, zoals onderkend in de loop van deze studie en het licht van de uitkomsten ervan, is voor de Kerk en voor de normatieve wetenschap die praktische theologie is een geëigend onderwerp van (toekomstige) onderzoek.

WORKS CONSULTED

Abbott, W. M.
    1966   *The Documents of Vatican II*. Piscataway: America Press.

Aetatis Novae
    1992   *Pastoral Instruction on Social Communications. Pontifical Council for Social Communications*.

Alinsky, S. D.
    1971   *Rules for Radicals: A Pragmatic Primer for Realistic Radicals*. New York: Vintage.

Althusser, L
    1971   "Ideology and Ideological State Apparatuses." In *Lenin and Philosophy and Other Essays*, ed. L. Althusser. London: New Left Books.

Argyle, M., and B. Beit-Hallahmi
    1975   *The Social Psychology of Religion*. London: Routledge & Kegan Paul.

Argyris, C.
    1983a *Increasing Leadership Effectiveness*. Malabar.
    1983b *Reasoning, Learning, and Action*. San Francisco: Jossey-Bass.
    1990   *Overcoming Organizational Defenses: Facilitating Organizational Learning*. Needham Heights, MA.

Ashbrook, J. B.
    1965   "The Relationship of Church Members to Church Organization." In *Journal for the Scientific Study of Religion* 5:397-419.

Ashby, Philip
    1955   *The Conflict of Religions*. New York: Scribner's.

Aubert, V.
    1963   "Competition and dissensus: two types of conflict and conflict resolution." In *The Journal of Conflict Resolution* 7 1:26-42.

Baart, A.
    1995   "The Unstable Authority of the Pastoral Leaders." In *(Dis)Continuity and (De)Construction*, ed. J. B. M. Wissink. Kampen: Kok Pharos.

Bakhtin, M.
    1986   *Speech Genres and Other Late Essays*, ed. M. Holquist, trans. C. Emerson and M. Holquist. Austin: University of Texas Press.

Baron, R. A.
    1990   "Conflict in Organizations." In *Psychology in Organizations: Integrating Science and Practice*, ed. K. R. Murphy and F. E. Saal. Hillsdale, NJ: Erlbaum.

Bartholomaus, W.
    1978   "Communication in the Church: Aspects of a Theological Theme." In *Concilium*, ed. G. Baum and A. Greeley, 111 1:95-110.

Bassett, W.
    1979   "Support of the Church by Freewill Offering." In *Concilium* 117 7:28-38.

Beals, A. R.
    1961   "Cleavage and internal conflict: an example from India." In *The Journal of Conflict Resolution* 5 1:27-34.

Beck, U.
    1986   *Risikogesellshaft: Auf dem Weg in eine andre Moderne*. Frankfurt: Suhrkamp.

Berger, P.
    1967   *The Sacred Canopy: Elements of a Sociological Theory of Religion*:
             Garden City: Doubleday.

Bernardin, J.
    1987   Address to Pope John Paul II, 16 September 1987. Published in *Origins* 17
             16:255-256.

Bernardin, J., and O. H. Lipscomb
    1997   *Catholic Common Ground Initiative: Foundational Documents*. New
             York: Crossroad.

Bernstein, C. and M. Politi
    1996   *His Holiness: John Paul II and the Hidden History of Our Time*. New
             York: Doubleday.

Bevvino, F. J., Jr.
    1995   "Proclaiming the Gospel: A Market Strategy for Catholic Evangelization."
             In *New Theology Review* 8 4:71-80.

Bisno, H.
    1988   *Managing Conflict*. Newbury Park, CA: Sage.

Blake, R., and J. Mouton
    1964   *The Managerial Grid*. Houston: Gulf Publishing.
    1973   "The Fifth Achievement." In *Conflict Resolution Through Communication*,
             ed. F. E. Jandt. New York: Harper & Row.
    1979   "Intergroup Problem Solving in Organizations: From Theory to Practice. In
             The Social Psychology of Intergroup Relations, ed. W. G. Austin and S.
             Worchel, pp. 19-23. Monterey: Brooks / Cole.
    1984   *Resolving Costly Organizational Conflicts*. San Francisco.

Bleistein, M.
    1988   "The Church in the Process of Social Communication: The Conflict over
             the Theology of Liberation in the German Press." In *The Journal of
             Empirical Theology* 2:51-63.

Blouin, F. X. et al.
    1998   *Vatican Archives: An Inventory and Guide to Historical Documents of the
             Holy See*. New York: Oxford University Press.

Boff, L.
    1986   *Ecclesiogenesis: the Base Communities Reinvent the Church*. New York:
             Orbis.

Boisen, A. T.
    1955   *Religion in Crisis and Custom: A Sociological and Psychological Study*.
             New York: Harper & Bros.

Bok, S.
    1979   *Lying: Moral Choice in Public and Private Life*. New York: Vintage.
    1984   *Secrets: On the Ethics of Concealment and Revelation*. New York:
             Random House.

Boulding, K. E.
    1962   *Conflict and Defense: A General Theory*. New York: Harper & Row.
    1966   "Conflict Management as a Learning Process." In *Conflict in Society*, ed.
             A. de Reuck and J. Knight. Boston.
    1968   "Preface to a Special Issue." In *The Journal of Conflict Management* 12
             4:409-411.

Bourdieu, P.
    1991 *Language and Symbolic Power*. Cambridge: Harvard University Press.
Briggs, C. L.
    1996 *Disorderly Discourse: Narrative, Conflict, and Inequality*. New York: Oxford University Press.
Briggs, K. A.
    1992 *Holy Siege: The Year That Shook Catholic America*. San Francisco: Harper.
Brown, G., and G. Yule
    1983 *Discourse Analysis*. Cambridge: Cambridge University Press.
Brown, P., and S. C. Levinson
    1987 *Politeness: Some Universals in Language Usage*. Cambridge: Cambridge University Press.
Brownlie, I.
    1971 *Basic Documents on Human Rights*. Oxford: Clarendon Press.
Buckley, M. J.
    1998 *Papal Primacy and the Episcopate: Towards a Relational Understanding*. New York: Crossroad.
Burke, K.
    1984 *Permanence and Change: An Anatomy of Purpose*, Third Edition. Berkeley: University of California Press.
Burns, G.
    1992 *The Frontiers of Catholicism: The Politics of Ideology in a Liberal World*. Berkeley: University of California Press.
Byrne, P.
    1995 "American Ultramontanism." In *Theological Studies* 56:315-326.
Byrnes, T. A.
    1991 *Catholic Bishops in American Politics*. Princeton: Princeton University Press.
Caldas-Coulthard, C. R., and M. Coulthard, eds.
    1996 *Texts and Practices*: *Readings in Critical Discourse Analysis*. London: Routledge.
Campion, D. R.
    1966 "The Church Today." In *The Documents of Vatican II*, ed. W. M. Abbott, 183-198. Piscataway: America Press.
Canon Law Society of America
    1983 *Code of Canon Law, Latin-English Edition*. Washington, D.C.: Canon Law Society of America.
Carney, T. F.
    1972 *Content Analysis*. Winnipeg: University of Manitoba Press.
Carpenter, S. L., and W. J. D. Kennedy
    1988 *Managing Public Disputes: A Practical Guide to Handling Conflict and Reaching Agreements*. San Francisco: Jossey-Bass.
Cereti, G.
    1979 "The Financial Resources and Activities of the Vatican." In *The Finances of the Church* (*Concilium*), ed. W. Bassett and P. Huizing. New York: Seabury Press.
Chadwick, H.
    1992 "The Early Christian Community." In *The Oxford Illustrated History of Christianity*, ed. J. McManners. Oxford: Oxford University Press.

Chatman, J. A. et al.
   1994   "Integrating Negotiation and Communication Research." In *Research on Negotiation in Organizations*, 3 139-164.

Chein, I.
   1956   "Research Needs." In *The Journal of Social Issues* 12 3:57-66.

Cheney, G.
   1991   *Rhetoric in an Organizational Society: Managing Multiple Identities*. Columbia: University of South Carolina Press.

Chomsky, N.
   1987   "The Manufacture of Consent." In *The Chomsky Reader*, ed. J. Peck, 121-136. New York: Pantheon.

Coleman, J. A.
   1978   *The Evolution of Dutch Catholicism, 1958-1974*. Berkeley: University of California Press, 1978.

Coleman, J. S.
   1956   "Social cleavage and religious conflict." In *The Journal of Social Issues* 12 3:44-56.

Collins, R.
   1988   *Letters That Paul Did Not Write*. Wilmington: Michael Glazier.

Congar, Y.
   1976   *Challenge to the Church: The Case of Archbishop Lefebvre*. Huntington: Our Sunday Visitor.
   1985   *Diversity and Communion*. Mystic: Twenty-Third Publications.

Cooke, B.
   1989   *The Papacy and the Church in the United States*. New York: Paulist Press.

Coppa, F. J.
   1998   *The Modern Papacy since 1789*. London: Longman.

Coriden, J. A.
   1999   "Church Authority in American Culture: Cases and Observations. In *Church Authority in American Culture: The Second Cardinal Bernardin Conference*, ed. P. J. Murnion. New York: Crossroad.

Coser, L. A.
   1960   "The termination of conflict." In *The Journal of Conflict Resolution* 4 4:347-353.
   1964   *The Functions of Social Conflict*. New York: The Free Press.
   1967   *Continuities in the Study of Social Conflict*. New York.

Cox, H.
   1988   *The Silencing of Leonardo Boff: The Vatican and the Future of World Christianity*. Oak Park: Meyer-Stone.

Crespi, F.
   1989   *Social Action and Power*. Oxford: Blackwell.

Cross, F. L. and E. A. Livingstone
   1988   *The Oxford Dictionary of the Christian Church*, Second Edition. Oxford: Oxford University Press.

Cross, J. G.
   1977   "Negotiation as a Learning Process." In *Journal of Conflict Resolution* 21 581-606.

Crowley, D., and Mitchell, D.

    1994   "Communication in a Post-Mass Media World." In *Communication Theory Today*, ed. D. Crowley and D. Mitchell. Stanford: Stanford University Press.

Curran, C. E.

    1986   *Faithful Dissent*. Kansas City: Sheed & Ward.

Curran, E., and R. E. Hunt

    1969   *Dissent In and For the Church: Theologians and* Humanae Vitae. New York: Sheed & Ward.

Dahrendorf, R.

    1988   *The Modern Social Conflict: An Essay on the Politics of Liberty*. Berkeley: University of California Press.

Danneels, G.

    1987   "Resolving Tensions in a Church That Is Universal and Local." In *Origins* 17 14:218-223.

    1999   "Real Reform." In *Church* 15 3:17-22.

Dawson, C.

    1960   *The Historic Reality of Christian Culture*. New York: Harper & Row.

Demerath, N. J., III, and P. E. Hammond

    1969   *Religion in Social Context: Tradition and Transition*. New York: Random House.

Deutsch, M.

    1969   "Productive and Destructive Conflict." In *Journal of Social Issues* 25 1:7-42.

    1973   *The Resolution of Conflict*. New Haven: Yale University Press.

    1991   "Subjective Features of Conflict Resolution: Psychological, Social and Cultural Influences." In *New Directions in Conflict Theory*, ed. R. Vayrynen, 26-56. London: Sage Publications.

Deutsch, M., and R. M. Krauss

    1962   Studies of interpersonal bargaining. In *The Journal of Conflict Resolution* 6 1:52-76.

Diesing, P.

    1960   "Bargaining strategy and union-management relationships." In *The Journal of Conflict Resolution* 4 4:369-378.

Dijk, T. A. van

    1994   "Discourse and Cognition in Society." In *Communication Theory Today*, ed. D. Crowley and D. Mitchell. Stanford: Stanford University Press.

    1989   "Structures of Discourse and Structures of Power." In *Communication Yearbook 12.* Newbury Park: Sage.

    1998   *Ideology: A Multidisciplinary Approach*. London: Sage.

Dijk, T. A. van, ed.

    1985   *Handbook of Discourse Analysis* (4 vols.). London: Academic Press.

    1997   *Discourse as Structure and Process*. London: Sage.

    1997   *Discourse as Social Interaction*. London: Sage.

Dobbelaere, K.

    1988   "Secularization, Pillarization, Religious Involvement, and Religious Change in the Low Countries." In *World Catholicism in Transition*, ed. T. M. Gannon, S.J. New York: Macmillan.

Dulles, A.
 1966 "The Church." In *The Documents of Vatican II*, ed. W. M. Abbott. Piscataway: America Press.
 1967 *The Dimensions of the Church: A Postconciliar Reflection*. New York: Newman Press.
 1974 *Models of the Church*. Garden City: Doubleday.
 1982 *A Church to Believe In: Discipleship and the Dynamics of Freedom*. New York: Crossroad.
 1985 *The Survival of Dogma: Faith, Authority, and Dogma in a Changing World*. New York: Crossroad.
 1988 *The Reshaping of Catholicism*. San Francisco: Harper & Row.
 2000 "The Papacy for Global Church." In *America* 183 2:6-11.
Eisenstadt, S. N.
 1966 *Modernization: Protest and Change*. Englewood Cliffs: Prentice-Hall.
Etzioni, A.
 1961 *A Comparative Analysis of Complex Organizations, Third Edition*. New York: The Free Press.
Fairclough, N.
 1989 *Language and Power*. London: Longman.
 1992 *Discourse and Social Change*. Cambridge: Polity Press.
 1995 *Critical Discourse Analysis*. London: Longman.
Fairclough, N. and R. Wodak
 1997 "Critical Discourse Analysis." In *Discourse as Social Interaction*, ed. T. A. van Dijk, 258-284. London: Sage.
Faulkner, J. E.
 1972 *Religion's Influence in Contemporary Society*. Columbus: Charles E. Merrill.
Fichter, J. H.
 1954 *Social Relations in the Urban Parish*. Chicago: University of Chicago Press.
 1961 *Religion as an Occupation: A Study in the Sociology of Professions*. Notre Dame: University of Notre Dame Press.
Filley, A. C.
 1975 *Interpersonal Conflict Resolution*. Glenview: Scott, Foresman and Company.
Fink, C. F.
 1968 "Some conceptual difficulties in the theory of social conflict." In *The Journal of Social Conflict* 12 4:412-460.
Finke, R., and R. Stark
 1992 *The Churching of America, 1776-1990: Winners and Losers in Our Religious Economy*. New Brunswick: Rutgers University Press
Fitzpatrick, J. P.
 1987 *One Church, Many Cultures: The Challenge of Diversity*. Kansas City: Sheed & Ward.
Foucault, M.
 1977 *Discipline and Punish*. London: Allen Lane.
 1981 *History of Sexuality*, Volume 1. Harmondsworth: Penguin Books.
 1984 "The Order of Discourse." In *Language and Politics*, ed. M. Shapiro. London: Blackwell.

Fransen, P.
    1982   "The Exercise of Authority in the Church Today: Its Concrete Forms." In *Louvain Studies* 9 1:1-25.
Fraser, N. M., and K. W. Hipel
    1984   *Conflict Analysis: Models and Resolutions*. New York: North-Holland.
Fray, H. R., Jr.
    1969   *Conflict and Change in the Church*. Boston: Pilgrim Press.
Galbraith, J. K.
    1986   "Power and Organization." In *Power*, ed. S. Lukes, 211-228. New York: New York University Press.
Gamson, W.
    1961   "A Theory of Coalition Formation." In *American Sociological Review* 26:373-382.
    1968   *Power and Discontent*. Homewood: The Dorsey Press.
Gangel, K.O., and S.L. Canine
    1992   *Communication and Conflict Management in Churches and Christian Organizations*. Nashville: Broadman & Holman.
Gannon, T. M.
    1988   *World Catholicism in Transition*. New York: Macmillan.
Giddens, A.
    1981   "Agency, Institution and Time-Space Analysis." In *Advances in Social Theory and Methodology: Towards an Integration of Micro- and Macro-Sociologies*, ed. K. Knorr-Cetina and A. V. Cicourel, 161-174. Boston: Routledge and Kegan Paul.
    1990   *The Consequences of Modernity*. Stanford: Stanford University Press.
    1991   *Modernity and Self-Identity: Self and Society in the Late Modern Age*. Stanford: Stanford University Press.
Glock, C. Y., and R. Stark
    1965   *Religion and Society in Tension*. Chicago: Rand McNally.
Goddijn, W.
    1975   *The Deferred Revolution: A Social Experiment in Church Innovation in Holland, 1960-1970*. Amsterdam: Elsevier.
    1983   *Rode oktober: Honderd dagen Alfrink*. Baarn: Ambo.
Goethals, G.
    1994   "Symbolic Forms of Communication." In *The Church and Communication*, ed. P. Granfield, 61-79. Kansas City: Sheed and Ward.
Goffman, E.
    1974   *Frame Analysis*. New York: Harper Colophon Books.
Goldman, R. M.
    1966   "A Theory of Conflict Processes and Organizational Offices." In *Journal of Conflict Resolution* 10:328-343.
Gramsci, A.
    1971   *Selections From the Prison Notebooks*, ed. and trans. by Q. Hoare, G. Nowell-Smith. London: Lawrence & Wishart.
Granfield, P.
    1987   *The Limits of the Papacy: Authority and Autonomy in the Church*. New York: Crossroad.
    1994   "The Theology of the Church and Communication." In *The Church and Communication*, ed. P. Granfield, 1-18. Kansas City: Sheed and Ward.

Greeley, A. M.
    1979   *The Making of the Popes 1978: The Politics of Intrigue in the Vatican.*
            Kansas City: Andrews and McMeel.
    1998   "Prospects for 'Evangelization.'" In *America* 178 2:8-11.

Hager, D. J.
    1956   "Introduction: Religious Conflict." In *The Journal of Social Issues* 7
            3:3-11.

Halliday, M. A. K.
    1985   Introduction to Functional Grammar. London: Edward Arnold.

Halliday, M. A. K. and R. Hasan
    1976   *Cohesion in English.* London: Longman.

Hanson, E. O.
    1987   *The Catholic Church in World Politics.* Princeton: Princeton University
            Press.

Hebblethwaite, P.
    1986   *In the Vatican.* Bethesda: Adler & Adler.

Heft, J. L.
    1999   *A Catholic Modernity? Charles Taylor's Marianist Award Lecture.* New
            York: Oxford University Press.

Heitink, G.
    1993   *Praktische Theologie: geschiedenis-theorie-handelingsvelden.* Kampen:
            Kok.

Hellwig, M.
    1990   "American Culture: Reciprocity with Catholic Vision, Values and
            Community." In *The Catholic Church and American Culture: Reciprocity and
            Challenge*, ed. C. Yuhaus. Mahwah: Paulist.

Henrici, P.
    1994   "Truth and Power in Ecclesial Communication." In *The Church and
            Communication*, ed. P. Granfield. Kansas City: Sheed & Ward.

Herman, E. S., and N. Chomsky
    1988   *Manufacturing Consent: The Political Economy of the Mass Media.* New
            York: Pantheon.

Himes, J. S.
    1980   *Conflict and Conflict Management.* Athens: University of Georgia Press.

Hinze, B. E.
    1996   "Reclaiming Rhetoric in the Christian Tradition." In *Theological Studies*
            57:481-499.

Hitchcock, J.
    1979   *Catholicism & Modernity: Confrontation or Capitulation?* Ann Arbor:
            Servant Books.

Hollenbach, D.
    1979   *Claims in Conflict: Retrieving and Renewing the Catholic Human Rights
            Tradition.* New York: Paulist Press.

Hoose, B.
    2001   "Towards the Truth about Hiding the Truth." In *Louvain Studies* 26 1:63-84

Hubbard, A.
    1997   "Face-To-Face at Arm's Length: Conflict Norms and Extra-Group Relations in
            Grassroots Dialogue Groups." In *Human Organization* 56 3:265-274.

Huizing, P.
    1971   "The Church and Contestation." In *Contestation in the Church*, ed. T. J.
            Urresti. New York: Herder and Herder.
Hume, Cardinal B.
    1999   *One in Christ: Unity and Diversity in the Church Today*. New York:
            National Pastoral Life Center.
    1989   "In Search of Wholeness." In *Louvain Studies* 14 3:179-194.
Hutjes, J. M. and J. A. van Buuren
    1992   *De gevalsstudie: Strategie van kwaliteitief onderzoek*. Heerlen: Boom.
Iedema, R. A. M.
    1998   "Institutional Responsibility and Hidden Meanings." In *Discourse & Society* 9
            4:481-500.
Iklé, F. C.
    1968   *How Nations Negotiate*. New York: Praeger.
Jacobson, W. D.
    1972   *Power and Interpersonal Relations*. Belmont: Wadsworth Publishing.
Jandt, F.
    1973   "Introduction." In *Conflict Resolution Through Communication*, ed. F.
            Jandt. New York.
Janis, I. L.
    1982   *Groupthink*. Boston: Houghton-Mifflin.
Janssens, L.
    1989   "The Non-infallible Magisterium and Theologians." In *Louvain Studies* 14
            3:195-259.
John Paul II
    1983   "Apostolic Constitution *Sacrae Disciplinae Leges*." In *Code of Canon
            Law: Latin-English Edition*, xi-xvi. Washington, D.C.: Canon Law Society
            of America.
    1985   "One Church, Many Cultures" (21 December 1984 address to Vatican
            officials and members of the College of Cardinals in Rome). In *Origins* 14
            30:498-502.
Kasper, W.
    1989   *Theology & Church*. New York: Crossroad.
Kennedy, G. A.
    1980   *Classical Rhetoric and Its Christian and Secular Tradition from Ancient
            to Modern Times*. Chapel Hill: University of North Carolina Press.
Kniss, F. and M. Chaves
    1995   "Analyzing Intradenominational Conflict: New Directions." In *Journal for
            the Scientific Study of Religion* 34 2:172-185.
Kolbenschlag, M.
    1986   *Authority, Community and Conflict*: Kansas City: Sheed & Ward.
Korobov, N.
    2001   "Reconciling Theory with Method: From Conversation Analysis and Critical
            Discourse Analysis to Positioning Analysis. In *Forum Qualitative
            Sozialforschung / Forum: Qualitative Social Research* [On-line journal] 2:3
Kriesberg, L.
    1973   *The Sociology of Social Conflicts*. Englewood Cliffs: Prentice-Hall

Krippendorff, K.
  1980   *Content Analysis: An Introduction to Its Methodology*. Beverly Hills:
         Sage.
Laclau, E. and C. Mouffe
  1985   *Hegemony and Socialist Strategy*. London: Verso.
Laeyendecker, L.
  1967   *Religie en Conflict: De zogenaamde sekten in sociologisch perspectief*.
         Tempel: J. A. Boom en Zoon.
  1988   "Van kardinaal Alfrink naar kardinaal Simonis." In *De Vernieuwingen in
         Katholiek Nederland: Van Vaticanum II tot Acht Mei Beweging*, 195-211,
         ed. E. Borgman, B. van Dijk and T. Salemink. Amersfoort: De Horstink.
Laghi, P.
  1983   "The Central Significance of the 'Ad Limina' Visits." In *Origins* 13 24:405-
         407.
Lambrecht, J.
  1987   "Power as Service." In *Louvain Studies* 12:54-61.
Lawler, P. F.
  1986   *How Bishops Decide: An American Catholic Case Study*. Washington, D.C.:
         Ethics and Public Policy Center.
Lee, R. and M. Marty
  1964   *Religion and Social Conflict*. New York: Oxford University Press.
Legrand, H., J. Manzanares, and A. Garcia y Garcia
  1988   *The Nature and Future of Episcopal Conferences*. Washington,
         DC.: The Catholic University of America Press.
Lemaire, A.
  1972   "From Services to Ministries: 'Diakoniai' in the First Two Centuries."*Office
         and Ministry in the Church*, 35-49, ed. B. van Iersel and R. Murphy.
         New York: Herder and Herder.
Lernoux, P.
  1986   "U.S. Bishops Can Help Seattle and Themselves." In *National Catholic
         Reporter* (11.7.86), p. 16.
Lewin, K.
  1948   *Resolving Social Conflicts*. New York: Harper & Bros.
Likert, R.
  1967   *The Human Organisation: Its Management and Value*. New York.
Loo, H. van der, and W. van Reijen
  1997   *Paradoxen van Modernisering*. Bussum: Coutinho.
Lubac, H. de
  1963   *The Splendour of the Church*. Glen Rock: Paulist Press.
Lukes, S.
  1974   *Power: A Radical View*. London: MacMillan.
  1986   *Power*. New York: New York University Press.
MacEoin, G. (ed.)
  1998   *The Papacy and the People of God*. Maryknoll: Orbis.
Mack, R. W., and R. C. Snyder
  1973   "The Analysis of Social Conflict -- Toward an Overview and Synthesis." In
         Conflict Resolution Through Communication, ed. F. E. Jandt. New York:
         Harper & Row.
Mackenzie, W. J. M.
  1978   *Political Identity*. New York: St. Martin's Press.

March, J. G., H. A. Simon and H. Guetzkow
    1966   *Organizations*, 8th Edition. New York.

Martinson, D. L.
    1998   "The Church and Public Relations: Some Important Lessons." In *America* 179 12:14-16.

Marzheuser, R.
    1995   "A Revitalized Theology of Catholicity: Toward Better Communication with Those Who Talk Differently Than We Do about the Church." In *New Theology Review* 8 4:48-55.

Maslow, A.
    1954   *Motivation and Personality*. New York.

May, J.
    1987   Text of address to Pope John Paul II in "Los Angeles Meeting of the Pope and U.S. Bishops." In *Origins* 17 16:254.

McBrien, R. P.
    1992   *Report on the Church: Catholicism After Vatican II*. San Francisco: Harper.

McClelland, C. A.
    1962   "Decisional opportunity and political controversy: the Quemoy case." In *The Journal of Conflict Resolution* 6 3:201-213.

McDonough, K. M.
    1997   "Diocesan Bureaucracy." In *America* 177 10:9-13.

McGuire, M. B.
    1997   *Religion: The Social Context,* Fourth Edition. Belmont: Wadsworth.

McKenzie, J. L.
    1969   *The Roman Catholic Church*. London: Weidenfeld & Nicolson.

McKersie, R. B., C. R. Perry, and R. E. Walton
    1965   "Intraorganizational Bargaining in Labor Negotiations." In *The Journal of Conflict Resolution* 9 4:463-481.

Mechanic, D.
    1962   "Sources of Power of Lower Participants in Complex Organizations." In *Administrative Science Quarterly* 7:349-364.

Melady, M. B.
    1999   *The Rhetoric of Pope John Paul II: The Pastoral Visit As a New Vocabulary of the Sacred*. Westport: Praeger

Mensching, G.
    1971   *Tolerance and Truth in Religion*. University of Alabama Press.

Merton, R. K.
    1949   *Social Theory and Social Structure*. Glencoe, IL: The Free Press.

Miles, M. B., and A. M. Huberman
    1994   *Qualitative Data Analysis. Second Edition*. Thousand Oaks: Sage.

Mintzberg, H.
    1979   *The Structuring of Organizations: A Synthesis of the Research*. Englewood Cliffs: Prentice-Hall.

Moore, M. C. and M. J. Moore
    1990   "Cooperation, Hierarchy and Structure." In *Research on Negotiation in Organizations*, ed. B. H. Sheppard et al, 2 207-217.

Moore, R. L.
    1994   *Selling God: American Religion in the Marketplace of Culture*. New York: Oxford University Press.

Morgan, G.
    1990   *Organizations in Society*. London: Macmillan.
Mouzelis, N. P.
    1967   *Organisation and Bureaucracy*. New York: Aldine de Gruyter.
National Conference of Catholic Bishops (U.S.)
    1989   "Doctrinal Responsibilities: Approaches to Promoting Cooperation and Resolving Misunderstandings Between Bishops and Theologians." In *Origins* 19 7:98-110.
Nichols, P.
    1982   *The Pope's Divisons: The Roman Catholic Church Today*. Harmondsworth: Penguin.
Nichols, T. L.
    1997   *That All May Be One*. Collegeville: The Liturgical Press.
Nicholson, M.
    1991   "Negotiation, Agreement and Conflict Resolution: The Role of Rational Approaches and their Criticism." In *New Directions in Conflict Theory*, ed. R. Vayrynen, 57-78. London.
Nielsen, M. E.
    1998   "An Assessment of Religious Conflicts and their Resolutions." In *Journal for the Scientific Study of Religion* 37 1:181-190.
Nisbet, R. A.
    1969   *Social Change and History*. London: Oxford University Press.
Noonan, J.-C., Jr.
    1996   *The Church Visible: The Ceremonial Life and Protocol of the Roman Catholic Church*. New York: Viking.
Nord, W. R. and E. M. Doherty
    1994   "Toward an Improved Framework for Conceptualizing the Conflict Process." In *Research on Negotiations in Organizations*, 4 173-240.
O'Brien, D.
    1994   *From the Heart of the American Church: Catholic Higher Education and American Culture*. Maryknoll: Orbis.
O'Connor, D.
    1986   "Ecclesiastical Intervention." In *Authority, Community and Conflict*, ed. M. Kolbenschlag. Kansas City: Sheed & Ward.
O'Grady, J. F.
    1984   "Authority and Power: Issues for the Contemporary Church. In *Louvain Studies* 10 2:122-140.
Parsons, T.
    1959   "General Theory in Sociology." In *Sociology Today: Problems and Prospects*, ed. R. K. Merton, L. Broom and L. S. Cottrell. New York: Basic Books.
    1960   *Structure and Process in Modern Societies*. New York: The Free Press.
    1965   "General Theory in Sociology." In R.K. Merton, L. Broom and L.S. Cottrell, Jr., (eds.), *Sociology Today I*, 3-38. New York.
Patchen, M.
    1970   "Models of Cooperation and Conflict: A Critical Review." In *The Journal of Conflict Resolution* 14 3:389-407.
Pecheux, M.
    1988   "Discourse: Structure or Event?" In *Marxism and the Interpretation of Culture*, ed. C. Nelson and L Grossberg. London: Macmillan.

Plas, M. van der and H. Suer
1967   *Those Dutch Catholics*. New York: Macmillan.
Pondy, L. R.
1967   "Organizational Conflict: Concepts and Models." In *Administrative Science Quarterly*. 12:296-320.
Prein, H. C. M.
1976   "Stijlen van conflicthantering." In Dutch *Tijds. v. Psych.* 31.
Primeaux, P.
1995   "Pastoral Organization and Decision Making." In *New Theology Review* 8 4:56-70.
Provost, J. H.
1989   "The Papacy: Power, Authority, Leadership." In *The Papacy and the Church in the United States*, ed. B. Cooke. New York: Paulist Press.
Pruitt, D. G.
1961   "An analysis of responsiveness between nations." In *The Journal of Conflict Resolution* 6 1:5-18.
Pruitt, D. G. and P. J. Carnevale
1993   *Negotiation in Social Conflict*. Pacific Grove.
Pruitt, D. G. and J. L. Drews
1969   "The Effect of Time Pressure, Time Elapsed, and the Opponent's Concession Rate on Behavior in Negotiation." In *Journal of Experimental Social Psychology* 5: 43-60.
Pruitt, D. G. and J. Z. Rubin
1986   *Social Conflict: Escalation, Stalemate, and Settlement*. New York: Random House.
Quinn, J. R.
1999   *The Reform of the Primacy: The Costly Call to Christian Unity*. New York: Crossroad.
1996   "The Exercise of the Primacy: Facing the cost of Christian unity." In *Commonweal*, 12 July 1996.
Rahim, M. A.
1986   *Managing Conflict in Organizations*. New York: Praeger.
1989   *Managing Conflict: An Interdisciplinary Approach*. New York: Praeger.
1990   *Theory and Research in Conflict Management*. New York: Praeger.
1992   *Managing Conflict in Organizations, Second Edition*. Westport: Praeger.
Rahim, M. A. and T. V. Bonoma
1979   "Managing Organizational Conflict: A Model for Diagnosis and Intervention." In *Psychological Reports*, 44:1323-1344.
Rahner, K. and J. Ratzinger
1962   *The Episcopate and the Primacy*. Edinburgh-London: Nelson.
Ratzinger, J. and V. Messori
1985   *The Ratzinger Report: An Exclusive Interview on the State of the Church*. San Francisco: Ignatius Press.
Rausch, T. P.
1998   "Divisions, Dialogue and the Catholicity of the Church." In *America* 178 3:20-29.

Reese, T. J.
    1986   "The Seattle Way of the Cross." In *America*, 9.20.86.
    1989   *Archbishop: Inside the Power Structure of the American Catholic Church.* San Francisco: Harper & Row.
    1992   *A Flock of Shepherds: The National Conference of Catholic Bishops.* Kansas City: Sheed & Ward.
    1996   *Inside the Vatican: The Politics and Organization of the Catholic Church.* Cambridge: Harvard University Press.

Roach, J.
    1983   "The Bishops and the Vatican: New, Positive Chapter." In *Origins* 13 24:402-407.

Robbins, S. P.
    1992   *Essentials of Organizational Behavior*, 3rd ed. Englewood Cliffs.

Robinson, J. A. T.
    1977   *On Being the Church in the World.* London: Mowbrays.

Roest, H. de
    1998   *Communicative Identity: Habermas's perspectives of discourse as a support for practical theology.* Kampen: Kok.

Roethlisberger, F. J. et al
    1954   *Training for Human Relations.* Boston: Harvard.

Rogers, C. R.
    1962   "Toward a Theory of Creativity." In *A Source Book for Creative Thinking*, ed. S. J. Parnes and H. F. Harding. New York: Scribner's.

Rondeau A.
    1990   "La gestion des conflits dans les organisations." In *L'Individu dans l'organisation*, ed. J. F. Charlat, 507-527. Quebec.

Rubin, J. Z. and B. R. Brown
    1975   *The Social Psychology of Bargaining and Negotiation* (New York: Academic Press).

Russell, B.
    1986   "The Forms of Power." In *Power*, ed. S. Lukes. New York: New York University Press.

Safranski, S. R.
    1985   *Managing God's Organization: The Catholic Church in Society.* Ann Arbor: UMI Research Press.

Salazar, A. J.
    1996   "Ambiguity and Communication Effects on Small Group Decision-Making Performance." In *Human Communication Research* 23 2:155-192.

Schaik, T. H. M. van
    1997   *Alfrink: een biografie.* Utrecht: Anthos.

Schellenberg, J. A.
    1982   *The Science of Conflict.* New York: Oxford University Press.

Schelling, T. C.
    1980   *The Strategy of Conflict.* Cambridge: Harvard University Press.

Schillebeeckx, E.
    1981   *Ministry: Leadership in the Community of Jesus Christ.* New York: Crossroad.
    1991   *Church: The Human Story of God.* New York: Crossroad.

Schreiter, R. J.
    1985   *Constructing Local Theologies*. Maryknoll: Orbis Books.
    1997   *The New Catholicity: Theology Between the Global and the Local*. Maryknoll: Orbis Books.

Segundo, J. L.
    1972   *The Hidden Motives of Pastoral Action*. Maryknoll: Orbis.

Seidler, J. and K. Meyer
    1989   *Conflict and Change in the Catholic Church*. New Brunswick: Rutgers University Press.

Shawchuck, N.
    1986a *How to Manage Conflict in the Church: Conflict Interventions and Resources*. Irvine: Spiritual Growth Resources.
    1986b *How to Manage Conflict in the Church: Understanding and Managing Conflict*. Irvine: Spiritual Growth Resources.

Simmel, G.
    1950   *The Sociology of Georg Simmel*. New York: Free Press.
    1959   *Sociology of Religion*. New York: Philosophical Library.
    1966   *Conflict and The Web of Group Affiliations*. New York: Free Press.

Snyder, G. H., and P. Diesing
    1977   *Conflict Among Nations: Bargaining, Decision Making, and System Structure in International Crises*. Princeton: Princeton University Press.

Sofer, C.
    1972   *Organizations in Theory and Practice*. New York: Basic Books.

Soukup, P.
    1996   *Media, Culture and Catholicism*. Kansas City: Sheed & Ward.

Soukup, P., F. F. Plude, and P. Philibert
    1995   "A Dialogue on Communication and Theology." In *New Theology Review* 8 4:5-25.

Stanley, A.
    2000   "God Is My Co-Pilot: Packing a Bible and Lolling With the Vaticanisti." In *The New York Times*, April 2, 2000.

Steiner, G.
    1970   *Language and Silence*. New York: Atheneum.

Stevens, J.
    1994   *In harmonie en conflict: Een multidisciplinaire benadering*. Den Bosch: Katholieke Bijbelstichting.

Stouthard, P. and G. van Tillo
    1985   *Katholiek Nederland na 1945*. Baarn: Ambo.

Stratton, G. M.
    1911   *Psychology of the Religious Life*. London: George Allen & Co.

Strauss, A.
    1990   *Basics of Qualitative Research: Grounded Theory Procedures and Techniques*. Newbury Park: Sage.

Strauss, A. and J. Corbin
    1990   *Basics of Qualitative Research: Grounded Theory Procedures and Techniques*. Newbury Park: Sage.

Suenens, L. J.
    1975   *A New Pentecost?* New York: Seabury Press.

Swidler, L. and P. F. Fransen
    1982   *Authority in the Church and the Schillebeeckx Case*. New York:
          Crossroad.

Szafran, R. F.
    1976   "The Distribution of Influence in Religious Organizations." In *Journal for
          the Scientific Study of Religion* 15 4:339-349.

Taylor, C.
    1989   *Sources of the Self: The Making of Modern Identity*. Cambridge: Harvard
          University Press.
    1999   "A Catholic Modernity?" In *A Catholic Modernity? Charles Taylor's
          Marianist Award Lecture*, 13-38, ed. J. L. Heft. New York: Oxford
          University Press.
    1999   "Concluding Reflections and Comments." In *A Catholic Modernity?
          Charles Taylor's Marianist Award Lecture*, 105-126, ed. J. L. Heft.
          New York: Oxford University Press.

Taylor, C. M.
    2000   *Abundance of Grace: The History of the Archdiocese of Seattle, 1850-2000*.
          Strasbourg: Editions du Signe.

Theissen, G.
    1982   *Sociology of Early Palestinian Christianity*. Philadelphia: Fortress Press.

Thomas, K. W.
    1976   "Conflict and Conflict Management." In *Handbook of Industrial and
          Organizational Psychology*, ed. M. D. Dunnette. Chicago: Rand McNally.

Thomas, S. J.
    1997   "After Vatican Council II: The American Catholic Bishops and the 'Syllabus'
          from Rome, 1966-1968." In *Catholic Historical Review*, April 1997,
          233-256.

Thompson, J. B.
    1984   *Studies in the Theory of Ideology*. Cambridge: Polity Press.
    1990   *Ideology and Modern Culture*. Stanford: Stanford University Press.

Thung, M. A.
    1976   *The Precarious Organisation: Sociological Explorations of the Church's
          Mission and Structure*. 's Gravenhage: Mouton.
    1996   "An Alternative Model for a Missionary Church: An Approach of the
          Sociology of Organisations.' In *Theology and Sociology: A Reader*, ed. R.
          Gill.

Tjosvold, D.
    1991   *The Conflict-Positive Organization*. Reading.
    _____, and D. W. Johnson
    1983   *Productive Conflict Management*. New York: Irvington.

Tracy, D.
    1987   *Plurality and Ambiguity*. San Francisco: Harper & Row.
    1991   *The Analogical Imagination*. New York: Crossroad.

Tropman, J. E., and J. L. Ehrlich
    1997   "Introduction." In *Strategies of Community Organization: A Book of Readings*,
          ed. F. M. Cox, J. L. Ehrlich, J. E. Tropman. Illinois.

Vaillancourt, J.-G.
    1980   *Papal Power: A Study of Vatican Control over Lay Elites*. Berkeley:
          University of California Press.

Vallier, I.

    1969   *Catholicism, Social Control and Modernization in Latin America*: Englewood Cliffs: Prentice-Hall.

Van Patten, J. J.

    "Religion." In *Conflict, Permanency, Change and Education*, ed. J. Van Patten, J. Roucek, M. Belok, and M. Schoppmeyer. Moti Katra: Satish Book Enterprise.

Väyrynen, Raimo

    1991   *New Directions in Conflict Theory: Conflict Resolution and Conflict Transformation*. London: Sage Publications.

Ven, J. A. van der

    1986   "Konflikten rond vrede: een gevaar voor de eenheid van de kerk?" In *Praktische Theologie* 13:312-331.

    1993   *Practical Theology*. Kampen: Kok Pharos.

    1996   *Ecclesiology in Context*. Grand Rapids: Eerdmans.

Walton, R. E. and J. M. Dutton

    1969   "The Management of Interdepartmental Conflict: A Model and Review. In *Administrative Science Quarterly* 14:73-84.

Watkins, C.

    1991   "Organizing the People of God: Social-Science Theories of Organization in Ecclesiology." In *Theological Studies* 52:689-711.

Weber M.

    1958   *From Max Weber: Essays in Sociology*, ed. and trans. by H. H. Gerth and C. W. Mills. New York: Oxford University Press.

    1962   *Basic Concepts in Sociology*. New York: The Citadel Press.

Weverbergh, R.

    1992   *Bouwen met beelden. Onderzoek naar theorie en praktijk van kerkopbouw* (Studies over kerkopbouwkunde 3). Baarn.

Williams, R. M., Jr.

    1947   *The Reduction of Intergroup Tensions*. New York: Social Science Research Council.

Wilson, B.

    1982   *Religion in Sociological Perspective*. Oxford: Oxford University Press.

Wilson, G. B.

    1999   "'Dissent' or Conversation Among Adults?." In *America* 180 8:8-12.

Yin, R. K.

    1993   *Applications of Case Study Research*. Newbury Park: Sage.

    1994   *Case Study Research: Design and Methods. Second Edition*. Thousand Oaks: Sage.

Yinger, J. M.

    1946   *Religion in the Struggle for Power*. Durham: Duke University Press.

    1963   *Sociology Looks at Religion*. New York: Macmillan.

    1970   *The Scientific Study of Religion*. London: Macmillan.

Young, L. A.

    1997   *Rational Choice Theory and Religion: Summary and Assessment*. New York: Routledge.

Zartman, I. W.

    1977   "Negotiation as a Joint Decision-making Process." In *Journal of Conflict Resolution* 21 619-638.

Ziebertz, H.-G.

    1993   "Konfliktbewaltigung in der Kirche." In *Diakonia* 24 2:118-126.

    1997   "Discontinuity and Continuity: A practical-theological reflexion on religion and modernity." In *The International Journal of Practical Theology.*

    1997   "Types of Church Leadership in the Context of Catholic Ecclesiology." In *Church Leadership*, ed. P. Hansson. Uppsala.

A Word of Thanks

Many persons made this work possible. Though I cannot name them all, I would be remiss in not naming a few who have made especially significant contributions.

Prof. Dr. Andries Baart, in his capacity as promotor, has shepherded this work from an early stage to its completion. His enthusiasm, tireless effort and far-reaching insights have benefited this work in more ways than I can say.

I am also grateful to the judgment committee: Prof. Dr. Jozef Wissink, Prof. Dr. Ruud Huysmans, Prof. Dr. Herman Lombaerts, Dr. Paul Minnihan and Dr. Melanie Morey. These persons have given a considerable amount of time to reading and critiquing this work. Their commitment and generosity are much appreciated.

In the course of carrying out the research I was fortunate to draw on the first-hand experience of two persons connected to the Hunthausen case. Mrs. Janice Wasden Price, a former employee of the Seattle Archdiocese, provided me with materials that were an invaluable aid to my research. And Very Rev. Michael G. Ryan granted me four hours of interview time that filled out and challenged my picture of the conflict events. This would be a lesser work without their offerings.

Finally, I could not have completed this work without the support of my wife, Janke de Groot. Though at times exasperated by the demands of the project, she recognized its importance to me and never wavered in her commitment to let me see it through.

Curriculum vitae

Timothy Peter Schilling was born on August 26, 1965 in Lafayette, Indiana, U.S.A. He graduated from Port Angeles High School, Port Angeles, Washington (U.S.A.) in 1983. In 1987 he completed a bachelor's degree in English at Princeton University. He subsequently earned BA (1990) and MA (1994) degrees in Religious Studies from the Katholieke Universiteit Leuven. From 1994 to 2001 he worked in parishes of the Catholic Archdiocese of Seattle as a religious educator and served as a collaborator and consultant on numerous archdiocesan projects. He is currently employed as a researcher by the Katholieke Universiteit te Utrecht and Actioma research institute, Den Bosch. Tim Schilling is married to Janke de Groot and is the father of Annegien.